Confessing
THE·FAITH

ALSO BY DOUGLAS JOHN HALL

Professing the Faith:
Christian Theology in a North American Context
(1993)

Thinking the Faith:
Christian Theology in a North American Context
(1989)

God and Human Suffering:
An Exercise in the Theology of the Cross
(1986)

Confessing
THE·FAITH

Christian Theology in a
North American Context

DOUGLAS JOHN HALL

FORTRESS PRESS
Minneapolis

CONFESSING THE FAITH
Christian Theology in a North American Context

Cover design: Judy Swanson/Craig Claeys
Text Design: David Lott

Library of Congress Cataloging-in-Publication Data

Hall, Douglas John, 1928–
    Confessing the faith : Christian theology in a North American
context / Douglas John Hall.
       p. cm.
    Includes bibliographical references and index.
    ISBN 0-8006-2547-1 (alk. paper)
    1. Theology, Doctrinal—North America. 2. Christianity and
culture. I. Title.
BT75.2.H33 1996
230'.097—dc20   96-31012
                                                     CIP

Manufactured in the U.S.A.   AF 1–2547

00   99   98   97   96   1   2   3   4   5   6   7   8   9   10

To

Walter Brueggemann

Aurelia Takacs Fule

Kosuke Koyama

C. S. Song

Phyllis Trible

If I profess with the loudest voice and clearest exposition every portion of the truth of God except precisely that little point which the world and the devil are at that moment attacking, I am not confessing Christ, however boldly I may be professing Christ. Where the battle rages, there the loyalty of the soldier is proved. To be steady on all battle fronts besides is mere flight and disgrace if he flinches at that point.

—Martin Luther

Friends! You drank some darkness
and became visible.
—Tomas Tranströmer

CONTENTS

CONTENTS

PREFACE

Years ago, when I was beginning to feel the compulsion to write theology, I sought the advice of one of my respected teachers, a well-known theologian and author. He said at once: "When you sit at your typewriter, keep in your mind's eye the faces of those for whom you write." It was the best literary advice I have ever received.

As I wrote this volume (and the two that preceded it), the "faces" I have tried to keep before me are those of the students I have taught, many of whom are now clergy or teachers of Christian theology; the ministers of many denominations in the United States and Canada whom I have met in my travels; and some of the "extraordinary ordinary" laypersons who have read, encouraged, and challenged me through the years. I hope that this work will be of interest to my colleagues in the theological academy as well; but "the faces" that have accompanied me at my computer have been those of persons who either are already or will become ministers or teachers, lay or clerical, of the once-mainline Protestant churches of the two northern nations of this continent.

It has been my good fortune as a working and itinerant theologian to meet a great many such persons in all parts of this geographic context. Not only that, but I have had the benefits of their discourse in the form of a steady flow of correspondence over a quarter century. The letters (and the essays, poems, plays, sermons, book manuscripts, videos, tapes, and so on that have often accompanied them) have been sources of reflection and inspiration without which I would have been deprived of a whole dimension of my awareness of those "faces." These communications—responses, usually, to something I had written—have not all been approving. This line from a letter that I received recently, one that expressed gratitude for my work, articulates some of the frustration that is felt by many parish clergy today: "You [seminary/university] faculty do have the security of a tenured position, and [I know many who] readily admit that they are glad they are not in the local parish."

It is not an easy time in which to be a Christian minister or priest. The great changes that are sweeping over Christendom are felt more keenly by parish clergy and their families, I think, than by anyone else in the churches. Often, men and women whose expectations and training for ministry have been based on conventional preconceptions of that calling find little resemblance between their earlier images of the ministerial office and their actual experiences of it. What could be assumed about ministry even three or four decades ago can no longer be assumed. The "end of the Constantinian era" is beginning to be very conspicuous in North America, as it has been for a much longer period in Europe. Though everyone who is serious about the faith is affected by this metamorphosis, it can be endured without much personal anxiety by the laity and (so far!) also by tenured theological academics. But, although there are certainly exceptions to the rule, many clergy in our context find themselves right at the biting edge of this "cold front."

That is why I have kept their "faces" in my mind's eye throughout this long exercise in contextual theology. (It pleased me more than anything when the Academy of Parish Clergy awarded the second volume of this trilogy their "Book of the Year" award.) I think that the only way this paradigm shift can be endured by those, especially, who are in this sense most vulnerable to it, is by reflecting on it, living through it—in a real sense, *living it*— theologically. And if one is able to live it with some theological *depth*, one will discover, I think, that it is not only something to be endured but an experience the like of which might have been accessible only to the *first* Christian diaspora.

To acquire such theological depth, however, we must all of us give up a great deal of what has been handed over to us as Christian theology—and especially Christian ecclesiology! For we have all been formed by some version or other of what Luther called "the theology of glory," and nowhere has this theology been more entrenched than in our conception of the church and ministry. The crisis through which Christendom is now passing becomes both intelligible and *necessary*—becomes, in fact, the "judgment [that] begins at the household of faith" (1 Peter 4:17)—only when it is regarded from the perspective of "the theology of the cross."

> The crisis of the church in present-day society is not merely the critical choice between assimilation or retreat into the ghetto, but the crisis of its own existence as the church of the crucified Christ. . . . the Christian church and Christian theology become relevant to the problems of the modern world only when they reveal the "hard core" of their identity in the crucified Christ and through it are called into question, together with the society in which they live. . . . The

crucified Christ himself is a challenge to Christian theology and the Christian church, which dare to call themselves by his name.[1]

To be a Christian today, and more particularly to be in some office of Christian leadership, is in my opinion an infinitely more interesting, challenging, demanding, and also, of course, often unnerving, lonely, and frustrating sort of venture than anything drawn from the long past of "business-as-usual" Christianity. As Moltmann quite rightly affirms in the above, the church is in a state of crisis. "Crisis," *krisis*, means judgment. None of us escapes this judgment; there is pain in it, and much uncertainty. But when we consider the "face" of the Judge, we know that the pain is only the pain of truth, and that the uncertainty can be borne because it is only the other side of trust (faith).

We may also come to know ourselves as Christians today to be, in a new way, part of that much longer "diaspora" tradition, the parental faith of the Jews, from whom and with whom we have much still to learn. Rabbi Dow Marmur of Holy Blossom Temple in Toronto wrote recently that as Jews and Christians meet one another today:

> They often come from the same realization that our society is, alas, no longer dominated by Christianity but by the neo-paganism that goes under the name of secularity. Both Christians and Jews find themselves in the Diaspora; because of their history, Jews are better equipped to live in it.
>
> Not long ago I spent an afternoon with a group of Bishops talking about what it is like to live in the Diaspora. It brought home to me the truth of how much we need each other—not for conversion but for comfort; not for politics but for testimony. This is, indeed, the time for all women and men of good faith to stick together.[2]

■   ■   ■

Writing of any kind is a lonely business. How many hundreds, perhaps thousands, of hours I have sat here alone with my computer—which, despite all the hype, is *not* a very interesting companion! But of course I have not really been alone. There were the aforementioned "faces"—and, perhaps more often than I could have wished, also *that* "face," the One who judges theologians, too, and usually, I suspect, finds them wanting.

---

1. Jürgen Moltmann, *The Crucified God: The Cross of Christ as the Foundation and Criticism of Christian Theology*, trans. by R. A. Wilson and John Bowden (London: SCM, 1974; Minneapolis: Fortress Press, 1993), 2–3.

2. Recorded in the "Newsletter/Communique" of the Canadian Theological Society (Spring 1995), 3.

Besides, I had always the companionship of my colleagues in the Faculty of Religious Studies of McGill University, from which, after twenty very good years, I have just retired—after a manner of speaking!

Also, my revered teachers—Reinhold Niebuhr, Paul Tillich, Wilhelm Pauck, Paul Scherer, Samuel Terrien, James Muilenberg, Robert McAfee Brown, J. Christiaan Beker, and many others—have never been far from me, as the many references to them in these volumes attest. To one of them recently deceased, John Coleman Bennett, along with another friend "of blessed memory," George P. Grant, I owe more than I can say.

Moreover, among my contemporaries in the academic disciplines of Christian theology there are more persons than I have perhaps suggested here and there in this book who share my strong feeling that professional theologians have a primary responsibility to *the church*. To five such persons, all friends of long standing, four of them companions since my student days at Union Theological Seminary, I have dedicated this volume.

Above all, there is Rhoda, without whom, despite all of the above, this would still have been a lonely work—without whom, in fact, it would not have been! This week I received a long letter from a young Francophone theologian in the University of Sherbrooke who said it all, really. In thanking me for "'your' theological work," he immediately qualified himself: "I say 'your,' but I am getting a little uneasy speaking of 'your' writings, understanding how much of a teamwork, a 'co-generation,' it is with Rhoda."

DOUGLAS JOHN HALL

Notre-Dame-de-Grâce,
Montréal, Québec

INTRODUCTION TO VOLUME THREE
Confessing the Faith

1. "Theology Matters"

This is the third and final volume of a series whose main intention has been to consider the whole substance of the Christian faith from the perspective of "a North American context." Two observations need to be made concerning this phrase from the common subtitle of the three books.

First, about contextuality. Since I began to use this term more than twenty years ago, it has become something of a cliché. Theologians are (or should be) very skeptical about such terms. Chances are that when they are widely used, they are used indiscriminately. They acquire a reputation for correctness among this or that segment of the community, and when that happens they no longer *connote* anything in particular, but only *denote* (for those "in the know") some vague feeling of approval.

For that reason, I have sometimes considered dispensing with the term "context" altogether; but it is such an important term that I could not bring myself to do so. Instead, I would urge the reader of this third volume to reread, in the light of the overuse and misuse of the term, what I wrote about it in detail in the first volume, *Thinking the Faith.* Like all other theological language, this term is not without its dangers; so I would ask the reader to consider that part of the discussion in that volume as well.[1]

---

1. *Thinking the Faith: Christian Theology in a North American Context* (Minneapolis: Fortress Press, 1991), chap. 1, §4, 110–26. See also my article "Contextual Theology" in the *Dictionary of Ethics, Theology, and Society,* ed. Robert Potts (London: Routledge, forthcoming, 1996).

It would also be salutary for anyone wishing to understand the meaning of contextuality in some depth to reflect on the following paragraph written by one of America's most seminal Christian thinkers, the late Joseph Sittler:

> We have been given, then, a Professor of Christian Theology. The poor man, unless he be a hod-carrier for a closed tradition or have a human soul carved of alabaster, will be alive and responsible to a double vocation: A vocation to work at the task of Christian Theology, and a vocation to citizenship in the twentieth century. The first vocation binds him to history, history in general and ecclesiastical history in particular. In obedience to this first vocation he must always look back and look down with responsibility, with gratitude, and in complete teachableness. In obedience to his second vocation (and this vocation is from God, too—for he was born a man on earth before he was called to a professorship on a theological faculty), he must look his day full in the face, participate in the joyous thud of ideas in collision, listen to its multiple voices, become creature of its vitalities and torments. But as a man of this day he cannot avoid coming to terms with the fact that what he has to communicate is so radically strange to the symbolical mentality of his time that he can scarce find hooks to hang it on, allusions to convey it with, or a matrix of association to bear it forth.[2]

The second observation, which is necessitated by a misreading of the subtitle on the part of some who may not have paid close enough attention to the text, has to do with the article in the phrase "a North American context." That I chose the *indefinite* article for the subtitle of all three volumes is by no means incidental. Had I set out to write a theology in dialogue with "the" North American context, I should have encountered from the start an obvious problem: Is there any such thing as "the North American context"? Is not the North American continent so diverse an entity that it defies *any* attempt, even the topological, at seeing it whole? Especially if one considers what lies south of the Rio Grande to be unqualifiedly part of North America in anything but geographic terms, one is confronted by historical and cultural differences that render any such unitary consideration impossible. Even excluding Mexico, the Central American states, and the Caribbean, however, there are distinctive contexts within the great land mass occupied by the United States and Canada, and to fashion a theology that addressed all of

---

2. "A Theology for Earth," in *The Christian Scholar* 37 (September 1954): 368. [Author's note: In this as in other direct quotations, I shall not attempt to alter the language to conform to the more sensitive and inclusive latter-day style. Those who knew Joseph Sittler (and this would be true of most of the other earlier authors I shall quote in this work) will realize that he would have been the first one to realize and correct the exclusivist tones such statements now bear for us.]

these contexts adequately and equally would be to court multiplicity verging on chaos.

Quite consciously, from the beginning, therefore, it has been my aim to speak out of, and to, "*a* North American context." But as the particular segment of our society to which this indefinite article refers is—historically, culturally, cultically, and in terms of its internal and external influence— more than just a segment among segments; as it encompasses a foundational culture[3] whose imprint is still clearly dominant in this society, the discussion throughout these volumes necessarily assumes a mode more expansive than would have been the case had I wished to address a less prominent aspect of our total continental context, for example, that of French Canada, or Hispanic America, or the Indigenous (First) Peoples, or the African American context. For good or ill, the cultural ingredient in this great admixture of peoples that has provided the matrix for its life is one that took shape chiefly in northern Europe and was deeply influenced by Protestantism—a statement that is largely true also of the Roman Catholicism that established itself in North America (as distinct from Catholicism of Latin America), for it was a Catholicism that had itself been altered by "the Protestant Revolt."[4] We have become a multicultural and religiously pluralistic society in recent decades; but until the present, although its dominance is now seriously challenged, the generative source of both American and Canadian societies has been and is the cultural, linguistic, organizational, religious, and general civilizational ethos emanating from Europe in its post-Reformation phase. That most of us still regard English as our principal if not exclusive language of discourse and commerce; that we organize our institutions of government, education, business, and social service along lines that reflect the pursuits of the European Renaissance and Enlightenment; that we combine corporate and individual rights and responsibilities in the way that we do, a way quite

---

3. See *Professing the Faith: Christian Theology in a North American Context* (Minneapolis: Fortress Press, 1993), 476.

4. This does not account, of course, for *contemporary* Catholicism, which has been affected by immigration from non-European sources. The fact that the latter segment is recent, however, makes it less weighty a factor in the present considerations. As a Catholic author recently has written, "the Roman Catholic community in the United States is still in some sense an immigrant church. After all the years of assimilation, there is still a sense of being guests in a host culture. Although the vast majority of Roman Catholics are second-, third-, or even fourth-generation immigrants, nonetheless that memory still pervades the mindset of most Americans who are Roman Catholics. The Hispanic population in this country is predicted to comprise about half of all Roman Catholics by the year 2000. However much the Irish and German of the middle of the nineteenth century may have assimilated to American culture, there is still a significant segment of the Roman Catholic population that perceives itself as recent arrivals on these shores." (T. Howland Sanks, *Salt, Leaven and Light: The Community Called Church* [New York: Crossroad, 1992], 12–13).

3

different from societies untouched by developments in Modern Europe; that, religious plurality notwithstanding, Christianity remains decisive for us even in its reduced and secularized contemporary expressions: all such observations demonstrate the extent to which our whole "New World" civilization presupposes the foundational impact of European Christendom in its stormy entrance into the modern epoch. Whether we adhere to a "melting-pot" conception of society, as U.S. Americans have done, or prefer considering ourselves a "patchwork quilt" or "vertical mosaic," as Canadians have preferred to do, neither of the two larger nations of the North American continent is explicable apart from the history of Europe, and explicitly of Europe as the flagship of Christendom at a decisive moment in the course of Christendom's evolution. The specific "context" that has exercised our attention in this trilogy, then, while it is by no means inclusive of *the whole* of what North America means or could mean, is one whose influence *within* the whole has been decisive. Even if its hegemony is now in the process of being challenged and changed, perhaps drastically, the three or four hundred years during which it has been dominant cannot be overlooked. Any possible alteration in the profile of this civilization would have to be a change in what *has been.*

Such a generalization is sometimes the stuff of which ethnocentric and even racist theories are made. But that can occur only where the character of this dominant ingredient in our society is regarded in an exaggeratedly positive light. Readers of these three volumes will agree, I trust, that such a perspective has not characterized this work. I am quite ready to believe and argue that great benefits have come to us, as a people, out of that particular European past—goods that the descendants neither of earlier nor of later immigrants to these shores would be willing to forfeit. But it belongs to Christian realism, and particularly to that Protestant critical vigilance that Paul Tillich named "the Protestant principle," to be wary of any tendency to elevate proximate achievements of the human species to positions of ultimacy. The European heritage that is our foundation is, like all human endeavours, a subtle mixture of good and evil; and the good, which in this case has seemed deceptively positive, is—here too—inseparable from the evil. Like the biblical wheat and tares growing up together (Matt. 13:24ff.), in the earlier stages of the growth of a culture, it is difficult to distinguish what is truly beneficial from what detracts and is dangerous. Some of the "tares" sown by Reformation and post-Reformation movements in Europe have only become visible as such in the later phases of their growth; and what is shocking to many of us is that they are so thoroughly intertwined with "the wheat"—for instance, that our vision of ourselves as masters of our natural environment, a vision that has undoubtedly given us much of what we con-

4

sider good, has issued finally in threats to planetary survival so profound that they may cancel out every other positive achievement of our civilization.[5]

Christianity as it has come to us and shaped us is thoroughly involved with this whole ambiguous side of our heritage. At the heart of the Christian dimension of the *problematique* of our European heritage is an unresolved paradox verging on contradiction. The Christianity that travelled to these shores with European adventurers, merchants, soldiers, missionaries, and settlers was a Christianity that had glimpsed, but not dealt with, the discrepancy between the imperial religion, Christendom, that had established itself in Europe from the fourth century onwards, and the original disciple community that, through the influence of reforming persons and movements over the space of two centuries, had become for many the very criterion of Christian authenticity.[6] The *sola scriptura*, although rightly described as the formal or methodological, as distinct from material and substantive, principle of the Reformation, was the medium of a niggling suggestion, introduced into Christian self-consciousness like a "thought that wounds from behind" (Kierkegaard), that Christianity as a triumphant, conquering religion, the cultic foundation of a militant and imperial civilization, might be fundamentally flawed, even a gross misunderstanding. If the Bible were to be adhered to, not only as normative for the meaning of gospel but also for its description of the community formed by and confessing the gospel, then could one justify the existence of . . . Christendom?

This disturbing theological insight, augmented by the experience of many whose flight to the New World was precisely a flight from a militant Christendom grown fierce and unforgiving under challenge, has lingered in the background of North American Christian history from its beginnings. But it has lingered as an unresolved dilemma, and one that for most of our history has not even been acknowledged openly. It has prevented Christians in both the United States and Canada from embracing European patterns of legal establishment, or sustaining them for any length of time. Yet it has not achieved sufficient critical prominence to discourage us from attempting, also on these shores, a type of Christianity victorious over and often contemptuous of all possible alternatives.

---

5. A film like the recent *Jefferson in Paris* graphically illustrates another aspect of the same point in its subtle combination of its subject's Enlightenment reasonableness with his unquestioning "use" of African American persons.

6. The most impressive "glimpse" of this discrepancy was of course vouchsafed to those who emanated from the Reformation's "Left" or radical wing. Their early history on this continent, however, demonstrates the truth of the generalization that this "glimpse" was "not dealt with." The attempt to perpetuate Christendom on these shores was only a variation on the European theme. (See "Dissent from Puritanism," in *Christianity: A Social and Cultural History*, ed. Howard Clark Kee et al. [New York: Macmillan, 1991], 616–18.)

Heretofore, the assumption of Christians that their faith would dominate as a matter of course, the vaunted separation of church and state notwithstanding, has been permitted because the Christian faith has been, in fact, the numerically and culturally dominant religion. But with the present century's turn to secularism and with the post–World War II advent of multiculturalism and religious pluralism, this situation has been changing visibly. One could say that now the newer Testamental situation, with Christianity as one of many faith-alternatives, has become our situation. The Reformers taught us to look upon the biblical description of gospel and church as normative; but only now has the sociology of our context sufficiently duplicated that of the newer Testament *koinonia* to enable us to achieve a better awareness of what is really involved in such a norm.

Among other things, two implications of what that norm entails are vital for the present study. First, in the pre-Constantinian situation, the Christian community was dependent upon Christian confession of the faith. What nurtured and sustained the church from Pentecost to the second decade of the fourth century was not an automatic and predictable translation of each new cohort of human beings into the Christian fold, but rather the decisions of individual persons to believe and follow the One whom they heard Christians confessing. In the pre-Constantinian situation, confessing the faith was an aspect of every Christian life. And this, I submit, is what now pertains also to us as we enter the post-Constantinian era.

In this situation, there is also another way in which we find ourselves mirroring the first three centuries of the church's history. Our identity as Christians is no longer given us, or preserved for us, by external agencies. Throughout the long history of Christendom, the definition of Christianity was, if not determined, then at least carefully guarded by the social and political forces that had adopted this cult as their own. The very first significant act of the Emperor Constantine, after he had given preference to Christianity politically, was to ensure that Christians were coerced into agreement concerning the principal focus of their belief, that is, what they believed concerning the nature of the deity (Nicaea, 325 C.E.). Prior to its adoption by the empire, Christianity had no such external guarantor of its identity and its unity. During the first centuries, all kinds of beliefs, systems, and forms of spirituality existed within the Christian movement. The church survived utter fragmentation narrowly and (so far as *human* agency is concerned) only because clear-thinking and responsible theologians such as Justin, Irenaeus, and Tertullian helped it to distinguish continuity with the Jesus-tradition from radical innovation, and to discern the practical consequences of heterodox theories.

In real if not always apparent ways, we are again placed in this same situation. Already we are conscious of innumerable voices insisting that what they stand for is Christianity, or that Christianity must be made conformable to this or that sociological "given." And there is absolutely no state or legal machinery, nor even strong cultural conventions, that will step in and cause Christians to clarify, purify, and unify their faith. Moreover, in Protestantism, there is no authoritative structure, such as the Roman Catholic *magisterium,* to distinguish "sound teaching" from its erosion or neglect. Only internally and in a fully participatory way can such refining and integrating work occur.

What this means concretely is that theology, which throughout most of its history the church has regarded as the rarified occupation of a small minority of scholars, is now once more the responsibility of the whole church, and is the only way Christianity will be preserved from such a chaos of meanings that it will eventually disintegrate. Theology—that is, disciplined rethinking of the faith in the light of contextual realities—will from now on be the condition without which the Christian community in North America, especially in its "mainline" Protestant expression, will sooner or later (and probably sooner) prove incapable of confessing the faith. In the words of a recent document of the Presbyterian Church (U.S.A.), "theology matters."[7]

Accordingly, the purpose of these volumes as a whole, and of this final volume in particular, is to help the churches and all serious Christians in North America to discern what is entailed in confessing the faith.

2. What Does It Mean to "Confess" the Faith?

In the English language, which is famous for fine distinctions that some praise as being wonderfully nuanced and others lament as the source of perennial confusion and misunderstanding, the verb "to confess" conjures up a bewildering variety of meanings. *The Oxford English Dictionary* offers no fewer than ten definitions. At least in popular usage, both secular and ecclesiastical, confession especially connotes the acknowledgment of wrongdoing: criminals confess their crimes, sinners their sins. It is no doubt bewildering that the same term Christians use to describe the frank admission of their human distortedness and alienation is also employed by them to describe what they are doing when they are most obedient to their calling.

If, however, we ask what, at bottom, is occurring in the act of confession, whether it means confessing what is wrong with one or what one believes to be right, we may easily perceive the common assumption of both. For both refer to the articulation of truth—or at least what one who "confesses" be-

---

7. Presbyterian Church USA, *The Minutes of the 206th General Assembly* (1994), Part I, pp. 87–91.

lieves to be true. To confess something is to own, avow, declare, reveal, or disclose what in the depths of the soul one considers truly to be the case.

It is not incidental either for etymological or theological discussion that this term implies the disclosure of something that, apart from the act it denotes, is in some vital sense *hidden*. The act of confession is not extraneous to the reality that is confessed. Until the criminal *confesses* his or her crime, "the *whole* truth" (to adopt the language of the courts) is witheld from all concerned. Until the sinner *confesses* his or her sin, the truth of the sin is incomplete, for the recognition of sin's reality on the part of the sinner is an indispensable dimension of the reality itself. The confession of a crime does not *establish* the crime, any more than does the open confession of sin *constitute* the sin; but until both are *owned* by their perpetrators, an entire dimension of their truth is missing.

This connotation of the word "confession" is particularly important for our deployment of that term in the present volume. Confession of "the faith," like the confession of sin, far from being incidental to the truth that the disciple community confesses, is itself an indispensable dimension of that truth. For the truth that faith confesses is always in some profound sense *hidden* apart from its disclosure to and by the confessing community of discipleship. It is hidden not only from the world at large, but also from the disciple community itself, which must always rediscover that truth as it manifests itself under the ever-changing circumstances of its historical sojourn.

Let us be quite clear: we are not claiming that it is the church's confession of the faith that *effects* the truth of what is confessed. Such a concept would be self-defeating. One could not take seriously anything whose truth one considered to be dependent upon one's personal recognition and articulation of it. The "I believe" [*credo*] of the historic confessions should be heard as affirming: "I believe this to be so, and I believe that it would be so even if I did not believe it were so!" Yet the confession of belief is by no means irrelevant to the reality thus testified to. For until this reality is received and appropriated, it has not yet attained its own internal aim and fullness.

Consider the Petrine confession (Matt. 16:16) that is historically and paradigmatically decisive for any discussion of this topic. To be sure, Jesus, according to the scriptures, was among his contemporaries and followers for a considerable length of time before anyone recognized him for what he was. Peter's confession at Caesaraea Philippi did not *make* him "the Christ"! Yet the church could only be "founded" and the purposes of God in Jesus could only begin to be effective when such a recognition occurred. Confessing the faith, while itself an act utterly dependent upon the "event" that precedes it, is nevertheless in "the economy of God" an integral dimension of that same truth. It is that serious a matter.

But what exactly does "confessing the faith" mean? Is one confessing the faith when one lists the various items of doctrine that one believes to be true? Is a congregation confessing the faith when it rises to recite the Apostles' or the Nicene Creed, or some more contemporary expression of belief? Are ministers confessing the faith when they preach their sermons, or theologians when they write their books and deliver their lectures? In all such instances, I think, most of us would only want to answer, "Perhaps." But why would we hesitate in that way?

We would hesitate because, in order to answer more definitively, we should have to know more about the total situation. One can imagine situations in which the simple recitation of the Apostles' Creed might be an act of genuine confession of the faith. Possibly that creed, or the Old Roman Creed from which it stems, originated under such circumstances. By itself, however, the recitation of any statement of belief does not necessarily constitute a confession of the faith—*even if it is an admirable statement, made with great sincerity.* If anything is to be regarded as confessional, it is not only the internal condition of the *confessor* that must be considered (for example, the question of sincerity) but also the external circumstances in which the act is undertaken. A devout person may be persuaded that he is confessing the faith when he stands on the street corner displaying some unquestionably Christian slogan—"Jesus is Lord!" or "God will judge!" But if, as it happens in most of our secular cities, there is a certain socio-psychic immunity to all such "fanatical" declarations, the likelihood of this being a matter of confession is slim.

This does not imply that confession is genuine only if it is received as such by the world. It does illustrate, however, something that must be taken seriously by the confessing community as it considers the nature of its witness: namely, that it belongs to the act of faith's confession that it wants to be heard by those round about. The confessing community desires to "disclose" the truth that has been vouchsafed to it, and to do so for the sake of *all* for whom this truth is intended.[8] In contrast, therefore, to gnosticism of

---

8. "It makes sense for Christian affirmations to have their truth tested in the public arena, for the Christian tradition affirms that God is at work in the *world*. It is there that the dramatic work of the triune God, which leads from creation to consummation through the unfolding of a covenantal vision of humanity, takes place. The test of the truth of Christian doctrine is that it should order the community of faith to participate insightfully and energetically in the *phronesis* of the *polis,* the 'fear and trembling' through which this divine dynamism works itself out in the search for justice and peace, and for the integrity of the creation itself. Doctrine participates in truth not only through its regulative function within the churches, but also by ordering the churches' instigative, shaping, interpretive work in the arena of human life." (Lewis S. Mudge, *The Sense of a People: Toward a Church for the Human Future* [Philadelphia: Trinity Press International, 1992], 210.)

every type, ancient and modern, Christian confession implies *worldly* witness, *public* testimony. Although it originates in the intimacy of the disciple community's relationship with God, it is intended for God's *whole* people; and therefore "'What I tell you in the dark, utter in the light; and what you hear whispered, proclaim upon the housetops'" (Matt. 10:27). Confession of faith is of the essence of the church, not only because Christians "cannot but speak of what we have seen and heard" (Acts 4:20), but because the Word of God is intended for "all."[9] And therefore the impulse to confess the faith is evoked not merely by theological and doxological but also by evangelical motivation; that is, confessing the faith is a matter of external, worldly *engagement* and not simply an internal compulsion of the believing community. The world may, of course, reject the disciple community's confession; and from both the biblical and the historical record of the "people of God," we may even conclude that rejection is the *characteristic* response of the world to the truth that faith intends to confess. But the point is that, in formulating its confession, the disciple community is under obligation to do so in such a way that its witness actually addresses its worldly setting, and not peripherally but at the heart of the matter—"the little point where the battle rages" (Luther).

Stated differently, confessing the faith is the quintessentially *contextual* task of the disciple community. In the first volume of this series, we demonstrated the thesis that "thinking the faith" is always contextual thinking, even when it seems not to be, even when it *intends* not to be! In the second volume, we recognized the importance of contexts in the formulation of the foundational doctrines of Christian "profession": every aspect of our received tradition manifests the manner in which specific historical conditions have shaped the evolving doctrine of Christendom.[10] For that reason, in order intelligently and faithfully to profess the faith today, we must distinguish the kernel of its essence from the husks of its cultural accretions, and rethink the former in relation to the particularities of our own situation. Our entire project is premised on the belief that recognition of the contextual dimension of Christian theology is vital to theological authenticity, and that its neglect in North American Christianity has fostered a kind of wooden and predictable religiosity which, whether in liberal or conservative dress, inhibits lively intercourse between church and society and robs Christian people of the intellectual and spiritual ferment that belongs to the best traditions of Christian

---

9. See Karl Barth's splendid sermon by this title—"All!"—in *Deliverance to the Captives,* trans. M. Wieser (London: SCM, 1959). The scriptural text for this sermon is Rom. 11:32: "For God has made all humans prisoners, that he may have mercy on all."

10. Lewis Mudge speaks of the "fateful choices by the early church of principles of institutional continuity inappropriate to its nature [which] must at last be confronted" (*The Sense of a People,* 69).

faith and discourse. From beginning to end, Christianity is a contextually sensitive faith.

But when we turn to the subject matter of this third volume we find ourselves at the root and core of this generalization. For to "confess the faith" means to have arrived at the place at which all reflection and forethought and planning and communal debate have given way to the thing that must be done; where words and deeds—words that *are* deeds; deeds that *are* words!—must and can be undertaken. (Anticipating the sixth chapter of this book, we might say, the place at which theology and ethics are simply one.) Everything else has been leading up to this. In its *thinking* of the faith, the disciple community has known from the first that it could not abide in the house of thought; that it would have to go out into the marketplace and *perform* the thought. In its *profession* of the faith, the community has understood throughout that it could not carry the whole vast system of Christian doctrine with it into the marketplace; that it would have to condense all this, to discover in its ruminations upon the *whole* of its belief the quite explicit message that was made mandatory by the here and now. Confessing the faith does not mean saying *everything*. It means "saying"—whether with words, or deeds, or sighs too deep for either—the one thing that *needs* to be said, then and there. That is why it represents a certain misappropriation of the tradition when congregational recitations of creeds, however hallowed by time, are labelled "confessions of faith"; they are in reality summaries of what Christians *profess*. No community of Christians ever arrives at the place of *confession* apart from an ongoing and disciplined struggle to comprehend the whole substance of what Christians *profess*. But when faith's profession is substituted for confession, the means have assumed the position of the end, and saying "everything" has become, in all likelihood, an excuse for saying nothing in particular.

But how shall the disciple community determine "the one thing that needs to be said, then and there"? To answer *that* question, we should have to subject our minds to every aspect of Christian thought and life—including the discussion of the previous two volumes in this trilogy; for such a "How?" necessarily leads the earnest inquirer into the whole life of Christ's discipleship. One important clue to the determination of obedient confession of the faith, however, is surely that it is necessarily related always to what the disciple community perceives as the most salient *danger* confronting the worldly context for which it has responsibility as steward of "the mysteries of God" (1 Cor. 4:1). The "good news" (gospel) is formed over against and in response to the "bad news" of the historical moment.

Anticipating this, when making the distinction between profession and confession in the previous volume, we stated that "We confess the faith when, through the process of contemplating our world in the light of that whole

11

heritage of meditation [that is, what Christians *profess*], *we are thrust into an active engagement with that which threatens the life of our world.*"[11] The precise wording of this sentence should be noted. At least three important claims are implicit: (1) The Christian community must be occupied with the biblical and doctrinal substance of its faith because this is its window on the world, the intellectual-spiritual perspective from which it "discerns the signs of the times" (Luke 12:56). (2) This professional contemplation of the world, when it is serious (and therefore not just "professional") *thrusts* the disciple community into an *active engagement* with the world; that is, far from providing a once-remove from history, the right profession of the faith already serves, on the contrary, to push the no doubt reluctant church ever more insistently into the actual life of the world. (3) In particular, such contemplation creates in the disciple community a vigilance for whatever *threatens the world's life.*

These claims, and notably the last one, should dispel once and for all a suspicion that may well lurk in the minds of some readers, namely that when we announce that we are going to discuss "confessing the faith," we mean to describe the ways in which the church may and should defend *itself* against whatever threatens it. That such a suspicion should exist is not surprising, for Christendom has seen to it that faith's "confession" has for centuries been associated with the defense of the church against all attacks from within and without. Church history is replete with tales of those who "confessed the faith," often to the point of martyrdom, by protecting Christ's true church against every manner of worldly insult and internal heresy. Henry the Eighth of England was awarded the distinction *Defensor fidei* by a grateful Pontiff who applauded the king's confession of the truth of there being seven sacraments over against the Lutheran insistence upon two only. (Incidentally, later, when the mercurial Henry was courting the favour of the Lutherans, he found it convenient to reduce the number of sacraments to three.)

We do not have to deny that the confession of faith may sometimes include the defense of the church, but we must certainly not allow ecclesiastical self-defense to become normative in this work. Such a conception of Christian confession belongs to Christendom, that is, to the triumphant church of the ages, which competed with the world and every worldly power, power against power, sword against sword, for preeminence. There is something incongruous about a church that is bent upon defending *itself.* For the "Head" of this "body" did not do so, and he forbade that impulsive apostle whom he named "the Rock" to use the sword even in his defense (Luke 22:51). Even on the cross, according to the record, Jesus was more concerned for his friends ("Woman, behold thy Son!"), his fellow-sufferers ("This day you will be with

---

11. *Professing the Faith,* 2.

me in paradise"), and his enemies ("Forgive them, for they know not what they do") than for himself. A church whose confession of faith is directed against worldly unbelief and scorn and toward its own self-preservation in the face of every threat is judged unworthy of this Example, who is more than example.

Not its own preservation but the preservation of *life*: this is the object of the disciple-community's confession of faith. Its discipleship is bound up with the *life*-commitment of the one whom it follows, who came "that they might have life" (John 10:10). Therefore it is vigilant for "that which threatens the life *of the world*"; and its confession, like the spear of St. George, is directed toward the "dragon" that is consuming the life-process, the élan and creaturely will-to-be, to the end that the creation-project of God may continue, and rejoice, and be fulfilled.

If now we attempted to *exemplify* Christian confession thus understood, there is one modern instance in particular to which every knowledgeable reader would want to direct us: Barmen. At Barmen-Wuppertal, in May of the year 1934, the so-called *Bekennende Kirche,* or "confessing synod" of the German Protestant church, issued an *Erklärung* ("Declaration") that is not only historically memorable but theologically instructive. For in relatively few words it did precisely what, as we have expressed it above, the act of confession must always do: first, it contemplated the received tradition with enough commitment and imagination to know that it could not remain at the professional level of detached reflection; second, it identified precisely[12] that which was threatening the life of the world—and this despite the fact that in 1934 few in Germany, including Christians, regarded the program of the Nazi Party as a worldly threat; and third, it thrust the "confessors" themselves into an active struggle against the evil thus named—even though, as

---

12. In the light of subsequent revelations, some have observed that Barmen's identification of "the bad news" was not precise enough, for it does not mention the Jews. I sympathize with this judgment, and therefore do not wish to become "romantic" about Barmen. Nonetheless, it is a remarkable model of Christian confession, and even this notorious omission may be instructive for future confessors of the faith.

The article by Victoria J. Barnett titled "Transcending Barmen: Confessing in Word and Deed" (*The Christian Century* 111, no. 16 [May 11, 1994], 495–98) states the matter well: "Barmen was not an inclusive statement. For those who took it most seriously, it was a very exclusive one. In May 1934 there was one issue that had personally affected all those present at Barmen: Nazism's ideologization of public life and private belief. The Barmen Declaration declared the church free from the demands of any ideology. In the midst of an ideological state that had turned conventional ideas of good and evil upside down, Barmen announced that not all theological views were welcome within the church. It stated further that there would always be a limit to Christian allegiance to any worldly authority. Christians could serve only one Lord, and that could not be a Nazi *Führer.*" It is for this reason, Barnett notes, that "it has been possible for Christians in such diverse circumstances as South Korea, the former East Germany, South Africa and Brazil to find significance in the words of the Barmen confession."

13

many have since observed, they did not "follow through" as faithfully as they might have done.[13]

It is especially important in this connection to recognize the centrality of the so-called *damnamus* [condeming clause] in the form of the Barmen Declaration. Each *positive* "article" (that is, each implicit "We believe . . .") of the *Erklärung* is followed by a consequent *negation*: "We reject . . . ." Thus the first and best-known article states:

> [We believe that] Jesus Christ, as he is attested for us in Holy Scripture, is the one Word of God which we have to hear and which we have to trust and obey in life and in death. . . .
> *We reject* the false doctrine, as though the Church could and would have to acknowledge as a source of its proclamation, apart from and besides this one Word of God, still other events and powers, figures and truths, as God's revelation.[14]

The *damnamus* ("We reject") is highly significant because it identifies concretely the nature of the threat—in this case, a political ideology setting itself forth as emanating from what its propagandists considered the very life-sources of a people (*Blut und Boden*—blood and soil), and claiming the kind of ultimacy and loyalty that, for Christians, only the transcendent Source of life, God, can require of human beings. If the "rejections" are eliminated from the Barmen Declaration, the confession is robbed of its *specificity*, that is, of its contextual pertinence. It becomes yet another rather pious and even perhaps innocuous Christian statement that—like the streetcorner evangelist with his sign that "Jesus is Lord!"—can without pain or even notice be absorbed into the general unconscious of the passers-by. Those whose faith is perceptive enough to know that Jesus' sovereignty ("Lordship") indeed implies a polemic against every other claim to ultimate sovereignty *may* deduce from that affirmation that they are to be on guard against idolatry (Nazism, in the case of Barmen); but such perspicacity cannot even be counted on within the churches, and outside them there are no existing links between the "religious" affirmation "Jesus is Lord," or "Jesus is . . . the one Word of

---

13. Including Barnett, who (rightly) concludes her article with this "instructive" statement: "The grace of history comes only to those who are willing to assume the burden of remembering Barmen in the context of Auschwitz." Ibid., 498.

14. Although the Barmen Declaration may be read in various sources, I recommend Arthur Cochrane's *The Church's Confession under Hitler* (Philadelphia: Westminster Press, 1962), which not only reproduces the Declaration in a good translation, with notes (Appendix VII, 237ff.), but also presents other relevant contemporary documents, including those of Nazi-sympathizing ecclesiasts calling themselves "Die Deutsche Christen," and sets them all within a lucid historical and theological discussion.

God," and the ethical imperative, "Be vigilant against tyranny and all pretentions to finality!" It is indeed probable that, had all the "rejections" been deleted from the Barmen Declaration, nearly everyone in Germany would have been able to endorse it, including the so-called *Deutsche Christen* [German Christian Movement], an organization sympathetic to Nazi goals.[15] As we have frequently had occasion to notice, in theological work the statement of the negative has very often a highly positive function.[16]

The example of Barmen has not been lost on the contemporary churches here and there. Yet while the *Barmer Erklärung* is singularly instructive on account of the clarity of its designation of the "threat" in the face of which the church's confession had to be made, it is also for that same reason limited. For rarely in history is it possible to be quite so clear about the "threat to the world's life." At least in reterospect, Hitler's program represents an almost classical threat—perhaps, as the late John Coleman Bennett used to say, it was the closest history has *ever* come to naked exposure to the demonic. Usually, evil is more ambiguous. For by far the majority of Christians in Germany in the 1930s, the evil represented by National Socialism was itself ambiguous, if not altogether submerged beneath an impressive number of "goods." Sometimes one has the impression that theologians and others who have been most influenced by the theologies that grew out of that particular historical cauldron are so thoroughly conditioned by the Barmen paradigm that they are always looking about for repetitions of that kind of "threat"; and often they are more than willing to turn far more complex phenomena (like Marxism or capitalism) into occasions for coming forward with another Barmen.

The characteristic *Sitz im Leben* of the disciple community, however, is that it is set down in the midst of bewildering social complexity. The demonic does not come with labels. Here too, the wheat and the weeds grow up together (Matt. 13:24f.). Evil frequently masquerades as great good—and, rather consistently, really *does* bring much that is beneficial and life-enhancing. Often the good that is ushered in by movements or systems that are ultimately dangerous is more conspicuous than their evil. Advanced technology, which has rendered countless human beings "permanently unemployable"[17] and may conceivably rob the human race of its "freedom and

---

15. "The Guiding Principles of the Faith Movement of the 'German Christians,' June 6, 1932" also warrants careful study by anyone considering the nature of Christian confession. Arthur Cochrane reproduces this in English in the aforementioned work, 222–23.

16. For a more complete discussion of this, see my essay, "Barmen: Lesson in Theology," in the *Toronto Journal of Theology* 1, no. 2 (Fall 1985): 180–99.

17. See Wendell Berry, *What Are People For?* (San Francisco: North Point Press, 1990), 123ff.

dignity" (B. F. Skinner) altogether, is perceived by an overwhelming majority of the planet's human inhabitants, including most Christians, as great and unquestionable good. The various ideologies that have grown out of the human rights consciousness of late modernity, ideologies that in North America now dominate the entire sociopolitical scene and, in the name of justice for special-interest groups, may banish altogether the idea of government for "the *common* good," are unconditionally lauded by forward-looking people, including the avant-garde in the churches, who celebrate them as liberation from the oppression of the majority.[18] How, in the midst of such admixtures of good and evil, is it possible to identify with sufficient clarity that which threatens the life of the world, and so confess the faith in the face of it?

The difficulty of achieving such clarity in our present context cannot be overestimated. Part of the enormous frustration of serious mainstream Christians in the United States and Canada today lies just here. While religious simplism[19] indulges in easy and vociferous "confession," because it can identify the threat to life with abortion-on-demand, or rampant homosexuality and AIDS, or "atheistic humanism," or "women's liberation," and so on, more circumspect Christians lack any clear conception of "what is wrong with the world." Unable to identify and to achieve consensus on the character of the "bad news," they are equally incapable of formulating "good news" in a manner approximating worldly engagement. Thus they drift "to and fro on the misty flats," for the most part as confused as the general public.

An alternative to such drifting is to fasten upon explicit problems ("issues") and to bring to bear upon them the weight of Christian concern and testimony. We could illustrate this by reference to various recent pronouncements and actions of church bodies including the World Council of Churches, Roman Catholic bishops in Canada and the United States, or denominational councils on such subjects as unemployment, human sexuality, ecology and the relation of human to extrahuman nature, war, and so on. This activist alternative is certainly preferable to neutrality born of indecision and confusion. But these and similar ethical issues, while not devoid of confessional potential, are more appropriately viewed as *consequences* of a deeper crisis; I shall refer to some of them as such in the chapter 7, on theological ethics. The trouble with fastening upon any or all such issues as Luther's "little point where the battle is raging" is that, in reality, they are symptoms of what is "raging" *at* the source, not the source as such.[20] Moreover, the liberal churches' involvement with such matters can usually be traced to

---

18. See in this connection Jean Bethke Elshtain, *Democracy on Trial* (Toronto: House of Anansi, 1993; New York: Basic Books, 1995).

19. See *Thinking the Faith,* 228ff.

20. See ibid., chap. 1, §3.3, 107–10.

motivations broadly sociological and humanitarian more nearly than to faith-motivation and concern. There is no question that Christians must involve themselves in (for example) the struggle and work of reconciliation involved in bringing to an end racial violence; but few churches in our context provide for their members an atmosphere of discourse that helps them understand why such involvement is mandatory *for Christians.* There is a conspicuous gap between the theological and the ethical, the indicative and the imperative. Or, rather, the theological *basis* of ethics is for the most part simply absent. People in churches, like people elsewhere, if they are thrust into vital causes, are for the most part involved in these causes for reasons unrelated or tangential to "the faith." Beyond vague references to "love" and "justice" and "liberation" and similar watchwords, they are hard-pressed to see connections between the religious belief they profess and the causes they have embraced. From the perspective of eternity, they may indeed be "confessing the faith," despite their theological innocence; and certainly it is more likely that such "activists" are confessors of Jesus Christ than are those who do know their doctrine and say "Lord, Lord" but remain Christians at the "professional" level (Matt. 25). Nevertheless, the confession of faith as it is conceived and exemplified in the tradition of Jerusalem assumes a foundation of *understanding,* or at least the earnest search for it; therefore it also assumes the potentiality, if not always the actuality, of *verbal* testimony; for, proverbs to the contrary notwithstanding, deeds do not, usually, speak for themselves. "Theology matters!"

How shall the church in our still-affluent, still-*somewhat*-Christian society discover and name the threat to life which must be encountered and countered by faith? How shall we find our way through all the noise and smoke of our strange warfare to the place where "the battle rages"? In the context of Barmen, the theological and the sociopolitical had come, almost, together: in the ideology of Nazism, with its "ruthless"[21] quest for world domination and its insidious theories of race and the like, the deepest spiritual malaise of the age had achieved transparency politically. If, in contrast, we want to locate the life-threatening sickness present in our North American context, we cannot, I think, identify it straightforwardly with any of the immediately visible problems of the day. We might *begin* with such specifics as the pollution of the natural order or the oppression of minorities; and we might, finally, *focus* our confession of faith on one or more of these "contributing crises,"[22] in this way lending it the necessary concreteness; but we would not even understand these explicit crises adequately if we did not try to get be-

---

21. One of the most common words in Hitler's speeches. See Walter C. Langer, *The Mind of Adolf Hitler* (New York and Scarborough, Ontario: New American Library, 1972).

22. See *Thinking the Faith,* chap. 3, 197ff.

neath them to the subtle anxieties and deeper movements of the collective spirit that brought them to the surface in the first place.[23]

Recognition of the extreme ambiguity and complexity of our cultural context may, however, blind us to the potentialities within our own faith tradition for discernment of our society's deeper crisis. There is a tendency in the churches and theological circles of mainstream Protestantism to become so conscious of the complicated character of contemporary life that lay persons and even clergy are discouraged from the outset from trying to understand it, let alone to judge, confront, and challenge it. This hesitancy is no doubt partly a consequence of the fact that these same churches comprise mainly middle-class people—the segment of our society in many respects most conscious of our societal ambiguity and complexity, most aware of social and economic problems, most in awe of science and technology, and least inclined to be critical of a "system" that on the whole still operates to their benefit.[24] On every side we hear of the enormous intricacies of every problem that is named. Who can understand the fluctuations of the economy? Who can follow the elaborate and conflicting reports about the depletion of the ozone layer? Who can sort out the reasons for the obvious disparities between the developed and developing peoples of earth? Who can understand the labyrinthine paths of the human psyche, or even of the body? This is an age of expertise and specialization. Even the experts and the specialists disagree—and even about naming the right questions, to say nothing of answers! How can ordinary Christians imagine that they have what is needed to get to the bottom of the witches' brew? Our normative traditions date to periods in history prior not only to the computer but to modern science and technology as a whole. Dare we think that we, on the basis of these ancient sources of wisdom and under the guidance of a Deity who is perhaps as anachronistic as the traditions, are able to discern both the problem and its resolution? Is this not the height of arrogance?

Perhaps. And the prospect of its being arrogance—or simply "foolishness" (1 Cor. 1:22–25)—is also an indispensable dimension of the act of "confessing the faith." Christians should not be dismayed by such a prospect; they need worry only when they sense no such possibility and think, on the contrary, that their witness is perfectly reasonable. All the same, there are ways, under the guidance of scripture, tradition, and the divine Spirit, of cutting through the complications even of postmodernity (whatever that may

---

23. See below, chap. 7, §30.2, "In Search of Depth."
24. See *Professing the Faith,* esp. 189–90, 292–95.

be!25) to the heart of the matter; and occasionally, perhaps almost accidentally, the disciple community actually does so.

That claim could be illustrated in many ways, for even the bewildering final decades of the twentieth century have not left Jesus Christ without faithful witnesses; but for sheer simplicity (not to be confused with simplism) I know of no *verbal* confession more apt as an instance of what I am suggesting here than the so-called "Contemporary Statement of Faith" produced by my own denomination in the 1970s. For our purposes, the first line of the statement suffices: "We are not alone; we live in God's world . . ."26

In this very simple affirmation, a highly insightful disclosure of the depths from which present-day humanity cries (Ps. 131:l) is glimpsed and responded to from the side of divine grace. Precisely the threat that is most detrimental to life in our historical moment, however camouflaged by cybernetic bravado and by a confusing battery of "contributing crises," is our pervasive, fearful, and melancholy sense that *we are alone:*27 there seems nothing "out there" to correspond to our persistent longing for companionship with the eternal. In Volume Two of this series,28 we saw that human being, according to the tradition of Jerusalem, is as such *with*-being: the quest for the counterpart, as Augustine insisted, is inherent in our being itself; and while that quest reaches out to others of our own kind and to otherkind, it is "restless" for the "eternal Thou" (Buber), whom it cannot identify wholly with any creature. We *are* being-with. Yet we have come to experience ourselves as being-alone.

Our newly experienced solitude contains more than merely "religious" implications. It robs us of any abiding sense of earthly purpose; it deprives us of any sustainable conviction of a meaningful vocation and destiny. In our middle years, if we are fortunate, we conceal our gnawing impression of randomness in work; but our youth face the prospect or reality of a jobless future, and the elderly live out their "retirement" in grim recognition of their

---

25. As is frequently noted in the current literature, the definition of *post*modernity depends upon one's understanding of modernity, and even here there is no clear consensus. See in this connection Hans Küng, *Theology for the Third Millennium,* trans. Peter Heinegg (New York: Anchor Books, Doubleday, 1988), 1–11.

26. The entire statement reads: "We are not alone, we live in God's world. We believe in God, who has created and is creating, who has come in Jesus, the Word made flesh, to reconcile and make new, who works in us and others by the Spirit. We trust in God.

"We are called to be the Church: to celebrate God's presence, to love and serve others, to seek justice and resist evil, to proclaim Jesus, crucified and risen, our judge and our hope.

"In life, in death, in life beyond death, God is with us. We are not alone. Thanks be to God. Amen."

27. See *Professing the Faith,* 480.

28. Ibid., chap. 6, §24, "Being and Human Being."

superfluity. Unlike our medieval precursors, we do not find the world shot through and through with mysterious intention; we find it haphazard, dysteleological, capricious, absurd. Unlike our modern forebears, the continued mimicking of the rhetoric of progress notwithstanding, we do not feel ourselves moving inevitably toward the realization of some heaven on earth. We have been abandoned by both sacred and secular epiphanies. While we noisily demand salvation of our successive governments, we do not expect redemption from either mundane or supramundane agencies. Our secularity is no longer the self-congratulatory affair initiated by the Enlightenment; it is a cheerless thing, which looks at best for entertainment and forgetfulness on the way to oblivion.

In North America we do not say so, openly or often, but we know as profoundly as do our European cousins that "we are alone"; and our characteristic incapacity to admit precisely this only makes its reality the more effective in our lives, personally and corporately.

In *naming* the experience of radical negation as it grasps our collective psyche, then, this "Contemporary Statement of Faith" makes the threat to our life concrete enough to earn the right to affirm faith's "nevertheless": "We are *not* alone; we live in *God's* world." By itself, of course, such a minute declaration by no means constitutes an adequate confession of the faith. As with every other formal creed or doctrinal statement, one would have to know a good deal more concerning any community engaging in such a confession if one were to ascertain anything at all about its authenticity. All the same, the *direction* indicated by this brief affirmation of faith is in my opinion the right one. It is, like Barmen, instructive for our learning; and, *beyond* Barmen, it adds the touch of subtlety that is required by Christians who live in gray times, when clarity of vision is difficult to achieve.

It is that direction that I intend to follow in this third and final volume of this halting attempt to articulate the Christian faith "in a North American context." I am increasingly persuaded that what Christians in this historical moment and place are required to do is to confess *the faith,* namely, faith *in God,* as God's reality and purposing are revealed in Jesus as the Christ. In the last analysis, despite the real complexity of our civilizational predicament, it is a very *simple* thing that we are asked, as disciples of the Christ, to do: having learned from experience how impossible it is to believe in God *and* how impossible it is to live without God [*a-theos*], we may be in a position now to hear the "nevertheless" of the Gospel of the Cross.

But this most simple confession must not be reduced to simplism and sloganization. Perhaps it can never be expressed adequately in the language of doctrine and piety. And certainly, if we are to risk it, we who despite everything continue to hover about these ancient ecclesiastical structures, we shall have to become far better acquainted than we are with the wilderness of disbelief and the forsakenness of Calvary. *This* confession can only be made in the environs of Golgotha.

3. The Plan of This Volume

Like the first two volumes, this book is meant to serve a dual purpose: first, to contribute to a critical and constructive theological perspective from which especially the so-called mainline Protestant churches on this continent, which are presently experiencing varying degrees of self-doubt, may be encouraged to rethink and renew their life and mission; second, to provide a basic intro-duction to the rudiments of Christianity, considered in the light of our spe-cific context, and accessible to serious students of the faith, whether profes-sional or lay. In other words, I have intended this series both for "seasoned" Christians who are concerned about the future of the Christian movement, and for those who may be at the beginning of their theological journeys and therefore need to be introduced to foundational teachings of the tradition.

While these aims are in some ways distinct, they seem to me, under the circumstances, to be inseparable; for the churches in question can be appro-priately challenged to renewal, I believe, only by a reminder of their own profound theological foundations as these are revisited in the light of present problems and possibilities. Too much of the literature that currently intends to critique the churches provides little of a positive *theological* nature aimed at enabling the ailing and often beleaguered communities of faith that are not part of the "Christian Right" to move toward a more decisive confes-sional stance than is proffered by the worn-out Christian liberalism whose ethos, reduced to truisms and sentimentality, they still cling to in the absence of anything better. It is easy to criticize empirical Christianity; the more difficult—and more urgent—task confronting serious Christians today is to present viable alternatives to the ecclesiastical status quo. In many of my previous works, I have been deeply critical of "the churches," although I have always done so as one who believes that there are possibilities for change and for faithfulness that are being missed by Christian institutions in their present forms. Here, however, I wish to be entirely responsible as a *church theologian.* I do not consider any professional expertise that I might have acquired in the course of the past forty years to be an end in itself; it is valid only if it is devoted to the service of the disciple community. Therefore I want to set out, in as transparent a manner as possible, not only what I feel are the problems that need to be faced by Christians as we enter the third millennium of Chris-tian history, but also the rudiments of Christian doctrine with respect to the areas assigned to this third volume.

Those areas, so far as their basic subject matter is concerned, are three: the doctrine of the church, or ecclesiology; the nature of the church's calling as a confessing body, or missiology; and the character of the hope to which the being and work of the church points, or eschatology. While these three areas of traditional Christian doctrine constitute the major themes of this book, the division of the material into four parts rather than three is necessitated by the peculiar circumstances of the Christian movement in North America today—circumstances that themselves require, in my view, an explicit and detailed consideration. The four parts of the volume may be introduced briefly as follows.

Part I: The Church. Confessing the faith presupposes the existence of a *community* of confession. Throughout this series, I have employed the term "disciple community" to designate this body. In doing so, I have joined the chorus of many other Christians in our time who have found that the simple designation "church" presents difficulties for those who want to retain the fullness of meaning that that word may once have conveyed. Like so many of the "great words" of the tradition, "church" is both so familiar and so vague a term that it connotes little that is of the essence of the faith, while *de*noting, unfortunately, much that is dubious or detrimental. Obviously, like most of the conventional terms in question ("sin," "salvation," "love," "hope"—even "God"), "church" must still be employed in Christian discourse; I am therefore retaining it in the title of Part I. Unless it is qualified, explained, and supplemented by less familiar terminology, however, "church" fails to communicate what is needful, and especially at a time when great clarification is required precisely concerning this term, or rather concerning the phenomenon it signifies.[29]

---

29. This problem has been almost universally recognized. Even the avowed "church theologian" Karl Barth had difficulty with the term *Kirche*: "It would be great gain, could Luther's urgent desire have been carried out and the word 'congregation' had taken the place of the word 'Church.' Of course we may find in the word 'Church' what is good and true, since Church means *Kyriake Oikia*, the Lord's House; or, derived from *circa*, a circularly enclosed space. Both explanations are possible, but *ekklesia* certainly means congregation, a *coming together*, arising out of the summons to the national assembly which meets the call of the messenger or else the sound of the herald's trumpet" (*Dogmatics in Outline*, trans. G. T. Thomson [New York: Harper & Row, 1959], 141).

Tillich, who drew upon the Reformation's "visible" and "invisible" church in his distinction between the "latent" and the "manifest" church, also introduced the interesting concept of the "Spiritual Community" "to characterize sharply that element in the concept of the church which is called the 'body of Christ' by the New Testament and the 'church invisible or Spiritual' by the Reformation" (162). "The Spiritual Community is determined by the appearance of Jesus as the Christ, but it is not identical with the Christian churches" (*Systematic Theology*, vol. 3 [Chicago: University of Chicago Press, 1963], 152).

Throughout the previous volumes, the disciple community—a designation inspired in particular by the work of Dietrich Bonhoeffer—has been a recurrent theme. It had to be, because Christian theology is after all a quest for integrated understanding—part, as it were, of a seamless robe. But heretofore we have not considered the subject of ecclesiology in a sustained way. Certain questions belong to this subject inherently and inevitably, as well as historically, and it is the task of the first part of this study to address them. The most important questions may be stated rather straightforwardly: What makes the church the church? What is the nature of the relation between Jesus Christ and the church? Between the church and the divine Spirit? Between the church and the churches? Between church and the "kingdom" or "reign of God" (*basileia*)? How does Christianity work out the always difficult dialectic of community and individual, the group and the person? What constitutes the Christian life? And, in that connection, how should we understand such traditional teachings as justification by grace through faith, sanctification, obedience, and *koinonia* (community, fellowship)?

Again, how does this community order its corporate life? What is ministry, and how does the organization of ministry relate to the mission of this community? Is the ministry of the whole community of Christians (*laos*) prior to that of individuals explicitly "set apart"? How may we think of specific ministries within the church today?

As the final question makes particularly plain, none of these and similar problems of ecclesiology can be treated in a purely abstract or ahistorical way, and particularly not during the present period of radical transition in the life of the disciple community. In any case, it belongs to our entire approach in this series to think about every aspect of the faith contextually; therefore throughout this first part, while it will be our object to cover "the basics" of ecclesiology, we shall be reminded at every turn of the manner in which all of these conventions are affected by the particularities of our specific time and place.

In some respects, however, these very ordinary and habitual problems of ecclesiology will inevitably *beg* questions more complex than can be considered under the nomenclature of ecclesiological "basics," for the context in which they must be discussed now is one that is itself so demanding of our undivided attention that it requires separate treatment. For that reason, as already intimated, we introduce at this point a second part, designed specifically to sort out the thorny problems of ecclesiology in a time of unprecedented change.[30]

---

30. Peter Berger, in a work that will figure more materially at a later stage in our deliberations, makes the important point that ecclesiological *doctrine* often falsifies the subject, "church," by failing to combine theological and historical-sociological reflection: "Very likely it

Part II: Metamorphosis: From Christendom to Diaspora.   For perhaps two centuries, Christendom as it was created by the political marriage of "Christ and culture" (H. Richard Niebuhr) from the fourth century C.E. onward, has been breaking down. This disintegration, while visible in Europe for more than a hundred years, has been obscured in North America by the peculiar nature of the Christian "establishment" in the New World. Indeed, there are locations on this continent still, particularly in the United States, where for all intents and purposes Christendom seems fully intact.

The reality, however, is otherwise. An immense change is occurring throughout the universal church, a metamorphosis so all-encompassing that the only other transition with which it can be compared adequately is the transition from the voluntary covenant communities of the first three centuries of Christian history to the establishment of the Christian religion under the Roman emperors Constantine and Theodosius the Great. Since, especially in our context, we are ourselves in process of being changed, it is difficult to chart this long-term alteration accurately. Here, as always, hindsight is more trustworthy! Yet the great and small changes that are occurring in the shape (*morphe*) of the Christian movement are so ubiquitous that no one can avoid them unless through deliberate and sustained acts of repression.

The character of the church tomorrow will be greatly affected, if not determined, by the readiness of Christians today to enter honestly and imaginatively into the realities wrought by this "paradigm shift" (Kuhn), and to seek to give it direction and purpose. The most irresponsible attitude toward this change is the refusal to admit it and to ask about its meaning. Such a refusal is strong among many Christians and even whole denominations of the church on this continent; yet there are minorities in all branches of once-powerful Christendom that are ready to face these eventualities and to rethink the nature and purpose of the church in view of them. The aim of this part of the work is to attempt a thoughtful and compelling description of the

---

is in a doctrine of the Church that theology would be most relevant to the problem of the social establishment. By defining what the Church ought to be and already is as the body of Christ, theology can provide the criteria by which the empirical reality can be evaluated. [But] another warning might be in place here. In this matter it is very important that theological articulation be accompanied by empirical perception. If the latter is absent (a common state of affairs), it is very possible that the theological doctrine is misunderstood as a factual description—and thus, from being a criterion of judgment, the doctrine becomes an instrument of rationalization. It is not enough, in other words, to have a doctrine of the Church. One must also have a sociology of the empirically existent churches. A Christian view of our situation can then emerge from the tension between theological doctrine and sociological diagnosis. The diagnosis without the doctrine may lead to resignation, which is bad, but the doctrine without the diagnosis almost certainly leads to illusion, which is much worse" (*The Noise of Solemn Assemblies: Christian Commitment and the Religious Establishment in America* [Garden City, N.Y.: Doubleday, 1961], 131).

character of Christian establishment as it has pertained in particular in Protestant North America, and to recognize in our effective *dis*establishment opportunities for authenticity of being and mission that will escape Christians as long as they try to perpetuate the establishment phase beyond its time.

At the same time, I wish in this part of the work to consider ways in which such a metamorphosis introduces alterations, not only in the structure and purposing of the church at large but in the Christian life as it may be lived in a post-Christian, multireligious and multicultural situation today and tomorrow. How does the changed sociohistorical context of the Christian life affect such traditional teachings as justification, sanctification, the primacy of Scripture, the biblical concepts of covenant and election, and similar themes? May we not discover in these doctrinal conventions, revisited in the strong light of Christendom's "humiliation" (Albert van den Heuvel), sources of courage and meaning that were often lost, or distorted, under the conditions of our establishment?[31]

Part III: The Forms of Faith's Confession. Here we turn from reflection upon the community of confession to the confession as such. In a real sense, the Christian community does not determine how, or when, it shall confess the faith, or what it may be required quite specifically to confess. "When they bring you to trial and hand you over, do not worry beforehand about what you are to say; but say whatever is given you at the time, for it is not you who speak, but the Holy Spirit" (Mark 13:11). Confession of the faith is always *responsive*: it is response to circumstances that are not ours to command, and to the Spirit who helps us, in our weakness, to find the appropriate witness— what the prophets called "the word from the Lord."

At the same time, this pneumatic dimension of the confession of faith must not lead to ecclesiastical presumption and sloth. The circumstances under which the faith is to be confessed are not only (and not even frequently) so extreme as those the author of Mark's Gospel had in mind in writing the foregoing advice. In a genuine sense, every moment is a moment with potentiality for faith's confession, and the Christian community must be prepared at all times to "give a reason" for its hope (1 Peter 3:15).

No reader of the newer Testament (and in this it is strictly continuous with the older) could overlook the fact that, for this tradition, confession of faith strongly implies language, discourse, address, persuasion—in short, words. While Jerusalem differs from Athens in many things, it shares with that other most significant founding tradition of our civilization a high evaluation of

---

31. Readers who already have a background knowledge of the "rudiments" of ecclesiology may want to consider Part II *before* they read Part I.

speech. As the late Jacques Ellul and many other commentators on our own society have pointed out, we are a people in process of jettisoning the word in favor of "the image";[32] and there is a strong temptation amongst Christians, especially those who are highly conscious of the priorities of the secular world, to capitulate in this struggle and abandon the word. Such an abandonment, however, would have to mean the abandonment of the faith itself; for only language, which is capable of subtle distinctions as well as breaking through the barriers of sense to the soul, can do justice to truth as this tradition conceives it. In our present context, there may be no more immediately vital point of *resistance,* which is always a dimension of faith's confession, than the refusal to permit the human psyche to be seduced by images— images that, without the critical power of the word, are always "graven." Among the forms of faith's confession, then, preaching and teaching within the congregation and direct address within the public sphere (evangelism, apologetics, and so on) must be given a prominent place, the more so in view of their seriously threatened status today.

No one, however, who has familiarity with the rudiments of this faith tradition would make the mistake of considering speech *alone* sufficient for faith's confession. In the first place, speech "alone," that is, the word separated from the act, is already a truncated understanding of language; for the Bible understands the word *as act:* "And God said . . . and there was" (Gen. 1). "And the Word became flesh and dwelt among us" (John 1). "To believe in the church means to believe that God's Word continues to make itself incarnate, to embody itself, to *real*-ize itself in the life of the world."[33] More than most ancient (and modern!) literature, the Scriptures of the Jews and Christians understand and teach that words "alone" are almost always deceptive. The word drives to embodiment; and, given an adequate background of linguistic confession, the deed by itself may also "speak." Confession of the faith is therefore by no means exclusively verbal, although Christian activism can too easily conclude from such a recognition that the verbal dimension is unimportant and superficial.

Beyond confession as word and deed, we shall explore here what I am calling confession as "stance." The very positioning of the Christian community vis-à-vis (for example) the state, a particular economic class, or a particular gender, race, or power grouping frequently constitutes a confession more effective than words and deeds combined. A congregation may speak much about Christian obligation toward the poor, and it may even anchor its words

---

32. See Ellul's important work *The Humiliation of the Word,* trans. Joyce Main Hanks (Grand Rapids: Wm. B. Eerdmans, 1985).

33. Douglas John Hall, *The Reality of the Gospel and the Unreality of the Churches* (Philadelphia: Westminster Press, 1975), 125.

in charitable deeds of an impressive nature; but if its posture in society is one that approximates the possessing classes and discourages any flesh-and-blood intermingling with the poor it rhetorically honors, its confession in word and deed will be compromised by the reality of its relationships.

Because faith's confession is usually related to specific moral issues, Part III also addresses the knotty question of the relation between theology and ethics. It is my perception that a great deal that transpires under the aegis of Christian ethics today begs the question of its theological foundations. In many ways, the Christian churches *reflect* and do not *engage* their host society, particularly in the sphere of morality. As there are conservatives, liberals, and radicals morally speaking in the larger culture, so the churches produce their conservative, liberal, and radical factions, which faithfully mirror society's stands on every conceivable issue, from abortion to euthanasia. Frequently, the only justification for considering a moral stand "Christian" is located in the vaguely religious or "spiritual" language that colors a particular document or position. If this language were removed in favor of more neutral terminology, would anyone find it especially "Christian"?

While such an assessment undoubtly applies more conspicuously to the liberal and moderate Christian groups than to the Christian Right, the latter segment is usually more explicitly biblical or doctrinal in its moral strictures only because it places a much higher value on proof-texting ideas that are, in fact, common currency among the most conservative North Americans of every stripe. Only rarely does one feel that the moral analyses and counsels emanating from the deliberations of the various ecclesiastical groupings have emerged out of a fresh encounter with Scripture and foundational theology.[34] Moreover, this situation grows increasingly problematic because so much of the more refined ethical reflection required of Christians, as of other responsible citizens of today's world, demands such expertise in nontheological disciplines such as medicine, law, business, and the like that those who take up the ethical "side" of Christian scholarship are, or seem, forced to emulate the specialists of the secular world simply in order to comprehend and communicate with their contemporaries.

---

34. In North America, perhaps the most consistent exception to this generalization is the Sojourners community of Washington, D.C., which regularly addresses social and personal ethical questions from a recognizably and "originally" Christian perspective. It is not accidental that this community consciously seeks to avoid all labels and sustains an ongoing dialogue with Scripture. A "draft manifesto" of the community states: "We call ourselves and our churches back to a biblical focus that transcends the Left and the Right. . . . We call the Christian community to carefully consider each social and political issue, diligently apply the values of faith, and be willing to break out of traditional political categories. By seeking the biblical virtues of justice *and* righteousness, the Christian community could help a cynical public find new political ground" (as quoted in "Grassroots America: The Christian Right Marches On," by David Wilson, *The United Church Observer*, new series 58, no. 11 [June 1995]: 26).

But ethics are only *Christian* if and insofar as they evolve out of Christian faith and the ongoing struggle of the Christian community to translate its faith into concrete forms of confession. An ethic is not Christian just because it has reference to "justice" or "liberation" or "love." There is a Christian understanding of (for example) homosexuality only where its advocates have shown how such an understanding arises out of the whole biblical and theological reflection upon human being as created, judged, and redeemed by the God of this confession. It may not always be possible, or even desirable, to demonstrate in detail how a specific ethical preference derives from foundational assumptions of the faith; but in the long haul, an ethic, in order to commend itself to the community of faith and enable that community to serve its confessional vocation, must be perceivable as the kind of "law" that emanates from "Gospel"—an imperative that truly belongs to that particular indicative. No "ought," no matter how immediately compelling it may seem to this or that social or religious faction, can stand on its own. If it is to have any sustaining power at all, it must be grounded in an "is"; and, at least where *Christian* ethics are concerned, that "is" must be one that can be recognized by Christians as belonging in an essential way to the core of their belief.

One of the greatest problems in liberal and moderate denominations in North America today stems from the failure of ecclesiastical policy setters, whether theologians or church leaders, to help ordinary Christians to move from foundational belief to ethical decision-making. Instead, the bureaucratic leadership in most of the churches addressed in the present work, being more "radical" in their views than the general membership, policies and attitudes are simply put forward as "Christian," and people in the pews are expected to assent. Ironically, while classical Protestantism objected to medieval Catholicism because faith had come to mean assent to *doctrines* decided upon by a few, contemporary "radical" Protestantism today seems to expect "the people" to assent to *ethical* agendas determined by a few. This problem can only be corrected by deliberate attempts to think *theologically* about the pressing issues of public morality in our time, and to do so "in the congregation."

Part IV: The Reign of God and Christian Hope. Eschatology is poorly conceived when it is translated as "the doctrine of last things." Although I am therefore reluctant to offer yet another statement of Christian systematic theology that ends with eschatology, I would ask the reader to consider the doctrinal areas treated earlier, and especially those discussed in Volume Two (*Professing the Faith*), and to ascertain the extent to which the eschatological dimension is one that conditions every other aspect of this faith tradition. If, beyond that, we also turn to eschatology as our final topic of investigation, it is only to clarify and specify assumptions about being and time that have already been informative throughout these volumes.

Such clarification and specification are made particularly necessary by the fact that in our sociohistorical context there are a great many currents of opinion, including quite explicitly and avowedly "Christian" opinions, that serious theological thought must regard as questionable and in some cases truly dangerous. "Future shock"—a socio-psychic phenomenon that has bedeviled North Americans at almost every level of daily life—has among other things rekindled in many the belief that this world really is, as Dwight Moody long ago announced, "a wrecked vessel," and that hope must now be thoroughly detached from history and linked to postcreational reality. The year 2000 beckons!

Even sane and sober persons, reduced to speechlessness by the cumulative effect of the daily news, are ready to abandon this world as a sphere of meaning and an object of well-doing. Violent public acts—virtual nihilism—are justified by reference to "the End." Dispensationalism and other forms of apocalyptic consciousness experience a new exhilaration with every new indication of the impossibility of a global future.

This trilogy, from beginning to end, has contained a strong critique of utopianism, and especially of its modern North American form (the American Dream). I simply do not believe in the inevitability of progress![35] I consider such a belief not only non-Christian but an *alternative* to Christianity. Yet my work has included an equally strong—and, I hope, even stronger— theme: that God, as I understand the nature of deity in the Judeo-Christian heritage, is a God who is committed in love to the good end and consummation of creation. From the start, therefore, and continuously throughout, I have interpreted the informing theological point of view in this series—the *theologia crucis*—as being in its most rudimentary expression a theology of "divine pathos" (Heschel) and covenantal faithfulness vis-à-vis this world. *This* is "the new covenant in my blood," whose "newness" is the more truly radical and rooted because it is an unconditional reaffirmation of the oldest of divine covenants, the Noachic.

An eschatology arising from this pre-understanding—an *eschatologia crucis,* let us call it—must of necessity have a great deal to say in such a context as ours today. It will be *by itself* a confession of faith if the Christian

---

35. As he often does, Kurt Vonnegut has captured the truth about progress and success in a lovely paragraph about a certain college library: "This library is full of stories of supposed triumphs, which makes me very suspicious of it. It's misleading for people to read about great successes, since even for middle-class and upper-class white people, in my experience, failure is the norm. It is unfair to youngsters particularly to leave them wholly unprepared for monster screwups and starring roles in Keystone Kop comedies and much, much worse." (*Hocus Pocus* [New York: Berkley Books, 1990], 33.)

community learns how, in such a context, to resist, on the one hand, the false worldly optimism of the religion of progress and, on the other, the false worldly pessimism of the neo-apocalypticists. How, without embracing unrealistic beliefs that run counter to all the scientific evidence, can the confessing church in North America today hold out to the human species and to poor, confused human individuals a hope that is not calculated from the very start to disappoint us? And how can Christians do so without at the same time losing touch with the traditions of transcendence (heaven and hell, the last judgment, and so on) that are also part of the historic confession of faith?

This final discussion in our contextual rethinking of the faith will attempt to engage contemporary thought not only at the level of history and culture at large, but also at the level of personal destiny. In an age that is again ready to flirt with every manner of theory and superstition about human immortality, the Christian confession of "the resurrection of the body" is easily misinterpreted. A present danger in North American Christianity is that Christian faith will be so thoroughly bound up with *personal* survival and the afterlife that what remains of public and global consciousness in the churches will be threatened even more severely than in the past. As public life and civilization become more complex (as they undoubtedly will), all religion will be tempted to take up residence internally, in the private human sphere—one reason, I think, for using the current language of "spirituality" with caution! There is a conspicuous and admirable modesty in biblical faith where our ultimate destiny as individuals is concerned, and this modesty must be preserved in any responsible theology because, particularly in apocalyptic times, the sphere of the personal may become so interesting to the religious as to cast every other aspect of the profession of faith in Jesus Christ into the shadows.[36]

At the same time, the fates of persons—unique and unrepeatable lives—matters profoundly to this tradition, and one has to be conscious of that other trend in our society, the cult of the "good death" (euthanasia), which is not only more sinister but in many ways more to be feared than the personalism that would prolong individual life as its most sacred trust. It is hard to refrain from pietism—and, in our context, sentimental pietism at that—when addressing a subject like the journey of the self ("soul"). One has to try to walk a narrow pathway between sheer dogma and mere egoism. None of us can contemplate his or her own end or the end of those we love without intense involvement, and while some degree of involvement is mandatory in all true theology, it must nonetheless also honor the Reformation's motto: *soli Deo gloria.*

---

36. Lewis Mudge speculates that "Modern religious privatism may eventually dispense with the decaying churches altogether" (*The Sense of a People*, 60).

PART I
THE CHURCH

CHAPTER ▪ ONE

The Confessing Church

1. Confession as the Church's Mode of World-Commitment

1.1. "We Preach Not Ourselves." In *Professing the Faith*, I identified as the meditative core of Christian theology the three doctrinal areas: theology (God), creaturely being, and Christology. These three, I argued, constitute the contemplative vantage-point from which faith considers the world. Some may fault me for not including the church in that classification. Others will recognize in my decision not to do so my quintessential Protestantism, a bias for which I do not apologize. "For what we preach is not ourselves, but Jesus Christ as Lord, with ourselves as your servants for Jesus' sake" (2 Cor. 4:5). While, as the third article of the Apostles' Creed insists, the church is always a subject of belief (if any aspect of the faith is a matter of faith and not sight, ecclesiology certainly is), it is not, in my view, part of what Christians profess.[1] The church is the professor and the confessor, not that which is professed and confessed. We may even say that the church is in a certain way indispensable to the purposing of God, but only because God freely wills it to be so. There are other possibilities! There should be no cause for presump-

---

1. Indeed, in the Apostles' Creed the "in" that prefaces the article concerning the Holy Spirit "is not repeated before 'holy catholic church.' The earliest texts of the Apostles' Creed, in fact, do not mention the church at all. Peter Hodgson, in his note on this subject in *Revisioning the Church: Ecclesial Freedom in the New Paradigm* (Philadelphia: Fortress Press, 1988), 113, writes, "It appears, then, that when reference to the church was added to the creeds, the church was first viewed as an instrumentality of belief, the place where the Spirit is at work; then it was to be 'believed' . . . but not 'believed in' in the sense that God is to be 'believed in'" (Lewis Mudge, *The Sense of a People* [Philadelphia: Trinity Press International, 1992], 237, n.23).

tion here. The "wild olive shoot" (Rom. 11:17) could be pulled away, easily enough, from the gnarled old tree onto which it is grafted.

It seems to me that Christians should now begin to take this very seriously, to think about it in relation to matters such as religious pluralism, and to speak about it openly with one another. Sixteen centuries of Christendom have conditioned all of us to indulge in quite fantastic assumptions about our importance in the scheme of things. Not only have we allowed ourselves to imagine that nothing could prevail against the church as Christ's mystical body, known only to its head; we have promoted very explicit and indeed exclusive forms of the empirical church as if they were eternal and inviolable. Some of us have clung so tenaciously to the promise that the "gates of hell" could not prevail against the church that we have virtually excluded God as well as Satan from interfering with our ecclesiastical arrangements, as Dostoevsky demonstrated so unforgettably in his "The Grand Inquisitor." At least since the Constantinian-Theodosian establishment, apart from radical experiments whose radicality consists chiefly in their earnest belief in the Holy Spirit, it has been considered rebellious and heretical to attack the church, as students of the Reformation do not have to be told. One must doubt whether anything as bold as Revelation chapters 2 and 3 (the seven "letters to the churches") could have been written even by the Apostolic Fathers or the Apologists of the pre-Nicene church; as for post-Nicene Christendom, its capacity for such forthright judgment and self-criticism has been so rare that people such as John Wycliffe, Luther, Kierkegaard, and Tolstoy must be singled out by church history as notorious exceptions. Had Scripture been truly normative in the life of Christendom, should not such persons, on the contrary, always have been considered normal, faithful church leaders? Who, imbibing seriously the prophetic tradition of Israel, the apostolic outspokenness of Paul's epistles, the Baptist's cutting judgment of the overconfident ("And think not to say within yourselves, 'We have Abraham to our father'. . . " [Matt. 3:9, KJV]); or who, living daily with the recorded sayings of Jesus of Nazareth, which are by no means harmless meditations on lilies and birds, would not assume that self-criticism, and radical self-criticism at that, is of the very essence of what we call "church"?

What I shall present in these pages should in my own opinion be thought a rather "high" doctrine of the church. No doubt some will find it too high. I am able to confess with the historic creeds that I do, indeed, "believe the church." I believe, in fact, that without the church (Christ's church, which is not simply to be *equated* with whatever calls itself church) there would be no confessing the faith at all. There would certainly be a living and active witness to God's redemptive presence in the world, for God does not lack for witnesses, and both in the religions of the world and in movements and persons who do not regard themselves as being in any way religious there are, *already,* "many whom the church does not have" (Augustine), who nevertheless testify openly or hiddenly to God—*our* God, who is certainly not only ours! But it would be false and imperious to name this testimony "confession of the faith." Only the church is called and enabled to do that; only the church would consider such a vocation in the first place.

But precisely as the *confessor* of "the faith," the church where it is faith*ful* knows that it is not itself that it either professes or confesses. It can only confess Jesus Christ as and when it refrains from the all-too-human propensity to the profession of self. For the Christ to increase, whoever confesses him must decrease (John 3:30). If this were understood, the humiliation through which Christendom is now passing would not be felt as failure but as a sign of grace and an invitation to renewal. That we can only experience our various reductions in these old denominations as defeats simply indicates that we have been pursuing the wrong theology, most of the time. It has been a "theology of glory" and not "of the cross." And it has been for the most part a very crass theology of glory at that, distinguishable from the glory and power sought by politicians and potentates primarily by its rhetoric of godliness.

Let us begin these reflections on the church, therefore, by renouncing all kinds of ecclesiastical promotionalism, ancient and modern. It is a hard thing to ask of contemporary North Americans, for self-promotion has become a veritable way of life with us. But this is where genuine discipleship parts company from the image-makers. "For what we preach is not ourselves, but Jesus Christ as Lord, with ourselves as your servants for Jesus' sake" (2 Cor. 4:5).

1.2. Confession as Necessity. Confessing the faith is not an option for the disciple community; *confessio* (from the Latin *com* [together] + *fateri* [to acknowledge]) is inherent in faith as such. It would be as unthinkable for faith to refrain from expressing itself as for the heart to suppress its own pulsations. The biblical word *necessitas* has already been alluded to in this connection: "For *necessity* is laid upon me. Woe to me if I do not preach the gospel. . . . I am entrusted with a commission" (1 Cor. 9:16). Paul's original Greek term, *anagke*, seems even stronger than the Latin *necessitas*. It has the connotation of "destiny." Significantly, it can also mean "distress" and "calamity," as it does in 1 Cor. 7:26—a nuance that at once links the confession of Christ with the *suffering* of the church, a theme to which we shall turn later, and effectively distinguishes genuine confession from the merely enthusiastic and celebrative associations religious self-expression has acquired in North American pietism of every variety. Christians who imagine that testimony to Jesus Christ is an unambiguously joyful and rewarding vocation demonstrate all too little familiarity with the Bible they characteristically claim as their own; for the Scriptures are well aware of the fact that part of the "*cost* of discipleship" (Bonhoeffer) is the affront of the gospel to our own preference for unimpeded *self*-determination and unclouded "happiness"! At the very outset of this study, therefore, we would do well to rid ourselves of our New World propensity to eliminate the shadow side of this (and most other) biblical-theological language.

The note of destiny—of "*having* to do it"—is, of course, part and parcel of the biblical conception of divine grace, which despite all the efforts of voluntarists, from Pelagius to Peale, does not permit of reduction to divine "niceness" and contains a strong element of both prevenience and irresistibility. For that reason, those who constituted "the confessing church" under Hitler were none of them pure romantics, engaging in Christian heroics in the face of manifest evil; they were, rather, persons who were driven to say and do what they said and did *in spite of* their own fear, sloth, reluctance, and preference for obscurity at a time when one dared to stand out from the crowd only at peril. They could not *not* confess the faith! They were living, like Paul, "under necessity."[2]

It is not accidental, therefore, that a few months after the promulgation of the Barmen Declaration, its chief author, Karl Barth, could tell a conference of Dutch theologians and pastors that the church "will *necessarily* be a *confessing* Church." Barth goes on to indicate precisely *why* the community of faith "must" bear witness to "what it has seen and heard" (Acts 4:20)— for even this alleged fideist did not consider the *necessitas* of confession a purely heteronomous thing, laid on from above, with no explanation given. He writes:

> *In relation to the world and to the error within its own ranks* [the church] will necessarily be a *confessing* Church, making its own confession along with the fathers [and mothers] in the faith, but, for the very reason that it confesses with them, *making its own confession and that also in the present.* In other words, in obedience to its Lord and therefore in obedience to the Scriptures, it answers

---

2. A particularly moving instance of this is the story of the German pastor, Paul Schneider, who "tried to withstand the National Socialist 'German Christians' in his congregation," and after "expulsion" by the church government returned to his parish because he "was convinced that his call to preach the gospel to this congregation was a divine command which he had to obey, and which took precedence over an expulsion directive from the German state." He had already been imprisoned in Buchenwald, tortured, and killed by July of 1939 (Jürgen Moltmann, *The Way of Jesus Christ: Christology in Messianic Dimensions,* trans. Margaret Kohl [London: SCM, 1990; Minneapolis: Fortress Press, 1993], 199f.). See also E. H. Robertson, *Paul Schneider: The Pastor of Buchenwald* (London: SCM, 1956).

clearly and consistently and fearlessly the questions put to it from moment to moment.[3]

This statement not only demonstrates what a consummately "contextual" theologian Barth himself was, his reputation for inflexible neo-orthodoxy notwithstanding, but it also delineates with precision *the reason that* the disciple community is and must be a "confessing" church. A threefold explanation is offered: first, the world must be addressed; second, the church must be corrected; third, theology and proclamation must respond to the here-and-now. A more definitive statement of the rationale of Christian confession could hardly be given in fewer words.

Of the three prongs of this rationale, the first is clearly the *governing* concept: the world must be addressed. Why "must"? Because it is the beloved of God. Because it is God's good creation.[4] Because its history is the scene of God's providential care.[5] Because God is faithful and wills to bring it to completion—to give it "abundantly" the "life" (John 10:10) that was intended before it gave itself over to death;[6] in short, because the biblical God is from beginning to end a world-orientated God, a geo- and anthropocentric God who will not abandon the world "prematurely" (Bonhoeffer) as the religious so regularly do! The Aristotelian "final cause" of the church's being a confessing church is that the One in whom its faith is placed is committed to this world. The church is the messenger and exemplar of this word of divine world-commitment.

Accordingly, the second prong of the rationale concerns the messenger: the church must be corrected. It must be trained and retrained for its *hermeneutical* vocation. It must be formed and re-formed through continuous attentiveness to the "Lord" who commissions and sends it out into the world (Matt. 28:19), and that means also (Barth notes) to "the Scriptures." *Semper reformanda!* It must indeed be *con*-formed to Jesus Christ (Rom. 12:2). The "error within its own ranks" must be identified and reproved—not, let us note, merely for the sake of doctrinal purity, but for the sake of its right apostolic witness within and before the world. When the confession of faith devolves into a concern for orthodoxy, order, or uniformity, or even unity within the church itself, such internal preciousness displaces the only legitimate rationale for theological vigilance, which is "that the world may believe"

---

3. *Credo,* trans. from the German; Introduction by Robert McAfee Brown (New York: Charles Scribner's Sons, 1962), 145. [Apart from the word "confessing" in the first sentence, the italics are mine].

4. See *Professing the Faith,* 79–82.

5. Ibid., 82–88.

6. Ibid., 88–90.

(John 17). Far too often, the most self-consciously "confessing" churches and movements have manifested an inordinate preoccupation with "doctrine." The only reason confession of the faith must also mean the correction of error within the confessing community itself is so that its trumpet call will be sounded with some clarity and confidence (1 Cor. 14:8).

Ironically, what has perhaps most frequently to be "corrected" by the church's confession is its own narcissism, including its substitution of internal matters for the welfare of the creation. Turning in upon itself, the disciple community fails repeatedly to follow the One who set his face steadfastly *toward* Jerusalem (Luke 9:53). Confession of the faith certainly entails the correction also of doctrinal, ethical, and other "errors" within the church; and the more "liberal" churches of this continent can no longer afford to overlook that necessity. But the end in relation to which this ecclesiastical correction is a means is that the church may reflect, in its life and work, the world-commitment of the God in whom its faith is placed; and this is what the more "conservative" and doctrinally careful denominations of our context should remember.

Third, the reason the church is a "confessing church" is that its confession has always to be discovered, grasped, and framed anew. It is not enough, as Barth says, that the church "makes its confession along with the fathers [and mothers] in the faith." The mere repetition of the confessions of yesteryear— the Apostles' Creed, the Nicene Creed, Heidelberg, Barmen—does not constitute confession. That is, at best, to substitute *profession* for *confession.* On the contrary, precisely as it pays strict attention to the creeds, confessions, and lively theologies of the tradition, the church "for the very reason that it confesses with them" has to strive for "its own confession and that also in the present."

We are at the heart of the meaning of *contextuality* in the tradition of Jerusalem. It is not without didactic potential that the theologian who more than any other in our century wrestled with *the whole* tradition, endeavoring to see and present it in its wholeness, insists here (as he does very frequently, in fact) that, when it comes to the church's *confession,* this confession is conditioned by the specifics of the here and now. "[I]n obedience to its Lord and therefore in obedience to the Scriptures, [the confessing church] *answers clearly and consistently and fearlessly the questions put to it from moment to moment.*" It has often been asserted that although Paul Tillich, the twentieth-century's great Protestant apologist, allowed "the situation" to determine the form of the church's "message," the kerygmatist Barth refused to permit the world to "set the agenda for theology." This is a partially true, but finally a very misleading simplification of the case. The truth is that both of these theological giants of the first half of the century, formed as they were in the crucible of their turbulent historical context, knew perfectly well that the church's "confession" had to address "the moment." If there is a difference between them in this regard, it may be that Tillich developed a systematic methodology for contextuality—which Barth, in spite of some of the things he *said* about theological method, applied more consistently than did Tillich![7]

If its *confession* of the faith is to reach the world for which it is intended, and to reach it as "gospel," the church must submit itself to the discipline of *thinking* and *professing* the faith; a thought-less and un-professional confession of *the faith* is a contradiction in terms. Conversely, thinking and professing the faith are "as nothing" (1 Cor. 13) if they do not lead to faith's confession.

1.3. The Precondition: Not of but in the World. There is, however, a condition that must be met by a "confessing church" beyond spiritual adherence to its living head and the scriptural testimony to that head. It is that this same community must be a conscious and sensitive participant in its own context. This has been our insistence already where the thinking and professing of the faith were concerned; but when it comes to faith's *confession*, this condition is truly a *conditio sine qua non*. There can be no possibility of faith's worldly confession unless the confessing community itself understands—stands under!—the questions, dilemmas, anxieties, and longings of the world for which the confession is intended.

In particular, this refers to that world's *problematique*, that is, what is wrong with it; and therefore the words that I chose in the previous sentence—questions, dilemmas, anxieties, and longings—were not chosen at random but with careful forethought. Christians know as well as anyone else that the world is more than a "problematic" place: that there are joys as well as sorrows, hopes as well as fears, fulfillments as well as unrequited longings, and so on. But Christians also know that the path of the human creature is always a precarious one. In fact, they are among the few today who are able to face this openly, without being unhinged by the experience. They do not have to endorse the false optimism of secular humanism, whose falseness is ever more conspicuous; for the authentic humanity they have glimpsed in the One through whom their faith has been evoked is a humanity that had to "suffer and be rejected" in order to find its peculiar glory. Human creaturehood, as the tradition of Jerusalem understands it, is certainly the most complex and difficult kind of creaturehood.[8] That this creature should be troubled, should question, even, its very existence; that it should experience pain, not only in

---

7. See, however, my critique of Tillich's "method of correlation" in *Thinking the Faith,* 362f. Tillich's term "the situation" carried with it his sensitive and informed understanding of the *times* in which he found himself, but his "*place*-consciousness" was governed too exclusively by his European experience to permit one to consider him a fully "contextual" theologian.

8. See the christological discussion in *Professing the Faith*, esp. §38.4, 543ff.

the moment of pain but in its anticipation; that it should long for what it does not, and perhaps cannot, ever achieve: such things are not surprising to Jews and Christian—they are part of our fundamental anthropology. Even apart from the doctrine of the fall and sin, the focus on anthropology provided by creation and redemption prepares us for an *imago hominis* (image of the human) that ought never to have allowed readers of the Jewish and Christian Scriptures to rush headlong into the inane and exaggerated promises of modernity. The "realism" (Reinhold Niebuhr) that is fostered by biblical faith and understanding is not and cannot be "pessimistic," because its fundamental assumption is the saving intention and deed of the Creator; but neither can it embrace the optimism that still enthralls the "successful" classes of our context, because a world that *needs* saving simply is not "the best of all possible worlds!"[9]

The confession of the church is always therefore related to what is wrong with the world—or, to put the same thing in terms that may be more palatable to those who are afraid of "negative" language—to what needs righting. But a church that is itself unfamiliar with that need; a church that is insulated against such need; a church whose very "faith" (!) keeps it from experiencing its world's real need at close range—such a church is in no position to *confess* its faith.[10]

Therefore it belongs to the life of faith itself (again, the shadow side) that it is *necessarily* a dialogue with faith's antithesis. To know profoundly anything worthy of consideration as "answer," the Christian community has to know profoundly also the question. And the question can only be known profoundly if it is a question that is not yet answered. Answers dispel, or at least take the edge off, questions. Christian answers (all those catechisms!) can very easily create an atmosphere of well-being that effectively isolates Christians from the very world they are commissioned to address in their confessions of faith.

In the United States and Canada today, we have the phenomenon of a large segment of the Christian population—certainly the largest, at least in terms of its public image—that is pathetically incapable of confessing the faith precisely because it is, or imagines itself to be, so very faithful, so confessional! I do not mean to be cynical or even merely ironic when I make this observation. I am quite convinced that many of those about whom I am thinking really *are* faithful people. Often enough, they know far better what they believe, are better acquainted with the Scriptures and traditions of the

---

9. For a splendid exemplification of this dialectical anthropology of biblical faith, see the work of the neglected Swiss Protestant theologian Suzanne de Dietrich, especially *Free Men: Meditations on the Bible Today*, trans. and with an introduction by Olive Wyon (London: SCM, 1961).

10. See *Professing the Faith*, 547–48.

church, are more earnest in their *desire* to confess the faith, than are those who, from the perspective of the more liberal or moderate versions of Christianity, criticize and ostracize them. But they cannot confess the faith because they are so protected by their religious certitude from the very problems and wrongs that constitute the social matrix of the confession that is needed. Instead of *confessing* the faith, they *profess* their answers. But for the most part their answers are not answers to the questions that plague our real world. Some of them may still answer questions of the first, or the sixteenth, or the nineteenth century. But the world's questions, whether openly asked or only implied and lived, are always new, even when they seem like "the same old questions"; and they will not be silenced by the old answers, and certainly not by people who are in fact using the old answers to shield themselves from all unanswered questions.

All of this is to say that which the Scriptures say in so many direct and indirect ways: that the confessing "people of God," which can only confess the faith if it is not "of" the world, must nevertheless be very decisively "in" it. They must be in the world, not only physically and factually (where else could they be?) but also spiritually and intellectually. That is, they must know the problems, anxieties, longings, and frustrations of their historical moment from the inside—as their own problems, anxieties, longings, and frustrations. Therefore they will understand, when they are *denied* answers and pushed over to the side of doubt and disbelief, that this is not only owing to their own weakness but that it belongs to the economy of God. They are being made participants in the world's questions so that they may listen anew for the answers that come from beyond both the church's and the world's storehouse of answers. And in this—precisely this!—they are being conformed to Jesus Christ, who was emptied and humbled in order that his name could be the source of exaltation for others (Phil. 2).

1.4. The Church's Confession as Act and Being. In the foregoing text, which, like most theological work, consists of words, the impression could easily be created that the church's confession is primarily a *verbal* affair. In a society (our own) in which words have become cheap and "plastic,"[11] it is contextually important to insist upon the indispensability and giftedness of language, and therefore to critique its reduction. In a real sense, words are all we have, and our disregard for and trivialization of language in this society is perhaps the most flagrant evidence of our cultural disintegration. The confession of the faith *is* a verbal affair, and even where it is silent words will be needed,

---

11. See in this connection the stimulating study of the linguistics scholar Uwe Pörksen of the University of Freiburg titled *Plastiko Wörter: die Sprache einer internationalen Diktatur* (Stuttgart: Klett-Cotta, 1988).

afterward if not beforehand, to interpret it. Jesus could be silent before Pilate because he had already spoken; and his silence was meaningful silence because of his words and the words that, after the event, his followers bequeathed us.

Yet, as we shall say more elaborately in Part III, it would be entirely wrong to *confine* confession to its verbal expression—to preaching, theology, declaration, proclamation, apologetics, and the like. Against the reduction of the Word to words, both contemplatives and activists are justified in their protests. What is revealed to faith in the face of Jesus Christ is not, to begin with, a "what." "It" is not an "it" but, as the blessed Martin Buber reminded us, a "Thou." To bear testimony to this "Thou," one must have recourse to something besides words.

One cannot even be satisfied with only words *and deeds*! The activists understand the importance of the deed as confession. They rightly point to the parable of the last judgment at the end of Matthew's Gospel (Matt. 25:1ff.) and warn us that mere words, pious speech, and right doctrine, may function as a *refusal* of confession. On the other hand, even *without* "the right words," some who do not know his name may bear witness to the Christ.

Yet deeds usually are also ambiguous. If they are "good deeds," as one supposes they would have to be to be considered "confession of the faith," they are never *wholly* good. Jesus (perhaps reluctantly) called into question the approach of the one who came to him asking what good deed he might do to have eternal life (Matt. 19:16f.). Deeds may sometimes "speak louder than words," but they do so far less frequently than is imagined in our so pragmatic society and churches. Most of our avowedly Christ-inspired deeds bear far more evident testimony to *ourselves* than to Jesus Christ. Not only their motivation but also the "messages" they contain for others are inseparable from our self-esteem—or perhaps from its lack. To be sure, the prospect that deeds may be misunderstood must not deter the disciple community from doing them. It remains, however, that deeds, like words, are only part of what is entailed in the confession of the faith.

Contemplatives stand for a corrective to neo-Protestant activism *and* to the verbalism of our whole Protestant ethos. They understand that silence is of the essence of true confession of the faith. Nearly all Protestants of every persuasion need to hear the message that I once discovered on a poster pinned, by some fortuitous accident, to the bulletin board of a liberal Protestant church: "Don't just do something, *sit there!*" It might just as pointedly have read, "Don't just *say* something, be quiet!" Words and deeds that do not presuppose silence are usually superficial, and often fatuous. Listening to sermons, and to the wordiness of our whole mode of worship in the churches of this continent, one frequently longs for silence. For the ease and quantity of speaking give little evidence of study, meditation, listening—let alone of "living, dying, and being damned" (Luther). They give even less evidence of exposure to the silence that robs us of our easy answers, our slogans, our imperatives, our "theologies-of." It may be that the best prescription for transforming North American churches into confessing churches would be to call a moratorium on speech. Deeds cannot and must not be halted, for there are many who have fallen among thieves! But perhaps we shall only learn to "speak the faith" in these old denominations of ours if we are first reduced to silence.

Confession of the faith implies, then, words, deeds, and silence. But it implies more than these "acts" of Christian people and congregations. It implies their *being*.

In the previous volumes, we have defined "being," Christianly understood, in a particular way. It is not just "existence," and it is not something that we "have." It is something we are always being *given*, like the "daily bread," and given in our being-with God, our own kind, and otherkind. Being, in the tradition of Jerusalem (we have said) *is* "with-being" (*Mitsein*). In place of the being-alone and being-against that *sin* means in this tradition, salvation means beginning to be *with* these others: a coexistence which is at the same time pro-existence.[12]

This is why the very *being* of the disciple community is—can be, must be, is being equipped to be—a *confessio fidei*. What more *appropriate* confession of faith could in fact be imagined, in the midst of our individualistic, me-first, acquisitive society than *a community*?

Of course, the *word* community easily takes on the function of "plastic words": it is to be heard everywhere in the world today. It signifies everything—and nothing. It connotes something universally good—and *denotes* nothing in particular. It can all too readily silence the real *quest* for community by making it seem that such a community actually exists!

Here too, therefore, we cannot depend on the word alone, nor on the deeds that issue from ecclesiastical "communities." But from time to time we may experience the actual *being* of community, and it is always "with-being." Without losing myself, I find or am found by the others. We shall consider this more fully when we turn to the Pauline metaphor of "the body" and its "members."[13] For the present, we only wish to underscore the thought that this com-unity, this "oneness-with," is itself integral to the confession of Jesus Christ in the world. In fact, without it, the words, the deeds, and even the silence of the disciple community would prove ineffectual and ultimately unreal.

The being-with of the Christian community is inexhaustible as to its potentiality for confession, but in order to be concrete and "contextual," we

---

12. See *Thinking the Faith*, 359f.; *Professing the Faith*, 147f., 157ff., 314–34.
13. See below, chap. 4, §6.

could at least consider this: What might it mean in North America today if churches really were communities in which human beings were being brought into *relationship* with God, with one another, and with the inarticulate creation? What kind of *confession* might be made if these communities really were characterized by sharing, cooperation, mutuality, openness-to-the-other, hospitality? In the impersonal and uncaring urban culture that we have become, might it not constitute a remarkable *confession of the faith* if the "new being" that is Christ's gift to his body were to extend itself into such worldly matters as public medicine, education, race relations, immigration, sexuality, gender roles, and the like?

This should not be heard only as a call to *act;* it is first and foremost a call to *be*—namely, to become what we are: a people being transformed from individualism to mutuality, from self-seeking to cooperation, from being-alone and against to being with and for. It is from the "new *being*" (Tillich) that we are being given daily that the speaking and doing, and contemplating arises. If that being is not present—that is to say, present as becoming—then the speaking, doing, and contemplating will lack any ontological foundation. They will be felt, always, as an imperative that has no indicative, an *ought* without an *is*, a command without a "reason why"—to anticipate the seventh chapter, an ethic without a theology.

Mention of the ontological *foundation* of the church's confession, however, brings us to the most important dimension of ecclesiology, and the condition without which the church devolves into another of the world's innumerable "organizations": the relational groundedness of the *koinonia* in Jesus, the Christ.

2. Christological Foundations of the Confessing Church

2.1. Brought to Live the Representative Life of the Christ. When in the preceding volume[14] we tried to think how best to speak today of the life and work of Jesus Christ, we explored, with several other contemporary theologians, the idea of representation. Representation is a concept with linguistic coinage in our society, being present not only in the political but in all areas of our common life. It is also a metaphor that can help us to recover the meaning of certain *biblical* terms (particularly priesthood) as well as some of the important christological ideas of historical theology that are otherwise either lost to us or present grave hermeneutical problems (particularly the idea of substitution). As well, we saw that representation can be a *binding* metaphor, keeping together the two sides of Christology (Christology/soteri-

---

14. *Professing the Faith,* chap. 9, §37, 506–48.

ology), which have always tended to separate and, in consequence, to divide the church; for, without shifting metaphors, representation may be applied equally and simultaneously to both aspects of christological doctrine.

Most important for our present consideration, however, is what we realized is yet another advantage of this concept:[15] namely, that it allows us to move from Christology to *ecclesiology* in a way that both does justice to the necessary connections between these two foundational areas of what Christians profess and, at the same time, gives access to an immediate response to the question, "What is the nature and calling of the church?" *The church,* we said, *is that community which is being brought to live the representative life of the Christ in the world.*

As we turn now to consider the ontological presuppositions of the doctrine of the church as a *confessing* community, we must draw out the implications of these preliminary observations. What *enables* the church to be a confessing community—and to be so not only in its speaking and acting but in its very being? What is the source of its life? What holds it together and gives it, at least from time to time, the possibility of making a common witness despite the conspicuous diversity of its membership? Is the church to be thought of as a "voluntary" community, whose members—let us say—have developed a particular attachment to Jesus Christ, or the Christ-ideal, or the teachings of Jesus, or "the biblical narrative," and the like?

Among mainstream churchgoers in North America today such a view is frequently endorsed or simply assumed. People think of themselves as having "joined" the church, more or less as one might join any other organization, except that this one is rather less well-defined. They "support" the church with their givings—"time, talents, and treasures." Where they are somewhat informed biblically and doctrinally, they listen without puzzlement or surprise to scriptural readings, prayers, or sermons in which various ideas and theological or doxological terms are used to describe the church—ideas and terms that, were they not so commonplace, might call in question their assumptions concerning the nature of the church and of their membership in it. On the whole, however, particularly in liberal or moderate Protestant circles, the largely unspoken working assumption about the life and work of the church is that it is dependent upon our individual and corporate commitment, energies, and promotion. And this working assumption is regularly and painstakingly reinforced by the whole machinery of our institutional churches, from financial drives to the generally exhortational mood of most preaching. It would be hard to sustain regular membership in the average Protestant congregation in North America and to avoid the belief that its

---

15. Ibid., 522–24.

basic enabling principle and the source of whatever vitality it has is the shared conviction of its members that the church is a very good thing!

Precisely this working assumption is what we must now question if we want to discover how the newer Testament as well as the most serious theological thought of all branches of Christendom understand the foundation and source of the church's life. Whether Catholic, Orthodox, Anglican, or classically Protestant, Christian doctrine assumes as its most *rudimentary* ecclesiastical presupposition that the source of the church's life is its relationship with Jesus Christ—or perhaps we should say its *relatedness to* Jesus Christ. For this ecclesiology begins with the "christological" assumption that the Christ is not only the "founding personality" of the Christian movement (an idea which was taken up by Christian modernism), but a living person, the risen Savior and Lord, reigning "at the right hand of God," *as* God "the Son," present to and in the church through Word and Sacrament and, in particular, through the life-giving Spirit of holiness. "Jesus Christ," writes the African American theologian James H. Evans, Jr., "is the center of the church. That is, the church is that community that is centered in Christ. It does not possess Christ, but it possessed by Christ."[16]

Today, for many Christians, the *language* employed by the tradition to describe this foundational relatedness of the Christ and the church is for a variety of reasons (including its sexism) problematic; but even those who deplore some of these linguistic problems would most of them want to retain the basic connection between Christology and ecclesiology: namely, that the church, far from being an organization like any other, is founded upon a relationship that it did not initiate and does not of itself sustain. For they recognize that if the church is thought to be dependent upon *us,* its membership, this not only flies in the face of Scripture and tradition, but (more existentially) it bodes ill for the church's future. It is always difficult to take seriously any undertaking that seems largely dependent upon the human will and from which any sense of a transcendent causation is missing. Today, as Christians in all denominations confront the realities of our de facto disestablishment, we need to recover some lively sense of the *christological* basis of the church. A Christian community laboring under the impression that its future is dependent upon its own effort to "stay alive" is in no position to resist the corrosive forces of post-Christian secularity, for that very assumption about itself is *of the essence* of secularity.

It is not easy for any of us to escape from the secular mindset, despite the evident failure of secularism as a system of meaning. It is perhaps as natural for us to bring to our thinking about the church, as to everything else, the

---

16. *We Have Been Believers: An African-American Systematic Theology* (Minneapolis: Fortress Press, 1992), 135.

pre-understanding of secularity as it was for our medieval forebears to assume a mystical, sacramental approach to the *corpus Christi.* From the Oxford Movement of the Victorian era onward, there have been those who attempted by sheer determination to banish secularity and reconstitute "the body of Christ" along lines that were not only premodern but pre-Reformation. This approach seems to me questionable, not only for the obvious reason that a Protestant cannot wish unambiguously to return to the Middle Ages,[17] but also and chiefly because it seems to me unnecessary. There are ways of recovering something of the biblical and traditional sense of relationship between Jesus Christ and the church that emanate from our own historical experience and do not require us artificially to adopt the worldview of a bygone age in order to acquire an ecclesiology that is less one-dimensional than the prevailing one. Moreover, such attempts are facilitated by the growing disillusionment of our contemporaries with secularism and their new openness to the transcendent.

One such way of thinking about the church is suggested by the language of representation. The church, we have said, is that community which is *being brought to live the representative life of Jesus Christ in the world.* This statement contains at least four implicit thoughts, which, to demonstrate our point, we must now make explicit:

First, it contains a *pneumatological* assumption. That the church is a community "being *brought*" to live that life means that our existence as such a community is dependent upon an influence distinguishable from and prior to our own individual and corporate determination. That such a community *is* at all, is a consequence of a spiritual impetus that cannot be accounted for in purely historical-empirical terms. It is certainly not the esprit de corps of *that community* that keeps it together! There is far more empirical evidence of division and discord in congregations, denominations, and the "universal church" than of anything resembling a strong will-to-unity. If despite this the church exists and—at least in its serious manifestations—*wills* to make good the unity to which it feels called, this must be attributed to a Spirit (*pneuma*) who creates and nourishes this community, and will not allow its internal disintegrative forces to destroy it utterly.

Second, the statement contains an explicitly *christological* assumption: the life that this community is being brought to live in the world is "the representative life of *Jesus Christ.*" The church is not asked to invent an identity for itself. In bringing it into existence, the divine Spirit gives it an identity: it is to live the life of Jesus Christ in the world. It may and must continuously ask

---

17. I say this despite the fact that many of us, like Paul Tillich, have learned to have a new respect for the Middle Ages as manifesting, in their best exemplars, a "theonomy" that was lost to the modern epoch—and already to much Protestantism.

itself what it means—concretely, ethically, confessionally—to live this life; but there is no question *what* life it is to live. The fundamental form and character of its life is present already in its formation by the Spirit. It is the life of Jesus Christ into which it is incorporated, and every re-formation of the church is and must be a renewal of its explicit identity with that One.

It is in this sense that Paul and other biblical authors employ the symbolic language of the church's being "clothed" with Christ (2 Cor. 5:4; see also Rev. 7:13–14). Christ clothes the church with his own past, and therefore also holds out to it *his* future. That past, with the cross at its center, is one for which the church as such can be given no credit; it is a past into which it is "being brought"; it receives that past, is "conformed" to it (Rom. 8:29), as a matter of sheer grace, "not in virtue of works" (2 Tim. 1:8ff.). The church neither created this past, nor does it on its own appropriate this past to itself. The past is there; the work "is finished" (John 19:30). Insofar as this past becomes the church's own point of departure, the locus of its new identity, it is only because it is already there as this past, this "finished" work, and because it is offered the church as an inheritance (Rom. 8:18) in which it may "partake" (1 Peter 4:13), to which it may be "made conformable" (Phil. 3:8), and into which it can be baptized (Rom. 6:3, and so on). There is here, in other words, no thought of that variety of *imitatio Christi* (the imitation of Christ) that would have us adopt this past as our model, consciously patterning our lives after "the Master" who walked the Way before us. We shall not in such wise be able to claim for ourselves the future that belongs to that past. *Conformitas Christi* (being conformed to Christ) upholds the pneumatological assumption noted in the first observation in a way that *imitatio Christi,* owing to its activist connotation in our context of the idea of "imitation," does not.

Third, the statement contains a *missiological* assumption: the church is called to live the *representative* life of Jesus Christ, and therefore (of course) to live it fully and responsibly *in the world.* We shall not repeat all that was said in the previous volume about the nature of Christ's representation, but here and in what follows it should be borne in mind that representation (in Christology as in everyday experience) involves a dual aspect. Jesus' representative life entailed both the representation of the creature before God and the representation of God before the creature. This life, into which the divine Spirit is bringing this community, is a life, not only of mediation, but of representation: that is, Jesus Christ not only stands "between" Creator and creature, but he stands "with" the Creator before the creature and "with" the creature before the Creator. In solidarity with God—as Emmanuel![18]—Jesus

---

18. See the discussion of "Emmanuel" in *Professing the Faith,* chap. 9, §38.1, esp. 528–29.

represents to us God's judging love, himself accepting the judgment that is and must be *in* this love. And in solidarity with "us," as our "high priest" (Heb. 8, 9), Jesus represents before God the pain and impossibility of our creaturehood, receiving in his own person, *pro nobis,* both the No and the Yes of God's response to our predicament.

To be brought into identity with Jesus Christ is to be incorporated into— to be made a participant in—just this representational life; and therefore it is to be sent all the more explicitly *into* the world precisely on account of our being given an identity that is not *of* this world.

Fourth, our leading statement contains an *eschatological* assumption: the church is that community which *is being* brought to live the representative life of Jesus Christ in the world. We are not speaking about a finished work but only about something that is "in the making." The work of Christ "is finished," but the church's participation in that work is not. The church's life is thus a "becoming," not a "being," and certainly not a "having." It is therefore a *communio viatorum,* a community "on the way"; it has not arrived! It prays, "Give us this day our daily bread." Daily, it is reconstituted; daily, it *needs* reconstitution, for it not only receives its new identity "in Christ" but it also rejects this identity and tries to have a different one, one of its own devising.

This eschatological dimension, as we shall see in a moment, is very important for the question about the nature of the relation between the church and Jesus Christ. Only where the eschatological dimension is neglected, or reduced to a species of "realized" eschatology, is it possible for the Christian community to regard *itself* as ultimate and therefore as part of what it professes and confesses.

The concept of representation does not overcome the difficulty that the secular mind experiences in grasping the christological basis of Christian ecclesiology, but it can help to locate the subject in a sphere of discourse less inaccessible to us than is the mystical-ontological language of the medieval world. No language can overcome our propensity as modern people to think of Jesus as a historical figure whose life is confined to the past. But if we can consider ourselves participants in a representational identity and work that is most lucidly communicated to us in the biblical witness to *his* life, we may discover a way into this subject that is less formidable than the substantialistic language of so much of the christological and ecclesiological tradition.

2.2. *Soma Christou:* The Dialectic of Identification and Differentiation in the Relation between Christ and the Church.

We have claimed that the church in its very being, as well as in its speaking and acting, is able to confess Jesus Christ, but that this potentiality is given it only as and insofar as it is "being brought to live the representative life of Jesus Christ in the world." Christ himself is the "chief cornerstone" of the church (Mark 12:10; Luke 20:17; Acts 4:11; 1 Peter 2:4ff.). The church *is* because and only because Jesus Christ both *was* and *is.*

This affirmation of the ontological dependence of the church upon the Christ, regarded from the side of *the church,* has yielded for some the concept of the church as "extension of the incarnation." Protestant theology has always exhibited a great deal of nervousness in the presence of such an idea, and the present discussion will not constitute an exception to the rule. It seems to me even more dangerous today than it was in the nineteenth century to pursue that route, because, given the facts of Christendom's "humiliation" (van den Heuvel), there exists a lively temptation to renew the ancient ecclesiastical triumphalism and imperialism of the past—and just at a point in the sojourn of Christianity in the world where new lessons in *modesty* are called for. Nothing now is less appropriate as a *confessio fidei* than an exclusivistic Christology in tandem with a triumphalistic ecclesiology.[19]

The rejection of the "extension of the incarnation" idea, however, raises for Protestants the question, "How *shall* we think of this relation?" If, on the one hand, we are not willing to reduce the whole subject to a matter of historical cause and effect, and, on the other, we are unwilling to indulge in an ecclesiology that makes the church itself the object of its confession, what alternative are we left with in sorting out this relationship?

In answer, we could turn to an exegesis of some of the key images or metaphors of the newer Testament that describe precisely this relationship— among them, that of the vine and the branches (John 15), the bride and the bridegroom (John 3:29; Rev. 18–22; Matt. 9:15; 25:1ff. and par.), and, above all, because of its historical importance, the Pauline term *soma Christou* ("body of Christ"). I will make use of these images, especially the Pauline term, but I will set them in a theological-philosophical framework.

There are two polar concepts between which the relation of Christ and the church has in fact been worked out in the history of Christian thought. We may name these concepts the principle of *identification* (or union) and the principle of *differentiation* (or distinction).

One side of the relation between Christ and the church for which there is ample biblical and historical-theological testimony is the emphasis upon identification. According to this principle, the relation between Jesus Christ and the church is not only a historical one—that is, it is not only that the church has been brought into being through the influence of this central

---

19. On Protestant rejection of the "extension of the incarnation" concept, see Claude Welch, *The Reality of the Church* (New York: Charles Scribner's Sons, 1958), 81f.

figure of the newer Testament's story, and is perpetuated by his memory. Rather, this relation is first and foremost a spiritual union. We have assumed this in discussing the second (christological) assumption in the preceding subsection.

It is this conception of a spiritual union that informs the Pauline "metaphor" (which is more than a metaphor, both for Paul himself and for subsequent theology), *soma Christou* (Latin: *Corpus Christi*, "body of Christ"). It also informs the frequent Pauline assertion that those who are "members" of this "body" are *en Christo* ("in Christ"). Through the hearing of the Word, through baptism, through the continuous activity of the Holy Spirit, and through the eucharistic celebration they are being constituted participants in the very life of the Christ. As we said earlier, the principle of *life* in the church is the Christ, mediated through the Holy Spirit. What sustains the disciple community is not the constancy and faithfulness of the members, but the faithfulness of the One "in" whose representative life and ministry the members are continuously being given a part.

Now, one branch of Christendom (in particular the "Catholic," including the Anglo-Catholic, branch[20]) has stressed this aspect of the relation between Christ and the church to the neglect, I should say, of the other "pole" in the relation, that of differentiation. Perhaps the most consistent, as well as

---

20. According to the late George S. Hendry (*The Gospel of the Incarnation* [Philadelphia: Westminster Press, 1958], 153ff.), the term "extension of the incarnation" seems to have originated in Anglo-Catholic circles. This tradition, writes Hendry, regards the church as "the institution founded by Christ to take over his mission at his departure and continue it throughout the succeeding ages of history." Hendry cites as the "clearest and most candid expression" of this position two stanzas of an Anglican hymn:

> His twelve apostles first he made
> His ministers of grace;
> And they their hands on others laid,
> To fill in turn their place.
>
> So age by age, and year by year,
> His grace was handed on;
> And still the holy church is here,
> Although her Lord is gone.

While we may agree with Hendry that this hymn expresses very cogently the ecclesiology we have in mind here, we must at the same time note that it gives clearer expression to one aspect of that ecclesiology, the *continuity* between Christ and the church, than to another aspect, the ontological or mystical *identity* between Christ and the church, upon which (I should judge) the historical continuity rests. Perhaps, however, that is simply an indication of the "logical difficulties (not to say incoherences)" with which the Anglo-Catholic ecclesiology is confronted and "from which the Roman Catholic is free . . . " (Lesslie Newbiggin, *The Reunion of the Church* [New York: Harper & Brothers, 1948], 56). For that reason, we shall follow Newbiggin's example (ibid.) and confine our remarks to the Roman Catholic treatment of the subject.

historically influential, statement of this position is found in the papal encyclical of Pius XII titled *Mystici corporis Christi.*[21]

"It is Christ," the encyclical declares, "Who lives in the Church, Who teaches, governs and sanctifies through her."[22] The church is "'the Mystical Body of Jesus Christ.' This title is derived from and is, as it were, the fair flower of the repeated teaching of Sacred Scripture and the Holy Fathers."[23] The encyclical exegetes four titles of the Christ through which the church is to be perceived as his "mystical body": Founder, Head, Support, and Savior. As Founder, through his victory on the cross, Christ "increased that immense treasury of graces which . . . He lavishes continuously on His mortal members" and "entered into the possession of His Church." Thus he "opened up to His Church the fountain of divine graces, which protect it *from ever teaching men false doctrine* and enable it to rule them for their soul's salvation through supernaturally enlightened pastors. . . ."[24]

The second title, "Head," is one to which we shall turn for our exposition of the other side of the dialectic of this relation, but so far as the encyclical is concerned it by no means yields a dimension of differentiation. On the contrary, this is where the Pontiff makes an explicit connection between the principle of identification and that of *authority*—to wit, papal authority:

> We must not think that He [Christ] rules only in a hidden or extraordinary way. On the contrary, our Divine Redeemer also governs His Mystical Body in a visible way and *ordinarily through His Vicar on earth.* . . .
>
> After His glorious Ascension into heaven, this Church rested not on Him alone, but on Peter, too, its visible foundation stone. That *Christ and His Vicar constitute one only Head* is the solemn teaching of Our Predecessor of immortal memory, Boniface VIII, in the *Apostolic Letters Unam Sanctum.* . . .[25]

Third, Christ is the "Support of the Body." Again here we could be led to consider the other pole in this dialectic. Obviously it cannot be wholly

---

21. I shall use the translation found in Anton C. Pegis, *The Wisdom of Catholicism* (New York: The Modern Library, 1955), 767ff.

I am, of course, conscious of the fact that, since the Second Vatican Council, this historically important encyclical can no longer be said to bear the authority that it possessed at the time of its composition. Already by the early 1960s a variety of Catholic discussions of the relation between Christ and the church had made their appearance (see, for example, Hugo Rahner et al., *The Church: Readings in Theology* [New York: P. J. Kennedy and Sons, 1963]). I employ the encyclical here, however, not as an instance of universal Roman Catholic teaching but only for the purposes of illustrating what seems to me the most explicit and sustained application of the principle of identification.

22. Ibid., 767.

23. Ibid., 773.

24. Ibid., 779–80. [My italics.]

25. Ibid., 882–83. [My italics.]

avoided, but the clear intention of the encyclical is to accentuate the principle of identification throughout; therefore, even under the rubric of Christ as "Sustainer [supporter] of the Body," we are given one of the most unqualified expressions of ontic continuity between Christ and the church:

> This naming of the Body of Christ is not to be explained solely by the fact that Christ must be called the Head of His Mystical Body, but also by the fact that He so sustains the Church, and so in a certain sense lives in the Church, *that it is as it were another Christ.*[26]

Fourth, in a similar vein, Christ's being "Savior" in relation to the church, an observation that necessarily points to his distinction from it, leads the writer of the encyclical to affirm that although salvation is certainly dependent upon Jesus Christ, "to us it has been granted to collaborate with Christ in this work of salvation."[27]

To reiterate: I do not intend to advance this as a sufficient account of Roman Catholic teaching on the subject. After Vatican II, it would be necessary (were this our intention) to enter at this point many objections to such an ecclesiology coming from Catholicism itself.[28] My intention here, however, is more limited: I only wish to show something of what happens, theologically, when the principle of identification is the one that *dominates* the discussion of this foundational relationship. While even here it is impossible entirely to exclude the antithetical pole of differentiation, the consistent *emphasis* upon the identity of Christ and the church makes it possible not only drastically to minimize the purely human, historical dimension of institutional Christianity, but to accentuate the exclusive salvific powers of the church and the authoritative ultimacy of the *magisterium.* There is perhaps no more transparent demonstration of the indelible link between a triumphalistic Christology and an imperialistic ecclesiology than is given in the context of this encyclical. Luther would surely have thought it a splendid example of the "theology of glory"!

It would be comforting to be able to assert that by contrast Protestantism, being fearful of such an *ecclesia gloriae,* has always been keen to embrace an ecclesiology "of the cross." Such, however, has hardly been the case. In fact, modern, liberal Protestantism, which tended to accentuate the principle of *differentiation* in its exposition of the relation between Jesus Christ and the church, in this manner denied itself the only real access to an *ecclesia crucis,*

---

26. Ibid., 788–89. [The phrase I have italicized replicates the teaching of St. Robert Bellarmine (1542–1621), a Jesuit theologian of the later phases of the Counter-Reformation.]

27. Ibid., 791.

28. For a discussion of the ecclesiology of Vatican II, see Mudge, *The Sense of a People,* 40–45.

for without some persistent sense of its *identity* with the crucified one, the life of the disciple community falls into the ethos of law and not gospel, and thus opens itself to yet another variety of the *theologia gloriae.*

To exemplify what I mean by liberal Protestant stress upon the principle of differentiation in this relationship, I will refer to aspects of the work of the great American exponent of the social gospel, Walter Rauschenbusch. There would be more sophisticated (Schleiermacher, Ritschl, Hermann, and others), as well as more straightforward (Washington Gladden, Harry Emerson Fosdick), exemplars of this principle; but I am choosing Rauschenbusch both because he represents a North American interpretation and because there is sufficient nuance in his understanding of this relation to discourage making of it a caricature.

In his best-known work, *A Theology for the Social Gospel,*[29] Rauschenbusch writes:

> If the Church is to have saving power, it must embody Christ. He is the revolutionary force within it. The saving qualities of the Church depend on the question whether it has translated the personal life of Jesus Christ into the social life of its group and thus brings it to bear on the individual. If Christ is not in the Church, how does it differ from "the world"? It will then assimilate its members, but it will not make them persons bearing the family likeness of the first-born son of God.[30]

At first glance, this may more readily seem to accentuate unity than distinction: the church "must embody Christ"; Christ must be "in" the church, and so on. But it soon becomes apparent that the language here and throughout—and, indeed, the whole thought-structure, with its recurring imperative, "must"—is poles apart from the language of ontic unity. Words like "embody" are not intended to convey ontological connection between Christ and the church, but point rather to a spiritual "affinity" that, Rauschenbusch stresses, the church "must" bear to Jesus. That the church must be exhorted to appropriate "the Christ-spirit,"[31] or "the law and spirit of Jesus,"[32] implies that such a spirit is not a "given" of its being as such. Indeed, it is clear that when Rauschenbusch considers the relation between Christ and the church, he is not thinking of a supernaturally initiated and endowed unity of *being,* but rather of a unity of *spirit and of purpose,* toward which the church "must" strive.

---

29. New York: Abingdon Press, 1917.
30. Ibid., 28.
31. Ibid., 128.
32. Ibid.

The Christ in this ecclesiology is "the historical Jesus." Jesus stands at the beginning of a new era. As one who in his own person "achieved a new type of humanity,"[33] Jesus is "the Initiator of the Kingdom of God."[34] "Within him the Kingdom of God got its first foothold in humanity."[35] His life marks "an epoch in the evolution of the race by the introduction of a new type and consequently new social standards."[36] By the force of his personal "consciousness of God,"[37] Jesus gathered others into his new vision of God and of God's purposes for society. For "Jesus not only achieved the kind of religious personality which we have tried to bring before our memory and imagination, but he succeeded in perpetuating his spirit. What was personal with him became social within the group of his disciples. His life became a collective and assimilating force and a current of historical tradition."[38]

Obviously, the dominant thought in all of this is the historical influence of the man, Jesus of Nazareth. Certainly, for Rauschenbusch, as for most others of the more "spiritual-pietist" branch of theological liberalism, this is not to be conceived in purely horizontal terms; it is not *simply* the impact of a Great Personality that is being presented here. *Jesus'* influence, unlike that of any other exemplary figure (for example, Socrates) is for Rauschenbusch to be understood within the framework of the divine immanence. It is not just that Jesus is "greater" than other historical luminaries; the difference lies in the fact that his life is the unique manifestation of a spirit, "the Christ-spirit," which has its ground in the will and mind of God.

While this ecclesiology presupposes a quite decisive *Theology* and *pneumatology,* then, the "christological" element is certainly more historical than ontological. Jesus is "the Initiator." As such, he is indispensable to the church, and the example that he sets is what the church again and again "must" try to live. But it remains that Jesus' person is confined to the past. There can be no talk here of his contemporaneity with us. His presence as "the Christ-spirit" is assumed, but the language of the church as the very "body" of Christ hardly fits this approach. The principle of distinction dominates the discussion of this relation: Jesus was "then and there," and we are "here and now." The distance between us is overcome by the divine immanence; but this spiritual presence transcends embodiment in the person, Jesus.

---

33. Ibid., 152.
34. Ibid.
35. Ibid., 151.
36. Ibid., 164.
37. Rauschenbusch's dependence upon Schleiermacher is here, as elsewhere, much in evidence.
38. Ibid., 164.

What we must now notice is that *both* of these approaches—the conservative Catholic emphasis upon identification and continuity between Christ and the church, and the liberal Protestant assumption of distinction and discontinuity—vitiate the biblical understanding of this relationship as a dialectic of identification-with-differentiation—that is, *as relational*! With Pius XII, the unity principle absorbs into itself the dimension of distinction that is necessary to any relation. For relationship presupposes difference: I *and* thou. The "extension of the incarnation" idea tends to dissolve this difference between Christ and the church, or to minimize its actual and potential impact upon the doctrine of the church. Because it is informed essentially by substantialistic and not by relational thinking,[39] this type of ecclesiology is content to regard the foundation of the church as its incorporation into, or appropriation of, the very *being* of Jesus. Over against this, biblically conditioned theology must say: the church *is* not Jesus, it is *with* Jesus, and Jesus is *with* it. Moreover, he is with it *as its "head,"* and therefore as that which is quite distinguishable *from* it and not possessible *by* it.[40]

On the other hand, liberal Protestantism vitiates the relational character of this relationship by failing to develop a sufficient sense of Jesus' own presence with and in the church. Here there are two—Christ, and the church. There is no danger of a merger of one into the other. They remain in fundamental isolation from one another. To repeat: Jesus was "then and there" and the church is "now and here." The church no doubt *remembers* Jesus, but it is not conscious of him as an abiding Presence, upon whose continuing (living) reality as its "head" "the body" depends as the very basis of its own life.

How does this juxtaposition of the two extreme ways of articulating this foundational relationship help us to formulate it in a manner that avoids their difficulties? Primarily, they demonstrate the importance of thinking *relationally* about this relationship that is crucial for all ecclesiology. Relationality—not only in the case of this, but in all relationships—presupposes both identity and difference, and the two poles must be understood in dynamic, dialectical tension one with the other. It would be possible to use the terms "relation" or "relationship" to describe the position taken in *Mystici corporis Christi* only in an organic sense, as one might speak of the "relation" between head and body in the human organism. In liberal Protestantism, the only manner in which these words could be employed is historical—the

---

39. See the discussion "Ontology" in *Professing the Faith*; for "substantialistic" conceptions of being, see esp. 202, 267, 510, 518. Extended discussion of this subject is also to be found in my *Imaging God: Dominion as Stewardship* (Grand Rapids: Wm. B. Eerdmans, 1986); esp. chap. 4, "The Ontology of Communion," 133ff.

40. See again the statement of James H. Evans, 46, n.16.

"relation" between a charismatic founding figure and the community that remembers him and seeks to promote his teachings.

In both instances, something drastic happens to the prominent newer Testamental insistence upon the *sovereignty* ("Lordship") of Jesus Christ in the church. In the "Catholic" alternative, the immediacy of the identification between Christ and the church (described by Pius XII, in Augustine's words, as "the whole Christ") virtually rules out the possibility of a radical sovereignty of the risen Christ that may call even the authority of the *magisterium* into question. In "liberal" thought, the effective remoteness of the historical Jesus makes it impossible to give existential weight to his sovereignty.

The Pauline idea of the *soma Christou* sustains both principles, identification and differentiation, and in a way that allows us to take the church very seriously but without according it anything like ultimacy. Because for Paul the church is "the body *of Christ*," it cannot be ignored or treated with condescension by those who "think the faith." Its "reality" (C. Welch) matters, its institutional forms matter, its conception of its mission matters, its future matters. Jesus Christ addresses himself to the world through the church; therefore *its* words are never separable from the Word that *He* "is." Jesus Christ acts through its actions; therefore its actions, although certainly a mixture of good and evil, can never seem to serious theology matters of indifference, Christ having "other sheep that are not of *this* fold," and so on. Jesus Christ lives in its life, is the source of its life; therefore, though its life is also informed by other, including antithetical, and even demonic, sources, the actual being of the church—for example, the question of its unity—is of immediate significance to a theology that places Jesus Christ at the center of its "meditative core." The church is *his* "body."

But he is "the head" of this body! And that—as is obvious from Paul's *metaphoric* deployment of this image that is more than *mere* metaphor—is not to be understood organically or substantially, but relationally. That is to say, "headship" in this case signifies both distinction from and ultimacy of authority in relation to "the body." Just as Paul is able on the basis of the body-metaphor to think of "the members" (feet, hands, eyes) as being different from one another and having different functions and contributions in relation to the whole, so he thinks of "the head" as being quite distinct from "the body," even though its office (authority) is oriented toward the body.

What is in this way presented to us as a kind of parable of this relation is, on the one hand, understood to be a dialectical *tension*; and there truly is *tension* in it, as there is in every authentic relationship. On the other hand, however, it is simply a *dynamic*, as distinct from a static, relation. That is to say, it is a *relation*—a *living* relation, in which there is continual change, growth, decline, movement, coming-closer, separating, reuniting, and so on and on.

We might also say therefore that it is an *eschatological* relationship: one whose *telos* is clear from the outset, namely, the perfect union and harmony of the two; but one whose *course* involves both union and disunion, harmony and discord, for it participates in both an "already" and a "not yet." This is one reason the "body" imagery should not be used exclusively to describe the relation between Christ and the church, but should be supplemented and qualified by other images that are less susceptible to noneschatological, static conceptualization. It is not that the imagery of "the body" lacks dynamism; yet in the history of theology, it has been too tempting for established Christianity to treat this imagery substantially, and it has served the purposes of the triumphant church to do so. Although in some respects the human body (which is Paul's paradigm), while it lives, provides a splendid model of identification-with-differentiation, the principle of differentiation is by no means as obvious here as it is, for example, with the Johannine imagery of the bride and the bridegroom. With the latter, one cannot avoid the thought that there are *two*; and indeed, the two have by no means become "one" in any permanent sense. "The bride," that is, the church, is Christ's *betrothed*, but the marriage has not been consummated and nothing is to be taken for granted in that respect. In fact, as some commentators have noted, it is often difficult to distinguish "the bride" from "the harlot" in the allegorical language of the *Apocalypse*.[41]

But we are attempting in this work to think *contextually*; and therefore the discussion of this relation should at last be applied to the particularities of our own ecclesiastical situation. I neither can nor do I wish to speak for *all* North American expressions of the Christian church. In general, it is my impression that the more "Catholic" denominations, despite the presence within them of post–Vatican II and other ecclesiologies that are implicitly and explicitly critical of the way in which this relation is presented in documents such as the one we have examined, still need to be conscious of the

---

41. "Here the church can by no means simply be identified with the bride of the Lamb who has made herself ready for the marriage (Rev. 19:7; 21:2). The perfect adornment (21:2, 10ff.) and readiness of the bride belong to the time of the consummation which is yet to come. Meanwhile the Church exists in the time of struggle and decision, for over against the figure of the bride is the figure of the harlot (ch. 17ff.), the enemy yet temptation of the church. The church is faced with the supreme choice between love and lust. The church is chosen to be the bride, thus chosen to choose Christ, and now exists in the tension of choosing between Christ and Satan (who has also chosen the church and is hardest at work in it). Judgment and transformation stand between the church and the marriage supper of the Lamb (ch. 21). . . . If then the church is the bride, it is the community which is yet coming to meet Christ in final fulfilment, a fulfilment which involves the entirety of the new heaven and the new earth" (Claude Welch, *The Reality of the Church* [New York: Charles Scribner's Sons, 1958], 132–33).

dangers of an ecclesiology in which the principle of identification is over-stressed.[42]

As for Protestantism, and particularly for the remnants of once-mainline Protestantism that are the primary concern of this work, it seems to me quite clear that the combination of liberalism and secularity has robbed us of the dimension of mystery that is requisite to thinking of the church as Christ's "body." Our tendency, as I proposed earlier, is to reduce the disciple community to organizational models that are hardly distinguishable, in the last analysis, from the ethos of clubs and corporations. Insofar as this is so, the contextually important emphasis that emerges from the consideration of this dialectic of identification and differentiation is the former pole. That such a concept as Paul's "body of Christ" is extremely difficult for the vast majority of Protestants is a truism. And it will not solve *our* difficulty to flout our own history and ethos and leap over into "Catholic" substantialism or sacramentalism.

By rethinking our own pilgrimage, however, from its Reformation expression onward, and by recovering the *biblical* mode of thought, which as we have seen is in its main *Hebraic* stream relational, we may also discover certain wrong turnings made by our liberal Protestant forebears—in particular, their too-easy endorsement of modernity, with its always implicit and finally explicit one-dimensionality. We are aided in this search, as well, by our growing unease with that same secularity, our wistful longing for mystery, and the new awareness of relationality that is brought to us by those who have suffered under the one-dimensionality of modernity, notably women. In feminist theology, as well as in Christian theology executed by those who have been "other," racially, ethnically, or sexually, there is a new appreciation for the dynamic character of relationality—for *both* difference and sameness, distinction and unity, and the potential mutuality of those who are different from one another. From these sources within our own context, as well as globally, we may be helped to overcome the "historicism" of our liberal humanism sufficiently to rediscover in the relation between Christ and the church something more than an abstraction.

2.3. The Holy Spirit: Reality as Becoming.   While it is Jesus Christ whom the church confesses in its speaking, acting and being, the possibility of its doing so is attributed by faith to the regenerative work of the Holy Spirit. The third article of the Apostles' and the Nicene creeds therefore groups belief in the church with belief in the Spirit, "the Lord and Giver of Life."

---

42. Mudge considers that "the notion of the church as mystical body is more fundamental to the underlying ecclesiology of [Vatican II] documents" than any other possible designations, such as the one that he prefers, viz., "people of God." *The Sense of a People,* 45.

"The Christian congregation arises and exists neither by nature nor by historical human decision, but as a divine *convocatio*."[43]

What is being claimed here becomes contextually significant only when one grasps what is being implicitly *rejected*. When faith professes that the life of the church depends upon the Holy Spirit, it is *denying* what, as we have seen, it is precisely the tendency of bourgeois Protestantism to assume, namely that the life of the church is dependent upon *us:* our enthusiasm, our "involvement," our activities, our "belief," our financial and other good works. The truth is, the first sign of existential disbelief is when people in congregations and denominations begin self-consciously to urge upon one another the importance of "getting involved." It would perhaps be possible to trace the decline of Christianity in North America, in part, by studying ecclesiastical documents and congregational literature from the end of World War II onward and observing the increase in promotional language, most of it mirroring almost exactly the promotionalism of the commercial society that is our host culture. Immediately after the war and throughout the 1950s, this approach seemed successful, for it could depend upon the positive determination of a society at the end of a tumultuous period of history, and it could concretize itself in the rampant church extension activity (the "building craze") that saw the erection of countless new church edifices, particularly in suburban locations. By the 1970s,[44] however, this ecclesiastical promotionalism had become hollow, and by the 1980s its essential nakedness was exposed for all but its own bureaucrats to see. When the life of the church is thought to be "our" responsibility; when people become concerned about "keeping the church alive," and "giving it a future," this can almost always be taken as a sign of the loss of any real sense of the presence of the Holy Spirit. A church that through the *testimonium Spiritus sancti internum* is being caused to live does not spend much of its energy upon its own preservation; it is too much concerned for the preservation of the world God loves.

To make such a claim is by no means tantamount to saying that there will be no self-concern, and even anxiety about itself and its future, in the church that is being given its life by "the Lord and Giver of life." For, again, we must remind ourselves that we are speaking of a process—an eschatological process. The "end" toward which this process moves is, truly, life; but this life is only partially realized, ever, and never in a way unchallenged by its

---

43. Karl Barth, *Dogmatics in Outline,* trans. G. T. Thomson (New York: Harper & Row, 1959), 142.

44. Unfortunately, as we shall argue later, the call for theological renewal of the churches that was particularly strong between 1960 and 1975 (in authors such as Don Benedict, William Stringfellow, Bill Webber, Stephen Rose, J. C. Hoekendijk, and many others) was not able to penetrate the structures of the churches, which were still too sure of their potential "success" to examine themselves critically with a view to renewal at depth.

antithesis. Where the real life of the disciple community is concerned, we may only say that it is *becoming* real.

Earlier in my career, I wrote a book titled *The Reality of the Gospel and the Unreality of the Churches*.[45] I composed the manuscript of that book under the impact of recent experiences of what seemed to me a "real" church. This was the church I experienced from 1972 onward in the German Democratic Republic (East Germany) and, to some extent, in other countries of the Warsaw Pact. Here, in a society officially hostile to religion, in which association with the Christian church was at least detrimental to social standing and vocational advancement, if not altogether dangerous, I had discovered Christian communities that seemed to me (it was the first word that sprung to my mind) "real." In an exceptional way, I found the reality of the gospel reflected in these churches. There had been a winnowing process: those whose membership in the churches had been perfunctory no longer found it useful to sustain that connection; those who remained were there because they wanted and needed to be, and because of decisions taken daily. The result was something quite "real."

By "real" I did not and do not mean anything like "ideal." On the contrary! Part of the *problem* with churches in North America is precisely that people expect them to be ideal, perfect—to be sure, according to very questionable yet ubiquitous conceptions of the ideal community. Therefore people can only accept these churches and retain their association with them by suppressing and repressing the unwelcome reality that is nevertheless there in them, underneath the surface. They may confess, in a rote manner, their sin; but they do not expect sin actually to manifest itself openly, unguardedly, in their midst. Through an enormous effort of will, tens of thousands of middle-class people in North America come together every Sunday morning, sit quietly listening to words that they either do not hear or comprehend only superficially, sing hymns whose content washes over them because the music is familiar enough to blot out any unsettling ideas the lyrics might contain, and then smile at one another in coffee hours afterward—all the while suppressing whatever intellectual misgivings and spiritual despair and human tragedy they may have carried with them into these "sanctuaries." *That* is unreality, and the only sane thing to do about it is to turn elsewhere for truth.[46]

---

45. Philadelphia: Westminster Press, 1975.

46. I suspect that this is a very common experience among churchgoing Americans and Canadians. Lewis Mudge speaks of "dysfunctional" churches: "The churches hold open social space in which the *question* of a beloved community of humankind can be asked. Yet, with their present structures and self-understandings, they are not able to account for the actual people-gathering work of the Holy Spirit in their midst and beyond. That is why I speak of the churches as 'dysfunctional.' It is not merely that as organized bodies they *mal*function, although that

Millions of North Americans of "Christian" origin have done precisely that in the past four or five decades. In fact, there is a kind of logic at work here that is as sure as it is institutionally devastating: the more insistent the controlling minority becomes upon keeping the "sanctuary" free of all that negates, the more those who look more for truth than superficial comfort are driven away.

It is the work of the Holy Spirit to "make real"—to "realize"—the individual and collective new identity that is being offered by, in, and with Jesus Christ. Too often, this process of realization (regeneration, to use the conventional expression) has been described by theologians and preachers in terms that are both unduly pious and intellectually innocuous. The older theologies were more honest. They knew perfectly well that the "new" identity (2 Cor. 5:17) could only be appropriated through an ongoing struggle with the "old"; that the "old nature" would not be "put off" without a fight; and that in the process, which would be a lifelong one, the "new nature" would certainly have to expose the "old" for what it was (Eph. 4:22ff.). Like the Psalms of Israel, the epistles of the newer Testament introduce us to communities of faith that are rife with human problems, from flagrant violations of the Ten Commandments to the most subtle kinds of human backbiting and treachery. These communities are not the "friendly churches" coveted by middle American Christians! Most of us would likely have preferred the old pagan cults, or the life of the baths and theaters. If such communities nevertheless continued and, in some cases, even flourished, it was because they offered something quite different from "friendliness"—but something that is also coveted by the human spirit at its best, namely authenticity. These communities must have been "real" in an unusual degree to have coped with letters like Paul's!

The Holy Spirit "makes real," and the reality that the Spirit brings cannot be possessed but only received; it cannot be stored up but must be ingested daily, like the manna of the wilderness; it cannot be accumulated, so that tomorrow I shall need less of it than today—it can only be lived.

In saying this, I am well aware of the fact that I am taking sides in a long historical debate. I am siding with Augustine against Pelagius, with Luther against some of the *Schwärmer*, with the Calvinist against the Arminian Methodists, and so on. The debate about sanctification is a complex one, but it is altogether too clear where the vast majority of North American Christians stand on the matter—for the most part, of course, without knowing anything at all about its history or its terminology. Anglo-Saxon Christianity

---

certainly happens. It is rather that their presuppositions prevent them from understanding, let alone manifesting, *the reality of the people whose possibility in the Spirit their institutional existence implies*" (*The Sense of a People*, 55).

in all its forms, with exceptions, has preferred to separate justification and sanctification and to regard the latter as a process of growth-in-grace beyond the initial phase of justification. John Wesley was simply carrying this preference to its logical conclusion when he developed his famous doctrine of Christian perfection. The preference greatly exceeds its Methodist expression.

In the New World, whose religious history, like its secular history, has been most deeply shaped by Anglo-Saxon preferences, in addition to this direct historical and doctrinal influence, sanctification has been thoroughly entangled with modernity's "Religion of Progress," to the extent that it matters little whether a denomination stems from Anglo-Saxon (for example, Anglican or Methodist) roots in the Old World or from continental European (for example, Calvinist, Lutheran, or Anabaptist) beginnings: the progressivism of the New World inclines church folk of all types toward a sanctification doctrine that insists upon gradual, almost automatic, improvement. The idea of our needing the grace of God as much at the end as at the beginning of a long life of sincere attempts at obedience is abhorrent to all but a few North American Christians. As a people, we think progress in all realms of life— even today, when quite different thoughts have begun to assail our collective psyche.

And precisely for that reason I will keep the doctrine of sanctification in close company with that of justification, as Luther did. Contextually speaking, nothing could be more important. Our society, like our churches, has practically been ruined by the assumption that time brings increasing good. Our "future shock" is nothing more than the intuitive recognition, late in time, that the future could be *worse* than the past, or at least that the bad things of the present might not easily submit to the technological and other "fixes" that we devise. Christianity, especially but not exclusively in its liberal expressions, has contributed more than its share to the illusion that has quite naturally ended with this incipient disillusionment—a disillusionment that has an increasingly cynical edge to it. A Christian faith that intends to be "confessional" must do whatever it can to correct the implicit and explicit corroboration of the religion of progress that has characterized our past. And a key element in that correction has precisely to do with the doctrine of sanctification.

It does not amount to pessimism and fatalism if one says that we are as much in need of divine grace at the end as at the beginning—that "we are beggars" (Luther) all the way through, "we" meaning both individuals and collectivities, including churches. It is in fact the only basis for truth-telling, and, consequently, for hope. If hope is dependent upon the gradual expulsion of the evil, sin, and death that still quite obviously characterize the life of "the regenerate," then it is a deceptive hope indeed. Deceptive and repressive hope has been the stock-in-trade of our white, middle-class Christianity on this continent. It constitutes, as such, an almost complete reversal of the informing concept of biblical faith, which was rightly identified by the Reformers as their "material principle," namely the idea of free, undeserved, nonpossessible grace. When this grace was made a very property of the time-process itself; when providence became progress; when sanctification became a steady, almost predictable increase in "holiness" ("successful living"!), the *sola gratia* of the Reformation was utterly compromised. From that moment on, the redemptive future depended on time—and on *us,* human beings, rational creatures who could "seize the time." But when time no longer unfolds itself in a manner unamibiguously beneficial to the allegedly rational creatures, as it no longer does, then there can be no other reaction from a society and church so conditioned than one of shock.

My purpose here, then, to state it in terms of the aspect of dogma under discussion, is to recover the eschatological character of the sanctification—the *"becoming* real"—that the Holy Spirit labors to bring to pass in the church. Like the labor of childbirth, this birthing involves pain. Not until we have learned that we only live daily by dying daily will we have a sound theology of hope.

On this note, we may conclude a chapter whose purpose has been to say why the church is and must be a confessing church and how, given the terrible ambiguities of its own life and history, it can dare to make such a claim. That possibility, we have said, exists only as and because "its own life and history" is continuously judged, infused, and supplanted by the life of the crucified one whom the divine Spirit causes it to represent in and for the world. "This then is the decisive work of the Spirit, that a man [woman, church] can no longer escape from Jesus, from the One who on the cross is able to let go of everything except his Father in heaven, so that in him the will of man and the will of God become one."[47] Some words of Simone Weil could thus be considered a statement of the confessing church at its most authentic:

> If it cannot be given me to deserve one day to share the cross of Christ, at least may I share that of the good thief. Of all the beings other than Christ of whom the gospel tells us, the good thief is by far the one I most envy. To have been at the side of Christ and in the same state during the crucifixion seems to me a far more enviable privilege than to be at the right hand of his glory.[48]

---

47. Eduard Schweizer, *The Holy Spirit,* trans. Reginald H. Fuller and Ilse Fuller (Philadelphia: Fortress Press, 1978), 79.

48. *Waiting for God,* trans. Emma Craufurd (New York: Harper & Row, 1973), 59.

CHAPTER ▪ TWO
Contours of the Church

3. The True Church: Parameters of the Discussion

3.1. Boundaries. The final paragraphs of the previous chapter introduce the subject to which we must now turn: the question of authenticity. What we want to ask in this chapter is in some ways a simple question, but history has made it complex, and its complexity is nowhere more conspicuous than in Protestant North America, where literally thousands of denominations and sects[1] and vague affiliations announce that they are the church. Our question could be phrased in this way: What may legitimately be regarded as "the Christian church?"

From ecclesiastical history, as well as the history of doctrine, we have inherited so many direct and indirect answers to this question that the result is rather bewildering. Perhaps, however, we can classify the answers in such a way as to facilitate our further reflections on the question. This history presents us, let us say, with two extremes, with a spectrum of possibilities between the two. On the one hand, ecclesiastical conservatism insists that the

---

1. In the United States (and similar observations could be made about Canada), from the 1830s onward, "a unique situation developed. The distinction of church and sect disappeared. The church had commonly been established, the sect disestablished, but now all religious groups in the United States were disestablished. Hence, from this point on, the American churches are commonly called not sects, but denominations. Again, the sect has frequently been dissociated from the culture, but the denominations in this country have created the culture. The Congregationalists did so in New England, the Anglicans in Virginia and the Carolinas, the Methodists in the Middle West, the Baptists in the South, the Lutherans in the central North, and the Catholics around the Great Lakes and in the old Spanish areas of the South." Roland Bainton, *Christendom: A Short History of Christianity and Its Impact on Western Civilization,* vol. 2 (New York: Harper & Row, 1966), 165–66.

boundaries of the true church may be drawn up quite strictly. It will, of course, depend upon the specific type of conservativism under consideration—for instance, whether it is of the conventional Roman Catholic or the fundamentalist-Protestant variety; but what is true of all such ecclesiologies is that the question of boundaries is really not a question. It has been determined in advance what the boundaries are and shall be; therefore the church need not concern itself with an ongoing attempt to *decide* where and what they are. Its identity is always quite certain. As with individuals who "know who they are," this is obviously a very satisfying, comfortable position for any institution to assume, and particularly for those who bear authority within such institutions. The agony of identity does not affect such churches, and this, undoubtedly, is part of their popular appeal.

The weakness of this position is also evident, however; and today it has become more obvious than in the past, to the point that many who have membership in such closely defined communities of faith find it increasingly difficult to sustain their own certitude. For in the pluralistic society they are bound to encounter others who, although "not of their fold," entertain many religious and ethical ideas disturbingly similar to their own; and this naturally raises for the sensitive among such communities the question of why their boundaries must be so *exclusive* of others. For such persons, the well-established, conventional limits of the "true church" begin to assume purely institutional, theoretical, or even artificial proportions. They appear to have little or nothing to do with substance, but only with form—perhaps only nomenclature. It was one thing to maintain the exclusive veracity of Latin or "Roman" Christianity when it occupied an almost monopolistic position in pre-Reformation Western Europe; it is something else to do so in a postmodern North America in which most of a person's waking hours are spent in company with others, the majority of whom do not share his or her explicit convictions.

At the other end of the spectrum we encounter the most broad-minded forms of Christian liberalism, which is as inclusive in its description of "church" as staunch conservatives are exclusive. In fact, historically as well as psychologically, the two positions often constitute reactions to one another. Appalled by the rigidity of an ecclesiology and church polity that insists that it alone is legitimate, Christian liberalism is driven toward a posture that is more and more universalistic. Correspondingly, as liberalism gains ground in churches, those who are fearful of the open-endedness of such a conception of the church become all the more adamant in their definition of ecclesiastical boundaries.

In our historical context, this particular polarization has been demonstrated very graphically during the past hundred years with the emergence of Christian fundamentalism. With the inroads made by historical-critical methods of biblical interpretation and other aspects of the Enlightenment mentality and scholarship, many conservative Protestants were drawn into a biblicistic reaction, culminating in the Niagara Conferences of 1895 and beyond, and issuing in the delineation of five so-called fundamentals by which the true church should be defined.[2] In turn, the continued growth throughout the twentieth century of fundamentalist or semifundamentalist forms of Christianity, including movements of the same within most of the once mainline denominations themselves, has inspired in those who could not accept such closed systems ever more inclusive, democratic conceptions of Christian boundaries, to the point of erasing boundaries altogether.

The apparent appeal of the latter position is signaled by two adjectives in the previous sentence: "inclusive" and "democratic." It belongs to the spirit of our present context to wish to appear as inclusive and democratic as possible. To exclude is bad; to include is good. That everybody should participate in decision-making is good; that decisions should be reserved for an "elite" is bad. In this respect, liberalism has become the order of the day—a reality that is regularly demonstrated by self-styled radicals who claim to despise liberalism while depending entirely on the language and tactics that religious and cultural liberalism introduced into our discourse. *Not* to be open, inclusive, tolerant, and democratic in such a society is to invite scorn from all sides of the popular culture. Consequently, a Christian liberalism that on the grounds of theological ideas such as the universality of the divine *agape* can both reflect and foster such values can seem reasonable, or at least inoffensive. Even where religious faith of every kind has become suspect, the secular mind is glad enough to find its predisposition to liberality corroborated by what can still be regarded as avant garde religion.

But this position is also becoming less viable. Even Christians of a basically liberal mindset are caused by the plethora of churches and sects all calling themselves Christian to wonder whether there are any limits whatsoever. As Bianchi and Ruether point out, "a dialogical church does not mean a debating society in which everything goes and nothing is decided or acted upon."[3] Whether overtly or covertly, a liberalism that is theologically nondiscriminating implicitly denies authenticity to Christian groups that are plainly restrictive. As for more serious Christians, they have long realized that the ultraliberal "position" ends by being no position at all. If there are no boundaries to the church—if everyone is to be included—then does the category "Christian" or "church" have any content at all? Is it not simply

---

2. They are: 1. the verbal inerrancy of Scripture; 2. the divinity of Jesus Christ; 3. the virgin birth; 4. a substitutionary theory of the Atonement; and 5. the physical resurrection and bodily return of Christ.

3. Eugene C. Bianchi and Rosemary Radford Ruether, *A Democratic Catholic Church: The Reconstruction of Roman Catholicism* (New York: Crossroad, 1992), 115.

a generalization covering humankind at large, humanity's actual differences notwithstanding? Is not such inclusiveness finally an absurdity? All are included—but in *what,* precisely?

As I have already indicated, these two positions do not exhaust the alternatives from which we may choose in determining how we should answer the question posed at the outset: What may be legitimately regarded as "the Christian church"? Nevertheless, the juxtaposition of these two extremes, which are not only theoretical but descriptions of actual positions operative in our context, establishes the parameters of the discussion. Our own response will be informed by these parameters. At least we know what we shall have to avoid.

On the one hand we shall want to avoid the kind of exclusivism that results from the perpetuation and hardening of conventional forms of orthodoxy which, however hoary with age, have their origins in very shaky biblical and theological premises, and are today falsely offensive—that is, they substitute the false scandal of arbitrary criteria of authenticity for the genuine *skandalon* of a gospel that offers any church "legitimacy" only conditionally and as a matter of "sheer grace."

On the other hand, we shall have to avoid the kind of *inclusivism* that has been imposed upon Christianity by liberal relativism, and which ends in the ridiculous spectacle of a system of "belief" that is both contentless and directionless—that is, indeed, no confessional stance at all but only a vague attitude of tolerance that is, ironically, incapable of taking seriously the views of the "others" whom it is so fearful of excluding.

Both of these extremes must be avoided by a theology of the church that insists that the church is a "confessing church"; because both are incapable of confession as we have understood it in the preceding chapter. Ecclesiastical conservativism is in danger of being so confined to its prescribed boundaries that it cannot go beyond them long enough to discover the world in which, and for the sake of which, its confession has to be made. Christian liberalism can be so devoid of boundaries that its flamboyant participation in the world makes no difference, finally. Professing nothing in particular, it can only repeat the opinions it already finds there. And since those opinions are in fact capricious and in constant flux, the church that is governed by such an orientation is pathetically bound to boundaries that are in the end more arbitrary than anything conceived by Christian exclusivism.

3.2. Indirect Self-Definition. By a process of elimination, we have arrived at the conclusion that if any community intends to be the church it must have some sort of self-definition, some sense of its own identity, some awareness of its boundaries; and that this must be derived from its own sources and not imposed upon it arbitrarily. From what already has been observed in the first chapter, we recognize that any discussion of the church's "own sources" must refer immediately to its God-given identity as the "body" of Jesus Christ, its "head"—an identity in which it is sustained by the Holy Spirit. We may speak of this as the church's "trinitarian foundation." If, beyond this, it is necessary to spell out the boundaries of the church more explicitly (and evidently it is), this must not be done in such a way as to minimize the significance of that one source and ground of its life. The danger of all very *direct* and *definitive* articulations of the boundaries of "the true church" is precisely that: that they will usurp this trinitarian source, if not in theory then certainly in practice, thus becoming criteria of authenticity that are no longer answerable to anything beyond themselves and their ecclesiastical guardians.

It is possible however to define the boundaries of the church *indirectly*. This may, of course, be done *via negativa,* by saying what the church is *not.* I shall make some use of this approach in what follows; but by itself it is not very satisfactory.[4] One may say that the church is not (for example) the religious dimension of the culture, or the established cult of the West, or a sectarian society, or "institutional religion," or a democratic "debating society" (Bianchi and Ruether), and so on; but unless one also risks defining the church more positively, these negative statements beg many questions. I shall take the risk.

There are, I think, two ways in which it is possible to offer the kind of definition of the church that avoids both conservative rigidity and liberal relativism—or, to put the matter more positively, that retains the dynamic character of the life of the disciple community as the body of the living Christ while providing certain regulative clues concerning its character. One of these ways—the more familiar of the two—is by discussing the so-called marks of the church as these are identified by the four qualifying adjectives in the third article of the Nicene Creed: "one, holy, catholic and apostolic." We shall treat these in the subsequent section, together with certain criteria insisted upon by the Reformers.

Another way of outlining the contours of the church indirectly is by considering its *relationships,* including its internal as well as its external relationships. All entities, including institutions and movements, are implicitly defined by their relationships. A nation is what it is as it stands vis-à-vis other nations, neighboring states, stronger and weaker peoples, enemy nations, empires or commonwealths or the trading blocs of which it may be part, and so on. Nations are also busy defining themselves in the manner in which they

---

4. Christopher Morse, in his recent *A Dogmatics of Christian Disbelief* (Valley Forge: Trinity Press International, 1994), 314–15, lists twenty-two misconceptions of the church.

work out their internal relations: how their citizens relate as individuals to the community; how different linguistic or ethnic or racial groupings within the nation treat one another, and so forth.

Similarly, the contours of the church are determined by its relation to entities external to itself with which it must necessarily enter into relationship: its host society, the state, other religions, and the like. And its boundaries are also being determined by its way of working out its internal relations: the relation of individual members to the whole community; the relation of the church to the churches; and, perhaps most important, the relation of the church to the "kingdom" or realm of God that it proclaims and anticipates in its life. The discussion of these relations will occupy the successive sections of this chapter.

In all of this, our intention is to describe the disciple community *theologically.* This is not an exercise in history or sociology but in doctrine. Since it is a *contextual* theology we are engaged in, we have, of course, to relate this doctrine to the empirical realities of church and society in our context. For the most part, this will result in a *critical* assessment of the church as we actually find it in our society, for (let me say this in advance) I do not see how we can contemplate the church *theologically* without being led repeatedly to the conclusion that what is, by grace, altogether *possible* for this community is being thwarted at nearly every turn by the actual patterns of ecclesiastical behavior in this transitional period in the life of "Christendom." Concrete discussion of the latter, however, will have to await treatment in chapter 4. Our present task is to pencil in the form of the church that is made possible by its trinitarian foundations.

4. The Marks of the Church

4.1. The Usefulness of the *Notae Ecclesiae.* In its usual form today, the third article of the Nicene Creed includes the affirmation, "And I believe [or believe in] one holy catholic and apostolic church. . . ."[5] Although they have been hotly disputed, the choice of adjectives is obviously not accidental. A Christian movement attempting to distinguish true from false expressions of the faith, as was the Council of Nicaea and subsequent deliberations, needed to find criteria of authenticity. These terms connote, in a remarkably concise yet suggestive way, precisely such criteria. In our treatment of them here, we

---

5. The "marks," which may not originally have included "holiness" (see John Burnaby, *The Belief of Christendom: A Commentary on the Nicene Creed* [London: SPCK, 1960], 142ff.]), were not much discussed until the Reformation period, when they became of particular concern to Catholic theologians wishing to refute Protestantism.

shall attempt to do justice to the positive, constructive theological reflection that informs each of the four adjectives.[6]

At the same time, we need to exercise a degree of critical acumen where these terms are concerned. It should not be overlooked that the church at Nicaea, and subsequently, was engaged not only in a necessary act of self-definition but, simultaneously, in equipping itself, under imperial command, to be the official religion of its host culture, Rome. Under such auspices, the quest for unity alone—to speak only of the mark of "oneness"—could hardly be thought a purely internal, theological matter. In considering each of the marks, therefore, we shall have to reflect on the shadow side of their application as well as their positive and useful intent.

It was partly because of that shadow side that the Reformation, while it could not and did not wish to dispense with the four traditional *notae ecclesiae,* felt that they were inadequate. It would be possible, in the view of the Reformers, to manifest conformity with all of these "notes of the church" yet fall far short of *being* the church. In the name of the primary authenticating sign of the true church, therefore, namely its foundation *en Christo* (in Christ), the Reformers proposed additional criteria. Principally, the Protestants insisted that the true church would be distinguished by the preaching of the Word and the right administration of the two sacraments that have biblical warranty. For instance, article VII of the Augsburg Confession states:

> It is also taught among us that one holy Christian church will be and remain forever. This is the assembly of all believers among whom the Gospel is preached in its purity and the holy sacraments are administered according to the Gospel. For it is sufficient for the true unity of the Christian church that the Gospel be preached in conformity with a pure understanding of it and that the sacraments be administered in accordance with the divine Word. . . .[7]

Luther, in his 1539 work *Von den Konziliis und Kirchen,* even spoke of *seven* marks of the church, one of which we shall consider later. Others wished to augment the list even further, but the process obviously lends itself to misuse, even to absurdity; so the Protestants tended finally to satisfy themselves with the twofold norm of Word and sacraments.

Is it important to identify such indicators of authenticity? Obviously enough, objectivity is impossible. To pretend to it is in fact blasphemous!

---

6. In my *The Future of the Church: Where Are We Headed?* (Toronto: The United Church Publishing House, 1989), 87–103, I have developed a more "popular" discussion of the marks of the church that may be considered supplementary to the "systematic" treatment of them here.

7. *The Augsburg Confession,* trans. and ed. Theodore G. Tappert (Philadelphia: Fortress Press, 1959, 1980), 12. See also Hendrikus Berkhof, *Christian Faith: An Introduction to the Study of the Faith,* 409; and Lewis S. Mudge, *The Sense of a People* (Philadelphia: Trinity Press International, 1992), 65–66.

Where ultimate truth of any kind is concerned, Christians must submit to divine judgment. God knows where the church is and where it is not. And here, too, "the first may be last." Yet without some serious concern for boundaries, and some measure of unity, we end with an ultraliberal diversity so devoid of any identifiable shape that it is indistinguishable from the cacophony of voices and positions crying for attention in the world at large. While neither the ancient (Nicene) nor the Reformation criteria of authenticity can be legitimately treated as if they were objectively verifiable tests (the truth is that in all cases they defy any such treatment inherently), they ought nevertheless to be considered serious points of corporate reflection, part of that process of critical self-examination that belongs to the "household of faith" (1 Peter 4:17). As norms, none of them were thrown into the dialogue of the Christian movement arbitrarily. They also have a history, a long one, and thus they constitute part of that "providential" dimension of what has been handed over: that is, they are provided to help Christians in each successive generation to distinguish the *esse* from the *accidens* of the Christian movement. And at a time when there is once again a strong danger that Christianity will disappear into a thousand factions with colliding emphases and ideologies, such traditions ought to be considered providential in a quite practical sense.

4.2. "One."   Behind the confession of the church's unity we should glimpse a whole substructure in which oneness, ergo integrity, is not only an aspect but in many ways the principal informing theme. The oneness of the church can be understood only if it is seen as a consequence, and a necessary one, of everything that is said about God, the Christ, creation, and redemption. As we have seen in *Professing the Faith,*[8] over against every temptation to polytheism, the early church struggled to sustain monotheism and thus its unbreakable ties with the parental faith of Israel. Again, in its christological debates, the Christian movement resisted (although with difficulty and never in a wholly satisfying manner) the tendency of many to present the Christ as a freak of duality, divine and human.[9] Despite its convoluted language, the Formula of Chalcedon is motivated by a desire to confess "*one* Lord Jesus Christ. . . ." Again, both the doctrines of creation and redemption accentuate the unity principle: all that is, is created, not only by the one God, but *from* the one basic "stuff" (*Adamah*)—humanity (*Adam*) no less than the other creatures, great and small. Moreover, the *telos* (inner aim) informing all creation, toward which the grace of the fulfilling *eschatos* (consummation) strives, is a reunification of all that is now divided, separated, and alienated,

---

8. Chap. 1, §2, "The Being of God," 51–71.
9. Ibid., chap. 7, §28, 370–93.

an ultimate harmonization of the whole that, without obscuring difference, overcomes the sting of difference under the conditions of sin and death. It would be extraordinary indeed if, given this multifold deployment of the principle of unity, we were to end with an ecclesiology that failed to reflect it.

In fact, on the basis of such assumptions concerning the foundational tenets of Christian profession, the unity that informs and even in some sense determines all of them would surely have to become the *foremost* mark of the community confessing such a faith. That community could hardly be regarded as the creation of the one triune God, living in discipleship vis-à-vis the "one Lord Jesus Christ," and in its life anticipating the ultimate reconcilation of all creatures, thus restoring the intention of their Creator, were it to consider its own unity incidental or merely desirable.

Precisely such an irony—that of a divided Christendom proclaiming unity—has been the chief negative motivation for the ecumenical movement that many, with Jürgen Moltmann, consider the most significant Christian achievement of the twentieth century.[10] If Christians are serious about their "ministry of reconciliation" (2 Cor. 5:18), then they cannot accept as normal a plethora of institutions and sects, divided and distrustful of one another, claiming to have been formed by the hearing of "the word of reconciliation" (v. 19). Such a situation is a scandal and a travesty. One is amazed, reflecting upon "our sad divisions," that anyone outside the churches would bother to take such a religion seriously. It may be that the discrepancy between the rhetoric and the being of the churches has done more than anything else in the last two hundred years to render the Christian confession incredible in the eyes of millions of people.[11] Not only have Christians permitted crass forms of disunity, and even thought them "natural," but they have introduced into an already disunited world countless additional causes of alienation. So overwhelming to sensitive souls is the fact that Christians have failed miserably to reflect the prayer of the Christ "that all may be one" (John 17), that the Christian message as one of forgiveness, compassion, peace, love and the recovery of genuine community can only seem a matter of woolly-headed idealism if not downright sham. To such persons (and in North America there are many), Christianity is compromised by the very fact of there being

---

10. "Christianity in the Third Millennium," *Theology Today* 51, no. 1 (April 1994): 75–89.

11. Albert van den Heuvel registers the shame that has been felt by most ecumenically minded Christians during the last thirty years: "It is a scandal to see the beautiful ecumenical documents which the churches drew up together far away from the place where God had set them and which were never applied at home. If somebody has sufficient courage to make a study of cynicism, he should buy the reports of all major ecumenical gatherings, read them, and see what the churches said together. Then he should go to the balcony of his house and look over his city at the churches that are standing there, from which steeples have risen to heaven since the Middle Ages, and see how nothing has happened to them" (*The Humiliation of the Church* [London: SCM, 1967], 51).

so many churches! If Christians in various denominations imagine that America is deeply Christian because church spires dot the landscape, they should consider again the visual message that is conveyed by these same spires to persons outside them who are actually given to religious thought.

At the very least, the existent disunity of those proclaiming unity ought to create in the mind of every sincere Christian and in the deliberations of every serious denominational council a deep dissatisfaction, and the determination to overcome it. At the same time (and here we must begin to consider the shadow side of this particular mark of the church), little genuinely constructive ecumenism can occur if the unity principle is turned into an ideal and treated as "a principle." The oneness that the church has *en Christo* is not an ideal, it is a reality; and it is not a principle but a gift, continuously being given.

In other words, we are sent back to our true foundations when we consider this mark of the church earnestly and in an informed way. Our foundations are not to be located in ideals and principles for which we strive, but in our identity with Jesus Christ through the ongoing labor of the divine Spirit. If we abstract the unity that is the fruit of this identity from the relationship that is its source, and if we then make of this unity a goal that we are to try to attain, then we have shifted the whole discussion from the realm of gospel to that of law, from faith to works, from grace to nature. Nothing, or little, can be as oppressive as the *command* to unite, when there is neither the will nor the way requisite to doing so. Confronting denominations with the imperative that they "get together" is as absurd and unfruitful as insisting that individuals become friends or lovers. Unity is either *given* or it does not exist. If it is forced, it is no unity, no matter how uniform it may become under certain circumstances.

With this observation, we return to Nicaea. It should not be forgotten that this important council of the early church was convoked and convened by the Emperor Constantine himself. Whatever else may be said about Constantine, it must be recognized by the historically informed that he was a very practical-minded ruler. As head of a highly vulnerable and incipiently disintegrating imperium, he recognized in the Christian religion a very "good thing." And at the center of that recognition, which has not been lost on politicians ever since, was Constantine's enormous respect precisely for the unity "principle" informing the whole Christian system of thought. Clearly, his object at Nicaea was to bring the Christians into line with their own stated preference for integration. Without that, the Christian religion could not do for Rome what needed to be done. The mere "message of reconciliation" could not prove the sort of cohesive force required; the message had to be embodied in a cultus, and the cultus could only become an official cultus if it achieved such unity in fact as well as in theory.

The same logic applied to subsequent rulers, Julian excepted, until with Theodosius the Great it reached its inherent goal: unity as law, both religious and civil. The Code of Theodosius (380 C.E.) tells the story very plainly:

> It is our desire that all the various nations which are subject to our Clemency and Moderation, should continue in the profession of that religion which was delivered to the Romans by the divine Apostle Peter, as it hath been preserved by faithful tradition; and which is now professed by the Pontiff Damasus and by Peter, Bishop of Alexandria, a man of apostolic holiness. According to the apostolic teaching and the doctrine of the Gospel, let us believe the one deity of the Father, the Son and the Holy Spirit, in equal majesty and in a holy Trinity. We authorize the followers of this law to assume the title of Catholic Christians; but as for the others, since, in our judgement, they are foolish madmen, we decree that they shall be branded with the ignominious name of heretics, and shall not presume to give to their conventicles the name of churches. They will suffer in the first place the chastisement of divine condemnation, and in the second the punishment which our authority, in accordance with the will of Heaven, shall decide to inflict.[12]

Later, in 381 C.E., the following:

> Let them be entirely excluded even from the thresholds of churches, since we permit no heretics to hold their unlawful assemblies in the towns. If they attempt any disturbance, we decree that their fury shall be suppressed and that they shall be expelled outside the walls of the cities, so that the Catholic churches throughout the world may be restored to the orthodox bishops who hold the faith of Nicaea.[13]

So long as Christendom held sway, the unity of the church was a powerful tool in the hands of both ecclesiastical and secular authorities. As Loren B. Mead comments concerning what he calls "the Christendom paradigm,"

> In Christendom there could be only one church within one political entity. To be *outside* that unity was unthinkable, impossible. To be outside the faith was to be outside the community. Heresy and treason were two sides of the same thing. In such a paradigm people who were disloyal to the faith or to the nation could be tortured, oppressed, or killed precisely because they were profoundly "other"; to be fully a human being was to be a Christian and a member of the Empire.[14]

---

12. Henry Bettenson, ed., *Documents of the Christian Church,* 2nd ed. (Oxford: Oxford University Press, 1963), 22.
13. Ibid.
14. *The Once and Future Church* (Bethesda, Md.: Alban Institute, 1991), 16.

The Protestant Reformation gravely threatened this law of unity; but inasmuch as the main Reformers did not seriously question the Christendom paradigm but rather sought alliances with other political entities (the emerging nation-states), they did not radically alter the effectively legal status of the unity principle. Only in the non-Establishment situation, which we shall discuss in Part II, is it possible to explore the meaning of unity as gift, not only at the theoretical-theological level but in practical terms of church polity and life. At their best, this is what both the ecumenical movement began by Protestants in 1910 and the Second Vatican Council (1962–1965) began to do. There is still, however, a strong propensity among Christians of all traditions to consider the oneness of the church from the perspective of law and not gospel. The sociological context of the Christian movement in its post-Constantinian phase enables us to think theologically about this mark of the church in a manner unique in post-Nicene Christian history. But until the lingering ethos of Christendom has been dispelled, we shall be haunted by the idea that unity is an imperative laid upon the church by cultural associations rather than an indicative implicit in its relationship with the triune God.

4.3. "Holy." That Christians confess the holiness of the church is not to be thought a boast, for this too is a gift, continuously given, and neither a spiritual quality of Christian persons and institutions nor a permanent feature of their life. It must be inculcated daily into the Christian community from beyond its own resources—more than that, from beyond its own intentions! For there is that within both the institution and the individuals composing it which resists precisely this vocation to holiness.

We speak of a *vocation* to holiness because, far from being a merely personal or moral quality, holiness, as it is applied in this connection, refers to the mission of the Christian community more directly than to its being.[15] This may be shown by considering the two connotations of the term "holy": first, that it refers to something set apart from ordinary usage; second, that it refers to the transcendent, to mystery.

That Christians dared to apply to themselves corporately an adjective normally reserved for the Deity, as in "the Holy Spirit," can only be explained if one realizes the manner in which they considered their purpose or calling in the world. The word *ecclesia* itself, as we have seen, contains the initially necessary presupposition: the church is a *koinonia* or gathering of those who

---

15. "Holiness has very little to do with asceticism, otherworldliness, or superhuman perfection. Rather, holiness refers to the persistent discomfort of the church with the unchallenged existence of oppression and exploitation in the world. Holiness also points to the commitment of the church to resist the defilement that toleration and complicity in human oppression bring" (James H. Evans, Jr., *We Have Been Believers: An African-American Systematic Theology* [Minneapolis: Fortress Press, 1992], 136).

are "called out" and "set apart." But as we have also been careful to point out whenever this insight has emerged, the setting-apart of the covenant people is not an end in itself but a means to their being *sent;* they are continuously redirected, as it were, back into the world out of which they have been called. They are more willing and able really to be *in* the world than, apart from their being called out of it, they should ever have been. They do not so whole-heartedly expend their energies now striving to get out of the world on their own terms. They are being enabled to say yes to the world, to their crea-turehood, to their solidarity with all other creatures—and in doing this, they are also being empowered to love and take responsibility for the others, both their own kind and otherkind.

And precisely in this they manifest the biblical meaning of holiness. They are set apart from the ordinary in their willingness to be among the ordi-nary—which, in a society that strives continuously to lift itself above the ordinary, really is extraordinary! Insofar as they make good this gift of earthly "compassion and solidarity,"[16] they exemplify the divine holiness that does not hold itself aloof but mingles with the apparently unholy—"tax-collectors and sinners."

Perhaps this has been understood best in Christian history by those mys-tics who, like Hildegaard of Bingen and Nicholas of Cusa, realized that true mystery lies not in what transcends the visible, the audible, the touchable, but in creation as such. That there is something and not nothing! That the life that shines through the eyes of creatures, guides their instincts, and makes their seeming dissonance and randomness a marvel of order: that this very ordinariness is so extraordinary, beyond telling! As another such mystic, Martin Luther, observed in his characteristically earthy way, "If you really examined a kernel of grain thoroughly, you would die of wonderment."[17]

This is not to suggest that the holy is *limited* to the physical world. Of course it is not. But so consistent has been the tendency of religion to deni-grate, despise, and seek escape from physicality (which some thinkers call the "Manichaean tendency") that critical theology needs constantly to reverse this habit and, in the name of a redemption that has creation as its object and not its obstacle, to insist that the holy is the here-and-now, this-and-that of everyday existence.[18]

---

16. See the recent work of Gregory Baum so entitled (*Compassion and Solidarity: The Church for Others* [Montreal: CBC Enterprises, 1987]).

17. *Works, Weimar Aufgabe* 19:46, 11. Cited by Heinrich Bornkam, *Luther's World of Thought,* trans. Martin H. Bertram (St. Louis: Concordia Publishing House, 1958), 182.

18. While I find Matthew Fox's way of setting the theology of creation *over against* the theol-ogy of redemption excessive and misleading, I can sympathize with his emphasis as a kind of strategic theology that is appropriate in religious circles where devotion and the pursuit of the holy really does mean flight from the world.

The vocation of the church is a vocation to holiness because the church is "the people of the cross." Discipleship under the aegis of a theology that is centered in God's determination not to abandon this world prematurely means being drawn ever more profoundly into the reality of the world, including its deepest negations. It is a "holy" people for the same reason that it is a "priestly" people (1 Peter 2:9): namely, because and insofar as it follows the Holy One, Jesus the Anointed (one "set apart") on his "journey into the far country" (Barth). It is holy because it does not fear and despise the real and reputed unholiness of the world but sees through it to the God-given core of its essential goodness. It is holy because it does not keep itself at a remove from life but plunges into the world with gratitude and expectancy. When we have understood this, we Christians shall have gone a long way toward redeeming the concept of the holy from its misuse both by ourselves and the secular world, which is uncommonly suspicious of just this concept—and for good reason![19]

But this introduces us once more to the negative or shadow side of the mark of holiness. If, where unity is concerned, that shadow side is associated with its misuse by powers and principalities that have their own reasons for stressing the unity principle, with holiness the shadow is cast by religion. Religion, as I am using the term in this context, refers to the Babel-quest for transcendence of creaturehood, for *securitas* and permanency beyond the flux, for control and finality. The religious drive for holiness is precisely the antithesis of a journey into the heart of the world and the darkness of the world; it is an attempted journey away from all that. It is Peter fleeing Rome. Against the ordinary, hum-drum, and secular, religion seeks the unusual, the ecstatic, the distinctively sacred. Its object is not "compassion and solidarity" vis-à-vis the creation, but proximity to the Creator—and for reasons that are never essentially different from those evinced by the Babel myth: fear and rejection of creaturehood, and the attempt to control the absolute. The *theologia gloriae* identified by Luther is at bottom a *religious* theology in this sense, in distinction from the *theologia crucis,* which is a theology of faith.

In the actual life of the churches, of course, faith and religion struggle with one another and are practically inseparable despite their theoretical distinctiveness. This struggle is nowhere more in evidence than in the two quite different preconceptions of holiness with which we have been contending here. For religion, as may be seen everywhere in our churches, holiness is associated with the symbols and rituals of the seeming sacred; for

---

19. In my book *When You Pray: Thinking Your Way into God's World* (Valley Forge, Pa.: Judson Press, 1987), I developed the consequences of such a conception of "holiness" for the meaning of prayer, which too often is presented precisely as a way of "getting out of the world."

faith, as may be seen in certain lives and movements today, as in the past, holiness is associated with the courage to abandon oneself to the other—to the poor, oppressed, and marginalized; to harassed and disappearing species; to those who hold no interest for society. These antithetical interpretations of holiness are probably permanent companions in the life of the church, which is after all a community of those who are simultaneously "justified and sinners." As Paul Tillich summarized the matter, "Where the church is, there is a point at which the ambiguities of religion are recognized and rejected *but not removed.*"[20]

What we must ask ourselves, however, is whether in the churches in our context there is even a sufficient recognition and rejection of "the ambiguities of religion." We cannot expect the negative connotations of the mark of holiness to be eliminated from the life of the churches; to entertain such a thought would be, once again, to turn this mark into a principle, law, or ideal. But we can expect, surely, that Christians and Christian communities would develop a sufficiently critical self-understanding to be able to distinguish the holiness that emanates from the religious quest from that which is given to faith as it seeks to express itself in Christ's true discipleship. Unfortunately, the contextual propensity to equate religion and faith, and so to assume that religious communities are necessarily also communities of faith, is such that it can only be altered by the most rigorously prophetic protest against religion; and in a society such as that of the United States, which still prides itself on its religiousness, this can only seem blasphemous.

4.4. "Catholic." Whether the adjective "catholic" in the Nicene Creed should be replaced by "universal" is a matter for local decision, but on the whole it would seem that ecumenism has advanced sufficiently in most areas of our geographic context to dispel the earlier Protestant suspicion of this term. That being said, it is indeed *universality* that is intended by this mark of the church, and by universality several things are meant: first, that the true disciple community transcends all natural and historical boundaries separating peoples, nations, races, ethnic groupings, genders, and political and other allegiances; second, that there is a shared confession of faith among all the scattered and varying expressions of the "one body"; and third, that the church, when it is true to its identity "in Christ," embodies an incarnational openness to all that is part of God's good creation—to the universe as a whole.[21]

---

20. *Systematic Theology,* vol. 3 (Chicago: University of Chicago Press, 1963), 173.

21. Lewis Mudge believes that "today we can discern in ecumenical discussion an understanding of catholicity more encompassing than anything found in the classical models. . . . Catholicity now begins to mean the totality of God's presence and people-configuring work in

This latter implication requires immediate clarification. It does not mean that the church accepts and embraces indiscriminately everything that is to be found in the world. When Paul wrote that in his freedom as an apostle of Jesus Christ he had been enabled, despite his own particularity, to "become all things to all people" (1 Cor. 9:18–23), he obviously did not mean that he now found everything equally right and acceptable, like a friendly modern sophisticate whose unbounded tolerance may be the consequence of nothing more profound than a pervasive boredom. He meant, rather, that to the Christian there is no strange or closed area of finite experience; everywhere, some common thread of compassion and discourse may be found.

> The intensive universality of the church is its power to participate in everything created under all dimensions of life. Nothing that is created and, therefore, essentially good is excluded from the life of the churches and their members. . . . There is nothing in nature, nothing in man, and nothing in history which does not have a place in the Spiritual Community and, therefore, in the churches of which the Spiritual Community is the dynamic essence. This is classically expressed in both the medieval cathedrals and the scholastic systems, in which all dimensions of being found their place, and even the demonic, the ugly, and the destructive appeared in a subdued role.[22]

The church that wishes to maintain control and exclusive glory, the *ecclesia gloriae,* sets definite limits to its associations and its concourse with the world; the church of the crucified one, who was numbered with sinners, prostitutes, and thieves, goes in and out of the world in all places and among all peoples. In the words of Gregory Baum, "The Christian Church must refuse to look upon itself as the white circle in the dark field of humanity, the house of light in the night of the world, the pillar of truth surrounded by ignorance and lies."[23] The universality of the disciple community in this third meaning, which should perhaps be considered *first,* is its sense of the "integrity of creation" and the breadth of the divine compassion.[24] There is something

---

the world. . . . The word catholicity now needs to refer to all [the] dimensions of inclusiveness and world involvement in Christian faith. It is not so much an attribute *of* the churches as it is a quality of God's reconciling work in which the churches are called to participate" (*The Sense of a People,* 179–80).

22. Tillich, *Systematic Theology,* vol. 3, 170.

23. In a private address delivered at McGill University on May 12, 1995, on the occasion of the retirement of the author and commenting upon the author's version of the "theology of the cross." Unpublished.

24. Commenting on "divine compassion" (from the root word *rechem,* or womb) and related concepts, Rosemary Radford Ruether writes: "In ascribing these qualities to Yahweh, Hebrew thought suggests that God has maternal or 'womblike' qualities" (*Sexism and God-Talk: Toward a Feminist Theology* [Boston: Beacon Press, 1983], 56). We are reminded in this way of the immense contribution that feminist theology has made to the reinterpretation, indeed the broadening, of the church's understanding of its "catholicity."

very moving about the famous sentence of John Wesley, who is sometimes falsely depicted as the essence of holy standoffishness vis-à-vis the secular sphere: "My parish?—it is the world."

To return to the first and second connotations of this mark of Christian authenticity, we ought to note that both contain implicitly critical assumptions, and not without reason. The first, in its recognition of the (may we not say) "global" character of the disciple community, warns against chauvinism of every type. To be "the true church" would mean to eschew every temptation on the part of specific embodiments of the Christian community to reserve *for themselves* the designation "true." As soon as a community claims (or assumes, silently) that it alone is worthy of the designation "church," it betrays its inauthenticity and invites correction. As soon as a community assumes that Christ's church must manifest the quite explicit characteristics and forms belonging to its necessarily limited appropriation of the life and mission of Jesus Christ in the world, it has opened itself to the *krisis* that begins at the household of faith.

Let us be concrete. Christianity has evolved mainly in what we call the West. To most observers, it is a Western religion—perhaps even *the* Western religion. The admixture of Western pursuits and presumptions with Christian teachings, an amalgam centuries in the making, is so subtle that distinctions between "Christ and culture" are very difficult. This incapacity to distinguish critically the sources of Western Christian belief is most pronounced, however, in the West itself. Although earlier (including nineteenth-century) missions beyond the West were frequently deceived by this admixture of "Christian" and "Western," and although today too there are situations in traditionally non-Christian parts of the globe where Christianity is promulgated *and received* without critical attention to the ambiguity of sources (especially where Western economic and technical values are coveted), the present century has nonetheless witnessed the development in Asian, African, and other contexts of a critical perspicacity on the part of the "newer" Christian communities, which are unwilling to receive imported versions of the Christian faith as though they were devoid of bias. It is a shock for most Western Christians when, through concrete exposure to contextual theologies developed in the younger churches, they are caused to glimpse the extent to which the originally Near Eastern faith of the Christian movement has been colored by assumptions and associations that have, in fact, little in common with the original. This lesson, wherever it is well learned, is a lesson in the meaning of catholicity.[25]

---

25. See, for example, the document titled *The Road to Damascus: Kairos and Conversion,* developed by Christians from seven countries and first published in 1989 by the Catholic Institute for International Relations of London, England.

The critique implicit in the second meaning of universality (that there is a shared confession of faith) in some ways offsets the danger that the critique implied in the first meaning will be exaggerated. Whereas Western Christians must learn that their professions of faith have been profoundly affected and altered by the circumstances of Western history, non-Western Christians who are tempted to dismiss theologies emanating from the West as inevitably imperialistic, racist, or untrustworthy are obliged by the confession of the church's catholicity to qualify their (perhaps understandable) prejudgment of the situation. There are Christians in the West, too, who know very well that "the judgment at the household of faith," and who are by no means apologists for a purely Western religion! The universality of the church means that the ongoing quest for an integrated and responsible theology and gospel belongs to the whole Christian community, globally. The necessity for contextual articulation of the faith, as at this point I should not have to remind the reader, is very great; not everything that should be heard and done in North America is appropriate for China, Argentina, or even Europe. But from the outset we have recognized that contextual theology, like every other approach to this discipline, has its peculiar dangers, one of which is the identification of ultimacy with what fits the here and now. This danger must be offset in communities of contextual discernment by an equally earnest attempt at ecumenical dialogue. Whatever the specifics of our *hic et nunc,* we all share both a past and a future: the past, moreover, is not limited to the Scriptures, and the future is not limited to the local or regional situation. The creeds and traditions of theology, for all their inevitable mirroring of contexts not our own, may be received by us as a living testimony to the search for universality informing the community of Jesus Christ from its inception at Pentecost, when persons of many different languages and traditions all "understood" (Acts 2:5-13). The future will obviously be a still more definitively common one, and therefore one requiring a common quest for integrating the truth by which we have been grasped. So long as there is history and geography, so long as there is particularity, the contextualization of the faith will be required; otherwise it would remain purely abstract—an ideology, and not gospel. But the mark of universality militates against the distortion of the contextual necessity through exclusivity and narrowness of vision.

Like the first two marks, catholicity, too, has its shadow side. We have glimpsed this quite explicitly in what we have noted concerning the tendency of Western Christianity to think *itself* universal. The universal that is the body of Christ, in which "there is neither Jew nor Greek, there is neither slave nor free, there is neither male nor female; for you are all one in Christ Jesus" (Gal. 3:28), stands as both a criterion and a judge of every *claim* to universality, and particularly where that claim is based on power: the power of history, the power of numbers, the power of possessions. Such power always seems to legitimate claims to universality. No powerful people, no powerful church, should be given immediate credence when it uses words like "all" and "global"; in all likelihood, it reads into such terms its own subtly imperialistic assumptions. The universality of the church, rightly understood, is premised on the assumption that the unity and ubiquity we glimpse but do not yet embody emanates from the cross and not from the throne.

4.5. "Apostolic."   The key biblical text for this fourth traditional mark of the church is Ephesians 2:19–20, which is addressed to the Gentile church: "So then you are no longer strangers and aliens, but you are citizens with the saints and also members of the household of God, built upon the foundation of the apostles and prophets, with Christ Jesus himself as the cornerstone."

With the movement of the disciple community out into the Gentile world came the inevitable mixing of a faith first enucleated under the auspices of Judaism with a great cacophony of religious, philosophic, and plainly superstitious practices, as well as political thought and intrigue. The question "What *is* Christianity?" informs nearly everything of significance in the ante-Nicene period. The answer toward which the majority of Christians were moved is the only one that is theologically reasonable, given the parameters of this particular faith (as, for instance, they are stated in the letter to the Ephesians), although it was by no means inevitable, for the power of such movements as Gnosticism and Montanism was very great.

That answer, first articulated in detail by Irenaeus of Lyons, turned the mind of the church toward its origins—meaning first and concretely to the Scriptures, especially the testimony of the Apostles who, Irenaeus declared, give evidence of nothing at all that is Gnostic. But, further, the practical question associated with this priority of the biblical witness was, of course, how that witness was to be ordered and by whom it could be safeguarded. As we observed in *Thinking the Faith* in our discussion "Authority in Faith and Theology,"[26] while Scripture has usually been given primacy among the "provisional authorities," its character as a diverse collection of narrative, history, doxology, exhortation, and predoctrinal reflection necessitates some kind of systematization, however ultimately unsatisfactory it may be. The many creeds and creedal statements that began in the second century C.E. to replace the pithy confessions of faith (such as "Jesus is Lord") that had sufficed in a simpler context are responses precisely to such a need. The so-called Apostles' Creed, which, as we noted earlier, evolved out of the old Roman Creed that was associated with the baptism of new converts, is undoubtedly the most important Western attempt of this kind, although it did

---

26. *Thinking the Faith,* chap. 6, §32, 427–49.

not assume its present form until much later.[27] What the creeds perform is really nothing more nor less than an ordered summary of what their formulators understood to be "the basics"; they are rudimentary systems of theology signifying what is believed to be the essence of *apostolic tradition.*

The further question of guardianship was answered by Irenaeus and others in a manner that must also be accounted altogether reasonable, given the historical basis of this faith tradition. Spiritual or pneumatic authority is by no means frowned upon by the writer of the *Adverses Omnes Haereses,* but without an objective or relatively objective test of spiritual giftedness, the community is at the mercy of many spirits (see 1 John 4:1). A faith whose foundations lie in historical event does not despise some organizational ordering of the community that attempts, through the passing on of the credentials of authority from one generation to the next, to safeguard the continuity of the present and future with the normative past. *Apostolic succession,* which for reasons yet to be discussed has been an offense to most forms of Protestantism, must nevertheless be understood as having the logic of history behind it. However haphazard, what better way is available to finite, ephemeral beings of sustaining a working relationship with the sources of their beliefs? Parallels are found in every system of thought that dares to locate its decisive breakthrough in some past event, figure, or movement. Socratic thought is to this day guarded by a rather small body of experts who devote themselves to the texts of that philosophic tradition. Marxism, despite its vaunted suspicion of ideology, made of the writings of Marx, Lenin, and Engels a tradition from which, in its doctrinaire expressions, deviation was not permitted; and the right interpretation of the sacred texts of that quasi religion rested with demigods whose machinations make the extravagances of Rome seem minor by comparison.

In order to appreciate the shadow side of this mark of the church, it is necessary, then, first to recognize its sheer *necessity.*[28] In the face of a multi-

---

27. See Williston Walker, *A History of the Christian Church,* rev. ed. (New York: Charles Scribner's Sons, 1959), 57f.

28. Wolfhart Pannenberg documents this necessity by pointing out—what in an age of rapid communications is easily overlooked—the importance of the "process of transmission" in the evolution of the idea of apostolic succession: "As vigorously as we call for a change from the authoritarian elements in the Christian tradition, we can nevertheless understand their origins and their strong hold upon the churches. The authoritarian structure of the Church before the Reformation and even afterwards until the eighteenth century was due to the special conditions of transmitting historical facts in the ancient and medieval world. Scientific knowledge was then thought to be restricted to the realm of general and timeless propositions. The particularities of history were regarded as foreign to scientific investigation. If eyewitnesses who could be questioned were no longer at hand, one was left with the decision to believe or disbelieve a tradition that was finally based on eyewitness evidence. In such a situation, everything depended upon the credibility of a particular tradition or of its present representatives. Any possibility of distortion of the *tradendum* in its course of being handed down to the present had to be excluded.

plicity of interpretations that threatens to wreck the ark of church altogether (which is what happened in the second century and the sixteenth century, and is happening again today), the recall to the original that begins with holy Scripture and leads to the ordering of Scripture's apparently dominant emphases (creeds, foundational theologies, and so on) really *must* end in the designation of an authoritative body of living persons who can demonstrate some genuine capacity for *connectedness* with the normative original.[29] This happened in the pre-Nicene church; in another mode, it happened in the Reformation churches, whose leading teachers grew to have great ecclesiastical and even temporal authority; and it is in process of happening again today—although it is unclear as yet how it will work itself out.

The logic of this pattern should not evade us just because we may dislike its empirical consequences, or some of them. A purely spiritual or transhistorical religion, whatever that might be, would find such a pattern both unnecessary and restrictive—which is, of course, the reason the more charismatic groupings in all three of the critical periods mentioned have found the apostolic paradigm oppressive. In some of the more radical or the protesting enthusiasms of the present time, it is evident that their objections are aimed not only at specific (for example, androcentric, hierarchic, racist, and so on) expressions of this paradigm, but at the paradigm itself. They want the whole process rejected in favor of a more pneumatic approach. But as previous historical experience of spiritualistic religion easily demonstrates, the ideal of such immediacy of authority regularly devolves into the reality of contending factions, the seizing of power by the most aggressive elements, and the subsequent fragmentation and disintegration of the community. The apostolic paradigm is not so readily written off by Christians who are clear-eyed concerning the historical moorings of revelation in this tradition.

That does not mean, however, that apostolicity is a problemless mark of ecclesiastical authenticity. To the contrary, it is perhaps the most vulnerable of the four marks, and its Achilles heel is not difficult to locate, however difficult it may be to remedy. It is that point (which, of course, is no specific moment but an ever-present temptation) at which the means for transmitting and guarding the truth assumes the posture of an end in itself. In other words,

---

Therefore Augustine said he wouldn't believe the gospel if he didn't first believe the catholic Church. A chief dynamic in the concern for apostolic succession of bishops was the desire to guarantee the reliability of the Christian tradition. In the ancient world, the identity and purity of the Christian tradition was secured only by authoritarian structures which regulated its process of transmission." (Wolfhart Pannenberg, *Theology and the Kingdom of God,* ed. Richard John Neuhaus [Philadelphia: Westminster Press, 1969], 94–95.)

29. Such a "capacity" entails both spiritual and intellectual gifts, as well as the church's recognition of these. Unfortunately, in practice, the "spiritual" gifts frequently were unaccompanied by intellectual ability and training, and of course the whole arrangement has been skewed regularly by the human impulse to power.

it is the temptation to reverse the order maintained, in a rather remarkable way, by Irenaeus and outlined in the foregoing, and for the priority of apostolic *tradition* as guide and norm for faith to substitute apostolic *succession*.

The latter, for reasons that are plain enough to anyone who reflects on the interplay of human weakness and the all-too-successful quest for power on the part of the few, has constantly overshadowed the end in relation to which it ought to have been seen as a very tentative if necessary sort of means. How often has it happened in the history of Christianity that those actually bearing the office of apostolic representation have been assessed on the grounds of their true presentation, in word, deed and stance, of the tradition of the apostles as it is testified to in Scripture and tradition? It is true that the protesting minorities that have appeared throughout this history, particularly at the end of the Middle Ages, have based their protests precisely on such an assessment. But the power of living, ruling, entrenched human authorities, backed as they normally are by all the pomp and circumstance of incumbency and, in most cases, brute force as well, outweighs without difficulty that of ancient writings and collective memory. Only when the power of the living authorities overextends itself conspicuously, or fails to give leadership at all, is the protest in the name of memory successful. It *was* successful in some genuine sense both in the second and the sixteenth centuries. Whether it will be successful in the twenty-first century depends, it seems to me, upon whether the theological and historical amnesia that is currently weakening once-mainline Protestantism can be in some measure overcome and a lively and operative collective memory restored.

4.6. The Protestant Addenda: Word and Sacraments. Where is the true church? It is there, answered the first Protestants, where the Word is truly preached and the sacraments duly administered. While "we must leave to God alone the knowledge of his Church whose foundation is his secret election," writes Calvin, and while "as Augustine observes, 'there are many sheep without the pale of the Church, and many wolves within,'" so far as the "visible Church" is concerned this is the rule we must follow as believers of the One who promised that he would be present where two or three are gathered in his name: namely, that "wherever we find the word of God purely preached and heard, and the sacraments administered according to the institution of Christ, there, it is not to be doubted, is a Church of God. . . . "[30]

From the perspective of nearly half a millennium of Protestantism and a continent that has seen the emergence of thousands of churches, most of

---

30. *Institutes,* book IV, chap. I, paras. 2, 8, 9 (trans. by John Allen [Philadelphia: Presbyterian Board of Continuing Education]).

them claiming legitimacy on these bases, one wonders whether this rule of classical Protestantism can be considered meaningful today. Hendrikus Berkhof, who in most things attempts to preserve Protestant traditions, is skeptical: "In our century [the four conventional marks] have completely lost their apologetic force. Already long before that the two Reformation marks had lost their discerning and sifting effectiveness, for each church thinks of itself as having true preaching. The time that the marks of the church could be used to make important decisions relative to the nature of a church seems definitely past."[31]

While granting the difficulty of redeeming these criteria for anything approaching objective verification of ecclesiastical authenticity, I am nevertheless of the opinion that they need to be contemplated seriously as defining characteristics of the disciple community. There are certain tendencies within liberal and moderate Protestantism in our context, as well as factors in our culture at large, that suggest the profitability of reconsidering these rather straightforward if hard to apply "tests" of Christian identity.

This is particularly the case with the preaching of the Word. In chapter 6, I shall pursue this subject in greater detail; for the present I wish only to draw attention to the way in which, in the older Protestant denominations particularly, preaching has suffered a conspicuous decline in the decades since World War II. The sermon simply does not have the prominence that it once had in Christian worship, and this is not due principally to the legitimate desire to enhance other elements of divine service. Jacques Ellul speaks of ours as a time "when preachers are as loath to preach as teachers to teach."[32] In issuing such a judgment, he does not mean (nor do I) to juxtapose the present with some golden age of preaching. I suspect that preaching has usually been less than "great." What marks the change in question is not so much the quality of preaching in the churches as public expectations and the attitudes of preachers themselves toward the preaching office. Congregations on the whole do not seem to expect much of the sermon—certainly they are willing to grant it far less time than in the past; and preachers, with exceptions, appear to have little confidence in what they are doing.

Many factors have contributed to this situation, but none, I think, is more immediately determinative than the influence of television. Television is not only the great educator of our populace, but it creates whole patterns of behavior that are incompatible with the modes of human communication that predate the invention of this "hot" (McLuhan) medium. Especially in North America, where commercial interests in programming guarantee that

---

31. *Christian Faith,* 410.
32. *The Meaning of the City* (Grand Rapids: Wm. B. Eerdmans, 1970), vii.

"entertainment" (Neil Postman) of the most immediately graspable sort will dominate, the public is increasingly conditioned to expect all attempts at communication, including private conversation, to conform to this pattern.

But the sermon as it was understood by both preachers and congregations in the past was conceived to be a type of meditation, reasoned persuasion, and spiritual conviction, and therefore a medium requiring both time and an attitude of contemplation. The sermon is addressed to the inner self, not to the senses. But in a society conditioned by image, spectacle, and the "one-liner," an atmosphere conducive to such address is extremely rare. The visible, audible restlessness of the average contemporary Protestant congregation, which seems as incapable of silence as of wholehearted participation, can be assuaged only by some attempt at simulating the "usual" posture of "the viewer."

When the children of Israel grew impatient with Moses and his "speaking" and "writing" God, they persuaded Aaron to put up a god they could see (Exod. 32:1f.). Aaron-like, the churches follow the law of supply and demand and give the people what they want—or try to. For the most part, ecclesiastical attempts to adapt to the world of images are not impressive. The "successful" churches in North America tend to be those that most nearly duplicate the sensory atmosphere of the television talk show or quiz program. The milieu is one of performance. Reading the sermons of Jonathan Edwards and others, one cannot doubt that their delivery involved something akin to drama. They were not, however, performances. The sermon, classically conceived, cannot be adapted to this approach. The milieu out of which it was born, the Hebrew prophetic tradition, is one that innately mistrusts image-making; it concentrates upon speaking and hearing for the precise reason that these activities defy the drive of human beings to possess and dispose, and require instead a participatory openness and waiting. The "preaching" that does continue to occur (it dominates the electronic church) is a far cry from the kind of address intended by the Reformers. It capitalizes, in fact, on the very *temptations* that responsible theology of preaching has always understood to plague this office: the cult of the preacher himself or herself, as a "personality," a "communicator," and the consequent displacement of the divine as well as the reduction of reasoned discourse and persuasion to harangue.[33]

In such a context, the Reformation dictum concerning the preaching of the Word could again be relevant as a point of critical reflection on ecclesias-

---

33. Neil Postman's provocative analysis of the role of television in our society ought to be prescribed reading for seminarians, and special attention should be paid to his discussion of religious TV. In his book *Amusing Ourselves to Death: Public Discourse in the Age of Show Business* (New York: Penguin Books, 1985), the relevant chapter (8) is titled "Shuffle Off to Bethlehem" (114–24).

tical identity. It is not as much a matter of asking whether this or that sermon is true to the Word of God as of reflecting on the question of whether the churches really need to emulate and cater to the society in the realm of faith's confession and communication. The real challenge that comes from this Reformation criterion of authenticity is whether the church can resist the society's demands for immediate intelligibility and "entertainment" and opt, instead, for a mode of confession and communication that is truly different. In almost everything, the remnants of the Constantinian church reflect rather than challenge our society. Must this be so also in the realm of worship and preaching? Ought the demand for popular appeal determine the character of divine service? Ronald Goetz once observed that "the true genius of Protestantism is to make extraordinary spiritual demands on very ordinary people."[34] Protestantism was bold enough to believe that human beings *qua* human beings were capable of listening, discerning, waiting for inspiration, understanding, being changed by words and thought. If that is "the true genius of Protestantism," what is one to say about a Protestantism that capitulates to the world of the image-makers?

It would be more difficult still to apply the Reformation test concerning the due administration of the sacraments. That insistence is bound up with the specific struggles of the church in the sixteenth and seventeenth centuries, and particularly with the question of whether a sacrament must be a practice instituted by Jesus himself and testified to as such in the newer Testament. The "due administration of the sacraments" for all the Reformers meant quite explicitly the observation of those two sacraments and no others. Beyond that, as soon as the Protestants began to investigate the meaning of those two sacraments, so many differences emerged that the question of their "due observation and administration" was already thrown into confusion.

It may, however, be asked of denominations and congregations today whether anything remains of the truly *sacramental* character of these rites. Given the fact that no uniform theology of the sacraments may legitimately be applied to all Christian confessions, one may still ask whether there has not occurred in this area too a species of secular levelling, removing from these ancient rites and ceremonies the whole dimension of mystery and participation in a realm of meaning and being that transcends the ordinary while employing precisely the ordinary (water, bread, wine).[35] Having been deliv-

---

34. "Protestant Houses of God: A Contradiction in Terms?" *The Christian Century* (March 20–27, 1985), 299.

35. This levelling process has, of course, been under way for a very long time. In 1948, Tillich noted it with great accuracy: "The decrease in sacramental thinking and feeling in the churches of the Reformation and in the American denominations is appalling. Nature has lost its religious meaning and is excluded from participation in the power of salvation; *the sacraments have lost their spiritual power and are vanishing in the consciousness of most Protestants;* the Christ is inter-

ered from the dangers of mere magic and superstition by the thoughtful probing of the Reformers and their successors, have we been delivered up to a
drab one-dimensionality that can only look upon these ancient acts of worship along the lines of "rites of passage," custom, or rote ceremonial? It is
often thought by high sacramentalists that Zwinglian and Anabaptist influences have robbed the sacraments of their depth; but could this not more
appropriately be attributed to the same secularizing forces that have reduced
reason to "calculative thinking" (Heidegger), art and music to contrivance,
and science to data? Neither the "memorial" approach to the Lord's Supper
nor the reservation of baptism for believers by themselves deprive these confessional traditions of awe. While "high-church" Christians may find nonli-
turgical traditions lacking in beauty and dignity, they are mistaken if they
believe that these traditions *as such* lack the capacity to grasp and communicate the depth, reverence, and mystery that belongs to the holy. At their best,
they represent another approach to the same spiritual transcendence that the
more liturgical serivces, at *their* best, embody.

It would constitute a major step toward serious ecumenical solidarity if
the denominations, instead of continuing to mistrust one another's theology
and practice of the sacraments, would realize that their common foe is a
secularity that has reduced human life in general, as it has reduced the whole
of creation, to a flatness that is devoid of transcendence and, indeed, of purpose. The question of whether the sacraments are duly administered, therefore, like the question of the true preaching of the Word, is not addressed to
the specifics of past confessional doctrine but to a broader and more existential concern, namely whether there is in the churches both a will and a mind
to resist the pressures of a society that has lost touch not only with the sacred
but with nature itself, which is fraught with "otherness" and eludes human
manipulation.[36]

4.7. "The Mark of the Holy Cross." Both the traditional *notae ecclesiae* and
the Protestant addition to these are, in effect, abstractions gleaned from a

---

preted as a religious personality and not as the basic sacramental reality, the 'New Being.' The
Protestant protest has rightly destroyed the magical elements in Catholic sacramentalism but
has wrongly brought to the verge of disappearance the sacramental foundation of Christianity
and with it the religious foundation of the protest itself. It should be a permanent task of Christian theology, of preaching, and of church leadership to draw the line between the spiritual and
the magical use of the sacramental element, for this element is the one essential element of every
religion, namely, the presence of the divine before our acting and striving . . . " (*The Protestant
Era*, trans. James Luther Adams [Chicago: University of Chicago Press, 1948], xxiiif.).

36. In spite of the ecumenical "breakthrough" represented by the World Council of
Church's *Baptism, Eucharist, and Ministry* (BEM) document (Geneva: WCC, 1982), it may be
asked whether the document adequately reflects either the one-dimensionality of Western secularity or the quest for transcendence that the failure of secular optimism has evoked. (See J.

summarizing, systematizing process of reflection on Scripture and tradition. As such, they are in their way both comprehensive and ingenious, which is undoubtedly the reason that, despite other influences, they have continued to inform Christian ecclesiology. If, however, we were to move from the doctrinal mode of abstraction to one of theological-biblical concreteness—that is, if, rather than seeking to derive from our sources general norms of ecclesial authenticity, we were to ask what the newer Testament actually says about the "true" church—we would discover one theme so prominent that one wonders how it could have been overlooked so consistently.

That theme is the suffering of the church. As Luther insisted, and as especially in our own epoch Dietrich Bonhoeffer exemplified both in his writings and in his life and death, the primary mark of the true church in scriptural terms is "the mark of the holy cross" (Luther). Not only is this the specific theme of whole documents (notably 2 Corinthians, 1 Peter, and the Apocalypse of John), but it looms large throughout the Gospels and Epistles. Despite the silence of historical Christianity on this subject, the motif of the church's suffering receives more attention in the Bible than does any other single ecclesiastical theme.[37]

It could hardly be otherwise, given the newer Testament's assumption of a basic continuity between the church and the "people of God" whose story is told in the older Testament; for not only in the Psalms and the prophetic and wisdom literature but in its more historical writings the Hebrew Bible assumes that Israel is elected to a role and mission in the world that will entail suffering. Moreover, the history of the Jews is a living-out of that theme—certainly not because the Jews extolled *suffering!* To the contrary, what they extolled and extol was and is *life,* creaturely life. But to be committed to life in a world that is marked by great ambiguity concerning just that subject is to encounter suffering on a regular basis. As I have put it in the title of an earlier book, "the stewardship of life in the kingdom of death" is a hazardous undertaking.[38]

Let it therefore be said at once: the suffering of the people of God is not and must not become an end in itself—something to be sought. The early church rightly warned those who were so tempted not to *court* martyrdom. Rather, suffering is a consequence of discipleship: namely, discipleship of the

---

Robert Nelson, "Baptism, Eucharist and Ministry," in *The Christian Century* 100, no. 27 (September 28, 1983), 846–48.

37. I first developed this thesis in my doctoral dissertation for Union Theological Seminary in New York City titled "The Suffering of the Church: A Doctrinal Study of an Aspect of the Nature and Destiny of the Christian Church." It was written under the direction of Daniel Day Williams, John Coleman Bennett, and James D. Smart, and is registered with the Copyright Office of the United States of America (Registration No. A 747982, Nov. 29, 1963).

38. *The Stewardship of Life in the Kingdom of Death* (Grand Rapids: Wm. B. Eerdmans, 1985).

one who said he had come "that they may have *life,* and have it more abundantly" (John 10:10). He did not say that he had come to introduce more suffering, or to make suffering a virtue. His object is life-giving, not death-seeking. But the life that he wills to give us, creaturely life, is a life that *we,* for our part, are forever seeking to transcend and avoid. Therefore there can be no gift of true, "abundant" *creaturely* life which does not entail birth pangs.[39]

That being understood, the newer Testament assumes that the disciple community *will* suffer, that it will do so in proportion to its real discipleship, and that it should "not be surprised" even when this happens in extreme forms; for this is simply part and parcel of the rebirth and new identity that, *en Christo,* it is being given:

> Beloved, do not be surprised at the fiery ordeal which comes upon you to prove you, as though something strange were happening to you. But rejoice in so far as you share Christ's sufferings, that you may also rejoice and be glad when his glory is revealed. . . . For the time has come for judgment to begin with the household of God . . .
>
> (1 Peter 4:12ff.)

The theology of the cross, which in the first volume I acknowledged as the "point of view" informing this entire study[40] would be a theoretical, doctrinal, abstract viewpoint indeed if it did not issue in an *ecclesiology of the cross.* For at the heart of the *theologia crucis* there is the cross of Jesus Christ, and therefore neither a theory (theodicy) nor an isolated story of one who suffered and was rejected, but rather the revelation of God's identification with suffering creatures.

It is precisely into this vicarious and healing suffering of God that the Spirit is bringing the community of Christ's disciples (Rom. 8:18ff.). "Jesus must therefore make it clear beyond all doubt that the 'must' of suffering applies to his disciples no less than to himself."[41] The new identity of which we have spoken in the previous chapter, identification-with-differentiation, is, after all, identity with one who "must suffer and be rejected"; therefore the *process* of identification, of "becoming real," *is* one of suffering: suffering both in the older sense of "letting this be" (as in the phrase "Suffer the little children to come unto me" [Matt. 19:14, KJV]), and in the sense of an active participation in the pain that is involved in the work of restoration to creaturely authenticity. The cross is that which the disciple community *must* "take

---

39. See Dietrich Bonhoeffer, *The Cost of Discipleship,* rev. ed., trans. Reginald H. Fuller and Irmgaard Booth (London: SCM, 1959), chap. 3, "Discipleship and the Cross," 76–83.
40. *Thinking the Faith,* introduction, §2, 22–39.
41. Ibid., 77.

up" (Matt. 10:38, 16:24; Mark 8:34; Luke 9:23; and so on) because there could be no identification with the crucified one, hence no "new crea-turehood," apart from such an act. But it is not first the church's act, and it is not first a commandment. The imperative "must" informing these and other biblical injunctions is grounded in a grand indicative ("are," or "were")—for example:

> Do you not know that all of us who have been baptized into Christ Jesus were baptized into his death? We were buried therefore with him by baptism into death, so that as Christ was raised from the dead by the glory of the Father, we too might walk in newness of life.

(Rom. 6:3–4)

We stress: the suffering of the church has nothing to do with masochism or a "martyr-complex" or any kind of legitimation of human pain.[42] It is in

---

42. As is well known, during the past decade certain American theologians working chiefly within a feminist frame of reference (Rita Nakashima Brock, Dolores Williams, and others) have raised serious questions about the function of central Christian symbols (the cross, suffer-ing, servanthood) in church and society. They point out that such symbols have served to legiti-mate the "nonredemptive" suffering of countless persons, especially women, children, and serv-ing peoples. "How do you justify teaching a people that they are called to a life of service," asks Jacquelyn Grant, "when they have been imprisoned by the most exploitative forms of service? Furthermore, how do you propose that we are called to service to Jesus, the one who has been sent by God to redeem us, when both God and Jesus have been principle weapons in the oppres-sive [white patriarchal] arsenal to keep blacks and black women in their appropriate place?" (June Christine Goudey, "Theologians Re-Imaging Redemption," in *The Christian Century* 107, no. 21 [July 11–18, 1990]: 675).

This type of criticism is deserved, pertinent, and potentially constructive. There is no doubt that "the cross" has been used to justify human suffering and therefore to lend weight to the power of those who profit from the suffering of others. Such "use" of the testimony to suffering that lies at the heart of the gospel is, however, the most flagrant *abuse* of it, and Christians are at fault not only for indulging in such misinterpretation themselves but for allowing it to occur unchallenged within the sphere of their social influence. The feminist, African American, and other criticism of such a questionable practice is therefore entirely appropriate and ought to inform all subsequent expositions of Christian doctrine.

When, however, the critique extends itself beyond the denunciation of misinterpretation and suggests that the cross, suffering, servanthood, and related aspects of the Christian narrative are *inherently* oppressive and nonredemptive, one must ask whether the exponents of such theories have not stepped outside the boundaries of Christian faith. This, in effect, is what Elisabeth Moltmann-Wendel has asked in her illuminating essay, "Is There a Feminist Theology of the Cross?" (Elisabeth Moltmann-Wendel and Jürgen Moltmann, in *God—His and Hers,* trans. John Bowden from the German *Als Frau und Mann von Gott reden* (New York: Crossroad, 1991), 77–91): "The women's concept of an absolutely non-violent religion," writes Moltmann-Wendel, "must ask itself whether it is overlooking reality in its dreams and taking refuge in a life-of-Jesus religion without perceiving the death of Jesus, and whether, remote from all criticism of religion, it is creating a transpersonal image of God as a power of life which no longer allows any paradox." Again: "There are two strident statements in the New Testament, in Mark, which are already harmonized in the later Gospels: Jesus' cry of dereliction on the cross and the flight of the women on Easter morning. They belong to the earliest Christian history. They cannot be harmonized, and they give us a glimpse into abysses. They cannot be removed morally. They fact the antithesis and antidote to the kind of preoccupation with self that informs the psychology of self-abnegation and the melancholy love of anguish. For to take up *this* cross is precisely to be delivered from the tyranny of the self through the grace of participation in something much larger than self: namely, the "pain of God" (Kitamori) and the "groaning" of creation (Rom. 8:22).

To express this in the language of a metaphor developed in the christological part of this study[43] and recalled earlier in the present volume, the suffering of the disciple community in its coming to be identified with Jesus Christ, is *representative* suffering. The Christ, we saw, suffered in consequence of *both* dimensions of his representational life: standing before God in behalf of the creation, and especially the "impossible creature" called *Homo sapiens,* he must hear the divine "No!" against human distortion of the creaturehood God intends; and standing before humanity as God's representative, he receives in his own person the human "rejection" of both Creator and creation that is the essence of what the Scriptures mean by "sin."

The disciple community is that community which is being incorporated into this representative life and therefore into the suffering that belongs to it—the end (*telos*) of which is healing and reconciliation and rejoicing: that is to say, *life.*

Unfortunately, the theme of the church's suffering, where it has been remembered at all, has too often been confined to its suffering at the hands of the "wicked world." The "Acts of the Martyrs" are filled with this theme. And it is indeed one side of the suffering of the church as this is depicted in the Scriptures:

> "Blessed are those who are persecuted for righteousness' sake, for theirs is the kingdom of heaven. . . . Blessed are you when men revile you and persecute you and utter all kinds of evil against you falsely on my account. Rejoice and be glad, for your reward is great in heaven, for so men persecuted the prophets who were before you."
>
> (Matt. 5:10–11)

This, however, is only one aspect of the vicarious, representative suffering into which the disciple community is beckoned as it is "knit together" (Col.

---

belong to the dark side of God and the dark night of the soul, without which the Christian religion, including feminist theology, is in danger of descending to a programme of psychological health or plans to change the world." There is not a symbol or concept in the whole realm of religion, Christian and otherwise, that cannot be used falsely—and few have escaped such misuse. But the cross is not an option for Christians. When it is abandoned in favor of a love that has no suffering in it, as we ought to have realized on the basis of nineteenth-century modernism, "Christianity" loses whatever depth it had.

43. *Professing the Faith,* Part III.

2:2, 19) by the life-giving Spirit. And when this side is isolated from the other, it gives a very false—a falsely "holy"—picture of the church. For it presents the church as a community unambiguously representative of the divine—"on God's side," so to speak—and it neglects its priestly representation of the human, indeed, of the "all-too-human." In and with Jesus, its "head," who in the wilderness was tempted, in the Garden "sweat great drops as of blood," and on the cross cried out in dereliction, the church is given the grace to enter into solidarity with sinful, broken, suffering humanity, and truly to *be* human before God.[44] Its own "transformation" (Rom. 12:2) is dependent upon its intentional priestly identification with the others who are "not of this fold." Out of the truth of the human condition, which it shares both in fact and in conscious identification, the disciple community presents itself before God. Thus its suffering, far from being only the suffering of the pure and holy, is the suffering of a humanity that refuses the purity and holiness that belongs to its *creaturehood* and can only—with and in Christ—"*learn* obedience" through self-emptying (*kenosis*) and the denial of the *doxa* that it covets.

Thus, in both aspects of the representative vocation to which it is called, the "mark of the holy cross"[45] is present; and where it is *not* present, then the apparent presence of all the other *notae ecclesiae* must be called into question. For to have unity, holiness, catholicity, and apostolicity in their true incarnational and trinitarian sense, *this* mark is indispensable.

And just here is where the whole history of Constantinian Christianity must seem, often, a mockery and charade. As Emil Brunner wrote,

> Luther contrasts the *theologia gloriae* as a false theology with the genuine theology, the *theologia crucis*. The whole history of Christianity, and the history of the world as a whole, would have followed a different course if it had not been

---

44. "The real and total and comprehensive task of a Christian as a Christian is to be a human being, a human being of course whose depths are divine. . . . And to this extent the Christian life is the acceptance of human existence as such as opposed to a final protest against it. But this means that Christianity sees reality as it is. Christianity does not oblige [the Christian] to see the reality of his historical experience of life in an optimistic light. On the contrary, it obliges him to see this existence as dark and bitter and hard, and as an unfathomable risk" (Karl Rahner, *Foundations of Christian Faith,* trans. Wm. V. Dych [New York: Seabury Press, 1978], 403).

45. "The holy, Christian Church is outwardly known by the holy possession of the Holy Cross. It must endure all hardships and persecution, all kinds of temptation and evil (as the Lord's Prayer says) from devil, world, and flesh; it must be inwardly sad, timid, terrified; outwardly poor, despised, sick, weak; thus it becomes like its head, Christ. The reason must be only this,—that it holds fast to Christ and God's Word and thus suffers for Christ's sake, according to Matthew v, '"Blessed are they that endure persecution for my sake."' . . . With this holy possession the Holy Ghost makes this people, not only holy, but blessed. . . ." ("On the Councils and the Churches," *Works of Martin Luther,* vol. V [Philadelphia: United Lutheran Publication House], 270–96).

that again and again the *theologia crucis* became a *theologia gloriae,* and that the *ecclesia crucis* became an *ecclesia gloriae.*[46]

In the North American context, this transmutation, neglect, and distortion of the theme of Christian suffering has been especially conspicuous, for, in addition to the usual ecclesiastical preference for a theology and ecclesiology "of glory," Christianity on this continent has been compounded with modernity's insistence upon progress, "happiness" and the elimination of all pain. Even to speak of suffering *positively* is to invite scorn, and not only on the part of non-Christian, secular society, with its incessant pursuit of the technological "fix," but on the part of Christians themselves. Indeed, in the United States and Canada it is by all odds the most prominent assumption of Christians and non-Christians alike that the role of religion in general and Christianity in particular is to *alleviate* all suffering—notably, that which cannot be alleviated by medicine, psychiatry, economics, and other human crafts and means. In the ears of people thus conditioned, to speak of suffering as an indispensable mark of the true church is to seem to endorse every form of oppression, from masochism to child abuse.

The tragic consequence of this insistence upon a pain-free world is the formation of a public that refuses to take into its consciousness the pain that is simply *there*—there in its own midst (for example, in the anxiety of over thirty million Americans without any kind of medical insurance coverage), there on the fringes of the imperium where "entire crucified peoples" are languishing,[47] and there within the soul of every human being who contemplates the harsh realities of life and death. When the church of Jesus Christ, the crucified one, adds its services to the efforts of all those agencies and institutions that have vested interests in keeping America "happy," it is a travesty beyond compare. Such happiness, which is in the first place ersatz, is bought at a very high price: the continuation and enhancement of pain in others, and the abandonment of truth in ourselves.

The cross is at the center—not, certainly, to *legitimate* pain and suffering, but to open our eyes and hearts to their reality, *and,* more importantly, to the reality of God's own participation in them, a redemptive participation whose object is the excruciating task of healing a world that is "sick unto death" without in the process destroying it. So long as human beings suffer, God

---

46. *The Mediator,* trans. Olive Wyon [Philadelphia: Westminster Press, 1948], 435.

47. See Jon Sobrino, S.J., "Awakening From the Sleep of Inhumanity," in *The Christian Century* 108, no. 11 (April 3, 1991): "The first thing we discovered in El Salvador was that this world is one gigantic cross for millions of innocent people who die at the hands of executioners. Father Ellacuria referred to them as 'entire crucified peoples.' And that is the salient fact of our world—quantitatively because it encompasses two thirds of humanity, and qualitatively because it is the most cruel and scandalous of realities" (366).

suffers, and so long as creation groans, the Spirit sighs. As the "body of Christ," the church is that community which is being enabled by the divine Spirit to participate in God's participation. The power of the resurrection is the grace given to the people of the cross to *be with* the suffering creation and creature, so that the sufferer is "not alone."[48]

In distinction from ideologies of triumph, whether religious or secular, the biblical tradition recognizes that, under the conditions of historical existence, suffering cannot simply be cancelled out. To cancel suffering—a thing that can in any case only happen in theory—would be to cancel creation itself, in all of its essential goodness.[49] What we call "church," if it is "true," is that sphere in which the suffering that belongs to creaturehood and the suffering that is the consequence of the human distortion of creaturehood is beginning to be borne—willingly. That is "the logic of the cross" (Reinhold Niebuhr); and that is why the only truly indispensable mark of the church is "the possession of the holy cross."

5. The Church and the Churches

5.1. The Old Problem—and Its New World Complications. The church, we have said, must have *some* sense of its own identity, and therefore some boundaries. When the boundaries are too rigidly fixed, they tend to deny in principle the trinitarian foundations of the church—that it is *God's* people, the body of the *Christ,* called into and sustained in its being by the *Spirit* who "blows where it wills." On the other hand, where there are no boundaries at all, the tyranny and confusion of the ever-changing agendas set for "religion" by the world are more problematic than the opposite danger.

The question immediately raised by these reflections is whether the boundaries of the church, Christ's church, are to be equated with the boundaries established and acknowledged by institutions called churches. Is the church (capital C, as it were) identifiable with the churches—and only with them? Is it necessary to be a member of one of the churches to be within the church of Jesus Christ? Does being in one of the churches *guarantee* that one is a member of *the* church? Are we to understand the old dogma that there is no salvation outside the church (*extra ecclesiam nulla salus*) to mean that those who are not members of the churches, or perhaps of *one* church in particular, cannot expect salvation?

This is a persistent question in Christian doctrine, partly inherited from ancient Israel, partly an inevitable problem for *any* movement that assumes

---

48. See the earlier discussion of "A Contemporary Statement of Faith," introduction, 20.

49. For a detailed discussion of this, see my *God and Human Suffering: An Exercise in the Theology of the Cross* (Minneapolis: Augsburg Publishing House, 1986).

an institutional status, and partly having specific pertinence to the *Christian* movement. Already, in the disagreement between the Jerusalem disciples and Paul, evangelist to the Gentiles, the problem concretized itself: Does membership in the *koinonia* of Christ's disciples presuppose Jewish birth, or at least circumcision? (see Galatians 2, 5, 6, and so on.). In another form, it is present in the Johannine literature: There are already those, apparently, who claim the status of Christian but whose fellowship is determined by "spirits" other than that Spirit that confesses Jesus Christ. In the Apocalypse, with its astringent "letters to the churches" (chaps. 2 and 3), we certainly encounter attitudes and assessments that would cause us to question any easy identification of Christ's church with the churches.

Very soon in its history, the young movement discovered that this incipient questioning of the newer Testament would have to become a major area of reflection and decision-making. It preoccupies the Apostolic Fathers, and the great Theological and christological decisions of the fourth and fifth centuries are almost impossibly intermingled with it. Who speaks for "the church"? How is the true church to be distinguished from heretical movements and sects? By now it is assumed by most thoughtful Christians, apparently, that there can be no question of an *equation* of the Church with the churches, or whatever may call itself "church" or the equivalent.

Thus begins the setting of boundaries—a necessary activity, but, in the end, perhaps far too successful! The early church tasted the potential and actual chaos that the boundary-less situation courts, and it reacted in the usual way: by drawing up boundaries, by bolstering them more and more, and sometimes by turning them into impenetrable bulwarks.[50] In the process, the *pneumatic* dimension of ecclesiastical existence was effectively curbed— and, in certain situations, altogether expelled—in favor of the institutional dimension. *The* church became *this* church, meeting such-and-such criteria of theological orthodoxy and observing such-and-such systems of government, worship, and so forth.

This equation of the church with *this* church quite naturally occasioned protest. The Great Schism of eastern and western Christendom is one consequence of the overdefinition of boundaries. The protesting movements of the late Middle Ages, culminating in the Reformation of the sixteenth century, constitute another. When institutional boundaries become inflexible and exclusive, the Spirit will raise up children to Abraham out of stones (Matt. 3:9,

---

50. Most notoriously, the Donatists of the fourth century, in the name of "holiness," wanted the church closed against all who had in any way apostatized during the persecutions, or even persons who communicated with *traditores* ("betrayers"). The statement of Augustine to which reference is made several times in this series ("Many who seem to be without are in reality within, and many who seem to be within yet really are without; from *De baptismo,* v. 38) was inspired by his opposition to the Donatist position.

Luke 3:8)—and peasants, and unheard-of scholars on the edges of the imperium.

But the vicious circle does not end there. In turn, the churches of the Reformation, tasting very soon the same chaos that was tasted by the pre-Nicene church, found it necessary to become definitive. And again, it was the *pneumatic* dimension that suffered most—both in the exclusion of those groups that were most affected by what they deemed to be the presence of the Spirit, and in the crystallization of dogma and form *within* the Lutheran and Reformed communions, resulting in the Protestant Orthodoxy of the seventeenth century and following.

And therefore, yet again, the pneumatic element had to assert itself over against the age-old institutional need to identify the church quite strictly with its institutional expression. And even the Augustinian-Protestant idea of the *ecclesia invisibilis* (church invisible) did not prevent this hardening from happening. In fact, one must ask whether the distinction between the "visible" and "invisible" church did not remain at the level of theory, and not praxis. It is comforting for the protesting element at the height of its protest against the rigidly defined and ordered church to cry that the true church is known only to God; but history intimates that as soon as the protest *becomes* the church, it is likely to behave toward *its* protesting elements in precisely the same way that it was itself treated.

In any case, this sad but perhaps inevitable history repeated itself, *mutatis mutandis,* in the protest of the Spirit-enthused pietistic, activistic, and other groupings of Christians against the established Protestant (and Anglican) churches, particularly in the eighteenth century. Many of them, like the Weslyans, wanted desperately to believe that the Spirit would still be welcomed *within* the well-bounded church—that the principle *semper reformanda* still applied. But the church that has determined in advance that its belief and its form and its polity are correct—are indeed of the very *essence* of church— is not easily moved; and therefore these later protestors and reformers had to form their churches outside the establishments, or as barely tolerated *ecclesiola in ecclesia* (little churches within the church).

And they in turn. . . . But there is no need to go on. We are *living,* in North America, with the consequences of these developments, and with further divisions and permutations bound up with our own continental Protestant history. The venerable problem of the church and the churches is accentuated in North America on account of the fact that the controls inherent in the old European situation, controls that evolved over centuries and were deeply entrenched, have been almost wholly absent in our religious history. As is well known, certain ecclesiastical bodies have *tried* very hard to import to these shores the kinds of ecclesial boundaries that took shape in their European histories, together with the systems of guardianship thereto pertaining.

But these efforts are foreign to the spirit of freedom and experimentation that has characterized our context from the outset.[51]

The historical and theological advantage of the legally disestablished or nonestablished status of the church in the so-called New World has been that the pneumatic dimension of ecclesial foundations has enjoyed a greater liberty here, for it was not continuously thwarted by strong church authorities backed up by even stronger states, armies, and executioners. The disadvantage of our situation is the other side of the same coin: without many effective institutional restraints, the boundaries of the church have been paper boundaries at best, giving no serious opposition to allegedly Spirit-inspired Christian movements and groups that insisted upon very different kinds of boundaries.

As a result, the ancient question of the relation between the church and the churches is augmented for us, and from time to time the augmentation assumes almost tragic proportions (Waco, Jonestown). It is not only the quantitative difference between the parental Old World and the New World in this respect (the fact that we have so many *more* churches); for here Engels' Law applies: at a certain point, a change in quantity introduces a change in quality. To have (as in western Germany) three of four churches claiming the status of church, most of them rather modestly so, is one thing; to have fifteen hundred or (according to some statistics) four thousand denominations making this claim, many of them without the least modesty, is something else! What it means, in fact, is that the setting of boundaries seems to almost everyone except the most die-hard fundamentalists an exercise in futility; for no boundaries whatever, under such circumstances, can be made to stick. Why bother, then, even considering them? Let it be! If it ends with every individual having his or her own private sanctuary, so be it. Is such individualism not in any case the general preference of our society?[52]

But serious Christian theology cannot let it be. For the fragmentation of the church is not only an institutional scandal, it is a theological scandal—a scandal of faith. This faith, after all, is centered in the belief that, through the judging love and loving judgment of God in Christ, reconciliation, mutuality, communality, "oneness" has been made possible.[53] The "dividing wall of hostility" (Eph. 2:14) has been broken down; we are able to respond in love to

---

51. Concerning the attempts of Anglican bishops from England to import to northern Canada the regulations they learned in the motherland, a witty Canadian clergyman, the late Ray McCleary, remarked in the presence of Reinhold Niebuhr: "Their gaiters did not go well with moccasins."

52. See their discussion "The New Voluntarism" in Wade Clark Roof and William McKinney, *American Mainline Religion: Its Changing Shape and Future* (New Brunswick and London: Rutgers University Press, 1987), 40ff.

53. See Mudge, *The Sense of a People*, 210.

love given. Unity here does not imply uniformity, but it does imply mutuality; and this gospel is rendered *incredible*, quite literally, unbelievable, in a situation in which Christians not only give no evidence at all of such mutuality but adamantly exclude one another, some openly, some more subtly. The question about the relation of the church to the churches, therefore, far from being passé in our context, is raised to existential heights never experienced in Old World settings, the wars, hostilities, and bloodshed of that European past notwithstanding. With so many *churches,* what can "the church" possibly mean? North American denominationalism is simply a *scandalon*— and not even a false scandal, but a real one. It literally betrays the gospel and makes a mockery of Jesus' high priestly prayer "that all may be one" (John 17).

Must we not conclude, moreover, that the scandalous character of this Christianity is particularly the responsibility of the older, formerly mainline denominations? While the absurdity of the situation may be more visible in the newer, "sectarian" groups, with their wild claims to ultimacy, the greater guilt for it must surely be laid at the doorstep of those from whose treasure houses of doctrine and experience wisdom might have been drawn—might still be drawn—to ameliorate this poverty of understanding. Instead, for the most part these denominations have tacitly withdrawn from the discussion, practicing a merely token ecumenism, and at bottom nurturing a "live and let live" liberality that, however admirable in its civility, has lost all touch with theological foundations and the wisdom they in some measure contain.

Let us attempt to outline something of that wisdom.

5.2. Church as Paradox.   If one asks concerning the church, as it is addressed in the newer Testament, "What is being assumed about this community by Paul and the others who are writing to it?" one is struck at once by two prominent facts: first, it is usually assumed that there is something wrong—or at least not yet right—about these little "fellowships." Second, it is assumed that they are nonetheless to be taken quite seriously as *ekklesia,* communities of those who are "called out" in order to be sent back "into" the world—that they are "the saints," "the church of God." It will be profitable for us to reflect briefly on this seeming paradox.

Concerning the first assumption, familiarity with the texts demonstrates that there is hardly a document in the newer Testament that does not contain or imply a critical note with respect to those to whom it is directly or indirectly addressed. In some instances, notably in the four Gospels and the Acts of the Apostles, the critique is certainly more by way of implication than it is straightforward. In a real sense, the very act of *writing down,* of *ordering,* the story of Jesus and his followers must be understood as a corrective activity, intended to curb misinformation and misinterpretation and the exponen-

tial growth of legends and "apocryphal" accounts. This already implies falli-
bility in the community—forgetfulness, readiness to listen to novelty, to be
titillated by the miraculous, tempted by the thought of special favor, and so
on. But even in the Gospels this indirectness not infrequently becomes rather
direct. It would be hard to read the "woes" of the Synoptics (Matt.18:7ff.,
23:13f.; Luke 6:24f., 11:42f.; and so on), or the parable of the kingdom at the
end of Matthew's Gospel (25:1ff.), or even the Beatitudes (Matt. 5ff., par.)
without feeling something of their chastening power. And nearly every parable of Jesus speaks as much to the lingering sins of the faithful—the propensity to self-righteousness (the publican and the Pharisee); the failure to "go
the second mile"; the thirst for power and greatness; the propensity to seek
retribution, and so on—as to the condition of the faithless. Surely the early
church could not remember Jesus' words to its alleged founding "rock"
(*Petros*)—"Get thee behind me, Satan!" (Matt. 16:23)—without asking itself
whether it had in fact exchanged "the mark of the holy cross" for something
more immediately desirable. We could go on.

When it comes to the Epistles and the Apocalypse, the questioning is more
immediate and insistent. For example:

> Examine yourselves, to see whether you are holding to your faith. Test your-
> selves. Do you not realize that Jesus Christ is in you? . . . Mend your ways, heed
> my appeal, agree with one another, live in peace.
>
> (2 Cor. 13:5f.)

> O foolish Galatians! Who has bewitched you, before whose eyes Jesus Christ
> was publicly portrayed as crucified? Let me ask you only this: Did you receive
> the Spirit by works of the law, or by hearing with faith? Are you so foolish?
> Having begun with the Spirit, are you now ending with the flesh? Did you
> experience so many things in vain? . . .
>
> (Gal. 3:1ff.)

> Come now, you who say, "Today or tomorrow we will go into such and such a
> town and spend a year there and trade and get gain whereas you do not know
> about tomorrow. What is your life? For you are a mist that appears for a little
> time and then vanishes. Instead you ought to say, "If the Lord wills, we shall
> live and we shall do this or that." As it is, you boast in your arrogance. . . .
> Come now, you rich . . .
>
> (James 4:13ff.)

> And to the angel of the church in Sardis write. . . . "I know your works; you
> have the name of being alive, and you are dead. . . . "
>
> (Rev. 3:1)

These and countless other texts of the same tenor do not contain the kinds
of sentiments that are addressed to congregations whom their authors con-

sider altogether genuine and blameless. There is no suggestion here of a satisfactory appropriation of grace, a completed journey. To the contrary! It is
not even certain that those so addressed are on the right road! Their behavior
might be so contradictory of the new identity they are being offered that, like
the nondescript church at Laodicea, they will have to be "spewed out" (Rev.
3:16). At very least, nothing at all is to be presumed about their future (1
Cor. 10). The "wild olive shoot" is not indispensable:

> If the root is holy, so are the branches. But if some of the branches were broken
> off, and you, a wild olive shoot, were grafted in their place to share the richness
> of the olive tree, do not boast over the branches. If you do boast, remember it
> is not you that support the root but the root that supports you. . . . For if you
> have been cut from what is by nature a wild olive tree, and grafted, contrary to
> nature, into a cultivated olive tree, how much more will these natural branches
> be grafted back into their own olive tree. . . .
>
> (Rom. 11:16bff.)

Yet, to speak to the second assumption, such warnings as these do not
stand alone. They have the impact that they do, in fact, only because these
same scriptures assume that the persons and communities so addressed have
been chosen as vehicles, messengers, and "stewards of the mercies of God"
(1 Cor. 4:1). Their "election" is apparently taken for granted, although their
faithfulness is not. The early church remembered the words of Jesus: "I have
called you friends, for all that I have heard from my Father I have made
known to you. You did not choose me, but I chose you and appointed you
that you should go and bear fruit and that your fruit should abide; so that
whatever you ask the Father in my name, he may give it to you" (John
15:15bf.).

Individual members of the *koinonia* may be severely castigated or even
excluded; but the documents continue to address these "little flocks" as those
whose "election" is unquestionable.

> Who shall bring any charge against God's elect? It is God who justifies; who is
> to condemn? Is it Christ Jesus, who died, yes, who was raised from the dead,
> who is at the right hand of God, who indeed intercedes for us? Who shall sepa-
> rate us from the love of Christ?
>
> (Rom. 8:33–35a)

> Remember that you were . . . separated from Christ, alienated from the com-
> monwealth of Israel, and strangers to the covenants of promise, having no hope
> and without God in the world. But now in Christ Jesus you who were once far
> off have been brought near in the blood of Christ. . . . So then you are no longer
> strangers and sojourners, but you are fellow citizens with the saints and mem-

bers of the household of God, built upon the foundation of the apostles and prophets, Christ Jesus himself being the chief cornerstone . . .

(Eph. 2:12ff.)

The "indicative" of the new condition (*en Christo*) is presupposed even by the most stringent "imperatives," all of which seem to counsel, "*Be* what you *are!*" It is almost an a priori of these scriptural letters that the community and its members will sin; but this "weakness" does not nullify the relationship with God. If confessed, it may even strengthen that relationship:

Since then we have a great high priest who has passed through the heavens, Jesus, the Son of God, let us hold fast our confession. For we have not a high priest who is unable to sympathize with our weaknesses, but one who in every respect has been tempted as we are, yet without sinning. Let us then with confidence draw near to the throne of grace.

(Heb. 4:14–16a)

These two assumptions give rise to a two-sided perspective on the question under discussion, that is, whether the "true church" can be thought continuous with the empirical church. We could express that perspective as follows: it can never be assumed that what identifies itself as church *is already* what it is called to be; and yet the profession of such an identity may not be regarded lightly. Otherwise stated, there is no absolute correspondence between the authentic "body of Christ" and the empirical communities called churches; and yet the churches should not be scorned, and those who bear responsibility within them may and must expect them to "be who they are."

This *perspective,* which of course predates the establishment of Christianity in the fourth century C.E., should be looked upon as the scripturally based background assumed by Augustine of Hippo when, in the *post*-establishment situation, he found it necessary *radically* to distinguish the empirical from the true church. Augustine's dictum, to which we have already made brief reference, was: "Many who seem to be without are in reality within, and many who seem to be within yet really are without."[54] For after the Constantinian-Theodosian arrangements with the Christian religion made it virtually illegal to be anything *other than* Christian, the problem of identifying genuine membership in the *soma Christou* was greatly increased for serious Christians.[55] The newer Testamental situation was thus enormously altered;

---

54. *De baptismo,* v. 38.
55. "In his [Augustine's] time Church membership was already, by a decree of the Emperor Theodosius, a statutory obligation. . . . His study of Paul had taught him something of the Pauline idea of the Ekklesia which referred to something wholly different from the all-inclusive Church" (Emil Brunner, *The Christian Doctrine of the Church, Faith, and the Consummation,*

yet the perspective provided by the two assumptions already present in that early context could be drawn upon to provide a way of maintaining some modicum of integrity in what was in fact a highly ambiguous and compromising situation for the Christian movement.

This is the scriptural and historical background of the Reformation distinction, *ecclesia visibilis* and *ecclesia invisibilis.* Because the boundaries of the "true church" are known only to God, the mere claim to being "the body of Christ" is no guarantee of the reality; indeed, presumption being the most unacceptable attitude of "the wild olive shoot," it is quite possible that the louder the *claim* to authenticity, the more questionable its truth! On the other hand, since the true church is not to be conceived as an ideal state already achieved but a community in transit (*communio viatorum*), a mixture of the sacred and the profane, of obedience and sin, the mere presence in churches of conditions apparently contradictory to the "new being" does not have to lead to the conclusion that such communities are inauthentic.[56]

This position obviously pits itself against certain alternative postures. Against those who insist that the church is coincidental with the churches (which in practice usually means with one particular ecclesiastical institution), one holding the typical Augustinian-Reformation view will insist that the boundaries of the true church are known only to God. In other words, the "body of Christ" is a mystery that should make all of us who claim membership in it very humble. Whenever we are tempted to equate our own denomination or fellowship with the true church, we had better remember that, in Jesus' recorded parable of the kingdom (Matt. 25), those who claimed all the proper credentials were excluded, while those who were invited to enter did not even know that they had been in such company! Jesus told some of his contemporaries that he had "other sheep who were not of this fold" (John 10:14); and although this statement was addressed to presumptuous Jews, it is as applicable to presumptuous Christians. There is too much in the tradition, both on the positive and the negative sides, to warrant an ecclesiology that does not leave much room for mystery and unpredictability when it comes to the identity of the authentic *koinonia.* Whether this mystery is sustained through a concept such as the "church invisible," or the "latent church" (Tillich), or "anonymous Christianity" (Rahner), is not so important as *that* it is sustained.

On the other side, it is obvious that the Reformation teaching does not intend us to *take refuge in the "church invisible."*

Dogmatics, vol. 3, trans. David Cairns and T. H. L. Parker [London: Lutterworth Press, 1962], 28).

56. "The paradox of the churches is the fact that they participate, on the one hand, in the ambiguities of life in general and of the religious life in particular and, on the other hand, in the unambiguous life of the Spiritual Community." (Tillich, *Systematic Theology,* vol. 3, 165.)

> The *koinonia* is neither identical with the visible church nor separable from the visible church. *Ecclesiola in ecclesia,* the little church within the church, the leaven in the lump, the remnant in the midst of the covenant people, the *koinonia* in the world—this is the reality which is the starting point for living of the Christian life and for our thinking about Christian ethics.[57]

There is a strong temptation among nearly all serious Christians today to decry the empirical church and even to abandon institutional churches. The churches frequently seem hopeless, anachronistic, and immune to depth of thought and action. Many of the most committed Christians in North America are driven to conclude that they shall have to exercise their commitment to Jesus Christ outside these ancient structures, which are so freighted with their own need to survive that they have lost sight of any mission larger than their survival. To feel *comfortable* in the churches, any of them, in our context, may be to be in danger of spiritual and theological myopia. It requires an enormous effort of will, not necessarily to *join* the churches but at least to remain within them, bear their preoccupation with trivia, and work toward their "reformation."

But the Augustinian-Protestant teaching of the *ecclesia invisibilis* should not constitute for us a theoretical escape from our calling within the churches. These institutions must be taken seriously, and perhaps *especially* at this "awkward" (Lindbeck) juncture of their unprecedented transition from the established to the disestablished position. Karl Barth's advice is still valid: "Take good note, that a parson who does not believe that in this congregation of his [or hers], including those men and women, old wives and children, Christ's congregation exists, does not believe at all in the existence of the Church." He continues:

> *Credo ecclesiam* means that I believe that here, at this place, in this visible assembly, the work of the Holy Spirit takes place. By that is not intended a deification of the creature; the Church is not the object of faith, we do not believe *in* the Church; but we do believe that in this congregation the work of the Holy Spirit becomes an event. The mystery of the Church is that for the Holy Spirit it is not too small a thing to have such forms. Consequently, there are in truth not many Churches but *one* Church in terms of this or that *concrete* one, which should recognize itself as the one Church and in all the others as well.[58]

This is a statement of the other side of the paradox of the church already present in the newer Testamental perspective; and it is probably the more important *side* of that paradox for our present ecclesiastical context, for now,

---

57. Paul Lehmann, *Ethics in a Christian Context* (New York: Harper & Row, 1963), 72.
58. *Dogmatics in Outline,* trans. G. T. Thomson (New York: Harper & Row, 1959), 143.

"at the end of the Constantinian era," with disintegrating and unstable churches all about us, it is difficult to maintain much confidence in the "church visible." The other side of the paradox should not be neglected, however, for the temptation to presumption has by no means disappeared with the disappearance of a confident form of Christendom. It is of the essence of the church that God permits it to participate in God's own judgment (*krisis*) of it—the *krisis* must always "begin at the household of God" (1 Peter 4:17). When this self-judgment is not present—when the critical function of theology and prophetic faith gives way to promotionalism and survivalism—something of the essence of Christ's church has been lost.[59]

Although the grace of God is by no means confined to "the churches," those who continue within them are therefore obliged to believe that the future of the Christian movement is very much dependent upon the present life, decisions, and actions of the churches. Christians do not believe that God has no other agencies in the world than these institutions! But they do believe that these institutions, so far as they will to retain the name "Christian," stand under the judgment and calling of God, and that as such they are constrained both by the *necessity* and the *possibility* of being made conformable to that calling.

6. The Body and Its Members

6.1. Community and Person in Pauline Perspective. The second internal relationship through which we may glimpse something of the contours of the church concerns the relation between the individual Christian and the *koinonia,* or community. We have already seen that the Pauline image of "the body of Christ" establishes an important critical and constructive theological perspective on the key question of ecclesiology, namely the relation between Christ and the church. But this image also tells us something very important about the manner in which Christianity attempts to work out what is undoubtedly one of the most difficult of human relationships, that between the person and the group. Tensions inherent in this relation are never wholly resolved, in practice; but Paul's metaphor reveals how he thinks the relation ought to be handled if its tensions are to be creative tensions.

Obviously "the body" has a certain priority in this relation, so far as Paul's ecclesiology is concerned, and in this respect at least Pauline theology would seem to speak for the early church at large. Gospel has to do with the overcoming of hostilities and alienation between persons; it centers in a reconcili-

---

59. "The critique of the house of authority and all that goes with it is also being mounted today from within the churches by thinkers who have the well-being of the faith community, not defense of the Enlightenment, in mind." (Mudge, *The Sense of a People,* 68–69.)

ation with the Creator that includes, at the horizontal level, reconciliation among creatures. It displaces the condition of sin (being-alone/being-against) with one of redemption (being-with/being-for). Under the serving "headship" of the Christ, human beings find one another, learn forgiveness and cooperation, are "knit together in love" (Col. 2:2). The maintenance of a strictly private life, and especially one that sets itself over against the community or attempts to impose its personal will upon the community, is thus incompatible with this vision:

> Let no one disqualify you, insisting on self-abasement and worship of angels, taking his stand on visions, puffed up without reason by his sensuous mind, and not holding fast to the Head, from whom the whole body, nourished and knit together through its joints and ligaments, grows with a growth that is from God.
>
> (Col. 2:18f.)

While the gospel of reconciliation contains a natural and necessary thrust toward communality, however, it does not do so *at the expense of* the individual person. For in the first place it is assumed—in accordance with the fundamental ontology and ethic of love—that the individual can only fulfill himself or herself through entering into a right relationship with others, and in the second place, this ecclesiology affirms that the community positively *needs* the contributions and talents of individuals, whose gifts vary and whose unique characters enable the community to achieve a measure of diversity and vitality that it would otherwise never know. Thus, in a famous passage, Paul warns against the exclusion of individual difference and implies that the "body" has a collective responsibility towards its "members," just as the reverse is true:

> For as in one body we have many members, and all the members do not have the same function, so we, though many, are one body in Christ, and individually members one of another. Having gifts that differ according to the grace given to us, let us use them: if prophecy, in proportion to our faith; if service [*diakonia*], in our serving; he who teaches, in his teaching; he who exhorts, in his exhortation; he who contributes, in liberality; he who gives aid, with zeal; he who does acts of mercy, with cheerfulness.
>
> (Rom. 12:4–8)

Not only are the individual members urged to use their unique gifts for the edification of the community as a whole, but the community is exhorted to treasure and support its members and to recognize that variety is necessary to this kind of community:

For the body does not consist of one member but of many. If the foot should say, "Because I am not a hand, I do not belong to the body," that would not make it less a part of the body. And if the ear should say, "Because I am not an eye, I do not belong to the body," that would not make it any less a part of the body. If the whole body were an eye, where would be the hearing? If the whole body were an ear, where would be the sense of smell? But as it is, God arranged the organs in the body, each one of them, as he chose. If all were a single organ, where would the body be? As it is, there are many parts, yet one body. The eye cannot say to the hand, "I have no need of you," nor again the head to the feet, "I have no need of you." On the contrary, the parts of the body which seem to be weaker are indispensable, and those parts of the body which we think less honorable we invest with the greater honor, and our unpresentable parts are treated with greater modesty, which our more presentable parts do not require. But God has so adjusted the body, giving the greater honor to the inferior part, that there may be no discord in the body, but that the members may have the same care for one another. If one member suffers, all suffer together; if one member is honored, all rejoice together.

Now you are the body of Christ, and individually members of it.

(1 Cor. 12:14–17)

The final sentence of this important passage recapitulates the argument succinctly: you (collectively) are the body of Christ, and you are this in such a way that the personhood of your various members is both honored and enhanced by membership within the community.[60]

6.2. Christianity, Capitalism, and Communism. Something of the timeliness of Paul's wisdom on this subject, as well as a clearer conception of what it involves, can be best shown if we contrast this early ecclesial understanding of the relation in question with its treatment in two contemporary political systems, capitalism and communism.[61]

Simply stated, capitalism is individualistic in its encouragement of the individual to assert himself or herself, to make the most of personal ambition and initiative, to climb, if possible, to the top. In the classical sources of

---

60. James H. Evans finds precisely this kind of dialectic at work in the African notion of "self-in-community": "This liberation involves the liberation of the self and the liberation of the community. If the collective aspect is emphasized to the exclusion of the individual aspect, there is the danger of the tyranny of the majority. If the individual aspect is stressed to the exclusion of concern for the group, there is the danger of the anarchy of the minority. The African-American church is based on the African notion of 'self-in-community.' The self has no being apart from the community, and the community is an abstraction apart from the collection of selves. The liberation of one implies the liberation of the other." (*We Have Been Believers: An African-American Systematic Theology* [Minneapolis: Fortress Press, 1992], 135.)

61. Elsewhere, I have applied this contrast to questions of justice in first- and third-world contexts. See *The Steward: A Biblical Symbol Come of Age* (Rev. ed.; Grand Rapids: Wm. B. Eerdmans, 1990), chap. 6, "Stewardship and 'the Worlds'—A Matter of Justice."

capitalist thought, this rugged individualism is mitigated by a sort of providentialism, whose theological roots are deistic. It is held that, in the last analysis, the gain of the individual accrues to the benefit of the whole community. Successful and wealthy individuals create the capital necessary to stimulate the economy, create jobs, and so forth. There is, as it were, an invisible hand regulating the gain of the rich and successful so that their individual enterprise ends by enriching the whole community.

The trouble is that today the "invisible hand" of this "theology" seems to have become inactive as well as invisible in our global economy. Those committed to the capitalist outlook, of course, insist that the theory applies internationally as well as within smaller, national units. This is advanced in the form of the so-called trickle-down theory: the rich nations, if not impeded by taxation and barriers to free trade, will eventually produce benefits for the poorer nations and peoples of the earth.[62] But the continuing disparity between rich and poor peoples calls such a global application of capitalist theory into grave question.

Thus it is felt by many today—and across a wide spectrum of economic and political philosophies—that the rampant individualism of unchecked global capitalism and the societies (such as our own) that it has bred have become dysfunctional. Not only are the so-called developing nations prevented from solving their economic problems because of the power of global capitalism, but technological *overdevelopment* among the "have" peoples of earth has produced in developed societies an underclass of permanently unemployed people.

From another perspective, the individual*ism* that these societies foster must be seen as ending in the loss of *individuality*. For these societies, which are leaders in the technological revolution, have ushered in "the universal homogeneous state" (G. Grant), that is, a mass culture, a "consumer society" in which everybody becomes like everybody else, coveting the same possessions, wearing the same clothes, being driven by the same sexual fantasies, valuing the same kinds of art, ignoring the same problems, and so on. While the drive to get wealth and power appeals to egocentric motives, the fruits of the capitalist enterprise also produce conditions in which it is very hard to remain an individual.

Marxism-Leninism starts with the opposite goal: it wants to put the community first. The rhetoric of communalism is not quite credible, now that we have so much evidence of the individualistic and elitist aggressiveness that it

---

62. It was reported that John Kenneth Galbraith in an Oxford University debate characterized this as "the horse and sparrow theory": the more you feed the horse, the more "you-know-what" the sparrow has to eat. See Galbraith's discussion of "The Prophets and Promise of Classical Capitalism" in *The Age of Uncertainty* (Boston: Houghton Mifflin, 1977), chap. 1, 11–42.

in fact cloaked in officially Marxist societies, but the *ideal* is plain enough: the communty precedes the individual, and individuals find their place and their meaning in the service of the community.

This ideal, as many have noticed, seems to come closer to the early Christian conception of this relation than does the capitalist notion of unchecked individual initiative. In fact, if Marxism is a Christian heresy, as many have said, it is visible as such especially at this point. For it rightly accentuates the well-being of the whole, desiring justice for all.

Yet precisely in the name of universal justice and equality, this philosophy of the *polis* almost inevitably ends by inhibiting or even crushing the individual. In the revolutionary stage, this can be "explained" as a necessary if unfortunate consequence of creating the new mentality requisite to the "classless society." Even at the ideational level, however, such an "eschatology" seems questionable: Does the end ("classlessness"—whatever that may mean) in fact justify the means (the suppression of the individual)? Will not such a means carry over into the end product itself? And when this questioning is transferred from idea to reality, as very recent history has demonstrated so devastatingly, does it not in fact imply that what such a "means" encourages is the coming forward of excessively strong and power-hungry individuals, who will justify all manner of wickedness by deploying the rhetoric of the ultimate paradise of perfect social harmony?

Biblical faith thus enters a protest against both of these ways of conceiving the relation between the person and the group. Communities that come into being through and are sustained by the reduction of individual uniqueness and worth in relation to the person's service to the community are rejected by this faith, because it understands that individuals *transcend* communities, even though they are personally impoverished without the community. When individual life is confined to the functions and limits that the community— *any* community—has for it, it will not be allowed to actualize its own potentiality for fulfillment, and the community itself, in the end, will be robbed of that contribution to its corporate life. It is not for nothing that Jesus is depicted in conversation with individual persons more frequently than with crowds; nor is it accidental that he chose particular individuals as his followers, calling them by name and responding, like a good mentor, to their quite different reactions to the new experiences into which he led them.

This biblical concentration on individual life (particularity) ought not, however, to be made the excuse for the kind of individualism that free enterprise, yoked with privatistic religion, has created in the North American context. For one thing, this very individualism, far from fostering the unique potentiality for transcendence and creativity in individual persons, has ended by giving us a society of conformists. Marxism-Leninism tried to *impose* uniformity—and created a very powerful backlash of individual and minority protest. Capitalism spawned individuals who were subtly conditioned to want the same things—and created a society of jeans-wearers! Ironically, technologized capitalism has proven a more effective route to the mass culture than has doctrinaire communism.

What historical experience on both sides of the former "iron curtain" tells us is that there is something delicate and important to the health of the human species in the *tension* between the individual and the group. As Eugene Zamiatin has so brilliantly shown, a people that can only say "We" and neither "I" nor "Thou" becomes an oppressive society, conspicuously deprived of the very things that can be brought to society only by individuals in their quest for fulfillment.[63] On the other hand, a people whose citizens can *only* say "I" will be equally and perhaps more pathetically deprived, for self-centeredness is of the essence of sin, biblically understood, and compassionate concern for others is of the essence of redemption.

This would suggest that Christian faith does stress the communal side of this dialectic, and we may certainly conclude, I think, that such an emphasis is at any rate the corrective that is required in our particular context. But this does not mean that the communal side may be pursued with vigor and without vigilance. Today, fired by the excessive individualism of our society and its churches, minorities in all the churches strive for a greater realization of community in both church and society. While that is a commendable goal, it needs to be seasoned by the knowledge that communities, too, may be oppressive. Even communities that are admirable in their original conception may give way to the intolerance of difference and the forfeiture of openness. The Geneva of Farrel and Calvin, especially in its first stage, prior to the expulsion of the Reformers in 1538, became such a community, as did Puritan New England. The very individuality that prompts the leaders of new experiments in community living to break with the patterns of their political environment tempts them to construct their new communities in ways that necessitate the subjection of others to their ideals. Perhaps no communities are so oppressive as those based on the high ideals of strong founding figures.

This leads to the nub of our argument: Christians are not asked to choose between individualism and communalism. These are not the alternatives with which the confessing community works. The corrective to individualism is not more communalism, and the corrective to communalism (including communism) is not more individualism. There is an ongoing, dialectical tension between the person and the group. We said earlier that it cannot be wholly

---

63. *We* (New York: Viking Press, 1972).

Pannenberg has observed, "The futurity of the Kingdom [or realm of God] guards the freedom of the individual from the power of social institutions while, at the same time, enabling the individual to commit himself to the society" (*Theology and the Kingdom of God,* 115).

resolved; now we may say that it *should* not be resolved. Resolving this tension invariably means killing the life of both individuals and communities by superimposing upon this dynamism a static pattern, usually in the form of some ideology (capitalism, communism, and so on), which in actuality does not resolve anything but only suppresses—temporarily—the inherent tensions of the relation.

What Christians need most to recognize is that biblical faith assumes another factor or dimension by which this whole relation, whether ecclesiastically or politically conceived, is profoundly qualified: namely, the presence of a transcendent source and arbiter of the relation. "The Body" with its "many members" presupposes *the Head,* to whom both the individual members and the corporate body are accountable. Where no such transcendent source of sovereignty is experienced, a struggle, always more or less destructive, almost inevitably occurs between the individual and corporate components of the relation. There will be a tendency either for powerful individuals to dominate the collectivity, or for the collective to suppress the initiative and potential for excellence within its individual members. In other words, in the absence of divine transcendence, an abortive human sovereignty will fluctuate between the two human poles of the relation. Stated otherwise, conflicts between the collective and its individual components, according to this tradition, are usually to be traced to an insufficient realization of the lordship of Jesus Christ.

The lesson for ecclesiology is therefore unmistakable: if we want to alleviate the *undue* frustrations that revolve around this ancient tension within "mainline" churches today, the point is not to evoke communality over against individualism or individuality over against mass culturism, but to attempt in whatever ways open to us to make more real and more concrete the presence of the One who will retain the legitimate headship of the body, wresting it from *whichever faction* seeks to possess it, and causing the tensions that inhere in this relation to contribute to the *life* of the church, rather than to its death.

6.3. The Place of the Sacraments in This Relation.   It is surely not accidental that the two biblical sacraments identified by Reformation theology reflect, in their juxtaposition, the two sides of the relation we have been discussing, thus affirming the necessity of both and also, by the very nature of the case, setting both within the context of that sovereignty which alone can make of their tension a creative one.

Baptism confirms and substantiates what has been claimed concerning the significance of the *individual* in Christian ecclesiology. It is not individualistic, because it is a communal rite, both in the sense that the congregation (in classical Protestant practice) participates in the act, and in view of the fact that the purpose of the sacrament is to receive individuals into the fellowship of the Body of Christ. This communal aspect of the Sacrament of Holy Baptism is, of course, vitiated when it is performed as a private ritual. While, therefore, there may be occasions when it cannot be a full congregational observance, it would seem mandatory under such circumstances for the congregation to be represented by persons other than the officiating clergy—as is indeed customary in denominations of the church stemming from the Reformation.

But while baptism is in this way also a communal act, it clearly concentrates upon the life of an individual person. Mass baptisms have sometimes been practiced by distorted forms of Christianity, but the whole point of baptism is the uniqueness of one life, which is there received by God and God's people, and brought into communion with Jesus Christ and his church. Here, it is claimed, the love of God, far from being impersonal and general, is intensely personal and specific. *This* man, *this* woman, whose name is here publicly announced—this quite particular, unrepeatable life—is forgiven, cleansed, reconciled, received, united with God and neighbor.[64]

Should we not also affirm, especially given the realities of our present context, that the union of the baptized individual extends to the extrahuman creation as well? Water, one of the four basic elements of the ancients, is, after all, the symbolic medium of this sacrament. As the "means of grace" by which the gift of new *creaturehood* is confirmed, baptism may be considered a sacramental enactment of solidarity with the whole realm of creaturely life and thus, while remaining an intensely personal rite, transcend the merely private. The sacramental dimension of this sacrament can only be enhanced if it is understood that here a solitary creature, living always on the verge of being-alone (alienation) and being-against (estrangement), both wills to be and is caused to be *with* all the others—God, humankind, and otherkind. Baptism thus accentuates the person—not by elevating the person above all others, but by locating the individual within the total sphere of the communion of creation. Therefore the congregation ought to consider itself, as in other dimensions of divine service or worship, a representative people: its reception of this one into its *koinonia* is a concretization of his or her reception by the Creator and by the whole creation; it is as if it were said to this one, "You are not alone. You have your place in the great community of the creatures of God."

The Lord's Supper or Eucharist of course speaks to the other side of the dialectic of person and community, individual and totality. Here the emphasis is upon the the latter. The community enacts its unity with its head and

---

64. Later (in subsection 18.5) I shall explain why the references here assume that the subjects of baptism are adults.

its members with one another. Partaking of the one cup and the one loaf, the members, "though many," as Paul says, affirm and are confirmed in their oneness.

This interpretation of the Eucharist calls in question all privatistic practices of the sacrament. The communion is a corporate act, and even when it must be administered apart from the worshiping community, the latter, as in the case of baptism, ought certainly to be represented. This corporateness seems to me more important than whether one regards the Eucharist from the vantage point of the tradition of transubstantiation, the mediating position of consubstantiation, or the Zwinglian symbolic or memorial conception. The critical question is not the substantialistic one (whether the bread becomes body, whether the wine becomes blood); it is, rather, the relational question: How does this sacramental function sustain the community?

For the community is always in danger of disintegrating. It is, after all, a tenuous, vulnerable affair. It is not kept together by blood ties, as are families, or by legal arrangements recognized by the laws of the land, as are civic communities; it is only sustained organically by the divine Spirit acting upon our weak and unstable wills. The relationship among us, even within a single, small fellowship, is never very solid. Again and again, families come first, individual needs assume priority, businesses and places of employment dominate. This "body" has to be *sustained,* and its sustenance is a matter of sheer grace. If we thought less about what is going on with the so-called elements (bread and wine) and more about what is transpiring among those who are imbibing them, we should come closer to the reality of the sacrament.

Thus, in both sacraments, what is central is the relational dimension, and this means first the relation with Jesus Christ, the foundational relation of the *ekklesia.* Only for that reason are these called sacraments and not merely rites or rituals. The Sacrament of Baptism does not signify first the willingness of a collectivity to honor and accept individuals into its midst; it is not merely an initiatory rite; it signifies the presence of the one who is "head," who once again moves this odd collective of persons, with all its ambiguity, tentativeness, and social hesitancy, to receive into itself yet another human being with a name, and to do so in a priestly (representative) manner. And in this Spirit-inspired movement, it also reaffirms its identity as the *body* of this head. Similarly, in the Eucharist it is not a matter of a group of people ritually enacting their collective "thanksgiving" (*eucharistio*); it is first and foremost the response of this community to One who again invites it to sup with him. This is one good reason that the old Protestant term "The Lord's Supper" should not be sacrificed to the more liturgical "Eucharist," despite the good and necessary connotations of the latter.

Thus both sacraments demonstrate graphically the point made in the preceding subsection, namely that *this* relation is not just a theoretical or practi-

115

cal give-and-take between two potentially and actually discordant components of human intercourse; rather, it is profoundly qualified by a spiritual
presence that is not visible in the two parties or polarities of the relation as
such.[65] It is this Presence that turns discord to concord. Baptism accentuates
the dimension of individuality, and the Lord's Supper that of communality;
but this interaction and mutual stimulation comes about not as a concession
of one side or the other, but as a gift of "the Lord" to each.

7. Church, Society, and State

7.1. Christianity and Culture: The Triumph of Christendom. We are attempting to describe the shape of the confessing church—indirectly, as we
feel it may best be done—by asking about the church's relationships. We
have considered two of its internal relations: that between the church and the
churches, and between the individual disciple and the disciple community.
We turn now to its most important external relations: in this section, society
and government, and, in the following section, other religious communities.

In the foregoing text, we have employed the term "host society" to describe the social, political, and cultural context of the Christian community.
This term itself already suggests a kind of response to the question, How
does the church relate to the public sphere in which it finds itself? For it
conjures up the thought of *distinction* between church and society, and (perhaps gratuitously!) assigns the latter the role of "host." The "host" has not
always acted in a gracious, hospitable manner, of course; but perhaps as
Christians enter a new and different phase of the relation in question, the
picture of society as "host" to the Christian religion could have a salutary
effect on Christians, if not on society itself.

The elaboration of such a tentative proposal must involve us in some general recall of the past with respect to this particular relation. As we noted
already in the first volume[66] for the first three centuries of its history, the
Christian movement (and the term "movement" is here the correct one) *was*
quite distinct from its "host society," and this distinction pertains not only to
its physical separateness vis-à-vis that society but to its self-consciousness as
being "different" from the latter. Given the time frame of nearly three hundred years (from the death of Jesus to the Edict of Milan), and the diversity

---

65. "Even more important than the Reformers' reduction in the number of sacraments [to
two], however, was their insistence on two basic points: first, the inseparability of Word and
sacrament; and second, the importance in both Word and sacrament of the working of the Spirit
and our faithful response. These emphases countered every quasimagical view of the nature and
efficacy of the sacraments" (Daniel L. Migliore, *Faith Seeking Understanding: An Introduction
to Christian Theology* [Grand Rapids: Wm. B. Eerdmans, 1991], 212).

66. See "The End of the Constantinian Era," *Thinking the Faith,* 200–207.

of a territory almost as large and diverse as the ancient Roman Empire, it is obvious that there must have been many ways in which, concretely, Christian congregations worked out their relations with the non-Christian majority; few enough of them are actually recorded or implied in documents. But one factor constitutes a given throughout this period, and it is that of distinction. Even in times and places when their movement was tolerated or relatively popular, Christians of these pre-Constantinian contexts would be conscious of their difference from the dominant culture and its institutions. And, of course, in periods of persecution, such as that which the great theologian Origen of Alexandria (c. 185–254) experienced in his late teens, the "difference" was raised to a point of high consciousness.[67]

All this was drastically altered during the course of the fourth century C.E. At the beginning of that century, despite the fact that Christianity had grown significantly, it is estimated that Christians could not have accounted for more than one-tenth of the population of the empire. In the short space of seven or eight decades, the Christian movement went from being a minority quite distinguishable from the majority culture to being virtually synonymous with the latter. In the process, Christianity ceased being a movement and became a highly organized institution—the official religion of the imperium, with power to control the destinies not only of individuals but in many respects that of the whole society.

This loss of distinction between church and society must be seen, however, more as a qualitative than as a quantitative matter—or perhaps we should again evoke Engels' law concerning the relation between quantity and quality, and note that this overwhelming change in the proportion of reputed Christians in the society introduced qualitative changes that far transcend mere quantities. In truth, the whole idea of *distinction* between church and society, the most prominent single dimension of the relation prior to the establishment, virtually disappeared. Even granting the presence of Christian minorities whose faith was too profound to allow them to identify "Christ and culture," the overweening impression history bequeaths of the post-Theodosian church is the high degree of *correspondence* between church and society. If there is difference, it is largely confined to the fact that the church sets the tone for cultic belief and ritual, moral standards and social acceptability: "Christendom" now *is* the society in its most respectable expression.

This is illustrated in a subtle way by the history of military service during this period. When the pagan critic and physician Celsus wrote his attack upon Christianity toward the end of the second century, he insisted that Christians ought not to be allowed to serve in the army. Because of their

---

67. See Robert L. Wilken, *The Christians as the Romans Saw Them* (New Haven and London: Yale University Press, 1984).

ambiguous and (in his view) probably seditious attitude toward government, they could not be trusted to defend Rome. By 438 C.E., the Theodosian Code, issued by Theodosius II, which decreed the death penalty for all who denied the Trinity or repeated baptism, also barred *pagans* from serving in the army. Only Christians could be counted on to take up arms for the defense of the Empire.[68]

While it required centuries before Christianity could penetrate and dominate the greater (northern) share of Europe, and while this process was never without opposition from those of other religious and political points of view (paganism, Judaism, Islam), the manner in which Christianity related itself to society begun under the reigns of Constantine and Theodosius the Great set the pattern for the future down to our own epoch. Naturally, in so-called missionary situations in which Christianity could not expect its "host society" to favor it, the original pattern of this relation, marked by distinction, has had to prevail—despite the continued efforts of many Christian missioners to realize, in these situations as well, the Constantinian model. We must also of course recognize that this model, like most, allows for a certain contextual adaptability. The most conspicuous adaptation to new circumstances came with the translation of many different European Christian groupings to our own continent from the sixteenth century onward. Because of the breakdown of Roman Catholic hegemony and the proliferation of churches stemming from the Reformation period, no one church was able permanently to achieve the status of legal establishment on this continent, although powerful attempts to do so were certainly undertaken. However, this did not signal the end of the Constantinian model, but only its (perhaps more effective!) transmutation into the trans-legal, cultural form that we shall consider in chapter 4. Thus neither the Reformation itself nor the removal of its sundry offshoots to the New World, greatly challenged this entrenched understanding of the manner in which the church ought to relate to its "host society."

If we ask why Christianity seems driven by that model (we may call it, with Loren B. Mead, "the Christendom paradigm"), which even in the late twentieth century and in our own highly pluralistic society must be regarded as easily the most prevalent preconception of this relation, we must probably notice at least three causes: (1) *A historical cause.* The idea of the Christian religion as the official cult of the official culture has endured for fifteen or sixteen centuries, has been the primary motivation for the expansion of the Christian religion through its association with imperial states, and has established itself so firmly that even the internal Christian critique of this model

---

68. See Roland H. Bainton, *Christendom: A Short History of Christianity and Its Impact on Western Civilization,* vol. 1 (New York: Harper & Row, 1964), 101.

(for example, that of Kierkegaard) has had little impact upon its momentum. (2) *A psychosociological cause:* Success is always a powerful persuader of the veracity of any movement. As the modern proverb has it, "Nothing succeeds like success," and no one can doubt the worldly success of the Christian religion *and* of most of the peoples who have adopted it. So persuasive has been the connection between Christianity and Western technological civilization that even today many non-Christian peoples are tempted to want this connection—for reasons essentially extraneous if not contradictory to the faith. (3) *A religious cause:* Christianity is, as we have seen, a missionary faith. It is the bearer of a message ("gospel"), and this message is intended for all. The so-called Great Commission that concludes the Gospel according to Matthew, a sentence attributed to the risen Jesus and cited repeatedly by those who wish to promote the Christendom concept, seems on face value to encourage this model and to *exclude* any other:

> "All authority in heaven and on earth has been given to me. Go therefore and make disciples of all nations, baptizing them in the name of the Father and of the Son and of the Holy Spirit, teaching them to observe all that I have commanded you; and lo, I am with you always, to the close of the age."
>
> (Matt. 28:18–20)

7.2 The Humiliation of Christendom. Even if the Great Commission belongs to the original strand of Jesus' remembered sayings (and that is by no means certain), and even if it is legitimate to interpret its meaning along Christendom lines (which is still more dubious), two factors have come to the fore within the past century or two that constitute a profound criticism of this model of the church's relation to society. They are (1) the breakdown ("humiliation") of Christendom in the very parts of the globe in which it has been dominant and successful, and (2) the search for and recovery of alternative ways of conceiving of this relation on the part of serious Christians who could no longer pursue the Constantinian model. Consideration of these two factors will help us to formulate our conception of the relation in question. In this subsection we shall treat the former, in the next the latter.

Long before the East German churchman Günther Jacob, then of Cottbus, "announced 'the end of the Constantinian era,'"[69] the process of Christendom's disestablishment had begun and, in many areas of the old European flagship, was very conspicuous. It would be possible to trace the beginnings of this process to the breakdown of the Middle Ages, "the Age of Belief," as this long period in Western history has been called. For while Christianity

---

69. Karl Barth and Johannes Hamel, *How to Serve God in a Marxist Land,* Introduction by Robert McAfee Brown (New York: Association Press, 1959), 64.

continued intact and even in some sense flourished beyond the effective de-mise of the Scholastic enterprise in the mid–fifteenth century, some of the ideas that eventually led to the end of the Constantinian era already made their appearance with Nominalism and the many-sided attack upon Western Christendom's mainstay, the Roman hierarchy. With the nominalistic con-finement of reason to particularities, the universal claims of revealed religion could no longer count upon corroboration from the side of liberated rational-ity. This, on the one hand, led the more venturesome to follow their "reason-ing" wherever it would lead, regardless of religious authority; on the other hand, it led religious authority to assert itself all the more aggressively, thus causing greater doubt concerning its *inherent* authority. With such doubt in the air, the social willingness to accept the long-standing concordat between the Christian religion and human society at large began to waver.

From the perspective of the history of this relation, the Protestant Refor-mation may be considered a kind of postponement of the inevitable. For, by a strange twist of historical providence, Protestantism managed to salvage from the wreckage of the medieval church new forms of Christian authority that enabled it to retain its hold on society—or at least on those (mostly Northern) European lands that were most affected by the collapse of the medieval synthesis of faith and reason. The "twist" that permitted this to occur was, of course, the emergence in those same lands of nationalist feeling and the concomitant rebellion against Rome's "Ultramontanism." Already with William of Ockham, John Wycliffe, and Jan Hus, we must see how *bibli-cal* authority, far from being a matter of pure faith, is made to serve as mortar for patching up the rent in the relation between church and society that was being created by the over-zealous demands of an ecclesiastical hierarchy whose authority was no longer automatically credible. This same kind of reinterpretation of the character of Christian authority served well the pur-poses of the later princes and governors with whom the main Reformers entered into negotiations; and so the bond between church and society was sustained after all—as it was, in other variations on the theme, in the counter-Reformational negotiations.

Thus the originating Protestants, whose *evangel* certainly contained the elements of a quite different understanding of this relation, perhaps unwit-tingly preserved the Constantinian arrangement at a critical moment. Their reworking of this arrangement, however, must, from our present perspective, be considered only a postponement. Their strong presentation of the *sola scriptura* was a convenient aid for ruling classes of nations coming to a new consciousness of their own worth and wishing for autonomy, but it could not detain for long the determination of these same classes to free themselves from the heteronomous influences of religion and to follow to its logical con-clusion the promises of rational autonomy.

The eighteenth century marks the victory of the rationality whose liberation was already glimpsed four centuries earlier. Now the structural consequences of this separation of reason and faith are enacted in the disengagement of society, or rather of its cutting edge, from Christian ties. If, in
spite of radical and even violent renunciations of these ties (especially the
French Revolution), the old *de jure* establishments of Christian Europe per-
sisted, with the possible exception of Poland they are in fact mere shadows
of their past glory, if not ludicrous and superficial imitations of that past.
The mechanism of the clock of Christendom has long since stopped, even if
the pendulum still swings of its own momentum. Even in the former West
Germany, where because 9% of one's income tax is designated for the
churches, both Catholic and Protestant churches are among the richest in the
world, only 5% at most of the populace is actively involved in church life.
The church is a convenience: it eases people over their "rites of passage"; it
cares for some of the young, elderly, and sick; it fosters a semblance of excellence in education and connectedness with the past; and so on. But it can in
no way be considered the genuine expression of society's cultic and spiritual
identity. It does not enter the daily thought of most citizens of these old
societies, or influence their priorities, or determine their values and goals. It
exists on the edges of the majority consciousness. Christendom's surviving
art and architecture guarantee that the church is for most people a pleasant
enough souvenir of a great cultural past; for others who are more informed,
it is a reminder of another way of being, thinking, and hoping; but only for
a few is it the very substance of private and social existence.

In short, *distinction* between church and society has re-entered the picture,
and if this distinction is so effective that it seldom even crosses the mind of
the secular European, it is prominent enough in the thought of those who
continue as active members of the Christian movement. To be a serious
Christian in nearly every part of Europe today is to be conscious of one's
"difference" from the majority.

This is also true in North America and other parts of the formerly Christian world that have had a sufficiently dominant and extended past to know
that the present is other than the past. But in North America, as we shall
see later, the consciousness of distinction between church and society is less
obvious than in Europe; and in the United States, especially, the current
resurgence of a militant form of Christianity that is at the same time ultra-
nationalistic greatly confuses the relation in question. Still, thinking Christians in our context also realize that the Constantinian arrangement no
longer holds. And wherever this realization is strongly present, it drives to a
rethinking of the relation of church and society and therefore to a reconsideration of this whole history, with special attention to biblical and other alternative conceptions of it that have been submerged by the dominant model.

121

7.3. The Quest for an Alternative Way of Conceiving of the Relation between Church and Society. The Pauline image of the church as Christ's body is indispensable not only because of its dominance in all types of historic ecclesiological dogma, but also for its intrinsic worth: it is, as we have seen, a holistic metaphor, joining together all or most of the aspects of the doctrine of the church, which are otherwise all too easily fragmented. We have said that it is for this reason more than a "metaphor." Yet it is also *only* a metaphor, and like all metaphors it has its limitations.

One of the most serious of these limitations is that it can lend itself to triumphalistic forms of ecclesiology, and, under the conditions of Christian establishment, it has regularly done so. If one considers, for example, the ecclesiastical bravado conveyed in the lyrics of the popular nineteenth-century hymn, *Onward, Christian Soldiers!* (especially when they are set to the militant tune by Sir Arthur Sullivan), and of the manner in which this hymn is able to incorporate the "body" metaphor to its advantage, one has a concrete instance of what I mean:

> Like a mighty army, moves the Church of God,
> Brothers, we are treading where the saints have trod.
> We are not divided, *all one body we—*
> One in hope and doctrine, one in charity.
>
> Onward, Christian soldiers . . .

Apparently not even the blatant fact of the scandalous divisions of Christendom in all the areas named (eschatology, doctrine, and ethics) deterred the author of these words from promoting the "one body" imagery, for it suited his purpose so well. A "mighty army" must be unified if it is to go "forward into battle" and "prevail" "against the foe" . . . and so on.

It tells us more than almost anything else about the character of Christendom that this image of the church not only dominated Christian imagination (a thing that could be thought reasonable enough in view of its exceptional development in the Scriptures) but that it seems to have excluded other images that present a very different picture of the Christian movement. We have already mentioned the Johannine image of the bride and the bridegroom, which in the Apocalypse leaves us with certain questions about the suitability of the "bride" (church). We have also alluded to the John's "vine and branches" imagery (chap. 15) which, when combined with the Pauline image of the grafted-on "wild olive shoot," introduces a radically critical dimension in the face of all Christian "boasting." But beyond these epistolary images, we may ask why the references to his "little flock" contained in Jesus' own recorded discourse of the Synoptic tradition have been so consistently ignored or trivialized.

In the Sermon on the Mount, which falls directly after the Beatitudes having to do with the blessedness of suffering (and themselves, as we have seen, explicitly instructive concerning the life of the disciple community in society), Jesus addresses his followers thus:

> You are the salt of the earth: but if salt has lost its taste, how shall its saltness be restored? It is no longer good for anything except to be thrown out and trodden under foot by men.
>
> You are the light of the world. A city set on a hill cannot be hid. Nor do men light a lamp and put it under a bushel, but on a stand, and it gives light to all in the house. Let your light so shine before men, that they may see your good works and give glory to your Father who is in heaven.
>
> (Matt. 5:13-16; par.)

Three things are remarkable about these statements from the vantage point of our present topic: first, both the image of salt and light refer to something small; second, both are intended to do something for the larger entity with which they are associated; third, both are capable of failing to do this and therefore may be judged worthless.

a. The Church as Minority. Salt was a precious commodity in the ancient world and well into our own period. So the fact that it is "small" in relation to the food that it is intended to season does not detract from its qualitative importance. All the same, there is no mistaking the fact that this is a minority image. One does not want a whole plateful of salt!

It is similar with the metaphor of light—although, in the age of hydro-electricity, this is more difficult for us to grasp. We are used to brightly lighted rooms, offices, public places. When we think of cities, we think of great centers of light. Our metropoloi are so ablaze with artificial light that they light up the sky for a hundred miles around. But Jesus and his followers did not live in such a world. Light for them meant a modest light, the light of humble oil lamps, surrounded by much darkness—as the Prologue of John assumes: "The light shines in the darkness. . . . " What is conspicuous, because it is so immense, is the darkness—"the encircling gloom" (John Henry Newman). Even a little light "lightens our darkness" (Cranmer); the deepest darkness cannot overcome even a candle (John 1:5). That is true—but only those who know the darkness know, profoundly, its truth. We should not therefore conclude that with the metaphor of light and the city of light we are led toward the imperial church! The light remains a little light, and the darkness remains immense.

123

For corroboration of this point, we could turn to two other images that Jesus employs—not, in these instances, to speak about his followers but about the greater reality at the center of the message to be broadcast by his followers, that is, the Reign of God. Even this reality, which greatly exceeds the disciple community as such, is likened to things that are by nature small in relation to that which they qualify: yeast (leaven), a mustard seed, one precious pearl, and so on (Matt. 13:31ff. par.) Only a little yeast is needed: as Paul notes on two occasions (1 Cor. 5:6; Gal. 5:9), "a little leaven ferments the whole lump of dough." The mustard seed is "the smallest of all seeds," although it becomes "a tree." The pearl metaphor, of course, introduces another main thought (value), but it is again a minority image. And we could find many others in this literature, for they all grow out of the language of election, the remnant, and the covenant.

That this is so is, of course, no accident. Jesus was a Jew! The whole story of Israel is the story of a minority, both in its ancient and its modern form. Israel is conscious of itself as "a few" in relation to "the many." It is "called out" from the nations—chosen. The covenant, as it is presented in the continuity of the Adamic, Noachic, and Abrahamic sagas, assumes the minority status of this people. So does the concept of election. When it is faithful, Israel does not understand its election as a matter of privilege but of responsibility, because it is essentially a *representational* concept:

> Now therefore, if you will obey my voice and keep my covenant, you shall be my own possession among all the peoples; for all the earth is mine, and you shall be to me a kingdom of priests and a holy nation.
>
> (Exod. 19:5–6)

—an affirmation repeated, this time about the church, in 1 Peter 2:9.

Out of this tradition of Jerusalem, Jesus quite naturally assumes that the "people of God" will be a minority in relation to the vast multitudes of earth's peoples, and that it will be *distinct.* Its distinction as such a minority is *by no means* an end in itself. To think so is to confuse the tradition of Jerusalem with that of Athens, which frequently thinks in elitist terms. "Elect" and "elite," as we have said before, are not synonymous, even though they both assume that "there only will be a few." The key question is: What is the *purpose* of this few? This leads to the second observation above.

b. The Christian Minority Exists for the Worldly Majority.　　For the tradition of Jerusalem that Jesus so faithfully represents in these sayings, there can be no question here: the election of the few is a means for the salvation of the many. "And by you all the families of the earth will bless themselves" (the Abrahamic covenant, Gen. 12:2–3).

We should not be surprised, therefore, that the images contained in the Synoptic verses cited above without exception convey precisely that message. The salt is for the food; the light is for the darkness; the yeast is for the dough; the seed is for the growing of a bush large enough for the birds to nest in; the pearl is for the enhancement and concretization of beauty, and so forth and so on.

The principle being invoked through these images (to reduce all this to abstracts which may, in the end, be far more constricting than the images themselves!) is one that is steadfast throughout the length and breadth of this tradition: *through the particular to the universal.* Or, to state the same thing in another way, *history is to be taken seriously.* Obviously enough, the God of this tradition wants to reach the whole creation, indeed to save "all" (a word which turns up again and again in that very literature, the Pauline, that develops most systematically the newer Testamental version of the concept of election and the covenant.) God's love is universal in its orientation—intended for creation in its entirety, and in the entirety of its existential distortedness. But God can communicate with "all" only through the medium of "some"—unless God would resort to an act of recreation that would in effect annul existing creation. The universal judgment and love of God must pass through the experience and vocation of particular people.

Is it essential, then, that there should only be a few such people? Without being adamant on the subject, we may nevertheless answer: Probably. At least, this same tradition is obviously very wary of majorities, especially powerful majorities. There are always empires *on the edge of Israel's existence,* and Israel itself, in the persons of some of its more ambitious kings, is tempted by the imperial dream—a fact that undoubtedly lies behind the prophetic critique of the whole concept of kingship. But Israel is prevented from achieving anything remotely resembling an imperial status—and there can be no doubt that its *God* has a hand in this! Even though Israel, with its wisdom, its self-knowledge, its organizational genius, its traditions of justice, its respect for "the stranger," and so on, certainly *deserves* the imperial status more than the mostly barbarian peoples that achieved it, it is prevented from realizing such an ambition. That way is barred—and not only by the greater nations round about. Why?

Because there is a prophetic wisdom at work here that recognizes very well *the temptations of power.* There are things that majorities cannot and will not do, and never have done. One of those things is that such majorities will not be vigilant against the oppression of minorities—will indeed *create* and *maintain* minorities, for their majority status is dependent upon that. Even at the level of *justice,* then, majorities cannot be trusted; and when it comes to *love,* the prospect of majorities being used in *that* service is beyond contemplation. Empires do not love. Perhaps nations cannot, either, and that is a thought entertained not only by Jesus and the Christians but already by the prophets of Israel itself. It is, by Jesus' own summing-up, precisely divine love (*agape*) that must be entrusted to human representation, and therefore it may well be that "there will only be a few." This, however, should not lead to mathematics! —as it does far too frequently with the guardians of the doctrine of election. The concentration here is not upon the messengers but upon the message. It is the quality of the message that has to be considered, not the quantity of the messengers.

c. The Tentativeness of the Church.   The last sentence is illustrated beyond my powers by Jesus' own words about salt and light: "But if the salt has lost its taste, how shall its saltness be restored? It is no longer good for anything except to be thrown out and trodden under foot by men." Again: "Nor do men light a lamp and put it under a bushel, but on a stand. . . ."

There is an assumption here that we have met before (for example, in connection with 1 Cor. 10 and the question of presumption): not only is "the people of God" for Jesus a minority concept, a people called out and apart, not only is it "there" for the world from which it is distinguished by its message, but if it loses touch with that message, as it may in fact do, it is no longer significant in the economy of God.

The ministry of the church is a public ministry. We have said from the outset that the gnostic temptation to privacy and ghettoization is anathema to this tradition. The *evangel* with which this community is entrusted is intended for "the world." To that end, as we saw in considering the mark of "apostolicity," the disciple community is "sent out." But it is sent out with a gospel that it has not learned from the world to which it is sent. To hear that gospel, it has had to be separated from the world, and to *sustain* its hearing of that gospel—a contextual gospel, about a love that is "new every morning"—it has *continually* to be called out, distinguished from the majority. Only so will it have salty salt; only so will its light be real and not ersatz light. To repeat, with high-sounding theological accents, the "plastic words" (Uwe Pörksen) that it has learned from its world will by no means prevent the church from being insipid.[70]

Here we have come to the core of the whole discussion of this relation: The recognition of the original disciple community concerning its distinction

---

70. "If the Christ and culture issue is not raised, then the gospel has become domesticated. There is no sense of distance between the church and its environment, no friction between what is and what might be that ignites the passions of repentance and transformation, no transcendent vision that illumines the dark places of the present while projecting a splendor yet to be. In other words, the gospel is betrayed and the church is boring." (Jack Stotts, *Insights* [Fall 1993], 4–5. See also Pannenberg, *Christian Spirituality,* chap. 4, "The Absence of God in Theological Perspective," 71–92).

from the rest of society, a recognition that is perhaps beginning once more to dawn upon the church at the end of the Constantinian era, is a consequence and aspect of a more significant recognition and reality: namely, that the *message* it has to proclaim is a *different message.* The distinction is not to be located in the church itself, that is, in these people, with their various peculiarities and propensities, their talents for this and that, their insights and crafts and capacities. They are for all intents and purposes no different from anyone else—with the possible exception of the fact that they may have begun to realize something of the distance between what they are and what they are called to be. When the case for "distinction" between church and society is based on the *church's* difference from the rest of society, it is a pathetic case, whatever it turns out to be. What distinguishes the church from the world of which it is a part is that it has heard, is hearing, and hopes to hear a Word that comes from *beyond* this world but is intended precisely *for* this world and will make all the difference to it. This Word alone makes the church distinct from society, and when adherence to this Word is lost there is no longer any distinction at all. The salt has become insipid, the light is hidden under a bushel.

The theo-logic of these three observations needs to be taken very seriously by churches (our own) that are being denied their ancient majority status vis-à-vis their "host society." As we shall argue in chapter 4, it is quite possible that their emergent *minority* status is opening to them a possibility they have scarcely if ever known heretofore. But this will only occur if they become infinitely more concerned to hear that Word than they have been throughout most of their history. That Word, if it is heard, will carry them, *in spirit,* farther away from their "host societies" than they have ever been (John 21:18). But, conversely, it will send them back *into* their same societies, *in the flesh,* in ways they have seldom undergone.

7.4. Church and State. The relation of the Christian church to the various states with which, in the course of its nearly two thousand year history, it has been connected follows more or less logically its interaction with societies at large.[71] There are, however, some particular nuances and problems associated with this relation; for the state, after all, is never wholly continuous with society. While the term "state" is a broad one covering many meanings, in its usual political, as well as theological, deployment (as in the phrase "church and state") it refers to the governing body within a given society; and government may or may not reflect the will and character of the society it governs. Even in democratic societies, there is usually a certain tension between the

---

71. See Eugene C. Bianchi and Rosemary Radford Ruether, *A Democratic Catholic Church,* 9–10.

ethos of society at large and its governing authorities; and in nations in which government is autocratic or despotic the tension is of course much greater. The state, in whatever form, represents not only *officialdom* but attitudes and objectives that are usually more decisive and cohesive than those of the greater society. The latter almost always contain more diversity than the former, so that even where governments have been hostile to the Christian religion Christians have usually been able to count upon the interest and support of minorities within the societies of which they were part.

This was certainly the case in the early church. Neither the Jewish state nor Rome, with which the Herodian dynasty collaborated, could officially tolerate Christianity. In the case of Judaism, this is a complex issue, for it involves not only Judaism's domination by Rome but also its co-optation by monarchic, priestly, and mercantile elements that rendered intertestimentary Judaism less than open to its own prophetic traditions. Obviously, significant numbers of *Jews* were open to the kind of message that brought the early Christian movement into being, for its first members were almost exclusively Jews; indeed, "Christianity" (as it was called only later) was at first and for a significant period of time thought by everyone to be a Jewish sect or a holiness movement within Judaism. One must at least wonder whether a Jewish state more independent of empire, less fearful of offending power, and more in touch with its own scriptural and theological roots would have been so threatened by the Nazarene as the rulers of Israel during his lifetime in fact were. Might they not have perceived in Jesus of Nazareth, and in John the Baptist before him, a clear if uncomfortable line of continuity with the prophets and purifiers (judges) of Israel?

However that may be, it illustrates the point that states do not reflect exactly the complex nature of their societies, including social *memory,* which often judges present government on the basis of criteria instituted by past states (consider, for example, the role of David in Jewish social thought).

As for Rome (and the church's relation with *that* state was and is still, in many ways, decisive for every other), prior to the Constantinian-Theodosian arrangement it seems almost inevitable that the Roman state would have found Christianity problematic. For, although Rome was intentionally tolerant of most religions, it had not yet encountered a religion of this type: namely, a religion that (a) transcended geographic, ethnic, linguistic, and class distinctions; (b) engaged in a lively and ecumenical missionary endeavor; (c) proclaimed a Deity utterly transcendent of *all* authorities, critical of the mighty and having "a preferential option for the poor"; and (d) thus created a climate of opinion potentially hostile toward precisely the pursuits of empire. From Paul onward (see especially Romans 13), the Christians anticipated that it would be necessary to defend themselves against the suspicion of bad citizenship or insubordination; and the second-century apologists made it their business to inform the state in detail about their attitude and actions vis-à-vis "the governing authorities"—how they were prayed for, and so on. But in fact Pliny[72] and the later accusers of the faith were in some ways more perceptive than the Christians themselves, for they intuited, partly on the grounds of the adamant nature of the Christians' *confessions,* that they were dealing with a new genre of religion, one which could not easily or for long maintain its piously passive stance vis-à-vis power.

Jesus, it was remembered, had advised his followers to "'Render to Caesar the things that are Caesar's, and to God the things that are God's'" (Mark 12:17), and under the *later* conditions of Christian establishment (as today) this can seem a rather pious saying. For the apparently genial relations between church and state make possible interpretations that, with variations on the theme, turn this statement into the innocuous exhortation to refer matters temporal and physical to the state and matters eternal and spiritual to the church. Indeed, in practice this advice has not been politically harmless at all, but it has been part and parcel of the (secular and religious) Establishment's very effective way of maintaining the status quo!

Jesus' own meaning (if the statement can be said to be his), like his acquiesence to the authority of Pilate, is surely much more subtle than this. Under any political circumstances, if it is seriously considered, the saying begs the immediate question "What precisely does belong to Caesar?" Given the general assumptions informing both the Theology and the anthropology of the tradition of Jerusalem, it would be hard to avoid the conclusion that, in reality, nothing at all can be said to "belong" to Caesar. "The earth is *the Lord's,* and the fullness thereof" (Ps. 24:1). Like Pilate, his underling, Caesar only "has" what God deigns temporarily to allow him (John 19:11). If one adds to this general presupposition of the tradition what we know of the explicit political context under which "the Christ event" took place, with hated Rome imposing its will upon a people gravely intolerant of tyranny, and some of Jesus' own followers involved, probably, in revolutionary activity, Jesus' statement about Caesar and God may be taken as an extremely sophisticated and pointed piece of practical wisdom. The coin that was presented to him by tricksters certainly "belonged" to Caesar. Israel's God would want no part of it! But it also represented to every thinking Jew a whole spate of absolutely false claims to sovereignty and ownership, and thus, even while it could not be used as evidence of his own revolutionary bent, Jesus' response to his tempters could be heard by sensitive Jewish ears as a confirmation of the usual prophetic condemnation of inauthentic authority. His sophistry saved him, for the moment. Nevertheless, the fact that the accusation brought

---

72. Governor of Bithynia, who wrote to the Emperor Trajan between 111 and 113 C.E. concerning the expansion of Christianity and its disruption of society.

against Jesus in the end could be that he was "setting himself up as King of the Jews" means that he never could wholly disarm those who felt his "program" had explicit political implications. So, to say the least, it is a piece of gratuitous pietism when Jesus' famous rejoinder to Pilate's suggestion of possible usurpation—"My kingship is not of this world" (John 18:36)—is turned into a proof of the nonpolitical character of the Christian gospel and movement.[73]

Yet it *is* political—in the broad and deep sense of that term; that is, it has to do with the *polis,* with "the city," with human community and its justice system, its economics, its way of working out the relations between individuals and society, and so on. How could it not be so? "Politics" are about ideas for the good ordering of human community, and every major concept of Christian anthropology (at least its anthropology!) contains implications for that ordering. If the Christians do not see it (and often they have not), the keen eye of the enemy does. And in that connection one of the most interesting figures in this history is one frequently neglected if not unfairly vilified by the Christians: Julian, the so-called Apostate.

Julian, a young prince of Rome who in 361 succeeded the Emperor Constantius, Constantine's son, had been brought up as a Christian. He therefore knew a good deal more about this religion than did the army officer Constantine, his uncle; and, no doubt for that reason, he understood rather well the discrepancies between the real pursuits of the Christians and the methods and goals of the imperium. Julian came to believe that Constantine had made a great mistake in assuming that the Christian religion would buttress his failing imperial project, and he set about to reverse the business (hence, "the Apostate"). Although in the short space of his reign (two years) he could not have succeeded in such a program, for Christianity was already too entrenched, the directions in which he moved are extremely perceptive for one so young (29, upon his accession). He asked the Alexandrians "whether their city had grown great on the precepts of the Galilean, who counseled turning the other cheek, rather than by the mighty deeds of their founder, Alexander the Conquerer." He also "forbade the Christians to teach the pagan classics and advised them to confine themselves to the exposition of the Gospels." Julian judged that, in any case, Christianity had become more questionable than it had been in its earlier, pre-established form. He regarded "the veneration of the bones of the saints, the exaltation of Mary, now called the Mother

---

73. The all-too-characteristic interpretation of the tribute money misses this subtlety altogether. An example: "'Jesus held that the claims of God are all-embracing. . . . but he does recognize that obligations due to the State are within the divine order' (Taylor). Loyalty to the emperor need not be inconsistent with loyalty to God although . . . there was to be a time when the two came into conflict" (Matthew Black, ed., *Peake's Commentary on the Bible* [London: Thomas Nelson, 1962], 813).

of God, and even the divinity of Christ [as] . . . innovations."[74] Such "innovations" were, in his view, very auspicious signs of the direction that was being taken by a religion whose piety and morality cloaked high public ambition. And was he not right in thinking that?

But here we must distinguish between two *kinds* of public involvement, the one belonging to that emergent Christendom insightfully mistrusted by the Emperor Julian, the other inherent in the original message of the Christ and his disciples. Christendom from the first quite naturally courted the kind of power that states must also quite naturally resist. For it is power of essentially the same nature as the power coveted by states; therefore the church, when it follows the Christendom pattern, invariably becomes a competitor with the state within whose jurisdiction it finds itself. Of course, Christendom will protest that it is by no means after such power, or that the power it seeks as means is, after all, directed toward noble and humane ends, or that it is only desirous of making common cause with the state, and so on. But the history of Christendom, and particularly of Catholic Rome (not because Rome is more culpable but because it has been so much more successful in this matter), demonstrates how little distinction lies between the two powers in question. States, too, have been capable of motivation by just and humane ends, just as churches and religions generally have been capable of tyranny.

This history also readily illustrates the manner in which powerful churches and powerful states are able, under certain circumstances, to cooperate one with another. Given the fact that the power they seek and, partially, possess is of virtually the same genre, this is not in the least surprising. The principle is already established with Constantine, and it is raised, almost, to a law of history by Theodosius the Great and the Theodosian Code. When each is able to do something beneficial for the other—the church with its spiritual "persuasion" and the state with its courts and armies—rivalry between the two is easily forgotten. Contemplating the history of religious warfare, who can suppress feeling the absurdity of it all when, time and again, embattled Christian factions are so intermingled with contending political parties that no distinctions of motive can be glimpsed by the wisest minds? And what shall we say of the many instances in which irreconcilable Christian elements could without compunction join forces to defeat Christian "insurrections" abhorrent to both of them (the Taborites of Bohemia, the Anabaptists of Münster, the Diggers and Levellers of Britain)?

This is the power that Julian "the Apostate" feared, and he was right to fear it. He was wrong, however, when he concluded that the quest for this kind of power was *inherent* in the Christian faith: that the church was ineluctably bound, bound by its very *belief,* to wrest power and glory from the state

---

74. Bainton, *Christendom,* vol. 1, 102.

wherever possible. Over against that conclusion, Jesus' insistence that his sovereignty is "not of this world" must be heard anew. For *that* insistence issues not from the logic of "Christendom" but from the logic of the movement that was born at Pentecost.

To reiterate: the pentecostal Christian Movement was not apolitical. Its goal, however, was not to seek power for itself but to represent, in the world, the power and sovereignty of *God.*

But let us take care! Before we leap to certain conclusions, we had better remember what we have said already about this God. We have *not* said that this God stands for ultimate power, power in its highest extremity, power-greater-than-which-none-could-be-conceived! We have *not* said that God's power competes with the that of sovereigns and potentates and states for the kind of ultimacy they all crave. We have, in fact, gone out of our way to discard that theistic fiction, the fiction of the "Almighty Father."[75] And we have faithfully carried this same theo-logic to our exposition of the second person of the Trinity, whose "dominion," we said, contrary to the Christen*dom* syndrome, had to be considered in another light altogether: the dominion of suffering servanthood, of the steward who claims nothing for himself, of the shepherd who lays down his life for the sheep, and so on.

How consistently that critique of power has been forgotten by Christendom! Putting itself forward as representative of the power and sovereignty of *God,* the church of the centuries (with a few great exceptions) has behaved as if the deity it had in mind were some other God than the one whose "thoughts" and "ways" are demonstrated in the continuity of the Testaments—and are therefore "not your thoughts" and "not your ways" (Isaiah 55:8). Historic Christendom has taken its election by and representation of God to mean that it had the right to scheme and fight for *greater* power than any state, its Deity, after all, being the apex of pure power.

We are, of course, once more glimpsing the visible consequences of the triumphalist theology of Christendom, the *theologia gloriae.* There is only one corrective to it, and it is the one that Luther named as its antithesis—although he did not always apply it very wisely in his own reflections on "church and state." Under the aegis of the *theologia crucis,* a very different conception of Christianity's public persona emerges, and with it a different conception of the relation of church and state. To represent the power of "the crucified God" in the public sphere is not only to foreswear competition with "the governing authorities [who] have their power from God" (Rom. 13); it is (as both Paul and Luther understood) to be ready to "obey" them. There is here no cause for ecclesiastical presumption or arrogance in relation to the state. Social order is necessary to human community, and governments are

---

75. *Professing the Faith,* chap. 2, 92–129.

usually lesser evils than anarchy. Therefore "pay all of them their dues, taxes to whom taxes are due, revenue to whom revenue is due, respect to whom respect is due, honor to whom honor is due" (Rom. 13:7). Those who think that revolution flows naturally from biblical faith have mistaken theology for ideology. They need to become more contextual! The *normal* posture of the disciple community in relation to government is not revolution, but respect—respect born of an appreciation for the tremendous responsibility undertaken by those who govern.[76] In this the apologists of the second century, as well as all who have argued for civic maturity on the part of Christians, are right.

There are, however, *contexts* in which this normal respect must give way to resistance. For faithfulness to the crucified one means, *concretely* speaking, a primary identification with "the crucified people" (C. S. Song). The Christian profession of faith does not bind us first to "the mighty" but to "the humble and meek," not to those who think they are righteous but to those who "hunger and thirst for righteousness," not to those who act as though they own the earth already but to "the meek [who] shall inherit the earth" (Matt. 5). That is to say, the cross of Jesus is for us not an empty symbol but a point of entry into the pain of the world, some sizable portion of which is caused by those who "lord it over" their own kind and otherkind (Luke 22:25).

The consequence of this "cross-consciousness" is the creation, in the "body of Christ," of a vigilance for oppression and injustice. And it is precisely this vigilance that is the immediate cause and goad of Christian *confession*. Not always, but normally, the confession of the faith arises just at the point at which Christian watchfulness recognizes that the powerful of the world have gone too far. The faithful church does not rise up in righteous indignation when *its own liberty or well-being* is threatened; it expects this to happen—it is "not surprised at the fiery ordeal" (1 Peter 4:12). But when the powerless are victimized—whether this means powerless people or powerless creatures of any sort, and whether this means physical victimization or more subtle types of oppression—then the faithful church resists. And not infrequently it is precisely the state that it must resist.

That is why the theology of the cross, contrary to its mistaken appropriation by pietism and personalism, is a fundamentally *political* theology.[77] It does not speak of a way to "get to heaven" ("through cross to crown"), it

---

76. "According to [Hannah] Arendt . . . 'the only reasonable hope for salvation from evil and wickedness at which men might arrive even in this world and even by themselves, without any divine assistance,' must be the imperfect working of government, the flawed actions of citizens among citizens" (Jean Bethke Elshtain, *Democracy on Trial* [Toronto: House of Anansi, 1993; New York: Basic Books, 1995], 123).

77. "In conventional piety there is no *necessary* relationship between Christian existence and ethics. If I am now loved by God, forgiven by God, and thoroughly established as his child in the community of the redeemed, then love for my neighbor may be an appropriate response, it may be the decent thing to do, but it is not a constitutive part of my being Christian." (Richard

speaks of a way of getting into the earth. The doorway to creaturehood, to the "true humanity" that sinful human beings renounce in their bid for deity or subhumanity, has a very low lintel. It is a cruciform doorway, a "narrow way," "the eye of a needle," and it does not lead to heavenly rest but to the "kingdom of God." That kingdom, according to John's Gospel, is preeminently a domain of *truth* (18:33).[78] It is a place of vantage from which the lies, the rhetoric, the hype and promotionalism of the world's kingdoms are seen for what they are, and where the *victims* of all "the kingdoms of this world and the glory of them" (Luke 4:5), so tempting even to the disciple community, become visible. Far from being "otherworldly," the theology of the reign of the crucified one is therefore radically *worldly*. It is only "otherworldly" in the sense that it is so very unlike this world to offer any such place of vantage!

> The kingdom of truth is . . . not the kingdom of some other world. It is the picture of what this world ought to be. This kingdom is thus not of this world, inasfar as the world is constantly denying the fundamental laws of human existence. Yet it is of this world. It is not some realm of eternal perfection which has nothing to do with historical existence. It constantly impinges upon man's every decision and is involved in every action.[79]

To speak of the *basileiou tou Theou* (reign of God) is of course to speak of another sphere in relation to which the church's countours become visible. We shall reserve this discussion, however, for the final part of this volume (Part IV), for this sphere contains, besides the recognition of the church's boundaries, other dimensions of the subject that must be addressed. For the present, suffice it to say that, in keeping with most classical Protestant sources, we must disclaim the view that the church either *is* the kingdom or moves without difficulty *into* the sphere of the divine reign. To speak positively, what we may say of this ultimate relation of the church is that the disciple community through faith *sees into* the "state of God," as Moses glimpsed the promised land from some distance, and therefore it cannot be quite pleased, ever, with worldly states—although it respects, in them, their always partial and mixed appropriation of whatever justice and truth they

---

John Neuhaus, ed., in Wolfhart Pannenberg, *Theology and the Kingdom of God* [Philadelphia: Westminster Press, 1969], 40.

78. Therefore "the Church has a vital critical role to play in society. The Church must always witness to the limitations of any given society. The very existence of the Church depends upon its playing this critical role. When this critical witness is abandoned, the Church becomes superfluous. In that case, the Church remains only as an institution catering to the religious needs of a fast-diminishing minority that needs that sort of thing" (Pannenberg, ibid., 83).

79. Reinhold Niebuhr, "The Kingdom Not of This World," in *Beyond Tragedy* (New York: Charles Scribner's Sons, 1937), 277.

embody. The church "sees into" that sphere by faith, and, by grace, it may even from time to time seem to be "taken up into" that sphere—as Paul, trying to describe in a roundabout way his conversion writes of being "caught up into the third heaven—whether in the body or out of the body I do not know, God knows" (2 Cor. 12:2). But when this happens—*if* this really happens—then the disciple community knows, once more, what Jesus already told its first cohort (Matt. 21:31), that this "heavenly" sphere is peopled, proleptically, by "many whom the church does not have" (Augustine).

8. The Church and the Faiths of Others

8.1. Jesus Christ, the Particular Who Opens Us to the Universal. Nothing is more frequently discussed in Christian academic circles today than the pluralistic character of our society. Religious plurality is particularly conspicuous in the North American context, and its visiblity (as represented in particular by the "visible minorities" in urbanized areas) makes it impossible to consider the question of the relation of the church to other religions a merely academic matter of theology.

This must be regarded, however, as a gain, for the greatest barrier to *theological* seriousness in the Christendom-dominated past has been the reduction of this important discussion to abstractions and theory. It is indeed still possible, particularly in the ethnologically monolithic cultures that are still extant in the old European flagship of Christendom, to ask about this relation without ever seeing *faces:* Jewish faces, Muslim faces, Buddhist faces, the faces of indigenous peoples. European theology has sometimes been very insightful with respect to the *secularization* of the West, but it has seldom spoken with wisdom where *pluralization* is concerned. The reason is obvious: with the exception of very large cities or special areas of meeting and confrontation such as the former Yugoslavia, most Europeans do not *live* in radically pluralized societies. Their theories of the manner in which Christianity relates to other religions, therefore, while sometimes containing important insights born of their older, deeper, and sustained theological reflection, lack the concreteness and compassion that can be avoided in North America only by deliberately isolationist-exclusivistic forms of Christian belief.[80]

---

80. See for example Richard John Neuhaus's account of Wolfhart Pannenberg's early meeting with the Harvard colloquium on Jewish-Christian relations: "Rabbi Arthur Hertzberg is among those who think it was largely an instance of insensitivity to the nuances of Jewish-Christian dialogue that have developed in America over the last several years. 'It is hardly fair to expect a European theologian to be alert to the nontheological mines that clutter the field of Jewish-Christian relations . . . '" (Pannenberg, *Theology and the Kingdom of God,* 33–34).

The way Christians understand their relation, as Christians, to persons of other faiths and specifically to the *faiths* of those others will depend to a large extent upon the degree to which they have been able to free themselves intellectually and emotionally from Constantinianism; or, to state this more positively, the degree to which they have been able to expose themselves to the Scriptures of the two Testaments and to the fundamental teachings of the Christian faith *without* bringing to these sources assumptions that were imposed upon them by the ecclesiastical imperialism and theological trium- phalism that accompanied the establishment of the Christian religion in the West. This is, of course, no easy accomplishment, for those assumptions are so entrenched as to seem veritable dogma, to be dispensed with only at the cost of leaving Christianity itself behind.

Included in these assumptions are such ideas as the following: (1) that it is the will of God, as expressed in Jesus' "Great Commission," to convert all human beings to the Christian faith; (2) that there is no salvation outside the church; and (3) that there is "no other name under heaven given among men by which we must be saved" (Acts 4:12). Central in all of these is, of course, Christology, although ecclesiology and missiology or the concept of evange- lism, as indicated by the first and second assumptions, are often extracted from the christological basis and introduce problems of their own.

Since Christology is central, however, we would do well to concentrate our attention there. The problem for any Christian who wishes to enter into *dia- logue* with other faith traditions is expressed in the above "no-other-name" quotation from Acts. The picture conveyed so graphically by this statement as it has been interpreted by popular evangelicalism is one of knowing the right name, like a password: people (souls!) are lining up to enter paradise, but only those who name *that* name are allowed inside. In more sophisticated versions, what is suggested by this imagery is that the explicit *acknowledg- ment* of Jesus Christ as Lord and Savior is required for salvation; ergo, those who persist in naming *other* names, and probably even those who have never heard of *that* name, are denied salvation. Against every version of divine grace that entertains the prospect that Jesus Christ may be present without being known, this kind of Christian exclusivism insists upon "*naming* the name that is above every name" (Phil. 2:9) as the prerequisite of salvation. In that case, of course, the contour of the church that is concerned with this aspect of ecclesial relations can be drawn with a heavy pencil: those who know the name constitute the church; all others are outside, beyond the pale.

Interestingly, the less sophisticated appropriation of this exclusivism seems often more susceptible to correction than do the more doctrinally hardened versions of the same position. Thus it frequently happens that ordinary

Christians on this continent, coming into contact with neighbors, shopkeepers, or casual acquaintances who embrace non-Christian faiths, are struck by the strangely "Christian" quality of the lives of these others, and even by parallels at the level of belief and morality. The battle against ecclesiastical bigotry in North America begins in earnest with this kind of humane recognition. Unfortunately, it too often fails to penetrate the more doctrinaire forms of this exclusivity; for doctrine, when it is bad doctrine, is a powerful form of insulation from life.

Several arguments must be brought to bear against the refusal, in Christ's name, to accept the authenticity of other faiths—which is the *sine qua non* not only of dialogue *with* these others but meaningful *discourse about* them. Most of these arguments come from the Bible itself, and all have biblical bases. This in itself demonstrates one of the common causes of religious bigotry in its "Christian" form—namely, what is commonly called biblical literalism. What this alleged literalism cloaks, usually, is the extreme arbitrariness of those who claim it for themselves. For despite fundamentalist claims concerning the literal authority of the whole Bible, what happens in biblicistic circles is that *some* scriptural passages—often only a very few, in fact—are lifted out of the context of the whole and become "proof texts" for iron-clad dogmas that are held a priori. The sole salvific capacities of a "Christ" understood *chiefly* not in the light of the Scriptures, but in the light of subsequent Chalcedonian dogma in sloganized and ritual versions, is one of these dogmas.

But supposing, instead of beginning with ready-made dogmas, we turned to the Scriptures themselves, and explicitly to their most direct testimony to *Jesus:* how, then, might the question of Christianity and other faiths have to be answered? As we have said in the second volume, before Christology there was Jesus, called by faith the Christ.[81] Surely it is pertinent for the outcome of this entire discussion to ask, And how did Jesus behave toward and speak about the "others"? Quite apart from what subsequent christological and other dogma made of Jesus and the question of salvation, does the Jesus of the Synoptic tradition—or even of John—convey the impression that only his name, explicitly acknowledged, will earn anyone salvation?

To the contrary! Liberalism may have romanticized Jesus, turning him into the first great liberal, but it was right, over against the dogmatists of the theological Right, to draw attention to the fact that the Jesus of the Gospels is astonishingly open to all sorts and conditions of human beings and human points of view. In fact, given the customs and strictures of his age, it is one of the most abidingly surprising characteristics of the Synoptic *imago Christi*

---

81. *Professing the Faith,* chap. 8, §35, 480–97.

that it not only breaks through the limits and conventions of Jesus' own age but all subsequent ages as well! Jesus is not, to be sure, a flower-child, or even "gentle Jesus meek and mild"; he knows how to make biting criticisms, and he can exclude. But if we ask *whom* he criticizes and excludes, we cannot possibly come up with the kinds of lists that "the religious" of the Christian ages have, in his name, devised. For he excludes above all precisely such excluders—the "righteous" ones who dissociate themselves from sinners and publicans and "have no need of a physician"; the officially designated religious authorities, who make their phylacteries broad but pass by on the other side when someone is lying hurt in a ditch; the law-abiding, who tithe mint and dill and cumin but do not observe the weightier matters of the law; the order-loving adults, who want to protect him from children; the practical-minded and officious men, who chastise spendthrifty women; the publicly chaste, who feel themselves so far above sin as to stone a too-openly generous woman; and all the rest!

More than that, and on the positive side of this same coin, if we ask about the way of Jesus in his exchanges with others who are excluded by his own people, we are even less likely to find scriptural warranty for identifying persons who are beyond the pale of salvation. For he not only welcomes sinners and tax collectors, but he tells of good Samaritans (Luke 10:29f.), an offense to the ears of his own people; he finds the response of a Syro-Phoenician woman, in a conversation quite precisely about our present subject, more insightful than anything he has heard from his disciples (Mark 7:24f.); he reminds his followers of the "other sheep that are not of this fold"; and so on and so forth. And why would he not do and say such things? He is, after all, himself a Jew; and the Jews have always known (except when they themselves forgot their covenant) that their mission was *inclusive.*

Does that mean, then, that Jesus himself (as evangelicalism claims) intended to include all others in *his* movement, to teach them all to say *his* name? Surely not! As we have seen, not only does he employ minority metaphors to describe the community that he intends to bring into being, but he even asks on at least one occasion whether there will be *any* faith when the Son of Man returns (Luke 18:8). The triumphalistic thrust *is* present in the newer Testament—but in Jesus' disciples, not in him, and it is consistently chastised.

We need not go beyond Jesus himself to refute the exclusivism that is fostered by those who most vociferously claim to represent him. All the same, there are other things to be said about this matter. *First,* the attempt to draw a clear line of distinction between "saved Christians" and "damned heathen" seriously damages the *central* biblical and Reformation insistence upon salvation "by grace alone." For it makes the *acknowledgment* of grace, and specifically of the grace designated by this name, the decisive dimension. One may call this acknowledgment "faith," and in this way seem to avoid the displacement of grace; but the Reformers were clear in their prioritization: grace precedes faith. We are not justified by "our faith"; that would turn faith into a religious work; we are "justified by grace through faith." And the faith "through" which grace becomes known to us is never in a straight-forward manner "ours," because it is the work of the Spirit within us. More-over, this is a lifelong process: we never "arrive," we are always "on the way" (1 Cor. 9, 10). Our acknowledgment of grace and its sufficiency is at best a sporadic thing, with continuous ups and downs. This, to say the least, already blurs the lines between Christians and others, not only persons of other faiths but even persons of no faith at all. Christians pray, "Lord, I believe, help my unbelief" (Mark 9:24), and in that prayer they acknowledge forthwith their solidarity with all sorts and conditions of people.

Second, if Jesus Christ is indeed "Lord and Savior," can serious Christians ever imagine that his sovereignty and salvation are limited to those who know about them and profess them openly? A sovereign, even in earthly terms, whose sovereignty depended upon the acknowledgment and approval of the citizens of her or his realm would be less than credible. Who is to confine this "Lord and Savior" to churches? Is that not the height of arrogance and presumption? Especially when, in the churches themselves, there is only a sporadic acknowledgment of his sovereignty and saviorhood?

In other words, there is a *cosmic* dimension implied in the concept of "the kingship of Christ," one of the three traditional "offices."[82] Christians have no right to claim that Jesus' sovereignty rules out the validity of claims that are made for the sovereignty of other deities; but if they in fact believe in the sovereignty of Jesus, they ought to be able to hear in the world, and in many places where they had not expected it, voices that remind them of the voice of the Good Shepherd. A wise statement of H. Richard Niebuhr's deserves endless contemplation in Christian circles in North America today: "I do not have the evidence which allows me to say that the miracle of faith in God is worked only by Jesus Christ and that it is never given to men outside the sphere of his working, though I may say that where I note its presence I posit the presence also of something like Jesus Christ."[83] It is not necessary for Christians to elevate the Christ; God does—and, as usual, "in mysterious ways." In their finally quite pathetic attempts to enthrone Jesus Christ along the usual lines—purely a habit of the theology of glory!—the excluding Christians only succeed in reducing him to a very tawdry type of monarch, a provincial potentate who in all his alleged grandeur is simply "too small" (Philip Watson).

---

82. See *Professing the Faith,* chap. 7, §31 ("Christus Rex").
83. "Reformation: The Continuing Imperative," in *The Christian Century* 76 (1960): 249.

Third, consider Luther's conception of the Christ who is "incognito," who is present in the neighbor who comes begging at my door at midnight, or the child who has been orphaned, or the widow without bread—who is ubiquitously among us. This picture of Christ needs to be expanded in the pluralistic context to include Christ's hiddenness in other religions and religious leaders. Such an approach could, of course, lead to a new kind of triumphalism, one that sees every other religion composed of cryptic Christians! But that does not need to happen. If we can let Jesus Christ be who he is, and not imprison him in our *Christologies,* we shall also find it possible to let the Buddha and Mohammed and Baha Ullah and all the others be who they are. The particularity of Jesus is a false scandal only if it is divorced from his actual person and reduced to dogma. As Paul Lehmann has written, "Too often . . . the [Christian] story has been told as though exclusiveness were the criterion on its particularity. But the contrary is actually the case. The Christian story . . . moves from its divine-human centre of freedom and fulfilment to its circumference from which nothing human is excluded."[84]

Christians, in short, are obliged by their own christocentric message, liberated from its Constantinian moorings and challenged by empirical pluralism, to rise to its potential for an inclusiveness that does not negate but builds upon its unique center and source. To say the very least, in the post-Christendom situation, the lines of demarcation between Christian and non-Christian cannot be drawn in indelible ink. We need not fear, however, that we shall lose the specificity of our confession through a greater openness to others. It is precisely through the specificity of *this* particular that we are learning such openness.

8.2. The Church as Movement and Religious Plurality.   Very simple questions, in theology as in life, are often the most difficult questions to answer. The question "What is truly the church?" is one of these. Most of the answers to this question that have come to us out of the past are only, at best, suggestive. To derive from them the wisdom that *we* need, it is necessary to distinguish their essence from many of the associations that have colored them historically. As we have noticed both in our discussion of the traditional "marks," including the Protestant addenda, and of the internal and external relationships by which the church has defined itself, everything has been affected by the primary sociological fact of ecclesiastical identity—the political extablishment of the Christian religion throughout by far the greater share of its history.

---

84. "The Indian Situation as a Question of Accountability," *Church and Society* (January–February, 1985), 59.

This fact, whose more detailed analysis will command our attention in chapter 4, is of particular significance for the question of the church's relation to other religions. For it means that, until our own period, except in missionary situations, Christianity has rarely related to other religious faiths *as a religion,* primarily; rather, it has confronted the others as a vast political organization whose worldly power made dialogue with the religions virtually impossible.

Wherever "the Christendom paradigm" (Mead) still pertains—or rather, can seem to do so—the same impossibility must be faced, and members of non-Christian religions should not be surprised if their desire for a closer communication with Christians in such contexts is not reciprocated. In North America today, for instance, wherever "the Christian Right" is dominant, we can expect little more than, at best, a polite continuation of the condescension with which powerful cults have always treated their minor rivals; at worst, there will be disturbing echoes of the Inquisition, Salem, and Auschwitz.

Such attitudes and actions, however, should not be attributed to Christianity as such, but to the Christian religion as a political entity—the remnants of Christendom. As the shell of Christendom is broken and Christian faith is liberated from the burden of institutional power, the institutional church may give way to the movement that Christian faith as such rightly generates. To a limited extent, this is already happening in the "Christian" West. And wherever it happens, it enables Christians for the first time to dialogue with other faiths *as a faith,* rather than as the guardian of a whole civilization and "way of life."

Christianity as movement—*communio viatorum*—has its own peculiar problems and limitations, as all movements do. But it also has possibilities that are inaccessible to more static forms of human community. Among these possibilities, that of friendship with those who are "not of this fold" is one. And perhaps it can be more than friendship. In a movement, belonging is by participation; and there are many levels of participation. As with the peace movement; the women's movement; and racial, ecological, and other protest movements of our epoch, in the Christian movement, some will be found at the center, some along the edges, some standing by with interest, almost persuaded perhaps, but waiting to see. . . .

And, as in all such movements, it happens that people discover others whom they did not expect to find there, some of whom may be "fellow-travellers" whose motives and understandings are quite different from one's own, so in the Christian movement that is perhaps the future church some will be involved whose identity seems at first puzzling. Perhaps they know more about the Buddha or Moses than about Jesus. Or perhaps they are only looking for some cause to which to give themselves, or have a vague desire to

141

help others, or are simply curious about "what is going on." In the movement, people discover one another, and they discover also the faith and the unfaith that have brought them together.

The Christian movement will have to take up what Christendom has regularly and quite predictably left behind: the cross. The first real steps in the movement that became "the people of the Way" were taken by One who started out along the Via Dolorosa to the Place of the Skull. He could carry nothing else except what was laid upon him by a judging, resentful, and profoundly needy world. And he could not even carry that by himself. The first one to join that movement (reluctantly, one supposes, although perhaps it was out of some kind of human fellow-feeling; what was he doing there in the first place?) was one commandeered to help that poor man bear his terrible burden. Simon Peter may have been the first one to confess the faith verbally, but Simon of Cyrene was the first to confess the faith by taking up the cross. Irenaeus reports[85] that the Basilideans, a Gnostic sect, taught that Simon not only carried Jesus' cross but was actually crucified in his place— a piece of their docetism that may, however, contain a parable of sorts. Simon Peter the confessor of the faith spurned the cross until the very end, it is said. As for Simon of Cyrene, who carried it, one is not told whether he was even a Christian—ever!

---

85. *Adversus Haereses,* I.xxxiv.4.

CHAPTER ▪ THREE
Mission, Message, and Ministry

9. What *Is* "the Christian Mission"?

9.1. The Confusion Surrounding Christian Mission Today. The ecclesiastical situation in North America today is confusing in many ways, but in no area of ecclesiology are the churches of our continent more bewildered than in what has been formally called their missiology.[1] On the one hand, old and new forms of evangelicalism, some of it *within* the once-mainline churches, press forward with strong mandates to "win the world for Christ," undaunted by pluralism, the "end of the Constantinian era," and many of the other contextual realities with which we have had to concern ourselves in this study. Campus "crusades" still seek to Christianize the universities, and the largest Protestant denomination on the continent, the Southern Baptist Church, engages in what is termed a "Bold Mission Thrust" aimed at confronting the entire globe with the claims of Christ by the year 2000. Indeed, the rapid approach of that apocalyptic thousand-year mark induces many, as it did in the year 1000, to entertain visions of unprecedented Christian triumph in or over the world.

On the other hand, the formerly mainline denominations, reputed inheritors of the major streams of the Protestant Reformation, are almost univer-

---

1. This is undoubtedly true for all Western expressions of the Christian religion, including Europe (see, e.g., Pannenberg, *Theology and the Kingdom of God* [Philadelphia: Westminster, 1969], 98.). The missiological confusion in the North American situation is particularly noticeable, however, because of the great variety of responses present among Christians here—all the way from the aggressive missionary zeal of the more conservative groups, which now seek to rechristianize Russia and other "lapsed" parts of the world, to an ultraliberal refusal of any type of missionary activity.

sally unsure what Christian mission (missions?) could mean. Neither their classical-Reformation past nor their nineteenth-century liberal past helps them to answer the question, "What precisely *is* the Christian mission?" For the Reformation occurred within a mostly Christian world—a world that, to be sure, the reforming elements felt had to be purged and made more authentically Christian, yet a world in which Christianity already had a long history and in which it could be assumed that certain foundational Christian concepts, symbols, and moral convictions were well and firmly rooted. That world is no longer the one in which Protestants find themselves.

As for the *liberal* past of most of these same Protestant denominations, it is in some ways even more remote where missiology is concerned. Nineteenth-and early twentieth-century Protestant liberalism was imbued with a strong sense of Christian mission. Indeed, what may have united the various schools and types of liberalism more than anything else was their shared belief in the necessity and possibility of decisive Christian missions. The great American historian, Kenneth Scott Latourette, concludes his book *The Christian World Mission in Our Day* with these words:

> We must aim at nothing less than winning all the nations to discipleship, incorporating them in Christ's Church, and teaching them to bring all aspects of their life into conformity with Christ's commands.

By 1954, when this book appeared, the earlier optimism that envisaged the twentieth century as "the *Christian* century" had been somewhat chastened by the actual events of the first half of the century; so we are not surprised to hear Latourette qualify this statement by appending the following thought: "Even though we know that, by a paradox, the goal is not to be attained within history, we must press forward toward it."[2] Yet even so qualified, the claim seems vastly remote from the present mood.

This belief in the fruitfulness of worldwide Christian missions was inspired in its liberal mode by a combination of renewed interest (born of historical-critical method in biblical study) in the "kingdom of God" as the very center of Jesus' own teaching and a strong (if, from our perspective, myopic) conviction of the advanced state of Western civilization. Under the impact of the modern West's "religion of progress," the kingdom of God seemed about to dawn. Evidence for its imminence was found in the vast increase of knowledge brought about by the scientific revolution and the technological improvements introduced by the application of science to existing problems. It is not accidental that so many of the Protestant missionaries who went off to

---

2. Kenneth Scott Latourette, *The Christian World Mission in Our Day* (New York: Harper & Brothers, 1954), 180.

China, India, Africa, and other "dark" places of the world were trained in both theology and medicine, or theology and agriculture, or theology and education, or engineering, and so on. The permanent influence of these missions, even in countries such as China, which eventually renounced them, attests to the humanitarian intent that was certainly a part of the overall enterprise.

But in the meantime, as Wilfred Cantwell Smith attests,[3] many Christians have also learned about the scandalous arrogance that was inherent in these missions. In particular, we have acquired a critical awareness of the naivete of the liberal churches of the West in imagining that they were bringing their high Christian civilization to backward peoples.

> "Many of us are still repenting a history of forcing our *beliefs* on those with less power. So how do we now share our joy in Jesus in a just and positive way? Can we go humbly to those outside our churches . . . who are open to mystery? Can we open our churches to them so that we can search together for answers and community, for faith?"[4]

The attitude reflected in this very representative statement, so different from that of a century or even a half century ago, is one almost of shame over Western "Christian" civilization. In the first place, we think that to have imagined it "Christian" was presumptuous, and in the second many are almost persuaded that it was demonic, or at least inferior to the more innocent, "primitive" cultures it displaced. The five hundredth anniversary of the voyage of Christopher Columbus to the New World has heightened the growing sense of guilt and self-criticism in both of the Americas and in Europe. To imagine that we could go off to "darkest Africa" today with messages of *salvation* is repulsive to many sensitive contemporary Christians. Our own North American culture does not seem to us terribly "advanced" any more, and many find it perhaps the most problematic of all human societies, despite (or perhaps because of!) its alleged "development."

If to this evaluational about-face we add (what was discussed in the previous chapter) the recognition of the legitimacy of other faiths, the loss of economic and other powers within these same once-mainline churches, the consequent preoccupation with their own housekeeping and their future prospects, and the general lack of confidence among their membership, we shall not be surprised at the disarray surrounding the question of Christian

---

3. Wilfred Cantwell Smith, *What Is Scripture? A Comparative Approach* (Minneapolis: Fortress Press, 1993), 83; 279–80.

4. Muriel Duncan, editor, *The United Church Observer* (*The United Church Observer*, 1993): 8; quoted by Reginald W. Bibby, *There's Got to Be More: Connecting Churches and Canadians* (Vancouver: Wood Lake Books, 1995), 34.

missions. These old churches may secretly envy the missionary successes of the younger and more enthusiastic evangelical bodies, and some among these churches will continue to urge their denominations to take up boldly that old missionary "thrust," whether in conservative or liberal forms; but, on the whole, that approach seems simplistic and naive—if not plainly imperialistic and arrogant. Apart from the support of established missions, now for the most part in charge of Christians indigenous to the lands in which they are found, the denominations in question manifest an embarrassed silence on the whole subject. Sometimes it seems as if the ending of imperial Christianity was so humiliating an experience for once-militant Christendom that it had determined, silently, to renounce any *hint* of behavior that could be accounted aggressive. The question implicit in this is whether, at the end of the Constantinian era, it will be possible for Protestants to discover a mode of Christian mission that is not implicitly imperialistic, racist, and destructive of cultures that may in important respects be superior to our own.

9.2. Mission Inherent in the Faith. The question should, I think, be stated in that rather stark way because the alternative being quietly entertained in our missiological entropy (namely, to forget the whole idea of there being a Christian mission) is not one that can be sustained within the sphere of a Christianity that is seeking to recover and rethink its biblical roots. Mission is not a concept superimposed upon the faith of the Christian movement from beyond its own internal drives, for instance, by Western empires and states that went out to conquer the world; it is inherent in the faith as such, as we have already observed in connection with Jesus' metaphors for the disciple community (salt, yeast, light, seed, and so on).

> The one thing must prevail: "Proclaim the Gospel to every creature!" The Church runs like a herald to deliver the message. It is not a snail that carries its little house on its back and is so well off in it, that only now and then it sticks out its feelers, and then thinks that the "claim of publicity" has been satisfied.[5]

From the start, the "people of the way" understood that the good news they had heard was to be shared—noised abroad, shouted from the housetops. They knew themselves to be denied the comfort of being only a "fellowship" (*koinonia*). The apostolic vocation, they remembered, had already been begun by Jesus himself, when he sent his followers, two by two, "into every town and place where he himself was about to come," saying to them, "'The harvest is plentiful, but the laborers are few; pray therefore the Lord of the

---

5. Karl Barth, *Dogmatics in Outline,* trans. G. T. Thomson (New York: Harper & Row, 1959), 147.

harvest to send out laborers into his harvest. Go your way . . . '" (Luke 10:1ff.). As Hendrikus Berkhof has noted, "all the appearances of the risen Jesus, with the exception of those on Easter morning itself, contain mandates for the work of missions which is now beginning (Matt. 18:19f.; Mark 16:20; Luke 24:49; John 20:21; 21:15–19; Acts 1:8) . . . ."[6] Despite the fact that the Jerusalem disciples had questions about Paul's mission to the Gentiles, they could not ultimately counsel against it, for they knew in their hearts that Paul had grasped the universal thrust of the message of reconciliation, and that Christians would have to be "ambassadors for Christ" (2 Cor. 5:20) in regions beyond the wildest dreams of Jewish fisher-folk. Paul merely made explicit what was already implicit in their own Pentecostal experience.

The rationale of the missionary direction of the faith is implied, we repeat, in the gospel itself. Far from conceiving of the revelation in Jesus as the Christ as a private or merely cultic illumination, the disciple community from the first believed that it was of cosmic significance—and not only, as we have already said in connection with other faiths, on the basis of people's recognition or acknowledgment of that significance, but as an "event," an occurrence, a new situation. As George Buttrick of Madison Avenue Presbyterian Church in New York City used to tell his students in homiletics: "Every sermon must articulate some expression of the message that *the most wonderful thing has happened.*" The "word of the cross" is not first an exhortation to make something happen, as is Karl Marx's *insistence* that the point of philosophy is "to change the world"; it is first an announcement (*kerygma*) that God *has already caused something to happen.* This is "the indicative" without which all Christian "imperatives" simply beg the question of their own *fundamentum* (ground).[7] But if this indicative is truly heard, heard in the depths and not merely with "the hearing of the ears," it will be understood to contain *within itself* a whole host of imperatives, among which the very first will be: "You must not keep this to yourself!" This gospel is not secret knowledge, to be purposely hidden and imparted only gradually and sparingly to the deserving or the curious. That is gnosticism and the way of the mystery cults. Discipleship of the Christ means participation in Christ's prior, universal mission, and not even as a second step but as part and parcel of the first— the hearing itself!

Confessio fidei is implicit in *auditio fidei.* With this conclusion, or rather this *premise,* Christians of many and varied doctrinal backgrounds may agree. Disagreement comes about, however, when it is asked, And what exactly does it mean to confess the faith, to engage in "evangelical" activity, to

---

6. *Christian Faith: An Introduction to the Study of the Faith,* trans. Sierd Woudstra (Grand Rapids: Wm. B. Eerdmans, 1979), 320.
7. See below, chap. 7, "Theological Ethics," esp. §29.

take up the apostolic vocation, to participate in Christ's mission? Here, sides must be taken, and there are *basically* only two sides, with variations on the themes. One side understands the object of Christian mission to be the conversion of people to an explicit faith in Jesus Christ and membership in the church. The other is more concerned for the implementation in the life of the world of the *will* of God as expressed in the Christ-event; it does not busy itself so much with the verbal acknowledgment of Christ's sovereignty as with the concrete consequences of that sovereignty for the here and now. The rest of what we shall have to say in this chapter will expand on this contrast.

9.3. The False Equation of Mission and Ecclesiastical Expansion. Biblical faith assumes that the Christian movement will grow, will expand—indeed, it assumes that this "must" happen, for if the *kerygma* (proclamation) is the message of a new situation affecting all the world, then it is vital that this good news should be heard by many people, and that there should be more and more people to participate in its telling-forth. Thus, the writer of the Acts of the Apostles is frequently impelled to inform his readers that some thousands were added to the community through the preaching of the apostles[8]—a testimony that, to the ears of *contemporary* Christians, can seem to justify every sort of evangelical endeavor!

The error in this assumption concerning the necessary expansion of the faith occurs when expansion itself becomes the significant reality—the end and no longer (what it clearly is in the newer Testament) the means to a far more important end, namely the spreading of the good news as such. Possibly the habit of turning the means into the end is already present in the testimony of Luke-Acts to these "increases"; certainly it is present prior to the establishment under Constantine, and understandably so. But it must nevertheless be asked whether, even before the Battle of the Milvian Bridge, it is not present chiefly as *temptation,* and whether, after its establishment and throughout most of its history, Christianity has not regularly confused its mission with its own augmentation.[9]

---

8. Acts 2:47; 4:4; 5:14; etc.
9. Loren B. Mead contrasts mission as understood within "the apostolic paradigm" with the later "Christendom paradigm." With the adoption of Christianity by Rome, he notes, "The missionary frontier on the edge of Empire now becomes the responsibility of the professional—the soldier's job for the political realm and the specially designated missionary's job for the religious realm. In addition, however, the missionary understands that winning souls to the Lord is the same task as winning nations to the Empire. . . .

"This new relationship between church and Empire changed the structures and form of mission immeasurably. The commitment of the ordinary person to the Lord undergirded the structures of society and strengthened and enlarged the Empire. . . . Imperialism and mission, in this paradigm, were inseparable" (*The Once and Future Church* [Bethesda, Md.: Alban Institute, 1991], 14–15).

If one studies the history of missions, especially as this subject is presented in nineteenth- and early twentieth-century literature, it is almost invariably assumed that mission *means* expansion. The so-called "great ages of Christian missions" are regularly identified with those periods in the history of the Christian movement when Christianity laid claim to more territory and more "souls" than previously. The nineteenth century itself is usually depicted in such terms.

It is never very clear in these studies whether any distinction is to be made between the sheer quantitative growth of the Christian religion and the quality of what is "noised abroad" and believed by Christian converts. Even today, when we are told so frequently that Africa, Asia, and Latin America are becoming the new centers of Christian demographic concentration, we are seldom informed in detail about the *character* of the "Christianity" that is growing in these regions of the planet. Questions of this nature are even discouraged because it is feared, in many centers of liberal Christianity, that such questions may imply standards of authenticity gleaned too restrictively from Western Christian sources. This is indeed a danger. But it does not relieve the ecumenical church of the responsibility for asking, always, what precisely "Christianity" means or is coming to mean. Two thousand-odd years of an ecclesiastical experience that is by no means exclusively Western have taught us that misinterpretations of many types easily evolve within communities calling themselves Christian, and that unless the faith is to proliferate impossibly and stand, in the end, for everything and nothing, there must be some *global* Christian vigilance with respect to the forms the church is taking. We have had centuries of experience, for instance, in the absorption of Christian teaching into preexisting religious forms, *some* of which have been altogether antithetical to biblical faith. Heresy—that is, misleading and unsound teaching—does not come to an end just because Christianity moves out of the religiously and philosophically complex world of the Europeans into societies that may be more humane, less aggressive, less individualistic, more given to consensus, and so on. The whole discussion of Christian expansion into non-European parts of the globe today is shrouded in the mists of Western liberal taboo and "political correctness," to the point that practices that would be intolerable in Western Christian contexts (for example, blatant patriarchalism) are accepted as Christian elsewhere. Surely this is little more than a contemporary liberal concession to the old expansionist concept of Christian missions.

The mission of Christianity in the world has to do with ecclesiastical expansion only tangentially. An expanded Christian movement *may* indicate the presence of a lively and authentic mission, but it may also indicate the presence of secular promotionalism and the gimmickry of technologically smart hucksters, or the naive desire on the part of so-called developing peoples to imitate the reputedly successful "values" of the West. Here too, and here especially, it must be said that the tests of authenticity are *not* quantitative ones. Genuinely *Christian* mission is not motivated by thoughts of gain, particularly *churchly* gain! John Macquarrie rightly asserts that "The abiding motive of mission is love":

> This always has been the fundamental motive for Christian mission, the history of which abounds in examples of sacrifice and martyrdom. But perhaps this fundamental motive has too often been combined with other motives which need to be looked at carefully. There has been too much thought of *gaining* converts, of *winning* the world, of *expanding* the Church. The Church, like the individual Christian and like Christ himself, is called to give itself. The end set before it is the kingdom, in which it will lose itself. The aim of the Church is not to *win* the world, but rather to identify itself with the world, even to lose itself in the world, in such a way as to bring nearer the kingdom in which the distinction of Church and world will be lost. What is important is the manifesting and propagating of Christ's self-giving love, and the awakening of this in ever wider areas of human society. But this may well happen without these areas becoming incorporated into the Christian Church or explicitly confessing the Christian faith. Here we have to remember that the Christian Church is continuous with a wider community of faith, and that wherever the love that springs from reverence for Being is active, there God has drawn near and revealed himself, and there christhood (by whatever name it may be called) is laying hold of human life and filling it with the grace of Being.[10]

But with this statement we are skirting the edges of the second way of considering the mission of the church, and therefore we shall turn to explore it directly.

10. The World-Orientation of the Christian Mission

10.1. God's Mission as the Presupposition of Ours. We have criticized the conception of Christian mission that equates mission with the numerical expansion of the church as such. We deem this an unworthy and inadequate interpretation of the "sending forth" of the disciple community into "all the world." The church may indeed grow. It always needs to grow, in fact, at least minimally; and there may be contexts in which its growth is of vital importance to its mission. But we believe that church growth is never to be identified as if it *were* the mission of the church, or elevated to the status of a Christian priority; and we recognize how very easily it can and does happen

---

10. John Macquarrie, *Principles of Christian Theology* (London: SCM, 1966), 393.

that church growth comes to be regarded as, or in lieu of, Christian mission. Congregations and denominations are regularly tempted to think themselves obedient missioners for Christ because they can boast of quantitative increases. But the test of authenticity in Christian missions, as in Christian life, generally has very little to do with quantities. It is entirely possible for "big" churches to be unfaithful and false representatives of the Christ, and conversely it is possible for "little," obscure, and apparently failing *koinonia* to be genuine witnesses to the reign of God. This "logic of the cross" has also to be applied to Christian missions.

The subject we have now to explore is that of the alternative to mission as ecclesiastical expansion. Earlier we characterized this alternative as follows: it is concerned for the implementation in the life of the world of the *will* of God as expressed in the Christ-event; therefore it does not busy itself so much with the verbal acknowledgment of Christ's sovereignty as with the concrete consequences of that sovereignty for the here and now. We shall attempt to describe the alternative by expanding upon this capsulization in three observations.

1. The first and most basic point to be made here is that this conception of Christian mission presupposes a *divine* mission as the foundation without which the mission of the disciple community would be literally impossible. The Christ-event (to use that particular nomenclature) both effects and reveals the "new reality" assumed by Christian evangelical work in the world. "The most wonderful thing has happened" (Buttrick)—to speak eschatologically, it has happened, is happening, and shall happen. Quite independently of *our* will and *our* work and *our* witness, God is active in the world, effecting the change that was introduced into history through Jesus Christ and that will in God's own time and manner be brought to completion.

This divine mission is not only prior to and definitive for the Christian mission, it is also infinitely more expansive. What Christians may see of it at any moment in time is only at best a fraction of its magnitude, the tip of the iceberg. In fact, deeply to sense *God's* mission in the world is to experience both awe and humility: awe at glimpsing something of the magnificence of that in which one is oneself involved; humility born of the recognition that one's own participation is infinitesimal and, quite possibly, so parochial as to be practically insignificant.

This intimation of the grandeur and boundlessness of the divine mission— an intimation that began to seize the better minds of Western Christendom early in the present century and, consequently, introduced a whole new conception of the nature of the Christian mission—injects a vital *critical* dimension into the theology of Christian missions. That dimension is of particular significance in the North American context today, and for at least two reasons. First, with their activistic mentality and their temptation to regard their own society as the pinnacle of civilization, North American Christian bodies have been prone to adopt a conception of the Christian mission that both underestimated the "prevenience" of the divine mission and frequently confused the character and content of the Christian mission with the propagation of their own cultural values and pursuits. We "New World" Christians have generally conceived of the missionary task in precisely those terms—as a task, an "endeavor," an "enterprise"—in other words something that we, with our much-touted initiative, daring, and "know-how," would carry out. We would take the gospel to Indonesia or Angola or Mongolia. We would "christianize" the pagan world. And we would do this impressively, because with our medical, educational, and scientific-technical prowess we would easily demonstrate the superiority of our faith. It was in part, after all, our faith[11] that engendered in us the will to develop our full human potential for knowledge and the dominion of nature. Why should we then question the obvious link between our faith and our culture? And why should not our mission incorporate the benefits of both? The idea that God might already be present in the "pagan" places to which our missionary enterprise would take us was an idea late in arriving on these shores, and it is still on the whole a very novel one. Even more novel—indeed, offensive, to most of us—is the notion that God might not only be present in those places but might wish, from the accumulated wisdom of human beings *in* those places, to enlighten *us*!

The second reason that the priority and immensity of the divine mission has critical significance for us today is related to the religiously pluralistic nature of our own society and of the entire globe. If it is sufficiently grasped both at the intellectual and the emotional level of comprehension, such an understanding of the prevenient mission of God can deliver Christians, such as we still tend to be, from our religious provincialism. The divine mission transcends our own "Christian" apprehension of it just as, and just because, the divine Being transcends our Theology. God is not equatable with any "doctrine of God," and what God is *really* doing in the world is not equatable with any conception of divine providence or salvation. To say this is no more radical than to embrace, at any point, Tillich's "Protestant principle." Just as we do not know what God's sovereignty means for the movements of the planets and the great "laws" of nature, but can only acquire, through study, some informed sense of awe over the vastness of these realities, so we are essentially ignorant of the manner in which the divine intentionality manifests itself in *historical* cause-and-effect. We do not have to be reduced to

---

11. See Lesslie Newbigin, "Can the West Be Converted?" in *The Princeton Seminary Bulletin*, new series 6, no. 1 (1985): 32–33. See also George R. Hunsberger and Craig Van Gelder, eds., *The Church Between Gospel and Culture* (Grand Rapids: Wm. B. Eerdmans, 1996), 26f.

total relativism to think this. We do not have to fear that our own little enterprise is insignificant, just because God's mission is so much more expansive and transcendent. But if once we grasp even a little the "mysterious ways" in which God moves, we shall be more open to the possibility that God may also be "moving" within religious and other movements that may at first glance appear to us strange, erroneous, or at odds with our own faith.[12] If the God of the Scriptures is able to use even tyrants and apparent enemies of the faith—and even Satan! (Job)—it is not improbable that God uses also those who do not "name the Name." Indeed, in view of the many biblical injunctions against presumption, one must reckon with the prospect that those who *do* "name the Name" may be ultimately less acceptable to God than those who do not.

The point is: Christian mission is premised upon the belief that the triune God is already present and active in the world and that the church can only *follow,* so far as possible, this prior, extensive, and only partially comprehensible mission of God.

2. The second aspect of the capsule description of mission indicated above is its world orientation. We affirm that the will of God expressed in the Christ-event is understood, in this way of regarding the church's mission, as being directed toward this world. As we have said in the discussion of the doctrine of Jesus as the Christ, it is the divine intention as revealed in this person and event to "mend"[13] the torn creation. The God of the Bible does not wish—openly resists, in fact—the temptation to abandon this world. Not that this world is *easily* accepted by God, or made the subject of God's "costly grace." It is a problematic world. But the primary cause of its malaise, so far as the tradition of Jerusalem is concerned, is that the world, God's creation, is so consistently and tragically *refused* by the creature who is its articulate center—the human being. This creature rejects and resists its own creaturehood, and attempts to bring about alternative creations of its own.[14] Salvation, far from implying deliverance from creaturehood (as in so much religion), for this tradition entails the human being's "yes" to its creaturely condition.[15] This "yes" will not solve all the problems of the the universe, because a created being contains conditions that are built into the process of life (death, for example) and are, although painful, in mysterious ways neces-

---

12. See my discussion of divine providence ("The Mystery of God's Dominion," in Douglas John Hall and Rosemary Radford Ruether, *God and the Nations* [Minneapolis: Fortress Press, 1995], 13–27).

13. From the Jewish term *tikkun.* See Emil Fackenheim, *To Mend the World: Foundations of Future Jewish Thought* (New York: Schocken, 1982).

14. Jacques Ellul, in *The Meaning of the City,* argues that the city is humanity's alternative to God's creation (Grand Rapids: Wm. B. Eerdmans, 1970).

15. See *Professing the Faith,* chap. 6, §25, 335–53.

sary to life. But whatever the salvific process means *ultimately,* for human beings in their present estate it means the peace (*shalom*) that comes from the glad acceptance of creaturehood. This acceptance is the necessary prelude to whatever else the consummation of the creation project of God will mean.

To recognize the world orientation of the divine mission is to be caught up in a quite different understanding of Christian discipleship, including its missionary dimension, from the one that has in fact dominated Christian history. We have spoken before of the "religious" temptation present in Christianity as in most religions. It is in the last analysis nothing more or less than the temptation to escape from the world and the worldly condition. Thus the most vociferous forms of Christian mission even today—the forms that everyone both inside and outside the churches immediately recognize— are variations on the theme of rescuing people from the world, snatching them as brands from the burning. Even where Christian missionary activity is not understood as gaining members for the church itself, it is often seen as saving "souls" from the torments of the present or the afterlife. Some of the most touching missionary tales are of human beings who, on their very deathbeds, were shown the light and could be confidently expected to enter the paradise that would otherwise have been denied them. The otherworldly orientation of the faith is perhaps nowhere more in evidence than in Christian missiology and evangelism.

What does it mean to take seriously a *this*-worldly orientation in Christian missions? Concretely speaking, there is no end to what such an orientation could mean, for (as we shall try to make clearer soon) different circumstances (contexts) suggest as many different ways of conceiving of and engaging in Christian mission. In general, however, we may observe that Christian mission oriented toward the "mending" of this world and its creatures would first hope, not that persons would be prepared for heaven, but that they would be enabled more fully to enter into the life of earth: to be more truly human; to be neighbors; to be *with* rather than *against* or *alone*; to be responsible for others; to lose their lives in causes greater than themselves; to manifest therefore less anxiety about their own circumstances; to cease needing enemies; to develop the *compassionate*, as distinct from the *possessive*, side of passion and sexuality; to forgive; to become sensitive to the pain and the needs of others; to exercise their capacity for depth of thought; to preserve and honor life in all of its myriad manifestations; to seek viable and just forms of human community; to overcome alienation and suspicion between races, genders, and species—and, of course, we could go on indefinitely.

The point is, Christian mission that is truly cognizant of the world orientation of the divine mission will always be found on the side of *life.* That will mean *this* life, which may indeed "go on" beyond this life (but that is God's domain), and it will mean that the realization of life, of "true humanity," will be more important to those engaged in such a mission than are the recitation of religious and theological formulae and ethical codes, no matter how significant are the latter in their own right. If the ultimate object is the fulfillment ("abundance") of life, then nothing penultimate, including the intellectual, spiritual, or physical processes by which this ultimate is arrived at, should be elevated to the status of the ultimate.

3. The third observation to be made concerning mission as conceived in this alternative is that its approach to evangelism, that is, the specific telling of the Christian story, is more likely to be indirect than direct. This follows from the previous observation, because if the object of the mission is the actual implementation or realization of Christ's worldly sovereignty rather than the verbal acknowledgment of that sovereignty, there is obviously a primary concern on the part of such missioners to foster whatever in the world may truly further the intention of God revealed in the Christ. Such missions cannot endorse as their chief end the explicit naming of the name. While they are themselves given the courage and imagination for their mission through their relationship with Jesus Christ, they do not make it their primary aim to bring others to the point of recognizing that name, for their main objective is rather to participate with others in the actual *work* of the Christ.

This should not be understood (although it invariably is!) as a neglect of evangelism. It is rather a means of making evangelism serve the mission, not vice versa. As such, it is partly a matter of strategy and partly a necessity implicit in the evangelical tradition itself, especially under the present contextual circumstances.

No doubt in its earliest manifestations, and no doubt in certain contexts today as well, the Christian community could legitimately begin straightaway with its central "story": Jesus, foretold by the prophets and law-givers of Israel; crucified, risen, and reigning "at God's right hand." The Acts of the Apostles as well, to a lesser extent, as do the epistles of the newer Testament, testify to this kind of directness of approach in the early church, and there are and always have been moments and situations in which the simple telling of the story suffices. One does not have to discount this approach.

But however it may be received in "missionary" situations in which Christianity is new or a relative minority, this direct approach to evangelism seems to me consistently to fail in our context, that is, a context in which Christianity has in the past dominated and in which churches are still numerous and active enough to have acquired a stereotypical image—to the point, indeed, of caricature. In such a context, with notable exceptions, to espouse a direct form of Christian evangelism is to court very obvious problems.[16]

---

16. Newbigin states the matter with accuracy when he writes that "What we have is . . . a pagan society whose public life is ruled by beliefs which are false. And because it is not a pre-

The problems are visible in two extremes particularly. On the one hand, when such evangelism is "successful"—as in contemporary forms of television evangelism—it creates communities of enthusiastic religious fervor that, with great regularity and (almost) predictability, come to serve ethical and political ends that responsible Christian faith can by no means endorse. It is not accidental that the most avowedly "evangelical" churches in North America today are aligned with the politics of the Right and the morality of the "moral majority." What this type of evangelism does for people, apparently, is to confirm in them their most deeply seated fears of any and every alternative to "the American way" and to stifle whatever critical consciousness may be native to their humanity.

Is this alignment of "evangelicalism" and the politics of the Right merely coincidental? I do not think so. For when evangelism means the telling of the story, even if (as happens only rarely) "the story" is told imaginatively and with personal involvement, it tends to remain within the private sphere and to function chiefly to adjust individuals to their dominant society—their acceptance by "God" or "Jesus" being enacted in their acceptance by the evangelical community. Not only is the larger sphere of the world's life left untouched, but the regnant values and goals of the host society are made to seem fundamentally sound. "Conversion," under these circumstances, becomes a rite of initiation into the existing culture; "Jesus" becomes a personification and legitimation of existing authority; and "the church" becomes a more loyal and enthusiastic microcosm of the social macrocosm.

At the other extreme, direct evangelism simply alienates most of our contemporaries—and (not incidentally) those especially whose intelligence and actual or potential maturity could be well used by the Christian movement in our time. Not only has our rampant secularity inured many to religion in general and the Christian religion in particular; not only has precisely the "evangelism" of the religious and political Right made it practically impossible to speak of "Jesus" and "salvation" and "prayer" and "faith" without courting ridicule; not only have recent revelations concerning the all-too-close association of Christian organizations and churches with unacceptable forms of sexual behavior and gender oppression left many with gnawing questions about even the traditionally more familiar forms of the Christian church; but even where it is possible for "tellers of the story" to rise above all such negative barriers to communication, there is an almost insurmountable

---

Christian paganism, but a paganism born out of the rejection of Christianity, it is far tougher and more resistant to the Gospel than the pre-Christian paganisms with which foreign missionaries have been in contact during the past two hundred years. Here, without possibility of question, is the most challenging missionary frontier of our time" ("Can the West Be Converted?" 36).

hiatus between *that* "story" and *our* story. The scandal of particularity still presents itself: why *that* story, in particular?

But, even more devastatingly, there seems to be a missing link: how does one get from the story of Jesus with his disciples, his encounters, his teachings and so forth, to the impartation of meaning in our lives here and now? It is not only, I think, that most contemporary preachers do not struggle intellectually and imaginatively enough to make a convincing transition; at a deeper level, it is our one-dimensionality, our incapacity for transcendence, and, at the same time, our sophistication. By the latter I mean that we have become hearers of many stories, not a few of which seem more moving, more immediately accessible and persuasive than the story Christians tell. Consider in this connection only one instance—the impact of contemporary films, some of them profoundly compelling and challenging.[17] The Christian story must now compete with these, and these modern tales have the advantages of novelty, contemporaneity, and contemporary technique. By comparison with the best of the contemporary stories by which our public is enthralled, the Christian story seems distant, stylized, and fraught with pious overtones and ecclesiastical promotionalism. Only rarely, I think, does it grasp the hearer apart from some context that may render the hearer in a state of readiness precisely for *that* story.

It is that context that must be borne in mind as we turn now to consider what I am calling here indirect evangelism.

10.2. World Commitment as *Conditio sine qua non.*   There has always been something terribly ironic about Christians who announce as the summation of their faith that "God so loved the world . . . " and so on while expending their missionary zeal rescuing souls from the world. If the theological presupposition of Christian mission is in truth God's "suffering love" for this *kosmos* (John 3:16), then the only convincing way of demonstrating this is by participating concretely in that suffering love. Our verbal witness to the divine *agape,* unless it arises out of and is grounded in a discipleship that is *more* committed to this world than would be the case apart from faith, only belies the message it intends to convey. If the effect of such a message is not to drive its *hearers* more unreservedly into the beloved world, then one must ask what the object of *proclaiming* it could possibly be. Discipleship of *Jesus Christ* means following him into the world, farther and farther, deeper and

---

17. Lewis Mudge observes that the challenge presented by popular film and other media includes the knowledge, much of it false, that is communicated concerning the Christian faith as such: "The community of faith may well discover that its own members gain more knowledge of their religious heritage from films, popular novels, and the evening news than they do from the religious community's own teaching" (*The Sense of a People* [Philadelphia: Trinity Press International, 1992], 71).

deeper into the heart of its darkness. A discipleship that functions to shield human beings from the reality of their human condition, that makes it possible for them to live on some plane of "tranquil self-righteousness" (Ellul) *above* the pain of history, that cushions every "shock of non-being" (Tillich) and enables people to maintain a splendid equilibrium in the face of all events: such is not discipleship of the crucified one. It may be Stoic, or peace-of-mind religion, but it has nothing to do with the one whose entry into creaturehood entailed *kenosis* (self-emptying) and "obedience unto death" (Phil. 2:8). To repeat: the object of the divine Spirit, biblically understood, is not to get us out of the world but to get us into it. This is the logic of the incarnation and the cross.

It is also the *conditio sine qua non* of the Christian mission. And that statement is to be understood both as one of *foundational* theology and as one of *practical* or *strategic* theology.

Let us consider first the character of this claim as one belonging to theological foundations. It is not merely a matter of strategy when we affirm that concrete participation in the life of the world is the condition without which mission is impossible; the affirmation belongs to the most basic assumptions of the tradition. To put the matter as directly as possible, we must say that the Christian mission *is* to "go into the world"—not (as has too often been understood on the basis of the Great Commission deftly extricated from its whole context) merely to "go into the world *proclaiming*," preaching, announcing, talking! It is to go *into the world*. If, indeed, as Matthew's version of the story insists, Jesus' final earthly command to his disciple community was to "go and make disciples of all nations," at the very least this must be understood as *Jesus'* command: that is, the command of one whose whole life, from Bethlehem to Calvary, was an unrelieved pilgrimage into this world—as Barth frequently phrased it, "the journey of the Son to a far country." This is not the command of a general who has surveyed the battlefield from some height and now commands his troops to rush in and claim victory! It is the command of one who has himself gone "all the way" into this world, as far as it is possible to go, identifying himself along the way with every sort of dilemma, every fond hope, every form of disappointment and failure. The Creed's declaration that "He descended into hell," baffling to modern ears, should be interpreted in that way: Jesus goes to the core of the human dilemma, beyond death itself to the "sting of death" (1 Cor. 15:55–56). He knows about this world from the inside. He understands humanity through and through—its expectancy, its ambition, its anxiety, its longing, its dissatisfactions, its foresakenness . . . "For we have not a high priest who is unable to sympathize with our weaknesses, but one who in every respect has been tempted as we are" (Heb. 4:15). Unless the Great Commission is heard by us as the conclusion of *such* a pilgrimage, it will be heard wrongly. It will be heard—it *has* been heard!—as a command to conquer, to "win the world for Christ," which, being translated, invariably means to gain power over others through persuasion, gentle or otherwise, and proselytization.

The precondition necessary to any form of word evangelization is identification with the *incarnate* Word. Verbal testimony to Christ that does not presuppose the process of becoming one with Jesus Christ in his "journey to the far country" is simply not to be trusted, no matter how clever or enthusiastic it may appear. If even a small percentage of the Christians who claim they are acting in obedience to the command to "Go and make disciples of all nations" were doing so out of a profound identification with the One who issued this command, both the church and the world would be different from what they are. As it is, many hear the Great Commission, and because it suits their temperament they go out to conquer; but few, I think, understand that such conquering is in reality a contradiction of the way of the one who issued this command. Only those whose discipleship is itself a matter of following Jesus Christ into the world are permitted, now and then, here and there, to "*make* disciples."

This, we repeat, is true at the level of Christian *basics*. It is not only a strategy for evangelical praxis. Its foundational truth has been obscured by the admixture of the Christian religion and the triumphal societies and kingdoms of the Western world. But today, as one of the fortunate dimensions of Christianity's release from its bondage to empire, this *foundational* truth becomes visible to Christians who seriously attempt authentic evangelization—evangelization that is *not* conquering; evangelization that is, in the best sense of the term, "saving." We must demonstrate "that witness (*marturia*) means not dominance and control but suffering."[18]

Such Christians recognize—often through painful trial and error—that *verbal* testimony to the Christ is in any case futile unless the lives of those who testify have in some real way established the conditions necessary to meaningful Christian *apologia*. Both negatively and positively, the struggles of the contemporary church have demonstrated the truth of this assertion. On the negative side, the hollowness and hypocrisy of so much *oral* enthusiasm for "Jesus" is embarrassingly exemplified by the scandals associated with many of those who have been most vociferous and ostentatious in their verbal testimony. No Christian should *gloat* over the exposure of televangelists, because none is without sin. But the lesson that all Christians and churches ought to take from these scandals is the obvious one that *affluent and self-indulgent lives* (not just sex!) invariably contradict any message recognizably related to Jesus Christ. The often crass and bizarre renditions of "the gospel" by ranting and media-conscious "evangelists" are patently incredible, not

---

18. Newbigin, "Can the West Be Converted?" 36.

only because of the absurd simplism they normally assume and evoke, but also and more conspicuously because they permit and foster such egomania, promotionalism, and opulence. The populace should not have *needed* these scandals to perceive the falseness of the message (and many people did not); but the scandals have made the obvious more obvious—inescapable, in fact, apart from deliberate and unrepentant blindness.[19]

But if the discrepancies between word and life on the part of some contemporary Christians demonstrate by negation the truth of the assertion that certain conditions of life must precede our verbal witness to the Christ, the same claim is more impressively exemplified, positively, by those contemporary Christians whose extraordinary participation in the life of the world has caused the world to be curious about their motivation. It is not, I think, a matter to be passed over lightly that the Christians of our epoch who have achieved the greatest credibility in the eyes of the world are not, in the first place, *speaking* Christians but *doing* Christians—persons whose faith has led them to involvement in life's darkest and most difficult situations. I do not want to oversimplify, and therefore I would remind the reader immediately, first, that speaking and doing are not to be taken as absolute distinctions but only as metaphors for two emphases that are distinguishable at least in theory; and, second, that the persons I have in mind are also, all of them, entirely capable of speech, and express themselves, in most cases, with great clarity and wisdom.

Invoking such names as Mother Teresa, Helder Camera, Jean Vanier, Martin Luther King Jr., Dorothy Day, Archbishop Romero, and others in the context of present discussion means recognizing the decisive correlation between participation in the life of the world and the establishment of the conditions necessary to authentic evangelization. For in every case it is precisely the depths of world involvement that causes others, who become conscious of these depths, to ask the question that is the only genuine *entrée* to evangelization: "Why?" *Why* did Archbishop Romero of El Salvador expose himself so openly to the powers he must have known could not stand for his type of honesty? *Why* did Martin Luther King Jr., despite his own obvious love of life, put himself into a position in which it was highly likely that he would lose his life? *Why* does Mother Teresa spend her life helping people who are of no account, according to worldy standards of worth—helping

---

19. It is interesting to note that the 1960 filming of Sinclair Lewis's *Elmer Gantry* was prefaced by a "Warning" to the effect that the producers were concerned that crass forms of evangelism were distorting the historic Christian faith. The warning also contained a clause advising parents that "sensitive children" not be exposed to the film. Thirty-five years later, few children would be shocked by a film with no explicit sex whatsoever; more to the point, however, it is highly unlikely that producers today would feel obliged to placate mainstream Christianity at the risk of offending the "evangelicals"!

them *to die*? What is the *reason* for this kind of behavior? Can it be explained on the basis of altruism or a reverse egoism or a bid for glory? No doubt some are satisfied with such answers; but, on the whole, the human psyche knows that such lives as these cannot be *sustained* by the desire for glory alone, granted it is probably always present to one degree or another. What, then, is the explanation?

This, I repeat, is the question—the world's question—without which Christian *answers* are on the whole superfluous. This is the world's *invitation* to the disciple community to "give a reason for the hope that is in it" (1 Peter 3:15).

It may be asked whether the disciple community must wait to be invited to do this; and I would like to answer, "In the West, with exceptions—yes!" I do not assume for a moment that this answer is pertinent to Christians in every time and place; I speak contextually. At least in the North American context to which I feel accountable,[20] however, Christians who are Christians intentionally and seriously must normally wait to be asked to "explain themselves." This invitation to "give a reason"—verbally to confess the faith—may be implicit or explicit; and it is probably never possible to know in advance the sincerity or depth of it. Few guidelines can be offered here, and more particularly because most of us have had so little experience of this "apologetic situation." We have inherited, and are ourselves the last remnants

---

20. No one can ever presume to encompass every actual or possible situation pertaining in a given context, and especially not one as large and increasingly diverse as that of the two northern nations of this continent. Contextuality in theology always drives to specificity, to particularity. A contextual theology inevitably moves toward *political* and *pastoral* theology, that is, toward praxis. Every generalization that must be undertaken in a work of this sort has to be adjusted to the specificity that prevails under the actual conditions of life. There are, however, as I have put it in the first volume (*Thinking the Faith,* chap. 1, 69ff.) *shared contexts.* Liberation theology is premised on the assumption that it is possible, despite variations, to articulate certain questions and certain answers in consequence of disciplined reflection on the character of the societies in which it has been developed; thus liberationists risk describing their context in terms of "oppression" and their gospel in terms of "liberation." It is certainly more difficult to derive a common language for North American theological analysis. There are specific and largely minority situations that cannot be greatly served by a theology that attempts to address the dominant middle classes of this continent. I have taken the risk, however, of assuming not only that such classes actually exist, and that they are still in some real sense "dominant" (historically and sociologically, if not always numerically), but also that it is possible to name the malaise ("sin," predicament, problematic) by which they are beset and, from the treasure-house of the tradition, to address it. I should not wish to claim for my analysis, either of "the question" or "the answer," that it is correct. It is the work, largely, of one mind, one life-experience, one attempt to "understand what is believed"; it is therefore limited, incomplete, no doubt in many places altogether inadequate, sometimes misleading, biased, and so on and on. My only *insistence* is that Christian theology is *obliged* to take such risks, and that our Christian North American caution and dependency has had the effect of limiting our theology either to academic pursuits or to minitheologies that revolve around this or that "timely" theme, issue, or group. It is precisely the *dominant* culture, and more especially as it is found in churches, that has suffered from this reductionism.

of, a situation in which Christians were expected to be fairly direct in their promotion of their belief system. The world, a "Christian" world (it was said), made a place for them, anticipated most of what they would claim and "stand for," and on the whole was never terribly surprised at their actual "witness." Christians in Christian lands, Christendom Christians, are entirely unused to being *invited* to address "the world."

And that is precisely why it is necessary for us now to wait for the invitation. The presumption and predictability accumulated over fifteen-odd centuries of Christian missions almost guarantees that uninvited testimony to Jesus Christ will fall on deaf ears. The realization of this new situation—which is in reality not terribly new, but which is made conspicuous today by the advance of secularity and religious and cultural pluralism—presents the churches with a whole new set of problems: How can we discern "invitations" to evangelism when they are issued? How can we respond to them without again becoming maudlin and predictable? How can we really enter into the *questions* that lie behind them, when we ourselves are shielded from so many of those questions by familiar and entrenched religious "answers"? And so on.

But while we must expose ourselves to such uncertainties concerning appropriate responses to the worldly "invitation to evangelism," it is by now *entirely clear* how we shall have to put ourselves into the way of becoming recipients of this invitation. There is in fact only one way, and it is to be profoundly and consistently enough involved in this world, and particularly at those places where it is most broken, to arouse the curiosity of at least a few of our contemporaries. If we love the world well enough and wisely enough, there will be among our contemporaries those who will ask (usually without actually *asking*!), "Why?" Then, and (with exceptions) only then, will it make sense to put into *words* the reason for our hope.[21]

---

21. In my three books on the theology of stewardship (*The Steward: A Biblical Symbol Come of Age*, rev. ed., 1990; *The Stewardship of Life in the Kingdom of Death*, 1985; and *Imaging God: Dominion as Stewardship*, 1986; all published by Wm. B. Eerdmans, Grand Rapids), I have attempted to expound in some detail the missiological thought developed here in a briefer and more theoretical manner. It is my conviction that stewardship, while not without its own problems, is nevertheless a timely and apologetically viable way in which contemporary Christians in our context may think of their mission and (to use the language of the above exposition) put themselves into the position where meaningful "invitations to evangelization" may be forthcoming.

The timeliness of the steward metaphor has little to do with the continued employment of that metaphor in ecclesiastical settings, which is almost wholly reductionist; it stems rather from the coinage the metaphor has acquired in our society, particularly (although by no means exclusively) on account of the environmental movement.

Biblically (as distinct from its ecclesiastical use and abuse), the idea of the human creature as a *stewardly* creature, both accountable to Another (God) and responsible for others (the cocreation), lends itself admirably to the quest for a new conception or "image" of the human by which sensitive persons throughout our society have been gripped. Over against the "owner-

11. The Mission as Message

11.1. "Be Prepared to Give a Reason. . . . " That the mission of the disciple community does have to do with "words," with reasons, with the conveyance of a "Christian *message*," has nowhere in the foregoing been denied. All that has been denied is that the words *are* the mission, and that they have priority. Words—preaching, teaching, writing—have always accompanied Christian mission and evangelism. The mission is inseparable from its articulation. Christians traditionally, like Jews and in the lineage of biblical Judaism, have high esteem for the word, spoken and written. Speech is perhaps the most sacred endowment of the human creature, according to the tradition of Jerusalem. The "speaking God" (*Deus loquens*) will have vis-à-vis Godself a "speaking creature" (*homo loquens*). And this gift of speech, far from elevating the human creature high above all other created beings, is precisely for the purpose of concretizing that creature's *solidarity* with all the others, for, in its speaking, it speaks *for* the others.

Not that the others actually *need* a spokesperson: their very being expresses their joy-in-being. But God, biblically understood, will have it so. God is a God whose very essence entails speech, whose communicative being (with-being) drives to incarnation of the Word. That this Creator fashions, makes covenant with, and beckons into the divine presence a representative *creature* who speaks is therefore not surprising. The anthropology follows from the Theology. And as for the rationale of the arrangement, it is as well perhaps to say only that God wills it for the sheer delight of the finely nuanced depth and beauty of life, to which only speech can do justice.

If we want to understand the biblical God, we must understand this divine penchant for and delight in speech. And we *can* understand it, at least partly,

---

ship" and mastery assumptions of secular modernity, the steward idea places humanity on the same level as all other creatures, for biblical stewards are simply servants among servants, and calls the human creature to account for its actions and attitudes in relation to all other creatures.

On the other hand, over against the contemporary tendency of affluent classes to abandon all responsibility for the earth and simply to enjoy, the steward concept demands that human beings actualize their potential for their peculiar type of creaturely care-taking—a potentiality that *includes* rationality and freedom as well as other "endowments" conventionally associated with the *imago Dei* concept, but not in such a way as to elevate the human above other creatures; rather, these gifts enable the human to become the responsible sort of creature-with-creatures whom God intends, reflecting God's own love and care for the world from a position *within* the creation itself.

My proposal, developed in different ways in the three books named earlier, is that stewardship, understood in this way as the kind of world commitment that Christian faith makes possible, can both *express* (for our context) the mission of the church and, when it is seriously undertaken, become the *occasion* for the more explicit sort of testimony that is conventionally associated with missiology and evangelism. (See in particular "Mission as a Function of Stewardship," in *The Steward: A Biblical Symbol Come of Age*, rev. ed., 245–58.)

because our own human experience reflects just this penchant and this delight. We know, if we reflect on it, how thoroughly our lives and our joie de vivre depend upon words. Thus children will ask for stories, the same stories, to be told again and again. And adults, even when they are themselves immediately involved in events and see, hear, smell, taste, and feel all that is accessible to the senses in these events, will insist upon *discussing* the events, endlessly turning them about in their minds and conversation, and finding ever new ways of "putting them [as we say, tellingly] into words."

It would be strange indeed, given this biblical concentration upon the word, if the mission to which the disciple community is called did not also have something to do with speech—with verbal and written testimony. To be sure, the Bible dismisses nothing more consistently than it does *mere* words: the easy words of false prophets who are always talking about "peace"; the flattering words of those whose object is to deceive or seduce (The Book of Proverbs abounds in instances of such); the falsely pious words of those who pray loudly so that others may hear them; the words of those who promise obedience and forget their promises almost immediately; the right and proper and "orthodox" words of the religious ones ("Lord, Lord"!) who do not recognize their Lord in the faces of the poor and needy; and on and on. The Bible is not naive about the human use of speech—its vital role in hypocrisy, the fickleness of tongue, that "little member [which] boasts of great things" (James 3:5f.). Those who set themselves to consider the subject of Christian missions should by no means neglect this side of the matter. The history of Christianity in the world is a *wordy* history, and this biblical wisdom concerning and critique of speech has informed far too little of it! If today Christian words are mistrusted or go unheard, this may be a judgment upon cheap speech—upon "evangelism" that does not issue out of participation in the suffering of the Christ and the groaning of the creation.

That having been said, however, we confront at once the opposite danger: the neglect of speech, the despising of words, the flight into feeling or act or experience—danger by no means hypothetical in contemporary North American Christianity. If on the one hand some (as we have seen) reduce the mission to "mere words," others in our midst reduce it to feelings, acts, and experiences without words—or without believing in the significance of words. No doubt the two forms of reductionism condition and beget each other: the tawdry, cliché-ridden, verbal testimonies of "evangelism" evoke in critical souls a kind of refusal of the word; and the activism or pietism of the latter drive the former to greater reliance on their sloganized and vapid precepts. What calls itself "conservative" Christianity in our context manifests a strong reliance upon words; what calls itself "liberal" an equally strong reliance upon deeds and experiences. Both emphases must be criticized by a theology that pays attention to the Bible and the best traditions of Christian thought. Each may represent a necessary corrective in relation to the other, but neither emphasis is acceptable and both distort the nature of the mission.

Enough has already been said in response to the identification of the mission with words. It is perhaps the greater task of a theology that consciously addresses itself to the more liberal (and especially liberal Protestant) churches of this continent to counter the tendency of these denominations, or of their "cutting edges," to despair of words and to reduce the mission of the church to deed. Many have remarked upon the "rampant anti-intellectualism" that stalks liberal Protestant Christianity today. This is perhaps an unfair accusation, for it by no means goes unchallenged in these same denominations, and in some respects it represents what may be a necessary stage in the transition from imperial to diaspora Christianity. Christian reliance upon "pronouncement" and the peculiarly Protestant temptation to think that the gospel ought simply to be "proclaimed" are certainly in part consequences of a Christian monopoly situation that no longer pertains; and those who achieve a heightened awareness of the changed situation are frequently led to distrust most of the verbal baggage that accompanied Constantinian religion. They—or some of them—rightly divine that our credibility as Christians now depends upon who we *are* and what we *do* more than it does upon what we say and write.

While this may represent a necessary transitional stage on the way to another, partly older and partly newer form of the Christian movement, however, it also contains the danger of missiological reductionism. Despite the North American predilection for pragmatism, deeds, including sacrificial deeds born of selfless love, do not usually "speak for themselves." The same act, externally viewed, may arise from many differnt types of motivation, some of them incompatible, and may communicate many different kinds of messages. A man who gives away his fortune to the poor may be acting out of Buddhist, Marxist, secular humanist, Christian, or many other forms of commitment; or he may be seeking notoriety, or exercising spite against his relatives; he may even be mad. The deed in itself, regardless of its rationale, is undoubtedly commendable also from a Christian point of view; but until it is explained, one does not know what its perpetrator intends it to communicate, if anything. Again, the same deed, uninterpreted by the doer, may "say" to one person that human beings are after all essentially generous, to another that egotism and the quest for publicity is terribly subtle, to another that riches are always tainted, to another that a radical, Scrooge-like conversion must have taken place, and so forth.

Similarly, as we know from the works of the second-century Christian apologists, certain practices of the early Christians persuaded some non-

Christians that these people were engaging in strange, elicit sexual orgies and other heinous rites, others that they were dangerous enemies of the state, still others that they were atheists, and a few that they must have been altered by some miraculous change of heart ("See how these Christians love one another!"). Today, Christians who identify themselves with (for example) victims of AIDS may elicit admiration from some, who are impressed by their courage; scorn from others, who may be of the opinion that this disease is in any case richly deserved; and from still others suspicion: perhaps those helpful souls are themselves morally questionable.

In short, the missionary deed, which is both ontologically and strategically prior, evokes and requires for its fullness the evangelical "word." It may not be either necessary or possible for the word to follow upon the deed with any great regularity. Sometimes the "invitation" to speech is not extended, or is long in coming. Sometimes those engaged in the deed are too thoroughly occupied with what they are doing to explain it to anyone. Sometimes others must explain it; sometimes it goes unexplained for years, decades, even centuries. Only now, with the most recent investigations into government and military affairs in Central America, can anyone say with authority what was involved in the deaths of the four American nuns and the Jesuit priests in El Salvador. Many of us are still trying to understand Dietrich Bonhoeffer. The life-testimonies of Paul Schneider, the Geschwister Scholl, Kurt Gerstein, and many others in the German resistence of the 1930s and 1940s are still shrouded in mystery. This illustrates how what we are calling here "the deed" (which is usually more than a single act) invariably transcends all explanation and renders verbal testimony forever inadequate. Yet on the other hand without any verbal testimony mystery is reduced to incomprehensibility and courts the sorry prospect that every manner of "message" will be imposed upon it.

The paradigm for this understanding of the relation between mission as participation (deed) and as proclamation (*kerygma*) or "message" (word) is, of course, the Christ-event itself. Unquestionably, what is prior in this event is Jesus' own life, death, and resurrection. Apart from this participatory, incarnational life-deed, the words about it would be empty and merely speculative. God's own mission, in Jesus, is Jesus himself: one "anointed" to enter into the world's darkness, to accept identity with suffering creatures, to go all the way into the terra incognita that we call "world," including the experience of death. As it happened, according to the newer Testament's own witness, there *were* words about precisely this divine intention beforehand—prophetic words, the words of the historians and law-givers of Israel. But even these words would be inadequate without the deed to which they point. The deed—the *incarnation* of the Word—is the presupposition also of *these* words.

Moreover, the deed—that is, Jesus' actual life, death, and resurrection—can never be summarized adequately, let alone definitively, in *any* words. His enactment of the divine mission, the ontological presupposition of *our* mission, cannot and must not be reduced to words—to "Christology" and "soteriology." The verbal aspect of the mission ("Go and tell . . . ") is not only wholly dependent upon the act ("Go and be!") but it is forever unable to interpret the act fully. The telling perennially falls short of the being.

And yet, the same Scriptures that teach us to recognize this transcendent mystery of the Christ's *life*-deed, command us to bear witness to it, and themselves are nothing more nor less than the first evangelical attempts to do precisely that. Moreover, this interpretational, explanatory, and in that sense evangelical work already commences with the Doer of the deed himself, according to this scriptural testimony, and not as a merely incidental aspect of his "doing" but as a necessary dimension of it. Jesus not only foretells what is to happen to him, but he explains to his disciples why it "must" happen and what its happening means.

This close correlation of deed and word, participation and interpretation, as it relates to the mission of God in the Christ-event is, then, the paradigm upon which all genuine Christian missiology depends. Where there is no prior participatory dimension, the interpretational or "evangelical" dimension begs the question of its ground and reality, and where there is no verbal dimension the participatory dimension, which may be commendable in itself, fails as communication. The two dimensions are distinguishable from one another, both in theory and (at least to some extent) in practice; but they nevertheless belong together and are incomplete in isolation one from the other.

For present-day liberal Christians who have learned the right lesson concerning the participatory dimension, it is necessary to accentuate the necessity of articulation. Liberal and moderate Protestants have allowed the evangelical dimension of the mission to atrophy. By default if not intentionally, they have turned the whole idea of evangelism over to the self-declared "evangelicals," as if it no longer applied to *all* Christian mission. In some cases they have substituted the language of the social sciences for that of the Bible and theology, or allowed political and other ideologies to become the interpreters of their "solidarity" with the world. This must be seen as a loss, because, while many human disciplines and viewpoints may and must be employed in the service of the Christian mission, there is a profound tradition of wisdom in Scripture and theology that should not (and finally cannot) be contained in the successive enthusiasms of human cultures. Unless Protestant liberalism is able to recover the genuine sources of its own evolution and develop an evangelical verbal testimony to accompany and interpret its right participation in the life of the world, it will continue to be driven by every wind that blows and end in a superficial humanism that, for all its "involvement," says everything in general and nothing in particular.

11.2. The Quest for "Gospel."   The Christian mission calls for words, but words, if they are "true," never come easily. Part of what is so distasteful about most of what boldly announces itself as evangelism in our context is the sheer glibness of its representatives. They speak effortlessly about God, Jesus, the cross, the resurrection, the divine Spirit, as if it were all second nature. Between their slickness and that of the hucksters of commercial products no appreciable distinction can be drawn. They even convey the impression that the Bible itself announces the things of God in a free and easy way, and that not to do so is a sign of doubt. But serious students of the Scriptures know that the words of the prophets were not dashed off in a morning. The Psalms, Job, and Paul's letter to the Romans give evidence of life long struggles with language. Luther worked for a quarter of a century perfecting his German rendition of the newer Testament—which for him meant getting it into words that stableboys and housemaids could understand. Calvin spent as much time reworking his famous *Institutes.*

Words that attempt to do justice to the Word have to be hunted down as if they were precious gems, hidden or lost in heaps of debris. Finding "the right words" is never an easy task for *any* human being who understands at some depth the inadequacy of all words to express truth, *any* truth; and the truth to which *Christians* are obliged and privileged to point—living Truth— defies every effort to articulate it with anything like adequacy. It *must* be articulated; that is its inherent demand upon us; but it cannot be articulated adequately. Above all, it cannot be articulated *permanently*—in words and thoughts that never change.[22] For this truth lives, moves, responds; this Word is incarnate. God allows us to speak of God; God permits Theology. But as soon as we think our God-talk is *itself* true, we have entered a state of delusion and, it is to be hoped, will find ourselves judged for our blasphemy, and repent of it.

This is why a certain caution has to be entered concerning the familiar use of the term "gospel" in Christian circles. Almost invariably, we preface this term with the definite article: *the* gospel. This perpetuates the impression that there is a never-changing entity, presumably in verbal form, to which credence must be given. It implies that what Christians are called to do as evangelists and missioners is to repeat, in some recognizable version, a definitive set of "truths," ideas, concepts, or dogmas that have been handed down from the past and must now be passed on intact to the future generations of Chris-

---

22. See the critique of *theologia eterna* in *Thinking the Faith,* chap. 1, §1, 69ff.

tians. Such a preunderstanding of *euangellion* (gospel; good news) flies in the face of the *livingness* of Christian truth, that is, of the one who said "I *am* the truth" (John 14:6). It also reduces the verbal testimony of the evangelist to formulae, doctrines, precepts, theories, and the like, which he or she may be thought to possess. If therefore the "seasoned evangelist" or the "professional theologian" seems to have achieved a high degree of articulateness about "the gospel," it is hardly surprising. Anyone who lives and works with any conceivable set of ideas long enough will be able to regurgitate the leading thoughts of that theory without hesitation. It is not difficult, after some years of practice, to detect the recurrence of certain questions, concerns, or biases in the discourse of others, and, in response to them, to draw forth from one's great storehouse of oft-repeated theories the appropriate rejoinders—and even to do so in what may seem a nuanced and clever manner.

But "gospel" is not possessible, is never mine or ours. It has to be heard, experienced, discovered—always newly. And it will only be discovered by those who are ready, daily, to listen. To listen truly is to pray (the reverse is also true), and to pray is to empty ourselves of whatever we think we possess and to become consciously, once more, the beggars before God that we really are. The genuine evangelist does not show up in the presence of God and "the neighbor" full of ready-made summaries of "the gospel"; the evangelist appears, rather, as one whose accumulated knowledge, however impressive it may be in some worldly settings, seems to him- or herself paltry and unsufficing to the living even of that one day.

This is said not in a merely pious or homiletical way, but as a statement of bald theological fact and the necessary correlate of everything else that has been said in these volumes. It is *of the essence* of a contextually understood faith in Jesus as the Christ. Without comprehending this, there will be no comprehension either of what is meant here by faith's *confession*. For the confession of faith, if it is real confession and not only a rote recitation of dogmas and well-worn notions, always entails forfeiture (*kenosis*, or self-emptying) and recovery; and this is no automatic process. Nothing *guarantees* that through the forfeiture of all of our practiced answers to life's conundrums we are going to be filled again with new and better answers. It is purely a matter of grace and of trust.

The theo-logic of this ongoing process of emptying and being filled, dispossession and rediscovery, deconstruction and reconstruction is impeccable, and can be stated in the following way: Every true articulation of gospel necessarily contains historical, sociological, linguistic, and other specific factors that, precisely *because* they make it "good news" for that particular time and place, render it inadequate for other times and places.

> It is hard for any church to separate the Christian message from the particular culture within which it is pronounced. In a sense it is impossible, because *there is no abstract Christian message.* It is always embodied in a particular culture.[23]

Time does not stand still, and history, despite certain recognizable patterns, does not repeat itself. God is the Creator and Sovereign of time, it is true, and may therefore be said to be above it, "eternal"; but God loves creatures who are *not* above it, and therefore there can be no "glad tidings" for such creatures that do not pass through the sieve of time and place—of context. The disciple community, as the ambassadorial representative of the love that God intends for such creatures, must therefore resist its own recurring temptation to rest in yesterday's confession of the faith. Insofar as it is really committed to its mission as hearer of and witness to truth, it must seek to withstand the powerful inner urge of all human insecurity to *have* truth as a permanent possession in relation to which it may achieve great familiarity and expertise. The seeming possessor of truth may indeed, on occasion, appear impressive, confident, helpful, articulate; and the one who waits for truth that cannot be possessed may, on the contrary, appear hesitant, tentative, "unprofessional." The strong-willed, true-believing Christian missionaries and evangelists who go out into the world with nary a doubt and are armed with persuasive arguments for every occasion will always impress many; and in contrast the Christians who are forever searching for understanding and for words will appear to many feeble or failed representatives of their faith. But, in the end, these last may well be first.

They *will be* first where truth really matters! Intuitively and occasionally, if not through repeated experience, every one of us knows the difference between personal encounters in which we have been heard, with all the joy or anguish of the moment, and those in which our presence was little more than an occasion for the expression of well-rehearsed phrases and constructs. The man who seeks out his pastor for counselling on some critical issue in his private life may find himself the recipient of an hour-long harangue on the perils of extramarital relations, or absentee fatherhood, or parental permissiveness, all of it delivered with great authority and skill, none of it vitally related to his actual situation. The truth of his life has not been taken seriously. In another pastor's study, the man may find himself doing most of the talking; and the pastor, when she speaks, may do so uncertainly, even apologetically, as though she were working through these kinds of human problems for the first time. The man may leave this encounter still doubtful about his future course, but knowing that the truth of his life has been shared with another.

---

23. Tillich, *Systematic Theology,* vol. 3 (Chicago: University of Chicago Press, 1963), 193.

Again, to illustrate the point: A professor of theology required to give a lecture on "the problem of evil" may without much travail of soul compose a splendid piece in which all the conventional aspects of the problem receive a fair hearing; and his audience, listening to him, will know that they are in the presence of a professional. Another professor of theology under the same obligation, although he too has been over and over these constellations of questions for years, finds that he must once again fight his way through all the knots and tangles of the ancient problem. He presents the final product with some visible sense of spiritual struggle upon him still. Some of his audience will be disappointed—they had hoped to hear an expert! But some will know that their own life-struggle with "the problem of evil" has been shared, and that they are not alone.

Or again: A Christian congregation under obligation (the obligation of discipleship!) to bear witness to Jesus Christ may be able to transmit the great truths of the Christian faith with a remarkable degree of knowledge and verve. Its leaders and people have been diligent in their study of the Scriptures and traditions of the ages. The congregation, modern skepticism notwithstanding, has achieved a rather favorable reputation for knowing where it stands and being able to communicate its belief persuasively. Its articulate preacher can be counted on to deliver interesting, inspiring, and informative sermons. Another congregation in the same community, whose leadership is equally capable and whose people are just as much aware of what Christians profess as are those of the first congregation, seems incapable of inspiring the same public confidence in itself. People of the community do not recommend it to one another. They are vaguely disturbed because the ethos of that congregation seems more one of asking than of answering. The sermons and discussion groups deal too often with "politics" and with disturbing contemporary issues whose solutions they rarely propose with alacrity. Citizens whose lives are relatively manageable feel they do not need that kind of "religion." Why should they distress themselves? But some, who *are* distressed, whether for themselves or for their world, will be found in that congregation and not the other.

What all three scenarios illustrate is the *quest* for gospel and the way in which faith's *confession* is bound up with that quest. It should not be assumed, of course, that the continued search for understanding and speech always and regularly leads to genuine confession of the faith: the pastor in the first illustration may just be inarticulate; the professor may really lack professional skill; the congregation may be too ingrown, too much swayed by this or that faction, and so on. These are not "case studies"; they are intended only to illustrate one point, namely, that if faith is really to be confessed and not only professed it entails an ongoing struggle and search for *euangellion*. They also illustrate, *about* this search, what was said earlier concerning the dimension of participation: in each instance, there is on the part of the faith-ful an entry—in some degree painful—into the unknown. Only to the extent that this unknown is entered, only to the extent that the reality of life is shared with those who experience its questions and contradictions in their always-specific forms, will there be something like a discovery of "gospel." And this will, I think, invariably mean a *shared* discovery.

In other words, confession of the faith occurs, or may occur, where the disciple community allows itself to become sufficiently involved in the life of "the world" to discover in and with its world (or some of its inhabitants) the good news that is intended for it. And it is not incidental that this good news *is,* in part, the fellowship that is the result of the shared experience of forfei-ture and recovery. The Christian mission is therefore not a one-way affair: Christians bringing something to others. It is a meeting in which the One whose mission precedes ours brings together for reconciliation and commu-nion those who are alientated one from another.[24]

Words belong to this meeting, because human beings are speaking ani-mals. They meet one another, it is true, through media other than the word, but only the word can do justice to both the alienation and the reconciliation that belong to their meeting. Where truth is at the heart of the encounter, the words, even though they may well be old, familiar ones, will seem fresh and full of significance—like the words "I love you" when they are spoken by those who have newly discovered their love for each other.

11.3. Wording "Gospel."   One of the recurring themes of Christian theologi-cal work during the past several decades has been the necessity of discovering new language for the communication of the Christian message. Characteristi-cally, this has entailed dissatisfaction with conventional terms of faith and theology. It was even suggested by some during the "death-of-God" epoch that a moratorium ought to be called on the use of the term "God." The search for novelty in theology, as in the arts, has its own allurements.

But linguistic alterations can be deceptive. "New" metaphors and analo-gies are not necessarily either authentic or effective as tools of communica-tion, nor are the old words necessarily outmoded. The entire second volume of this trilogy was devoted to the importance of what has been handed over (*tradere*). *None* of the "great words" of the faith should be discarded; *all* must be taken with the greatest seriousness, pondered, meditated upon, entered into both intellectually and spiritually. To lose touch with a concept such as that of sin, as, for instance, late nineteenth-century modernists did, is to lose touch with a key to life itself, not only to the Christian tradition. Its absence from the human vocabulary will require someone later on, if not one of the

---

24. See Mudge, *The Sense of a People,* 209–10.

faithful then one of "the stones" (Luke 3:8), to reintroduce it—as Karl Menninger did with his timely book, *Whatever Became of Sin?*[25] Something similar could be said for all the other words, some of which are more and some less essential.

It would be a misreading of the previous subsection, therefore, if the idea of "forfeiture" was interpreted to mean the intentional neglect of well-established concepts and terms of the tradition. What has to be forfeited is not the *memory* of the tradition, with its "great words," its doctrines and dogmas, its systems of thought, its stories and litanies, hymns and collects; rather, what has to be given up is our *reliance* upon all that. What must be lost, and not once but again and again, is our habit of offering "all that" as if it were gospel. In other words, we are required to stop using faith's *profession* as if it were the *confession* of the faith.

The Christian mission, as to its verbal dimension, entails a transition from the professional to the confessional mode. And while this way of expressing the matter makes it seem little more than a changed manner of address (say, from the dispassionate descriptive to the engaged exhortative), the truth is that, where it is genuine, the change is a profound, existential one, in which something like crucifixion and resurrection are undergone.

For what the contemporary missiological situation means for faith is that reliance on what is *professed*—on *what* is professed!—must be exchanged for a newly realized, naked reliance on the One *whom* faith professes. The substance of what is professed—what we called in the second volume the "meditative core" of belief[26]—is certainly preparatory to this moment of transition; in fact, it is requisite to it. But until our reliance upon that meditative core has been sacrificed to a renewed reliance upon the Presence to whom our professional meditation is seeking to point, faith's *profession* will never give way to its *confession*.

The character of the transition must also be considered from the perspective of those for and to whom the confession is intended. The evangelical mission contains an immense barrier and is self-defeating when it remains at the professional level of communication. For all it can then convey, even when it is undertaken with great skill and sensitivity, is that Christians enter the presence of others in the manner of those who "have" approaching those who do not "have."

Let me illustrate this experientially. As a theologian, with a relatively expert professional knowledge of Christian doctrine, I find myself in the com-

---

25. Karl Menninger, *Whatever Became of Sin?* (New York: Hawthorn Books, 1973). An excellent illustration of my point concerning the continuing importance of traditional Christian categories is Ted Peters' recent study *Sin: Radical Evil in Soul and Society* (Grand Rapids: Wm. B. Eerdmans, 1994).

26. *Professing the Faith*, 1.

pany of non-Christians—let us say, of people in a sickroom, in which a young acquaintance is dying of cancer. There is, in that context, an implicit "invitation to evangelism." I am not invited outright to "answer" the situation, as a Christian; but in view of my identity as a religious person, I am conscious of the fact that everyone present is looking to me for something—an explanation? Comfort? Or perhaps only a convenient scapegoat for understandable outrage? What shall I do?—say?

Some Christians would not hesitate to tell me what to do; they would do it themselves, under the circumstances. They would have me pluck up my courage and tell everyone present the whole story, or as much of it as time and decency permitted: sin, forgiveness, atonement, salvation, the cross, resurrection, life beyond the grave, and so on. If I were able to do this well, it might even seem to "work." Perhaps there would be a sufficient memory of some of the words I used, in some of the persons present, that certain meaningful associations could be drawn and some comfort given. Perhaps I would leave the hospital room feeling that I had done something rather worthy: people had been helped, and the call to discipleship had been heeded. I do not deny such a possibility. Who could do so?

Yet it would remain true, all the same, that the whole encounter had occurred at the level of faith's profession—namely, *I* had professed *my* belief. *I* had given something to *them*. It had cost me very little, besides the initial embarrassment, and even that could disappear, with practice.

What would be required to turn this moment to one of *confession*?—to accept the invitation to genuine *evangelism*? This: It would be required of me that I die a little. I would have to share the dying that was in progress in that room. I would be asked (by God!) to experience, according to my own particularities, something comparable to the ending that was being entered into there—by the dying one, and by his friends and relatives. I would have to feel deprivation and loss. Otherwise there could be no real communication—no communion—with those others. We would remain entirely apart: I living and full of answers, they dying or facing death and full of questions. Somehow, their situation would have to become mine too.

How? I could not, except superficially, put myself directly into their shoes—certainly not into the shoes of the dying one; but not into those of his friends and family, either, for their sorrow stems from years of friendship and close communion with him. But in the situation I come to know how I shall have to come to share their . . . context: I shall have to lose my ready-made answers. I shall have to forfeit my expertise. I shall have to become, with them, another human being waiting to be comforted, waiting for God, waiting for words (Simone Weil). Perhaps if I am allowed in this way to participate in their state of waiting I, too, shall be met again by love and the peace that passes understanding. Perhaps if I am made to ask once more, out of the particularities that belong to my own life, the human *question,* I shall be able to hear once more the divine *answer*—rather, the divine Answerer; the One who, in raising questions, *is* the Answer. Perhaps if I am once more reduced to silence, my easy speech and prepared responses rendered sorely inadequate, I shall learn the words that must be said *here and now.* Perhaps! It is not a foregone conclusion.

But it is a promise.

If it occurs; if I am given words to speak, they may well be . . . the old words. Some of them will be, in all likelihood. Or if the words are not old, familiar words (sin, grace, forgiveness, the cross, "nothing can separate us from the love . . . ," and so on,), what lies behind them will be the old, old story. Reflecting on the encounter afterward, I shall be able to say that what I had spent years learning to *profess* was absolutely necessary to what, in that moment, I was enabled by grace to *confess.*

All the same, the old will have become new—and not only for "them," the others; for me, too. Together, we shall have been ministered to by the One whose mission precedes ours.

A dramatic and sensitive exemplification of the "process" of forfeiture and recovery that I have sought to describe here is presented in the recent film *Dead Man Walking.* In contrast to the practiced professionalism of official religion, represented here by the prison chaplain, Sister Helen Prejean finds herself drawn into the whole complex admixture of good and evil that has brought about the condemnation of the prisoner she is counseling. This is the "loss" that she must experience in order to be able, finally, to walk with the "dead man walking." But this loss is also paradoxically a gain; for in identifying with the humanity of the condemned man she herself recovers an awareness of the reality and sufficiency of grace.

11.4. Mission and the Context. Let us attempt to apply these reflections on mission drawn from pastoral experience to the larger question of the church's mission in our contemporary context. It is not difficult to identify the two leading principles entailed in the pastoral illustration; they are *identification* (participation, solidarity) and *concretization* (particularization, specification). And their relation can be stated in this way: *the concretization of "gospel" presupposes identification with those for whom it is intended.* The possibility of *wording* the Christian "evangel" may be given the disciple community only as it undergoes existential identification with its worldly context. The transition from profession to confession of the faith is effected by the divine Spirit as the church is led out of its ideational sanctuary into the secular wilderness, the marketplace, the spiritual "open spaces" of its worldly environs, and learns from that vantage point of unguarded participation in its world the character of the human predicament that must be addressed. Faith cannot presume that its participation in the human question will issue in a renewed capacity to bear witness to the divine response. It can, however, *trust* that it will be given, in the moment of its need for them, "the right words" (Mark 13:11). One thing it can know with certainty: that unless it risks exposure to the question, the words it offers as "answer" will miss the mark.

We are again at the heart of Christian theological contextuality. Every theology of our time that has gained insight into the mission of the church in the contemporary world has done so through undergoing, in some observable manner, the process about which we are thinking: participation and concretization. The so-called "theology of crisis" or "dialectical theology" that challenged theological liberalism and the optimism of secular modernity in the early decades of this century did so because its leading thinkers (Barth, the Niebuhrs, Tillich, Bonhoeffer, and others) found themselves participants in a world very different from the one that their liberal progenitors described and assumed. Contrary to common interpretations of the whole movement, it was not a simple *reaction* against liberalism, it was the quest for "gospel" on the part of Christians who knew they were no longer part of the world to whose perceived conditions their liberal teachers had responded. That is why it is misleading to name this movement "neo-orthodoxy"—a term that suggests reaction and romantic reversion to an earlier point of view (Protestant Orthodoxy). If earlier expressions of the Christian faith were appealed to by Reinhold Niebuhr and the others, it was only after they had experienced both the failure of liberalism *and* the specifics of the new era they had entered (for example, Henry Ford's Detroit).[27] With the questions they derived from their participation in that new and different worldly context, they found they had to go to Christian sources "back behind" liberalism to find guidance in the process of confessing their faith.

Although movements that have followed in the *second* half of the twentieth century have often produced emphases very different from the theological reformulations of the first half of the century, they have usually manifested the same process of identification and concretization. Thus, liberationists in Latin and Central America and elsewhere have been persons who found themselves in a world quite foreign to the one assumed by the Catholic or Protestant doctrinal-moral conventions of their immediate background. As these thinkers entered more and more deeply into the condition of the poor, that is, the *majority* of human beings in their situations, they had to discard even the questions attributed by church convention to the human condition,

---

27. See in this connection Gary A. Gaudin and Douglas John Hall, eds., *Reinhold Niebuhr (1892–1971): A Centenary Appraisal* (Atlanta: Scholars Press, 1994), in particular the essay "The Thought of Reinhold Niebuhr and the Twilight of Liberal Modernity in Canada," by Terence R. Anderson.

to say nothing of the familiar ecclesiastical answers. The questions they discovered to be existential ones among the people with whom they now began to find solidarity were not questions about guilt and longing for immortality but about oppression by economic and political forces and longing for the freedom to live in a decent, human way. With these "new" questions, the Christian thinkers who became liberationists had to search the Scriptures and traditions of the faith for "answers" that were not to be found in the regnant conventions of theology, liturgy, and the religious life. Like the "theologians of crisis," who were in many cases helped by existentialist analyses, the liberationists were aided in their search for "words" by Marxist social analysis.[28]

Similarly, black theologians in North America, confronted by the growing refusal of African Americans to have not only their lives but also their faith determined by the dominant, white society, through a more "conscientized" participation in the actual life and struggle of their own people, found it necessary to discard much that had been presented to them as "*the* gospel." Only by rejecting (forfeiting) ready-made professions of faith could they learn how to confess their faith in authentic ways.[29]

Perhaps the most far-reaching of all these movements, Christian feminism has challenged the whole "reading" of the human condition in the predominant traditions of the faith on account of the androcentric bias evident in these. As Christian women have found themselves consciously reflecting upon the experience of women, including their own experiences, they have discovered different questions and were thus driven to search for different answers.[30]

The process that is at work in these theological movements and in many more theological and paratheological trends that could be instanced is vital for all genuine Christian confession. For without participation and concretization, entailing forfeiture and rediscovery, there can be no act of faith's confession. The process is not always as dramatic or conspicuous as it is in the examples I have cited here, but it is always present wherever there is a significant confession of the faith. It has been there in the great transitions of the Christian past—conspicuously so in the Reformation period—as it is in our own period. In the pages that follow, we will need to become increasingly

---

28. See Robert McAfee Brown, *Theology in a New Key* (Philadelphia: Westminster Press, 1978).

29. See Gayraud S. Wilmore, *Black Religion and Black Radicalism: An Interpretation of the Religious History of Afro-American People* (Garden City, N.Y.: Doubleday, 1972); James H. Cone, *For My People: Black Theology and the Black Church* (Maryknoll, N.Y.: Orbis, 1984).

30. The prologue and opening chapter of Isabel Carter Heyward's *The Redemption of God: A Theology of Mutual Relation* (Lanham, Md., New York, London: University Press of America, 1982), 1–23, constitutes a moving documentation of this search.

explicit about what this process involves for us in the context to which we are trying to speak—namely, a North American context, with special reference to the remnants of classical Protestantism in and around the formerly main-line churches of the two northern nations of this continent.

So as not to become lost in particulars, however, we should here try to provide some statement of general direction for Christian mission in the context in question. What would it mean for the disciple community working among dominant cultural groups traditionally served by the once-mainline churches of this continent to undergo the process of participation and concretization that we have been considering here? Presupposing the analyses already partially developed in the previous two volumes, we may respond to that question briefly in the following summary way.

Serious Christians in this context will have to begin by questioning the depth of our present *participation* in the culture with which our history has associated us. How well do we know even the classes (chiefly, the middle classes) from which our members are gathered and to which we still attempt to address ourselves? What is assumed by most of us in these churches to be participation in that "context" is perhaps more likely to be the retention of a cultural construct, a category called "middle class," which is nourished by the expressed needs of *some* within that class, and publicly rehearsed by the media. The middle classes today are in a state of transition and confusion, for they have been the creation of an ideology that is plainly under attack. The segments within this class that are clinging most tenaciously to the cultural-economic status that historical providence has assigned them are those most eager to have cultic ("religious") support in their struggle to survive. But it is likely that the *real* needs of these nonpoor/nonrich classes are quite different from the demands that are articulated by those elements within them that still look to religion for sustenance and legitimation.

Because the formerly mainline churches have been historically and culturally atuned to the expressed needs of these religiously oriented segments, they are often blind to the actual condition of the larger social classification. It has seemed to me, in fact, that the churches are for the most part engaging in a supply-and-demand religious enterprise, which positively necessitates falsification *both* of the social context *and* of the Christian message. Their (largely unconsidered) assumptions concerning the character and needs of the "constituency" they hope to address are for the most part based upon conceptions of the middle classes that are patently dated, and are kept alive by commercial and other influences that have vested interests in perpetuating them.

The ideational background of these preconceptions of the human situation is a worldview that many in our time have probed. I have attempted to understand it throughout most of my career as a theologian, and have written about it in every publication of mine since my earliest published essay, "The Theology of Hope in an Officially Optimistic Society."[31] This worldview first made its appearance in the Renaissance; it was honed into philosophic form by the Enlightenment; it was organized for mass production through the industrial revolution; and it entered its highest state of influence with the technologization of Western society in the twentieth century. In the latter stage, however, this conception of the human has also demonstrated the flaw that was in it from the beginning. For it was informed by the idea of human mastery, and that *imago hominis* (image of the human) cannot be indulged, finally, without delusion and without pathos—as Christians ought to have known all along! The consequence, which has been anticipated by the wise for a very long time but has only in these latter decades of the twentieth century become visible enough for less sensitive observers of the human condition to see, is that humanity *itself* has become victimized by its own implementation of its self-appointed vocation to rule. Starting out to master nature and eliminate chance (G. Grant), human beings have at last begun to realize that they would have to be mastered themselves, being part of the nature they hoped to subdue. "Man's mastery of nature turns out in the end to be nature's mastery of man. We have been conned by the oldest trick in the book. Marching triumphantly forward we failed to notice the jaws of the trap closing behind."[32]

The classes that were brought into being by this conception of the human have begun to realize the "trick" by which they have been "conned." It is, I think, not more than the beginning of self-knowledge, and it is so abhorrent to the average citizen of our two countries that few are willing or able to pursue the insight beyond its initial, shocking stage. People draw back from the full realization of what has happened because, of course, if entered into more reflectively it would spell the demise of their own way of being in the world. They therefore repress and suppress this knowledge as long as possible.

And unfortunately (with exceptions!) the *churches* in question are helping them to do so—unwittingly. That is what I mean by supply-and-demand religion. The very classes with which these established denominations are historically and sociologically bound up represent the people in our context who feel most keenly the effects of the changes through which we are passing, who have the most to lose, and who therefore cling most tenaciously to their preconceptions and "values." They *demand*—often quite literally—that the

---

31. *Religion in Life* 40, no. 3 (Autumn 1976).
32. Newbigin, "Can the West Be Converted?" 34.

churches confirm them in their accustomed lifestyle and help them to resist the dis-illusionment that is being visited upon them by economic recession, job losses, chronic unemployment or underemployment, and the general overtones of decline by which our society is now enthralled. They *demand* of their religious cultus, when everything around them seems to be failing them, that it should assure them, Sunday after Sunday, that all is well. They *demand* that "the gospel" must mean the legitimation of their whole undertaking, as if the gospel is to say to them, "The enterprise in which you are engaged—your work, your ambitions, your relationships—is the one that God approves. Do not be discouraged by critical voices and events and 'future shock.' God is with *you.*"

This "demand," of course, increases in proportion to the increase in the forces of radical change at work in our midst. Moreover, it is *exceptionally* hard for even conscientious clergy and church leaders in the North American situation to resist the demand for legitimating religion, because, with our particular financial arrangements (particularly clerical salaries), those who do not supply this demand but pursue the more painful path of truth can be summarily dealt with. Besides, Christianity in this context has been so thoroughly coopted by the "positive outlook" ("official optimism") that it would be difficult to pursue the kinds of questions this situation necessarily evokes in thinking people, even if churches arranged their finances differently. It is not accidental that the most "successful" congregations are those that can continue to provide persuasive combinations of Christian love-rhetoric and the American dream. The familiar language of mildly liberal pietism can still "work" where economic and other material-spiritual conditions have not become too threatening to be swept beneath the carpet.

All the same, the dis-illusionment of the classes under discussion continues apace; it is felt by more and more people; it can be avoided only through the expenditure of much emotional energy. Daily the public is reminded of the national debts of both the United States and Canada; daily we learn of the closures of large firms, with thousands rendered jobless; daily we confront the prospect of further cuts in government spending, social programs, the arts, pension funds, and more. By now, there is an entire category of human being called "permanently unemployable," and even skilled workers and persons in "middle management" can no longer assume job security. (Some analysts now claim that within two or three decades only 20% of the workforce will be needed to supply global demands.) We are told by experts in many disciplines (and most of us no longer need to be told!) that our children and grandchildren will not be allowed to enjoy the same standard of living that we have attained. And while these hard economic factors unfold, we are also conscious of the less tangible but perhaps more unsettling social and personal problems by which, in particular, these same expectant classes are most affected: marriage failure, violence against women and children, suicide, and so forth.[33]

All such experiences contribute to the state of insecurity increasingly felt by the very classes with which these "older" denominations have been associated; and, while many in these classes may indeed *want* the churches to continue to "stand for" all the allegedly positive things sought by the more affluent elements of the society, truly to *participate* in the condition of these classes today is precisely to resist such 'demands' and to enter more critically and truthfully into the actual experience of the people who constitutes these classes. Their anxiety is all the more dangerous to themselves and to society at large because, for the most part, they cannot express it or even admit to it. There is nothing more pathetic in the realm of human experience than despair that must be cloaked as "happiness" and well-being!

The question that cries out to be addressed in our churches, therefore, is whether we can let go of middle-class *religion* long enough to become real participants in the present-day plight of the middle classes. If we cannot, then any talk of Christian mission is premature and purely rhetorical. We shall continue to offer the Christian message as confirmation of the bourgeois quest for transcendence and "happiness," for the first requirement of missions will have been pushed aside.

Sadly, one fears that, apart from exceptional acts of courage and imagination, this requirement *will* be pushed aside as long as the churches in their present condition are economically viable; and—such is the vicious circle in which we find ourselves—they will be economically viable so long as the segments of society on which they depend need them to perform the services of legitimation and comfort to which we have referred.

---

33. Thirty years ago, in a response to Pierre Burton's news-making book, *The Comfortable Pew* (Toronto: McClelland and Stewart, and Philadelphia: J. B. Lippincott, 1965), Elizabeth Kilbourn, a writer, broadcaster, and art critic, and a member of the Anglican Church in Canada, wrote movingly of her awakening to the desolations of her world and her class: "I suddenly realized in anguish that though I possessed all that the world rightly calls good—husband, children, friends, comfort, even a newspaper column with my picture at the top—I was not one of the ninety-nine sheep safely in the fold. I was the hundreth sheep clinging to a cliff overhanging the abyss in the dark night, with nobody hearing my cries, or, if they did, powerless to help.

"And I was not alone. How many times in a darkened bar have I heard human beings confess that they can't feel love? Or that life is meaningless or flat or just plain hell. What about all the masks and defences and status symbols we parade around to hide from each other that paralyzing insecurity beneath? How does a church which claims that God is love say anything to a generation which not only cannot beleive in God, but is terrified of love as well?" (William Kilbourn, ed., *The Restless Church* [Toronto and Montreal: McClelland and Stewart, 1966], 4.)

Such "intimations of deprivation" (George P. Grant) are articulated only by a few, but they are felt by many; and in the thirty years since these words were written, the many have increased

That fear leads some of our contemporaries who long for Christian support for vital contemporary causes to despair of ever receiving it. In an insightful essay, "God and Country," Wendell Berry laments this seeming fact. As one deeply concerned for the fate of the natural environment within technological societies, Berry find himself hoping for Christian support:

> The subject of Christianity and ecology . . . is politically fascinating, to those of us who are devoted both to biblical tradition and the defense of the earth, because we are always hankering for the support of the churches, which seems to us to belong, properly and logically, to our cause.[34]

However, ecclesiastical support is seldom forthcoming. The churches "have shown little inclination to honor the earth or to protect it from those who would dishonor it." Why? asks Berry. Because, he answers,

> Organized Christianity seems, in general, to have made peace with "the economy" by divorcing itself from economic issues, and this, I think, has proved to be a disaster, both religious and economic. The reason for this, on the side of religion, is suggested by the adjective "organized." It is clearly possible that, in the condition of the world as the world now is, organization can force upon an institution a character that is alien or even antithetical to it. The *organized* church comes immediately under a compulsion to think of itself, and identify itself to the world, not as an institution synonymous with its truth and its membership, but as a hodgepodge of funds, properties, projects, and offices, all urgently requiring economic support. The organized church makes peace with a destructive economy and divorces itself from economic issues because it is economically compelled to do so. Like any other public institution so organized, the organized church is dependent on "the economy"; it cannot survive apart from those economic practices that its truth forbids and that its vocation is to correct. If it comes to a choice between the extermination of the fowls of the air and the lilies of the field and the extermination of a building fund, the organized church will elect . . . to save the building fund.[35]

Actually, the situation is even more desperate, I think, than Berry suggests in this statement. The churches' failure to take up "causes" that would seem, as does the environmental problem, to be implicit in their faith, is not owing only to their "necessary" endorsement of the capitalist economy; it is owing to their commitment to an "upbeat" message that leaves little room for issues

---

in number. What serious Christians must ask, however, is whether the churches have increased in their awareness of this despondency within the very classes they seek to serve.

34. *What Are People For?* (San Francisco: North Point Press, 1990), 95.
35. Ibid., 95–96.

that are as potentially *critical* as this one. So long as the churches serve that segment of middle-class America that is trying so desperately to hold on to "positive values" that it refuses negative thoughts, little by way of either truth or justice can be expected of them.

These words, however, are addressed to people in churches who have crossed the threshold of the realization that such a religion of comfort no longer comforts even the middle classes. There *are* such people in the churches, and it is my perception that their numbers are increasing. There also exists, therefore, a growing potentiality for informed participation in the actual condition of those to whom we are being sent.

This participation does not—should not—manifest itself straightaway in an "answering" faith-stance. For it to do so is to fall back into the repressive mold demanded by those who disdain critical reflection. The point is not to answer all the questions that abound in this age of rapid change, but to become the place where the questions can be asked, and the realities they probe confronted, as honestly as possible. The Christian faith, whose meditative core is the story of One who entered the heart of this world's darkness, does not provide answers; it points to an Answerer. And it does so by taking us, in the company of that One, farther into the questions to which any life that is really reflected upon inevitably leads us. A theology of glory wants to answer all questions, to silence doubt, to suppress anxiety. The theology of the cross opens itself to the questions that are simply *there* and cannot be magically dispelled. The gospel of the cross does not want to dispel them, but rather it invites us to enter more profoundly still the darkness that our questions conjure up. It does not provide the certitude that all our questions will be answered, but it provides the confidence we need in order to ask them openly and to wait for . . . the Answerer.

To positive religion, this may be thought a counsel of despair; but in fact it is the first necessary stage in the process of *concretizing* the Christian message, and particularly in a sociocultural context such as ours, in which what most oppresses the human spirit is its fearfulness of everything that negates or seems to negate. In such a context, nothing is more needful than the permission to consider and discuss openly and in the company of others the personal and social negations that modern expectations have conditioned all of us to repress. It is already a concretization of "gospel" when middle-class people, who have been trained from their youth up to maintain a "happy face," feel they are invited to share their anxieties openly with others in an atmosphere of acceptance and mutuality. In this way we see that the process we are calling here "participation and concretization" are not two separate steps but a single process. Because of the solidarity of Christians with those to whom they wish to bring the message of truth and hope, the first and most basic stage in the making concrete of the Christian message has been taken.[36]

From this position of mutuality, further concretization of the message will occur. It will above all be *concrete,* and therefore generalization is more difficult here. But if our earlier analysis of the human predicament as it is experienced in our context is true, concretization of the Christian message will usually have something to do with the discovery of human *meaning* beyond, and differentiated from, the meaning that has been bound up with the materialistic and acquisitive goals pursued by the dominant classes of our society. It will concern the recognition of our creaturehood, of its glad acceptance as the sphere of our appropriate glory, and of our consequent solidarity with and responsibility for all other creatures of God. It will be a matter of being set free from the distorted ("sinful") pursuits of human creatures who attempt to rise *above* their humanity (pride) *and* of those also who attempt to live *below* the responsibilities and possibilities of humanity (sloth, sensuality). "Gospel," whatever its particularized form, will therefore come to us— as always—as judgment and as renewal and life. We will not find our *status quo* legitimated by this message, but we will find our *life* legitimated.

12. Ministry: The Empowerment of Mission

12.1. The Ministry of the "Whole Church" in the World. The ordering of our thought in this chapter is deliberate and should not go unnoticed. The church's mission, which consists in the proclamation and enactment of a message ("gospel") in the world, is the presupposition and basis of the theology of ministry. In practical terms, this means that when we speak of ministry we are not speaking in the first place of the "order of ministry" *within* the church, but of the ministry of the whole church (*laos,* "laity") in the world. If this priority were maintained, the knotty historical and theological question of the nature of ordered ministry would prove less frustrating; for it would then be seen for what it is—a *secondary* consideration, whose determination follows from decisions that have already been taken concerning the ministry of the whole "people of God."

---

36. The conclusion of Elizabeth Kilbourn's statement (see n. 24 above) is appropriate here: "The Church I know is a small community of human beings who have caught the contagion of Christ's freedom and among whom I can be accepted for myself as I am: all of them ministers who, with their own wounds bound, are free to go out into society, sensitive to the cries of other humans in their multitudinous needs. I cannot forget that the first person who encountered Jesus risen was not Peter, the man of action, or John the intellectual, or James the organizer, but a weeping needy woman whose only resource was persistent love" (William Kilbourn, ed., *The Restless Church,* 5).

But there is also an a priori conditioning our understanding of the ministry of the whole people of God, namely the ministry of the Christ—or, as we termed it earlier, God's mission in Christ, which precedes and makes possible, as well as mandatory, that of the church. In order to grasp something of the significance of this christological presupposition of Christian ministry, we should again remind ourselves of the key concept or metaphor that was introduced in our discussion of the person and work of Jesus Christ in *Professing the Faith*—that of "representation." One of the advantages of that metaphor that we noted again in our discussion of the church is that it enables us to move from Christology to ecclesiology without introducing a whole new set of concepts, and thus it preserves the necessary *relationship* between these two aspects of Christian doctrine. To state this relationship directly in connection with the question of ministry, *the church's ministry in the world is its participation in the representative life and ministry of Jesus Christ.*

This statement must be understood pneumatologically, otherwise there is a danger of losing sight of the priority of Christ's ministry by regarding it as little more than a kind of pattern for the disciple community to follow. Jesus said "Follow me!" not "Follow a model-for-ministry that I am leaving behind for you." It is not as if the church were a voluntary community of altruistic persons who thought it good to behave in the world as Jesus behaved; rather, it is a community gathered by the Holy Spirit and made participant in the life and work of the crucified and risen Christ. The *church* does not "extend" this representative life of the Christ into a world in and to which the Christ himself is no longer present; rather, it is carried by the divine Spirit into the sphere of *the Christ's* representation. There is, to be sure, an element of volition involved in this (surely it is not necessary with the stricter adherents of divine determination to eliminate the human *response* to grace), but our decision to follow is not what is prior. The emphasis here falls upon the priority of grace, that is, of *Christ's* representative ministry and of our being "carried" (John 21:18) into a work that is already well underway before we are in any way involved in it. To state it in terms of a distinction introduced earlier, the church's ministry is not a matter of *imitatio Christi* but of *conformitas Christi:* we are not simply "doing ministry"; it is something being done to us and through us—often enough, we know, in spite of ourselves.[37]

When this priority of grace is grasped in its full application to the theology of ministry, we may go on to speak about the manner in which the metaphor

---

37. "The Christian life begins, 'not because men chose Christ . . . but because Christ has chosen them.' It is not because 'Christians choose to go out into the world that they went there, but because Christ sends them there" (James Y. Holloway, ed., *Introducing Jacques Ellul* [Grand Rapids: Wm. B. Eerdmans, 1970] 48). (The quoted phrases are from Ellul's *The Presence of the Kingdom* [New York: Seabury, 1967].)

of representation informs the church's ministry.[38] Representation, as we recognized in the christological discussions, always involves two sides, because it is essentially a mediatorial position or office. In political life, where representation is a prominent concept, individuals in government represent their constituencies to the governing bodies and the decisions of the latter to their constituencies. This dual aspect of representation makes it particularly adaptable christologically and soteriologically.

Representation (as distinct from substitution) permits us to explore *both* sides of the life and work of Jesus Christ: his representation of the divine before the human, and his representation of the human before the divine. It will be recalled that we found this a more satisfactory way of speaking about the human and the divine in Jesus than the conventional "two natures" terminology, because it enables us to consider both the person and the work of the Christ *relationally* rather than substantially. We formulated our relational Christology/soteriology in this way: that which the tradition calls "divine" (*vere Deus*) in the Christ impels him toward the human, and that which is "human" (*vere homo*) in him impels him toward God. In moving toward the creation, in solidarity with all creatures, Jesus represents the Creator who continually yearns for full communion with the creation; and in moving toward the Creator (as, for instance, Jesus is shown doing in the high priestly prayer of John 17) he represents the creature, which even in its separation from God yearns for reconciliation and communion with God.

Following this christological basis through into our theology of ministry, we may affirm that the ministry of the church to the world, as does its participation in Christ's ministry, involves the disciple community in this same two-fold life of representation. With and "in" Christ, the church his "body" represents (re-presents) God to the world and the world to or before God. That is to say, insofar as the church *realizes* ("makes real") its identification with its head, it finds itself being moved, with and in him, to greater communion with both the creature and the Creator.

There is an implicit polemic in this innocent enough claim, and it should not be passed over lightly. The Spirit-initiated identification with Christ which is, as we have seen, an ongoing process in the life of the disciple community, involves greater communion with *both creature and Creator.* Pietistic and ecclesiocentric conceptions of the mission of the church concentrate exclusively on the latter, that is, the greater communion of the church with the Creator. But if it is understood that it is *the Christ's* ministry into which the

---

38. For an application of the metaphor of representation in current North American Catholic thinking on the restructuring of the church, see Eugene C. Bianchi and Rosemary Radford Ruether, *A Democratic Catholic Church: The Reconstruction of Roman Catholicism* (New York: Crossroad, 1992), 254f.

disciple community is always being carried, then it must be recognized that this means greater communion with the creature as well as with the Creator. For, as we have just reminded ourselves, it is precisely that which has its source and ground in *the divine,* in Jesus Christ, that impels him toward the world. As God's representative, he has to become "Emmanuel"—*God-with-us.* It would therefore be impossible for a disciple community that had found itself, through the grace of this relationship, in greater communion with God, to avoid a simultaneous sense of greater communion with God's beloved world. If God, in the theology of this tradition, is by definition oriented toward the world, and if it is precisely this orientation that the revelation of God in Jesus as the Christ concretizes, then any community claiming identity with this triune God would by definition be a community irresistibly impelled toward God's world.

This is indeed the basis for our earlier claims for the worldly orientation of the church and its mission. If the church is prevented from "enjoying" the kind of religion that is happy always to distinguish itself from the world; if it is disallowed the comforts of that type of "fellowship" in which only those who "belong" matter; if it is "sent out" (*missio*); this is because the One whose body it is, is representative of a God who is turned toward the world. It is precisely what the tradition calls Christ's *divinity* that drives Jesus toward the world—toward Jerusalem (Luke 9:51)! And it is precisely as the church is seized by this same *divinity* or divine impulse that it becomes entangled with the life of the world. Those who associate the divine with *otherworldliness* have not yet understood this fundamental principle of biblical Theology.

To reinforce the point, let us state the same thing via negativa. When Christian community finds itself being led away from the world; when it begins to accentuate the goodness and godliness of its own fellowship (*koinonia*); when it refuses to become "mixed up with politics" and worldly issues, and pursues instead what it may be pleased to call (with Paul—2 Cor. 4:18)) "the things that are unseen"; then it had better ask itself whether precisely the *divine* impulse had perhaps gone out of its life. The disciples on the Mount of Transfiguration desired, in the name of what they imagined to be "the Holy," to remain aloof from the world of political and religious conflicts and human suffering and struggles of every sort. "Let us build here three tabernacles," urged the spokesman, Peter (Mark 9:5). But Jesus led them down the mountain into the midst of crowds crying for truth and healing. The Holy One tabernacles with humanity—even unholy humanity.

If that which is divine in Christ's body drives it into the world that the religious always try to avoid and evade, that which is human in this body—that is, that which is becoming "*truly* human" (*vere homo*)—drives it to greater communion with God. And this humanity is *representative* humanity, because it is the humanity that is Christ's gift to his body. It is not anthropocentric-egocentric humanity but a humanity that looks for its center in the Other—in God, and therefore, as we have just seen, also in other creatures. For though we are speaking about a dual orientation the process as such is unified: impelled toward humanity and the creation because of the gift of identity with the divine, the disciple community finds itself simultaneously impelled toward the divine because of its gift of new, authentic humanity.

The church's turning-toward-God, we reiterate, is a representative turning; that is to say, it is a priestly act. The church that tries to orient itself toward God in an exclusive way, that is, in a manner that suggests utter distinction or separation from the rest of the world: such a church is a contradiction in terms. It is not its own cause, well-being, and destiny that the body of Christ brings into the divine Presence—not, at any rate, if it is making good its identity as *Christ's* body; rather, it comes before God *in behalf of* the creature. And today we must make it clear that "the creature" in this case does not mean *only* the human creature but the whole, groaning creation—the disappearing species, the polluted rivers and lakes, the overburdened ecosystem. It is the church's mission as that body in which Christ's mission is being extended in history to be before the source and ground of all life in a priestly way: to represent to God the terrible pain of the world, the longing of all creation for the fulfillment of the promise it contains.

If it is the divine impulse in the new identity that Jesus Christ gives to the church that sends it out into the world; if, in other words, the church's representation of God is the basis of the Christian *ethic,* then we may say that it is the human impulse in this gift of identity that sends the church into the sanctuary—that is the basis of its *worship.* The church's mission is not only its going out but also its coming in—its standing-before God, representatively.

To sense this is to acquire a perspective on worship that is almost diametrically opposed to worship as it is commonly understood. For in its conventional expressions, nothing that the church does is regarded as more *private* than its worship. Worship is seen as the intimate communion of "the chosen" with their Lord, the event of the inner sanctum, the almost-hidden, utterly personal discourse between Christ and his little flock. But if it were understood that precisely in this undoubtedly intimate act all of creation is to be represented, with all of its pain and longing, the entire character of worship would be altered. Not only would there be a greater emphasis upon *intercessory prayer* (that is a truism), but every aspect of worship would be transformed. For then we would understand ourselves to be "there," not merely for ourselves alone, but—as Jesus was in Gethsemane—for a great multitude of beings, including especially *human* beings, whose creaturehood is in the first place a rather impossible sort of thing, perhaps a tragic thing. If our representation of humanity were *true,* we could not listen *easily* to the decla-ration of sin and forgiveness that is at the heart of the sermon; it would not be an automatic process for us—sin (point 1), forgiveness (point 2). It would be *skandalon*—and it might also be "gospel"! For we would be hearing all this with the world's ears and not only our own. If then we became filled with gratitude, which would certainly distinguish such worship from the usual, it would be the representation of a gratitude far broader and deeper than our own: the gratitude for being that is found in every creature according to its kind, and also in fallen humanity, hiddenly.

Participation in Christ's ministry is the missionary vocation of the *whole* church. Here there can be no distinction between clergy and laity. Every Christian by virtue of his or her faith inherits the ministry of Christ in the world, and all Christians together, not only singly but as "body," perform this ministry. This ministry of the whole "people of God" is the presupposition of all questions concerning special ministries within the disciple community. The representative life and work of the Christ in the world can only be under-taken corporately, although each "member" of the "body" brings her or his gifts to this calling.

This was the most important insight of the 1956 study *The Purpose of the Church and Its Ministry,* undertaken by H. Richard Niebuhr in collaboration with Daniel Day Williams and James M. Gustafson.[39] This investigation, prompted by the perceived needs of theological educators at a point in time when the great transition from Constantinian to post-Constantinian forms of the church began to be visible to some on this continent, insisted that a new conception of ministry was emerging. In the study, the investigators emphasize repeatedly that they cannot as yet determine the character of this new model, but they find at the heart of it a growing consensus within all the denominations and seminaries studied that ministry must be understood as the ministry of "the whole Church."[40] This aspect of the report is as true today as it was forty years ago, and the report's rather hesitant designation of this as the heart of the "emergent" model of ministry has certainly been demonstrated, by succeeding decades, to be accurate. What was not, I think, anticipated by this important document were the *problems* that would be attendent upon the broadening of ministry thus conceived. In a real sense, precisely the good and necessary opening up of ministry to "the whole church" has created new occasions and needs for special ministries *within* the church. And, as I shall attempt to show in the succeeding subsection, the

---

39. H. Richard Niebuhr, in collaboration with Daniel Day Williams and James N. Gustaf-son, *The Purpose of The Church and Its Ministry* (New York: Harper & Brothers, 1956).

40. E.g., ibid., 85.

most misleading aspect of the report with regard to these latter is when it identifies the desirable "new" conception of the minister as "pastoral director."

12.2. Ministry Within the Disciple Community. The ministry of Jesus Christ is the presupposition and evocation of the ministry of the whole church, and the ministry of the whole church is the presupposition and evocation of ordered ministry within the church. I introduce the word "evocation" in this connection in order to convey the belief (which is certainly not mine alone) that ordered ministry is a necessity implicit in the concept of ministry as the vocation of the *whole* church. For, from the outset, it has been the experience of the Christian movement that the ministry of the whole people of God required "ordering." We have already affirmed that the original idea of the disciple community is more accurately conveyed by the term "movement" than by the words "organization" or "institution." But even a movement, and perhaps especially a movement, must order itself if it is to function—if it is to *move*!

This ordering should be traced to Jesus' selection of the original twelve, and, behind that, the ancient Hebraic sense of the election of the "twelve tribes." Moreover, although Protestants have been (rightly) hesitant to assign primacy to the apostle Peter, the whole idea of primacy being, on newer Testamental grounds, a questionable one, it is clear from the Gospel accounts that Jesus occasionally chose some from among the twelve for this or that particular responsibility.

At the same time, in order to prepare ourselves for later observations that will have to be made in this connection, we should already note that the biblical record in its totality introduces a strong prophetic critique of dangers that almost inevitably accompany the naming of special offices within the community. Not only is the human temptation to special status (primacy) specifically warned against; not only are those named to particular duties warned against presumption and instructed in the difficult lessons of learning to bear office in the manner of *servanthood* and stewardship; not only is the *prophetic* office precisely instituted to be a constant reminder to the offices of priesthood and kingship that their authority is strictly "provisional";[41] but we are also presented throughout both Testaments with a *pneumatological* understanding of ministry within the *koinonia*—an understanding that is always potentially at loggerheads with legislated or established authority (and in that sense with "ordered" ministry). The prophetic office, particularly as it is filled by Amos and others among the prophets who do not possess even the right *prophetic* credentials, is itself part of this pneumatological under-

---

41. See *Thinking the Faith*, §32.

standing of ministry; and in the newer Testamental accounts, the original apostles themselves, as well as Paul, are seen in their own historical contexts as unauthorized religious figures who nevertheless, from the point of view of the faithful, are the true bearers of God's mission in the world. This pneumatological alternative has always been felt as a threat to established forms of ministry, and in the situation of Christian establishment particularly it was never a live alternative for any who feared for their lives. Even with the Reformation it only gained ascendency sporadically and among the most persecuted elements of the protesting bodies. At the end of the Constantinian era it becomes again in some sense viable. But it too contains dangers, and should not be romanticized.

These dangers are already in fact visible in the community that emerges from the post-resurrection experiences, and as such they constitute the negative rationale for the ordering of ministry that already begins to occur in the early church. For it is soon recognized that, apart from some ordering of the life of the movement, it will be immobilized by potentially and actually destructive dimensions within itself. How, apart from some at least rudimentary organization, will any action at all be undertaken?[42] How will disorder and chaos be averted? Who will prevent the faith from being interpreted in all manner of ways, some of them quite fantastic, some (as Paul's letters plainly tell us) the very antithesis of "the way of the cross"?[43] Who will make sure that the "spirits" are tested? Human history (and not only *ancient* human history!) abounds in spirits, and in powerful "charismatic" representatives of spirits. No doubt all authority is from God, but are there not tests of pneumatic authority, and is it not necessary for some to be vigilant in their application?

Thus even for negative reasons it may be said that the ministry of the whole people "evokes" special ministries within the whole. But there are also positive reasons for this evocation. The past must be remembered, the apostolic tradition preserved. "Apostolic succession," as we have seen, is an organizational concept intended to serve the preservation of apostolic teaching. Besides, the mission must be organized, decisions have to be made, funds and properties and alms have to be handled. The diaconate is a response to that aspect of the community's life in particular.

---

42. "The church exists in contradictions and conflicts, and it must organize itself as the visible community of believers against the impeachments of this world of violence, so that it may show the world God's alternatives" (Jürgen Moltmann, *The Way of Jesus Christ*, trans. Margaret Kohl [London: SCM, 1990; Minneapolis: Fortress Press, 1993], 55).

43. "It would be naive to advocate pluralism and decentralization in the reshaping of the Catholic Church without considering the dangers of fragmentation and factionalism. Communities do not exist in some tensionless, pure state. There are always conflicts over theory and practice, based on the convictions of different interest groups" (Bianchi and Ruether, *A Democratic Catholic Church*, 257).

There can, I think, be no question therefore that ordered ministry—ministry within the *koinonia*—is assumed by these biblical sources. What *can* and must be questioned is whether the Bible authorizes a particular *type* of ministry. That such types eventually emerged, that one particular type came to *dominate* in Western Christendom, is obvious enough. But it is not at all obvious that biblical warrant can be found for any one form of ordered ministry, including the one that came to dominate in the West.

What the Bible seems to give us in this whole area is a theology of ordered ministry that is very much in line with the contextual approach we are taking in this entire study: namely, that the ordering of ministry is determined by the mission of the church and therefore subject to the particularities pertaining in this or that given situation. If therefore a considerable *variety* of forms of ordered ministry can be discerned in or on the basis of newer Testamental evidence, as many maintain, this is not surprising. For the needs of the mission in one context are not necessarily the same as those in another; and, so long as *the mission* is served, it is not terribly important, given this approach, how ministry is ordered. Adjustments in its ordering can be instituted as and when they are needed. In short, the priority established in this chapter's title ("Mission, Message, Ministry) is the one that seems to be honored here.[44]

Just because this is the case, however, it is all the more necessary for Christian communities to inform themselves and to struggle with the *whole* tradition and practice of ordered ministry. Instead of being fixated upon this or that form, the church that assumed biblical authority as foremost among the "provisional authorities" of the faith would continuously ask itself whether the patterns of ministry to which it was *historically* tied were still capable

---

44. An insightful study undertaken by the United Presbyterian Church in the United States of America in 1961 makes the same point: "Every aspect of the organization of the Church should be understood in this way. On every level, and at every stage, order has a single purpose: *to enable the Church to deploy its forces most effectively in its assigned mission in and for the world.*

"But here we run into a snag. For rather than recognize the astonishing flexibility and adaptability in the New Testament understanding of 'orders,' there are always those who want to 'freeze' the process and insist that subsequent generations of Christians must reproduce exactly the 'orders' of the New Testament Church.

"In the New Testament, we read of apostles, prophets, teachers, evangelists, workers of miracles, healers, leaders, helpers, administrators, speakers in various kinds of tongues, pastors, bishops, elders, deacons, and many more as well.

"But these 'offices' are *not* being reported to us as permanent, inflexible 'orders,' a conclusion that is inaccurate and misleading at best. They are, rather, displayed to us as the ways by which the Early Church deployed *its* forces in the light of the particular campaign on which *it* was embarked in *its* historical situation.

"This means . . . that every effort in subsequent centuries to use the Bible as a book of canon law, or manual of polity, inevitably lapses either into frustration or into nonsense" (Robert Clyde Johnson, ed., *The Church and Its Changing Ministry* [Philadelphia: Office of the General Assembly, United Presbyterian Church in the U.S.A., 1961], 21). (Italics are part of the original text.)

of serving the church's present mission faithfully. Protestants have seldom hesitated to propose to Catholics and Anglicans that they were tethered to theologies of ministry that were historically but not biblically grounded, but Protestants have rarely applied to themselves the critique they applied so liberally to these older traditions. Obviously, the episcopal form of ministry *evolved*, and did not emerge ready-made in the ministry of Christ himself. (Even Richard Hooker, attached as he was to the threefold order of ministry, believed this to be so.) But so did every other conception of ministry evolve. And may there not be contexts in which the episcopal form of ministry really does serve the mission of the church better than other forms might do? Could it not be, in fact, that congregational and presbyterian forms of ordered ministry are in many cases less than helpful today, precisely where *mission* is concerned? In churches in which leadership is lacking or confused because of constantly fluctuating offices and the kind of "democracy" in which "everybody's business becomes nobody's business," it may well be asked whether elected bishops are not the most contextually responsible kind of ordering of ministry.

This leads to the question posed at the end of the previous subsection regarding the problems that emerge when the ministry of "the whole church" is accentuated and, through changed social and ecclesiastical circumstances, becomes more concretely realizable. That the ministry of the entire people of God is not only a desirable end but one that is implicit in an ecclesiology that is christologically based has been affirmed in the foregoing subsection. The primary reasons that that conception of ministry has been so consistently neglected in the history of the Christian movement is that, under the conditions of "Christendom," most Christians were so only officially and nominally, and the church could therefore simply mirror in its internal government the patterns of government and authority of its host society. As we shed the Constantinian mode of Christian existence, both of these conditions are significantly altered: more and more of those who remain within the church do so out of conviction, and as the church is relieved of its duties as the cultic dimension of official culture, it is freer to pursue its own internally determined forms of governance and authority. As these conditions are realized, there is a natural movement toward what secular reason would describe as a more "democratic" type of internal structuring, with the *laos* as a whole participating in all aspects of ecclesiastical life.[45]

---

45. This is perhaps best appreciated in the churches that most reflect monarchic and hierarchic forms of government and ministry, especially Rome. The present struggles of the Roman Catholic church are most of them consequences of a historic battle between those who have been moved by the cultural and political disestablishment of the church to explore more demo-

It belongs to the general tenor of the ecclesiology developed in this study to laud these developments. The "democratization" of the churches is long overdue! But to approve of these developments does not mean to close one's eyes to the problems that they, in turn, produce. There is no problemless ecclesiology. Even a theology of ministry in which, at last, the whole *laos* is stressed has its attendant dangers; and the study of the transition in ministry to which reference was made in the preceding subsection seems to me not to have been very conscious of these. This is no doubt in part attributable to the fact that, in societies such as ours, in which "democracy" has been my-thologized and romanticized, the very emergence of greater participatory forms of governance and authority can seem an unquestionably praisewor-thy matter.

Thus the study in question proposes that in the new situation, in which ministry is the prerogative of "the whole church," the task of ordained minis-try can best be thought of as that of a "pastoral director."

> The call to the ministry is not for our contemporaries first of all a mystic matter enacted in the solitariness of lonesome encounter; it is rather a call extended to social man, the member of a community, through the mediation of communi-ty. . . . Young men and women today feel themselves challenged to identify themselves with the community and institution devoted to the service of God rather than with an ideal; the human need of which they are made aware is one that only the community can minister to; the words through which they hear the Word of God addressed to them are likely to be words of the Church. As the conception of the work of the ministry changes into the idea of the whole Church ministering so the conception of call changes into the idea of the called and the calling Church.[46]

One does not doubt that this represents an accurate reading of the "emerg-ing" conception of ministry in the 1950s in Canada and the United States; nor can one doubt, in the light of subsequent development, its prophetic character. What one misses in the study is some forewarning of the pitfalls attendant upon such a view. Not only does the idea of the minister as "pasto-ral director" mirror almost slavishly the managerial approach of the business and professional world,[47] but it is wholly inadequate as a conception of minis-

---

cratic forms of authority in all phases of ecclesiastical life and those, on the other hand, who are driven to cling all the more tenaciously to the established forms.

46. H. Richard Niebuhr et al., *The Purpose of the Church and Its Ministry*, 85.

47. C. S. Calian writes: "Today's pastor is increasingly captive to the *manager-enabler* model of ministry. This style sees the minister as the manager or pastor-director who participates within the congregation as an enabler. Mission through management and wise planning is the key. The framework views the pastor as the hired executive of the parish, employed to give a sense of direction to the whole planning process. Hence pastors are following the example of the corpora-tion executives and mastering such terms as management by objectives, goal-setting, priority

try equipped to deal with problems that are bound to arise—and have arisen—with the democratization of ministry.

In the latter I include the following: the tendency of the democratized church to mistrust all authority and to rely on majority opinion even in matters on which the majority are not qualified to make decisions; the consequent and growing inability of congregations and denominations of the church to use expertise;[48] the resultant alienation of Christian scholars from the larger body of believers; the consequent loss of theological depth and intellectual rigor in Christian communities generally; the tendency, as a result, to be "blown about by every wind of doctrine," every new "theology of," every trendy "issue"; the general fear of leadership and the resultant danger that de facto leadership will be seized by powerful personalities and lobbies; and so on. These, I think, are not hypothetical risks in the last decade of the century (although they were no doubt more hypothetical in 1956); they threaten to capsize the ship of our Protestant church!

And "the minister as pastoral director" will by no means prevent that disaster from happening. If we are thinking of ordered ministry *contextually,* at least in the once-mainline Protestant churches of North America today, we shall have to entertain a quite different image of the minister. Our churches do not need managers, they need thinkers! They need people whose knowledge of the Scriptures, traditions, and contemporary Christian scholarship is *more* deeply developed than has been required of clergy in the past. They need teachers, resident theologians, teaching elders, rabbis: learned persons who can prevent the faith from being reduced to platitudes and ethical truisms and pious reflections of the regnant "values." They need persons who

---

determination, evaluation objectives and support systems. I suspect that Jesus would find such terminology strange. Life is said to be much more complicated today than it was during the world of Jesus, but is it really? Have the essential aspects of living changed? Is the manager-enabler the type of pastor who will reach greatness and bring the church to a higher vision? A whole new corps of church consultants has emerged, promising to bring pastors and people to a new threshold of service through carefully planned management and forecasting. . . .

"The pastor who primarily seeks to serve as the manager-enabler will not be able to help the congregation see beyond their crisis of objectives; the pastor's role is to provide theological guidelines in furthering the mission and vision of the congregation in their local community and beyond.

"The manager-enabler model of ministry is tempted to dilute the biblical norms into a 'theology of the feasible.' What is feasible may in retrospect prove to be not only bad theology but serve as a definite barrier in that church's search for identity under God. . . . It is about time that the laity who understood our business culture so well stop their pastors and inform them of the limits of the manager-enabler style of ministry" (*Today's Pastor in Tomorrow's World*, rev. ed. [Philadelphia: Westminster Press, 1977], 32–33).

48. For an elaboration of my meaning here, see the essay "The State of the Ark: Lessons from Seoul," in D. Premen Niles, ed., *Between the Flood and the Rainbow: Interpreting the Conciliar Process of Mutual Commitment (Covenant) to Justice, Peace, and the Integrity of Creation* (Geneva: WCC Publications, 1992), 34–48.

know the literary and artistic traditions of Western civilization well enough not to be duped by cheap art, and who understand the technocratic society sufficiently to understand that it must be resisted![49] And they do *not* need "communicators" who know all the "skills" of modern communication but have nothing to communicate beyond these methods and skills. Ours is a time for *prophetic* ministry, not for "pastoral directors." We have been so busy producing pastors—and, for the most part, pastors who are more "director" than "pastor"—that the entire prophetic and sapiential (wisdom) side of ministry has been vitiated. The ministry of the "whole church," if it is truly to reflect Christ's ministry today and not just bourgeois religion in its lowest-common-denominator expression, calls for the ministrations of *learned* clergy—not, it is to be hoped, men and women who are made pompous by their learning, but persons in whom those who hunger and thirst for truth will be able to recognize something approaching depth of understanding and curiosity. There is already such a slide toward anti-intellectualism and religious *kitsch* even in these remaining representatives of classical Protestantism that the trend can be altered only with the greatest effort. Perhaps for the majority it *cannot* be altered. Nevertheless, the effort must be made, because the alternative is the further trivilization of the faith and, finally, its relegation to sheer religious froth. And that is a fate too melancholy to contemplate for a faith that could move the intellects of an Augustine, an Aquinas, a Calvin, a Simone Weil, and countless others.

Whether such a prophetic ministry can be nurtured *within* the churches or has to be developed alongside them; whether, in particular, it can be achieved under the conditions of stipended ministry: these are questions that must be addressed by every serious seminary, theological college, and denomination. There is already enough evidence to suggest that education for ministry must be prolonged and constantly renewed, and that there must be a return to basics and less emphasis upon what we have been pleased to call "practical"

---

49. I have in mind the sort of ministry that the late Jacques Ellul, the lay theologian, describes in the following autobiographical statement: "I have given myself to the task, on the one hand to deepen my theological and biblical knowledge and, on the other hand, to continue with a sociological analysis of the Western world. I have sought to confront theological and biblical knowledge and sociological analysis without trying to come to any artificial or philosophical synthesis; instead, I try to place the two face to face, in order to shed some light on what is real socially and real spiritually. That is why I can say that the reply to each of my sociological analyses is found implicitly in a corresponding theological book, and inversely, my theology is fed on socio-political experience. But I refuse to construct a *system* of thought, or to offer up some Christian or prefabricated socio-political solutions. I want only to provide Christians with the means of *thinking out for themselves* the meaning of their involvement in the modern world.

"Such is the essential goal of my work. It ends, necessarily, in a Christian ethics—but *only* therefore an ethics that is indicative" (Holloway, ed., *Introducing Jacques Ellul,*, 6).

subject matter.[50] If the practice of ministry truly does belong to the "whole Church," then clergy ought *not* to be trained to *do* the whole work of ministry! There is also enough evidence to suggest that we do not absolutely *need* full-time *paid* clergy. Many alternative patterns have been proposed for years, and occasionally attempted—sometimes with excellent results. If, in the pattern of the synagogue and the rabbinate, Christian ministers really were trained to be teachers within the congregation, leaving more of the priestly and pastoral work to others, the "full-time" concept would in any case not be as mandatory as it now is for our "pastoral directors"![51]

We have only begun to explore the surface of the changes through which the churches are passing as they emerge from their Constantinian cocoon, and, in ordered ministry, where so many "vested interests" are to be found, we are even slower than in other areas of ecclesiology to reflect on the possibilities that open out to us in the changed status of the Christian movement. If we can keep before us the prioritization to which this chapter has pointed—namely, that the purpose of ordered ministry is to serve the ministry of the whole church, which in turn is to serve the ministry of Christ in the world—we shall be in a position spiritually and intellectually to consider radical alternatives in the field of ordered ministry. Present generations of Christians may still be too physically and materially tied to old patterns of ministry and priesthood actually to undertake the changes that are now possible, but if we can even entertain them seriously at the intellectual level, the way will be prepared for later implementation, which in any case will be *necessitated* by material/physical realities.

But in this as well as many other aspects of the doctrine of the church, its mission and its ministry, we have been anticipating greater questions of the transition through which the Christian movement is passing, and to those questions we must now direct our attention.

---

50. What James Smart wrote on this subject in 1959 is still eminently true: "It is surely clear that one of the drastic needs of the present is the recovery by the practical disciplines of their thoroughgoing theological character. The task of theology is the investigation of the question of truth and error in every aspect of the Church's life. It is possible for the Church so to preach, so to teach, so to act, so to deal with individuals that it is no longer the Church of Jesus Christ but something else, some other kind of institution. The Church is in constant danger of unconsciously becoming something other than that which it was founded to be, the body of Jesus Christ, in which He continues to live and speak and act among men" ("The Minister as Pastor," in *Canadian Journal of Theology* 5, no. 3 [1959]: 182).

51. I developed this line of thought in considerable detail in my *Has the Church a Future?* (Philadelphia: Westminster Press, 1980), chap. 6.

PART II

METAMORPHOSIS: FROM CHRISTENDOM TO DIASPORA

CHAPTER ▪ FOUR

Disestablishment and the Crisis of Mainline Protestantism

13. The Changed and Changing Status of the Christian Movement

13.1. At the Crossroad.   No one during our lifetime manifesting serious interest in Christianity can overlook the reality to which this second part of our study is addressed. During the past two centuries or more, the Christian religion has been undergoing such an immense transformation that even those who refuse to consider it are profoundly affected by it. Their very refusal, like the denial of death that is one of the typical stages through which terminally ill persons pass, is symptomatic of the reality in question. Very much of the behavior of Christian individuals, congregations, and whole denominations today can only be understood if it is realized that in the face of *this* death, the death of Christendom, denial, whether active or passive, is the most characteristic response of the present. This is especially the case in the North American context that is our particular concern in this series.

Such denial is, of course, understandable. It is understandable first because the death in question constitutes a complete reversal of expectations. We have been conditioned by centuries of Christian domination and expansion to assume that the future would see more of the same and, in the end, achieve the global victory that the "Constantinian" reading of the newer Testament taught us to anticipate. It is understandable, second, because without any theological basis for reflection upon failure, especially Christian failure, the only alternative to denial seems to be disbelief: if Christianity does not "succeed," it must be internally flawed. Since most Christians are reluctant to take such a plunge into the nether regions of renunciation, and since in our context particularly theological grounds for the contemplation of failure at *any* level of human experience are rare, denial seems the only recourse.

A third reason for such denial in our context, notably in the United States, is the fact that apparently persuasive evidence can be mustered to demonstrate that the death in question is by no means immanent or inevitable. Indeed, it can be made to seem that "America" has escaped the general decline of Christendom that is readily documented in so many other parts of the world, including Canada. Thus the impulsive denial that is adduced in the first and second explanations is often emboldened by the insistence that there is really no need to acknowledge this alleged death in the first place, so that denial here is elevated to refutation.

The greater one's knowledge of history and society, however, the more one knows that neither refutation nor denial are appropriate responses to the Christian present and immediate future. Not only is this so, but such responses are the very stuff out of which the churches today are courting a reduction still more dramatic than the present one. Only a disciple community that has the courage, trust, and theological wisdom that are needed to enter into the experience of Christendom's dying will be able, under God, to pass through this dying to something like newness of life.

To risk another metaphor, the Christian movement is standing at a crossroad: the most momentous decisions of its history are before it. But if Christians are unwilling even to acknowledge this fateful intersection, assuming instead that there is still only the one way and that one "ever upward," they will not only very soon find themselves in a cul de sac but, more importantly, they will have missed the road that *is* opened to them just at this juncture.

That road is undoubtedly a narrow one—a country lane or footpath compared with the broad thoroughfare Christendom has been travelling since the fourth century C.E. And here we glimpse a fourth reason that many Christians, both individuals and churches, opt for denial: the alternative future seems to them so bleak as to be as good as death. But if, instead of reading the newer Testament as if it were describing the humble beginnings of a journey that would later on become interesting, we considered it a permanently accurate roadmap for the *communio viatorum,* we would not be surprised, surely, about finding ourselves on a narrow way (Matt. 7:14)!

That, in a manner of speaking, is the hypothesis I shall develop in this part of our study. To speak less metaphorically, I want to demonstrate that, with an appropriate ecclesiology (the *ecclesia crucis,* or ecclesiology of the cross), the present transformation through which the Christian movement is passing does not have to be denied or refuted, but may be participated in knowingly and even joyfully; because the future that divine Providence is holding out to this movement is nothing less than new life for an old institution that is really on the verge of collapse.

To present such an argument, I shall move through four stages: (1) a discussion of the decline of Christendom in the broader sense, noting some creative responses to the change (section 14); (2) a consideration of the North American situation in particular (section 15); (3) the task of disestablishment as opportunity (section 16); (4) reflections on being a "diaspora" in the midst of an allegedly "Christian" culture. First, however, a brief digression is required in order to situate this whole discussion in our larger inquiry.

13.2. Why This Subject Requires Separate Treatment. Why is it necessary to devote a separate part of our study to this matter, which on the surface has more to do with history and sociology than with theology? The answer is multifold, but two particular observations are of immediate significance.

First, the very complexity of the metamorphosis in question, including not only *what* it is but why we have such difficulty with it, is such that every systematic theology today must try to come to terms with it. Such an attempt is even more needful for a theology that intends to be contextual, for there is no more salient factor in our ecclesiastical context than this vast transition. It is not enough to make mention of it from time to time, or even to permit it the status of a recurrent motif, as I have done in all three of the these volumes. This is because a transformation of these proportions must be reflected upon in a sustained and thoughtful way—as, almost, a thing in itself. Simply to *understand* it, one must give one's undivided attention to it and seek to work out a reasonable conception of what it means.

In numerous previous works of mine, to some of which I shall refer in what follows, I have attempted to acquire just such an integrated overview of this transformation. In connection with the present work, I reviewed many of these earlier writings and, in doing so, I realize that each one represents a further attempt to fit together the many pieces of this theological-historical puzzle. I will not claim that the present contribution sees the last piece put into place, for the attempt of the Christian community to deal with the end of the Christendom phase of its life and to enter the next stage is one that must endure, literally, for generations. I do feel, however, that the years of wrestling with this whole *problematique* (something required particularly in my Canadian context) have resulted in the production of something like a reasonable overview and a work not only of critical but also of constructive ecclesiology. The net result of the deconstruction of Christendom into which my historical context has thrust me is, I believe, a very *positive* conception of the church of the future—one that can commend itself to those who both honor the *sola scriptura* of our Reformation past and require of the *future* church, therefore, that it be a faith community of public witness and responsibility, however "humiliated" in relation to its reputedly glorious history. It takes time to come to terms with this metamorphosis. I have taken that time, and I wish to share the results, for whatever they are worth, with those who have also devoted some thought and concern to this very complex matter.

A second reason that a separate section is devoted to this subject is related to the first, although it adds a dimension. The fate of Christendom and our total response to that fate affects every aspect of Christian *doctrine*. Not only the doctrine of the church, which is most directly influenced by the change and our way of interpreting it, but every other aspect of what Christians profess and confess will be touched by the manner in which, today, Christians actually deal (or do not deal!) with this transformation. If the reader will review the contents of the first two volumes of this series in the light of this claim, it will, in fact, be seen, I believe, that my discussion at every point has taken account of the transformation in question. I have treated such subjects as reason and revelation; theology, Christology, and soteriology; and creaturely being in the ways I have partly because I feel strongly that it is not valid for Christians to make "Christendom" assumptions in any of these areas any longer. The whole informing point of view in this trilogy—the *theologia crucis*—is in considerable measure the consequence of my having concluded, over the years, that a movement that could no longer either pretend to be or desire to be imperialistic would certainly have to find a different way of describing its gospel and living its life—different from the theological triumphalism that has in fact provided the imperial church with the *theoria* it needed for its whole worldly conduct.

In the present part of this volume, then, it is my intention to make explicit the assumptions concerning this metamorphosis that have been implicit and partial throughout the discussion heretofore.

14. Change and Response to Change: An Overview

14.1. "As It Was in the Beginning . . ." Christianity entered the world as a minority faith, a "missionary movement"[1] that most people who knew of it regarded as a sect of Judaism. Through the missionary endeavors of Paul and others, small Christian fellowships or *koinonia* were established in many cities of the Mediterranean world. They constituted a "scattering" (*diaspora*) of believers, most of whom were drawn from the lower classes.

---

1. See Elisabeth Schüssler Fiorenza's instructive discussion of Christian origins in her book *In Memory of Her: A Feminist Theological Reconstruction of Christian Origins* (New York: Crossroad, 1992), chap. 5, 160–204.

Although it grew numerically and geographically during the first three centuries of the Common Era, the Christian movement did not achieve anything like the status of a "major" or "world" religion until the fourth century when, in the short space of approximately eighty years, it attained cultic dominance in the most powerful empire of the age. From the end of the fourth century onward, while peoples on the European edges of Christendom were being converted well into the early Middle Ages, and while submerged pagan, Jewish, and Muslim faiths precluded a universal victory of the Christian religion, the church continued to dominate Europe and, from the sixteenth century, its colonies in the New World.

This situation began to be altered, however, at that imperceptible point in Western history when the age-old human propensity to doubt began to apply itself openly to Christian verities and weakened, gradually, the hold of the Christian religion upon the soul of the West. In contrast to the first great metamorphosis of Christianity, its transformation from diaspora to religious establishment, the second, from establishment to diaspora, has not been imposed from without but has evolved from within. The first great change can be dated, even though it required centuries to effect: the Edict of Toleration of 311 C.E., "allowing Christians the right to exist again and to set up their places of worship; provided always that they do not offend against public order,"[2] marks its decisive beginnings. No such possibility attaches to the dating of the second metamorphosis, the one of which we are part. Nevertheless, it *is* possible to discern a certain progression of thought leading eventually to the effective disestablishment of this religion.

The first stage must be associated with the late Middle Ages, as we have recognized at various points in our work heretofore. The medieval synthesis of faith and reason, based on the Augustinian sense of continuity between the human quest for truth and the divine gift of truth in the Christ, had faltered under the impact of the new Aristotelianism, revived by Jewish and Muslim philosophers and made interesting because of the general intellectual climate of the age. Albertus Magnus and his more prominent student, Thomas Aquinas, saved the synthesis from capitulation to the new rationality by laying hold of Aristotle for Christian use. But the Thomistic synthesis, unlike that of Augustine, Anselm, Bonaventura, and the Platonist Christians generally, left faith and reason separate and separable sources of truth. Indeed, from the perspective of the older synthesis, that of Thomas is not a synthesis at all but a kind of willed mutuality that can endure only as long as there is a general willingness to have it so. The synthesis breaks down the

---

2. Henry Bettenson, ed., *Documents of the Christian Church* (Oxford: Oxford University Press, 1963), 15.

moment someone (or rather, majority opinion) insists that human reason, basing itself on empirical data logically considered, leads to conclusions that are not only different from those of allegedly "revealed" truth but discontinuous with them.

That "moment" was, in fact not long in arriving, and with it came the breakdown of the whole medieval scholastic endeavor. The nominalists of the late Middle Ages were still, of course, serious Christian believers. William of Ockham, perhaps the most famous of them, was a Franciscan monk. They were not about to discredit the faith! Yet their way of pursuing both reason and faith betrays the fact that by now the course of European civilization had gone far enough to permit, in the midst of a Christendom still powerfully protected by the political machinery of its host culture, another manner of viewing truth and authority. A camel's nose of doubt had clearly poked its way into the tabernacle of established religion. As reason became increasingly bound to "the evidence of the senses" and the knowledge of particulars, revelation was made increasingly dependent upon ecclesiastical authority for its credibility. It is indicative of the extent of the segregation of faith and reason that John Duns Scotus, another Franciscan, for whom "much in theology is philosophically improbable,"[3] was able to become the first major theologian to defend the idea of the Immaculate Conception. Faith that is no longer fully supported by reason is at liberty, apparently, to pursue exceptionally suprarational precepts! But if faith is free to speculate, so is doubt free openly to entertain the antithesis.

What I am suggesting is that the interior condition necessary to disestablishment, that is, skepticism concerning what has been established, precedes *by centuries* the more discernible facts of disestablishment. The breakdown of the Middle Ages was not just, and not even primarily, a transition to another phase of Christendom; it was the beginning of Christendom's humiliation. For Christendom at base depends not only upon the readiness of the political establishment to befriend the Christian religion, but upon the willingness of society at large, beginning with its intellectual "cutting edge," to tolerate (at least tolerate!) this religion as beneficial if not true. The doubt that begins to manifest itself with the nominalist's readiness to give reason an independent role and to make faith less accessible to rational investigation and more dependent upon its own authority structures is a doubt that has never ceased to grow in the Western world, despite the obvious fluctuations of the Western spirit.

But this interior or collective spiritual condition preparatory to Christian disetablishment was of course accompanied by external factors that could

---

3. Williston Walker, *A History of the Christian Church* (rev. ed., New York: Charles Scribner's Sons, 1959), 251.

only aid and abet the process. It is very significant that the greatest nominalist of the fourteenth century, Ockham, was also persona non grata with the papacy in Avignon. In fact, that the papacy was in Avignon in the first place reminds us that the disestablishment of Christianity is bound up with the machinations of a church that was not content to be the official *cultus* of empire but desired imperial status for itself. The ambition of Christendom, represented by a figure such as John XXII (1316–1334), the pope with whom Ockham quarrelled, seems almost a classical case of pride going before the fall. The whole pathetic tale of Christendom's hubris and its consequences could be told by considering the history of the Franciscan movement, for no prominent historical Christian ever embodied the *antithesis* of Christendom's triumphalism more graphically than did Francis of Assisi, and John XXII, of whom it is said that "'he possessed in his nature not one single feature in common with St. Francis',"[4] could well represent the spirit of a Christendom that would only find abhorrent the simplicity of the Franciscans whom Ockham supported (the so-called Spirituals). Precisely at the point at which implicit doubt has been permitted to enter the halls of the theologians, then, the behavior of the political leadership of the church provides more than enough evidence to give wings to doubt.

If it is significant that William of Ockham, the Franciscan nominalist, quarrelled with the most powerful ecclesiast of his day, it is equally interesting for this account that the first vociferous pre-Reformer, John Wycliffe, was Ockham's younger contemporary, and that, a little later, Martin Luther would refer to the Franciscan originator of the *via moderna* as "my dear teacher Ockham." What I am pointing to in this is, of course, the Reformation, with its long, preparatory stage—a stage frequently overlooked by enthusiastic Protestants! Although, as we have noted earlier, the main Reformers did not seek to disestablish the Christian religion, they certainly did unsettle Christendom. The fact that they sought or were drawn into political arrangements that in some ways mirror the pre-Reformation establishment of Rome should not blind us to the manner in which the Reformation must be considered a milestone on the way to Christendom's demise.

It is this in two ways. First and most obviously, the Reformation introduced such divisions into a Christendom that, apart from the Great Schism, was remarkably unified that it wholly compromised the very principle that, as we have seen, appealed to Constantine and all his successors: the unity principle. Neither imperial commands, nor councils, nor wars could piece together the humpty-dumpty of Christendom after the sixteenth century, and the establishments that now had to be worked out on the basis of national

---

4. Tony Lane, *The Lion Concise Book of Christian Thought* (Tring, Herts., England: Lion Publishing, 1984), 99.

identities, international alliances, and the religious choices of the ruling elites (*cuis regio, ejus religio*) were never able to overcome the great ambiguity lodged in the fact that they were now establishments—plural! The same religion, established under a multitude of mutually suspicious and warring peoples, does not impress itself upon the public consciousness as a cult sufficiently binding to warrant its high position. (A common observation about the two world wars in our own time, especially the first, namely that human beings were seen killing one another in the name of the same deity, illustrates the point memorably.)

The second reason the Reformation must be considered a milestone on the road to Christendom's ending is that it reintroduced a *theology* that, when it is entertained seriously and imaginatively, is incommensurate with establishment. All the *primary* teachings of the Reformers (justification, Scripture, the priesthood of all believers, the covenantal basis of the church, and so on) contain implicit if not explicit criticism of the very idea of Christianity as an official religion—indeed, as Barth maintained, of religion as such. If in spite of that criticism the main streams of the Reformation were fashioned in establishmentarian forms, the reasons must be sought in areas other than theological. While the careers of Luther, Zwingli, and Calvin manifest a strong sense of public responsibility, they also manifest a consistent ambiguity with respect to "the ruling authorities." And why would they not? For in each of them there are profound spiritual assumptions, representative of their "ultimate concern" (Tillich), that simply are not consistent with the religious quest for temporal power. *Soli Deo gloria!* (To God *alone* belongs the glory!) Ergo, the struggle of the ruling classes for preeminence cannot legitimately locate any sort of support for itself in the *theology* of classical Protestantism, however amenable it might have found some of the avowed Protestants. At best, there can only be a kind of gentleman's agreement with power, and a very tentative one at that—which is precisely how one should regard Luther's "two realms" theory.

If, beyond the characteristic theological emphases of the Protestants, one considers, as I have done in this trilogy, that the heart of the Reformation is to be found in the "key signature" (Moltmann) of its theology, the *theologia crucis,* the theoretical impossibility of a Christian establishment is still more obvious. For such a theology, in the name of the divine commitment to *the world,* enters a permanent critique of every attempt of human government to possess the world on its own terms. A theology of glory may—usually does!—seek alliances with powerful human agencies, for without them its triumphalist theoretical claims lack substance. But while the theology of the cross is forever prepared to serve human agencies in their quests for justice and peace, it cannot become the basis of a quest for power without implicitly contradicting itself. The place of the *ecclesia crucis* is not in the imperial household but among its subjects and its victims.

If this spiritual core of the Reformation was seldom applied to Protestant relations with powerful governments and classes—if it remained dormant at the ethical level and hardly even entertained theologically—it was nonetheless there at the center, waiting to assert itself and, here and there, be grasped with conviction and imagination. The assumptions and allures of establishment have been such, however, that apart from individual and small group claims upon this "thin tradition,"[5] Protestantism has preferred to limp through most of its history following two paths, ultimately divergent: the path of political quietism or noninterference, and that of personal piety. The cross could sometimes be a meaningful symbol for the latter, but not for the former.[6] Protestantism as the favored religion of Northern European states and their missionary offshoots has been obliged and content to hide even from itself the critical political and social implications of its theology of the cross. Only with its nineteenth and twentieth century decline and disfavor has mainstream Protestantism begun to know a posture sufficiently outside the walls of power to be able, if and where it is willing, to apply its theology more consistently to its worldly relationships. This will be the subject of our later deliberations in the present chapter.

But first we return to the earlier discussion of the gradual divorce of faith and reason. For this, I am convinced, is the interior rationale of the breakdown of Christendom. Had the West remained satisfied with the Augustinian, or even the Thomistic, synthesis of these two sources of religious belief and piety, no amount of turmoil on the surface of Christendom could have brought about its decline. For lively systems of meaning, even if they contain incongruities and gaps, can so long as they are responsive to the most basic human questions and needs withstand the foibles and misdemeanors of their chief representatives. In our own time, this has again been demonstrated by state Marxism, which fell not because of the evils of its leaders, even of Stalin, but because of its internal contradictions—contradictions that could no longer be camouflaged by propaganda or silenced by terrorism. The displacement of Christianity from the center of Western civilization is likewise owing to its inability to quell doubt (the natural child of human reasonable reflection upon the conditions of life) that the Christian religion answers and satisfies all human questions and anxieties. Or, to state the matter differently,

---

5. See my *Lighten Our Darkness: Toward an Indigenous Theology of the Cross* (Philadelphia: Westminster Press, 1976), chap. 4, 115–37.

6. Schüssler Fiorenza asserts that even Paul does not pay sufficient attention to the political concreteness of Jesus' crucifixion (*In Memory of Her*, 188).

Christianity failed as an established religion because it is at bottom a religion of faith and not reason. Unwilling to admit this about itself, it found no way of incorporating into its life a real *dialogue with doubt.*

The logic of this failure was not long in working itself out, as soon as reason was released from the burden of corroborating "revealed religion." There is an obvious line of continuity from the *via moderna* through the Renaissance to the Enlightenment. The more autonomous reason becomes, the less obliged are its leading representatives and spokespersons to uphold even the more accessible truths of the Christian religion. Indeed, doubt concerning the veracity of Christianity had become, by the eighteenth century, almost a law of serious intellectual investigation. It would be impossible earnestly to subject oneself to the main sources of philosophic thought from the seventeenth century onward and not to realize that Christianity would be incapable of surviving its Constantinian mode. In the late twentieth century, many have fallen victim to the supposition that the intelligentsia has little influence upon society at large, but this is a pseudo democratic fiction that will not stand the test of history. To read the treatises of Hobbes, Hume, Descartes, Locke, and numerous other philosophers of modernity, or even to study carefully the plays of William Shakespeare, is to know that already by the seventeenth century the days of Christendom were numbered. And for those who know the signs, the graphic arts and music tell the same story. Long before Kierkegaard conducted his famous "Attack" on Christendom; long before Overbeck announced that the whole Christian establishment had been a gross misunderstanding; long before the new apologists, such as Schleiermacher, began to address Western humanity in the knowledge of its real estate of secularity; and certainly long before 1963, when, according to Hauerwas and Willimon, the opening of the Fox Theatre of Greenville, South Carolina, on a Sunday evening announced the fact to the still-religiously Christian U.S. South, "the end of the Constantinian era" had been well prepared for by centuries of increasingly confident, independent rational thought—thought that not only did not require the incarnation of the Word, but did not even need the "hypothesis" of deity.

It is a kind of advanced folk wisdom in North America today that Christianity has been "done in" by secularism, multiculturalism, and religious pluralism. When this argument is advanced by Christians, it is usually a convenient way of avoiding the deeper questions that must be raised about a religion that allowed (and still allows) itself to be established, and the yet deeper questions concerning the reason it had to fail as such. Secularism is not the cause of the displacement of Christianity from center stage, it is a consequence of it; that is, secularism is a nineteenth-century "philosophy" that, in the vacuum created by Christendom's effective although not yet clearly perceptible demise, sought to encourage human beings to avoid despair by taking charge of their own destiny.

As for multiculturalism and religious pluralism, although their recent conspicuousness in Western societies has made the facts of Christian disestablishment the more obvious, they are by no means its cause. Christians have always known about the existence of other cultures and cults, and this knowledge did nothing at all at the height of European Christendom to deter the sense of Christian superiority and finality, as witness the Crusades. Even today, wherever the remnants of Christendom persist, the actual presence of strong communities representing other cults and cultures fails to deter true-believing Christians from assuming the same attitudes, although fortunately not always the same actions, as their medieval forebears, toward "the unfortunates" who have not yet "come to Christ." In short, although the global character of local societies may indeed make the mentality of Christendom harder to sustain, it is naive to think that the Christian religion has been and is being dismissed from its position as official *cultus* because of the presence and influence of "the others." We must finally come to terms with the fact that Christendom crumbled for reasons internal to its own character and history. It was not mortally wounded by some enemy; it became terminally ill for intrinsic reasons. This is the nature of the death through which we must pass if we are to discover the life that is possible through and beyond it.

14.2. Creative Responses to the Reduction of Christendom. Typical North American responses to Christendom's decline, as we proposed in the introduction of this chapter, demonstrate anything but a willingness to enter, contemplate, and learn from the experience. They range, rather, from a deliberate rejection of the whole notion that Christendom is ending to the determination to recover it with all haste. In the United States, where Christendom may often appear fully intact, only a minority seems interested in exploring a Christian future conspicuously different from the one that Christendom has taught us to expect. We shall discover reasons for this in the subsequent section. First, however, it is important to recognize that within the larger ecumenical scene there have been responses to this metamorphosis that are not only realistic but creative. They take us through the experience of Christendom's demise to a future that, although by no means problemless, holds out possibilities of *discipleship* that were denied most expressions of the Christian religion in the past precisely on account of its established status.

Before turning specifically to three of these responses, however, it would be well to remind ourselves that most serious Christian theology throughout the present century has presupposed this "paradigm shift," in most cases simply assuming its reality. Given the tone of such earlier works as Schleiermacher's *Speeches on Religion to Its Cultured Despisers,* one is tempted to think that that assumption predates the twentieth century and that Kierkegaard, although notorious for his blatant castigation of Christendom's pretense, is after all not alone.[7] At the same time, nineteenth- and early twentieth-century liberalism, with its quest for "the Kingdom of God in our time," seems to have been thoroughly imbued with the spirit of Constantinian religion, aided and abetted by the general aspirations of the modern West in the full cry of the Age of Progress.

Beginning with the "theology of crisis" in the second decade of this century, however, the open or implicit assumption of the leading theological movements of the present century is surely that essential Christianity must from now on be strictly distinguished both from the ethos of the once-Christian civilization of the West and, for the most part, the ecclesiastical remnants of Christendom itself. Even much twentieth-century Roman Catholic theology (and, as we shall see, this includes Karl Rahner and not just critical theologians such as Hans Küng and the Latin American liberationists) manifests this tendency. In the Protestant world, it is usually still more conspicuous. The vast output of Karl Barth takes on a more radical aspect if it is viewed as an attempt of a Christian scholar in an age of rampant disbelief ("a-theism") that is often cloaked by false belief and "religion" to preserve the essence of the faith, and to do so for the sake of the church that is coming to be. Paul Tillich is less interested in the church and more in sustaining meaningful dialogue with the existentially doubting world; but from first to last, he assumes that the only way in which such a dialogue can be kept going is if Christians cease imagining that their religion will automatically renew itself and enter with sufficient empathy into the world's post-Christian anxieties to discern genuine points of communication.

Similarly, although largely within another sphere of influence (the political), Reinhold Niebuhr addresses his contemporaries as being, for the most part, thoroughly secular men and women, whose best efforts at justice and

---

7. Kierkegaard's irony is wonderful and unsurpassed, but beneath it there is an indignation that comes straight from the prophets of Israel! To wit:

"How tiresome to make such a fuss about nothing at all; why can't he behave like the rest of us who are all Christians? . . . and if he happened to be married, his wife would say to him: 'Dear husband of mine, how can you get such notions into your heart? How can you doubt that you are a Christian? Are you not a Dane, and does not the geography say that the Lutheran form of the Christian religion is the ruling religion of Denmark? For you are surely not a Jew, nor are you a Mohammedan; what then can you be if not a Christian? It is a thousand years since paganism was driven out of Denmark, so I know that you are not a pagan. Do you not perform your duties at the office like a conscientious civil servant; are you not a good citizen of a Christian nation, a Lutheran Christian state? So then, of course you must be a Christian.'" Quoted by John Coleman Bennett in *Christians and the State* (New York: Charles Scribner's Sons, 1958), 218.

human responsibility are ostensibly unrelated to religious interests, although they are frequently more profoundly religious than are the avowedly religious.

Dietrich Bonhoeffer may be considered in some ways the model theologian of the end of Christendom, for, having to confront as he did the most absurdly reduced vestiges of Constantinianism, he staked out for future generations of Christians a theology and ethic of resistance that was also a luminous revisitation of discipleship in the biblical mode.[8] A similar claim, *mutatis mutandis,* must be made for theologians working for half a century behind the Iron Curtain—such persons as Johannes Hamel of Naumburg; Joseph Hromadka of Prague and his students Milan Opocenski, Jan Milič Lochmann, and others; Heino Falcke, the Probst of Erfurt; and others. Even more than in the Third Reich, Christians in officially atheistic states could no longer behave as if *Christianity* could claim any "standing" at all; therefore, they discovered possibilities of responsible witness and service that were as old as the first diaspora, and ought to be studied far more carefully than they are by contemporary Christians who ask after the Christian future.[9]

In the second half of this century, theology has gone even farther in assuming a position outside the Christian and political establishment. The most widely publicized movements—Black theology, liberation theology, Christian feminism—by their very nature as movements in solidarity with dispossessed or marginalized groups have reinforced the perception that Christian civilization is not only a present misnomer but a past fiction as well; that authentic faith can only enter into alliances with majorities by betraying its innate responsibility toward minorities; and so on. Something similar could be said of the various theological postures inspired by the ecological crisis; concern for global justice; the plight of ethnic, sexual, racial, aboriginal, economic and other minorities; and so on. Moreover, programs such as the World Council of Churches' "Justice, Peace, and the Integrity of Creation" are indicative of the fact that such post-Christendom theologies do find their way into the life of the churches. At the same time, the criticism that they also meet within and around the churches indicates the extent to which the latter are ill prepared for the vocation of resistance and life on the edge of empire.

---

8. People are attached to Bonhoeffer for many different reasons. Isabel Carter Heyward speaks for many when she writes: "In 1967, I did not understand what Bonhoeffer meant, but it moved me. Something rang true for me. Still now, I make no claim to understand fully Bonhoeffer's paradoxical affirmation of a God both with us and absent. But I know there is something here, something that has hounded me for years, something that has sought articulation and serious, active, attention" (*The Redemption of God: A Theology of Method Relation* [Lanham, Md., New York, London: University Press of America, 1982], 8).

9. See especially Johannes Hamel, *A Christian in East Germany,* trans. Ruth and Charles C. West (London: SCM, 1960).

While we may conclude with some confidence, then, that serious theology has for a long time assumed the end of the Constantinian era, we must nevertheless underscore, in my opinion, the fact that it has done so largely at the level precisely of *an assumption.* On the whole, professional theology has been of little service in interpreting this metamorphosis to the churches, or of helping those within them whose dissatisfactions with the status quo render them open to such instruction, to acquire a thoughtful and hopeful attitude toward this immense change—a change that, apart from such reflective assistance, can be truly confusing and discouraging. Professional theology is, in any case, as we have noted heretofore, frequently disdainful of the churches; and in no area of Christian experience today is this more unfortunate than in connection with the need, on the part of serious lay and clerical members of the *soma Christou,* to understand what is happening to once-powerful Christendom—that is, to them personally and corporately. As with every other sort of dying, people can be expected to enter into this death only if they can be helped to believe that exposure to so painful an ending can become both meaningful and productive of hope. Something comparable to the intellectual-spiritual journey of the theologians themselves must be made available to those who do not have the benefits of years of professional training and full-time study. To *assume* the end of Christendom, to speak out of that assumption and to presuppose that it is both self-evident and purposeful: this is clearly not enough.

It is particularly inadequate—indeed, it is counterproductive—when, on the basis of solidarity with this or that minority, the voices of theological professionals convey to Christians traditionally associated with the dominant culture that in any case they could not understand the whole affair, being, as they are, denizens of the establishment. It is one of the limitations of the most publicized theologies of the second half of the present century that, unlike that of the Barths, Niebuhrs, and Tillichs of the first half, they appear to many so hostile to the old mainstream Protestant or Catholic Christianity that they fail to effect in the latter the conscientization that might otherwise be possible. If—in North America particularly—ordinary Christians and congregations are so confused by Christendom's reduction that they can only repress the awareness of it or, alternatively, run after the latest promotors of "church growth," some of the responsibility for this must be laid at the doorstep of the professional theologians, who have abandoned the churches in favor of professional dialogue or discourse with others who share their particular interests.

This said, it must also be acknowledged that a few Christian and other academics *have* attempted to interpret the end of Christendom in ways comprehensible to nonprofessionals, and, in order to set the tone for what follows in this chapter, I wish to outline three such attempts—one by a renowned journalist and lay Christian; one by perhaps the most significant Roman Catholic theologian of our epoch; and one that comes to Christians from the perspective of Jewish experience as a diaspora people.

a. Malcolm Muggeridge. In two popular lectures delivered at the University of Waterloo (Ontario) in 1978, the late Malcolm Muggeridge, in his usual brilliant and somewhat satirical style, offers a no-nonsense approach to our topic.[10] He begins by noting the obvious, but an obvious that is rarely noted: "Christendom . . . is something different from Christianity." He identifies the former as "the administrative or power structure, based on the Christian religion and constructed by men." It may be a form of Christianity, or an attempt to institutionalize it; but to identify "the everlasting truth of the Christian revelation" with any such institutionalization is like identifying laws with justice or moral codes with goodness.[11]

Christianity is not only different from Christendom, Muggeridge insists, it is incompatible with Christendom. "The founder of Christianity was, of course, Christ. The founder of Christendom I suppose could be named the Emperor Constantine." He continues:

> Christianity began with the Incarnation, that stupendous moment when, as it is put so marvellously in the Apocryphal book of Ecclesiasticus, "While all things were in quiet silence and the night was in the midst of her swift course, Thine Almighty Word leaped down from heaven, out of Thy royal Throne. . . . "
>
> Christendom, on the other hand, began when Constantine, as an act of policy, decided to tolerate, indeed positively to favour, the Church, uniting it to the secular state by the closest possible ties. . . . A parallel situation which might easily arise would be if the revival of Christianity in the U.S.S.R. reached a point at which the ruling oligarchy, the Communist Party, decided to absorb it into the state as an alternative ideology to Marxism, in the same sort of way that under the Czars the Russian Orthodox Church was absorbed into the state.[12]

But as such an absorption illustrates, it constitutes a terrible distortion of Christianity, so that "You might even say that Christ himself abolished Christendom before it began by stating that his kingdom was not of this world."[13]

Muggeridge does not doubt that Christendom "has played a tremendous role in the art and literature, in the mores and jurisprudence, in the architec-

---

10. Malcolm Muggeridge, *The End of Christendom* (Grand Rapids: Wm B. Eerdmans, 1980).
11. Ibid., 13.
12. Ibid., 14.
13. Ibid.

ture, values, institutions, and whole way of life of Western man during the centuries of its dominance in the world."[14] But as the West itself declines, its official *cultus* "comes to have an evermore ghostly air about it, to the point that it seems to belong to history already, rather than to present-day actuality."[15]

Foremost among the factors contributing to this decay, in the view of the former editor of *Punch,* is "a sort of death wish at the heart of [Christendom], in the guise of what we call liberalism":

> Previous civilizations have been overthrown from without by the incursion of barbarian hordes. Christendom has dreamed up its own dissolution in the minds of its own intellectual elite. Our barbarians are home products, indoctrinated at the public expense, urged on by the media systematically stage by stage, dismantling Christendom, depreciating and depricating all its values.[16]

Christendom, for Muggeridge, is a human civilization, and like Gibbon, Toynbee, and many others, he believes that "civilizations wax and wane."[17] That this has been happening to Christendom should not surprise us: "Why should anyone expect Christendom to go on forever, or see in its impending collapse a cosmic catastrophe?"[18] He reminds his hearers of Augustine when he was told of the sack of Rome. Augustine was not pleased about Rome's fall; he was a Roman! But he told his congregation: "All earthly cities are vulnerable. Men build them and men destroy them. At the same time there is the City of God which men did not build and cannot destroy and which is everlasting."[19]

For faith, moreover, the collapse of civilizations is sobering and instructive, "for it is in the breakdown of power rather than its triumph that men may discern its true nature and in an awareness of their own inadequacy when confronted with such a breakdown that they can best understand who

---

14. Ibid., 16.
15. Ibid., 16–17.
16. Ibid., 17. Martin E. Marty had something similar in mind when he wrote about "The Golden Age That Never Was" in an editorial for *The Christian Century* 111, no. 11 (April 16, 1994): 367: "Self-hating white tribespeople in the American academies regard as innocent the Maya and Aztecs and the other people whose paradise Columbus' people encountered. But the encountered people were not all that gentle and nature-loving. The Golden Age romantics necessarily overlook the tens of thousands of human sacrifices that the native peoples perpetrated, their constant warring, and the despoiling of environments from which they had to move on. But let someone claim that there was a Golden Age when the goddesses ruled, or when there was 'harmonic convergence' or when the tribes had their way, and many respond with suspicionless affirmations."
17. Ibid., 21.
18. Ibid.
19. Ibid., 22.

and what they are."[20] With the end of Christendom, the disciple community is able to discover again its real and true foundation, which is only tangentially related to Christian civilization: "amidst the shambles of a fallen Christendom, I feel a renewed confidence in the light of the Christian revelation with which it first began. I should hate you to think that this view that I've put before you is a pessimistic view. Strangely enough, I believe it to be the only way to a proper and real hope."[21]

We shall hear echoes of these very same sentiments from our second exemplar of creative responses to the demise of Christendom, especially the disclaimer that this is not and must not become an occasion for pessimism. It is important in that regard to grasp that, so far, Malcolm Muggeridge has been considering Christendom's end. His hope is not reserved for what this ending makes possible only, but it is associated nevertheless with the ending as such; for, as he says, there is truth in such an ending—truth about the nature of "power," and truth about the misalliance of faith with power. The termination of a duplicitous and misconstrued experiment, however interesting or productive of some beneficial side-effects it might have been, contains a kind of satisfaction for those who had hoped for something more authentic.

But of course the real source of Muggeridge's hope is that Christendom's ending makes possible a new beginning for Christ's discipleship. The second lecture, presupposing the title of the first ("The End of Christendom") is, "But Not of Christ."

We should not, however, be naive. This is the more difficult part of the subject! Standing at the beginning of a new phase of the Christian movement, none of us is very wise concerning the form that it might take or even ought to take. As Loren Mead has written, "We are surrounded by the relics of the Christendom Paradigm, a paradigm that has largely ceased to work. But the relics hold us hostage to the past and make it difficult to create a new paradigm that can be as compelling for the next age as the Christendom Paradigm has been for the past age."[22]

In view of this reality, one is not surprised that Muggeridge's second lecture lacks the concreteness of the first. He spends most of his time telling his audience about what has happened in the U.S.S.R. Writing in 1980, he may be forgiven for assuming that the renewal of Christianity in "the countries that have been most drastically subjected to the oppression and brainwashing and general influence of the first overtly atheistic and materialistic regime to

---

20. Ibid., 23.
21. Ibid.
22. Loren Mead, *The Once and Future Church* (Bethesda, Md.: Alban Institute, 1991), 18. Mead's suggestion that the old paradigm was "compelling" is undoubtedly true; but I am made somewhat nervous by his juxtaposition of this with the "compelling" character of what he hopes may replace it!

exist on earth" is "a wonderful sign that has been vouchsafed us." The future both of the Russian state and Christianity within it has not been so splendid ("the most extraordinary single fact of the twentieth century"[23]) as it could seem to be in the 1980s. This does not invalidate, however, the testimonies of Russians known to the journalist Muggeridge, including the authors Aleksandr Solzhenitsyn and Anatoli Kusnyetsov, whose Christian faith was immensely deepened by their experience of life in a state ruled by ideology and tyranny. It would not be the first time that absolute negation has served the positive force of truth and life. "The only possible response to absolute power is the absolute love which our Lord brought into the world," Kusnyetsov told Muggeridge. And Muggeridge himself, who had been critical of Christianity, acknowledges in this lecture that he became a Christian because of his disillusionment with the world of "fantasy, in which my own occupation [as a journalist] has particularly involved me."[24]

Although he does not tell us, then, what kind of future we should anticipate and prepare for, Malcolm Muggeridge does remind us of what, as Christians, we must consider the central reality of our reflections as we look toward that future; it is signified by the name Jesus Christ:

> The shadow in [Plato's] cave is like the media world of shadows. In contradistinction, Christ shows what life really is, and what our true destiny is. . . . By identifying ourselves with Christ, by absorbing ourselves in his teaching, by living out the drama of his life with him, including especially the passion, that powerhouse of love and creativity—by living with, by, and in him, we can be reborn to become new men and women in a new world.[25]

Thus in a way that many learned theologians miss, the journalist Muggeridge turns the mind of the church to its source, the body to its head. We may not know the shape of the future. All of our anticipations and experiments may fail. But we may and must know that source, and the present neglect of Christology (rather, of Jesus Christ!) by professional theology and by the churches may be, therefore, the most basic reason that we are having such difficulty with our ecclesiology. For Muggeridge, the breakdown of Western Christian civilization is the occasion that makes possible—and necessary—a return to this one foundation:

> Let us then as Christians rejoice that we see around us on every hand the decay of the institutions and instruments of power, see intimations of empires falling to pieces, money in total disarray, dictators and parliamentarians alike non-

---

23. *The End of Christendom*, 38.
24. Ibid., 53.
25. Ibid., 53–54.

plussed by the confusion and conflicts which encompass them. For it is presently when every earthly hope has been explored and found wanting, when every possibility of help from earthly sources has been sought and is not forthcoming, when every recourse this world offers, moral as well as material, has been explored to no effect, when in the shivering cold the last faggot has been thrown on the fire and in the gathering darkness every glimmer of light has finally flickered out, it's then that Christ's hand reaches out sure and firm. Then Christ's words bring their irrepressible comfort, then his light shines brightest, abolishing the darkness forever.[26]

Such doxological language may jar the sensibilities of professionals, but it is too close to the language of the Scriptures for *Christian* professionals to ignore. It is, besides, the language of faith's *confession.*

b. Karl Rahner. The second exemplification of a creative response to the metamorphosis of the Christian movement comes from a source that is in some respects surprising. That Karl Rahner, one of the most trusted Roman Catholic theologians of our time, should have written about the Christian future in the way that he did in his *Mission and Grace* is surprising, not because it is inconsistent with his other views, but because it is so very different from the past that Rome, more than any other branch of Christendom, has "enjoyed"—and from the future that many of Rome's present-day ecclesiastical leaders would like to bring about.

"My thesis," writes Rahner under the general heading "Christians in the Modern World,"

> is this: Insofar as our outlook is really based on today, and looking towards tomorrow, the present situation of Christians can be characterized as that of a *diaspora;* and this signifies, in terms of the history of salvation, a "must," from which we may and must draw conclusions about our behaviour as Christians.[27]

The diaspora status and mandate of Christianity may not be what we wish for, or even what God wills; but it is nonetheless a reality: "there are no longer any Christian countries. . . ; Christianity (though in very varying proportions) exists *everywhere* in the world, and everywhere as a diaspora. It is effectually, *in terms of numbers,* a minority *everywhere.*"[28]

Presumably the great Rahner knew very well, when he wrote this, that many Americans, and perhaps Poles, would dispute the fact. But he will not qualify the statement:

---

26. Ibid., 56.
27. Karl Rahner, *Mission and Grace: Essays in Pastoral Theology,* vol. 1, trans. Cecily Hastings (London: Sheed and Ward, 1963), 20.
28. Ibid., 25. (Rahner's italics.)

On the contrary, the Christendom of the Middle Ages and after, peasant and individualistic petty-bourgeois Christendom, is going to disappear with ever-increasing speed. For the causes which have brought about this process in the West are still at work and have not yet had their full effect.[29]

Like every other "earthly institution," the church wants to be successful—to achieve "total victory." But this was not what "her Founder" promised. Christ did promise that his church would endure "until the end of time," but he also promised

> that his work would also be a sign of contradiction and persecution, of dire and (in secular terms) desperate combat; that love would grow cold; that he, and his disciples, would be persecuted in the name of God; that the struggle would narrow down to an ever more critical point; that the victory of Christianity would not be the fruit of immanent development and widening and a steady, progressive leavening of the world, but would come as the act of God coming in judgement to gather up world history into its wholly unpredictable and unexpected end.[30]

The "must" of the church's participation in the suffering of the Christ was obscured during the Middle Ages, the high point of Christendom, when the only persecution came "from outside [the] closed culture" of Western Christendom, which was "the result of temporal, secular combinations of historical forces [and] a fact of cultural history rather than of theology." But with the advent of the modern world in the Reformation, Renaissance, and Enlightenment, the church finds herself "surrounded by non-Christians," and "living in a culture, in a State, amidst political movements, economic activity, science and art which are conducted *not* simply and solely by Christians"— a *"diaspora everywhere."* [31]

In this situation, certain consequences accrue for the Christian life. (1) Faith "is constantly threatened from without." Christianity can count on little or no support

> from institutional morality, custom, civil law, tradition, public opinion, normal conformism, etc. Thus . . . each individual must be won to it afresh, and such recruitment can appeal only to personal decision, to what is independent and individual in a man, not to that in him which makes him a homogeneous part of the masses. . . . Christianity ceases to be a religion of growth and becomes a religion of choice. Obviously Christians will still give institutional form to

---

29. Ibid.
30. Ibid., 26–27.
31. Ibid., 32–33. (Rahner's italics.)

their lives, over and above the institutional element in the Church herself; they will try to transmit to their children the faith that they themselves have won in a personal decision, they will develop and try to preserve Christian habits of morality, customs, practices, associations and organizations. But by and large the situation will remain one of choice, not of natural growth; of a personal achievement constantly renewed amid perilous surroundings.[32]

(2) Christians will have to learn to live within the larger culture, and they will realize that—contrary to ecclesiastical "propaganda"—it is not composed only of disintegration and decay. (3) "If it is to remain alive at all," the diaspora church will have to be "a church of the laity," who "will have ecclesiastical duties . . . as they did in the early church." Rahner even suggests that, "*sociologically* speaking, the Church of the diaspora has the character of a sect, in contrast to that of a Church of the vast mass of people, a Church *in possession*"; and, as such, "the diaspora Church has the advantage that her 'sect' character gives her, and the duty constantly to overcome the dangers inherent in it."[33] (4) It will no longer constitute a matter of privilege and status to be a member of the clergy.[34] (5) The relationship of Church and State will be much less confrontational. In the past, this characteristic feature of Christendom was due to the fact that a rivalry between church and state was built into the situation in which nearly everyone was a member of both simultaneously.[35]

According to Rahner, we "must" accommodate ourselves to the diaspora situation, and this "must" emanates not only from our actual, empirical condition, but from the same gracious sovereignty that is contained in the journey of Jesus toward the cross. But we must and may do this *joyfully*. But note: the condition necessary to such an attitude is that we cease striving for "total victory": "We have still not fully wakened from our dream of a homogeneous Christian West. It often leads us to react furiously and in a false context when something happens to shake us out of the dream. . . . I had better refrain from giving examples."[36]

When we say that we have the right to make a cool, dispassionate reckoning with the fact that the Church is a *diaspora,* we mean, understanding it rightly, the very opposite of resignation and defeatism. If we once have the courage to give up our defence of the old facades which have nothing or very little behind them; if we cease to maintain, in public, the pretence of a universal Chris-

---

32. Ibid., 33–34.
33. Ibid., 36.
34. Ibid., 37.
35. Ibid.
36. Ibid., 38.

tendom; if we stop straining every nerve to get *everybody* baptized, to get *everybody* married in church and onto our registers (even when success means only, at bottom, a victory for tradition, custom, and ancestry, not for true faith and interior conviction); if, by letting all of this go, we visibly relieve Christianity of the burdensome impression that it accepts responsibility for everything that goes on under this Christian top dressing, the impression that Christianity is *natura sua* a sort of Everyman's Religious Varnish, a folk-religion (at the same level as folk-costumes)—*then* we can be free for real missionary adventure and apostolic self-confidence. Then we should not need to sigh and say, "We *still* have 15 percent;" we could say, "We're up to 17 percent already." Just where is it written that *we* must have the whole 100 percent? God must have all. We hope that he takes pity on all and will have all indeed. But we cannot say that he is doing so only if we, meaning the Church, have everybody.[37]

Again,

Let us get away from the tyranny of statistics. For the next hundred years they are always going to be against us, if we ever let them speak out of turn. *One* real conversion in a great city is something more splendid than the spectacle of a whole remote village going to the sacraments.[38]

It is tempting to ask why the analysis of this great Catholic scholar has been so little discussed by the hierarchies of his own and other churches. It is even more tempting (and for Protestants more appropriate) to ask why such an analysis is still unheard of in North America. Is it really pertinent only to Europe? We shall return to this question presently.

c. Irving Greenberg. For the third exemplification of creative response to the transformation of Christianity I turn to a non-Christian source—to a Jew; and I do so for reasons that ought to be evident to readers of this trilogy. For I do not regard Judaism as another—and certainly not as a rival—religion where Christianity is concerned, but as the parental faith, whose far longer experience in the world (not least of all the world of Christendom!) is instructive for Christians at every point. This may be especially true where ecclesiology is concerned. If with Rahner we consider the Christian future to be the future of a diaspora, what better source of understanding is available to us than that people that has in fact existed as a diaspora throughout the greater share of its history? Although Judaism has not understood itself to be a missionary faith in the newer Testamental sense, and certainly not in the Constantinian sense of "total victory" (Rahner), it has understood itself

---

37. Ibid., 51.
38. Ibid., 48.

to be a witness in the world to God's humanizing work; and in the long run that may be precisely the best and most faithful kind of mission for Christians also to assume, now that we have tried the way of "total victory" and found it wanting.

In an essay that is really about the prospects of a new kind of trusting relationship between Jews and Christians in the post-Holocaust situation, the U.S. theologian Irving Greenberg draws upon Jewish history to offer Christians a proposal that may, at this critical stage in the history of Christianity, be one of the most original and compelling challenges to be put forward. Clearly, for Greenberg, as for a few perceptive Christian thinkers,[39] the Holocaust is that moment in time when the Constantinian form of the Christian religion reveals itself in all its potential and real violence, a violence that is finally more *self*-destructive than it is destructive of Judaism. Very modestly, Greenberg writes: "One might suggest that the Holocaust has its primary impact on Judaism. Nevertheless, as a Jewish theologian, I suggest that Christianity also cannot be untouched by the event."[40]

Christianity "cannot be untouched by the event" because, in the ghastly light of Auschwitz, Christians must (and some have) come to know that the supersessionistic assumptions of their faith as it has been practiced historically are based on an ideological triumphalism (in our terms, a *theologia gloriae*) that drives to the extinction of other religions, beginning with the parental faith.

> The supersessionist interpretation continually tempted Christianity into being neither the gospel of love it wanted to be, nor the outgrowth of Judaism seeking to reach out and realize Israel's messianic dream that it could have been. Christianity was continually led to become an otherworldly, triumphalist religion that put its own mother down; it spit into the well from which it drank.[41]

Wherever this is recognized, Christians are caused to understand that their faith has to undergo a radical transformation. Irving Greenberg's proposal is that at this point in its history "Christianity will have to enter its second stage."[42]

What does "second stage" mean? It is a reference to Jewish history: with the destruction of the Second Temple in 70 C.E., Jewish faith moved to the

---

39. In the essay ("The Relationship of Judaism and Christianity: Toward a New Organic Model," in *Quarterly Review* 4, no. 4 [Winter 1984]: 1), Greenberg mentions Alice and Roy Eckhardt, "whose fundamental critique of Christianity is surely one of the most sustained and devastating moral analyses in its history," as well as Paul van Buren, Rosemary Ruether, and Eva Fleischner.
40. Ibid., 10.
41. Ibid., 5.
42. Ibid., 10.

synagogue and to its rabbinic phase. Christians interpreted the destruction of the temple as the sign of God's rejection of the Jews (see Matt. 24:1–2), but "The Christians were wrong. Judaism did not disappear, the Jews did not disintegrate."[43] The rabbis taught that, while the destruction of the temple was "punishment for sins," it was also the means of a new way for the Jewish people to move into the future: "The lesson of the destruction was not that God had abandoned Israel, but that God was deliberately hiding in order to evoke a greater response, a greater participation in the covenantal way."[44] The religion of the temple was a religion of the sacred and of God's awesome power and majesty, by comparison with which that of the synagogue could be interpreted "as a kind of 'secularization' process":[45] "The synagogue is the place you go to when God no longer speaks to you."[46] But God's silence does not mean God's absence: "The deepest paradox of the rabbis' teaching was that the more God is hidden, the more God is present."

> The difference is that in the good old days one did not have to look—the divine illumination lit up the world. Now, one must look. If one looks more deeply, one will see God everywhere. *But to see God everywhere, one must understand. The key to understanding is learning.* The Jewish people, in biblical times an ignorant peasantry, awed by sacramental, revelatory experiences in the temple, were trained by the rabbis to learn and study. Now that God no longer speaks directly, how would you know what God wants? The answer is to go to the synagogue; there one does not see God visibly, but one prays and asks God for guidance. . . . [47]

The "transformation of Judaism" that Greenberg calls its "second stage" was "the triumph of the rabbis"; and its special genius was its creation among Jews of a sense of "greater responsibility" for the world. The covenantal basis of the faith is reaffirmed and renewed in rabbinic Judaism—"Indeed, the rabbis came to the conclusion that they had lived through events comparable almost to a reacceptance of the covenant." For now the God-centered, "sacramental" aspect of the faith was complemented by a human "participatory" and "'laic'" response, which was of course basic to the covenantal idea from the outset.

When therefore Greenberg suggests that Christianity, having experienced the effective ending of what we have called its Christendom phase, in the aftermath of the Holocaust "will have to enter *its* second stage," he has some

---

43. Ibid., 7.
44. Ibid.
45. Ibid.
46. Ibid., 8.
47. Ibid. (My italics.)

quite specific things in mind. *First,* the otherworldliness that has been Christianity's temptation would be set aside in favor of a greater sense of responsibility for this world—what Dietrich Bonhoeffer called "responsibility for history."[48] "In this stage, Christianity would make the move from being out of history to taking power, *i.e. taking part in the struggle to exercise power to advance redemption.*" Thus Christianity would manifest in this stage "a greater 'worldliness' in [its] holiness."[49]

Second, the second stage of Christianity, if it were patterned on the rabbinic experience, would accentuate "learning and understanding" in place of "hierarchy and mystery." It would involve *the laity* in a faith that "seeks understanding," rather than one that accepts, on the authority of hierarchic governance, what is deemed truth and obedience. It would substitute for the "mystification" of sacerdotalism and vapid "spirituality" (the latter, I think, is what Greenberg means by "mystery" in this context) a discipleship that entails study and reflection—not the detached and academic approach that may be sugested by these and similar terms, of which Greenberg is just as critical as I; but engaged thought—thought that is also prayer.[50] Judaism survived *its* apparent ending (the destruction of the Second Temple) because it became a *thinking* faith. "Learning and understanding" in the diaspora situation could no longer be the pursuits of the few wise ones whose relative leisure and aptitude made such activity possible; it had to become the survival strategem of a people, *all* of whose members must at some level of seriousness devote themselves to disciplined recall of the tradition as it impinged upon the problematic of the present.

Greenberg's remarkable essay is a challenge to Christianity as it faces the destruction of its own long-established sacerdotal and triumphalist form. Stating the challenge in a single question, we may ask, Can the church that has been temple now become synagogue? It does not mean, necessarily, that such a church would lose touch with the grandeur, beauty, and true mystery of "the temple"—Judaism never has. But it does mean that it would have to cease relying on the power, authority, and mystique that the temple in both its Judaic and its Christian expressions represents; it would have to become

---

48. The reference to Bonhoeffer is not accidental. In an insightful discussion of the similarity between Greenberg and Bonhoeffer, Larry Rasmussen notes that both thinkers call for a break with a "religious" past that used religion as an excuse for noninvolvement. God's sovereignty must not become the rationale for human passivity. The covenant involves the human partner in a greater concern for "the fate of the earth" (J. Schell) than, apart from its relationship with God, humanity either has or wishes to have. (See Larry Rasmussen with Renate Bethge, *Dietrich Bonhoeffer and His Significance for North Americans* [Minneapolis: Fortress Press, 1990], 120.)

49. Ibid.

50. See my *When You Pray: Thinking Your Way Into God's World* (Valley Forge: Judson Press, 1987).

a genuinely covenantal community, both in terms of its understanding and its acting in the world.[51]

Greenberg shares with many of us the sense that we are living at a time of "great destruction," and therefore one in which any faith that lays claim to "the tradition of Jerusalem" must "summon up an even greater response of life and of re-creation."[52] A church that seeks *its own preservation* in such a time can only be "a part of the problem." A church that discovers God's presence in the suffering world, relinquishes its quest for "total victory" *over* the world, and follows its Lord *into* the world, may contribute much to the world's renewal.

15. Establishment and Disestablishment in North America

15.1. The New World Variation on the Christendom Theme. In introducing this chapter, I observed that it would be hard to live in the world today— and indeed for some time past—and be oblivious to the great transformation through which the Christian religion is passing. There are parts of the United States of America, however, where it seems quite possible to believe still that Christendom is alive and well, perhaps even flourishing.[53] *And precisely this constitutes a source of profound frustration for all informed and thinking Christians attempting to confess the faith within this context.*

It is indicative of the tenacity of the New World variation on the Christendom theme that most American Christians would find the previous sentence surprising, perhaps even deeply offensive. Should not all Christians, whatever their particular affiliation or theological stance, rejoice that so many American citizens still announce themselves as Christians, and "born-again" Christians at that? Is it not perhaps the chief source of America's greatness that this is so? While an atheistic empire dramatically collapses, the other

---

51. In my *Has the Church a Future?* (Philadelphia: Westminster Press, 1980), 117ff., I drew upon this same distinction between temple and synagogue (similar to cathedral and parish) to suggest a practical model of ecclesiastical life for the church of the future.

52. Ibid., 10.

53. This is much less true of Canada, though in recent years there has been a certain "spill-over" of American-based evangelicalism in parts of Canada; in considerable measure this is due to the ubiquitous influence of television. Like most northern peoples, Canadians manifest a strong penchant for skepticism. "True belief" does not sit well with a people whose literature revolves around the theme of "survival" (Margaret Atwood). The assessment of the Canadian church historian, John Webster Grant, as reported by Robert T. Handy, seems to me an accurate one: "Conservative evangelicals generally still worked for a Christian nation. For example, from his Canadian perspective, Grant declared that they 'now seem to constitute the only important segment of the church that seriously believes in the continued existence of Christendom . . . not to the European version but to the rurally based Protestant piety of North American Bible belts'" (*A History of the Churches in the United States and Canada* [Oxford University Press, 1977], 421).

great imperium of the modern world endures: is its endurance not due precisely to its godliness? While the nations of Western Europe, once the flagship of Christendom, flounder spiritually and embrace godless philosophies, America clings to its sense of purpose and mission in the world of the nations as to a divine vocation; is this not evidence of the depth and sincerity of its Christian faith? And is it not a betrayal of Christianity itself, as well as of Christian America, when someone actually claiming to be a Christian, announces that just this "Christianity" is a source of deep frustration?

I shall defend the assertion, but first it is necessary to enter a caveat: the critique of Christian America is not aimed at individual believers, or even at churches and denominations. Individuals are drawn into states of belief or credulity by a great variety of influences upon their lives, and if some of these influences are questionable from a theological point of view (for example, the sheer power of convention in a self-consciously "religious" culture), the problem cannot be attributed straightaway to the individuals concerned. Likewise, churches and whole denominations may be driven by a cultural ethos that demands nothing by way of critical thinking; they follow the law of supply and demand, and the trajectory of their own histories. One may wish that the faith-sources that such churches honor, particularly the Scriptures, would break through the barrier of religion and raise questions about the compatibility of Christianity with even so humane an empire as the United States; but one has to recognize how cultural forces greater even than the influence of the Bible, which is interpreted largely on the basis of hermeneutical principles drawn from the social fabric itself, can sway entire denominations.

The judgment that precisely American's high incidence of "Christianity" constitutes a source of frustration for serious faith is directed, then, against those cultural forces and not against persons and institutions wholly or partially in their thrall. Thus the purpose of this exercise in critical theology is not merely to define and denounce but, it is hoped, to illuminate. For only as Christians, individually and corporately, are prompted to inquire critically about the real condition of Christendom in its New World variation will there be any impetus within and around the churches to explore alternative forms of the church. As Loren Mead has rightly asserted, we are so laden with the relics of Christendom that we have enormous difficulty contemplating what might replace it.[54] I would venture even farther and say that only a minority of Christians in our context manifest a sufficient dissatisfaction with the Constantinian status quo to think alternatives necessary!

How can such a state of affairs be understood? It is, after all, a very strange situation when the country that is the world leader in applying all the as-

---

54. Mead, *The Once and Future Church*, 18.

sumptions and achievements of secular modernity, as well as manifesting most graphically modernity's malaise, is at the same time perhaps the last bastion of Western Christendom. How can this be accounted for? And why is it so problematic for faith's *confession* in our context?

In the subsections to follow, I shall offer brief responses to these two questions. The reader is encouraged to supplement them by consulting other works, including the sources I shall cite.

15.2. "Culture Religion."   The fact that the Christian religion was not permanently established in either the United States or Canada in the legal sense of the term, as occurred in Europe, has obscured the reality of Christianity's informal, cultural establishment in the New World. The truth of the matter is, surely, that our type of establishment, precisely because it is not an arrangement at the level of law but at the level of society's fundamental self-understanding, has been far more effective and enduring than any other form of Christian establishment known to history. The old, legal establishments of Europe, existing today as mere vestiges of the past, could be set aside easily enough when the arrangement was no longer useful or particularly meaningful. Forms may remain, but they are mostly devoid of existential content. In Germany, for instance, church taxes are still collected with income tax, and, although this may be changing, most citizens are willing to go along with the custom, since it does have some marginal benefits; but less than 5% percent of the population maintains an active membership in the church. This shows that legal arrangements (as we see in connection with marriage in our own context) can be effectively altered without great difficulty; covenants of a less precise, more internal character, such as longstanding friendship or the intermingling of a particular religion with the whole history of a people, are infinitely more complex and hardly susceptible to surface alterations of the legalities that may be involved in them (for example, church property taxation, prayer in public schools, references to God in public life, and so on). In short, an establishment at the level of *content,* such as Christianity in New World experience has been, is more resistant to change than one that is first and foremost at the level of *form.* The former has been aptly labelled "culture religion."

In the last half of the 1950s and the 1960s, beginning perhaps with Will Herberg's *Protestant—Catholic—Jew,*[55] a number of studies attempted to interpret and explain the phenomenon of "culture religion" in the United States. While this endeavour has not been set aside altogether, it has certainly been displaced as a lively concern in American and Canadian theological work. The reason for this is complex and could be worth pursuing. For the

---

55. Will Herberg, *Protestant—Catholic—Jew* (Garden City, N.Y.: Doubleday, 1955).

present, we may say simply that it has something to do with the prominence, during the past two or three decades, of internal ecclesiastical struggles and conflicting trends within the churches that have distracted us from the larger question of their relation to society. More recent approaches to the latter question, while often applying sociological skills with greater specificity, lack the theological-historical perceptiveness of the earlier studies.

In order to respond to the question how the tenacity of Christian establishment in our context may be accounted for, I shall return to one of these earlier discussions: Peter Berger's *The Noise of Solemn Assemblies.*[56] This work deserves to be taken up again today, for it was in advance of its time and it has not been adequately followed through.[57]

The subtitle of the book, "Christian Commitment and the Religious Establishment in America," implicitly contains Berger's thesis. Writing of "The Nature of the Religious Establishment," Berger notes the same "religious paradox" mentioned at the outset of this section: the continuing popularity of religion in a highly secularized society.

> There can be little doubt about the prominence of the religious phenenomon in America. Religion occupies a conspicuous place in American society, is accorded considerable social prestige, and appears to be a matter of active interest to large numbers of people.[58]

The author recognizes that this is not new. European commentators from de Tocqueville onwards have noted it.[59] (Indeed, de Tocqueville went well beyond recognizing the fact of American religiousness. He believed it to be a major cause of the paucity of *thought* in the nation.[60]) What is new (or was in 1961), however, is "the paradox that this religious establishment . . . is to be found in a highly secularized society."[61]

---

56. Peter Berger, *The Noise of Solemn Assemblies: Christian Commitment and the Religious Establishment in America* (Garden City, N.Y.: Doubleday and Co., 1961).

57. It is unfortunate that Berger "is often regarded as a theological right-winger." This, as a critical review of his *A Far Glory: The Quest for Faith in an Age of Credulity* (New York: Free Press, 1992) insists, is a serious misunderstanding. Berger's "entire theological effort . . . is to carry out the liberal Protestant program that runs from Kant and Schleiermacher to Troeltsch and Tillich: i.e., to correlate the content of Christian faith with the best insights of the Euro-American enlightenment" (Ralph C. Wood, in *Dialog* 33 (Summer 1994): 207).

58. Berger, *The Noise of Solemn Assemblies,* 31.

59. Ibid., 32.

60. "'The majority draws a formidable circle around thought. Within its limits, one is free: but woe to him who dares to break out of it.' Religion, he saw, was a major element in the formation of this circle. He believed there was no country in the world where the Christian religion retained a greater influence over the souls of men than in America" (Martin E. Marty, *Righteous Empire: The Protestant Experience in America* [New York: Harper Torchbooks, 1970], 90).

61. Berger, *The Noise of Solemn Assemblies,* 34.

But what is the nature of this religiousness? If examined, Berger responds, it is seen to be a strange combination of public symbol and private affair.[62] The "values" that it inculcates in individuals are not generated by its own internal content and rationale; rather, "it ratifies and sanctifies the values prevalent in the general community."[63] "Usually the most that can be said is that the church members hold the same values as everybody else, but with more emphatic solemnity."[64] Theology, which "is rather a bad word" not only among the laity but with most clergy, scarcely functions in this process of value-transference; in fact, "the intellectual in the religious institution is as much a marginal man [sic] as he is in the culture at large. Seminaries for the training of religious functionaries, with some noteworthy exceptions, are frankly 'professional schools'. . . ."[65]

The establishment of Christianity in America, so different in this respect from the Church of England or the Lutheran Church in Sweden, consists, then, in the identification of Christianity with the values commonly held by Americans:

> American society possesses a cultural religion that is vaguely derived from the Judaeo-Christian tradition and that contains values generally held by most Americans. The cultural religion gives solemn ratification to these values. The cultural religion is politically established on all levels of government, receiving from the state both moral and economic support. The religious denominations, whatever else they may believe or practice, are carriers of this cultural religion. Affiliation with a religious denomination thus becomes *ipso facto* an act of allegiance to the common political creed. Disaffiliation, in turn, renders an individual not only religiously but also politically suspect.[66]

The conclusion to which Berger is led in his analysis of the Christian establishment in the U.S.A. is stark indeed: it is that *"The social irrelevance of the religious establishment is its functionality."*[67] That is, "It is functional precisely to the degree in which it is passive rather than active, acted upon rather than acting." In other words, the Christian establishment is important to America, including the state and all dominant institutions, precisely because it *contributes nothing distinctively its own* but serves as an excellent medium for conferring upon successive generations the "optimistic ideology"[68] of the society.

---

62. Similar claims were brought forward a year after the publication of Berger's book by William Stringfellow in his *A Private and Public Faith* (Grand Rapids: Wm B. Eerdmans, 1962).
63. Berger, *The Noise of Solemn Assemblies*, 41.
64. Ibid.
65. Ibid., 45.
66. Ibid., 63.
67. Ibid., 103. (Berger's italics.)
68. Ibid., 104. (My italics.)

"The failure to see this," Berger concludes, "makes impossible any meaningful Christian thinking about the American situation."[69]

Later, we shall return to the second part of Berger's analysis, "The Task of Disestablishment." For now, we shall close by drawing attention to a very significant question and answer that he includes in an "Interlude" between the two parts of his essay.

The question could be asked, Berger acknowledges, of whether "there is any real reason for concern." "So what?"—What does it matter, what is lost, if Christianity serves such a "function" as this? What is left out by a Christian establishment of this kind? "Our answer," the author responds, "will be quite simple: It leaves out the Christian faith."[70] If a people is ready to look upon religion in this way—as an aid to social stability, a mode of "symbolic integration,"[71] a "sort of conscience which allows the society to get along with a minimum of policemen,"[72] so be it.

> Our churches can then be accepted as an essentially harmless ingredient of a social reality that we are willing to live with. There is one crucial assumption, however, that we must be willing to abandon—namely, *the assumption that these churches have anything to do with the message of the New Testament and the historic experience of the Hebrew people.*[73]

15.3. A Matter of Truth.   Peter Berger's discussion of the nature of the Christian establishment in the United States of America is a response to our first question, how to account for the continuing existence and power of Christendom in this context. It is not, in our outline of it, a detailed response; but it is still in my opinion one of the clearest and most challenging to date. We shall acknowledge later that it is in some important respects "dated," but in essence it seems entirely pertinent still, and in some ways more immediately so than when it was written some thirty-five years ago.

With the concluding observations from the "Interlude," however, we have entered the sphere of the second question announced earlier: Why is this form of establishment, even more than the *de jure* establishments of Europe at their height, a source of profound frustration to serious Christians? Berger's answer is very straightforward: because it "leaves out" Christian faith! In what follows, I shall maintain essentially the same thing, but I shall do so according to the mode of discourse adopted throughout this study. I shall say, in effect, that our kind of establishment on this continent, especially but

---

69. Ibid.
70. Ibid., 112.
71. Ibid., 51.
72. Ibid., 72.
73. Ibid., 112. (My italics.)

not only in the United States, makes it extremely difficult actually to *confess the faith.*

There is a sense in which it is the perennial function of religion in human life and society to inspire contentment while keeping before human beings a vision of what might be. The human spirit is wonderfully prone to melancholy and resignation. Given the human condition as we have considered it in the second volume, that is hardly surprising.[74] A creature that not only is a creature, but knows it and reckons daily with the awesome boundaries of that condition, cannot be expected to be both content and expectant. All religion, in one way or another, counters the sorrow engendered by the naked knowledge of our vulnerability through the presentation of reality as a larger and friendlier prospect. As a religion, Christianity is heir to this perennial role, the purveyor of peace and hope.

As we observed in the first volume, however, there is a limit beyond which the hope that religion fosters must not go—or rather, if it does exceed it, which religion regularly does, it leads people, through *false* expectation and self-deception, to forms of delusion more ultimately harmful than their perhaps "natural" predisposition to disillusionment.

That limit, as we heard from Ernest Becker,[75] is the indecipherable and no doubt constantly moving boundary line between "creative illusion" and the fabrication of visions that have literally lost touch with this world. The difference between what Becker calls *"creative* illusion" and mere illusion—the spinning of beautiful worlds or afterworlds out of thin air—is the difference between truthfulness and neurotic repression. The creative illusion provides people with a framework of meaning necessary to their exposure to the real terror and pathos of life, the ecstacy as well as the agony; they are enabled by such a "metaphysic of hope" to be *more honest* about the real world than, without such a frame of reference, they could ever have been. The fabrication of ideal states, on the other hand, only functions to assist those who cannot or will not face their actual condition to do so more successfully—and, in the process, to court neuroses in themselves and pain in those round about them, on whom they inflict their repressed consciousness of the negations that their belief systems cannot wholly dispel and cannot absorb.

Christian faith, when it is genuine, Becker believes, constitutes such a "creative illusion." That is, it permits the kind of hope that is an open dialogue with hope's antithesis. What I have called "the data of despair" does not have to be banished from Christian consciousness. Indeed, writes Becker, quoting Paul Tillich's *The Courage to Be,* "the bold goal of [Christian] courage is to absorb into one's own being the maximum amount of non-being." While

---

74. *Professing the Faith,* Part II, 187–362.
75. *Thinking the Faith,* esp. 179–89.

truth in its fullness ever eludes finite creatures, the Christian, through faith, is delivered from the frantic pursuit of "half-truths or even organized delusions."[76] Christians do not have to lie about life, with all of its ambiguous mixture of good and evil, pleasure and pain, in order to sustain hope.

This is the real, indeed the only, answer to Marx's otherwise quite correct dictum that religion is humankind's "opiate." Religion will be an opiate where it functions as an ideology enabling a flight from reality; furthermore, as the downfall of the Soviets dramatically illustrates, Marxism itself, like other very positive political ideologies, easily degenerates into such a religion. But faith, as distinct from religion in this sense, where it is most at work in the lives of individuals and Christian communities, drives them farther and farther into the dark places of public and private existence (consider Bonhoeffer) and enables them, here and there, now and then, to see the light that shines only *in* the darkness.

It is for this reason that Christian triumphalism, the *theologia gloriae,* has been the object of our primary critique throughout this series; for in its various forms and guises, the "theology of glory" is always such a fabrication. Capitalizing on the all-too-human desire for quick and easy hope, it exaggerates the positive and minimizes "the data of despair." It is nothing more or less than an ideology of triumph, drawing roughly upon the more obviously triumphant elements of the Christian story, and serving the human instinct to banish from view all that negates. Its repressive capacities, when applied to powerful peoples, naturally express themselves in *oppressive* ways; for the modicum of truthfulness that even the cleverest ideology cannot destroy will lead to disbelief unless the source of contradiction can be located outside the system in some "enemy." Far from being an innocent agent of calm and stability, therefore, the theology of glory contains a high potentiality for aggressive behavior. Like every other ideology, and more fiercely than most secular illusions, it drives its adherents to try always to *make* the world conform to its theory. This drive, which was tragically manifested in the brutality of the Nazis and the Stalinists, is found in less virulent but not less driven forms in all those Christians past and present who were and are determined to make the world Christian—to "conquer" it for Christ.

Christendom as a political phenomenon, "a fact of cultural history rather than of theology" (Rahner), by definition requires a theology of glory. And Christendom in its American form, although significantly different from the classical Constantinianism of Old World history, is in this respect no exception to the rule. It is not accidental that the most "successful" churches and denominations in the United States are institutions that proclaim simple, positive messages in which there is room for neither dialogue nor doubt; and

---

76. Berger, *The Noise of Solemn Assemblies,* 10.

it is not accidental, either, that these same bodies have come to occupy the favored place among the present-day conservative political leadership of the nation, even though in order to do so they have had, in many cases, to relinquish their sectarian pasts and their cherished sense of being holy remnants in a lost and wicked age.

It also belongs to this scenario that the older, once-mainline churches that are unable to embrace straightforward versions of this same positive religion are increasingly edged toward the social periphery. As we shall argue presently, they *are being disestablished* despite their vain efforts to remain at center stage, because, at a time when the imperium is in special need of unqualifiedly positive religion, the religious who do not or cannot supply this demand have moved beyond Berger's state of "social irrelevance" to political superfluity and, in some cases, suspicion. We shall return to this.

That the so-called Christian Right has risen to political prominence in the U.S.A. within the past two decades can be no surprise to anyone who understands the dynamics of the relation between Christendom and the theology of glory. Like imperial Rome in the earlier part of the fourth century, when it was still powerful but inwardly suffering from the diseases that would eventually lay it open to the barbarians, the U.S.A. is today in conspicuous need of self-confidence and a renewed sense of its high purpose. Lacking an external enemy upon which to visit its repressed sense of unease, it is ready to listen more attentively to those who locate the enemy within. The Christian Right, with its inherent religious certitude, its apparent moral rigor, and (especially!) its well-known facility for enemy-imaging, is supplying what the majority culture demands in a way that the old remnants of classical Protestantism cannot or (to their credit) will not. The Christian Right sees the rebirth of a strong America and the rebirth of Christianity in America—and, through a strong America, the rebirth of Christianity in the world at large—as part of the same process. That it trivializes both American democratic ideals *and* Christianity belongs to its role as official cultus of an imperial people. *Theologus gloriae dicit malum bonum et bonum malum* ("the theologian of glory calls evil good and good evil"—Thesis 21 of Luther's *Heidelberg Disputation*)—which is simply a sixteenth-century way of remarking that Christian triumphalism always *must* oversimplify and trivialize, because, like all "pretensions to finality" (Reinhold Niebuhr), it has to exaggerate the ultimacy of its answers and push aside every question that will not be silenced by them.[77]

---

77. Recently an engaging and much-read study, Stephen Carter's *The Culture of Disbelief: How American Law and Politics Trivialize Religious Devotion* (New York: Doubleday, Anchor Books, 1993; paperback edition, 1994), castigates critics of the religious "renewal" in America. The present climate among intellectuals in the U.S.A., the author argues, fears the influence of religion, and especially the Christian Right, in the political sphere. The critics use the separation

To Christians who want to sustain the best Christian traditions of a commitment to hope that is simultaneously a commitment to *truth* (that "calls the thing what it is"!), the captivation of Christian America by combinations of religious and cultural-political triumphalism can only be a source of immense frustration. Compared with the task of distinguishing Christian faith from an officially atheistic political credo like Marxism-Leninism, that of distinguishing Christian faith from an almost-official religion called Christianity is infinitely more complicated. In our analysis of both Muggeridge and Rahner, we have seen how creative response to the demise of Christendom has to begin with the recognition that there is a vast difference between Christianity and Christendom, and that no matter how closely linked the two have been throughout most of Christian history, it is necessary to the survival of classical Protestant Christianity today that this difference be grasped. That, however, is just what our form of Christian establishment makes it difficult to do. To confess the faith in this context, one has frequently to sound like an enemy of the faith!

15.4. The Virtual Disestablishment of "the Mainline."   Rereading Peter Berger's *The Noise of Solemn Assemblies* more than three decades after its initial publication is instructive, not only because the book so pointedly discerns what is wrong with Christian establishment, American style, but also because the exercise demonstrates graphically the shift that has since occurred in filling the establishment role. Berger's critique is directed almost exclusively to the Protestant mainline:

> We have found it necessary to say several times that our remarks refer principally to middle-class Protestantism. It is this group of churches, which Carl Mayer has called the "central core" of American Protestantism, with which we shall be mainly concerned throughout this essay. . . . We would contend that this "central core" is the main locale of the cultural religion discussed here.

---

of church and state clause of the First Amendment to back their warnings about the encroachments of religion in government. But in fact, says Carter, the original intention of the separation clause was to protect religion against state interference, not the other way around. There is every reason that Christianity, which is a source of meaning for more people in the United States than in any other nation of the Western world, should make itself felt in the culture at large, including politics. The "philosophical rhetoric that treats religion as an inferior way for citizens to come to public judgment" and the general trivialization of religious devotion in this "culture of disbelief" must be countered.

The book deserves serious consideration. What its Episcopalian author does not tell us, however, perhaps because he does not entertain the thought, is that the alleged trivialization of religion on the part of the "intellectual" critics of religious America is at least in some cases a response to the greater trivialization of religion *on the part of the religious themselves,* and especially of the more vociferous "Protestants," who represent neither classical Protestantism's political realism nor its nuanced theological traditions.

Here the fusion between religion and culture is strongest, for historically understandable reasons.[78]

This is where Berger's analysis obviously dates itself. For although it is still true that the *aspirations* of the Protestant mainline reflect their historic role as official *cultus*, the reality of their position in American and Canadian societies is another matter. Quite to their own surprise and chagrin, these older, historic denominations are being dispatched from their position at the center. The extent to which they have already been "sidelined" can be grasped very directly by reading a work such as Berger's, in which they are so unquestionably still *the* religious establishment.[79]

A historic comparison helps to concretize this shift. When the Interchurch Center (the so-called God-Box) was dedicated in New York City in 1960, President Eisenhower himself came from Washington to do the honors. When President Bush launched the Persian Gulf War thirty-odd years later, the religious leader whom he invited to the White House that night was Billy Graham. The head of the President's own Episcopal Church was engaged in a demonstration against the war.

Many factors have contributed to this change. Some of them, including the one implied in the above illustration, ought to be considered gains by any Christian who, like Berger, Muggeridge, and Rahner, wishes to see a greater resemblance between the empirical church and the biblical picture of the prophetic minority of the God who desires to humanize the world. Since the 1960s, there has been a much higher probability than would have been the case earlier that members of the churches designated "mainstream" or "mainline" would be involved in demonstrations against war and nuclear testing and for human rights and similar events and causes. It is even the case, fortunately, that some of those Christians are leaders in their churches. In the quest for world peace, for justice, for human dignity, for equality of women and men, for the full humanity of persons regardless of their sexual orientation, for the reduction of violence, for the health of the environment,

---

78. Berger, *The Noise of Solemn Assemblies*, 50.

79. According to the 1991 study, *Christianity: A Social and Cultural History* (Howard Clark Kee et al., eds. [New York: Macmillan Publishing Co., and Toronto: Collier Macmillan Canada]), the situation of the mainline churches in the U.S.A. may be summarized as follows. Those "that dominated America's religious life before the Civil War (Congregationalists, Episcopalians, Presbyterians and Methodists) are in decline." Between the years 1940 and 1986, there was an increase in the population of the United States from 130 million to more than 240 million, a rise of 83%. "Denominations defined by their European origins—for example, Lutherans and Mennonites—have grown at rates roughly comaparable to the rise in population. Most of the older Protestant denominations have had rates of growth considerably below the rise in population, and some of the mainline denominations actually lost membership in the 1970's and 1980's" (731).

for racial and ethnic rights and many other causes, the churches of the historic mainline have gradually, over the past thirty years, manifested a disproportionate concern and involvement. It may be claimed rightly that this was their inheritance from Christian liberalism, especially the Social Gospel movement; but it would also have to be said that the ethical thrust of the gospel embedded in the theology of the Reformers, perhaps especially of the Calvinist tradition that has been the primary historic religious influence in U.S. history, prepared the way for this flowering of Christian world responsibility.

For the purposes of our present discussion, however, what has to be recognized is that precisely this passion for social justice is what constitutes the alienating factor where establishment religion is concerned. The very attempt to implement justice in human and creaturely life is perceived by officialdom and the dominant classes and economic influences within our First World society as countercultural activity. And they are right to perceive it so! The Canadian sociologist Reginald Bibby, although he is writing to churches that are bent upon recovering their status and numbers, must nevertheless lament the fact that social involvement detracts from the chances that such a recovery will occur: "It's a sad commentary that Peter Wagner [an American church-growth "expert"] finds himself reminding growth-minded churches, 'To the degree that socially involved churches become engaged in social action, as distinguished from social services, they can expect church growth to diminish.'"[80]

I do not, of course, imply that once-mainline churches are wholeheartedly and unanimously active in divisive social issues. We are speaking of minorities. But they are significant minorities, both because they tend to be heavily representative of the leadership of these churches, and because they include the churches' most vocal theological and ethical segments. As such, they play an important role in the displacement of these churches from their formerly unquestioned status as the religious dimension of the dominant culture.

A second factor in the effective displacement of the same churches, ironically enough, is a consequence of the spirit of tolerance and liberality that has characterized them at their best. For such a spirit militates against the kind of decisiveness and certitude that is wanted in a historical moment conspicuously lacking the same. A large part of the demand that the religions are asked to supply in the age of "future shock" is precisely a demand for clear, unambiguous, and simple expressions of conventional social verities. But the liberal and moderate Christians know that such expressions are both simplistic and, in most cases, implicitly exclusive. In a religiously pluralistic

---

80. Reginald Bibby, *There's Got to Be More: Connecting Churches and Canadians* (Vancouver: Wood Lake Books, 1995), 148.

society, to claim without nuance—without explanation, even—that "Jesus saves" is to imply that the Buddha, Allah, Elohim, the Manitou, and others do not. The Christian Right, whose representatives are by no means bothered by such an implication, is thus much better equipped to become the supplier of the societal demand for certitude than are Christians whose traditions of openness have made them relatively (relatively!) sensitive to the faiths and practices of others.

A third factor in this effective disestablishment is the shadow side of the second. The Protestant mainline is on the whole open, but it is also theologically vague and forgetful. It does not indulge in aggressive missionary programs that ride roughshod over the religions of others, but it is also notoriously unclear and indecisive—in its present-day form—about the teachings of its own tradition. It has produced a significant minority of persons with an unusual sense of social responsibility, but it is uncertain how it did so, and why such responsibility is mandatory for Christians.

In fact, this question continually presents itself today: what *is* Protestantism? According to Berger's analysis, it is the absence of anything decisive, anything distinct from the culture whose *cultus* it is, and its "function" is just that—to absorb and transmit the culture's values and not to challenge these from any potentially alien or critical perspective. Perhaps it is here that the changed situation is most conspicuous. For what the culture now wants and needs from religion is not just solemn confirmation but exhortation. It looks to religion to add something that is missing—enthusiasm, credibility, "true belief." And mainstream Protestantism seems, to increasing numbers of people, itself so lacking in such qualities that it is for all intents and purposes indistinguishable from the secular world. Secularism has thoroughly invaded and captured these old structures; and while that may have been the source and secret of their former social prominence, now that secularism itself has failed and its survivors are in the market for "spirituality," it is a commodity not found in these churches. It may be found in Christian evangelicalism or—for another class of citizens—in New Age religion, but few find it in the once-mainline churches.

A fourth factor contributing more, I think, than is usually thought to the peripheralization of the mainline church is related to the second and third observations, but presents another aspect of the matter. Contemporary communications technology, particularly television, has enabled Protestant biblicist-evangelicalism to become by far the most conspicuous form of Christianity on this continent. Christianity for most North Americans is now virtually *defined* by televangelical religion. This is owing to the ideal combination of this particular medium with the type of Christianity that most readily lends itself to sloganization and spectacle. The Protestant mainline, whose pathetic attempts at televization only reinforce this judgment, simply could not have matched such a performance! I accentuate *could not*. It is not just that the remnants of classical Protestantism have not availed themselves of these technologies, as if they had forgone the opportunity because of a lack of will or wherewithal; they *could not* have competed with the evangelicals for this dubious honor, for the media themselves are compatible neither with the "friendly faith" of suburbia nor with the complex *kerygma* of classical Protestantism. The latter is particularly incompatible with television as it has developed in our context. Even in Europe, where television programming is much less determined by commercial interests, it is rare for representatives of the most sophisticated versions of the Christian faith to find an outlet through this medium. The antics of a lively televangelist may qualify as entertainment, but apart from the occasional public television documentary, who could imagine a program designed to explain the doctrine of justification of grace through faith, or to communicate the importance of thinkers such as Reinhold Niebuhr, Paul Tillich, or Rosemary Ruether in the political and religious life of America? It is even difficult for privately operated television systems to achieve a hearing unless they, too, give way to popular formatting.

In short, everything seems to conspire to reduce the centrality of "the Protestant core" to a shadow of its former self. The culture upon which it depended has itself significantly changed, requiring now fewer intellectual demands, less social engagement, and more direct exhortation than the older denominations can or will supply. And at the same time these churches are torn by internal divisions, with vocal minorities in all the denominations pursuing "radical" courses that are quite beyond the mild religious conventions of the majority and clearly incompatible with the role of the "culture religion."

By now, the displacement of the Protestant mainline can scarcely be ignored by any within it who care deeply about its future. There are concrete realities: dwindling finances, congregations dominated by senior citizens, church closures, a shortage (or in some cases an overabundance) of clergy, humiliating divisions, moral scandals and legal suits going back to a previous generation, failure of ecclesiastical polity and the structures of authority, and so forth. While exceptions are certainly to be found, these churches do not enjoy, as they once did, the trust of the communities and classes with which they are associated. They are not depended upon now for social cohesiveness and moral integrity, as they were, say, in 1930 or 1950. Their clergy are not automatically regarded as community leaders, even if they are still sought out occasionally for civic ceremonial purposes. Belonging to one of these churches does not enhance one's job prospects or chances of promotion, does not guarantee one's respectability, and does not ensure the continuance of marriage and family life. In some cases, given the presence of the aforementioned "radical" elements in all of the denominations in question, membership in such churches may well be reckoned against one.

At the end of a century that was ushered in with the mainline Protestant boast that it would become "the Christian Century," all such evidence of "decline" (for that, on the whole, is how it is received both within and outside of the churches) is ready at hand and may not be dismissed lightly. On balance (as I have said elsewhere[81]), I agree with the judgment of George Lindbeck that we who belong to the formerly mainline Protestant churches find ourselves today "in the awkwardly intermediate stage of having once been culturally established but . . . not yet clearly disestablished."[82] Yet even in the decade since those words were published, it seems to me, we have moved rather closer toward de facto disestablishment. The question that confronts us is how we ought to regard this eventuality.

16. "The Task of Disestablishment"

16.1. Disestablishment as Opportunity. There can be little doubt about the ways in which the majority within the denominations under discussion in fact do regard their churches' displacement. They consider it a matter of failure, a case of grave misfortune, an unacceptable reversal, even perhaps a calamity. They look about for someone to blame, and frequently blame themselves: they have not been diligent enough as missioners, promotors of their own cause; they have not packaged their "product" attractively; they have been insensitive to the religious and human demands of their potential clientele; they have been stuck in the past instead of being atuned to the present and future; they have lacked appeal for the young, despite the introduction of guitars! "It is a case of sin," a highly placed officer of one of the major American denominations explained to me; and it was clear that he did not mean transgression of the law of God but of the law of supply and demand.

Naturally enough, the immediate impulse of those who go so far as to lament the situation (often because it affects them personally) is to seek to reverse the trend. No group of ecclesiastical advisors is so greatly sought after today as those who have devised various schemes and techniques for recapturing the market for religion—a market that, as most of these experts are quick to demonstrate to their eager audiences, is in fact *greater today than in living memory!* Not all of those who peddle such wares are to be

---

81. *An Awkward Church,* Theology and Worship Occasional Paper No. 5 (Louisville, Ky.: Presbyterian Church [U.S.A.]), 1994.

82. George Lindbeck, *The Nature of Doctrine* (Philadelphia: Westminster Press, 1984), 134.

scorned by conscientious and informed Christians, and certainly not by the Christian professionals and academics whose abandonment of the churches is partly to blame for the prominence of these technicians and promotors. Among the more biblically aware of them, there is an undercurrent of recognition that "success" is not an unambiguous criterion of authenticity for a faith whose central symbol is a cross. "Growth as such," writes Reginald Bibby in the work quoted earlier, "is not synonymous with ministry."[83] Yet even in the most theologically aware of the technicians of growth, there is a common and unassailable assumption: namely, that Christianity is intended to be numerous, appealing, and influential, and that apart from some measure of quantitative and quantifiable increase, if not a veritable recovery of Christendom itself, Christianity can only expect to become less and less important in the scheme of things and, eventually, disappear. In other words, "the Christendom paradigm," as Mead calls it, persists, even when it is otherwise labelled. Unfortunately, this is the operative assumption of the majority of the membership of the once-mainline churches.

As such, it is indicative of two realities that must be recognized by anyone wishing to challenge this assumption: the entrenched character of Constantinian religion, and the dearth of biblical and theological knowledge and reflection in the churches concerned.

Of the two, the former is the more forgiveable. Any religion whose longest and most formative historical experience has been that of a majority faith, a faith firmly "established" in either of the two ways discussed above, cannot fail to have gleaned the impression that its only truly genuine expression is one that *sustains* its majority status. No matter how humble the beginnings of the Christian movement, what counts in ecclesiastical self-understanding is the fact that Christianity achieved something like "total victory" (in the West; but, of course, this can easily be universalized). It achieved majority status, moreover, relatively early in its historical pilgrimage, and, as we noted elsewhere, the very translation from humble beginnings to dominant religion can and does feed the image of success more deliciously than would have been the case had Christianity been successful from its very beginnings.

The trouble is, the psychological-religious effect of this historically based assumption greatly impedes any attempt to overcome the second reality mentioned above: the lack of biblical and theological awareness in churches today. For even when scholars and others may succeed in demonstrating that, in its original conception, the Christian movement was not pictured in any such world-conquering terms, the mythos of success is well able to accommodate such data. Especially in the American context, with its Horatio Alger

---

83. Bibby, *There's Got to Be More*, 151.

syndrome still intact, the idea of a suffering, struggling minority at last being vindicated by the kind of recognition given Christianity in the fourth century is particularly appealing. It confirms, in fact, the whole assumption that Christianity was meant from the start to conquer. Conversely, it militates *against* any attempt to hold up the biblical model of the people of God as being *permanently* valid. Hearing the "Great Commission" at the end of Matthew's Gospel, almost all Christians, conservative and liberal alike, are induced to put behind them any inclination they might have had to give serious consideration to the biblical metaphors of salt, yeast, and light! The fact that the Christians once *did* succeed in making their world Christian, even if it were only nominally and officially so, proves that those modest beginnings were only beginnings; that their *telos* (inner aim), from the beginning, was the conversion of the nations—just as the *telos* of the little acorn is to become a gigantic oak tree.

It is the opinion of the author that, in our context particularly, such thinking is not likely to disappear unless and until there is a corresponding termination of the host society's own inflated conception of its glorious future; and that does not seem imminent. Thus the Constantinian model of the church will continue to be a source of frustration to sound teaching for the foreseeable future. The only hope for inculcating alternatives to "the Christendom paradigm," so far as mere earthly planning and wisdom are concerned at any rate, lies in the *fact* of Christendom's decline, and in the recognition of this fact on the part of thoughtful persons and minorities within the churches that can least avoid the knowledge of it. Even if we are all profoundly conditioned by Constantinian religion in its various expressions (and we are!), some at least among us will be driven by the increasingly bald fact of our disestablishment to ask whether, in the first place, establishment is the only way in which Christians are permitted to think of their faith and seek obedience to their Head.

At the point of such questioning (and I believe it to be more common than is thought among ecclesiastical policy-makers), it is possible to introduce the interesting thought that the effective and irreversible disestablishment of once-mainline churches may be perceived as opportunity and not as defeat, and be acted upon accordingly.

16.2. Active Disestablishment. The second half of Peter Berger's 1961 study, as I indicated earlier, is titled "The Task of Disestablishment." If the first part of his book ("The Nature of the Religious Establishment") was all too quickly set aside after its initial impact among the more critical elements of Protestantism in North America, this second part was, it seems to me, almost ignored from the outset. Perhaps it was just not understood. Or perhaps it was too easily lumped together with the "neo-orthodoxy" that Berger cautiously commends in the book, which was itself scarcely understood in our context.

The very fact that Berger regarded disestablishment as a "task," something to be taken on and engaged in actively by Christians, is still today a very radical concept. Even those who are critical of the identification of Christianity with "the American way" (or its paler Canadian version) are most of them ill disposed to consider it the obligation of serious Christians to dismantle, intentionally and consistently, the whole substructure of Christian establishment—and to do so with a joyful heart and sense of mission! Stanley Hauerwas may command the attention of many disaffected churchfolk, but most of them cannot overcome the suspicion that he is only half serious.

There is no question about the seriousness of Berger. It will be remembered that he concluded his analysis of the nature of New World Christian establishment in an "Interlude" in which he posed the question of whether the cultural establishment he had analyzed should concern anyone: What would be lost if that were the only form Christianity in our context could take? And he answered: Christian faith would be lost. Active disestablishment is therefore, for him, as for Rahner, a "must," since as a serious Christian he is not prepared to see Christian faith reduced and dissipated through its captivation by a culture. An establishment that "is designed to prevent the encounter with the Christian message"[84] has to be challenged and dismantled. That "shattering message" of the newer Testament[85] is the veritable antithesis of the "'O.K. world'"[86] that the culture religion confirms and fortifies.

> To say the least, it is difficult to imagine how the religiously mature, socially respectable, and psychologically adjusted church member in our situation can come to terms with the naked horror of Calvary or the blazing glory of Easter morning. Both his religion and his culture compel him to sentimentalize, neutralize, assimilate these Christian images.[87]

Christian tradition, Berger notes, has always known that "conversion" is the only doorway to a genuine encounter with the message of Jesus Christ, and even if "this is . . . a dangerous term to use in America, evoking associations with hysterical revivalism," "little would be accomplished if we tried to think up another term to replace the traditional one."[88] The task of disestablishment is precisely one of "conversion," including the recovery of genuine *theology*. I shall return to the latter subject in the following subsection.

---

84. Berger, *The Noise of Solemn Assemblies,* 115.
85. Ibid., 117.
86. Ibid., 118.
87. Ibid.
88. Ibid., 114.

But before doing so, I should like to point out again the difference that thirty-five years may have made in respect to "the task of disestablishment." In many of my other writings on this subject, I have insisted that the message of the divine Spirit to the churches today is to "disestablish yourselves." It is not necessary simply to wait passively and *be* disestablished—pushed to the sidelines by a society that now cries out for more spectacular (although infinitely less "shattering") religion. We are called to assume, I believe, an active role in this process, and so to give it meaning and direction—or rather, to realize the meaning and direction that are already, providentially, present in it.[89]

This is in fact very close to Berger's counsel. But it is also significantly different. Berger's whole discussion in the second part of his study, a discussion with whose major elements I wholeheartedly concur, is offered in an attitude of (almost) disbelief in the possibility of its ever occurring. Obviously enough, the reason for this is that the establishment he is personally so conscious of is still deeply entrenched, intact; he can only set forth the alternative that, as a believer, he entertains as a vision he hopes some may eventually be able to share. Significantly, he addresses this part of the essay explicitly to "the concerned Christian student."[90] He is no doubt well aware that "the religiously mature, socially respectable, and psychologically adjusted church member" will find his descriptions of authentic Christianity and his prescriptions for arriving at it as unpalatable as the thought of "conversion" itself. After all, the entire decade preceding the writing of his book was one of unprecedented "church growth" and the seemingly interminable building of new churches!

In the interim, however, something has happened that materially alters all this: the facade of Christendom that was still rather believable in 1960s-style North American suburbia has become conspicuously less so. Among the denominations Berger addressed, as I have maintained above, it is simply not as easily achieved today as it was in the era of postwar church-building to ignore the de facto disestablishment that has been underway since the Enlightenment and earlier. While, as we have acknowledged, there are exceptions to the new realism about "the end of the Constantinian order," and while few enough are willing and able to envisage anything different from it, there are by now significant numbers of persons in all of the denominations under discussion who *are* ready to consider alternatives to Christendom, for

---

89. See Douglas John Hall and Rosemary Radford Ruether, *God and the Nations* (Minneapolis: Fortress Press, 1995), chap. 3, 44–61; Douglas John Hall, *The Future of the Church: Where Are We Headed?* (Toronto: United Church Publishing House, 1989); Hall, *Has the Church a Future?*; *An Awkward Church; Ecclesia Crucis* (Chicago: Chicago Community Renewal Society and St. Paul's Church, 1980); and so on.

90. Hall and Ruether, *God and the Nations*, 114.

they can no longer foresee its continuation or, in the more daring, can they condone its rectitude.

It is possible, therefore, today, in my opinion, to expect that some *will* hear and heed the message to "disestablish yourselves!" and will accept "the task of disestablishment," not as an impossible ideal but as a necessity and possibility (a "must," in Rahner's terms) confronting the whole people of God.

16.3. Disestablishment as a *Theological* Task.   Although the mood of Berger's discussion of the task of disestablishment mirrors the conditions, cultural and religious, of his historical moment, the means that he proposes for the working out of this task are as right today as they were then; and so is the object of the task, about which we shall think in the next subsection.

The means are first of all and preeminently *theological.* Despite the fact that "the milieu of our establishment is not favorable to theology," theology is essential to the life of the Christian community. As

> the intellectual articulation of the Christian faith, . . . it provides criteria by which both the institutional and the personal aspects of the Christian life can be evaluated. In the absence of theological criteria, two very dangerous criteria will tend to take over—in the institutional area, the criterion of expediency; and in the personal area, that of experience.[91]

Expedience has been the rationale for most institutional activity in American Christianity, and it is "a direct consequence of intellectual inertia."[92] One does not ask, "What is the truth?" but, "How can we use this?" or "How can I preach this?" In the area of personal faith, "the consequence of the abandonment of theological criteria for the Christian life is the cult of experience."

> When an individual ceases to grapple intellectually with the problems posed by his religion, feeling takes the place of thought. . . . The individual no longer asks, "What is the truth?" Instead, he asks, "What do I feel?" . . . . Emotional pragmatism now takes the place of the honest confrontation with the Christian message. The way is opened for the attitude of the religious consumer, who shops around the denominational supermarket for just the right combination of spiritual kicks and thrills to meet his [sic] particular psychological needs. The question of truth loses all significance.[93]

---

91. Ibid., 124.
92. Ibid., 125.
93. Ibid., 126.

Disciplined theological work and construction is the only way in which the hold of expedience and experience upon North American Protestantism can be broken, Berger affirms. He is at pains to guard against the misinterpretation that he is referring only to a greater emphasis on "doctrine":

> Theological construction means neither a return to empty traditional formulas nor the concoction of glittering pronunciamentos with which the religious institutions can make a splash in the publicity media. It means rather a return to painstaking and passionate intellectual effort, the willingness to confront the Christian faith with all the critical faculties of the mind and to find the means to articulate this faith in our own historical moment.[94]

While such theological work "requires the *expertise* of some," it can by no means be left to the experts; it must become in some sense the vocation of every Christian if the "task of disestablishment" is to be achieved in this way. Moreover, there needs to be a strongly objective dimension in such theological reflection if the habit of turning theology into psychology, and hence of reverting to the criterion of "experience," is to be avoided:

> We would contend once more that it is imperative in this context to elaborate theologically the nonmystical and even more, the nonpsychological character of the Christian faith. . . . The exegesis of the Old Testament is perhaps even more important in this connection than that of the New.[95]

And Berger is constrained to conclude that "as far as the theological critique of our establishment is concerned, we would strongly advocate a *theologia crucis.*"[96]

These prescriptions seem to me more pertinent, indeed more imperative, today than they were when they were written. What we can now add to them, on the basis of both negative and positive historical experience, is something like "the reason why." On the negative side, we have accumulated more than enough evidence of what occurs when the (largely unwilled and unacknowledged) process of disestablishment is allowed to proceed without the benefit of disciplined theological reflection. On the one hand, the congregations,

---

94. Ibid., 127.

95. Ibid. A sentiment with which Walter Brueggemann, Phyllis Trible, and all the students of James Muilenburg and Samuel Terrien would certainly concur!

96. Ibid., 133. Although this statement by itself, to say nothing of what has preceded it, seems to confirm that the present author has taken his entire program from *The Noise of Solemn Assemblies,* I must admit in all honesty that my early reading of this work when it first appeared was so superficial, and my own theological predisposition at that time so different from this, that I can see no conscious link between Berger's directive and the work that I have undertaken.

confused and anxious in the face of their depletion and decline, turn to technicians of growth and the like, who are often not only deficient in biblical and theological awareness, but have their own market and other theories to demonstrate and their own careers to make. On the other hand, among religious activists and trend-setters, all kinds of innovative and "far-out" theories and spiritual experiences and experiments in worship are put forward as "Christian," and in the absence of both theological wisdom and the courage to apply it, people are swept into movements that bear, often, a startling resemblance to the most dangerous experiments of the past—but, here too, an unremembered past that is repeated with all the pains thereto pertaining, and more.

On the positive side, the past three or four decades have only reinforced the insistence of Peter Berger that disestablishment has to be a task of theology. At least for Protestants, the great distinctions that are to be made between Christendom and Christianity, particularly in the North American context, are not at the level of polity, structure, authority, or form. Christendom assumptions are present in all types of churches—episcopal, presbyterial, congregational, free; conservative, liberal, radical, and so forth. Nor are the great distinctions clearly discernible at the level of racial, ethnic, gender, sexual, economic, or other social identities and concerns, important and sometimes illuminating as these may be. It is quite possible to pursue the typical values of North American culture religion in minority situations, as James Cone for one has pointed out,[97] even though such situations *can* be schools of discernment for those who acquire the necessary "criteria."

The point is, where an establishment is, such as ours, a *cultural* establishment—an establishment at the level of shared convictions and values; an identification of Christianity with "our way of life"; and so on—the only possible way of *dis*establishing Christianity is by acquiring a new or renewed understanding of the genuine foundations of this faith and reflecting on these scriptures, doctrines, traditions and ecclesiastical journeys as they encounter the regnant goals and values of our culture; that is to say, serious and disciplined theological reflection. If Christianity or Christian faith is to be disengaged from its long and effective absorption into the evolving culture of this society, there is no shortcut. It will be necessary for the churches (and not only a few professionals) to become knowledgeable about the Christian faith in a way that has not occurred in North American heretofore, that is, they must achieve not only a breadth but a *depth* of theological awareness, and not only a depth but a sense of commitment, and not only commitment but

---

97. See esp. Cone's *Speaking the Truth: Ecumenism, Liberation, and Black Theology* (Grand Rapids: Wm. B. Eerdmans, 1986), 150–51.

a willingness to embark on critical thinking of the kind that is (as we heard from de Tocqueville) foreign and even offensive to the "nice" Christianity of the Protestant middle classes.

This may appear an impossible requirement. The alternative, however, is one that serious Christians cannot permit themselves to entertain. It is that the process of disestablishment, which has, as we have shown, been underway for a very long time, will simply continue apace, and that soon its most vulnerable casualties, liberal and moderate Protestant denominations, will be so far excluded from social discourse and policy making that their existence will hardly be noticed. The point is not to capitulate to that process, but to admit its reality and irreversibility, embrace it as opportunity, grasp it with the awareness and conviction of Christians who have begun to know who they are, and make it serve God's purposes in the world—a world that is larger than "our" world. Only a *theological* awakening can make this possible.

16.4. The Object of Disestablishment: Mission and Service! We have considered many of the issues surrounding the task of disestablishment in our context: its complexity; the necessity of intentionality in relation to the task; the fact that in such a context this must be primarily a theological undertaking. But we have not addressed the most important question: Why?

To what end are Christians asked to disentangle their movement and message from the cultures with which they have been identified? What purpose is served by the deliberate disengagement of the Christian faith from the values and pursuits of the dominant culture in North America? Why would anyone feel that the message of the divine Spirit to the churches in our field of concern is to disestablish themselves, rather than waiting to *be* disestablished, further "sidelined"? After all, any such deliberate dissociation must prove, in practice, a painful thing. Like any divorce, Christian efforts to define the church *over against* the culture will inevitably introduce disquiet and tension into what has been, all things considered, a rather comfortable if on the whole innocuous relationship.

Why, then, should it be undertaken at all? Could one not just let the matter be, assuming that it will happen in the future, as it has in the past, that here and there, in spite of everything, a few individuals will make their tortuous way through all the bric-a-brac and tinsel of the Christian religion to the gospel that originally inspired it?

This is the first temptation, and it is an insidious one. For most of us who get so far as to entertain such thoughts know that breakthroughs of that nature do occur; that for all its falseness, Christendom has always been the bearer of treasures that transcended its sins. Besides, we are reasonable people, not fond of conflict, craving acceptance and by no means wholly disinterested in the progress of our own careers! There is not a preacher alive who would not prefer to hear approving comments after his or her sermons, rather than being told Sunday after Sunday that the sermon was disturbing— or even "thought-provoking."

An allusion to the sermon in this connection is not incidental, for if the task of disestablishment is one of theology, then, given the character and program of most congregations, the sermon will have to be one of the primary occasions for the implementation of such a task. Similar necessities, however, are laid upon other lay and clerical officers who have responsibility for shaping the future of the churches. And in all of us the temptation to hesitate, to wait, to carry on in the usual way—in short, inertia—is strong. In all honesty, we must face the probability that one of the main reasons that the task of disestablishment has been so long delayed is that human beings such as ourselves are always sorely tempted to refrain from instituting any significant changes in the status quo until there is no other alternative—that is, usually, until it is too late.

Here again, however, Rahner's "must" confronts us. The Spirit of God may be resisted, and regularly is. But there is also something called irresistible grace, and not infrequently it takes the form of the niggling awareness that *not* to act may be to miss the one real opportunity for "doing the truth" that shall ever come one's way.

Those who overcome the temptation to passivity are sometimes confronted by a second and greater temptation. This is to undertake the task of disestablishment with a vengeance, relishing this exercise in "rightly dividing the word of truth" (2 Tim. 2:15, KJV), enjoying "the judgment [that] begins at the household of God" (1 Peter 4:17), perhaps even taking pride, secretly, in one's own purity, thinking oneself God's scourge, almost another Christ, driving out the tax collectors and corrupters of the temple.

This response is not as infrequent as may be thought. There is a palpable anger against the churches today. It is conspicuous in society at large, highlighted by court cases and lawsuits amounting to millions of dollars in many denominations. But it is also present within the churches, where it is often hard to distinguish personal hurt from legitimate complaints about institutional injustices. In addition, there are many whose depth and sincerity of Christian conviction engender in them a terrible impatience with "bourgeois Christianity." They can only castigate or dismiss false Christendom. Such an attitude is easily mistaken for enthusiastic participation in "the task of disestablishment." But all it accomplishes, usually, is the alienation of the self-appointed judges from those in relation to whom a more compassionate witness to *God's* judgment could have made a difference.

A third temptation, the most subtle of all, is a refinement of the second. Perhaps it could be described as an objectification of the latter, an exercise whereby subjective distaste for empirical Christianity is qualified by reputedly objective theory—by theology! One may have recourse to the Reformation's concept of the church invisible, for instance. Or one may want to turn to the prophets, who "hate and despise your feasts and take no delight in your solemn assemblies" (Amos 5:21). With a little scriptural and doctrinal knowledge, this temptation can seem the very command of God.

What I am referring to is, of course, the approach that understands the disestablishment of Christianity from Christendom as an end in itself: pure Christian faith must be separated from the chaff and dross of religious history. "Come out from among them, and be ye separate, saith the Lord." (2 Cor. 6:17, KJV). "What has Jerusalem to do with Athens?" (Tertullian). God is *totaliter alliter* ("wholly other") (R. Otto, K. Barth). If American culture, this strange combination of personal charm and imperial aggressiveness, has contorted the image of the Christ, giving him the aura of a figure out of Disneyland, or the Pentagon, or both, then "Christ and culture" (H. R. Niebuhr) must be decisively separated. The political implications of the religious clause of the First Amendment must be supplemented, from the side of faith, by theological implications: Jesus Christ has nothing in common with "the American way"; Jerusalem has nothing to do with Washington, Hollywood, or the countless "theme parks" devoted to "Christian America." The purpose of disestablishment is simply—to disestablish! What has been falsely joined together must be parted without sentimentality or regret.

This is the great temptation of serious faith in our social setting today, and it is not to be attributed lightly to self-righteousness on the part of those who succumb to it. Whoever considers deeply the culpability of *Christians* in our context—their active or passive embrace of economic policies that oppress the two-thirds; their acquiescence to racism, sexism, and bigotry of many types; their silence and conformity in relation to consumerism; the exploitation of the natural environment; the destruction of species and natural processes; and so on—whoever contemplates earnestly even Christian sins of omission, to say nothing of our positive compliance with the whole course of First World greed, may well be driven to the conclusion that Christendom as such is beyond redemption; that the only possible course of action is to shake the dust off one's sandals, take leave of the moral Sodom and Gomorrah that our civilization has become, and seek among the misfits and victims of our society, here or abroad, the true church. In short, disengaging itself from a corrupt and perhaps damned culture, its alleged "Christianity" included, is itself the only justification needed for the act.

Biblical as well as historical precedent may without difficulty be found for such a position. Are not many of the words attributed to Jesus himself reminiscent of it? And in every age there have been Christians who have followed that path: the stricter monastics, the Donatists, the Cathari, Savonarola, some among those whom Luther called the "*Schwärmer*" (enthusiasts), holiness sects in our own time. Perhaps ironically, as the formerly sectarian, pietistic, and Bible-Christian separatists move toward greater identity with the dominant classes and structures of authority (the aforementioned Christian Right), not a few within the once-mainline churches are experiencing such estrangement from those classes and structures that they are increasingly attracted to separatist postures vis-à-vis their former hosts. Did not even Rahner speak of the "sect" quality of the diaspora church?

Understandable as this may be, I do not think that it is biblically or theologically defensible. As an exercise in *strategic* theology, that is, as an interim measure geared to equipping the *koinonia* for more faithful discipleship, it may be both justifiable and, in some situations, necessary. But the danger is nevertheless always present in such an approach that it will so absolutize the command of Christ not to be "of" this world that it will cease to hear his equally absolute command to "go into" the world—a command which, as we have seen, decisively qualifies the first, for it is nothing less than the inner aim (*telos*) of the command to "come apart and be separate."

There is only one legitimate rationale for the task of disestablishment, and that is to enable a new and different *kind* of relationship with those persons, classes, and institutions from whom and from which some kind of independence of identity is sought. As I have put it elsewhere: the purpose of disengaging the disciple community from its host culture is nothing more—and nothing less!—than to re-engage that same culture.[98]

Let me emphasize: *that same culture.* It is no doubt a great temptation for those who have been smitten by the gospel and by the often abysmal differences between the beliefs and lifestyles to which Christ calls us and the pursuits of white middle-class North Americans—a temptation to look upon one's own people as the enemy. I intend to question in this connection no one's ministry; yet precisely because many of the most clear-thinking and committed Christians in our context have in fact or in effect abandoned their own white middle-class culture and its historic cults, the process of the latter's decline has been denied the benefits of the kinds of purposing that it might otherwise have received. This is even more noticeable among professional theologians than where clergy and active laity are concerned. Those among our middle-class professionals who have not wished to be detached academicians and "religionists" have often turned to liberation theologies of the Third World, or concentrated their attentions on minorities within our own society, rather than engaging in the steady, difficult work of attempting to bring about in our dominant culture and its Christian expressions a metanoia of spirit and mind that might, in the end, make a far greater difference also where "the victims" are concerned.

---

98. See *An Awkward Church*, 14ff.

This certainly does not imply that ministry among the poor, marginalized, and oppressed is invalid when it is taken up by white middle-class Americans or Canadians. Such an idea would be patently absurd. What I lament is the fact that so many of those most equipped by their personal background, training, and faith to minister to the culture and *cultus* that has reared them have failed to concentrate their insights and energies on the "conversion" (Berger) of that same element. It is not that all whom I have in mind have abandoned that context physically. Removal to other parts of the world applies only to a minority, and in most cases, in my experience at least, these persons seem genuinely called to such mission and service abroad. But there is a way of abandoning the whole by concentrating on this or that part of the whole—taking up this or that cause, identifying with this or that particular interest group and, in the process, often not only failing to keep the larger society and church in mind, but coming to perceive it as "the problem," or as being insensible of judgment and inured to change.

Too many promising seminary graduates leave academia with the impression that they have become utterly different from the people who nurtured them. They are ready to repeat Isaiah's complaint that he dwells in the midst of "a people of unclean lips," but not his acknowledgment that he is himself one of them (Isa. 6:5). Too many clergy mount their pulpits quietly believing that the people they are about to address are incapable of sharing their profound critical insights—and believing, too, that the people are unaware of this attitude in their preacher! Too many pastors, having failed to learn the distinction between the *skandalon* of the gospel and "false scandals," imagine that they have struck the very core of the gospel's offense when their congregations object to their uncompromising use of inclusive language or take umbrage over their sexual preferences and moral conduct. It seems to many Christian professionals, who have got hold of the latest disavowal of some central Christian doctrine or symbol, that their very vocation in the church is to shock and ostracize every middle-aged male, every conventional housewife, every entrepreneur; and to uncover the latent homophobia, racism, sexism, and so forth that is allegedly rife in the whole WASPish institution (WASPS being the only remaining group who may be scorned publicly). A certain disappointment is to be noted in some clerical circles when evidence of middle-class generosity and compassion is brought forward. In view of the almost universal denigration of "typical" North American Protestantism that is found in the theological works most widely read by seminarians, it is perhaps no wonder that such attitudes are as prevalent as they are. Educationally, the great disservice that has been done by liberationism, especially when it is taken up by the relatively affluent, is that in its necessary concentration upon the plight of victimized peoples and groups, it has left the impression that the only thing to be said about the nonvictims is that they are victimizers. I do not take this to be a fault of the theologians of liberation, especially those working in "developing" world contexts; it is the fault rather of the educators and the educated in our own context who are naively prepared to leave the whole task of theology to those who represent oppressed minorities. So long as that particular context called "dominant culture," or "middle-class Protestantism," or "WASP," or whatever else it may be named is left out of the theological spectrum; so long as the only "interesting" theology, biblical interpretation, ethics, and practical theology is done by persons outside or inside that context who view it only from the vantage-point of its more blatant sins (which are many!), we shall continue to produce clergy and teachers of the faith who are so conditioned to disdain their congregations that their only function will be to participate in the "deconstruction" of the church as an end in itself.

By comparison with the theological literature and pedagogical influences that have dominated the professional Christian ethos in North America since approximately the mid-1970s, much of the earlier theological work of this century, including many now almost forgotten works of the 1960s and early 1970s, managed to combine deconstruction with creative reconstruction, and to do so in relation to the churches of "the dominant culture." None of this theology was easy on the churches. Neo-orthodoxy, a misnomer (as we have seen) for a movement whose aim is hardly to be confused with the desire to rekindle in Christians a passion for "orthodoxy," was at least as critical of the ecclesiastical endorsement of capitalism and the class system as liberation theology—and often more contextually relevant. All of the major exponents of that movement were accused of socialism—and they were socialists! Drawing upon biblical criteria, the "neo-orthodox" confronted conventional Christianity with the discrepancy between the Bible's radical conceptions of sin and salvation and the church's bland reductions of both. Although its leading representatives may all be criticized for having failed to develop feminist, ecological, racial, interfaith, and other themes that have since become mandatory, they all (in their responses to war, Stalinism, technology, anti-Judaism, and countless other issues of their epoch) demonstrated very concretely the necessity for what has since been named "contextuality" in theology, and for a *praxis* that was by no means all theory.

And they called the churches to account for their failure to do so. The theological memory of the churches, including their academic "wing," is extremely short. Each generation of scholars also manifests a certain, no doubt human need to chastise its forerunners for their omissions and shortcomings. But even in many areas in which they are currently accused of failure and myopia the major theological voices of the first part of this century were hardly as neglectful as a later generation [preferring to pass along unexamined stereotypes of past schools of thought instead of reading original works] makes them out to be.

For instance, Karl Barth's creation theology still has much to teach the ecologically minded theologians of today, and Tillich's conception of "the spiritual community" may be the most fruitful background for those who are newly conscious of religious pluralism. As for feminism, it is unfortunate that many of the women who were actually working alongside men in the World Council of Churches and elsewhere (to name only a few, Suzanne de Dietrich, Olive Wyon, Ellen Flessemann-van Leer, Ursula Niebuhr, Hulda Niebuhr, Charlotte von Kirchbaum, Marie-Jeanne Coleman, and Dorothy Sayers) seem to have been forgotten or categorized as compliant and lacking in gender-consciousness. In most areas of human concern, the theological community of the period between World War I and 1960 could be regarded, in fact, as setting a high example for the humanization of private and public life. Moreover, the example was felt within the churches because, while it was critical of them in ways that might astonish even the more disdainful of ecclesiastical life today, this community demonstrated a remarkable and consistent sense of responsibility toward the churches, as the very existence of the World Council of Churches testifies.

More lamentable than neglect or ideological caricaturing of the earlier theologians whose impact and literary output guarantees that they are not wholly forgotten even when they are seldom carefully read, is the fate of the Christian writers of the period from 1960 to ca. 1975. These persons, of whom many were Americans (William Stringfellow, Stephen Rose, Gibson Winters, Bill Webber, Don Benedict, Harvey Cox, Joseph Haroutunian, Joseph Sittler, Peter Berger, Hans Hoekendyjk, Albert van den Heuvel, and Paul Lehmann, to name only a few) were in almost every instance particularly concerned about the doctrine and life of the church. They wrote excellent and often poignant ecclesiological studies and tracts that combined biblical, doctrinal, and sociological-practical perspectives and insights in a way that is exceptionally rare today, when a more specialized approach has come to dominate the literature that actually reaches the churches—one, namely, that is particularly weak both biblically and theologically. Like their teachers and forebears, with whom they often quarreled but from whom they had learned much,[99] they made the churches their special focus—not chauvinisti-

---

99. For example, in his *God's Revolution and Man's Responsibility* (Valley Forge, Pa.: Judson Press, 1965), 10, Harvey Cox writes, "We all stand today in the shadow of Karl Barth. That is why there is such an emphasis in this book on man's responsibility responding to God's holy initiative."

cally, because they had the kinds of concrete concerns for *society* that demanded more of the churches than they were giving—but expecting the churches, nevertheless, to be capable of change.

Why has this work been neglected—some of it forgotten? The short answer is that it was displaced by the dramatic, media-catching movements—the theology of the "death of God," of liberation, black theology, feminist theology. But there is no reason it could not have been combined with most of these movements (as it was in Martin Luther King Jr., for example) to produce a more holistic theology than any of them by themselves could possibly achieve. Surely the deeper reasons for the neglect of this earlier and truly contextual work have to do with (*a*) the unwillingness of North American churches and their leadership[100] during the same period to subject themselves to so explicit a critique, and (*b*) the abandonment of the churches by academic theology, much of it newly admitted into the universities and colleges, which could live its own life apart from the churches by fixing its attention upon issues that, despite their seeming concreteness, were in many cases more adaptable to abstraction than were the concerns of the earlier authors.

Be that as it may, the body of literature produced between 1960 and approximately 1975, much of it dealing with the *problematique* of the Christian movement at the beginnings of its contemporary North American awareness of the metamorphosis we have discussed here, really did set the tone for reforming the church along the lines of a new appreciation of its mission and worldly service. It knew that Christendom was ending and that Christianity could only emerge out of the ashes of that form of the church through much painful purgation. But it did believe that Christianity could emerge out of those ashes, and therefore it took very seriously the existing ecclesiastical structures.

Peter Berger, although perhaps more articulate than some because of his expertise in both theology and sociology, is nevertheless representative of much of this literature. For that reason I have devoted considerable attention to his *The Noise of Solemn Assemblies.* And while, as I have already pointed out, his analysis naturally dates itself at some points, its basic challenge seems to me still entirely relevant.

Nowhere is its relevance more pertinent than in connection with the present subject, the "Why?" of the task of disestablishment. I have expressed my own answer to that question in the formula: disengage in order to re-engage.

---

100. It should be noted that this period (1960–1975) was also the era during which, following the corporate model, head-office church bureaucracies began to expand exponentially and the "secretariats" of the denominations began to assume leadership, filling the vacuum of leadership on the part of the courts of the churches.

Berger, using the language of freedom that he may have learned from the school of Barth and Ellul, makes essentially the same point:

> What is required in our situation is a new sense of the freedom of the Church. A free Church does not mean a community that is radically detached from culture, a sort of un-American enclave living on the margins of society. But a free Church *will* mean a measure of disestablishment. In relating to the culture, a free Church will pick and choose. Neither its affirmations nor its denial of cultural values will be absolute. In such an attitude of freedom, the Christian community *can then engage itself with the social dynamics of the rapidly chang-ing American situation.* Such social engagement may not lead to dramatic changes in the nature of society. But it will mean a change *from the passive to the active mood in the churches' relationships with the society.* In the measure that this happens, the functionality of the religious institution previously ana-lyzed will be damaged. As, indeed, it should be from the viewpoint of Chris-tian faith.[101]

Or again:

> As Christians free themselves from the bondage of the take-for-granted reli-gious establishment, they become free to engage society at all of its focal points. *Disestablishment is the very opposite of a retreat into a Christian ghetto.* It is rather the presupposition to a fully contemporary and fully conscious Christian mission in modern society.[102]

The parallels with what I have written both here and elsewhere will be ob-vious.

17. On Being a Diaspora in a "Christian" Context

17.1. The Problem: How to Avoid Both Ghettoization and Absorption. The first Christian communities were minorities within majority and often hostile cultures. In its various missions outside the protective environs of Western Christendom, the church has also frequently known itself to be a scattered and fragile minority. In Japan, Christians account for less than 1 percent of the total population. In Eastern Europe, during the three-quarter century of Communist rule, Christians again experienced the diaspora situation. During the early 1970s, I sometimes worshiped in tiny *Gemeinde* (congregations) in the Erz Mountains of East Germany and elsewhere in East Germany, where only little children and the grandparental generation dared to worship regu-

---

101. Berger, *The Noise of Solemn Assemblies*, 138–39. (My italics.)
102. Ibid., 157. (My italics.)

larly; youth and wage-earners had too much to lose. Today in western Europe, even where churches remain relatively prosperous and are thought harmless, the minority status of congregations is often conspicuous. Although the remnants of Christendom are clearly present in buildings, laws, and lore, proportionately few regularly attend churches.[103] There are also places in North America (certainly in Quebec and in the larger cities of both Canada and the United States) in which something approaching this also pertains. In such situations, the churches sometimes manage to take stock of their societal position realistically and devise innovative ways of engaging in mission and service.

But how shall the church in "Christian" America live faithfully as a diaspora? We have already noted that few Christians in this context are willing or able to recognize their actual disestablishment. When it is recognized, however, there is a concomitant realization of the problem inherent in any minority conception of the Christian church in this society: how can one be Christian in a "Christian" context—concretely, how can one be Christian in a context (the U.S.A.) in which 85 percent of adult citizens describe themselves as Christians? How can one be Christian in a society where Christianity at its most vociferous and powerful has become a militant and self-righteous crusade against nearly everybody else—in which "an estimated 50 million evangelicals and conservative Catholics" are poised for political action of the most unforgiving nature?[104] How can one be Christian in a society that identifies Christianity with its own history, values, morality, and global mission?

To refine the question: Can Christian communities that know that they live at an "awkward" (Lindbeck) time and in a place where Christianity still means Christendom avoid the two obvious dangers that pertain to such a context—on the one hand the danger of ghettoization, on the other of continuing absorption into culture religion?

Probably the latter danger is the greater where Christian institutions and the structures of denominations are concerned, for the patterns of relating to the culture have been centuries in the making, and precedent changes very slowly at the institutional level. Much of what ecclesiastical committees and

---

103. For instance, "In England fewer than one in ten adults regularly participate in corporate worship. The years 1960–1982 saw a decline in baptisms and confirmations, and less than five per cent of the English population may properly be regarded as members of the Established Church. They are, therefore, a minority of the religiously active, outnumbered in aggregate by Roman Catholics, Muslims, and members of Free churches. A survey carried out in 1989, and published in 1991, revealed that 'attendance at Sunday services in English church had fallen at the rate of one thousand people a week over the previous ten years'" (Ian Bradley, *Marching to the Promised Land: Has the Church a Future?* [London: John Murray, 1992], 4.

104. David Wilson, "The Christian Right Marches On," in *The United Church Observer,* new series 58, no. 11 (June 1995): 21–26.

bureaucracies plan (or leave unplanned!) is premised on the assumption that, quite naturally, our "Christian" civilization will be open to the pronouncements and promptings of the church.

This attitude is still prevalent in the older Protestant denominations, whose historic links with this civilization and its structures of government, education, and commerce function to assure church leaders that the opinions they hold still matter. Denominations whose ties with the society are more recent may not be as likely to harbor this assumption, but among the "Protestant core," the expectation persists that the close associations of Americanism and Protestantism over centuries more or less guarantee the continued readiness of civil authorities, as well as the public at large, to pay attention to the church.

The danger of absorption is fostered by this attitude, for until church leaders and denominational structures cease behaving as if they had a *right* to be heard, they will only continue to convey the impression both to their own membership and to the society at large that they regard the church as an integral part of the establishment, and are quite content to have it remain so.

When the church relinquishes its vestigial Christendom assumptions; when it stops being afraid that its voice will not be heard; when it ceases putting itself forward, promoting itself, or wishing to "have its commercial at the end," and demonstrates its readiness to serve the world for the world's own sake, then and only then it may be distinct enough from the world to begin to appear interesting. For then it will cease being part of the world's own system and strategem—yet another of the many collectivities clamoring for attention, yet another segment with its own vested interests—and its very "strangeness" may then become its point of contact with the world.[105]

For the world is made curious by those who give themselves to it unconditionally. This has always been the precondition of genuine mission, as it was of Jesus' own ministry, and in the post-Christendom "second stage" (Greenberg) of the Christian mission it is doubly so. For a church that has been preoccupied with *itself* for so many centuries has to go more than the second mile to persuade anyone having some familiarity with its history that it has overcome its well-known penchant for expecting special treatment.

It must be said at once, however, that this is very different from the liberal-humanist idea of Christians entering and blending with society simply as enlightened human beings offering themselves in worldly service. One should not lightly decry such Christian humanism, for there has been little enough of it! But there is by now, surely, more than enough evidence that a Christian humanism that ceases to rehearse *for itself* the explicitly Christian *reasons* it

---

105. See Daniel Jenkins, *The Strangeness of the Church* (Garden City, N.Y.: Doubleday, 1955).

is so concerned for humanity can soon become indistinguishable from the other good people and good causes that are (fortunately!) present in our civilization.

But should that matter? Is it not perhaps the very aim of the love that Christ inspires in us to lose itself, to *be absorbed* into the greater whole, to cease desiring anything for itself, not even the memory of why we are doing this?

With exceptional individuals, rare saints, such an ideal may be thought admirable. But as a strategy for the whole "people of God" it is naive. One is not "naturally" a Christian, even though in unusual individuals Christian behavior may become or seem to become habitual (Simone Weil? Dorothy Day?). Even where this occurs, however, closer attention to the lives of those involved will usually reveal a foundation of meditation, prayer, and study that provides the spiritual source of their worldly solidarity. Often, indeed, such examinations reveal the struggle of a soul that is by no means as automatically "kenotic" as it may seem to others.

As for the disciple *community*—a community of faith that is also, let it be remembered, a community of doubt—the more exacting its determination to involve itself in the life of the world, the more needful it will be for the community to remember, contemplate, and celebrate the sources of its world orientation. We should not overlook the concrete image that is contained in the concept of *diaspora*. Diaspora means dispersion, a scattering: the seed is sown over a wide space; it falls, almost at random, here and there, among many other types of growth. And, as Jesus' parable of the sower (Matt. 13:3ff.) beautifully illustrates, the fate of the seed is uncertain, precarious. It must be tended, nurtured, "watered" (1 Cor. 3:6–8) if it is to survive. Although the diaspora church may be composed of Christians who are more seriously committed than occurs in the Christendom situation, it finds itself *more* in need of constant nurture through study, dialogue, and worship than was ever the case in established churches. For one thing, nothing in its environment positively supports the life of discipleship, and much, on the contrary, militates against it. As Rahner has said, membership in such a body entails decision constantly renewed. Besides, there can be no point in the life of Christ's discipleship at which everything that can be gleaned from the sources of this life, historical and transcendent, has been gleaned. Not only are the challenges that come to it every day unpredictable and complex, but the wisdom that may be found for the meeting of these challenges requires diligence and discipline—a point we have made early in this series by drawing attention to the etymological link between discipleship and discipline.[106]

---

106. *Thinking the Faith,* 58ff.

It is, of course, this very demand for ongoing sustenance of an explicitly Christian identity and meaning, over against the danger of absorption, that can lead to the antithetical danger: ghettoization. Particularly when the fear of losing such an identity and meaning is constantly present—as it is especially in the culturally "Christian" context in which so much that is *not* so can seem Christian!—there is a perennial temptation for the diaspora to feel that it can only maintain its faith by devising exceptionally stringent means of distingushing itself from its social milieu. Following this path, lines of demarcation are plotted between church and society, and subtle gradations are introduced into the life of the disciple community itself, with some being stronger and others weaker in the observation of distinguishing marks. Then it may happen that the Christian message itself begins to seem so distinctive, so precious, that it can no longer be compromised by worldly discourse and interaction.

These are not hypothetical dangers. The temptation to ghettoization has beset every Christian group that ever seriously contemplated the real discontinuity between the foolishness of the gospel and the vain wisdom of the world (1 Cor. 1–2). Whenever today Christians of the once-mainline churches grasp something of this discontinuity and seek to make the transition to the diaspora situation, they would do well to study the history of sectarian Christianity. What such a study yields is the knowledge of a logic that leads inexorably from a partitioning of the church to a partitioning of grace itself. The gospel, bracketed off from life, almost becomes the church's possession; and salvation is seen as being accessible only to those who can claim full membership in the church thus delineated. *Extra ecclesiam nulla salus.*

It is this logic that concerns me in the work of Stanley Hauerwas, despite my appreciation for and agreement with much of what he affirms. In his *After Christendom,* Hauerwas even titles a chapter "Why There Is No Salvation Outside the Church." In it, he criticizes Reinhold Niebuhr's interpretation of Augustine's "two cities." Niebuhr, he says, "read Augustine as justifying a 'realist' account of church and society":

All is sin. The best the Christian can do is achieve the lesser evil, knowing that justice achieved will only be the basis for future injustice. The church is politically relevant only as it provides the account of our existence necessary for the creation of liberal democratic regimes that are capable of acknowledging the limits of all politics. Our awkward situation is no surprise for Niebuhr, as that is exactly the politics we should desire.[107]

---

107. Stanley Hauerwas, *After Christendom* (Nashville: Abingdon Press, 1991), 40.

In addition to being a rather shoddy reduction of Niebuhr's views, this becomes the foil against which Hauerwas renders his own (it seems to me questionable) interpretation of Augustine:

> There is no doubt that Augustine's account of the worldly city invites a Niebuhr-like interpretation. Yet missing from Niebuhr's account is Augustine's equally strong insistence that the church is the only true political society, because only in the church are we directed to worship the one true God. Only through the church do we have the resources necessary for our desires to be rightly ordered, for the virtues to be rightly formed.[108]

Hauerwas grants that "the standard response to those who emphasize Augustine's account of the church is that such an emphasis on the church confuses the church with the city of God." He himself, however, seems to endorse the *extra ecclesiam* as if the church were in fact that divine "city," urging that "the church's main task is to be what we are—*God's salvation*."[109] One wishes that he had studied Rahner's exposition of the matter:

> Why should we not today alter to our use, quite humbly and dispassionately, a saying of St. Augustine's: Many whom God has, the Church does not have; and many whom the Church has, God does not have? Why, in our defeatism, which springs from a muddled feeling of pity for mankind, do we forget that it is not the truth but a heresy that there is no grace outside the Church?[110]

To walk between the dangers of absorption and ghettoization is to walk a very narrow way, but it is not an impossible one. What is wanted is clear enough: a believing church with a strong sense of public responsibility. It will be a confessing church only if it continually reviews and renews its own identity with Jesus Christ through prayer, disciplined study, and nurture of the membership. And it will be a confessing church only if it continually confesses Jesus as Christ in the specific and ever-changing sphere of public life. Confession involves both inward- and outward-turning. Without the inward-turning that is its spiritual-intellectual discipline the community's outwardness will lack the mark of its discipleship of the crucified one; it will be indistinguishable from other voices, and, eventually, incapable of grasping and articulating even for itself the "reasons for its hope." But without its outward orientation, the wisdom that it may have gleaned through its life of

---

108. Ibid.
109. Ibid., 44.
110. Rahner, *Mission and Grace,* 51–52.

listening and spiritual renewal will be lost to the world for which it is intended.

17.2. The Future of the Christian Movement in Our Context. Will Christianity in the North American context follow the path suggested by people such as Muggeridge, Rahner, Greenberg, Berger, and others whom we have cited in this chapter? Will Christians especially in the formerly mainline Protestant denominations come to acknowledge their effective displacement, learn to regard it in a providential light, and in the spirit of the Reformation seek to re-form themselves accordingly? Will leadership within the churches begin to insist with greater frequency than is presently the case that it is time for those who are in earnest about the faith to *think* it, learn to *profess* it, and so put themselves into a position where it may actually be *confessed*?

Or can we expect the process of disestablishment to continue unnoticed— that is, more or less deliberately ignored? Or will the threat of collapse and extinction, a threat that is bound to increase in the years and decades ahead, drive the old churches of our no longer very "new" New World to seek still greater means of supplying what the culture seems to demand, imitating, perhaps, on the one hand, the New Age spiritualizers and on the other the hucksters of televangelistic religion? Will the hunger for numbers and finances drive the churches to adopt yet more desperate, market-oriented, gauche, and "gimmicky" programs of church growth, "packaging" the "gospel-product" in increasingly sloganized and unthinking ways that will alienate thoughtful people even more conspicuously than at present? Will Christianity finally be defined unqualifiedly by the formerly sectarian groups, many of which were regarded as late as three decades ago as "the lunatic fringe"? While the Christian religion experiences something of an upsurge in Africa and Asia, will the churches in the United States and Canada follow the patterns of European establishments, becoming empty forms and architectural points of interest for tourists? Will the old Protestant denominations still exist a hundred years from now? Two hundred?

Our purpose here is not to predict the future. Prediction is only a very minor—and almost an incidental—dimension of the prophetic tradition that is part of the scriptural heritage of Christian theology. Sensitivity to context does involve recognizing apparent trends and asking where they might lead. One notices, for instance, that interesting realignments are occurring within all the churches today, such that moderate and thinking conservatives who feel estranged from their more authoritarian and biblicistic denominational norms are able to make common cause with moderate liberals who sense the loss of theological foundations in their own churches. Such factors naturally stimulate the speculative side of faith, which is not to be scorned because it is the breeding ground of new visions that may give new life even at the eleventh hour.

But prediction and speculation do not constitute the major thrust of theology's prophetic aspect. The prophets, taking their cue from their awareness of God's suffering-presence in the midst of history ("divine pathos"), asked first of all what the divine Spirit seemed to be seeking within the worldly context. They dared to assume that they understood something of God's intention—a dare that would be very close to blasphemy except for one of its conditions: that whoever ventured such an assumption would be given the responsibility of suffering with God, and therefore of bearing human and creaturely suffering at a depth beyond the human alone.

It has been the presupposition of this chapter, and indeed of this trilogy as a whole, that God's intention is that the church should have a future. Going beyond that presupposition, which is itself strictly a matter of faith, to the point perhaps of sheer presumption, I have written all this in the belief that the form of the church called by sixteenth-century Christians "Protestant" would also, in God's intention, have a future: that it would continue to represent, not the whole truth but a highly significant dimension of the truth that cannot be contained but only pointed to; that "the Protestant principle" would inform not only churches called Protestant but all serious forms of Christian community; that this particular emphasis upon the priority of divine grace, justifying faith, and obedience to Jesus as the Christ "in life and in death" (the Barmen Declaration) would not be lost in the cacophony of history but would continue to exercise its critical and constructive powers indefinitely, outlasting, undoubtedly, most of the institutions to which it had given rise.

The church, I believe, has a future, because God, I believe, wills to give it one—not, certainly, because of its own worthiness! But I also believe that the future that the church can have is not the future that approximately sixteen centuries of Constantinian religion has conditioned it to want and to expect. Beyond that, I should say that the future that God wills to give the church is one that it can have only if it gives up trying to have that other future!

But when we speak about the church, "the people of God" (Mudge), the *koinonia,* "the people of the cross," "the body of Christ," or however we may name it, we are speaking of a *covenant* people—a people whose faith means a particular form of *relationship* with God. And the covenant, as the Jewish theologian Irving Greenberg has reminded us, involves the strong participation of this people who, although they did not initiate it, said yes to it.

God is not going to give the church a future automatically, irrespective of the church's own response to divine grace and providence. Do we still imagine that God is dependent upon the churches? There can be no room for presumption in this relationship (1 Cor. 9–10)! If there is to be a "second stage" for historic Christianity—if out of this ending there is to emerge, phoenix-like, a new beginning—then the gift of a future will have to be met by a new, cheerful, and disciplined readiness on the part of Christian individuals, congregations, and "churches" to take responsibility for its implementation. That is, the church will have to become "the disciple community" all over again, and in great earnestness.

And for the churches in the United States and Canada, it seems to me, that means one thing in particular: they will have to seek to *deepen*. And they will only deepen if they are ready to become communities of *theological* struggle, contemplation, and dialogue. "Formal religious thought," writes Mark A. Noll in the final section of *Christianity: A Social and Cultural History*,[111] and he here seems to mean theology, "has never been of utmost importance in the history of Christianity in America." Precisely! But, if "Christianity [Christianity—not just Christendom!] in America" is to have a future history and not only a past and present, if it is not to be absorbed into the general cultural milieu of "religious America" or become indistinguishable from every other vague "spirituality," or devolve further into thousands of quarrelling and individualistic sects, or suffer any number of other fates that could only cause serious Christians profound sorrow, then it shall have to begin to find "thought" (forget the "formal religious") the *conditio sine qua non* of survival. *Thought* is of the essence of the cross that North American Christians today are called to pick up and carry!

---

111. Mark A. Noll, in Howard Clark Kee, et al., *Christianity: A Social and Cultural History,* 745.

CHAPTER ▪ FIVE

Christian Life in a Post-Christian Context

18. Sojourners

18.1. The Loneliness of Christians in Post-Christian Cultures. Wherever it occurs conspicuously, the end of the Constantinian era is inevitably accompanied by a phenomenon that affects individual Christians personally and is often a source of melancholy. Whether suddenly or over a period of years, serious Christians find themselves alone much of the time—not physically but spiritually, that is, in their innermost selves. The new identity they feel they are being given *en Christo* is not able to discover the companionship that, in itself, it both promises and craves. Not only in their places of work, but in their wider social contacts, they are again and again brought to the realization of their solitude. They cannot assume that their most rudimentary beliefs are shared by those around them. Not only with respect to God, Jesus Christ, the Spirit, and other foundational aspects of faith, but also where the more immediate and practical consequences of Christian belief are concerned, they frequently sense their "otherness" vis-à-vis the majority of those who constitute their circle of acquaintance.

To take an obvious example, Christians are unable to assume any public support of their belief that the Scriptures of the older and newer Testaments have special meaning and authority for life. Even to think that these ancient writings are known is to indulge in unwarranted innocence about the contemporary world. In most settings on this continent, although the Bible will almost certainly have been heard of, it is an unknown book so far as its content is concerned. It may even be, here and there, an object of exceptional re-

265

spect—after all, it can still be used in courts of law to reinforce people's promise to tell the truth. But it may just as readily be treated as an object of jest, and all who honor it may well be lumped together in a category only slightly more respectable than those who follow the horoscopes in popular media. The idea that the Bible should be studied in depth, and might even become the subject of a lifetime of scholarly contemplation, is a very strange notion to most of our contemporaries, including many who remain in the churches. And it does not help (to the contrary!) that in our context there is a large contingent of "Bible Christians" who revere the Bible to the point of idolatry.

But perhaps the experience of their otherness comes to most Christians most noticeably where ethical questions are concerned. Although Christians themselves are deeply divided over issues like abortion, euthanasia, homosexuality, and similar topics of human behavior today, the very fact that they find it necessary to consider such issues theologically, to weigh them over against Scripture and tradition, and to seek to arrive at their positions on grounds that are recognizably Christian—all this is bound to seem foreign to persons who approach such matters without any conscious prior commitment to any overarching system of meaning. Christians may legitimately suppose that people of other faiths, as well as those who subscribe to various nontheistic systems, would understand the need to consider moral questions in the light of a professed tradition, but for the majority of our contemporaries on this continent the only basis for moral decision-making is personal freedom. Any extrapersonal factors impinging upon individual choice, including the laws of the land, are regarded with suspicion. Even the language of "values," which has replaced the classical language of "the good," can seem oppressive to those whose values (whose "rights"!) are incommensurate with the expressed values of the majority. That anyone should feel obliged to work out his or her attitude to abortion, for example, in relation to a system of belief that imposes millennia of tradition upon the free-floating individual seems to most "moderns" absurd. But if profession of Christian faith means what we have claimed it means,[1] then precisely such an obligation is built into faith itself. As a Christian, one is responsible to what has been handed over (*tradere*) and accountable to a community that honors that tradition. This responsibility and accountability separate one from the culture of autonomous freedom. Hence, in situation after situation, Christians find themselves ethically and spiritually estranged from the majority.

This experience would not be so unnerving were it not for the fact of its apparent novelty. Such loneliness does not belong to the long history of Christendom, or to the expectations that history has conditioned us to enter-

---

1. *Professing the Faith,* introduction.

tain. For centuries, as we have seen, Christianity *was* the majority culture in the West. During its heyday, the church virtually determined not only acceptable morality but truth of every kind. Under the regime of Christendom, those who were alone with their ideas were not law-abiding Christians but, on the contrary, persons driven by their conscience or intelligence to explore further the world that the Christians had so definitively and authoritatively circumscribed. Galileo!

Rather suddenly—in historic terms, at least—all this has changed. The change, we have seen, began to occur perhaps two hundred years ago, but in North America its appearance has been retarded. Even well into our own period, Christianity in this context has enjoyed the role of pacesetter in matters of ultimate truth and morality. The trial of John T. Scopes in July 1925, is perhaps the most famous single instance of a Christian religious establishment, late in time, prescribing what was acceptable teaching concerning the physical universe; in terms of moral rectitude, the supremacy of the Christian religion still prevails, or seems to prevail, in many parts of this continent. And yet Christians who look beneath the surface know that morality, too, for the vast majority of North Americans, has by now passed well beyond ecclesiastical control.

Where *does* control lie, where public morality is concerned? Perhaps there is no control at all, but only moral or amoral drift. As for religion, once the primary guardian of morality, we have already suggested that it may well be that most institutions of religion simply *reflect* social trends and mores that have been determined with little or no reference to the historic teachings of any faith-tradition. This, to many observers, seems patently so where liberal and moderate Christianity is concerned. Patterns of sexual behavior, for example, are almost the same inside as they are outside the once-mainline Protestant churches, and even the Roman Catholic Church now experiences a conspicuous discrepancy between the very decisive and stringent rules upheld by the magisterium and the actual practices of Catholic Christians.[2] Where lifestyle, domestic expectations, child-rearing, fashions, and the daily round are concerned, little distinction exists between church folk and others within the same economic brackets. It is said with justification by critics within the churches that they are among the first to be affected by new social trends.

This introduces an important nuance in our reflections. The loneliness of the contemporary Christian is not necessarily assuaged by his or her associa-

---

2. A poll of Christian attitudes in Canada in 1993 indicates that Roman Catholics are "overwhelmingly at odds with official church teachings on premarital sex, contraception and the ordination of women." Also, a surprisingly large percentage of Roman Catholics (68%, as compared with only 38% of conservative Protestant churches) "support changing the Canadian Human Rights Act to give gays and lesbians legal protection from discrimination." (*Maclean's* 106, no. 15 [April 12, 1993]: 32–42).

tion with the church. In fact, inasmuch as many churches have failed to grasp the new situation that we described in the preceding chapter but continue to reflect "establishment" identity and pursuits, it should not surprise anyone that Christian congregations often accentuate, rather than relieve, the alienation of those who have become earnest in their faith and their search for understanding. It is an irony of contemporary Christianity—although it was long ago experienced and painstakingly described by Søren Kierkegaard!—that the Christian can be lonelier in church than in the world at large. For one hears, in that context, some reminiscence of the very things that have made one Christian: the Scriptures are read, prayers are said in the name of the crucified one, the sacraments are observed, symbols of the faith are found in every nook and cranny. Yet the depths and heights that these things have produced in one seem, in that setting, to engender nothing out of the ordinary: nothing that excites the mind, nothing that moves the spirit, nothing to challenge the bourgeois lifestyle that is reinforced by every television commercial and situation comedy.

The phenomenon of the lonely Christian, whose loneliness is perhaps enhanced by church attendance, has to be reckoned with in a discussion of the Christian life in a post-Christian society. Certainly it has to be a subject of concern in a theology desiring to be contextual! For it is not a rare phenomenon in our context but a very common one. One seldom finds oneself in the company of other thoughtful Christians without some reference to their common sense of alienation vis-à-vis "the church" being voiced.

Just as rarely is this a matter of shallow criticism. It is usually accompanied by a sense of regret, even of anguish. For the alienated Christian seldom accustoms himself or herself to the fact that this feeling of isolation probably will not be overcome by the gathering of the *koinonia*. Although disappointed again and again, the lonely Christian wants to believe that the answer to her or his quest for communion truly is, or could be, the body calling itself "church." Just here, he or she hopes to find "membership" and a place of belonging. This is, after all, what the sources of the faith assure one; and this is what the language of worship and Christian hospitality evidently intend to make available. But rarely do these promises actualize themselves in churches.

Even more discouraging, the lonely one frequently discovers that it is precisely one's faith, and the hope that it engenders, that stands in the way of churchly fellowship. If only one did not take the faith so seriously! If only one did not insist on actually *discussing* the Scripture lessons of the morning! If only one would refrain from drawing all those radical conclusions from the Lord's Prayer: that the coming of the reign of God "on earth as in heaven" would have to mean such wholly altered human behavior and motivation! If only one would join in the convivial banter of the coffee hour in-

stead of wanting to pursue some terribly demanding—possibly even contro-
versial, even political—subject of discourse! . . . To be lonely in the "friendly
church" in the midst of the "fellowship of believers": is this not a travesty?
As Peter Berger writes, however, "he who would freely encounter truth must
pay the price of being alone."[3]

18.2. Waiting. If, however, the reflections of such Christians carry them far
enough into the Scriptures and deeper traditions of the faith, their loneliness
will not seem unusual after all. Christendom greatly altered Christian expectations also in this respect. The early church appears to have assumed that
the experience of alienation would be both common and normal for individual Christians and for the "little flocks." On the basis of newer Testamental
evidence, Christians should not expect to find their thoughts and deeds, let
alone their baptismal identity, confirmed at every turn. On the contrary, if
the Gospels and epistles are considered normative, we should have to assume
that ostracization and the experience of being considered strange, intense,
perhaps even "mad," as Paul was (Acts 26:29), are highly probable where
disciples of the Christ are concerned.

Nor is risk due only to the unpopular, demanding paths of truth and obedience the disciple of Jesus Christ is expected to walk. It has been the conceit
of the stricter Christian sects and cliques to imagine that it is their higher
morality and piety that sets them apart from the sinful world. But this claim
to distinction has more in common with the Pharisees and others with whom
Jesus quarreled than it does with the Christ himself. Certainly the solitude
of the Christian is in part the consequence of his or her obedience to a Voice
that the world does not hear; but it is more than that. It has to do with the
character of faith itself.

Faith has an inevitable future thrust. It hopes for what it does not yet see
(Rom. 8:24–25). It wants to be *replaced* by sight! It longs to see "face to face"
and no longer "through a glass darkly" (1 Cor. 13:12, KJV). It desires to
experience fully the love, purity, justice, peace, and contentment that it now

---

3. *The Noise of Solemn Assemblies: Christian Commitment and the Religious Establishment
in America* (Garden City, N.Y.: Doubleday and Co., 1961), 120. Elaborating on the point later
in his text, Berger says, "If we would now subject the American values previously analyzed to a
theological critique, we dare say that their identification with the Christian faith will appear as
an impossibility. This-worldliness [read: secularity, consumerism, etc.], moralism, success, activism, conformity to cultural norms, suppression of metaphysical concerns—all these are values
that must be in tension with the Christian view of the human condition. . . . We suspect that it
is a theological task in our situation to elaborate the eschatological character of the Christian
faith against the this-worldliness of American religiosity, to set justification by faith against our
pervasive legalism, to explain the meaning of the cross to a culture that glorifies success and
happiness. And we would argue once more that such an understanding of the Christian faith
will of necessity lead at least to a measure of alienation from the culture" (133).

knows only sporadically and in a token fashion. It presses forward to the finish line, to use Paul's analogy of the race (1 Cor. 9:24; *cp.* Heb 12:1). In relation to the communion (being-with) that it anticipates, the unimpeded fellowship of the realm and reign of God, it can never be fully satisfied with that of the church.

In other words, faith *waits.* And this waiting for the fulfillment of what is promised introduces into the life of the Christian and the Christian community an aboriginal sense of longing.

> I wait for the Lord, my soul doth wait, and in his word do I hope.
> My soul waiteth for the Lord more than they that watch for the
>   morning:
> I say, more than they that watch for the morning.
> (Psalm 130:5–6, KJV)

Paul Tillich used this text, together with Romans 8:24–25 (Paul's distinction between faith and "sight"), as the scriptural basis of a brief sermon that he called, simply, "Waiting."[4] The sermon is insightful not only for its exegesis of this important biblical theme but for its contextual wisdom, for Tillich was well aware that North American Christians have little time for waiting! Instant gratification is our wont in every aspect of life, and it is nowhere more in evidence than in our version of Christianity. Everything that the world denies us, we expect our religion to provide.

But waiting, Tillich declares, describes the very character of faith:

> The condition of man's relation to God is first of all one of *not* having, *not* seeing, *not* knowing, and *not* grasping. A religion in which that is forgotten, no matter how ecstatic or active or reasonable, replaces God by its own creation of an image of God. Our religious life is characterized more by that kind of creation than anything else. I think of the theologian who does not wait for God, because he possesses Him, enclosed within a doctrine. I think of the Biblical student who does not wait for God, because he possesses Him, enclosed in a book. I think of the churchman who does not wait for God, because he possesses Him, enclosed in an institution. I think of the believer who does not wait for God, because he possesses Him, enclosed within his own experience.[5]

To wait for God is hard. It is comparable to the posture of the beggar, who possesses nothing, is dependent, and is constantly made conscious of his

---

4. Paul Tillich, *The Shaking of the Foundations* (New York: Charles Scribner's Sons, 1953), 149–52.
5. Ibid., 150.

inadequacy. The Christian preacher who waits for God feels bereft in the presence of those who look to him for religious answers to all their questions; his expertise appears bogus; he does not command the respect accorded to those who possess authority in their fields. Yet, who other than superficial persons can give credence to those who speak and act as if they already possessed . . . God?

> I am convinced that much of the rebellion against Christianity is due to the overt or veiled claim of Christians to possess God, and therefore, also, to the loss of this element of waiting, so decisive for the prophets and apostles. Let us not be deluded into thinking that, because they speak of waiting, they waited merely for the end, the judgment and fulfillment of all things, and not for God Who was to bring that end. They did not possess God; they waited for Him. For how can God be possessed? Is God a thing that can be grasped and known among other things? Is God less than a human person? We always have to wait for a human being. Even in the most intimate communion among human beings, there is an element of *not* having and *not* knowing, and of waiting. Therefore, since God is infinitely hidden, free, and incalculable, we must wait for Him in the most absolute and radical way. He is God for us just in so far as we do *not* possess Him. The psalmist says that his whole being waits for the Lord, indicating that waiting for God is not merely a part of our relation to God, but rather the condition of that relation as a whole.[6]

Waiting for God, one of the great themes of another seminal thinker of our time, Simone Weil,[7] is not a matter of "despair,"[8] but it is a matter of "hoping for that which we do not see" (Rom. 8:24–25), of longing for fulfillment, and hence of an abiding sense of separation: the loneliness of Augustine's "restless heart" languishing for its "repose" in God. Our being-*with* God, which is the basis of faith, contains (as we have said before) an inherent drive to being-*in* God. We walk along "the Way," at the best of times, "with patience" (Rom. 8:25), yet also hoping to reach our destination—which should *not* be interpreted to mean death and the afterlife but the fullness of creaturely life, the resurrection of "the body," the consummation of *history.*

18.3. The Transformation of Alienation. Evidently, what we encounter in the two previous subsections are two different types of Christian loneliness.

---

6. Ibid., 151.

7. See the collection of Simone Weil's writings titled *Waiting for God,* trans. Emma Craufurd (New York: Capricorn Books, 1959). In the Introduction, Leslie Fiedler writes: "Here [according to Weil] we must be content to be eternally hungry; indeed, we must *welcome* hunger, for it is the sole proof we have of the reality of God, who is the only sustenance that can satisfy us, but one which is 'absent' in the created order" (36).

8. Tillich, *The Shaking of the Foundations,* 152.

The first is a loneliness that is historically conditioned, one of the many consequences of the breakup of Christendom; the second is an existential solitude that belongs to the life of faith and is present under all sociohistorical conditions. The question we are led to ask on account of this juxtaposition is whether, through the present contextual experience of loneliness, Christians individually and corporately may recover something of the component of "waiting" that is an essential aspect of faith itself and thus transform the negating loneliness of life in our "secular city" into a meaningful solitude that may contribute to faith's genuine confession. To phrase the question in another way: Can North American Christians at this point in their history come to know something of the meaning of the "eschatology" of faith?

Tillich was right, in my opinion, in identifying one of the marks of inauthenticity in the typical Christianity of this continent as the refusal to "wait," the insistence upon "having" God—and all that that Name stands for—here and now. It belongs to the brand of *theologia gloriae* by which all forms of Christianity in our context have been enthralled, to exploit everything in the tradition that can seem to confirm the immediacy of the fulfillment that, in Scripture, is offered only proleptically. Faith thus becomes credulity: faith as trust is exchanged for faith as sight, or interpreted as the possession of unshakable truths. Hope, which in the Bible is a dialogue with despair, as faith is a dialogue with doubt, is absorbed into modern optimism concerning the realizability of every fond wish. As for love, which in the tradition of Jerusalem is, in its historical realizations, always partial and frustratingly mixed with its counterfeits and antitheses, it becomes in popular liberal as well as pietistic Christianity an unambiguous and immediate achievement of the Christian life. The same logic makes facile distinctions between good and evil, which is why moral self-righteousness has seldom been imaginatively detected in Christian circles and "justification by grace through faith" seldom understood; it tends to equate church and kingdom, showing always a clear preference for what modern theology named "realized" eschatology, and in liberal and conservative versions alike what we have had of doctrine and theology consistently courts what Reinhold Niebuhr called "the menace of finality."[9]

That this kind of immediacy ("possession," "finality") should have been so dominant in all aspects of North American Christianity is not accidental. In part, it may be the result of the relatively nonreflective piety, activism,

---

9. Ursula M. Niebuhr, ed., *Remembering Reinhold Niebuhr: Letters of Reinhold and Ursula M. Niebuhr* (San Francisco: HarperSanFrancisco, 1991), 398. (Writing to Niebuhr in 1960, British labor minister John Strachey quotes with appreciation Niebuhr's dictum: it is "a good thing to seek the Kingdom of Heaven on earth but very dubious to claim to have found it" (ibid.).

and literalism that was perhaps an inevitable consequence of the leveling of Christianity in the New World context. Not only did North America provide a haven for many varieties of folk Christianity that were expelled from the parent continent, but in one degree or another all Christian churches on this continent were free of the kind of vigilance and critique provided in Europe by longstanding traditions of theological authority and intellectual rigor. The "religious simplism" that has become particularly influential in our own time is not without its precedents.

The more powerful reason for the accentuation of finality and immediacy in the Christianity of this continent, however, is the one we have already identified in these volumes: the modern vision, which itself eschewed ancient skepticism about the realizability of the good. The religions that have always been most "successful" in the United States and Canada are those that could most readily be adapted to the underlying cultural religion, the religion of progress. That is the character of our establishment. And if, in these latter days, the formerly mainline denominations are being pushed to the sidelines while the more sectarian churches are assuming something approaching majority status where the Christian population is concerned, this is not unrelated to the fact that the remnants of classical Protestantism are increasingly critical of dominant cultural patterns, while the more conservative denominations now provide the unquestioning support powerful political and economic forces in the society want and need. Even if conservative Christians insist upon doctrinal and personal ethical tenets that are hardly amenable to the majority, they do not question the fundamental economic and political structures of the society, but on the whole presuppose their rectitude; thus they perform the role that established Christianity in this context is "supposed" to perform.

By the same token, the remnants of older, classically Protestant bodies that are being displaced in this process experience the loneliness of the dispossessed—or, rather, seeing that, as institutions, they try still to retain as much of their former status as possible, let us say more modestly that they become increasingly a context for alienation on the part of individuals and small groups. Part of the "awkwardness" of which, as we saw earlier, George Lindbeck speaks is just this phenomenon. Individuals who throughout their lives and the lives of their parents and grandparents have been conditioned to expect that being (for example) a Presbyterian or a member of the United Church of Canada was of the essence of social respectability are now discovering that their churches do not, after all, represent what is socially dominant or unqualifiedly acceptable. Or perhaps they themselves, having been moved by some aspect of "radical" thought present in their ecclesiastical background, no longer find themselves "at home" in *either* their church or their accustomed societal niche.

Unfortunately, the historic patterns of religious affiliation on this continent being what they are (namely, if you don't feel at home, join another church, or start one of your own!), one fears that the occasion for reformation present in this displacement and alienation from the majority is not being grasped. The establishmentarian assumptions of once-mainline Christianity are so strongly embedded that it seems to occur to relatively few Christians that their personal experience of alienation might become an entrée into postestablishment forms of the church.

To state this more directly, through the experience of "not belonging" or "difference" or "separation," as it comes both to individuals and to groups within the churches, it should be possible to recover something of the *existential* loneliness that belongs, as we have seen, to faith itself; and, through it, to be led gradually to another way of being the church in the world.

That way may be called the way of the sojourner.[10] The Christian as sojourner expects to feel, always, a little out of place. She is not a complete foreigner or a visitor from another planet; but she does not find that this "city" is her final destiny. That is to say, the status quo is not the end she seeks.

Sadly, religious otherworldliness has conditioned all of us—upon hearing such language—to assume that the city the sojourning Christian seeks is the celestial city—heaven, accessible only to the dead! Thus people are led to forms of world-loathing that biblical faith simply cannot endorse. As Simone Weil put it:

> This world is the only reality available to us, and if we do not love it in all its terror, we are sure to end up loving the "imaginary," our own dreams and self-deceits, the utopias of the politicians, or the futile promises of future reward and consolation which the misled blasphemously call "religion."[11]

That for which the sojourning Christian waits is not a supraworldly state of being but the City of God, which is to say God's transformation of the *civitas terrena* (earthly city), whose kingdoms shall yet become God's kingdom.

In the contemporary experience of being denied full membership in the dominant culture, including its religious institutions, Christians are being offered a spiritual and intellectual entrée into this ancient experience of the sojourning, "wandering," unsettled, scattered—in short, this diaspora people of God—a people that, because it knows the world be to be God's world, cannot accept the world as it is but waits for its renewal.

---

10. And if this term conjures up the community of that name centered in Washington, D.C., I shall not object!

11. Weil, *Waiting for God,* 37.

With this by way of introduction, we shall now ask how such an experience of the Christian life in a post-Christian context can become the matrix for discovering new meaning in some of the oldest symbols and doctrines of the faith.

19. Resources for the Journey

19.1. Crisis as Opportunity. Crises are moments of radical change, when danger to life and the renewal of life struggle with each other. With wise remedial medicine, a heart attack in the life of an individual who has been suffering unknowingly from heart disease may be a blessing in disguise—a means to the kind of knowledge and preventative action that can lead to a healthier life. Of course, the patient may also die—and no doubt will die, if there is not careful attention paid to his condition.

The history of the Jewish and Christian peoples in the world demonstrates that periods of change and uncertainty are often occasions for the rediscovery of ancient wisdom, wisdom that is literally vivifying. In its "settled" condition, ancient Israel almost always gave way to life-threatening temptations. These temptations were not only the obvious inclinations of the prosperous, such as presumptuous glorying in wealth, or anxious lusting after ever greater power on the part of Israel's monarchs; the more dangerous of them were temptations to untruth. Sedentary Israel, as the prophets never ceased to remind it, continually "forgot" its sojourner status in the world. In exchanging tents for houses, Israel succumbed to fictions of permanency that gave the lie to the human condition and turned the heart of the people away from the God who alone could lead it into the unknown country of the future. It was usually in their "established" state that the children of Israel were drawn to gods that did not challenge them to venture further into paths of truth and justice but, rather, tempted them to imagine they had already "arrived." The prophets therefore constantly reminded Israel of the poor—not only because they were concerned for the poor, but because they knew that the poor are those who must bear the consequences of such metaphysical lies; not only for reasons of justice, then, but also for reasons of truth.[12]

Ecclesiastical establishment, whether legal or cultural, is the peculiarly "Christian" form of this same quest for *securitas*. "Settlement" has been even more damaging to the people of the newer covenant than to the older people of God, because, unlike Israel, which, despite the pretentions of some of its more ambitious elements, was never allowed to *become* "empire," the Chris-

---

12. See Samuel Terrien, *The Elusive Presence: Toward a New Biblical Theology* (New York: Harper & Row, 1978), chap. 5, "The Prophetic Vision," 227–77.

tian church, through its association with successive imperial peoples, often virtually achieved what Israel could only long for—the appearance of glory. Hence, by adopting a political posture incommensurate with their foundational theology, the faith of Christians has been far more consistently distorted than that of Israel. Moreover, the prophetic critique of Christian settlement has been a far less central aspect of the faith. Christianity's alignment with political power has guaranteed that the potential for such a prophetic critique would be muted and could never become what it was for biblical Israel: almost the *dominant* expression of faith, which kings and priests could ignore only at their peril. Even the Reformation, which Protestants with some justification regard as the most significant historic Christian outbreak of prophetic faith against entrenched religion, represents a relatively short-lived victory of the prophetic. It soon gave way to new forms of religious settlement that were just as inhospitable to the prophet as the old Roman forms of Christian imperialism had been.

What periods of upheaval, and notably the sixteenth century, do demonstrate, however, is the manner in which the unsettling of the church's relation to powerful political and social structures drives minorities within the Christian movement to recover biblical and other dimensions of its sojourner status in the world, dimensions that were either lost or rendered innocuous through the status of establishment. Crisis—unsettlement, disorder, alienation, and confusion—in the life of churches can therefore be turned to great advantage, given sufficient imagination and wisdom on the part of a prophetic few. Even chaos can be "creative chaos" (Tillich). The sense of loneliness that grips many serious Christians today as they undergo the great transition that marks the end of the Constantinian era could be the occasion for reclaiming basic dimensions of the tradition that can turn rote profession of the faith into its genuine confession.

In what follows in this chapter, I shall discuss several such basic dimensions as spiritual-intellectual resources available to persons and congregations who find themselves at the cutting edge of this momentous transition from the imperial to the diaspora church. I shall group them in two categories. In the present section, I shall consider certain key teachings that come to us particularly out of the Protestant Reformation, and address the inner life of faith in both its personal and its communal reality. These are (1) the so-called material principle of the Reformation, justification by grace through faith; (2) sanctification and the doctrine of the Holy Spirit; and the formal principle of the Reformation, the primacy of (3) Scripture and (4) the sacraments. Subsequently (sections 20, 21, and 22), I shall consider certain more public aspects of the Christian life—aspects of the tradition that describe the bases upon which the disciple community conceives of its relation to the world: (1) the covenant, (2) the doctrine of election, and (3) the ethics of resistance and responsibility.

My intention throughout this discussion is to ask about the significance of these traditions for the Christian life in this context of radical change in the status of Christianity in the world. I do not intend this as a full discussion of any of the doctrines or themes that I have just named, each of which warrants a book in itself; rather, they are presented as responses to the problem I broached in the first section. The question to which I wish to respond is, How can reflection upon these subjects help to transform the experience of alienation that we feel as individuals and communities undergoing this historic transition so that it may become for us a way into the future rather than the impasse that it seems, for many of us, to be?

19.2. Justification by Grace through Faith. "For by grace you have been saved through faith; and this is not your own doing, it is the gift of God—not because of works, lest anyone should boast" (Eph. 2:8–9). "Justification by grace through faith": this claim and "slogan" of the Reformation was its primary way of summarizing the content and thrust of the Christian message, especially as it applied to the living of the Christian life. The justification teaching developed in particular by Luther was never without its dangers, and, despite the general Protestant endorsement of the teaching, it was never taken up in an unqualified way even by non-Lutheran Protestants, to say nothing of its reception by the Roman Catholic Counter-Reformation.

Two salient dangers attach to the teaching, and they were recognized from the outset. First, because of the attendant polemic against "works-righteousness," it could be heard as a way of dismissing all claims to the significance of Christian obedience and discipleship. For Luther, who came to this *sola gratia, sola fide* by means of the hard road of monastic discipline and merciless self-examination, the Pauline declaration that the just shall live by faith and not "good works" was the soul of gospel: we do not have to make ourselves righteous, and in fact we cannot; God accepts us in our state of inevitable unrighteousness, considering us acceptable for the sake of the One who was righteous. This was personal liberation and life for Martin Luther. But for others less reflective, more opportunistic, or simply looking about for a way of doing what they pleased, the idea of our being acceptable to God regardless of our sin was a very convenient escape from both guilt and the call to discipleship. Grace, as Bonhoeffer taught us to recognize, really could become "cheap grace"—grace as a principle, as a justifying substance rather than the establishment of a relationship setting us on the road to a quite different kind of life.[13] The relational ontology developed earlier in this trilogy is nowhere more important than here.

The second danger present in this teaching was and is that of turning faith into yet another religious work. The formulation "justification by faith," which is unfortunately the more common way in which this teaching has been transmitted to subsequent generations of Christians, actually encourages such a misinterpretation. For both key terms—"faith" and "justification"— are regularly abstracted from their relational framework (namely, from "grace" as the active outreach of God toward humankind) and become qualities or activities more or less within the reach of those who truly desire them. Faith, whether it means assent to doctrinal truths (as for many conservative Christians) or a belief-ful attitude (as in liberalism),[14] accentuates human initiative; and justification, which (where it has been understood at all!) is popularly associated with morality, makes it even more "natural" to assume that what the dogma is after is some spiritual effort of ours that will render us morally acceptable. And such an interpretation defeats the whole intention of Luther in considering this teaching so central to his confession of faith.

Part of the reason that the doctrine of justification as Luther and his followers understood it was never enthusiastically embraced by Catholics, Anglicans, many pietists, and even Calvinists (excluding Calvin himself) is no doubt associated with these dangers. Insofar as that is the case, the hesitance of these Protestant and other bodies is historically justifiable; for the dangers of the slogan, received as slogan, have been amply demonstrated by subsequent history.

But this, I fear, only accounts for one side of the hesitance in question. The other side has more to do with the caution of the religious in the face of all bold declarations of grace. "Justification by grace through faith" is rightly called a *radical* teaching: that is, it not only goes to the deepest roots (*radix*) of the Christian profession of faith, but it presupposes a context of extreme, truly basic need—as one could appropriately say, a genuinely *confessional* context, when "all other helpers fail and comforts flee." The assumption without which the justification dogma one way or another becomes dangerous is that all purely human, religious efforts at self-salvation

---

13. "Cheap grace means grace as a doctrine, a principle, a system. It means forgiveness of sins proclaimed as a general truth, the love of God taught as the Christian 'conception' of God. An intellectual assent to that idea is held to be of itself sufficient to secure remission of sins. . . . Cheap grace therefore amounts to a denial of the living Word of God, in fact, a denial of the Incarnation of the Word of God" (*The Cost of Discipleship,* trans. R. H. Fuller, with some revision by Irmgard Booth [London: SCM, 1959], 35).

14. See *Thinking the Faith,* 248ff.

have failed. Only in a beggarly position is it possible to hear that one is "accepted" (Tillich) without hearing this either as easy acceptance ("cheap grace") or as tacit approval of one's actual or potential "faith-righteousness."

And for most people during most epochs of church history, this radical *context* has been missing. The settled state, which has been the normal state of Christendom, militates against such a drastic reading of the human condition. Established religion rarely addresses human beings in the naked truth of their situation: that they are wretched and lost, proceeding toward death, and wholly dependent upon the mercy of God. Established religion cannot do this, except in formulary and doctrinaire ways, because the very conditions under which life is lived, including conditions sustained by religion itself, convey a quite different message: that, basically, all is well; that the necessary safeguards are in place; that those who live lawfully and with respect for social institutions will survive, will perhaps even prosper, and so on. Established religion offers milder analyses of the human malaise and gentler prescriptions for its cure. What Rome found so offensive about the "wild boar" Luther and his following was not only their renunciation of entrenched authority and doctrine, but their uncouth, "drunken German" exaggeration of both sin and redemption. The Council of Trent is best understood if it is seen as the attempt of established religion to restore *balance.* The teaching concerning justification by grace, with its dismissal of the ultimate significance of human and ecclesiastical achievement, threw aside all the carefully calculated rites and urbane regulations of the temple and demanded of human beings that they face the real impossibility of their situation and receive their lives again, after judgment, as gifts of pure grace.

While there are probably always individuals for whom this kind of stark *kerygma* is immediately arresting, the wider accessibility of such a message normally, I think, assumes a social context of critical proportions, in which the customary safeguards both of culture and cult do not function to insulate human beings from the shock of self-awareness. Most people are not prepared to hear that they are justified by grace *alone,* as long as they can feel they are also upheld by other, worldly forms of security, including the security offered by well-regulated religion.

The multifaceted crisis of our culture—and, for many Christians, particularly the insecurity created by the effective *disestablishment* of the Christian religion itself—may therefore be the occasion for grasping this central claim of the Reformation existentially and in original ways. Let us reflect on the justification teaching with this possibility in mind.

Luther described it in these terms:

Der Artikel von der Rechfertigung ist ein Meister und Fürst über alle Arten von Lehre und er regiert alles Gewissen und die Kirche. Ohne ihn ist die Welt fade und lauter Finsternis.[15]

Of course Luther did not mean to reduce the whole faith to this one formulation. Despite his high assessment of it, not even he believed that the justification teaching could stand alone. Without the christological presupposition —*per Christum solum* (through Christ alone)—the *sola gratia* and *sola fide* are incomplete and misleading. Moreover, as we have seen, all three components of the slogan (justification, grace, and faith) require careful interpretation if they are to convey what the Luther intended them to convey and not end in distortion.

Yet, as a way of expressing what is basic or definitive, this doctrinal symbol is one whose comprehensiveness and lucidity cannot be overlooked without loss.[16] To begin with, justification by grace through faith should not be construed simply as "a doctrine." Rather, it cuts across all major doctrinal dimensions of the tradition and attempts a confessional summation of them that is at the same time theoretical and practical—today we could speak of it as *praxis.* For this reason, Tillich called the teaching also "a principle":

> I call it not only a doctrine and an article among others but also a principle, because it is the first and basic expression of the Protestant principle itself. It is only for unavoidable reasons of expedience a particular doctrine and should, at the same time, be regarded as the principle which permeates every single assertion of the theological system. It should be regarded as the Protestant principle that, in relation to God, God alone can act and that no human claim, especially no religious claim, no intellectual or moral or devotional "work" can reunite us with him. . . . In this sense the doctrine of justification is the universal principle of Protestant theology. . . .[17]

---

15. "The article concerning justification is master and prince among all types of doctrine, and it rules over conscience and church. Without it, the world is flat and sheer darkness." Kurt Aland, ed., *Lutherlexikon* (Göttingen: Vandenhoeck & Ruprecht, 1983), 269.

16. "While the doctrine of justification was the centerpiece of the theology of Luther and has been called 'the article by which the church stands or falls' [Carl E. Braaten], it would be a mistake to suggest that all Christian doctrine can be reduced to this single truth. The fullness of the event of Jesus Christ does not find expression simply in the doctrine of justification" (Daniel L. Migliore, *Faith Seeking Understanding: An Introduction to Christian Theology* [Grand Rapids: Wm. B. Eerdmans, 1991], 175–77). Migliore goes on to admit that it would nevertheless "be folly to think that this doctrine is an outmoded teaching." Yet his assessment is mistaken in one important matter: justification by grace through faith is not primarily "a doctrine," or, rather, if it becomes "a doctrine," as it tends to do with Melanchthon's interpretation of it (see Wilhelm Pauck, *From Luther to Tillich: The Reformers and Their Heirs* [San Francisco: Harper & Row, 1984], 51), the point of its being (in Migliore's term) Luther's "centerpiece" is missed.

17. Paul Tillich, *Systematic Theology,* vol. 3 (Chicago: University of Chicago Press, 1963), 223–24.

As Tillich's statement implies, the justification "principle" articulates the Christian message both positively and negatively. *Via negativa* (and we may begin there because, historically, that *is,* in a real sense, the beginning), it enters a permanent criticism against legalistic, moralistic religion. Such a critique is perennially necessary, because the essence of the "religious" heresy is the human propensity to acquire divine (and human) acceptability through allegedly "righteous" or "just" behavior. In fact, Hendrikus Berkhof, in a wonderfully informative small-print discussion of the history of the justification principle, proposes that "the reason for the early demise of [Paul's justification teachings] in the history of the church, without leaving much of a trace behind them" is related precisely to its debunking of presumed righteousness. "The morally blameless man [sic] considers it an offence that his righteousness before God should rest totally on the righteousness of Christ."[18]

The principle of justification by grace through faith is by no means, however, a category of critical theology only; it makes a highly positive statement both about God and humanity. It insists that the fundamental posture of God in relation to the creature is one of unambiguous favor; that the Absolute vis-à-vis whom our lives are lived is not only "with us" but also "for us" (*pro nobis*). Although we are unworthy of it, we are pursued by a love that will not let us go, that will indeed sacrifice itself rather than permit our self-destruction. From the perspective of human worth, a more positive conception of deity could hardly be imagined.

As for humanity, while the justification principle assumes (on the negative side) the universality of sin and the helplessness of the sinner, on the positive side it presupposes a capacity for *fiducia*—that is, for a trust that is stronger than alienation and can live toward reconciliation. This trust (faith, *Vertrauen*) is not "natural" to us, according to the Reformers, but it may nevertheless be achieved by the divine Spirit working within us; it may become in some genuine sense ours—not as a permanent possession, but as a gift and struggle continuously renewed.[19]

---

18. Berkhof finds the Pauline theology of justification by grace through faith surfaces only *rarely* in the history of Christian thought—to wit, in Augustine, Luther, Calvin (to some extent), Wesley, the nineteenth-century Reformed theologian H. F. Kohlbrugge (1803–1875), and Karl Barth. He also relates that, according to a certain tradition (which he does not identify), "Luther, at the end of his life, referring to the doctrine of justification, said, 'Soon after our death this doctrine will be obscured.' That [Berkhof continues] has indeed happened, not only then, but after each subsequent explosion, also in our own century. To live as a sinner from the faith that salvation is purely God's free gift is something which in the long run proves too demanding" (*Christian Faith: An Introduction to the Study of the Faith,* trans. Sierd Woudstra [Grand Rapids: Wm. B. Eerdmans, 1979], 438.

19. "Luther, at the same time that he speaks of faith as a work of God, has also described faith as a continuous and persistent struggle, and has spoken of its bold *dennoch,* its 'nevertheless.' Faith exists as a militant and praying faith, which can exist and continue only by being

In order for Christians today to appropriate this radical message of salvation by grace alone, through faith, we have not only to be conscious of the historical dangers associated with the principle but also of the limitations of the language in which the teaching was expressed at the time of the Reformation. Tillich (rightly, in my opinion) suggested that the whole conception of justification may be virtually incomprehensible to our contemporaries, even to most church-going Protestants and theological scholars![20] For one thing, justification by grace through faith was conceived under the impact of a historical context redolent of an abiding sense of guilt before God and of fear concerning one's eternal destiny; and if, as I also argued in the second volume,[21] the anxiety prevalent in contemporary Western society is not that of guilt but of purposelessness (in Tillich's designation, "the anxiety of meaninglessness and despair"), a gospel that addresses the guilty will not engage our culture at its heart. Perhaps even Tillich's own "translation" of the justification principle into the language of "acceptance"[22] is not quite appropriate to an age that since Tillich's death in 1965 has increasingly demonstrated an incapacity for entertaining the significance of human creaturehood.

This is by no means to imply that the principle of justification by grace through faith is outmoded. Because guilt continues to assail many people, it may even be possible often to express it almost directly in the language of Paul, or of Luther and his contemporaries. But the teaching is too important to be reserved for those who are burdened with that anxiety, and to address the anxiety most prevalent in our context, it must be interpreted in other language.

Let us attempt to find a language in which the essence of this principle may be expressed in such a way as to meet the predicament of human beings

---

constantly won anew. There is always something of this element in faith: Lord, I will not let you go until you bless me" (Gustav Aulén, *The Faith of the Christian Church,* trans. Eric H. Wahlstrom and G. Everett Arden [Philadelphia: The Muhlenberg Press, 1948], 320).

20. "Protestantism was born out of the struggle for the doctrine of justification by faith. This idea is strange to the man of today and even to Protestant people in the churches; indeed, as I have over and over again had the opportunity to learn, it is so strange to the modern man that there is scarcely any way of making it intelligible to him. And yet this doctrine of justification by faith has divided the old unity of Christendom. . . . We have here a breaking-down of tradition that has few parallels. And we should not imagine that it will be possible in some simple fashion to leap over this gulf and resume our connection with the Reformation again" (Paul Tillich, *The Protestant Era,* trans. James Luther Adams [Chicago: University of Chicago Press, 1948], 196).

21. *Professing the Faith,* 529ff.

22. See Tillich's sermon "You Are Accepted," in *The Shaking of the Foundations,* 153ff. Some regard this as Tillich's greatest sermon. In their official biography, Wilhelm and Marion Pauck relate that, in the corner of the manuscript of this sermon, Tillich had written, "For myself." The sermon was written at the time of his sixtieth birthday. See Wilhelm and Marion Pauck, *Paul Tillich: Life and Thought* (New York: Harper & Row, 1976).

undergoing the anxiety typical of the great transition we have described here. Luther and his contemporaries were laboring under a legalistic system of religion in relation to which they could not feel "justified." The truth is, they were living with a failed system of meaning—a system that retained only its external forms without the vision and life that had brought them into being. The forms, even when they were pursued as rigorously as sincere monks untrammelled by the usual cares of laypersons could pursue them, did not give life. On the contrary, the more seriously they were taken, the more thoroughly they failed to make good the promises they held out. Before the Deity testi-fied to by these rules, rituals, and dogmas, the most obedient could only feel increasing guilt, rejection, and condemnation—in short, death and not life.

Our situation as North American Christians at the end of the twentieth century is very different, but in one respect it is similar: we too find ourselves the victims of a system of meaning that no longer gives life. Both in its secular and its religious expressions, the modern vision that promised the inevitable unfolding of purpose to all who gave themselves to the pursuit of knowledge and technique has failed. The more sincerely persons attempt to achieve "success" according to the formulae of modernity (mastery over nature and the elimination of chance), the more conscious they are of being caught in a vicious circle, a "Catch-22." The modern vision does not give life, it takes it. Increasingly, we have argued, the end toward which it moves seems to be death and not life.

Sixteenth-century Christians found deliverance from the moribund system of legalistic religion when they discovered—rather, were discovered by!—the God who justifies the self-condemned. The guilt-ridden, religiously inhibited Luther "came to life" (as we may say) when he was found by the "gracious God" whose real, life-giving presence the spent, penitential system of medieval monasticism denied him. "Justification," for Luther, to express it in nonconventional terms, meant the opening out of the future: his life could go on beyond the impasse of condemnation, and it would be something approaching real life, "abundant life"—"The dream I had lately, will be made true; 'twas that I was dead, and stood by my grave, covered with rags. Thus am I long since condemned to die, and yet I live."[23]

But let us pursue this a little. It is true that the justification teaching conventionally exegeted has rarely made very much of the language of life, which is nevertheless a definitive component of the Pauline formula itself. In fact, scripturally, this language is absolutely central, and precisely so in the texts

---

23. Thomas S. Kepler, ed., *The Table Talk of Martin Luther* (New York and Cleveland: World Publishing, 1952), 320–21.

to which the Reformers turned for help in their expositions of this principle. While the usual promulgation of the justification teaching emphasizes "justification" and "faith" (with "grace," as we have noted already, frequently being virtually left out of account in the formula), there is good reason to think that the Bible places *its* emphasis upon "life." Thus, what we read in both Romans (1:17) and Galatians (3:11), and in their common background in Habakkuk (2:4), is not that we are "justified by faith" but rather, as the RSV actually translates the Greek, "He who through faith is righteous *shall live.*" In other words, the object of the whole experience is not the "religious" aim of believing in God and therefore qualifying as a candidate for ultimate salvation; rather, the object is to be set free for life. That which prevents, inhibits, and demeans life; that fear and caution which holds us back from entering joyfully and gladly the terrifying but wondrous creaturehood that is God's gift to us: just *that* is being set aside by the gracious God, who liberates us for life.

Whoever knows the commitment to life—creaturely life—that informs the tradition of Jerusalem from beginning to end will not be surprised by such a formulation. As we have already argued in the second volume, the whole purpose of the creating God is to have vis-à-vis Godself creatures who not only *are* creatures, but know that they are creatures, and are ready willingly and expectantly to enter into the possibilities and responsibilities of their peculiar creaturehood. When the justification doctrine (doctrine!) is turned into a forensic device by means of which, although wholly unworthy, we are rendered acceptable to God, without pursuing the horizontal and ethical end to which this acceptability ought to lead, it does a terrible injustice to this life-affirming tradition. It makes "righteousness" (justification) a religious concept, and as such an end-in-itself, whereas, biblically understood, "righteousness" is a very earthy idea, and a means—a means to life.

It is almost impossible in our context to use the word "righteousness" without casting it under the abysmal shadow of a holier-than-thou prudery; in ordinary parlance, the term is practically inseparable from the idea of *self*-righteousness. But its scriptural meaning is quite different. It has to do with what today we might well call authenticity. The "righteous" one is "for real"—is one whose behavior is genuine and not "phoney," whose goodness is deep, internal, and not "put on" or hypocritical. Jesus was in this sense "righteous"—"*Truly* human," in the language of Chalcedon.

"Righteous*ness*" is therefore the condition of being authentic, real, genuine—of being right for who one is a human being, neither more nor less; of being right for the vocation to which one is called, for the kind of life one is given, for the loves and labors that are one's responsibilities: of being truly *human. Menschlich!* Joseph Sittler graphically illustrates my meaning here in likening the biblical "righteousness" to a hammer, whose heft and balance is "just right" for the function it has been made to fulfill.[24]

Justification, accordingly, means being "righted" for such an end—being righted for life: *ho de dikaios ek pisteos zesetai*—"By faith the just [*dikaios*] shall *live*" (Gal. 3:11). It is assumed that something stands in the way of our being what we are called to be and doing what we are called to do; therefore this inhibiting factor (in Luther's case, his obsessive guilt) has to be removed. This process of rectification is "by grace" because liberation for life, the removal of that which inhibits life, cannot be achieved by us—that would be like people pulling themselves up by their own bootstraps, or like insomniacs repeatedly telling themselves that they had to get to sleep! And grace, in the justification formula of the Reformation, is a relational term, as we have understood all key biblical terms to be; it means nothing more or less than the presence of God in our lives, establishing a "right" relationship with us, or, conversely, our "righting" our relationship with God.[25] And, finally, faith is that trust which grasps and holds fast to God's gracious offer of "new life," appropriating the divine gift in our relationships with others (the aforementioned horizontal-ethical thrust of the teaching).

What is it that has to be removed if *we* are to "live" in this biblical sense? We, who find ourselves, unsettled and alienated, at the end of an era; we who are products of a system of meaning that promised so very much and does not deliver what it promised?[26] Luther, together with many in his generation, had to be liberated from his inordinate guilt and fear of condemnation. If my analysis of the human condition today in North America has any truth in it,

---

24. "The man at the hardware store had a whole case of hammers. All of them were within the formal statement of what a hammer is: a wooden handle with a piece of steel attached at one end. The function of a hammer is to hit things with—and all of them would presumably do that.

"But one doesn't buy a hammer in the same way he buys a picture. I bought the one I did, not by visual selection, but by tactile instinct. I picked it up, got the ingratiating masculine heft of it, made a couple of tentative passes at the nail-heads in proleptic imagination. The thing was so justly balance, proportioned, that it was a literal extension of my striking arm. As a tool it constituted so effective a transposition from vision to form as positively to invite pounding.

"The hammer is an incarnation of a function. It is, in biblical language, *righteous;* it establishes a right relation between the arm and the nail. If the Lord God made hammers, they would be righteous hammers in that sense" ("Hammer, the Incarnation, and Architecture," in *The Christian Century* (March 27, 1957): 394–95.

25. "In both testaments, 'to be justified' means to be brought into right relations with a person. It can be used both of man to man, and man to God. In the case of man to man, justification is everywhere possible; but there is nothing man can do to secure justification before God" (N. H. Snaith, in *A Theological Word Book of the Bible,* ed. Alan Richardson, D.D. (London: SCM, 1950), 118.

26. See Walter Brueggemann, *Finally Comes the Poet: Daring Speech for Proclamation* (Minneapolis: Fortress Press, 1989), chap. 3, 79–99.

what we shall have to be freed from, if we are to live again, is our sense of futility, purposelessness, and superfluity.[27] We no doubt also need "a gracious God" who will forgive; that is a perennial need. But more than forgiveness or even "acceptance," we need an animating, vivifying God who will inspire—who will make these dry bones live, enabling us to discover in our very creaturehood, for all its limitations and terrors, a vocation[28] that is more than sufficient to fill us with a sense of purpose and direction.

At the level of language, then, "justification by grace through faith" may not mean for us today what it meant for our forebears in the Protestant tradition five hundred years ago. Neither their physical nor their spiritual context duplicates ours. But the *essence* of the principle of justification can certainly speak to us as it spoke to them, for its essence is the process of transformation by which the human spirit, fearful of the unlikely creaturehood that is its true destiny and its glory, is being righted for life.

Let us accentuate the word "process" in the preceding sentence! We are speaking, after all, of the recovery of a dogmatic tradition that is fit for sojourners. The fullness of life for which divine grace prepares us is never wholly appropriated by us. Its mode of appropriation is faith, and faith is not only not sight but it contains in itself a persistent consciousness of the unfulfillment of the very thing it wills to realize. Faith waits and longs for the *truly* new life that it glimpses in Jesus and knows only sporadically and as a matter of hope. That is why Luther accompanied his justification teaching with the insight *simul justus et peccator* (simultaneously justified and sinner). That which holds us back from life—in a word, sin—continues to inhibit the life of those who are being "righted." This is a doctrine of pilgrims, for those who are on the way; it will not do for those who believe they have already arrived. Therefore it is precisely a resource for the journey.

19.3. The Sanctification of Life by the Divine Spirit.   Many expositions of the "time-honored traditional term 'sanctification'"[29] speak of sanctification as a process. Therefore, if justification by grace is itself understood as a process, it is somewhat artificial to make a hard and fast distinction between *justificatio* and *sanctificatio;* and in view of the fact that we have understood justification in just that way, we shall not draw such a distinction in what follows. Perhaps it is useful to follow the Protestant scholastics who described justification as the *terminus a quo* (point or end *from* which) and sanctification as the *terminus ad quem* (end *to* which) divine grace moves the human

---

27. *Professing the Faith,* chap. 5, 253–300.
28. Ibid., chap. 4, §15; chap. 6, §25.
29. Hendrikus Berkhof, *Christian Faith,* 450.

spirit. However, even this manner of expressing the relation between the two terms raises certain questions, and if we are to reclaim the idea of sanctification for the living of the Christian life in our post-Christendom context we must by all means address ourselves to the historic as well as to the contextual problems associated with this concept.

Two questions present themselves to anyone who is somewhat familiar with both the traditional and the peculiarly North American understanding of this biblical theme: first, How can one think about sanctification without conjuring up the entire Pandora's box of misconceptions connected with that reputation for exceptional, affected piety that—justifiably or not—colors religion in general and Christianity in particular in the context of this secularized society? Sanctification and sanctimony are not only linguistically but cultically far too close for comfort in the perceptions of our contemporaries. And it has not helped to rectify this misleading association that those who pursue the doctrine of sanctification with the greatest zeal in our context are often the kinds of Christians whose behavior does betray a certain hint of the sanctimonious.

Historically speaking, the second question is even more important: Can sanctification be described approvingly without ending in the sort of concentration on human response or achievement that in effect nullifies or seriously compromises the insistence on justification by grace through faith, and produces odious distinctions in merit that in turn feed precisely the religious impulse to sanctimony?

A third problem, which is so much part of the two preceding questions that I shall develop my own response to it through endeavoring to address the latter, is how to do justice to the inherently *ethical* dimension of the doctrine of sanctification without being caught up in the too personalistic and moralistic connotations of "growth in grace" that churchly practice and personal piety have associated with this doctrine.

To establish a framework necessary to informed reflection on these and other questions, we should first consider briefly the biblical and historical background of the sanctification concept. Sanctity is a derivative of the Latin word for holy (*sanctus*), and the Bible associates holiness with God alone (Pss. 99:9, 111:9; Josh. 5:15; and so on): "Holiness is God's fundamental nature, what distinguishes God from everything that is not God. God is the Holy One, who has made Himself known to His people as such, and therefore can be called 'The Holy One of Israel.'"[30] Sanctification or "making holy" is therefore God's activity and prerogative: God confers holiness; it is not an

---

30. Emil Brunner, *The Christian Doctrine of the Church, Faith, and the Consummation* (Dogmatics, vol. 3) trans. David Cairns in collaboration with T. H. L. Parker (London: Lutterworth Press, 1962), 290.

achievement or possession of creatures. For prophetic faith, what the divine gift of sanctity evokes in human beings is not an "egocentric" conviction of their own holiness but an "ex-centric"[31] concern for others: that is, the consequence as well as the authentication of sanctifying grace is ethical (see, for example, Hab. 1:13; Isa. 6:3, 5).

This older Testamental conception of the holy is adapted to the christological and ecclesiological as well as the Theological reflections of the newer. Here, the divine holiness (*hagiasmos*) is of course revealed in and conferred through the Christ, and its reality in the life of those who are "in Christ" may even be considered an accomplished fact: "you were washed, you were sanctified, you were justified in the name of the Lord Jesus Christ and in the Spirit of our God" (1 Cor. 6:11); "we are bound to give thanks to God always for you, brethren beloved by the Lord, because God chose you from the beginning to be saved, through sanctification by the Spirit and belief in the truth" (2 Thess. 2:13).

At the same time, the newer Testament can speak of sanctification as a condition or state that awaits fulfillment and requires of believers their ardent participation: "Since we have these promises, beloved, let us cleanse ourselves from every defilement of body and spirit, and make holiness perfect in the fear of God" (2 Cor. 7:1); "For just as you once yielded your members to impurity and to greater and greater iniquity, so now yield your members to righteousness for sanctification" (Rom. 6:19).

This dual aspect of the newer Testamental presentation of the subject may be a source of later historical confusion, for some could accentuate the soteriological actualization of sanctification exemplified in the first, and others the necessity for human response and obedience in the second usage. The ambiguity is clarified, however, if one understands that the two emphases belong to the familiar (especially Pauline) juxtaposition of indicative and imperative statements; that is, as if it were said, "In and through Jesus Christ you are already sanctified [indicative]; therefore live according to your new sanctity in him [imperative]. Be what you are!" Such a connection at the same time accentuates the interrelatedness of justification and sanctification, as aspects of a "unitary process,"[32] and reinforces the earlier observation that (as J. K. S. Reid has stated it) "It appears . . . that sanctification stands nearer to Justification than is often supposed. If, as must be the case, it be rescued from immersion in bare moralism, it will occupy a position nearer to the initiation of the Christian life, and *ipso facto* to Justification."[33]

---

31. Berkhof, *Christian Faith,* 450.

32. John Macquarrie, *Principles of Christian Theology* (London: SCM, 1966), 305–6.

33. Richardson, *A Theological Word Book of the Bible,* 218.

With the near disappearance of the Pauline theology of justification in the postbiblical period of church history, however, sanctification tended increasingly to be associated with the imperative side of this couplet. Jesus Christ was the exemplar and source of holiness, but it was the responsibility of Christians to emulate him through the accumulation of "good works" and "merit." Although for Paul, as later for the Reformers, sanctification is a matter of *conformitas Christi* (that is, being conformed to Christ through the internal, regenerative activity of the Spirit), sanctity in the Middle Ages was characteristically based upon the concept of *imitatio Christi.* While the latter by no means eliminates the restorative work of the Spirit, and while it was accompanied in medieval piety by all manner of sacramental, ritual, and other aids to the achievement of true sanctity, there can be no doubt that it emphasizes the determination of the believing subject. Such an emphasis may not be questionable where it can be assumed that the "indicative" (gospel) dimension is its theological foundation, but this can usually never be assumed, and the danger that sanctification-praxis will degenerate into a type of religious moralism is by no means only theoretical. There can be no doubt that the *imitatio Christi* of the Middle Ages in a (perhaps inevitable) trivialized form laid the groundwork for the whole vast system of legalistic, penitential, and sacerdotal *cultus,* culminating in a corruption of the idea of indulgences, which had to be attacked by all those inside and outside the Church of Rome who remembered the gospel of free grace.[34]

The Reformation's view of sanctification begins, in fact, with justification, and this—in theory at least—precludes its reduction to the "works-righteousness" castigated by Luther and others. For the main representatives of the Protestant protest, sanctification can only signify the ongoing realization, in the life of believers, of the transformation begun through the experience of justifying grace. Nevertheless, Protestantism has been far from unani-

---

34. Emil Brunner argues with some justification that classical Protestantism lost something when it abandoned the emphasis upon personal responsibility for sanctification. "As everyone who is free of theological prejudice knows, there are degrees of approximation to the goal of complete union with the divine will and of transparency to the divine light. It seems to us that in preserving this clearly Biblical insight, Catholicism—eastern as well as western Catholicism—has an important advantage over Protestantism, although on the other hand the declaration of sainthood by the Church, canonization, is something problematic. . . " (*The Christian Doctrine of the Church, Faith, and the Consummation,* trans. by David Cairns in collaboration with T. H. L. Parker [London: Lutterworth Press, 1962], 293).

Brunner has a point. There are dangers on both sides of this question. In my opinion, however, the greater danger is always that grace and gospel will not be understood, whereas "law" and "good works" are immediately accessible (almost "natural") and are easily mistaken for the essence of religious belief. It is not surprising that, as we shall see, the Reformation's emphasis upon justification and sanctification as, both of them, gifts of grace itself, soon gave way to the more "natural" religion of tit-for-tat—and especially in the North American context!

mous on this question. Tillich's breakdown of Protestant views on sanctification into three types seems to me particularly helpful.

First, for Calvin and his followers, "sanctification proceeds in a slowly upward-turning line; both faith and love are progressively actualized. The power of the divine Spirit in the individual increases. Perfection is approached, though never reached." Tillich believes this to be a consequence of Calvin's teaching concerning the third use of the law, namely, that besides its preventative and revelatory functions, the law also serves to guide "the Christian who is grasped by the divine Spirit but who is not yet free from the power of the negative in knowledge and action." Thus "growth in grace" is possible, even though the good Calvinist would never endorse Wesley's belief that *perfection* is possible.[35]

Tillich's second group, the radical evangelical reformers, were ready to push Calvin's nuanced position on sanctification beyond the limits set by the Geneva reformer. They rejected his belief that perfection could not be reached,

> and reaffirmed the concept of the perfect ones but in such a way that the paradoxical character of Christian perfection becomes invisible. Actual perfection is demanded and deemed to be possible. In the selected group the holiness of the whole and the saintliness of the individuals are actual, in contrast to the "world," which includes the large churches. Obviously, the situation became rather problematic when the holiness sects themselves became large churches. Then, although the ideal of the unparadoxical holiness of every member of the group could not be sustained, the perfectionist ideal remained in force and produced the identification of the Christian message of salvation with moral perfection in the individual members.[36]

Third, Luther's position on sanctification, according to Tillich, must be distinguished from both the previous two. He did not accept the upward thrust of either Calvin's qualified or the Evangelicals' unrestrictive progress-in-holiness theory:

---

35. Tillich, *Systematic Theology,* vol. 3, 229–30. An interesting and well-worded recent instance of what seems to me an impeccably Calvinistic position on sanctification is found in Daniel Migliore's *Faith Seeking Understanding:* "The term *growth* must be used with care in reference to the Christian life. Any suggestion of an organic process of development or an ordered sequence of stages should be avoided. There is real movement in Christian life, but it is not predictable and does not take place in neatly identifiable stages. If we respect the freedom of God's grace and the limitless disguises that sin assumes, we will avoid oversimplification in our portrayals of the process of growth in Christian life. Still, in the environment of the Spirit of God, growth in Christian faith, love, and hope does occur" (178).

36. Tillich, *Systematic Theology,* vol. 3, 230.

In Lutheranism the emphasis on the paradoxical element in the experience of the New Being was so predominant that sanctification could not be interpreted in terms of a line moving upward toward perfection. It was seen instead as an up-and-down of ecstasy and anxiety, of being grasped by *agape* and being thrown back into estrangement and ambiguity. This oscillation between up and down was experienced radically by Luther himself, in the change between moments of courage and joy and moments of demonic attacks, as he interpreted his states of doubt and profound despair. The consequence of the absence in Lutheranism of the Calvinistic Evangelistic valuation of discipline was that the ideal of progressive sanctification was taken less seriously and replaced by a great emphasis on the paradoxical character of the Christian life.[37]

Tillich admits that the Lutheran position on sanctification left Lutheranism open to certain problems—particularly, during the period of Lutheran orthodoxy, "the disintegration of morality and practical religion against which the Pietistic movement arose."[38] Calvin's position, by comparison, he affirms, "is more realistic, more able to support an ethical theory and a disciplined life of sanctification."[39] On the other hand, however, Luther's "ecstatic," "up-and-down" treatment of the doctrine is "full of creative possibilities in the personal life:

> Luther's experience of demonic attacks led also to a deep understanding of the demonic elements in life in general and in the religious life in particular. The second period of romanticism, in which the existentialist movement of the twentieth century was prepared, could hardly have sprung from Calvinist-Evangelical soil, whereas it was genuine in a culture permeated by Lutheran traditions.[40]

This analysis is particularly useful for any discussion of sanctification in a North American context, for a rather simple reason: Calvinism and evangelicalism, both of which could relate fairly positively to older, Catholic sanctification theology, have set the tone for our whole understanding of this concept, and Lutheranism, which in its postclassical phases itself often gave way to pietistic and orthodox Protestant corruptions of its earliest expressions, has had very little influence in this respect. The consequence, theologically speaking, is that the whole notion of progressive growth in obedience and holiness, with legalistic and moralistic overtones, has dominated the religious life of this continent.

---

37. Ibid., 230–31.
38. Ibid., 229.
39. Ibid.
40. Ibid., 231.

That it could do so was, of course, also in part the consequence of the sociopolitical vision that inspired the New World altogether: that which throughout this study we have named, with George Grant, the religion of progress. In fact, it is hard to imagine how any other version of the Christian life could have prevailed in this context, so long as the Christian churches wished to be "established" in the manner already discussed. What could be more fitting for a culture based on growth than a *cultus* promising growth in grace? Luther's nonprogressive, up-and-down conception of the process of Christian living simply does not fit with a worldview that is consistently up-and-up!

But what happens when the ever upward-and-onward worldview founders? It is true that, in such circumstances, some will find *religious* assurances of progress even more needful. They will be comforted by the thought of personal growth in grace, and will seek the solace of this faith all the more ardently because their world does not offer them such solace. But what of those whose physical-material or spiritual-intellectual conditions prevent them from pursuing a religion that embraces comfort at the expense of truth? Tillich states that Calvinistic sanctification theology is "more realistic" than Luther's; but surely this "realism" refers to its capacity for ethical pragmatism and not to realism in the contemporary sense. Luther's recognition of the "up-and-down" character of the Christian life, as of life in general, is surely the more realistic in the latter sense; and in historical contexts that aggravate the *fluxus* character of personal life through great fluctuations in the public, global sphere, such realism is surely necessary to the very survival of persons and peoples—and churches! Unless justifying, sanctifying grace helps us to become honest about the world, or about the church, religion will only function in precisely the way Karl Marx said it would, as "opiate"; and the *terminus ad quem* of that kind of holiness-quest is not life but death.

In this way we are led to an initial insight in our contextual reconsideration of sanctification theology: namely, that sanctification will undoubtedly and perhaps inevitably lead to the undoing of justification by grace through faith if it indulges in a spirituality of progressive growth in personal or ecclesiastical holiness that must leave the experienced world behind. By the experienced world, I mean both the great world of political, economic, and cultural life (the macrocosm) and the world of our own personal experience as human beings who share with all other creatures the vicissitudes of existence. For Christians, there can be no embracing of a holiness that makes it necessary for one either to lie about that experienced world or to take flight from it. Luther's justification theology, which is a dimension of his undergirding *theologia crucis,* does not impose such a necessity upon the believer, because it accentuates divine grace and pictures human appropriation of this grace as a faith (trust!) that is in dialogue with its antithesis; the antithesis is still

present, because sin is still present (*simul justus et peccator*). Luther's sanctification doctrine does not contradict or weaken this justification concept,
because it too remains grounded in the theology of the cross and does not
quietly wander over into Christian triumphalism. The process of sanctification remains *a process,* and does not court the heady notion of progress.
Salvation continues to be *per Christum solum, sola gratia, sola fide.*

Why is this so important? Not, surely, for the purely doctrinal reason that
it sustains the christological basis of Christian soteriology, and not even because it sustains this basis according to a *theologia crucis* that consistently
resists doctrinal and ecclesiastical triumphalism. If we would discover the
fundamental reason for *all* of this—the Christology, the theology of the cross,
the justification and sanctification theology that resists progress, and so on—
then we must recall once more that most rudimentary ground-concept of the
tradition of Jerusalem: that this world "must not be written off prematurely"
(Bonhoeffer), must not be abandoned, must be "mended" (Fackenheim); that
"grace," in this tradition, is nothing more or less than "divine pathos"—that
is, God's suffering love for the creation; that the "making holy" to which the
God of grace is therefore dedicated is a *worldly* holiness,[41] that is, a sanctification of creaturehood.

Luther did not always say this—nor does anyone else, not even Bonhoeffer, who among us all came closest to it. Every one of us is sufficiently
conditioned by certain forms of piety and presuppositions about the sacred
to resort, sometimes, to language and actions that appear sanctimonious.[42]
But Luther (and the type of Christian he exemplifies) understood intuitively—almost, I feel, at a visceral level—that faith in Jesus Christ, if it
means anything at all, must mean commitment to life: God's life-
commitment, and therefore (the ever present "death-wish" notwithstanding!)
also ours. *That* is the ground-concept of the whole of his theology of the
incarnation and the cross.

Sanctification, therefore, cannot mean other than the sanctification of *life*
by "the Lord and Giver of Life." It has (we reiterate) nothing at all to do
with getting out of the world and everything to do with getting into it. It
shuns altogether the "religious" impulse to supranatural holiness and growth
in that well-known kind of piety that lives two feet above the ground and
wills to ascend even higher! The life that the divine Spirit will give us, our
strenuous objections notwithstanding, is the same life that the creating God
already gave us and the justifying God already secured for us: creaturely life!
If this pneumatic "process" leads us on a merry ride; if we are carried

---

41. See Greenberg's discussion of Christianity's possible "second stage," chap. 4, §14.2.

42. Bonhoeffer's *Life Together* indulges in a good deal of this language! See the new translation by Daniel W. Bloesch (Minneapolis: Fortress Press, 1996).

"whither we would not" (John 21:18, KJV); if our lives are a *fluxus* of ups and downs, ecstasies and depressions, it is only because it is by no means an easy matter even for the triune God to make us *truly* human. We still want to be gods, or, failing that, we would still be content to be happy animals; but God wills to sanctify us with human being, and through our regenerated humanity to sanctify also what we have sullied by our pride and sloth.

This life-oriented interpretation of sanctification, which could well be exemplified by many "lives of the saints," ancient and modern (including many who do not look like saints!), addresses both of the misconstruals of the doctrine named at the outset. The first, the tendency to equate sanctity and sanctimony is addressed directly: the point is not to become *unworldly* but, on the contrary, to become worldly. The second, the idea of increase in sanctity that threatens, if pursued, the theology of justification by grace, requires only one more observation: It is, of course, absurd if someone denies *any* kind of growth. The whole exercise undertaken in this and other studies of Christian theology, for instance, takes it for granted that Christians may increase in their knowledge of the faith and in their recognition of its meaning for their lives. My polemic against the "growth-in-grace" syndrome is contextually inspired: it is far too entrenched in North American Christianity of every variety, and it is productive of the kind of personal pietism that is all too ready to leave the world behind so long as one may save oneself (Berkhof's "ego-centrism").

But even if this were not the case, contextually, I would opt for Luther's theology of sanctification, because it allows one to be honest about life's grave *un*sanctity while believing, hoping, and living under the *necessitas* of a Spirit-directed grace that drives one into the world, the macrocosm and the microcosm, to find one's true sanctity there among the creatures.

And, not incidentally, this may even help to overcome that alienation one feels as a serious Christian about the church. Even the church, for all its unholiness, may be a candidate for the sanctification of the life-giving Spirit.

19.4. "People of the Book." The Reformation of the sixteenth century was a response to the breakdown of an epoch, the Middle Ages, and the vacuum of meaning and authority that was entailed in this crisis. Already with the so-called "pre-Reformers," Wycliffe and Hus, and with late scholastics (especially Ockham) who shared their mistrust of ecclesiastical authorities that had become all the more insistent in their decadent state, a single source of meaning and authority begins to assert itself: the Bible. Through reacquaintance with the original witnesses, these scholars and their later, more prominent successors believed that the Christian movement could find its way through the ending that was affecting every aspect of its life to a new beginning. The shaking of the foundations of the nearly thousand-year period we call "medieval" proved an opportunity for Christian revitalization through a fresh encounter (virtually the first momentous encounter) with the Scriptures of Israel and the early church.

Something like this *could* happen, and so far, to a limited extent, is happening, in our own time. It is almost inevitable that this should be so, because during periods of crisis or "paradigm shift" (Kuhn), human movements and institutions are driven by their present uncertainties to re-examine their foundations, and the Bible is the primary and unique documentary evidence of Christian foundations. If there is to be any recovery of purpose and direction; if there is to be any sifting of wheat from chaff; if there is to be any doctrinal and ecclesiastical housecleaning; in short, if there is to be any genuine confession of the faith in the face of contemporary threats to the life God intends, it must perforce pass through the sieve of these writings. Not only are they the original sources to which the evolving doctrines and practices of the church must be traced, but they are the only reliable witnesses that we have to the events that brought the disciple community into being in the first place, and to the interpretation of these events that fired its resolve to become a messenger-community.

Like the parental faith, Christianity, as we have had many occasions to recall in these pages, is a historical faith. As soon as one says (with Paul) "Jesus Christ and him crucified," one commits oneself to history—and therefore to the Bible. The Reformation was a re-forming of the church around its original model, so far as this could be discerned and emulated a millennium and a half later. This original model means, of course, the scriptural model; and therefore the *sola scriptura* principle of the Reformers, while not the *first* principle of their confession of the faith (they did not counsel us to believe *in* the Bible, but *through* it) is inseparable from that first principle, which is their witness to the grace of God in Jesus as the Christ, received by faith.

There is growing evidence of the necessity for such a recovery of scriptural knowledge and authority in most churches on this continent today. If the transition through which we are passing is as significant as many have claimed it is, comparable only to the transition that marks the beginning of Christendom in the fourth century, then it is even more important for our present generations of the disciple community to rediscover the Bible than it was for sixteenth-century Christians. This necessity manifests itself today in all of the major bodies of the church, and for a variety of reasons.

For one thing, among minorities in all of the churches in North America, there is by now a sufficient awareness of the crisis through which we are passing both as church and society that many sense the need for direction. "Future shock" naturally orients human beings to the past: if we have become so confused as to have to contemplate such a future, how did this happen? Where have we come from? Where did we go wrong? For many Christians, both lay and clerical, this intuition of the need to return to "basics" is vague and unformed, for, as was suggested in the introduction to *Professing the Faith,* the "basics" (including the Scriptures) to which it is felt we must return are not sufficiently familiar to enable many to become more explicit concerning what is lacking.

At the same time, in these same denominations there exist groups that feel quite confident that they *do* know what is lacking, and, as self-appointed guardians of "the Bible," they create in congregations and church structures an atmosphere of antagonism that is often very destructive. In the name of the Scriptures, they offer vigorous resistance to every progressive decision and new alliance of their denominations, and frequently end by driving their more thoughtful contemporaries away from the very "book" they purport to know and revere. If the churches are to be preserved from the machinations of biblicistic elements within and beyond them, those who are *not* familiar with the Bible are going to have to become so.

Not only does this *need* for biblical knowledge and authority make itself felt today, however, but there is as well an *opportunity* for such a renewed acquaintances with our sources. I do not mean only that the crisis is itself the opportunity; I mean also that we are the inheritors of several *centuries* of biblical study, and have in our midst many who possess an expertise in biblical interpretation undreamed of by our Reformation forebears. This vast accumulation of biblical scholarship and expertise exists in the manner of a colossal fortune bequeathed to the church, of which the beneficiary is unfortunately unaware, or of which it has heard only rumors. Luther and Calvin, who were in the nature of the case theologians and reforming spirits, had themselves to become—so far as they were able—biblical scholars; for apart from a few (notably, of course, Erasmus) who were linguistically and historically equipped to decipher such complex problems as which versions of the ancient texts were most reliable, they had little assistance. We, on the contrary, can depend on literally centuries of refined and intensive biblical scholarship and a cadre of scholars to help us to glean from this treasure house what is most significant for our needs.

Yet there are barriers in the way of the church's access to the Bible, and if it is to become a resource for the sojourning people of the Way, these barriers will have to be faced and ways found of removing them. I shall name four such.

a. Biblicism. The aforementioned guardians of the Bible, due to their excessive zeal and, on the other hand, the relative ignorance of the Scriptures on the part of the majority in the mainline churches, have created a certain image of Bible Christianity that discourages many others from the attempt to familiarize themselves with these writings. Fundamentalism may not be the greatest evil in our ecclesiastical and social context, but it is nonetheless an evil; for it has established itself as the only appropriate way of approaching the Scriptures. Its adherents are characteristically so adamant, so "knowledgeable" (at a superficial level of "chapter-and-verse"), and so intimidating to the weaker and more modest church folk, that they have been able to discredit—in the minds of most laypersons—even the best biblical scholarship. Whatever does not accord with their own literalistic-rationalistic way of receiving these ancient texts, they attribute to "modernism" and plain unbelief.

The success of this element in North America has been phenomenal. Although their movement is only a century old, and although it was and continues to be chiefly a *negative* movement—a reaction against liberalism and what is usually identified as "humanism"—it has succeeded in creating the impression that it, and not "mainstream" Protestantism, is the true successor of the Reformation, as well as the only trustworthy representative of true biblical faith.

That this has been possible in North America (it has not happened in Europe) is not only owing to the promotional cleverness of the biblicists themselves; it is far more a consequence of the *political* reality that this kind of Christianity, which in kind resembles individualistic capitalism and is conveniently negligent of the social critique that prophetic faith ought to bring to bear against the rich and powerful, is entirely amenable to the economic and political forces of the dominant culture and therefore allied with them, whether intentionally or by default. Nothing is more pleasing to the ear of those who benefit most from the status quo than a religion that addresses itself to the disturbances of private souls and leaves untouched the societal ills that are behind most of the disturbances in question. Here, in other words, we encounter once more the absolute need for responsible Christianity to distance itself from the dominant culture if it is to make the slightest difference even *to* the dominant culture.

The victory of biblicistic Christianity is also owed, however, to two of the further barriers to a renewal of biblical knowledge and authority in the churches, and both of these, being within or in close proximity to the churches, can—if Christians have the will for it—be more readily dealt with.

b. Liberal Sentimentalism and Selectivity. If biblicism has attained the power that it seems to have on this continent, a major reason for this is the virtual abandonment of Bible study and authority on the part of major groups within all of the once-mainline denominations. Historically speaking, the liberal movement of the nineteenth and early twentieth centuries made it possible for Christians to *study* the Scriptures in the more disciplined sense of the term "study." That is to say, the spirit of liberalism enabled Christians to approach the Bible as a historical source, the work of human beings, and as such susceptible to scholarly investigation and deconstruction of the scope achieved by feminist and other biblical scholars in recent decades. Without questioning that the writers of these documents were inspired persons, liberalism nevertheless lifted the Bible out of its imprisonment as a "holy book" that simply had to be believed and not investigated in the manner of other ancient works.

But the course of liberalism in theology and church proves the truth of the saying that "a little knowledge is a dangerous thing." Those who have pursued far enough the kind of biblical scholarship made possible by liberalism (and this is true of all serious students of the Bible today) know that such scholarship renders the Bible even more important for faith than it would otherwise have been. But the public impression created by "a little knowledge" of liberal attitudes toward the Scriptures has left by far the greater majority of mainstream Protestants with the impression that the Bible is so immersed in history (ancient history!), so bound up with prescientific worldviews, so subject to human error, and withal so internally inconsistent, that it cannot be regarded as profoundly authoritative as it was for our Protestant forebears. Its authority is at most relative, and at worst diffuse: one can make it say what one wishes!

The resultant attitude permeating the liberal and moderate denominations has been one of neglect. And this neglect, combined as it has been with an abhorrence of fundamentalism and the old orthodoxy, has left the field of biblical knowledge and authority wide open to the biblicism of the Christian Right. Liberal and moderate Christians continue vaguely to "revere" the Bible, and therefore (often secretly) to admire the very biblicists they criticize; but they do not know what is in it, apart from a few, well-worn verses and usually oversimplified ideas (such as that God "is love" and that we too should "love one another.") In place of biblical awareness and authority, which the scholarly wing of liberalism intended to illuminate, the bourgeois ecclesiastical ethos most influenced by liberalism has ended by apotheosizing certain sentimental "truths" roughly gleaned from the Bible, but so thoroughly abstracted from their historical-theological context as to perform no office beyond the confirmation of the bourgeois transcendence already held in these circles.

c. The Malfunctioning of Biblical Scholarship. The one factor that might have countered both the easy victory of biblicism and the neglect of the Bible in liberal and moderate North American churches is biblical scholarship.

Beyond that, the overcoming of the two barriers designated above will depend, to a large extent, on the emergence of a new attitude toward biblical
scholarship on the part of both churches and scholars themselves. But while
there are some hopeful signs that such a new attitude is already taking shape,
the problems here are in my opinion very serious indeed.

These problems can perhaps be summarized from two angles: persistent
anti-intellectualism in the churches, and detached professionalism among the
"guild" of the scholars.

So thoroughly has "religion" been relegated to the realm of private feeling;
so averse is the average middle-class congregation to the kind of disciplined
study requisite even to minimal awareness of the Scriptures; so reluctant are
these same congregations to entertain particularly the critical and "discom-
forting" aspects that are an inevitable part of any serious encounter with the
Bible; so consistently have liberal Protestant preachers capitulated to ser-
monizing of the sort that entails a minimum of biblical exegesis, that one
sometimes despairs of the possibility that the Protestant ideal of faith as a
thinking faith can ever be approximated on this continent.

This kind of discouragement is itself partly to blame for the other side of
the *problematique* under discussion: professional distancing from the life of
the churches. When there seems to be so little demand for scholarship in the
churches, those who have pursued the truly difficult linguistic, historical, and
theological disciplines requisite to biblical scholarship seldom feel that their
work is needed and appreciated by the churches. A few scholars—I am thinking of Walter Brueggemann, Phyllis Trible, and Walter Wink, for example—
are themselves sufficiently committed to the churches *as scholars* that they
persist in their efforts to communicate with "ordinary Christians" without
the kind of condescension that is sometimes involved in this attempt.

A much greater number of professional biblical scholars, on the other
hand, being themselves caught up in the often finely nuanced aspects of their
craft (*and,* one must admit, in the highly competitive academic guild of which
they are part), pursue their scholarship with seemingly little regard to its
actual or potential usefulness to the churches. Some come to feel themselves
part of a community of scholarship whose aims are so objective and whose
methods are so demanding of a value-free approach to truth that it would be
something like a betrayal of their "science" either to write and lecture for the
community of believers or even to concern themselves overmuch with the
pertinence of their studies for Christian belief.

C. H. Dodd remarked on this phenomenon already in 1928:

> The Bible has suffered from being treated too much as a source of information.
> The traditional theory valued it as giving authoritative information, in the form

of dogma, upon matters known only by special revelation. The critical method has too often issued in treating it as a collection of information for the anti-quary.[43]

Already more than sixty years ago, the great English scholar who was himself a luminary of the guild of biblical scholars had concluded that "the reaction against the old dogmatic use of the Scriptures has in some quarters gone too far."[44] The very discipline that could have established a new understanding of the *genuinely* authoritative character of Scripture for the disciple commu-nity, thus circumventing its cooptation by both dogmatic fundamentalism and liberal sentimentalism, served instead to render it less accessible to the nurture of the church than it had been in earlier periods.

This barrier, I would humbly suggest, has not yet been overcome, despite the heroic efforts of some to do so. It can only be altered by the growth of congregational and clerical concern for sound teaching and by the willing-ness of more of the professionals to serve the churches more directly. It seems to me one of the ironies of our present situation that such a large percentage of the limited personnel and monetary resources of the Protestant churches is expended on biblical scholarship that benefits the churches themselves so little. Clergy who are still, in many cases, minimally indoctrinated into the Greek and Hebrew languages as well as the latest methods and insights of scriptural exegesis, by the time they have been in their parishes for five years, draw (most of them) hardly at all upon that scholarly exposure. They too often capitulate, just as their senior colleagues have done, to "topical" preaching of the most predictable sort. After a hundred years of historical-critical method, few indeed are the "people in the pew" who have the slightest understanding either of the method or what it makes possible by way of enlightened wisdom concerning the very sources upon which the whole faith hangs. There is something quite wrong about this!

d. "Spirituality." A fourth barrier to the recovery of the *sola scriptura* in Protestant Christianity is the appearance, particularly noticeable in the past two decades, of what must be regarded, I think, as a substitute for biblical (and most other forms of) authority. This phenomenon is in reality not new; its antecedents are ancient, in fact, and it contains a sufficient element of

---

43. *The Authority of the Bible* (1929; reprint, London and Glasgow: Collins [Fontana Books], 1960), 270.
44. Ibid., 271.

authenticity, Christianly understood, to render both its detection and its problematic character difficult.

I am referring to what is now increasingly named "spirituality"—a term that does not emerge naturally from classical Protestant sources and is in fact in some ways inimical to these, but has its roots in religious mysticism, whether Christian or pagan. It is, of course, strongly encouraged by the general atmosphere of our late phase of modernity, with its (albeit ambiguous) reaction against materialism and its search for stronger expressions of the subjective and mystical aspects of human experience. It is also, quite obviously, a Christian heritage from the whole pneumatic dimension of the faith, which has been scandalously suppressed by all forms of ecclesiastical orthodoxy, as we have already had occasion to recognize.

As such, this amorphous and ill-defined phenomenon of "spirituality" should not be regarded by responsible theology and faith *only* in a critical vein. It is a necessary corrective to all three of the problems outlined above: the literalism of the biblicists, the doctrinalism of the orthodox, and the obscurantism of the scholars. Wherever the Spirit is smothered, it will breathe freely in other quarters!

But however grateful we may and must be for the spiritual-charismatic revitalization of Christianity here and there, we shall nevertheless have to recognize that it cannot as such be a basis for the nurture and edification of the Christian community. To identify the Christian faith too exclusively with spiritual receptivity and aliveness is to abandon trinitarian tradition for a unitary religion of the Spirit; and when this happens, as the history of the church amply attests, one does not know *what* spirit is alive and at work in the congregation. In fact, that history causes one to suspect that it will usually be a spirit that is carrying its devotees far away from Jerusalem!

Undoubtedly, such a direction is preferred by many. Given the history of mysticism in general and Christian mysticism in particular, one would not be surprised to discover that many who adhere to the churches do in fact covet for themselves the kind of immediacy and emotional ecstacy that spiritualism offers and trinitarian faith resists. But we should be quite clear that if, today or tomorrow, the churches should move uncritically in that direction, they would have moved out of the orbit of the Judeo-Christian tradition into something quite different.

For the tradition of Jerusalem is, as we have continuously stressed in these pages, a *historically* oriented faith.

Christianity is thoroughly committed to the view that God reveals Himself in and through history. It is no doubt paradoxical to affirm that our knowledge of eternal and necessary truths of religion depends upon contingent truths of

301

history. Christianity accepts the paradox. Mysticism in its more extreme forms dismisses the historical order as irrelevant. *Christianity cannot do so, while it uses as the symbol of its faith a creed which recites events "under Pontius Pilate.*[45]

These four barriers to the recovery and updating of the *sola scriptura* principle must be understood and struggled with, not only in order that the disciple community should find its legitimate sources of authority in a time of uncertainty and crisis, but in order that it should be equipped truly to "confess the faith" in a cultural context that is far more gravely threatened than is generally thought.

In spite of everything that has been said heretofore, some readers may suppose that the "threat" to which I am referring is one or other of the great physical instabilities—economic, environmental, and other increasingly visible problems—by which our society is confronted. These, however, must in my opinion be regarded as consequences of what is really threatening our civilization, not causes. For causation, we have to look to deeper attitudinal—and, in the best sense, spiritual—dimensions of our social malaise. These dimensions are many, and they cannot be lumped together into a single slogan or description; but one of the most visible of these invisible sources of malaise is surely the loss of memory that has gripped the North American peoples, and the consequent failure of vision and hope.

Memory is indispensable to civilization. This is perhaps the single most important assumption binding the two founding cultures of Western civilization, Athens and Jerusalem. The two did not remember the same things, nor did they even regard the process of remembering in the same way, but both assume that memory is the basis of culture, and that without it there can be no culture. As Reinhold Niebuhr put it,

> Human communities have one thing in common with persons. They are historical entities who have reacted to unique historical events. Their memory of these events is one of the basic forces of community. They express their consciousness of their uniqueness by their devotion to heroes, who represent dramatic and poetic embodiments of the peculiar "genius" of the nation. Thus Washington and Lincoln have a special position in the national "myth" which expresses the self-consciousness of our nation. The memory of critical events such as the granting of the Magna Carta and the Declaration of Independence and Lincoln's Gettysburg Address, are also capable of sustaining and giving consistency to the "spirit" of the community.[46]

---

45. Ibid., 9. (My italics.)

46. Reinhold Niebuhr, *The Self and the Dramas of History* (New York: Charles Scribner's Sons, 1955), 39.

At one level, what this observation means for our present subject is the quite obvious fact that the loss of *biblical* memory is a serious cultural loss, and not only a religious one; for the Bible really is "the great code" without which neither our history nor our literature, art, and music can be understood profoundly. The very heroes and documents referred to by Reinhold Niebuhr in the foregoing quotation, to mention only these, are themselves inconceivable apart from some acquaintance with that "code." For this reason alone, Christian forgetfulness of this primary source is a cultural loss, and informed Christian testimony to the Bible is a cultural gain.

But that is merely a surface observation beside the one that needs to be drawn here. What lifts the necessity of a new encounter with the Scriptures of Israel and the church above the realm of cultural edification and preservation and places it in the realm of confession is the fact that there is a colossal threat to our civilization originating with what we regard as our highest achievements. Our technological genius has produced means of communication that, while appearing to foster the process of memory, in fact destroy it. We are fast becoming what a brilliant American teaching novelist, Daniel Quinn, calls "cultural amnesiacs."[47]

I am, of course, referring to modern media, and particularly visual media. Through television and its related technologies, it is possible to communicate the data of civilization to vast numbers of people. One can not only hear the Gettysburg address read by a competent actor but simultaneously "visit" the site on which it was delivered, view rare historical pictures of those involved, receive interpretations by leading experts on the subject, and so on. This seems to many to be an enormous leap forward in communication and education; and under certain circumstances, it may in fact be so.

But one element is missing in the process, and if it is not supplied by other resources (and, for the majority, it is not!) the audiovisual medium alone will not only not supply it but will rob its recipients of the *habit* necessary to its development. We may call that habit reflection, or contemplation, or meditation, or simply thought. All of these words, and others that could be employed for the purpose, refer to a vital dimension of the process called memory: that is, the absorption of experience, so that what the senses take in becomes the raw material of an ongoing inner dialogue within the self and

---

47. See Quinn's fascinating "novel" *Ishmael,* which is more like a contemporary socratic dialogue (New York: A Bantam/Turner Book, 1993). Quinn distinguishes between the "Leaver" (hunter and gatherer) and the "Taker" (industrialized, "developed") peoples of the earth. The former "are still passing [their accumulated tradition] along in whatever form it came to them. But we're not. . . . We [Takers] have no such consciousness. For the most part, we're a very 'new' people. Every generation is somehow new, more thoroughly cut off from the past than the one that came before." And "Mother Culture [Quinn's term for the dominant structure of our society] says that this is as it should be. There's nothing in the past for us. The past is dreck. The past is something to be put behind us, something to be escaped from" (200–201).

within the community. The excitement of the senses alone does not cause this to occur. In fact, when the chief medium of communication in a society is one that presents an endless flow of visual images, nicely framed and controlled, and seldom accompanied by sustained interpretation, the habit of reflection necessary to the creation of memory is systematically discouraged. The mind is constantly occupied by ever new images, which, unless they are ordered and evaluated by some perspective brought to them from beyond themselves, exercise a tyranny of randomness and numb the imagination. It is not for nothing that one of the prohibitions in Israel's most succinct expression of the Torah forbids the making of graven images, and that the whole sensory accent in Hebrew thought falls upon the sense of hearing, not of sight. When the sensory impressions by which one's life is dominated are visual images created *for* one (and, as we noted earlier, by economic forces whose whole object is to move one to become the consumer of their products), the imagination is in grave danger of ceasing to function at all, and, with it, what we call memory.

I am proposing that there is today a new reason for Christians to remember that they are "people of the book." More than that, I am suggesting that their intelligent and informed appropriation of "the book" in question is in itself already an integral aspect of Christian confession. If the definition of confession I have offered in this trilogy, namely, that it is the witness to which Christians are called in the face of explicit contextual threats to the life that God intends, has merit, then the recovery of the *sola scriptura* in the North American context today comes very close to confession, and is at least the penultimate phase and presupposition of every other explicit act of confession. For "television may represent a threat to our culture analogous to the threat of atomic weapons to our civilization."[48]

Of course we cannot simply take up the sixteenth-century methods and associations of this "formal principle" of the Reformation, and if this is not already obvious to us, then the attempts of fundamentalism to represent the Reformers in that respect ought to forewarn us of the wrongness of the approach. But we do not have to repeat the past—and, in fact, we can only repeat what is significant about that particular past if we refuse to repeat it! To quote again C. H. Dodd, "even supposing we had before us His [Jesus'] own words, they would need 'translation' out of their historical setting before they could be directly applied to our own case."[49] To communicate faithfully "what the Bible says" one cannot simply repeat "what the Bible says." Biblical authority only occurs when, through human discipline (scholarship, preach-

---

48. Reinhold Niebuhr, *The Irony of American History* (New York: Charles Scribner's Sons, 1952), 59.
49. C. H. Dodd, *The Authority of the Bible,* 265.

ing) and the "internal testimony" of the divine Spirit, one is grasped by the *Logos* (Word) to which the Bible points and cannot in itself contain. We should, however, be in a better position today than were our progenitors in the sixteenth and seventeenth centuries at least to meet the first criterion, human discipline. Precisely that is part of the *discipleship* to which these volumes have tried to speak. The second is not ours to control.

At the conclusion of his imaginery and prophetic treatment of the problematic future being courted by our "forgetful" society, the story he called *Fahrenheit 451,*[50] the American writer Ray Bradbury depicts a community of latter-day monastics who inhabit a wilderness area in hiding from the authorities. It is the task of these refugees from a society of control similar to the one depicted by every antiutopian writer since Samuel Butler to keep alive the literary and other traditions of the past. The particular responsibility of the main protagonist of Bradbury's tale, interestingly enough, is to memorize the Book of Ecclesiastes, and to repeat it over and over again so that the burning of books[51] will not destroy this testimony to human wisdom from the past.

There are new and compelling sociohistorical reasons for the revival of the Reformation's *sola scriptura,* as Bradbury's story in its way illustrates. While it seems likelier that books of every type will simply be set aside in favor of the electronic media rather than burned, the important question is whether the kind of reflective wisdom (not only knowledge) that has been transmitted by print and the necessarily slow process of reading can be retained. For Christians, beyond being the sole historical witness to the events upon which faith is based, the Bible is the indispensable source of that wisdom (*sophia*). As the Christian movement leaves its "settled" state and ventures once more, like Abraham and Sarah, into the unknown land of the future, the Bible will have to be taken down from the shelves, lecterns, and end-tables on which it has been displayed more frequently than it has been "read, learned, marked, and inwardly digested"; it will have to become again what it was for the first disciples and the reforming Christians—our primary guide on "the Way."

19.5. The Sacraments. Our concern in the present discussion is to explore certain foundational teachings and practices of the tradition that, under the conditions of transition to the diaspora form of the church, may be appropriated by the disciple community in new, or at least newly meaningful, ways. The subject of the sacraments, on account of its history and the quite differ-

---

50. Ray Bradbury, *Fahrenheit 451* (Paris: Denoel, 1955).
51. The temperature indicated by the title of the book is the temperature at which paper burns.

ent ways in which sacraments are understood and practiced in the various ecclesial families, is an especially complex one. We shall not be able to avoid all of the problems associated with this subject; however, in keeping with our main intent, we shall concentrate here on one question: What could the coming diaspora status of the Christian movement mean for our understanding and practice of the sacraments?

As background for the consideration of that question, we must review briefly some of the aspects of the subject that will of necessity affect our answer. We may begin by recognizing that the term "sacrament" (*sacramentum*), which as such does not appear in the Bible, "was taken to be the translation of the NT word *mysterion* and was used for many elements in the faith and ritual of the church."[52] If one consults a lexicon, biblical word book, or concordance, one discovers that *mysterion* (mystery), a term used most frequently by Paul, usually refers to the core of the gospel: its revelation (Eph. 6:19), the awareness of the divine purpose now made known in Christ (Rom. 16:25f.), the mystery of the fact that the Gentiles are included in the divine plan of salvation (Rom.16:26; Eph. 3:3–6; Col. 1:27), and so on. In other words, *mysterion/sacramentum,* as employed in the newer Testamental writings, is not linked directly with the sacred acts that we call sacraments, although indirect connections may be drawn. Yet the practice of considering *mysterion/sacramentum* as a general term for specific sacraments began to develop early in the church, perhaps under the historic influence of the mystery religions. Tertullian (160–225 C.E.) applied it especially to baptism.

It would surprise many contemporary Christians to learn that the number of specific rites designated sacraments has varied all the way from two to thirty (Hugo of St. Victor [d. 1142] listed thirty sacraments).[53] Not until the thirteenth century did the Catholic Church of the West settle on seven sacraments (Baptism, Confirmation, Eucharist, extreme unction, priestly orders, and marriage). The Eastern Church accepted these. The Protestant Reformers, however, reduced the number to two (Baptism and the Lord's Supper[54]), basing their decision on the apparently explicit institution of these by Jesus (Matt. 28:19; 1 Cor. 11:23–26). In other words, here as elsewhere they were guided by the *sola scriptura* principle. In doing this, however, they were also

---

52. Berkhof, *Christian Faith,* 347.

53. Quakers and the Salvation Army do not practice any sacraments.

54. As noted earlier, I find the nomenclature "The Lord's Supper" preferable to "Eucharist" or even "Holy Communion." The latter is perhaps a rather neutral term, but Eucharist too easily shifts the focus from "the Lord" and that "supper" that is the foundation of this sacrament, to the celebrating clergy and parishoners who are "giving thanks." As Moltmann writes, "By using the expression 'the Lord's Supper' we are . . . stressing the pre-eminence of Christ above his earthly church and are calling in question every denominationally limited 'church supper'" (*The Church in the Power of the Spirit,* trans. Margaret Kohl [London: SCM, 1977; Minneapolis: Fortress Press, 1993], 245.

following a long-established understanding that Baptism and the Eucharist held a special place among the sacraments as being "ordained by Christ."

When we ask about the meaning historically assigned to "sacrament," we are bound to realize that the defining of something that connotes the deepest mystery poses insurmountable problems. A defined mystery is an oxymoron! Augustine considered the sacraments "visible words," and this idea was appealed to by the Reformers, who, as we have already seen, insisted that "Word and sacrament" belong together.[55] The catechism of the (Anglican) Book of Common Prayer provides the following well-known definition of sacrament: "an outward and visible sign of an inward and spiritual grace given unto us, ordained by Christ himself, as a means whereby we receive the same and a pledge to assure us thereof." The underlying thought in most explanations of the meaning of the term "sacrament" could be stated tentatively in this way: the mystery of the Christian life, the life "in Christ," is both expressed in and sustained by ritual enactments in which there is an objective component of a symbolic nature—"symbol" being understood here, not as an arbitrary "sign"[56] but as an object or token that participates in what it symbolizes: for example, water is used in baptism because it was used by John the Baptist in the baptism of Jesus, with whom one is being identified in baptism; bread and wine are the substances of the Eucharist or Lord's Supper because they were distributed by Jesus at his final meal with his disciples. The very "elements" carry association with the events to which they refer us—provided, as the Reformers would insist, that the sacrament is accompanied by the Word, including both preaching and teaching.

The presupposition of such an understanding of "sacrament" is that the Christian life *is,* or at least involves one in, a realm of mystery that transcends mere rational or verbal explanation. It therefore requires such symbolic practices to sustain our existential connectedness with our foundations—to sustain our "with-being." In participating in sacraments, the disciple community, led by the divine Spirit, renews its awareness of and communion with the source of its life, Jesus Christ, a communion that, like the communion of familial love or profound friendship, can never be adequately grasped and articulated in concepts and words but requires symbolic enactment.

This presupposition of transcendent mystery, when it is no longer present, robs *specific* sacraments of their depth and meaning. They become flat, rote, routine ceremonies, having for some a certain nostalgic or sentimental value because of their associations with the past, but conveying little of their

---

55. See Robert Jensen, *Visible Words: The Interpretation and Practice of Christian Sacraments* (Philadelphia: Fortress Press, 1978).

56. Although Thomas Aquinas used the term *signum* ("the sign of a sacred thing in so far as it sanctifies men").

spiritual-symbolic meaning. They may *remind* us of the events upon which our faith is based, but without the presupposition of transcendent mystery, they do not *connect* us with those events or renew our sense of belonging to the "body of Christ." Is it due to the one-dimensionality and fact orientation of our technological civilization that the sacraments are experienced by so many of us as rituals lacking in wonder, depth, or even interest?

Paul Tillich argued that although the Reformers were justified in attacking Roman Catholic sacramentalism, with its tendency to "distort the sacraments into non-personal acts of magical technique," Protestantism itself, because in the end it experienced "the disappearance of sacramental thinking," lost touch with the "religious significance" of the sacraments that it did retain. The "larger sense" of the term "sacrament," he writes, "denotes everything in which the Spiritual Presence has been experienced. . . ." In the "narrower sense," "sacrament" refers to "particular objects and acts in which a Spiritual community experiences the Spiritual Presence." But the latter, he insists, is dependent upon the former: "If the meaning of 'sacrament' in the largest sense is disregarded, sacramental activities in the narrower sense (sacramentalia) lose their religious significance."[57]

This brings us a little closer to the point at which we may begin to respond to the question announced at the beginning of the discussion: What could the coming diaspora status of the Christian movement mean for our understanding and practice of the sacraments? For, if modern and contemporary Christians have lost touch with "sacramental thinking"; if they have little capacity for the contemplation of mystery; if they live their lives in a cause-and-effect world in which "rationality" means "technical reason" (Tillich) and contemplation is called "day-dreaming," the world of "the great god Fact" (Ellul), this only indicates the extent to which they, like nearly everyone else, have become quite detached from the spiritual-intellectual tradition in which they are supposed to stand. They have become part of a *secular* society from which the sacred has been banished.

But this captivation by secular one-dimensionality is in reality only an aspect, indeed a consequence, of the greater problem that must be confronted by anyone who asks about the sacraments today. The unavoidable truth of the matter is that in the situation of Christian establishment it is always in large measure the *society* and not the community of faith that sets the tone for the church's theology and practice of the sacraments. If in the medieval church sacramentalism verged on magic and was used to sustain the power of the priestly hierarchy, this cannot be separated from both the public anxieties and aspirations of the age and the political functioning of the medieval church. And if in the Reformation period Zwingli and others were able to

---

57. Tillich, *Systematic Theology,* vol. 3, 121.

achieve a hearing through a more rationalized or intellectualized version of the Lord's Supper, this cannot be separated from the early humanism of the epoch and the desire of the middle classes to achieve autonomy. And if in our own period church-going people (and perhaps not only Protestants!) tend to look upon the sacraments as rituals that are important only, or chiefly, as "rites of passage," this cannot be separated from the general secularity of our era—a secularity that nonetheless, in some of its representatives, still hopes to retain a modicum of ceremonial dignity and decorum.

To speak plainly, although it would be an absurd exaggeration to claim that the sacraments have *always* been distorted throughout the history of Christendom, it must nevertheless be recognized today, as we emerge from that long period of our history, that under the conditions of establishment, the sacraments—and perhaps one should say *especially,* of all Christian practices, the sacraments—have suffered a reduction of meaning because they have had to function culturally and politically as *social* rites and not primarily as symbolic enactments of Christian faith.

This is particularly conspicuous where Baptism is concerned. (It is also true of Confirmation, marriage, burial, and other sacramental or parasacramental rites, but since Protestants have not regarded any of these as sacraments in the full sense of the term, it is Baptism that requires our attention here). Many and various arguments can be and have been put forward for infant baptism, most of them broadly theological, some claiming implicit scriptural grounds; and there can be no question that some of these arguments (such as the argument from prevenient grace) are meaningful as generalizations *about the faith.* But none of them conclusively demonstrates that infants should be baptized, and certainly none demonstrates that infant baptism should be *normative.*

Quite apart from the pros and cons of infant or child baptism, however, what must now be recognized by serious Christians of all ecclesial groupings is that infant baptism, which *has* been the normative form of Baptism in most denominations of the church, is perhaps the most obvious visible indicator of the Constantinian form and functioning of the Christian religion. So thoroughly coopted is the sacrament of Baptism by its service to society that many of those who still today bring their infants to churches or clergy for baptism have absolutely no ties with Christianity, or, what is more pitiable, that adults wishing to receive baptism on the grounds of their conversion to the faith must feel embarrassed because they were not baptized as babies!

It is not possible in this place to enter into the details of this subject, particularly its practical aspects;[58] but I register this concern about Baptism

---

58. In chap. 2, §6.3, I have already expressed my opinion on the subject of the elements in the Lord's Supper. As the practice of infant baptism is the most concrete indication of our

for the same reason that Karl Barth did in an early booklet on the subject[59]—namely, because as a very explicit and conspicuous indication of our failure to critique the confusion of Christianity with Christendom, it is also a "little point" (Luther) at which we may begin to reconsider that whole confusion and, in consequence, achieve a sacramental understanding that is something more than and different from a vaguely sacerdotal response to the quasi religious demands of our host culture.

We Christians have come to a moment in our history when it is possible, if we are willing, to explore both the "larger" *and* the "narrower" (Tillich) meaning of sacraments on the basis of *internal and recognizably Christian presuppositions,* and without being concerned in a primary way about the needs of society. The needs of society can be met, and should be met, in other ways. The disciple community has its own needs, and among them is the need for sacramental depth. This cannot be achieved so long as the sacraments are serving the purposes of "rites of passage" or ritualized nostalgia or secular quests for ceremony and dignity.

In proposing such a radical rethinking of the sacramental life of the church, I am fully conscious of the barriers it confronts and also of the misunderstandings it may generate. Among the latter, one that I wish to dispel forthwith is that I speak from a liberal or neoliberal or in any case non-sacramentalist kind of Protestantism that does not properly understand mystery. On the contrary, I am trying to preserve the sacramental life of the Christian community for the real mystery that it involves, and therefore to rescue the sacraments from the cloying secularity with which, in the establishment mode of ecclesiastical existence, they are necessarily and inevitably entangled. Both meaning and mystery will be recovered if the sacraments become what in the best traditions they have always been intended to be: part of the divine service (worship) of the "committed congregation" (Moltmann), enabling it to recover its always tenuous and vulnerable identity with the crucified One in whose risen power it "goes into all the world."

Obviously such changes as would be necessitated by this rethinking of the sacramental dimension of the church's life could only be instituted gradually, and with great compassion. Individuals—including ordinary, "unchurched" parents who bring their new baby for baptism—should not be caused to bear

---

captivation by the Constantinian form of the church, concentration on "the elements" in the Eucharist is the most concrete indication of our captivation by substantialistic thinking. The very terms that are used (transubstantiation, consubstantiation) draw attention to this preoccupation. Instead, I have suggested, we ought to consider both of the biblical sacraments relationally. The question, then, as it pertains especially to the Lord's Supper, is not what happens to the bread and wine but what is happening to and among the people who are imbibing them—in their relation to God, to one another, and to the whole creation.

59. Karl Barth, *The Teaching of the Church Regarding Baptism,* trans. Ernest A. Payne (London: SCM, 1948).

the burden of decisions and alterations that need to be undergone by *the churches* in their courts and theological classrooms. I am in complete agreement with Jürgen Moltmann's position in the following:

> The way to a new, more authentic baptismal practice will be the way from infant to adult baptism. By adult baptism we mean the baptism of those who believe, are called and confess their faith. The usages of centuries cannot be suddenly altered. The path proposed means a learning process for the Christian church which has many implications.
>
> As a first step the time of baptism should be made a matter of free decision left to the parents. Church law and church order would have to be altered in this sense. The clergy and the church's "full-time workers" should not be forced to have their children baptized either. But for their part they must not compel anyone to postpone baptism, or prevent parents from having their children baptized. They should preach and teach the Christian meaning of baptism and make it comprehensible, and not only at the baptismal services themselves. . . .
>
> Infant baptism should be replaced by the blessing of the children in the congregation's service of worship and by the "ordination"—the public and explicit commissioning of parents and congregations—for their messianic service to the children.[60]

As with most aspects of the biblical and theological traditions in which we stand, the coming diaspora situation of the church could witness the inauguration of a sacramental life for the Christian movement that has seldom been experienced by a millennium and a half of Christendom.

20. The Covenantal Basis of the Disciple Community.

20.1. A Neglected Theme. As Christian communities find themselves adrift in the world, with long-established ties between church and society severed or strained, observant Christians wonder whether anything can be assumed about the moorings of the church. For many centuries—indeed, for most of its history—it has been possible to take for granted the place of the Christian

---

60. *The Church in the Power of the Spirit,* 240ff. The entire section ("Suggestions for a New Baptismal Practice"), while emanating from a European context, is very evocative also for the North American context.

In connection with baptism, see also Letty M. Russell, *The Church in the Round: Feminist Interpretation of the Church* (Louisville, Ky.: Westminster John Knox Press, 1993): "Many feminist and liberation theologians also argue that the important symbolism of conversion and exodus into freedom in Christ is better served through the practice of adult baptism. This also helps to make clear that, although the gift of grace in baptism is based on God's free choice in Christ to welcome all God's children into the household of God and is administered only once, baptism is a response to that gift through a lifelong process of struggle for life in covenant relationship with God and our neighbors" (141).

religion in society. Its foundations have been deeply embedded in Western civilization, and apparently guaranteed by the legal or cultural ties designated by the term "establishment." But precisely these are the foundations that have been and are being shaken. As the fabric of Christendom disintegrates and it becomes apparent that little can be assumed about the church's rights and standing in society, many are prone to ask whether the church has any foundations at all. Is it perhaps so contingent, so purely voluntary an entity, that it stands on nothing more substantial than the will of a sufficient percentage of the human population to associate with it? Is Christianity like the "values" of which people now speak, whose reality is entirely dependent upon their retention as such in the minds of enough people to represent them?

What the technical and almost abstract term "disestablishment" designates, quite concretely, is just this experience of lost or crumbling foundations. By contrast with the security that the "major denominations" of Christendom have known throughout the histories of most of them, the Christian life in its corporate manifestation now seems terribly uncertain. This uncertainty is made painfully conspicuous by the frequency of legal action that is now taken against individual church authorities or whole denominations. Every new charge of sexual harassment, child abuse, or exploitation laid against clergy or ecclesiastical bodies in North America reminds us that our former *status* in this society can not only not be depended upon today but may constitute a background of unwarranted privilege for which present-day Christians shall now be held accountable. A significant dimension of the alienation Christians feel today must be attributed to this sense of the loss of social foundations.

As we are deprived of these sociopolitical foundations, we are thrown into a position where we may discover our theological foundations—and not only at the level of rhetoric and piety, but at the level of praxis and polity. The "charter" of the church is not the Edict of Milan or any of the successive agreements drawn up, or assumed, between churches and governments or peoples. The only legitimate basis of the disciple community is the theological charter that the Bible calls "the covenant."

In the most established of Christian churches, this is a charter that has been sadly—but predictably—neglected. While it was never been wholly lost sight of,[61] the covenant-theme of biblical faith has for the most part been

---

61. It was present to a limited extent in the thought of Augustine, and it became a significant concept in the theology of Calvin and the Reformed Tradition generally. As such it has also had a prominent place in secular as well as ecclesiastical history on this continent. See Allen Miller, ed., *A Covenant Challenge to our Broken World: A Study Carried out by the Committee on Theology, Caribbean and North American Area Council, World Alliance of Reformed Churches* (Atlanta: World Alliance of Reformed Churches, 1982).

relegated to the spheres of doctrine and piety. It has rarely achieved in Christian churches the highly practical and political connotations that it has in the Scriptures. The reason for this neglect and trivilization (or "spiritualization") of the prominent biblical concept is not difficult to detect: as long as the most conpicuous practical foundations of ecclesiastical existence have been the various legal and cultural arrangements with empires, nations, and classes, the covenant basis of the disciple community did not lend itself to Christian praxis. It could be treated as a sacred concept of biblical history and faith without its seeming to imply any directives for the day-to-day living of the Christian life. Even in denominations that for historical reasons gave covenant theology a prominent place in theology, liturgy, and church polity (notably the Reformed tradition), few believers have thought that the foundations of the church were quite literally to be located in its covenant with God, "sealed in the blood of the Christ." For this theological truth has been obscured by the more obvious marks of belonging and status that constitute "establishment." Only the churches that have been denied the status of establishment have a sufficient background experience of alternative assumptions concerning Christian foundations to lessen the shock created by Christendom's effective disestablishment. Not incidentally, some of these have quite intentionally exploited the biblical theme of the covenant.[62] From such excluded groups, the formerly mainline churches may learn much today.

Disestablishment, that is, the retraction of seemingly permanent sociopolitical foundations, could prove the condition necessary to a Christian recovery of our genuine grounding, both theoretically and practically speaking, in the covenant, christologically understood. Biblically considered, only one reliable foundation exists where the disciple community is concerned, and that is the one of which (as the early Christians put it) Jesus Christ is the "chief cornerstone":

"Have you not read this scripture [asked Jesus of the chief priests and scribes and elders, who demanded to know the source of his authority]:

> 'The very stone which the builders rejected
> has become the head of the corner;
> this was the Lord's doing,
> and it is marvelous in our eyes.'"
> (Mark 12:10–11[63])

---

62. One such group that is the so-called Covenanters, dissenting Presbyterians of the sixteenth century who refused Charles I's attempt to bring the Church of Scotland into line through the introduction of the Scottish Prayer Book of 1637, and so on.

63. Ps. 118:22–23; see Acts 4:11; 1 Peter 2:7.

In both Judaism and Christianity, "covenant" is the primary metaphor of biblical faith for the foundational charter of "the people of God." It is the Bible's most common expression for describing in a single term the nature of the relationship of this "people" to God, who alone calls it into existence and causes it to stand. Covenant is really a very complex concept, for all the apparent simplicity of its pious usage; it is difficult to do justice to it without much textual and sophisticated theological-political investigation. Its complexity, however, is not owed to the term itself, although it is to modern ears rather arcane; it is complex only because it tries to designate a highly complicated relationship, the relationship between God and human beings. In interpreting this term as one to which, in its present context, the Christian community might at this point in its sojourn return for guidance in the corporate living of its life, I shall concentrate on those aspects of covenant theology that can in my opinion speak meaningfully to our context.

I shall make four observations, and I shall state them in the form of theses, which I shall then elaborate in the four subsequent subsections. (1) As a conceptual vehicle for understanding Christian foundations, covenant is a supremely relational term, combining in a unique way the biblical themes of divine initiative (grace) and human freedom (faith). (2) In locating its "cornerstone" in Jesus Christ, the Christian community necessarily affirms its indelible ties with Israel, the "older" and "newer" covenants being manifestations of the same providential or salvific process. (3) As the authentic basis of the church, its covenant functions critically in relation to other relationships of Christian corporate life. (4) Ethically, the covenant combines in a unique way the two polar concepts of freedom and responsibility, and our informing concept of "discipleship" is the consequence of this combination.

20.2. Covenant: The Divine-Human Relationship. *As a conceptual vehicle for understanding Christian foundations, covenant is a supremely relational term, combining in a unique way the biblical themes of divine initiative (grace) and human freedom (faith).* Our discussions of the doctrines of God and human creaturehood in *Professing the Faith* leave us with at least two important presuppositions where the question of the relationship between God and humanity is concerned: (*a*) that both chief actors of this biblical drama, Creator and creature, are free: God is not *bound* to love and redeem humanity, and humanity is not bound or "programmed" to love and serve God; (*b*) that it is nevertheless in the nature of both Creator and (human) creature to be oriented toward the other, and to be in a real sense diminished by the frustration of this orientation: the human creature is gravely impoverished and distorted when it is not "turned toward" God, and even God suffers a parental sense of sorrow and longing on account of humankind's disorientation.

If, given such assumptions as these, one asks what kind of relationship were possible between the two, certain forms of relatedness that often pertain both in human and religious terms would have to be ruled out. The first and most obvious would be a relation imposed from the side of the stronger subject, God. Biblical faith presupposes (and it is largely a *pre*supposition) that God could, if God chose to do so, simply overrule human freedom and so alter the will of the creature that it would *necessarily* "image" that of the Creator. But biblical faith is committed to human freedom. Its commitment is not an ideological one; that is, it does not, with modernity, cherish human freedom as an end in itself, but only as a necessary means to the kind of relatedness that it finds desirable: love. Therefore it resists such a mode of relatedness; and all later doctrinal positions that favor strong concepts of divine, irresistible grace must wrestle with this resistance or else risk resolving the dilemma implicit in the divine-human encounter in a too-facile manner. To speak differently, the "heteronomous" or other-imposed (Tillich) resolution of the matter must be rejected.

So, however, must the antithetical resolution, which has been the preference of all voluntaristic theologies: namely, the notion that the human being, on account of its "natural" inclination toward the divine, will itself, with some encouragement (law, exhortation, example, and so on) turn toward its Creator. This ("autonomous" or self-directed) resolution overlooks not only the radical character of the estrangement between Creator and creature ("the fall") but the equally radical biblical assumption that the creature, however distorted by the fact, is nevertheless free to live in the state of alienation. From the outset, the optimistic anthropology that believes that human distortedness will right itself naturally through eventual enlightenment or gentle persuasion is ruled out.

This leaves a third possibility. It is, I think, what Paul Tillich has in mind when he coined the term "theonomy" as an alternative to either "heteronomy" (imposition) or "autonomy" (voluntary association).[64] This alternative presupposes that the initiative in restoring the relationship between Creator and creature rests with the Creator: it is a matter of divine grace. But this grace, although "prevenient," does not and must not simply overrule the contrary will of the creature; rather, in making itself available to the creature in ways that are compatible with the creature's own existential reality, divine grace so acts upon the will of the creature as to elicit the response that it wills—and wills not only for the Creator's but for the creature's own sake and "wholeness" (*salus* = salvation).

---

64. Tillich, *Systematic Theology,* vol. 1 (Chicago: University of Chicago Press, 1951), 83–85; vol. 3, 249–68.

Covenant theology presupposes and is an expression of this latter, "theonomous" conception of the divine-human relationship. The covenant concept, at least as it relates to that relationship, is to be distinguished on the one hand from the kind of relationship established by the strong over the weak (as in despotic or monarchic government) and on the other from the kind of relationship that is strictly voluntary (as in superficial or decadent forms of democracy). It assumes an initiating and a responding partner. It honors the freedom of the responding partner while at the same time assuming that that partner's positive response is advantageous to itself—is even essential to its life—and may be experienced as such. And it presupposes that the agreement, once entered into, is binding on both partners.

20.3. "Old" and "New" Covenants. *In locating its "cornerstone" in Jesus Christ, the Christian community necessarily affirms its indelible ties with Israel, the "older" and "newer" covenants being manifestations of the same providential or salvific process.*

The covenant as understood in the older "testament" ("testament" being the Latinized expression for covenant first introduced by the Vulgate) upholds and exemplifies the principles described in the first thesis.[65] It is initiated by Yahweh, whose commitment to the creation entails a persistent determination to establish relationship with the human creature through the "elect" people, Israel. Thus "the character of this covenant is succinctly stated by Jeremiah, 'I will be your God and ye shall be my people' (Jer. 7:23; 32:33)."[66] The "new covenant" or testament,[67] the term that Jesus, according to the tradition, uses in distributing the wine to his disciples at their last meal together (Mark 14:24; Matt. 26:28; Luke 22:20; 1 Cor. 11:25,[68] is not new *conceptually.* The same Jeremiah already names and describes it (31:31f.), and what he describes is not discontinuous with the "old covenant"; it is rather an internalization of "the covenant I made with their fathers" (v. 32): "'I will put my law [Torah] within them, and I will write it upon their hearts; and I will be their God, and they shall be my people" (v. 33).

What is being described, in other words, is a new way of achieving the divine intention that is already present and accounted for in the faith of Israel's prophets and law-givers. The law (Torah) itself already assumes this way, but the desire of the human community (represented by Israel) to keep God

---

65. The most important instances of covenanting between God and Israel are the Noachic (Gen. 6:18; 9:8–17), the Abrahamic (Gen. 15, 17, 22), the Mosaic Sinaitic (Exod. 19), the Levitic (Num. 25:10–13), the Davidic (2 Sam. 7:8–17; 23:5; Pss. 89 and 132), and the new covenant (Jer. 31:31-34).

66. Richardson, ed., *A Theological Word Book of the Bible,* 55.

67. "Testament" is the Latinized expression for covenant first introduced by the Vulgate.

68. See also 2 Cor. 3:6; Heb. 7:22; 9:15–20.

at a distance frustrates the Torah by externalizing it, objectifying it, separating it from its Giver and manipulating it in legalistic and moralistic ways. This process of externalization, which was the source of Jesus' quarrel with the Pharisees and others, is by no means a Jewish problem, as simplistic Christian critics of Judaism frequently assert; it is a human problem, faithfully demonstrated by the people elected to represent humanity before God. Moreover, this representation of humanity's flight from God is just as faithfully undertaken by the Christians, who, almost from the inception of the church, did the very same thing as those legalistic and ritualistic Jews who resisted Jesus: that is, they too externalized the ethical and religious principles of their apprehension of the will of God, and perhaps more thoroughly than Israel had ever done! To move from the newer Testament to the Christian writings of the second century is to discover how quickly and successfully this externalization of faith occurred. All the same, the "strategy" of God is clear in both Testaments, and the whole doctrine of the Trinity, far from being a breach with Israel, is at its core the Christian church's attempt to say *how* God achieved the process of internalization ("I will write my law on their hearts!") necessary to the fulfillment of the covenant that is already anticipated in the earliest writings of Israel.

20.4. The Critical Function of the Covenant. *As the authentic basis of the church, the covenant functions critically in relation to other relationships of Christian corporate life.* When the apostles Peter and John were taken before the authorities and warned not to speak or teach in Jesus' name, they responded, according to the record, in a clear but subtle way: "Whether it is right in the sight of God to listen to you rather than to God, you must judge; for we cannot but speak of what we have seen and heard" (Acts 4:19). These apostles, "uneducated, common men" (v. 13), were certainly responsible to the governing bodies that charged them to be silent; and, as the Apostle to the Gentiles would certainly have confirmed (Rom. 13:1, 2, 3a), they ought to have been

> subject to the governing authorities. For there is no authority except from God, and those that exist have been instituted by God. Therefore he who resists the authorities resists what God has appointed, and those who resist will incur judgment. For rulers are not a terror to good conduct, but to bad. . . .

But although Peter and John did not possess Paul's learning, they had grasped an aspect of their discipleship that Paul, in composing that particular portion of his letter to the church at Rome, unfortunately did not take sufficiently into account: namely, that the covenantal relationship with God has priority over all other social contracts, including those of citizenship and the law. In fact, the divine covenant exercises a critical function where all other relationships are concerned.

Walter Brueggemann has named this the "subversive" dimension of the covenant. "The central affirmations of covenant stand against and subvert the dominant forms, patterns, and presuppositions of our culture and of cultural Christianity."[69] It was because the reformers of the sixteenth century took this biblical priority seriously that they gave us what Tillich called "the Protestant principle": nothing conditional and contingent should assume the position of the unconditional and absolute. The covenant with God means that ultimate loyalty cannot and must not be given to any other relationship.

This does not immediately translate into the posture of revolution. The apprehended apostles left it to the authorities to decide whether (as they slyly put it) it was right for human beings to obey human institutions when it meant disobeying God. They would take the consequences—and they did. They did not intend to turn their relationship with God into the basis for an ideological rejection of state and society. But their sense of the priority of their foundational relationship—the "new covenant in my blood"—gave them the possibility of *humanizing* their other social relationships. It is precisely this humanization of all social contracts that constitutes the basis of the indubitable relation between biblical faith and democracy.

But the critical principle included in the covenant concept goes more deeply still. For, as Brueggemann points out, the disciple community not only believes the covenant with God to be its own charter but it sees it as the divinely intended pattern for all human relationships. "Covenanting . . . is the way all of society is intended to be with its markings of justice, freedom, abundance, and compassion."[70] The *krisis* that the disciple community brings to bear upon existing social structures is not only its refusal to grant them the ultimacy they covet but its intention to alter them, to make them conformable—so far as possible—with the covenantal pattern of relationship revealed in the history of Israel's and the church's covenanting.

Thus the covenant is not a private arrangement, affecting only the disciple community itself, but it is also perceived as the basis and paradigm of its social ethic. As such it is grounded in commitment to the creation. What we have said of the theology of the cross—that it is about God's abiding commitment to the world—is reaffirmed in the covenant imagery. The "theonomous" pattern of God's relating to those called out to represent creation before God, the "elect," is the pattern that God intends for relationships

69. Walter Brueggemann, "Covenant as a Subversive Paradigm," in *A Social Reading of the Old Testament: Prophetic Approaches to Israel's Communal Life,* ed. Patrick D. Miller (Minneapolis: Fortress Press, 1994), 43.

70. Ibid., 51.

within the creation itself. Neither relationships of mastery (heteronomy) nor relationships of caprice or arbitrary individualistic choice (autonomy) belong in the creation, but relationships of mutuality—mutuality and not "equality" (an innocuous term, and the source of great misunderstanding!). It is assumed by the community of the covenant that such relationships are both desireable and possible—at least as "proximate goals" (Reinhold Niebuhr) or approximations of God's own manner of relating to creatures.

Therefore, writes Brueggemann, "perhaps . . . the most important and most subversive thing that the church can now do [is] to refuse to give up on the world and its promised transformation." The community of Christ which discovers that its own alienation can be its opportunity for discovering the meaning of reconciliation knows, with Hosea, that "a condition of alienation and displacement is not our final destiny; that the world is not closed, fixed or settled; that institutions can be changed and transformed; that communities of people can be practioners of other ways of living."[71]

If the covenantal foundations of Christian existence were grasped in this fundamental, practical way rather than being relegated to the sphere of religious rhetoric, it might even be that that sacrament which in liberal and moderate Protestantism has become so sacrosanct and (for many) purely formal, namely the sacrament of "the new covenant in my blood," would acquire depth and vitality. Perhaps it is not wholly due to rumor and mob ignorance that some of the misunderstanding of the early church to which the apologists of the second century tried to speak centered in the Eucharist. Perhaps the Lord's Supper really was, in some sense, the point at which the community of faith rediscovered its distinctive foundations and recognized its different vision of creaturehood. Thus, Brueggemann concludes his essay by proposing that the Lord's Supper is the ultimate subersive act of the church:

> Whenever we eat this bread and drink this wine, we engage in a subversive minority report. Precisely because of being broken and poured out, this bread and wine will never be fully accommodated to the interests of the old age. . . .
>
> Undoubtedly covenantal discernments will become more dangerous in time to come as resources shrink, as we grow more fearful, as our public world continues to disintegrate. And therefore it is very important that we do not lose heart.[72]

20.5. Discipleship: Consequence of the Covenant. *Ethically, the covenant combines in a unique way the two polar concepts of freedom and responsibility; our informing theme of discipleship is the consequence of this combination.* The

---

71. Ibid.
72. Ibid., 53.

"theonomous" nature of the biblical concept of covenant manifests itself concretely in its ethical implications. Over against the kind of morality that is forced upon people by agencies more powerful than they are, whether these be divine or human agencies, the covenant describes a relational context of ethics in which the role of the initiating partner, God, is not to impose morality upon a reluctant creature but to evoke the good toward which the creature, as creature, is already oriented, and in relation to which its actual behavior must be seen as a *dis*orientation.

This has seldom been understood, even by sincere Christians. The almost natural impulse of the human will, partly because of its inherent (sinful) inclinations and partly because of sociohistorical conditioning, is to assume that "law" always entails the superimposition of the will of another: I am commanded to do what I neither wish to do nor am really capable of doing. This general attitude toward law informs people's reception also of biblical law. Such a thing is bound to happen when the law (say, the Decalogue) is extracted from the relationship that it assumes, biblically speaking, and becomes an independent code of behavior. Given the gracious relationship that God establishes with God's people, the divine law should be seen as the concrete evocation of possibilities for the true humanity for which grace liberates us.

Otherwise expressed, the divine law is not law in the usual sense of being rules devised by some higher authority, but rather is the concretization, in exhortational terms, of the very being for which we have been created. Thus, while God's Torah as expressed in Scripture is usually stated prescriptively, it will only be understood aright when it is first heard descriptively. For its intention is to answer the question, What would it mean to be human according to God's intention? Thus, by assuming the constructive and positive response to this question, certain types of behavior are quite naturally excluded—for example: as God's creation and covenant partner, the human being is one who preserves life (therefore does not kill); who honors the other (therefore does not steal); who loves truth (and therefore does not lie); who is faithful to earthly commitments (therefore does not commit adultery); who is content with his or her lot (therefore does not covet), and so on. The prescriptive expression of the Torah is dependent upon the implied description of authenticity out of which it emerges. To state the matter in other terms that we have employed heretofore, the imperative ("Thou shalt") arises out of the indicative ("Thou art")—meaning the indicative of our human reality as creatures of God. As we are liberated by grace to *be* such creatures as, *essentially,* we *are,* this same grace continues to evoke from us the actual behavior that belongs to our "new being." If this is understood as evocation, it will help to dispel the common idea that God's law, too, is simply imposed upon us.

But if the idea of the *nomos* as imposition of the good ("heteronomy") is here rejected, so is the assumption that the good will simply be chosen by us—perhaps with a little persuasion or through moral enlightenment. Biblical realism concerning human sin rules out the prospect that the Torah (*nomos*) will ever be obeyed spontaneously (*autos*). According to its essence as God's creature, the human being is oriented toward the good and exists in a state of disorientation when it chooses evil instead. But it may choose evil (that is its creational birthright), and it has done so; and evil, once chosen, contains its own logic and necessity. Therefore covenantal theology assumes that the creature, trapped in its unfreedom, must be liberated for obedience to God—that is, for adherence to its own essential being. What we call "gospel," as Christians, is just this process of being freed to be *truly* human, or, in other words, to be obedient.

But the word "process" is not used loosely here. Biblical faith assumes that this "freeing" is an ongoing reality of active grace. It is not a once-and-for-all event, but a continuous aspect of the covenantal relationship. If, therefore, the Torah must still be stated in prescriptive terms; if (to say this in the language of the *newer* Testament) the "new law in Christ" has still to be given in the imperative mood (as, for example, Paul constantly does), this is because the process of liberation for the good is an eschatological one, containing both an already and a not-yet. Already those *en Christo* are "new creatures"; but the "old Adam" in them also continues to resist their new being. *Simul justus et peccator.* Therefore the newer Testament or covenant does not mark the end of the law, as antinomians have always wished to have it, but a spiritual intensification of law as both possibility and necessity. Through the liberating work of the triune God, obedience to God's *nomos* becomes newly possible and, because of this, it is also newly necessary (Rom. 6). Freedom and responsibility are not two separate and separable aspects of the Christian life but rather the same process seen from two perspectives.

It is unfortunate that the main stream of the sixteenth-century Reformation tended to divide the two inseparable movements of this process. Lutheranism, which rightly stressed the justifying grace by which the human being is freed for fullness of life, failed to develop sufficiently the necessity for responsibility that was the other side of this new freedom. The Reformed tradition, on the other hand, characteristically cautious and mistrustful of freedom, so accentuated the responsibility laid by grace upon "the elect" that it regularly devolved into legalism and moralism. Lutheranism tended to err on the side of autonomy where the redeemed are concerned ("the freedom of the Christian person") and Calvinism on the side of heteronomy. Both streams of the Reformation failed to develop the covenantal basis of the Christian ethic with sufficient consistency. While Calvinism used the language of the covenant copiously, its prior emphasis upon divine sovereignty guaranteed that it would understand the covenant in a way that verged almost naturally on heteronomy. Lutheranism seems to have been so preoccupied with the initiatory aspects of the divine-human relation that it did not pay sufficient attention to the character of the relation thus initiated. In both cases, Christian life as discipleship was diminished.

For discipleship requires both gospel and law, both freedom and responsibility, if it is to be conceived biblically. The disciple is not only the unquestioning follower but the participant—the "friend," in fact, whose relationship with the one who leads frees her to take initiative, to develop her skills and test her intuition, to see what requires doing and to do it. Stewardship is a useful category for the theology of discipleship, because the steward in biblical terms is one who, given the task and the freedom to manage a household, takes responsibility upon himself. Without going to the householder for every small matter, he makes decisions and carries through on them; for he knows what the householder intends and he knows that he is trusted to implement the householder's intentions.

But the other side of this same coin is, of course, the accountability factor. It cannot be assumed that the steward will be a *faithful* steward. It cannot be assumed that the disciple will appropriate the gift of friendship wisely and well. Without the concretizing factor of law, gospel too easily leads to generalization. Gospel frees us for others but law leads us to their doorstep.

The diaspora church that is and is coming to be will need to explore and exploit the covenantal basis of Christian community in order to withstand both the external and the internal threats to its coherence and its integrity. There can be no question of a flawless application of the theology of covenant, but there are self-corrective checks and balances within this theopolitical conception of the nature of relationships that can, if faithfully and imaginatively reflected and acted upon, prevent the worst aspects of alienation from becoming ultimately destructive of Christian community.

21. The Doctrine of Election

21.1. "I Have Chosen You. . . ." The doctrine of election is an aspect and consequence of the foundational concept of the covenant. The disciple community with whom God enters into covenant is conscious of itself as a community called or elected by God, the God "who gives life to the dead and calls into existence the things that do not exist" (Rom. 4:47b). Its covenant partnership with God implies its "singling out": as Israel believed and believes itself to have been "chosen," so the Christian community regards its existence as response to its divine election.

This ancient belief, too, can be a source of courage at a time in its history when its acquired historical foundations are being shaken. If it is able to recover the sense of being called and chosen by *God,* the church may find the courage to endure the loss of its social and political election and privilege. Indeed, unless the church does recover the consciousness of its divine election, it will continue to lack the confidence that is needed to exercise responsible discipleship in the world.

But the doctrine of election is not easily recovered, for it is associated with certain ideas that render it less than helpful for these purposes, if not altogether repulsive. In order to reclaim divine election as a vital dimension of its existence and vocation, therefore, it is necessary to dissociate the doctrine from these unfortunate historical connotations. I shall attempt to do so by setting forth the following four propositions. (1) Election is a necessary implication of the biblical concept of grace. (2) Election belongs to the theology of representation and is distorted when it is separated from that theology. (3) Election is primarily a communal and not an individual calling. (4) Election as it applies to ecclesiology is to be understood as means and not end, and therefore to be distinguished sharply from the concept of an elite. I shall treat the first proposition in this subsection and the other three in the three subsequent subsections.

First, then, we consider the proposition that *election is a necessary implication of the biblical concept of grace.* In the discussion of justification, we affirmed the priority of grace: we are not justified by our faith but by the grace that evokes trust (faith) from our spirits. Likewise in the discussion of the covenant, we recognized that God is the initiating partner. Again, whenever we have considered the subjects of the divine love, or forgiveness, or judgment, and particularly in the entire discussion of Christology, we have had to acknowledge that the tradition assumes as its most basic theological assumption that everything depends upon the prior decision and action of God. God loves—and therefore we may love. God forgives—and therefore we may also "forgive those who trespass against us." God comes to be "with us" in Jesus Christ—and therefore we may become neighbors of one another. And so on.

That both ancient Israel and the early church developed a concept of "election" is therefore by no means surprising. It would have been surprising had such a concept or dogma not been developed. For it is nothing more— or less!—than an extension of the theology of grace that is the foundational theology of the entire tradition. It would be absurd, in fact, if the presentation of both God and humanity in the foundational documents of the Judeo-Christian tradition were to lead to the belief, on the part of Christians, that we ourselves have elected to become what we are, that the church is *our* enterprise, that we have chosen God. Not only is God presented in the continuity of the Testaments as "the God who acts"—and whose action is prior—but humanity is presented there as being continuously resistant to the divine overtures of "friendship" and reluctant to participate in anything that God wills to initiate.

Not only does this apply to "the natural man" in general, to use the language of the Reformers, but it also applies to those who are called—to Israel and the church. Far from being eager volunteers, those who are singled out by God are forever excusing themselves from any such association or vocation. The whole story of Israel is a story of resistance and reluctance, and, lest Christians naively congratulate themselves on their being quite different in this respect, let us remember again the central "moment" of the Gospels, when "they all forsook him and fled." This "moment" is not a once-upon-a-time occurrence; it is symbolic of the continuing reluctance of the disciple community to assume, willingly and gladly, the life to which it is called.

Jesus, in John's interpretation, therefore makes the position entirely clear: "You did not choose me, but I chose you . . . " (15:16). There is no need to interpret this as if it implied that the disciples, to whom it is addressed in this pericope, have no choice in the matter whatsoever. A strict determinism is ruled out: philosophic determinism and divine grace are not at all the same thing! After all, the same disciples are depicted as having responded positively to Jesus' call to "Follow me," and on at least one occasion, in the same Johannine record, they decide precisely *not* to go away when other followers have in fact done so: "Lord, to whom shall we go? You have the words of eternal life" (6:68). Yet the decisive thing is not their decision but Christ's: "You did not choose me, but I chose you. . . ." If philosophic determinism is not to be equated with divine grace, biblically understood, neither is philosophic voluntarism appropriate to this relationship. The initiative rests with God, and God's decision is not thwarted by human indecision and rejection, for God's "call" cannot easily be brushed aside—and not because God is so very powerful, but because the call, once heard, implants itself in the human psyche in such a way that it is not readily dismissed. For it is, after all, only an invitation to become who we are, essentially.

The "courage to be" (Tillich) can only come to human beings as they acquire some reminiscence of the trust that their being is not a random thing but is purposed. The courage to be *the church* in the post-Christian era can only come to congregations and churches if and when they begin to sense that their existence is the consequence of a choice that is greater than their own individual and corporate choices, and precedes both their negative and positive responses to it. Nothing short of some clear consciousness of *having to be* will deliver the post-Constantinian church from its morass of arbitrariness and indirection. The congregation that wavers between "carrying on" and "giving up" has not yet been grasped by the only decision that creates the disciple community, the grace of the one "who gives life to the dead and calls into existence the things that do not exist" (Rom. 4:17).

21.2. Elected to Representative Existence—Not to Privilege. The second proposition regarding election is that it belongs to the theology of representation and is distorted when it is separated from this theology. Indeed, perhaps the greatest misappropriation of the doctrine of election occurs when it is separated from the vocation of "the elect." Both Jews and Christians have frequently indulged in the habit of assuming that being a "chosen people" is tantamount to being a "choice" people—that of all the peoples of the earth, only they are worthy of being singled out. We shall see in the fourth proposition that this is related to the confusion of the doctrine of election with the concept of an elite, to which attention was also drawn in earlier parts of this series. For the present, our only concern is to set election within its proper context, which is the calling of the people of God to a peculiar vocation.

If election is not understood as being inextricably bound up with the vocation of the elect, then it is certain to be misunderstood. Israel and the church are *elected to* an office and work in the world, not *selected out of* all the world for some higher form of existence or because of their superior character. God's choice of Israel, like Jesus' choice of the disciples, is not purely arbitrary, but the Bible is unanimous that it has nothing to do with allegedly superior righteousness, intelligence, holiness, or other qualities that may be possessed by those so chosen. For God's purposes, the details of which are shrouded in the mystery of deity, these particular people seem to have qualifications that suit them to the task. Perhaps they are chosen for qualities usually considered undesirable—because they are so stubborn, for example, or so skeptical, or so irreligious! The name "Israel" means "the one who struggles with God." Given the specifics of the biblical story, a better case could be made for such seemingly odd reasons than for the pious reasons conventionally associated with divine "choice." But, in any case, the explanation of God's choice is neither the business nor the prime concern of theology; what has to occupy our attention is the question, "To what end?"

And where that question is concerned, I think there can be no hesitation: people are elected for the glory and service of God in the world. They are not elected for separation from the world but for mission to the world. Or, to be more precise, if separation is present in their election, it is for the sake of their vocation. The word "election" itself (in Greek, *eklegomai, eklectos*) suggests that the "calling out" or choosing of some on the part of God already contains the missionary impulse to which we have paid some attention—that is, that they are called *out of* in order to be sent *back into* the world.

If, as our proposition suggests, the doctrine of election is understood within the theology of priesthood or representation, it is prevented from devolving into a matter of status. Those who are "chosen" are chosen as "a kingdom of priests and a holy nation" (Exod. 19:5–6; 1 Peter 2:9), through whom "all the families of the earth shall bless themselves" (Gen. 12:3). There is an end in view that far surpasses the means by which it is to be brought about. We have presented this end in the second volume as being nothing less than the redemption of creation,[73] and, in Part IV of the present volume, we shall develop that theme more fully. The creation itself, which "waits with eager longing" (Rom. 8:19), is to be fulfilled. All creatures are to be brought into the harmonious state that the Creator has intended for them from the outset. And God's manner of achieving this end, although it seems strangely indirect to those who would prefer an omnipotent God who simply overrules the laws and the limits of the creation, is to choose, out of all the world, those who may represent God before all the other creatures and all the creatures before God. Through the struggle of God with these few, and the "yeast" of their work and witness, an alternative way of being will be introduced into the course of the world's history that will prepare for the consummation— that "kingdom," when God will truly be "with us" and we, with all our kind and otherkind, will be God's beloved (Rev. 21:3).

The posture of "the elect" is not, therefore, a particularly privileged one. In fact, it is regularly perceived by the chosen ones themselves—when they understand what it really involves—more as burden than as privilege. They are singled out, not for special favor but for the particular attention of a God who is not able easily to accept fallen humanity, and they are caused to bear God's Word to a fallen humanity that is not able easily to accept God. Amos, who makes a great deal of election, also understood fully this burdensome aspect of God's choice of Israel:

> You only have I known
>   of all the families of the earth;
> therefore I will punish you
>   for all your iniquities.
>   (Amos 3:2)

The "punishment" is meted out, not because Israel alone is sinful, but because it is "known"—called to a relationship of intimacy in behalf of all the others. The struggle between God and humanity is keenest and most poignant where it is most intimate.

---

73. *Professing the Faith,* §26.2, "The End as Consummation," 356–59.

Considering election under the aegis of the theology of representation implies the assumption, which Karl Barth developed most consistently (perhaps too consistently!), that God's "choice" is really a choice for humankind as a whole; that in choosing the anointed one, "the man Jesus," God implicitly chooses all those for whom Jesus stands as high priest, ergo, for humanity in toto. Barth's christological approach to the doctrine of election may seem unnecessarily convoluted, but he ends (or begins?) at the right place, in my view: namely, with God's intention to redeem the totality.[74] Anything less than this will end by pitting the doctrine of redemption *over against* that of creation, and we have already stated our reasons for avoiding such a non-Hebraic conclusion.

21.3. The Election of "a People."   Our third proposition concerning election affirms that it refers primarily to a communal or corporate calling rather than to individuals. This observation is needed because a significant cause of confusion in election theology lies in the individualistic approach that it has received in the more pietistic-personalistic ecclesiastical settings of Christendom. These have abounded in North American Christianity, and have drawn upon reductionistic forms of Calvinism combined with the individualism indigenous to our social ethos to produce intensely privatistic versions of the doctrine of election. The extreme form of individualistic election doctrine found in contemporary dispensationalism, with its dramatic idea of individuals being "raptured," is only an intensification of the widespread assumption that election or predestination applies primarily if not exclusively to individuals. In the past, and in more conservative evangelical circles still today, this assumption has been the cause of untold personal anxiety; for, apart from the few who were hardened against such a thing through ironclad doctrine

---

74. For example: "The ontological determination of humanity is grounded in the fact that one man among all others is the man Jesus. So long as we select any other starting-point for our study, we shall reach only the phenomena of the human. We are condemned to abstractions so long as our attention is riveted as it were on other men, or rather on man in general, as if we could learn about real man from a study of man in general, and in abstraction from the fact that one man among all others is the man Jesus. . . . Every one who bears the name of man is to be addressed as such in the name of Jesus, and therefore . . . he stands in an indisputable continuity with Him which is quite adequate as a point of contact. . . . There is not one for whom He has not done everything in His death and received everything in His resurrection from the dead." (Excerpts are, respectively, from *Church Dogmatics,* as collected by Helmut Gollwitzer; *Karl Barth's Church Dogmatics,* trans. G. W. Bromiley [Edinburgh: T. & T. Clark, 1961]; and "The Determination of Man," 162–72.)

In his recent ecclesiological work, *The Sense of a People,* Lewis S. Mudge tries to "re-invent the idea of a universal church": "The church is that part of the human whole which conveys to that whole *its* destiny as the space of God's reign. The church is a community in which the whole of humanity may see signified *its* calling to become a people of God" (Lewis Mudge, *The Sense of a People* [Philadelphia: Trinity Press International, 1992], 52.)

or personal certitude of spirit, most human beings harbor sufficient self-doubt to question their election to salvation, and many have been driven to despair by the thought of eternal damnation.

It would be better to dispense altogether with the doctrine of election, as Macquarrie suggests,[75] than to retain it in this distorted form. For the ultimate intent of the doctrine is not to create anguish and insecurity but, on the contrary, as we have maintained in the first proposition, to provide a foundation for faith and life in something more solid than social acceptance or personal determination. When it is individualized, election theology is inevitably transmuted into an instrument of fear and—on the part of the falsely secure—of presumption and oppression. Besides, individualization completely redirects the emphasis of the doctrine, exchanging for the biblical stress upon God's choice and intent as the electing one a disconcerting preoccupation with those elected. The question, "Am I among the saved?" makes of election an egocentric rather than a theocentric and geocentric dogma.

Part of what is involved in the correction of this religious egocentrism in its North American manifestation is the association of the doctrine of election with *a people.* As Daniel Migliore writes,

> *The goal of election is the creation of a people of God and not, in the first instance, the salvation of solitary individuals.* The doctrine of election is not intended to cater to excessive self-concern but precisely to open us to the blessings and responsibilities of life in community. Election is the expression of God's will to create a community that serves and glorifies God.[76]

The point in this is not only to save individuals from the anguish of unknowing, but to render the doctrine in its appropriate biblical perspective. Individualistic interpretation of election almost invariably shifts the whole concern of the doctrine to a supernatural goal: "Am I among the elect?" means "Am I going to go to heaven?" "Heaven," which we have yet to discuss, is not uninteresting to biblical faith; but it is not its primary interest. Its primary interest is this world—creation; heaven itself is part of the created order, and the strategy of God that is intended by the concept of election is a strategy for the redemption of the whole of what God has made. This strategy can be served by the creation of a people—a priestly people whose task is (as Migliore affirms) to serve and glorify God. It cannot be served by "raptured" individuals!

21.4. Elect, Not Elite. Our fourth proposition was that election as it applies to ecclesiology is to be understood as a means and not an end, and so to be

---

75. John Macquarrie, *Principles of Christian Theology,* 302–03.
76. Daniel Migliore, *Faith Seeking Understanding,* 77. (Italics are present in the original.)

distinguished sharply from the idea of an elite. The most damning distortion of the theology of election—so insidious as to cause one to despair of its being redeemable—is the habit of regarding election as an end, indeed *the* end, rather than a means to a greater end. Perhaps this is a "natural" heresy; certainly it is a common one.

Whether it begins with the recognition that so many—the majority!— seem unmoved by the gospel, or with the antithetical observation that relatively few are deeply moved, this position stems from a preoccupation with the objects of election ("the elect") rather than the electing Subject, God, and the object or aim of God's electing. For reasons that are never without a goodly portion of presumption or even prurience, advocates of this position are usually intrigued by the relatively small number of the seeming "elect"— hence their common attachment to Jesus' statement, "For many are called, but few are chosen" (Matt. 22:14). Whenever such consciousness of "the few" predominates, there is a concomitant temptation to look upon these as those for whom the entire enterprise has been undertaken. Creation has labored and has brought forth this chosen few, the golden ones.

This logic, which is at work in Stoicism, Neoplatonism, and many other ancient and modern systems, and in secular forms is found in nearly every political ideology, seems (as I said earlier) an almost natural heresy. It is especially tempting to the luminaries and leading spirits of religious and other organizations that manifest conspicuous distinctions between the most serious advocates of the system, who are normally few in number, and the larger numbers of those who are carried along for uncertain reasons. The latter, the many, seem to exist for the few who may emerge out of their numberless ranks.

This is, of course, elitism. It is "natural" because it is the simplest solution to the question (which regularly and inevitably arises from historical experience), "Why are there only a few (a few who understand, a few who are earnest, a few who are ready to sacrifice, and so on)?" The most immediate answer to this question, as the whole course of intellectual history attests, is that the majority are incapable of the superior qualities demanded by the system in question; that its perfection can be attained only by a minority; that it must therefore be for the sake of this minority that the system itself exists.

Surely this is, in part, what explains the preferences of John Calvin, the student of classical literature, in his explication of the doctrine of election. It is not that Calvin arrived at his "dread decree" by following Seneca and others, but surely that background rendered the "decree" less abhorrent than, on biblical grounds alone, it would certainly have been. Given Calvin's austere, monarchistic theology and his unbending insistence upon the total incapacity of human being for the pursuit of the good, it was inevitable that he would have to turn the doctrine of election into a predestinarianism so precise as to distinguish between the eternally saved and the eternally damned.[77]

Another answer may be given to the question, "Why so few?" It is the answer that is, it seems to me, implied when it is not openly stated, scripturally; and it assumes what we have already said about the "people of God" as a priestly or representative people. This answer assumes that the intention of God, which we have affirmed has at least universalistic *implications,* requires the service of the few *for the sake of the many.* This implication is present, as we have seen, in all of the metaphors that Jesus employs for the signification of the disciple community, the "little flock"—its being "seed," "salt," "light," and so on. This is no innovation of Christianity; it is part of the logic of election already with the people of the older covenant. It belongs to the same prophetic consciousness and "wisdom" that recognizes the limitations of omnipotence (the very thing Calvin did not and would not recognize![78]), given the fragility of the creature. God, if God loves and will save, must ("must"!) do so indirectly; otherwise God will destroy, in the process, the very thing God wills to save. "Divinity may terrify man. Inexpressible majesty will crush him" (Luther).[79] God's hidden, indirect, and "mysterious ways" are not, in the end, either odd or capricious; they manifest a profound "wisdom," although it is not the wisdom of the world, which proceeds from assumptions of power; it is the wisdom of one whose power is voluntarily submitted to the stronger impulse of love (1 Cor. 1, 2). "God chose what is low and despised in the world, even things that are not, to bring to nothing things that are, so that no human being might boast in the presence of God" (1:28). Paul is speaking of the mission of the elect—a few unimpressive and even "foolish" ones, whose stewardship of God's mysterious faithfulness to creation mirrors and makes concrete the character of *God's* dominion, which is the dominion of love and not of power.

Election thus conceived belongs to the theology of the cross, and when the doctrine of election is removed from those auspices it invariably becomes

---

77. Calvin's own exposition of predestination reaches its climax in the following excerpt: "Whom God passes by, therefore, he reprobates, and from no other cause than his determination to exclude them from the inheritance which he predestines for his children. . . . Hardening proceeds from the Divine power and will, as much as mercy (*Institutes,* Bk. III, Ch. 23, Para. 1). "It is an awful decree, I confess; but no one can deny that God foreknew the future final fate of man before he created him, and that he did foreknow it because it was appointed by his own decree. If any one here attacks God's foreknowledge, he rashly and inconsiderately stumbles" (ibid., Para. 7).

78. In the same context as above, Calvin expresses indignation over the thought of those who maintain that Adam had free choice: "If so weak a scheme as this be received, what will become of God's omnipotence, by which he governs all things according to his secret counsel, independently of every person or thing besides?" (*Institutes,* Bk. III, Ch. 23, Para. 7).

79. Christmas sermon, Hugh T. Kerr, *Readings in Christian Thought* (Nashville and New York: Abingdon Press, 1966), 157.

a "dread decree"; for then it necessarily falls under the aegis of the antithetical theology of glory. It may be thought a "glorious thing" if the sovereign Deity stoops to save a few from the flames that all deserve (even if their deserving them has been prearranged by the same sovereign Deity!); but it may not be thought a thing belonging to the glory of the God of Abraham, Isaac, and Jacob, the Abba of Jesus the Christ. The great error of Calvin in this respect (and it shows up in other places as well) must be traced to the subtle but not inconspicuous presence of the *theologia gloriae* running throughout his exposition of the faith as a kind of *tentatio* (temptation). His biblical language too often cloaks a theology and an ontology that owes more to Athens and Rome than it does to Jerusalem.

If it can be managed by Christians at the end of the Constantinian era to think through their election by God under the aegis of the theology of the cross, the result may be quite surprising. In the foregoing chapters, we have taken note of the humiliation and, in places, decimation of formerly powerful Christendom: we are becoming fewer, weaker. There are temptations in this, and they are not being resisted well in North American churches. It is hinted, and sometimes openly declared, that this historic sifting is a kind of earthly anticipation of the separation of the sheep from the goats; that those who come through the winnowing process will have the comfort of knowing themselves "the chosen ones." However it is phrased, this is nothing other than the usual pomp and boasting that belongs to triumphalistic religion.

Instead of yielding to that temptation, the critical moment in which we find ourselves affords serious Christians the opportunity of recovering the other, more hidden but more faithful reason that "there are only a few": that the few are there for the many; that there are things the few can do that the many cannot and will not do—precisely because they are many, and have power, and are driven by a logic of domination, and therefore can neither love nor serve.

One of the most pressing theological-historical needs of the church as it moves into the post-Christendom stage is to learn how to distinguish between the character of an elite and that of an elect; for as the church finds itself reduced, the greatest temptation of some Christian groups will be to comfort themselves falsely with the thought of their spiritual superiority. As we have said before, the two constructs, elite and elect, have in common a particular consciousness of "the few," the comparative minority. But that is all that they have in common. They are absolute opposites when it comes to the question, "Why?"

22. The Ethic of Resistance and the Ethic of Responsibility

22.1. Recovering the Protest in Protestantism. We have seen that there are foundational theological dimensions of our heritage upon which, in the inhospitable climate of post-Christendom, the Christian individual and *koinonia* may discover sources of meaning and courage. We must now explore the more specifically ethical side of our tradition from the same perspective. As we have already frequently affirmed throughout this series and shall reinforce in the subsequent chapter, "Theological Ethics" (chap. 7), Christian theology when it is true to its biblical and best historical traditions, is already ethics; therefore it has proven impossible to discuss the basic doctrinal matters of the previous sections of this chapter without at every juncture introducing their ethical thrust. There are, however, certain explicitly ethical directives in our Protestant heritage that ought to inform the Christian life as the disciple community takes leave of its establishment status and moves into a diaspora situation that is bound to seem strange and produce in most of us a sense of confusion and loneliness.

Without pretending to exhaust the possibilities, the two ethical directives I wish to develop in this connection could be understood as principles or guidelines for an attitude and posture of the disciple community in diaspora vis-à-vis its host culture. As such, they stand in a certain dialectical relation—therefore a certain tension—with one another, chastening one another, so to speak, while at the same time informing one another. As the subtitle of the section indicates, the two principles are, first, the belief that, in relation to the pursuits of the classes and forces that chiefly determine our social context, it will be necessary for the disciple community in its disestablished state to draw upon the prophetic tradition of resistance; second, that as the bearer of a gospel that is grounded in God's "suffering love" (*agape*) for this world, the disciple community is obliged to develop an ethic of public responsibility as the undergirding rationale of its resistance.

We consider first the ethic of resistance.[80] Resistance ought to be a familiar theme to Protestants, and the fact that on the whole it is not only indicates how very respectable Protestantism soon became, and remained. If the emphases in our pronunciation of the word were removed from the first syllable and placed on the second (Pro*test*ant), we would come closer to our origins; for the term was first used (at the Diet of Speyer, Germany, in 1529) to designate the minority of princes who were "against the proceedings of the emperor and the Catholic princes."[81] Unfortunately, about the only aspect of

---

80. See Ched Myers, *Binding the Strong Man: A Political Reading of Mark's Story of Jesus* (Maryknoll, N.Y.: Orbis Books, 1988), "Resistance," 452f.

81. Owen Chadwick, *The Reformation* (Harmondsworth: Penguin Books, 1964), 62.

this heritage that remains in most Protestant circles is that the word "Protestant" has a distinctly anti-Catholic connotation; but while the original protest, as well as much subsequent activity on the part of Protestants, was directed against Rome, the significance of the nomenclature theologically has little to do with anti-Catholicism. As Wilhelm Pauck writes in *The Heritage of the Reformation,*

> Protestantism is a spiritual attitude, grounded in the living faith that God has made himself known in the person of Jesus of Nazareth and expressing itself ever anew in ways of life and thinking which reflect this faith as a proclamation of the glory of God transcending all human limitations and sufficiencies. *The Protestant spirit is a spirit of prophetic criticism. Its norm is the gospel of the God of love who liveth in a light no man can approach unto and yet is nearer to us than breathing, closer than hands or feet, and who has disclosed himself in Jesus who was born in a manger, had no place where to lay his head, and died on a cross.*
>
> No form can adequately express this content of the faith in revelation. No liturgical or ecclesiastical or theological form of this idea of revelation can be final.[82]

As Pauck's excellent summation indicates, Protestantism, historically and classically understood, implies an a priori polemic against all pretension to finality of doctrine and understanding; and just this is the reason that Paul Tillich spoke of "the Protestant principle" to which, at various times, we have made reference in this series.

But Protestantism is not only a protest against doctrine put forward as final truth, it is also a protest against power masquerading as ultimate. In the name of the Ultimate, Protestantism resists the contingent, finite, and penultimate that pretends to ultimacy. The ethic of resistance has its foundation in this determination, which Pauck rightly links with the traditions of "prophetic criticism."

The voice of resistance has never quite been silent in the Christian church. Had it been consistently repressed, the very act of "confessing the faith" would have been practically impossible, for, as we have defined that act, it always entails the recognition and denunciation of that which threatens the life of God's beloved world. The dimension of resistance is therefore inherent in faith's confession. As we have noted in Part I, even where the confession may appear harmless to the uninitiated ("Jesus Christ is Lord") it implies a polemic ("ergo Caesar is not!"); and with some historic confessions, of which the Barmen Declaration, as we saw, is one, the negating or critical or resisting aspect is made quite explicit: Jesus Christ is Lord, and therefore *der Führer*

---

82. Wilhelm Pauck, *The Heritage of the Reformation* (Glencoe, Ill.: The Free Press; and Boston: Beacon Press, 1950), 142f. (My italics.)

is not. Fortunately, the ethic of resistance, and therefore of the right, timely confession of the faith, have never been wholly suppressed or repressed. The diaspora of today and tomorrow may draw upon this critical history, much of it submerged, as in fact minorities throughout the universal church have been doing today.

But let us not imagine that the broad history of Christianity (including Protestant Christianity) in the world has been the history of a resistance movement. To the contrary! Resistance has been the way of minorities, whose critique was usually directed not only against secular and other agencies of power but against powerful Christendom itself. And the reason this has been the case is one that we have considered at length in chapter 4: religions seldom resist when the social office they have accepted is to legitimize and confirm, or (as Peter Berger said of American Christianity) to refrain from offering any alternative to, the status quo. That is, so long as Christianity functions as an establishment, whether in the legal or the cultural sense, it is inhibited by its own relationship with power from pursuing an ethic of resistance. Especially where power seems favorably disposed toward the Christian religion, as appears still the case with us in North America, the whole idea of resistance is one that most Christians, being also decent people and loyal citizens, find difficult if not abhorrent.

Just here we must register a nuance, or perhaps an irony. The very history of resistance that is part of the lore of Christendom—all the way from the acts of the early martyrs to the resistance against fascism in the 1930s and 1940s, and in more recent times against the police regimes of Central America, South Africa, South Korea, and elsewhere—functions to discourage resistance in the less "dramatic" situations that are more regularly the context of the Christian life, as is the case with us in North America today. We tell ourselves that the apostles, saints, and martyrs of the faith were living under conditions wholly intolerable to both faith and reason. In this way we help to convince ourselves that the conditions of our own context do not warrant any such protest, for, by comparison with the extremes of life under Nero, or "Bloody Mary," or Stalin, or the death squads of El Salvador, ours is a context of peace, tolerance, and humanity.

The resisting voices of our context, however, think otherwise. While we may not have the obvious evils of death camps and gulags and the strict censorship of literature, they would say, we belong to a system and a world that creates oppressive conditions for many both beyond and within the boundaries of our nations. The social, political, and cultural realities that we have to resist are certainly less obvious than those celebrated in the sacred history of resistance, but they may be even more insidious for all that. It does and will require greater subtlety, vigilance, and insight to detect them. And it does and will require, especially, concern for the victims who are not seen, some of whom may even appear to be well off.

In all of the once-mainline denominations within the United States and Canada today, there are such protesting voices. Their protest cannot be ignored; for some reasons which I shall mention presently, it has achieved a remarkably sympathetic hearing within all of the churches concerned. But it is also rejected by many within these churches. There is a resistance against the resistance. It seems to many to be exaggerated, excessive.

This resistance of the resistance is the inevitable harvest of centuries of Christendom, augmented by the mythology of American innocence, decency, and good will. We should not be surprised if the resistance is resisted—that Pro*test*ants on the whole, through the elevation of their forms of Christendom to the position of established religion, have little sympathy for any sort of protest.

Nevertheless, the resistance has made a greater impact upon once-mainline Protestantism in these past two or three decades than could have been predicted in (say) 1950. With the breakdown of Christendom, the ethic of resistance becomes a live option for more and more of those who remain within these formerly most established of the denominations. As members of these denominations recognize their effective distancing from the source of power and policy-making, they are also grasped by a new sense of freedom: they may pursue avenues of thought and action that are significantly different from the opinions and pursuits of the majority. Realizing that they are no longer obliged to confirm the "conventional" morality, they are ready to explore ethical questions from the perspective of their own faith. It may be difficult to "swim against the stream." Most of those about whom we are thinking had or have little or no experience of real resistance. Unlike the experience of twentieth-century European Christians, there has been no dramatic history of resistance in the established churches of this continent, although the antinuclear protest, the Civil Rights movement, the Sanctuary movement and some more recent forms of resistance have influenced minorities in all of the churches. Still, for many who begin to feel the necessity and the possibility of the way of resistance, it seems an entirely new approach to the Christian life. In congregations in which this new way achieves a certain momentum, there are usually divisions.

As with the whole matter of our transition from Christendom to diaspora, there is also at present a serious lack of informed Christian leadership helping people to locate in the Scriptures and theological traditions of their faith a rationale for the ethic of resistance. Significant numbers of laypersons in our liberal and moderate denominations are prepared to engage in some kind of protest—for instance, against the growing power of a new kind of "conservativism" that celebrates individual initiative to the point of leaving the powerless to their own devices. But this readiness to resist is seldom sufficiently informed and empowered by Christian reflection. The result is that in the absence of such Christian tutelage the incipient resistance that informs many congregations today has to look for its rationale and for sheer encouragement to sources that are external to the faith. The Christian protest is thus caught up in other movements of resistance that, although they may share certain proximate goals with Christianity, also usually incorporate assumptions and strategies that are not compatible with Christian obedience. Thus the potentiality for developing a more genuinely confessional church through a thoughtful, disciplined discipleship remains unrealized.

We are again brought face to face with the priority of *theology.* For without any theological basis and corrective, that is to say, pursued as "an ethic" or "way of life" or "lifestyle," resistance may become as questionable an approach as conformity. It may become little more than conformity to the program of some countercultural ideology. But this leads to the second principle, which, in my view, may act as a corrective to that tendency.

22.2. Discipleship as Worldly Responsibility. The posture of resistance must be held in tension with another aspect of the Christian life that will prevent Christians from abandoning the stance of confessor for that of ideologue. That other aspect is the worldly responsibility that discipleship of the Christ entails. Discipleship is not a program, a lifestyle, an agenda. Christians are disciples *of Jesus Christ,* therefore of One who lives, who commands, who is committed to the life of the world, and who for all these reasons refuses to be encased in any system or moral code or "theology of." Discipleship as worldly responsibility means obedience to the living Lord in the midst of a living, changing world; the ethic that belongs to this life is a thoroughly contextual ethic. What is required today may differ much from what is required tomorrow; what is commanded here may differ much from what is commanded there.

Certainly, in obedience to Jesus Christ, the disciple community may be called upon to resist, and we have seen that resistance, according to the Protestant faith and experience particularly, is a highly probable dimension of every faithful act of Christian confession. But Christian obedience is not to an ethic of resistance, it is to Jesus Christ.[83] "The Protestant principle" has also to be applied to the ethic of resistance!

---

83. "Christ is not a principle in accordance with which the whole world must be shaped. Christ is not the proclaimer of a system of what would be good today, here and at all times. Christ teaches no abstract ethics such as must at all costs be put into practice. . . . For indeed it is not written that God became an idea, a principle, a programme, a universally valid proposition or a law, but that God became man. This means that though the form of Christ certainly

For when protestation becomes a way of life, it is just as guilty of usurping the ultimacy of the Ultimate as any other system or code of behavior. The ethic of resistance becomes an ideology when the source and the object of resistance have been obscured by the style of resistance as such. Protest as a means has been transmuted to protest as an end in itself. The source of *Christian* resistance is a Christ who wills not that the sinner should die but that he should turn from his wickedness and live; not that the evil world should perish but that it should be transformed. In short, life and not death is the object of this resistance; therefore, although the threat to life has to be resisted, that which enhances and sustains life has at the same time to be supported, fostered, edified. Resistance of evil without reinforcement of the good is incomplete. It is because good is possible that evil must be resisted. Because of the possibility of justice, injustice must be named and stopped. Because of the possibility of peace, war and war preparations and the mentality of violence must be confronted and converted to a statecraft and mentality of peace. Because of the possibility of creaturely harmony, the disintegrating forces at work in the biosphere must be resisted and other ways found of sustaining and enriching life. Resistance of evil is for the sake of the good; and the good is not a theoretical good, but one that has been revealed, lived, and is always being concretized; a good that has "already" triumphed although it is "not yet" fulfilled.

The responsibility of the church as the disciple community of Jesus Christ is thus a broad and complex worldly stewardship that, in practice, is extremely difficult to exercise wisely and with integrity, yet prevents many of the excesses and dangers of "easier" versions of morality. While it assumes that Christians will be especially critical of "powers and principalities" that try to acquire worldly sovereignty, and vigilant for the victims of these powers, its resistance will be tempered by the recognition that both oppressors and oppressed are human beings; therefore it will attempt to avoid divisions of the world into camps of good and evil—divisions that, however appealing to the ideological spirit, are simplistic and unredemptive. And while it must be assumed that the disciple community will seek and find others with whom (through the recognition of "middle axioms," perhaps) it may make common cause, it will also recognize the variety of motivation and goal with which people band together for specific purposes, and it will continue to listen to, and depend for courage and sustenance upon, its own particular Source and sources of wisdom (the point of our whole discussion of "Resources for the Journey").

---

is and remains one and the same, yet it is willing to take form in the real man, that is to say, in quite different guises" (Dietrich Bonhoeffer, *Ethics,* ed. Eberhard Bethge, trans. Neville Horton Smith [London: SCM, 1955], 22).

To exemplify the latter: Christians who participate in the universal *agape* of God in Christ will know today that "the world" for which they have responsibility includes the nonhuman creatures and the natural processes that are threatened by human folly and greed. They will therefore be impelled by divine love to cooperate with all who share this concern for "otherkind." They will enter into such covenants knowing, however, that as Christ's disciples they are not permitted to embrace outlooks and actions that reputedly "save" some species and natural processes by jeopardizing the future of others, including humanity. In other words, the holistic or integrated concern for *life* to which faith in Jesus Christ leads precludes the kind of specialized moral concentration that leads to myopic and exclusivist positions that in their preoccupation with parts no longer ask about the whole. As Rosemary Radford Ruether writes, "We need a much more nuanced perspective, one that can acknowledge that the sources of [the ecological] crisis are complex, not unilinear from one source [Gen. 1:28]. . . . What we do not need is the simple either-ors that write off entire cultures and groups of people as discardable, a way of thought that is all too obviously the reversed product of that same dualistic culture that feminists and deep ecologists deplore."[84]

The holistic nature of the "responsibility for history" (Bonhoeffer) that discipleship of Jesus Christ entails means that Christians will normally be denied the satisfaction of feeling that their actions have wholly succeeded—that the dilemmas to which they addressed themselves have been met and resolved. On the contrary, they will understand that the ultimate resolution of any specific dilemma will await the larger resolution of history as a whole—in short, they will know that resolution as such is an eschatological category. The resolution that history awaits is contained for Christians in the symbol of the divine reign or "kingdom." While approximations of the "peaceable kingdom" are possible in the midst of history, and therefore disciples of Christ *resist* what others think is inevitable, neither do they court utopian ideals that so often prove the most implacable tyrants in their attempts to impose perfection upon life. Life is movement, and the object of the disciple community is to move into the future with "the Lord and Giver of Life," doing what it can today to implement the promise of that future, and realizing that much will remain to be done tomorrow.

We are speaking about the Christian life, and what we have just observed about it is a reminder of an aspect of the theology of the cross that is also, with the rest of that "thin tradition," almost totally unheard of in the "estab-

---

84. Douglas John Hall and Rosemary Radford Ruether, *God and the Nations* (Minneapolis: Fortress Press, 1995), 86.

lished" situation of the church. It is that the Christian life is a "hidden" life.[85] "For you have died," writes the author of Colossians (3:3), "and your life is hid with Christ in God." Far from being a clear-cut and transparent life that is dedicated to a recognizable program and mode of behavior ("the Christian Right," "the Left," fundamentalism, liberalism, and so on), the life of discipleship is one that may involve many different and even apparently incompatible approaches, and may bring one into the company of many different and sometimes strange combinations of persons and groups. While the ethic of resistance suggests a typical stance, attracts predictable supporters, and repels equally predictable critics, the ethic of responsibility bears about itself a certain unpredictability that may to some seem capricious and to others flexible. This is because it flows from discipleship. It follows and does not lead. It is content to obey, so far as understanding and volition allow, the One who shepherds it, and so to do what must be done "this day," and to trust that it will be used for good. It is a matter of faith and not of sight. "For *thine* is the Kingdom. . . ."[86]

In the diaspora situation, where Christianity is no longer something altogether evident and predictable, the hiddenness of the Christian life that is part of our Reformation heritage will be newly meaningful. If Christianity is not a program; if it involves one in the world in an unprotected and unfamiliar way—the way of the sojourner; if verbal confession of the faith is meaningful only where it can presuppose solidarity with the world on its own terms, then we shall have to discover not only the traditions of the hidden God, the ubiquitous Christ, and the anonymous Christian, but also Luther's concomitant teaching concerning the "incognito" character of the Christian life itself. The strict lines of demarcation between Christian and non-Christian disappear in the post-Christendom situation. This is undoubtedly a confusing experience for those who have been conditioned by establishment forms of the faith—as we all have! But, in the concept of the hiddenness and

---

85. "God is a hidden God, faith is the evidence of things that do not appear, the life of the Christian is hidden. These three statements belong together in the most intimate way. One follows from the other. . . . Why is the life of the Christian a hidden one? Very simply because it is a life of faith. . . . The Christian life is an object of faith and, as such, it is hidden. What we see is never the real thing; only God and faith see this innermost core" (Walther von Loewenich, *Luther's Theology of the Cross,* trans. Herbert J. A. Bouman [Belfast: Christian Journals Limited, 1976], 114).

86. "In explaining the beginnings and the course of the Reformation to the people of Wittenberg after his return from exile in Wartburg castle, [Luther] said: 'All I have done is to further, preach, and teach God's word; otherwise I have done nothing. So it came about that while I slept or while I had a glass of beer with my friend Philip [Melanchthon] and with Amsdorf, the papacy was so weakened as it never was before by the action of any prince or emperor. I have done nothing; the word has done and accomplished everything. . . . I let the word do its work'" (Wilhelm Pauck, *From Luther to Tillich,* 9).

anonymity of the Christian life, we may discover a way of absorbing this experience into a theology of discipleship that frees us for obedience.

In introducing this segment, I affirmed that the ethic of resistance and the ethic of responsibility qualify and correct one another. Each contains its temptation to which the other may apply itself. We have seen that the danger of the ethic of resistance is that it becomes under certain conditions a whole way of life with its own rationale and its own satisfactions. It needs to be constantly reminded that faith is not faith in a style of life or a posture vis-à-vis "the dominant culture," but faith in One who lives and moves within a living and changing world.

The danger of the ethic of worldly responsibility, on the other hand, is that it will devolve into a mystical attraction to the whole that fails to address itself to the parts—that it will become an abstract commitment to "life" that is apt to overlook the specific threats to life that must be resisted by any confession of faith.

In the tension between the two (which are, of course, not two separable ethical positions but two dimensions of the one covenantal relationship), the church that is edged out of its established relation with its host culture may work out a manner of existing vis-à-vis its "world" that is both critical and constructive; or, to use the language we adopted in the fourth chapter, a mode of disengaging that enables meaningful re-engagement.

PART III
THE FORMS OF FAITH'S CONFESSION

CHAPTER ▪ SIX

Christian Confession as Word, Deed, and Stance

23. The Forms of Faith's Confession

23.1. The Pneumatic Dimension. In the two previous parts of this study, we have been concerned with the community that confesses the faith; now we direct our attention to the character of confession itself. Of the two chapters devoted to this subject, the first asks broadly about the ways in which the disciple community bears witness to "Jesus Christ and him crucified"; the second discusses theological ethics, thus both cementing the connection between theology and ethics and making visible the assumption of the author that ethics, Christianly conceived, constitute a concretization of faith's worldly confession. In both chapters, the particularities of our context will continue to inform the discussion.

The plural form of the initial noun in the title of this part (and the first heading that follows) indicates that, in my view, there is no one fixed form to which Christians must adhere if they are to confess their faith. I have already stated, and will presently elaborate on the presupposition that faith's confession usually entails language. It would be hard to imagine a confessing church that never spoke, and almost as unthinkable to conceive of the speaking of such a church that did not employ certain familiar terminology and affirmations. Yet faith's confession is certainly not limited to language, and the mere use of language, including that familiar language, by no means guarantees that the faith is being confessed.

Are there *any* limits to the forms that the confession of faith may assume? It would be presumptuous, I believe, to say so. Professional theology is pre-

343

disposed to limit confession of the faith to the spoken or written word; but even the most scholastic theologians are obliged by the core of their meditative work to recognize that words may obscure the truth more often than they succeed in pointing to it, and that wordless deeds may indeed "say" more than all the tomes of the erudite. Even things to which the nomenclature of the deed or act can hardly be applied—even sighs and silences and gestures; even simply being present in a given situation—may constitute an act of confession.

Theoretically, it is questionable to prescribe what forms faith's confession may take, and the reason is not only that, in practice, it has taken innumerable forms, but that confession cannot be engineered and manipulated by anyone. There is always an element of unpredictability in the Christian life, as we have noted in the previous chapter. Those who set out quite explicitly to be "confessors of the faith" may succeed only in impressing others of like mind. In their solitude they may come to know that they have achieved little by way of genuine confession—perhaps they have not succeeded in transcending the mode of faith's *pro*fession. On the other hand, without intending it or even thinking the thought, it may sometimes happen that what one said, or did, or refrained from saying or doing, is received by others as a statement of faith.

This unpredictability of the act of confession tells us something about our subject that we have not stressed heretofore, namely that faith's confession involves others besides the ones making the confession. We are prevented by the actual history of the confessing community from claiming that Christian confession is authentic only if it is heard and received. The history of the Christian movement abounds in tales of those who bore witness to the truth and were not heard! Yet this familiar image of the *confessor fidei,* the unheeded and despised martyr to truth, too easily obscures and distorts the character of faith's confession. For it suggests that what is important in the whole matter is that Christians ought to manifest the courage of their convictions, regardless of the consequences.

And that is undoubtedly true; but it is not the whole truth. For in the economy of God the goal of faith's confession is not its demonstration of the faithfulness of the confessors so much as its effect upon those who hear. The whole witness of the church, indeed its very existence, is understood by the Scriptures as having its rationale in the divine desire "that the world may believe" (John 17:21). The God who is committed to creaturely life and seeks its fulfillment could hardly entertain as the divine "plan" a movement of martyrs ready to give themselves over to suffering and death. As I have claimed throughout, the proper end of faith's confession is life and not death; therefore what ought to dominate the church's collective thought is not the building up of a phalanx of stalwarts ready to suffer and die for their convic-

344

tions, but rather the edification of a faithful company of witnesses who care enough for the life of others, and of the world itself, to want to share their "good news." The very term *martereo,* from which the English word "martyr" derives, has as its primary meaning the thought of pointing (witnessing) to something beyond oneself. The blood of the martyrs, it was said, is the seed of the church. The object is not the dying but the living that may be made possible through—if it must be—such a death.

There is, consequently, a dimension of unmanageability in the confession of the faith; for no one, not even the most adept manipulator of human emotions, can cause others to receive his or her confession; nor, conversely, can anyone prevent others from receiving as confession of faith what was not necessarily intended as such. Confession no doubt remains confession even if it is not received. Yet the object of the act is to be received as witness, and therefore its fullness depends upon the response of those who are to be found in the vicinity of the act, and not only upon the act itself.

Almost any Christian biography illustrates the manner in which individuals come to faith—initially, through chance occurrences, snatches of conversations, remembered phrases out of books or plays, the looks or gestures of persons long since absent remembered in the light of new occurrences, and so forth. George P. Grant, whose works have been cited frequently in this series, describes how, going to work as a farm laborer in England during World War II, he pushed his bicycle through a gate and realized, suddenly, that he believed in God. No doubt countless words, acts, pictures, music, relationships, and experiences of every kind all contributed to that moment of insight and change (*metanoia*). But it was neither predictable nor managed. The element of surprise, as for C. S. Lewis, was strong in it.[1]

What such experiences of "hearing" illustrate is that faith's confession is normally a process far more random, eclectic, and unintentional than is usually imagined by the writers of books of doctrine. Or does it not demonstrate, rather, that there is an invisible Presence at the center of this act, able to use both our willed and our unwilled testimony to Itself? A Presence quite independent of us while allowing Itself to be in a certain sense dependent? If

---

1. "When [Grant] wrote to his mother . . . he spoke to her of a spiritual journey and of being born again. . . . 'It is just not a journey that one could call up or down. It is merely to a different plane of existence. Spiritually it has been so far that it is as if it wasn't the same person who started out . . . there is no fear for my mental health as just recently I feel as if I had been born again. Gradually I am learning there are unpredictable tremendous forces—mysterious forces within man that are beyond man's understanding driving him—taking him along courses and over which he has no or little control . . . ' On Christmas Day he felt 'like a piece of stick being carried by the strength of the current. . . . So many Christmases one does not have the time to think of Christ, though we are crucifying him now—more and more I understand the glory of him'" (William Christian, *George Grant: A Biography* [Toronto, Buffalo, London: University of Toronto Press, 1993], 86).

we dare to speak of the forms of faith's confession, then, we shall do well to remember this; and if we remember it we shall not allow our professional penchant to categorize to go unchallenged.

23.2. The Intentional Dimension. While confession of the faith occurs in ways that defy human deliberation and management, it must also be recognized that the disciple community knows itself to be called to a life of witness, and insofar as it does know this, it *intends* it, and insofar as it intends this, it plans and works for the realization of this calling. The disciple community cannot command, at will, the occasion of confession; that remains the domain of the Spirit. But the community learns how to recognize the occasion, and in its ongoing reflection on the tradition that it professes it continually readies itelf for the confessional moment.

We should pause to consider the thought of "the occasion." Confession of the faith is occasioned by the inherent compulsions of apostolicity[2] as these are stimulated by specific events and situations in the actual life of the church in the world. The Barmen Declaration did not come to be as the result of an ecclesiastical decision that there should be some new articulation of Christian belief. It came to be in response to a particular, open-ended sequence of historical circumstances. These circumstances, acting upon the minds and consciences of some who seriously professed the faith, exerted such an influence that the latter were driven to confess what they professed. Their confession was occasioned by events over which they had no control. Barmen thus, as we saw, contains a conspicuous element of urgency and necessity. It is a necessity that, like Paul's, is "laid upon" (1 Cor. 9:16) the confessing body; it is not in any simple sense voluntary, and it is certainly not arbitrary.

This way of conceiving of faith's confession is very different from the sort of Christian witness that emanates from individuals or religious communities unbidden. For many Christians in North America, the idea of confessing the faith is naturally associated with the kind of Christianity that feels obliged to deliver itself of its message on every occasion and all occasions, irrespective of circumstances. Such confession arises habitually, without any prompting from the side of the context. It is assumed in such circles that faith must always be announcing itself; and, apart from stereotypical preconceptions of the human condition, it feels no obligation to articulate itself in response to what is actually occurring in its theatre of witness.

By way of contrast with this familiar approach, we are assuming here a contextual framework of faith's confession. The confessing community is *not* at liberty to engage in the act of confession without reference to its context.

---

2. See the discussion of apostolicity in chap. 2, subsection 4.4.

It understands that its confession has to be called forth, evoked, by specific realities in its situation, and that its *form* will be determined by those realities. The *content* of the confession emanates from a Source and sources that transcend the context; but the form of the confession will be dependent upon what is "going on" in the environs of the confessing community. Apart from this formation, the community will not make the "breakthrough" into a truly confessional mode but at best will remain within the mode of faith's *profession*.

This point is again readily illustrated by dramatic occasions such as the circumstances that precipitated the Barmen Declaration. Had the confessing church not allowed the specifics of Adolf Hitler's program to shape its response, its confessional activity would have been in the literal sense merely professional—and we should probably never have heard of it! While this applies in an obvious way to such dramatic and critical situations, it is true also of the more placid or "gray" circumstances that are—at least in our context—the more common *Sitz im Leben* of the Christian community.

Today in the United States and Canada, the context in which confession is to take place seems, by comparison with Barmen and numerous other critical moments in the history of the Christian movement, uneventful; some would even say tranquil. But if one probes a little beneath the surface of our life, as we have tried to do in this trilogy, one discovers crises that in the long run may be more decisive for the future than those that occasioned the confession of Barmen. And even where such crises are held in abeyance by affluence, or custom, or inertia, or the vigilance of the few, the disciple community is obliged by its world-commitment to mold its confession in response to them. Even the Sunday sermon, which, as I shall insist presently, is one of the forms of faith's confession, must be fashioned, thought by thought and word by word, in response to the actualities of private and public life, probed and illuminated by a faith that "seeks understanding." And every conscientious preacher knows that, while the regularity with which Sunday makes its appearance demands of him or her a high degree of intentionality, there is also a strong dimension of the unpredictable and the unmanageable in this office; for the concrete circumstances to which the preacher must speak are always transcendent of his or her invention and control.

So far as confession of the faith is intended by the disciple community, and can be anticipated and planned, three types of activity suggest themselves: speech, action, and positioning (or what I shall call "stance"). That is to say, we prepare to bear witness to Jesus as the Christ through direct address, through deeds inspired by faith, and through the general posture that we assume vis-à-vis others. Few if any Christians would want to regard these three forms of faith's confession as alternatives; they are, rather, dimensions of the life of the church that, as such, will be present in every *koinonia* even if, gifts being diverse, they are not all present in every Christian individual. There is an obvious interdependence of the three types of activity: words without deeds, deeds without words, words and deeds without the assumption of positions commensurate with them—such are self-contradictory. The three belong together.

It is nevertheless true that we may and must distinguish these different forms of faith's confession, and it is also true that occasions will evoke, often, one of them more insistently than the others. Remembering, then, their interdepencency, we shall discuss the three forms of faith's confession separately in order to explore the possibilities of each. I am devoting two sections to confession as address because, of the three intentional forms, it is the most complex and also, historically and doctrinally, the most important.

24. Confession as Address: Preaching the Faith

24.1. The Contemporary Reduction of the Sacrament of the Word. The confession of faith, we have said, normally entails speech; and one of the traditional forms of speech in the Christian community is preaching. Preaching is by no means the only form of confession as direct address, but, for Protestants especially, it is of high importance both historically and theologically. My thesis in what follows will be that preaching is also contextually vital to the church's confession of faith, and that precisely this potentiality is little realized and exploited by today's preachers and congregations.

Preaching, which for the Reformation tradition was the lifeline of the church, seems to have fallen on evil times.[3] A great variety of factors has brought this about. During the countercultural "revolution" of the 1960s and early 1970s, preaching shared the fate of every other activity that required the prominence of one person whose training and vocation had been thought, earlier, to qualify him or her to stand before others and "speak with authority." The so-called Age of Aquarius introduced a vast distrust of all authority, and especially that of supposedly authoritative individuals. No doubt this distrust had been brewing for a very long time, and no doubt it

---

3. Already in 1959, James D. Smart, commenting on the Niebuhr-Williams report on the ministry and theological education, writes: "The report comes in from every quarter that our Protestant preaching is in a very bad way, that larger numbers of our ministers, in spite of three years in seminary and classes in homiletics, do not seem to know why they are in the pulpit, and that from these pulpits sounds a babel of gospels that is strangely and disturbingly like the confusion of tongues in the eleventh chapter of Genesis. . . . Why is there this chaos in our preaching? It is certainly not unrelated to it that there has been a neglect of critical theological investigation and definition in homiletics. We have stumbled into chaos in our engrossment in practical and technical concerns" ("The Minister as Pastor," in *The Canadian Journal of Theology* 5, no. 3 (1959): 181). The only change in this "chaotic" situation since Dr. Smart's article appeared is that the chaos has increased.

was in some ways merited. Preachers, like many professors, politicians, and other authority figures, mostly masculine in gender, had too frequently been immodest, presumptuous, and more concerned for themselves and their reputations than for the well-being of those whom they addressed. It was in many ways salutary for all such figures to learn that their alleged "right" to speak with authority was a right granted them by their hearers, and that not permanently! They would have to earn the right by dint of hard work, if not of consistent inspiration.

Yet the effect of this perhaps necessary chastisement of the authoritative preacher has been, it seems to me, excessive. Combined with other factors operative in our context, it has tended to rob Christian preachers of the confidence that this office requires—*confidence* (*con* = with, *fide* = faith), not certitude. Certitude in preachers is more destructive than in most people, for it gives a falsely secure image of the life of faith and understanding. But confidence is necessary to preaching, for it is a reflection of the very trust (*fide*) that the preacher commends in his or her verbal testimony. Such trust enables one to speak with authority—not *as* authority, but as one who is "under authority" (*cf.* Matt. 8:9), who is "sent" (*apostellein*) by Another, and is there before his or her co–human beings to *represent* that Other. Here, too, the informing metaphor of representation is of vital importance. The man or woman "in the pulpit" is there, not just as this man or this woman, but as priest and witness to *God's* Word.

The chastisement of authority that was part of the countercultural critique two or three decades ago seems to have had a permanent effect on preaching. In the moderate and liberal denominations of our context today, it is very hard to find preachers who will dare to speak with anything that could be called authority. Even though in many (although not all) cases they may be said to possess the necessary "credentials," most contemporary preachers hesitate to assume any such posture as that suggested by the very verb "to preach" in its original Greek form: *kerusso* = to announce or proclaim. With exceptions, when today's preachers are unable to fill the "sermon period" with dialogical, meditative, or narrative material, they approach their task cautiously, suggestively, and indirectly, introducing as many disclaimers of their own expertise as possible, and being so conscious of "inclusivity" of every variety that one is left wondering whether there is any particular person behind the robe of office!

This is not always the fault of the individuals concerned. The mood of the churches in question naturally calls forth such individuals and discourages persons who "stand out." And this seems to be an aspect of the age itself, which militates against individuality while fostering a rampant individualism. Such an age discourages those with daring messages. To read the sermons of the earlier part of this century, or of the Reformation period, or of the Bible itself (for example, Stephen's sermon in Acts 7) is to find oneself in a quite different milieu. Apart from the neo-evangelicals, whose preaching manifests more of certitude than of confidence, preaching on the order of St. Stephen, or John Knox, or Harry Emerson Fosdick would be thought terribly aggressive by today's standards. But the price that is paid for our caution and tentativeness is also evident.

If a *thinking* faith is what the context calls for, contemporary preaching on the whole will do little to supply such a demand. The most "successful" preachers are not those who stimulate depth of thought, especially not "thoughts that wound from behind" (Kierkegaard), but those who entertain. This, too, as we have already noted in passing, has a sociological explanation, and indicates the extent to which, instead of engaging the society, the churches tend to mirror it.

For in an age when human expectations with respect to public address have been reduced to entertainment; when slow argumentation and the reasoned presentation of ideas has been replaced by the shallow magic of the one-liner or the three-minute "clip," and when individuals, if they are allowed to speak, speak as human beings whose natural endowments are "enhanced" by the technics of sound, light, makeup, and all the rest, the person who dares to stand before others simply as a human being before human beings, attempting to sway them by mere language, knows the meaning of naked finitude. This, of course, applies to lecturers, politicians, and all passionate, articulate citizens just as much as it does to preachers; but preaching is still— perhaps by force of habit—central to the life of Protestant Christianity; and when it can scarcely rise above the mundane, the consequence is that the Christian community is deprived of this source of energy, understanding, and depth.

To accommodate themselves to the new expectations of a television-educated laity, preachers surround themselves with whatever accoutrements of *la technique* they can commandeer, and (what is more devastating so far as preaching is concerned) they attempt to mimic the quick pace of the talk shows and newscasts, thus often reducing faith's confession in this form to trivia. The sermon came to be what it was in Protestant history because the Reformers and their successors believed human beings to be capable of some depth of understanding, and they felt that the symbols and rituals of late medievalism were depriving human beings of their potentiality for wisdom and understanding.

Beyond these secular influences and "attacks" upon the office of preaching, there has been a slow but effective internal ecclesiastical dry rot. In part, this aspect of the malaise may be traced to the liberal Christian preference for "topical preaching," and, in another version, to the conservative Christian preference for a kind of Bible-based preaching that, however, did little to encourage thought. Both the Reformers themselves and those who were educated in the linguistic, historical, and theological traditions of classical Protestantism looked upon the sermon as the occasion for meditation of the most disciplined and serious nature. It is not accidental that preachers such as Edwards, Wesley, Spurgeon, Fosdick, Scherer, and others of their epochs were persons of great learning, and not only "communicators." If preaching today strives to be entertaining or "helpful," rather than edifying, convincing, and convicting, it is at least in part because so few preachers are themselves immersed in the theological and other disciplines that make for "wisdom"— a term that is too often today associated with the kind of "spirituality" that is indifferent to learning. If preachers do not aim for such wisdom themselves but for conviviality, sincerity, and "communications skills," they cannot expect their congregations to derive from their sermons anything different from what is available twenty-four hours a day in their own homes—and, probably, in more interesting forms.

This is said passionately and critically because it seems to me quite obvious that unless there is some theological renaissance within the once-mainline Protestant churches of our context they are not going to survive the next century; and such a renaissance, so far as congregational life is concerned, could and perhaps must begin with preaching. Since we have spoken about the need for churches to disengage in order that they may re-engage the culture with which they have such long historical ties, one of the most salient points of disengagement ought to be a revolution in preaching: namely, the refusal of preachers and congregations to make of preaching a mirror image of the "information highway" or the entertainment industry, and a recovery of some of the depth of "the sacrament of the Word" as it was conceived by the Reformers. It is simply untrue that *everybody* in the churches would turn away if preachers engaged in such a revolt. The fact is, "many whom the churches do not have," as well as a significant number of those whom they "have," are waiting to see whether anything approximating wisdom can come out of Nazareth!

24.2. The Word as Sacrament. "The Word is the audible sacrament and the sacrament is the visible Word"; so wrote a Lutheran theologian, Johannes Rupprecht, in 1925.[4] Protestantism, as is well known, did not use the term "sacrament" lightly, or allow its application to various and sundry acts of worship and ritual hallowed by centuries of observation or decreed by those in authority. We have seen that the Reformers insisted upon two sacraments only. Yet the Reformers, and particularly Luther and his associates and fol-

---

4. As quoted by Karl Barth in *The Doctrine of the Word of God*, trans. G. T. Thomson (New York: Charles Scribner's Sons, 1936), 79.

lowers, conceived of the preaching of the Word in what is clearly a sacramental way:

> The preaching of the New Testament is naught else but an offering and presentation *of Christ* to all men out of the pure mercy of God, in such wise that all who believe in Him receive God's grace and the Holy Spirit, by which all sin is forgiven, all law is fulfilled. . . . Therefore St. Paul . . . calls the New Testament proclamation *ministerium spiritus,* a ministry of the spirit, i.e. a ministry by which the spirit and grace of God are presented and offered to all who by the law have been burdened, killed, and made to long for grace.[5]

For Luther, preaching was "the highest office in the Christian Church."[6] The preaching of the Word may even be said to have priority over the administration of the sacraments; for (as Rupprecht stated the matter), "'The Word is the first and will remain the first. It does not say, Heaven and earth shall pass away, but my sacraments shall not pass away; but it says, But my words shall not pass away.'"[7]

How is this extraordinary sense of the sacramental character of the preaching of the Word on the part of the Reformers to be explained? In part, it is a consequence of their new encounter with the Scriptures as the primary "provisional" authority for faith, and, on the Reformed side, this is of course bound up with the humanist movement's sense of the importance of language. It is also in obvious ways related to the Germanic mysticism of the "concrete" (Tillich) variety, by which Luther was deeply influenced. But its foundation lies with the faith of Israel. The God of Abraham, Isaac, Ruth, and Deborah is a speaking God (*Deus loquens*), as we have frequently reminded ourselves in this series; and that creature whom this God fashions to be representative of all the creatures is, correspondingly, a speaking creature (*homo loquens,* as we have said before, is a far more biblical way of thinking of humankind than the preferred term of the Renaissance, *homo sapiens*). The very ordinariness of language takes on another meaning when it is viewed in the light of this Creator-creature relationship.

The speaking God is not captured in the words either of Scripture or of preaching, so far as the tradition of Jerusalem is concerned. Truth transcends all truths and the Word transcends all words: this is understood from the outset, and it is fairly represented by Karl Barth's "threefold form of the Word," which acknowledges the relativity of the Word written and the Word preached in relation to the Word incarnate. Only of the latter form of the

---

5. Martin Luther, *Works,* Philadelphia edition, vol. 3 (Philadelphia: Muhlenberg Press, 1930), 355.

6. Luther, *Works,* vol. 4, 84.

7. Barth, *The Doctrine of the Word of God,* 79.

Word can it be said, unequivocally, This is God's own Word. Yet words that witness to that living Word may be caused by the divine Spirit to become its vehicles, and there is a strong intimation throughout the literature of the Reformation, which can be supported in this sense scripturally as well, that when all is said and done the Word can only be communicated through words, and that it seeks, as it were, the *appropriate* words, always, in which to manifest itself. Moreover, the appropriateness of the words is directly related to the question that has driven our whole endeavor to think the faith contextually, that is, "What needs to be said *here* and *now*?"[8] The sense of "occasion," which belongs to this sacramental understanding of the office of preaching, stems from this contextual awareness: the moment has about it a sense of urgency. There is a human need to be met, hunger for meaning to be fed, longing for truth and direction to be filled; God is ready to encounter human beings in all the particularity of their here and now; and the preacher is to be God's representative, as much here as at the communion table and the baptismal font.

This accentuation of the Word does not imply a diminution of the two sacraments; on the contrary, if Protestants still speak of "the ministry of Word and sacraments" it is in a real sense because both aspects of the "ordered ministry" participate in the same coincidence of the concrete and the transcendent. The concrete—which, in the case of the sacraments, means the quite elemental substances of bread, wine, and water, and in the case of the Word, means words—becomes the vehicle of the transcendent, the visible/audible through which the invisible is conveyed.

But unlike Catholicism, which was prepared to extend the sacramental dimension to many aspects of life but continued to look upon preaching chiefly as instruction, exhortation, or homily, Reformation theology found in the Word, and therefore in both Scripture and preaching, a *ministerium spiritus* more transparent even than the sacraments; in fact, reading the literature of classical Protantism, one can have the impression that the writers understand the Sacraments because they understand *better* the sacramental character of the Word, without which, in any case, the administration of the sacraments, they felt, regularly devolves into magical or superstitious practice. For them, in other words, the connectedness of the concrete with the transcendent is more transparent where preaching is concerned than it is with the sacraments of Baptism and the Eucharist. Bread, wine, and water do not necessarily and inherently participate in the transcendent realities that, in the sacramental act, they are caused to make concrete; the assocation of those

---

8. See my essay, "The Diversity of Christian Witnessing in the Tension Between Subjection to the Word and Relation to the Context," in Peter Manns, et al., *Luther's Ecumenical Significance: An Interconfessional Consultation* (Philadelphia: Fortress Press, 1984), 247–68.

elements with those particular realities is a historical one, instituted by Jesus among his disciples. But between words and the Word there is more than a merely historical tie. In addition to the whole background of the prophetic, doxological, and sapiential literature of Israel, there is the universal human experience of the relation between language and meaning. Perhaps if Luther and Zwingli had quite explicitly taken that approach at Marburg, their philosophic and personal differences notwithstanding, they would have found greater agreement than they did when they tried to discuss the Lord's Supper independently of their theology of the sacramental Word.

For the Reformation tradition, the act of preaching is thus an exceptional event in the life of the disciple community. It has nothing to do with oratory or histrionics, pomp or stained-glass accents. Yet it participates in the numinous, and is by no means just ordinary discourse or public speaking. Teaching is a dimension of preaching, but the sermon is not conceived primarily as an educational event. It is even less a display of "communications skills" on the part of an individual! Although Luther often criticized preachers for addressing the high and mighty and learned instead of ordinary peasants and untutored folk (his *Table Talk* abounds in such criticism[9]), he would have been equally if not more greatly offended by the contemporary attempt to render preaching as close to ordinary discourse as possible—a friendly chat with one's parishoners! For, in a way similar to the Catholic or Anglican priest who so reveres the Eucharist that it creates in him or her a certain holy fear (*mysterium tremendum et fascinans*), so the preacher in the tradition of the Reformation is apt to feel a particular sense of unworthiness, or even dread, at the prospect of addressing other humans with so awesome a message. Jacques Ellul speaks precisely out of this tradition when he writes that

> the one who speaks is absolutely committed as he faces others. Only his word can explain a given action or attitude and make it acceptable or despicable. Only by his use of language can such a person's authenticity be demonstrated. . . . Thus we are told that everyone will be judged according to his words; and again, "as I hear, I judge" (Jn. 5:30). These are surprising statements for people eager for action! Yet Jesus says, "By your words you will be justified, and by your words you will be condemned" (Mt. 12:37). This reminds us of the ultimate seriousness of words. Here we are far removed from the modern scorn for words, far from phrases that commit no one and mean nothing. . . .
>
> Precisely for this reason preaching is the most frightful adventure.[10]

---

9. For example: "Cursed are all preachers that in the church aim at high and hard things, and, neglecting the saving health of the poor unlearned people, seek their own honour and praise, and therewith to please one or two ambitious persons" (*The Table Talk of Martin Luther* [New York: The World Publishing Co., 1952], 253).

10. Jacques Ellul, *The Humiliation of the Word,* trans. Joyce Main Hanks (Grand Rapids: Wm. B. Eerdmans, 1985), 108–9.

That a sober French Reformed layman can express himself in this fashion should dispel every attempt to explain classical Protestant attachment to preaching by reference to its "intellectualism" or its penchant for didactic. At bottom, this conception of preaching belongs to the *mystical* dimension of the Protestant tradition, and therefore to a mysticism that abhors what is usually called mysticism and honors the labors of the intellect while knowing full well that truth transcends the intellect. The fundamental conviction behind this sacramental understanding of preaching must be located in the pneumatology of the Protestant tradition, namely, in the belief that here, in this human and therefore entirely fallible act, it may be that the eternal shall once more invade the temporal and human souls glimpse once more their true origin and destiny.[11]

It may be! It will not *necessarily* be. Protestantism at its best was never presumptuous here. The words of the preacher may be words only—the preacher's words; "words, words, words," as said Shakespeare's *Hamlet*. Nothing resembling the *ex opera operato* of medieval Catholic sacramentalism ever achieved a foothold in the classical Protestant theology of preaching. For the "hearing" that is faith's presupposition and the sermon's object cannot be manipulated by human skills, however impressive. It is the Holy Spirit that causes one to hear the divine Word, and "the Spirit blows where it wills."

Yet "faith comes from what is heard, and what is heard comes by the preaching of Christ," and "how are they to hear without a preacher?" (Rom. 10:14ff.). Protestantism at its core did not court the kind of spiritualism that settled for ecstasy. It did not despise passion, as the critics of Calvin constantly assert; but it believed that the deeper passions are aroused by truth and that truth involves the struggle of the mind as well as the soul. Perhaps it seems ironic that the man who called reason the devil's harlot (Luther) expected preachers to present their witness in the most carefully reasoned way—not in "lofty words," to be sure, but in clear and thoughtful terms that ordinary mortals could grasp. But Luther's quarrel, after all, was not with reason as such, but with the wayward human will, which easily succumbs to the "devilish" use of reason for its own (rationalized) ends. What has to be changed is not the human capacity to think, but the propensity of the will to think what it wants to think. This alteration (*metanoia*) can only occur through the purging, renewing presence of the divine Spirit. But the Spirit, while sovereign and not manipulable, is for Luther bound in promise to the

---

11. See in this connection Karl Barth, *The Holy Ghost and the Christian Life,* trans. R. Birch Hoyle (London: Frederick Muller, 1938). A particular value of this study is Barth's documentation of his treatment of the subject by extensive references to the writings of the chief Reformers.

Word—to Jesus Christ, the incarnate Word, but also therefore to the Word faithfully preached. Without the internal testimony of the Spirit, the Word both of Scripture and sermon remains mere "letter"; but, as the one who testifies to Jesus Christ, the Spirit is also dependent upon the Word, and will not leave either the speaking preacher or the listening congregation comfortless.[12]

24.3. The Need to Recover the Protestant Theology of Preaching. Is it possible to recover anything of this classical Protestant understanding of preaching? It is my belief that if we cannot do so, we shall have lost not only an important aspect of the Reformation but the prospect of a future for "mainline" Protestantism as such; for preaching is not incidental to this tradition, it is of the essence of it. As Emil Brunner wrote in 1962, "today the crisis of the Church is most evident as a crisis of preaching." In Reformation Christianity, "the sermon, that is, the exposition of the words of Scripture by a theological specialist who is called the minister of the divine Word (*verbi divini minister*), has been without doubt the centre, the authentic heart of the Church." And in spite of "the powerful movements for the renewal of theology [in 1962], these movements . . . have not succeeded in bridging the gulf which yawns between contemporary man and every kind of Church preaching."[13]

If in 1962, and in Switzerland, Emil Brunner believed that preaching, the core of Protestantism, was in a crisis that threatened the very life of the

---

12. Luther's view of the relation between the Spirit and the Word is complex and justice cannot be done to it in the present context. The explanation here, however, intends to be a faithful representation of Regin Prenter's lengthy exposition of this relation. The following paragraph from the latter is helpful: "When the living Christ himself is the Word, then the outward Word as such, whether we find it in the Bible, in the sermon, or in the sacrament, can never directly be identified with God's own Word. Only when the Holy Spirit makes Christ present in the Word does it become God's own living Word. If this does not happen the Word is only a letter, a law, a description of Christ. From the opposite point of view it is true that the Spirit, when it undertakes to make Christ present, is not able to work independently of the Word. For Christ is indeed the incarnated Logos in the person who appeared in history, Jesus of Nazareth, who by the Old and New Testament writings is proclaimed as the Christ. It is therefore only by the Word depending on Scripture that the Spirit can make Jesus Christ present. A spirit who would work independently of this definite outward Word about the incarnated Logos would not be the Spirit of Jesus Christ. We are always referred to this definite Word. But we are not referred to it as our guaranteed possession, but as the place where we expect the Spirit to make Jesus Christ present for us. Without the work of the Spirit the Word may continue to be the Word which speaks of Jesus Christ, but it is not the Word which bestows Christ on us" (*Spiritus Creator,* trans. John M. Jensen [Philadelphia: Muhlenberg Press, 1946], 106–7.)

13. Emil Brunner, *The Christian Doctrine of the Church, Faith, and the Consummation* (Dogmatics, vol. 3), trans. David Cairns in collaboration with T. H. L. Parker (London: Lutterworth Press, 1962), 99–100.

church, what would he make of the situation in 1995 in the United States and Canada? To exemplify: Recently I attended an event at a well-known seminary in the United States in which a newly installed professor of liturgics lectured on the subject of worship today. To highlight her community-centered conception of worship she presented slides depicting a congregation gathered in the seminary chapel some thirty or forty years earlier, when it was still essentially a neogothic church. In sharp contrast to the present-day "homey" arrangement of the sanctuary, one diapositive depicted a congregation sitting in pews and listening to a sermon. "This looks like a lecture situation," commented the professor. Her audience of seminarians and others chuckled their agreement. I realized, looking at the somewhat blurred picture, that the person in the pulpit could well have been Paul Tillich.[14]

Has the sacramental conception of preaching been so far lost to North American Protestantism that even to ask about the possibility of its "recovery" is naive? Clearly, many factors militate against any such understanding of preaching. We have always been a pragmatic people, and the pragmatism of our conventional culture has been augmented in the past half century by a technologism, of which television is only one aspect, that has rendered us even more one dimensional and lacking in a sense of wonder than we already were. In the churches, the preachers who appear to succeed are "great communicators," that is, persons who can transmit uncomplex ideas with the minimum of effort and the maximum of humor or conviviality. The almost total absence of silence in our urbanized life, and the abundance of incessant and often vacuous chatter, almost guarantees that more talk from the pulpit will be classified along with all the rest.

Meanwhile, a kind of experimental liturgicism has invaded Protestantism, and with it a definite suspicion of the sermon. Eucharistic, artistic, participatory, and many other allegedly innovative approaches to worship have become fashionable, and preaching, as we observed earlier, being the monologue of an individual, seems to many undemocratic. ("This looks like a lecture situation.") This "liturgical" and "participatory" model is at the same time reinforced by the the "group" approach that is popular, not only because of television's preference for involving as many people as possible in the discussion of any subject, but also through the influence of psychotherapeutic methods that have a built-in suspicion of individuals who "need" to dominate.

---

14. Anyone who heard Tillich preach, or has read his four books of sermons, will realize the significance of his name in this connection; for whatever his fame as a philosophic theologian may have been, he was thoroughly imbued with the Lutheran sense of the mystery of preaching, and his entire demeanor in the pulpit, as well as the content of his sermons, was one hundred and eighty degrees removed from the concept of "a lecture." On Tillich as preacher see Wilhelm

Preaching of any sort, under these conditions, seems an outmoded activity. Can one hope, then, that a sacramentally understood form of preaching would be able to find an opening in such a context?

Like so many of the questions that pertain to the present transitional time of the church, such a question defies easy answers, whether negative or positive. We shall have to live with this as with many other questions for a longer period of time before we can answer wisely. One response that may be given immediately is that in view of the general malaise of preaching, the only kind of preaching that *could* find an opening would have to be one different enough from the status quo to arouse attention; and that the sacramental conception of preaching is different from the status quo in North America today seems to me self-evident.

There is, however, an aspect of the problem that has not yet surfaced in this discussion of preaching, although it has been central in our deliberations throughout this volume. We may introduce it with a question: What, if anything, has our culturally established status to do with the crisis of preaching, and how might that crisis be affected were we to explore, in this "awkward" (Lindbeck) stage of our relations with our host culture, the approach proposed in chapter 4: disengage in order to engage?

Interestingly enough, in his discussion of the crisis of preaching that was cited earlier, Emil Brunner, when he tries to unearth the reasons that "people have so little interest in the preaching of the Church and so little understanding of it," comes to the conclusion that contemporary persons do not feel that they are being addressed as human beings, with all the particularity of their individual lives. Rather, they are being "'preached at'" by "an institution" that has a definite and all-too-familiar point of view that it wants to reinforce, and, in addition to the absence of personal concern in the sermon, Brunner notes, there is no "fellowship" surrounding the act of worship, so that the individual feels wholly ignored. Rather naively, it seems to me, Brunner proposes that European churches should learn from "the American Free Churches" how to create a sense of community that could offset the individual's feeling of isolation. That may in some wise answer the lack of fellowship in European Protestantism, but it is not an answer to the problem of the sermon and preaching—at least in the North American context.

More important is Brunner's intuition (which he seems not to develop in this part of his *Dogmatics*) that the boredom, disinterest, and alienation that parishioners feel in relation to most preaching has something to do with its "institutional" character:

---

and Marion Pauck, *Paul Tillich: His Life and Thought*, vol. 1: *Life* (New York: Harper & Row, 1976), 228ff.

A Church which meets [the "modern man"] only as an institution, which exists for the sake of this so-called Word of God and is organized exclusively for this purpose, which accordingly neither includes him in a fellowship nor has anything of importance to say to the problem of creating fellowship, is suspect in his eyes from the start.[15]

This statement too assumes a European context, but what Brunner notes concerning people's sense that through the sermon they are being spoken to by "an institution"—a part of their society with its own role to play, but nevertheless an institution of society—this, I believe, ought to be taken to heart. So long as the Christian church sustains, or wills to sustain, or does nothing to alter a fifteen hundred year old history that sustains this well-known relationship with its host culture that is called "establishment," its preaching will be received as the voice of "an institution." For many people in our particular context, that is indeed the primary function of preaching: to communicate—yes, of course, the verities of the Christian faith, "the gospel"; but to do so in such a way as to reinforce at the same time the values and pursuits of "the American way." So that, sitting for fifteen or twenty minutes[16] while the preacher delivers himself of his message is for many an extension of the elementary and high school "pep talks" they once heard from other voices representative of "the system," naturally with "greater solemnity" (Berger) and a language suitable to neogothic architecture and organ accompaniment.

Even where preaching is less blatantly noncritical and continuous with other articulations of the culture; even where it may be somewhat questioning of the morality of the dominant classes; even where it approaches "alternative thinking," perhaps, so long as the fundamental relationship with "Mother Culture"[17] is unchanged, preaching will "cast shadows not its own"; for it will be heard as the testimony of "an institution," part of the great complex of institutions making up our social fabric, and not as the confession of a Way that is fundamentally different from (for example) "the American Way"—different, not necessarily opposed, but different.

In sum: if preaching is to become the genuinely *confessional* office that it can be and has sometimes been, the changes that must be made are not *first*

---

15. Brunner, The *Christian Doctrine of the Church,* 101.

16. I am informed that seminarians are now being advised to limit their sermons to ten or even to five minutes. A *bon mot* of the great American preacher and homilitician, Paul E. Scherer, comes to mind: "Sermonettes make Christianettes."

17. I borrow this term from Daniel Quinn's *Ishmael* (New York: A Bantam/Turner Book, 1993) to refer to the "dominant culture" or "the establishment."

of all in preaching but in the self-understanding both of preachers and those who listen to them. If we are to "preach Jesus Christ and him crucified" (to use Paul's summation of the matter), we must above all cease confusing that message with the messages that we *shall* be communicating, willy nilly, if we do not attempt to alter the nature of our foundational relationship with our society: disengage in order to engage. Of course, such a socioecclesiastical change also assumes changes in the style and content of preaching, for, as we have argued here, the sermon must become a primary contributor to the deeper change. In the final subsection on this subject, we shall pursue this latter claim.

24.4. In What Sense Preaching Is *Confessio Fidei.* Even in its decadence, preaching is a quite unique undertaking. This is perhaps truer today than in the past. In former times, when anyone who wished to capture public attention had to do so through direct address and in person, preaching could be considered a specialized form of a much more inclusive genre—public address. Apart from the occasional political meeting or public lecture, however, very little if anything in our present society resembles the ritual that occurs Sunday after Sunday in congregations throughout this continent and around the world: a human being appearing before other human beings, face to face, with words.

The uniqueness of this act may in some respects have contributed to its downfall: it can appear an anachronism. And when it is approached by contemporary preachers themselves as if it were not only archaic but slightly embarrassing, its absurdity can seem almost palpable. On the other hand, its uniqueness can—could!—be considered a positive asset: Where else in the world today does anything like this occur? Where else is such direct address still possible? Where else can a speaker engage so small and compact a gathering of his or her own kind, with a message meant for *these particular persons*—not for millions of anonymous "listeners" or "viewers," but for individuals who are at some level known, and for whom the speaker has an ongoing (pastoral) responsibility? Such uniqueness, if it were fully appropriated, could by itself alter the attitudes both of preachers and congregations. It will be appropriated, however, only by those who possess a sufficiently critical social awareness to know the extent to which, in the technological society, such an act is not only unique but potentially full of meaning *just as such an act.* The contextual background of the act—a background of impersonality, anonymity, and the profound alienation of human individuals—lends to the act in itself, if it is realized by those engaged in it, an *almost*-confessional potentiality.

If this potentiality is to be actualized, of course, the form will have to become the occasion for content of a particular character. In our context, such content, including the approach or mode of discourse that accompanies it, is rare. In those ecclesial communions that have accentuated the liturgical aspect of worship, preaching has been understood as edification of the faithful or "homily" (from *homilos* = assembly); and, because of the predominance of an exhortatory approach in so much preaching in all branches of the church, the very terms "preach" and "sermon" conjure up an attitude of tiresome moral harangue. Obviously neither the homily nor exhortation qualify as confession in the sense discussed here. Protestantism in its classical expression, however, regarded the sermon as confession of the faith, and for at least two important reasons:

First, because what is required of preaching is that it should *always* be *kerygma,* that is, the proclamation of the Word. It is not law but gospel. It is not exhortation but the promulgation of "glad tidings." It is not first imperative but indicative. (We shall encounter this distinction again in the next chapter, on theological ethics, where it will convey the same differentiation between gospel and law). Therefore the dominant *linguistic* "mood" of the sermon is not the imperative ("You must do such-and-such!") but the indicative ("The most wonderful thing has happened!"[18]) The first requirement of the preacher is to interpret the Scriptures, and the main thrust of the Scriptures, moralism in the history of Christianity notwithstanding, is not the laying down of precepts and rules for living but the declaration of God's unmerited grace and love. Edification of the faithful, the building up of the Body of Christ, is certainly part of the intention of this act, as of all other aspects of worship; but it is not its primary function. First and foremost, preaching is confession.

As such it is the confession of a particular human being, the preacher, but a human being whose very presence in that place, before that people, is representative. The preacher is before the people as one of them: he or she represents what it means to "fall into the hands of the living God," to wrestle with the Word as it shines through a particular biblical text, and, Jacob-like, to insist upon being blessed with understanding. The preacher is also before the people as one sent (*apostellein*) to them: he or she represents before them the God who wills to bless them, too, with trust and understanding.

And this "drama" (for it is more art than craft!) is to be played out in every sermon. As countless homiletical studies insist, the preacher ought over the course of the years to entertain every manner of human subject and question, as well as every portion of the Scriptures. And this will be the case, if

---

18. The wording, it will be recalled, is that of George Buttrick, the famous Scottish preacher of Madison Avenue Presbyterian Church in New York City, who attempted to counteract the moralism native to his North American ministerial students by altering their fundamental mood, including their actual language, from the imperative to the indicative.

the preacher really does live "between text and context." Nevertheless, *every* sermon—in the Protestant conception of the matter—constitutes a return to basics, even if through an infinite variety of specific concerns. Every sermon is confessional.

The *second* reason the act of preaching must be considered confessional is that, in the classical Protestant understanding of it, those who listen need to *hear* what is basic over and over again. For they are not only "the faithful"; they are also "the faithless." They are—to appeal once more to Luther's excellent phrase—*simul justus et peccator* (at the same time justified and sinner). Thus the radical *metanoia* that is the aim of all confession of the faith applies quite explicitly to preaching. In fact, the aim of "conversion" is more directly applicable to congregational preaching than to the church's worldly witness, because the temptation to disbelief is stronger where there is incipient or even earnest belief than it is in the world at large.

If preaching is to be confessional in content as well as form, we must recover something of this Reformation sense of the existential character of faith, with its "ups and downs" (*fluxus*). Luther's teaching concerning the simultaneity of belief and unbelief has seldom been understood profoundly, and in the Anglo Saxon world, with its pragmatism and its preference for progressive sanctification over radical justification, it can seem almost heretical—capitulation to doubt! But faith, we have said, when it is genuine, *is* an ongoing dialogue with its antithesis.[19] When faith is artificially divorced from doubt (and the divorce is always artificial) it becomes credulity. When the preacher assumes, as in our context preachers are wont to do, that his or her congregation already "believes" in a fundamental way, a way that is inimical to radical doubt, the best purpose that the sermon can serve is teaching or edification: the foundational belief of the congregation is now to be built upon. But this ignores the distinction between faith and "sight," and the entire dynamic of faith. The negation—including the disbelief, rejection, resentment, and estrangement from God and one another—that is actually there within the believing community is not taken seriously. In other words, the *reality* of the community is not taken seriously! Thus the sermon, along with the rest of the service of worship, silently confirms an illusion (not to say a lie!)—the illusion of belief in which there is no unbelief.

Moreover, this occurs at a time in the history of the Christian movement when less, much less, can be assumed about the faith of congregations than, possibly, at any other time in the past. Except in unusual situations, congregations of the once-mainline Protestant churches today not only *know* less about the Christian faith than they did a century ago, but they are far less confident about its veracity and their own "belonging" to it. Far in excess of

---

19. See *Thinking the Faith*, 251, 293, 354ff.

the experience of their forebears, they are subjected to lively alternatives to Christian belief on an hourly basis, and indeed to pressures detrimental to any kind of sustained coherence. In brief, within the moderate and liberal Protestant denominations, we are now dealing with a laity whose need for gospel is not in the least theoretical, but absolutely concrete. *Conversion* and not merely the edification of "the faithful" is what is required if the church is to avoid further confusion or absorption into the general cultural milieu. And conversion will not result from convivial homilies or even well-intentioned discourses on the pressing issues of the times.

Conversion is, in any case, for the *classical* traditions of the Reformation, a continuous process: "continuing baptism." The language of conversion has become the property of evangelicalism, and given the stylized and often truly gauche expressions of that biblical concept in our context it is, admittedly, very difficult for the more reserved Christians of the middle ground to reclaim the idea of "preaching for conversion." But that is precisely what Reformation theology assumes about preaching, and it is precisely what is needed in mainline Protestantism in North America today. There is no reason, beyond class consciousness and sheer pride of person, to allow this perfectly biblical concept to languish under the bizarre and crude auspices of "born-again" manipulative emotionalism. Both biblically and in the more profound traditions of the faith, conversion has to do with the mind and the will, not only with the "heart" and the "soul." Augustine was converted—several times; indeed, continuously. Blaise Pascal, the great mathematician and philosopher, recorded his conversion in 1654 on "a scrap of paper . . . sewn into the lining of his coat": "FIRE! God of Abraham, Isaac and Jacob; not of the philosophers and scientists. . . . "[20] Simone Weil was converted, although not in the bizarre, emotional way that that term unfortunately connotes. The fact that conversion has been defined by its assocation with thought-less and thought-poor and slogan-ridden religion ought not to prevent us from discovering once more the profundity of the experience. Without the recognition of a radical change of heart, faith itself, in the biblical mode, is unthinkable, and the bulk of the Judeo-Christian tradition makes little sense. Moreover, in the post-Constantinian situation, when people are no longer Christians by birth, this "second birth" will have to be the normal mode of entry into the Christian movement.

But as such it need not and should not be based on any established pattern, whether that of American fundamentalism, or Wesley, or Luther, or Paul, or any other prominent figure or movement. The transformation intended by this language of "rebirth" and "conversion" will assume, in the future as in the past, many forms; for it is always the transformation of partic-

---

20. See J. S. Whale, *The Protestant Tradition* (Cambridge: At the University Press, 1955), 19.

ular, unique, and unrepeatable lives. The point, however, is not that mainstream Protestantism should mimic the more "evangelical" expressions of Protestantism in our midst, but that it should try to recover authentic insights of the Scriptures, the Reformation, and other (often submerged) periods in the history of Christian thought, and adapt them to the specifics of the present context. Where preaching is concerned, the Reformation's insistence that preaching is *always* confession aimed at the radical transformation both of those who hear and those who speak is an insight that is not only needful for the church in our context but may well be indispensable to its continuance.

25. Other Verbal Forms of Faith's Confession

25.1. Direct Public Witness.   Christians engage in verbal confession of faith in many ways other than preaching within the congregation. Some of these we may categorize as direct public address. Preaching itself may be considered "public" address at least indirectly, both because those addressed are citizens and because, normally, assemblies of Christians are open to the general public. Yet preaching is also, as we have seen, a specialized type of address. It is a form of confession intended for those who have already *pro*fessed the faith or are in some proximity to that kind of relationship with the Christian movement. There are other types of verbal confession that do not and cannot make the assumption of openness to the faith, but on the contrary must reckon with the prospect of skepticism, opposition, or even persecution. We may refine this category by identifying three activities that might be so described: evangelism, apologetics, and the addressing of specific questions or issues.

a. Evangelism.   By evangelism I mean any attempt of the Christian community to proclaim the gospel in the public realm. Tillich identifies evangelism with the church's endeavors to reclaim its lapsed adherents: "Evangelism by preaching . . . is directed toward people who have belonged or still belong to the realm of Christian civilization but who have ceased to be active members of the church or who have become indifferent or hostile toward it."[21] This seems to me somewhat restrictive. Perhaps it reflects the world of its author, which by comparison with the present was more monocultural— more nearly still Christendom. In the multicultural and religiously pluralistic society that we have become, it would be difficult if not impossible to confine evangelical preaching to lapsed or "cultural" Christians, especially when contemporary means of communication not only reach into the lives of millions

---

21. Tillich, *Systematic Theology,* vol. 3 (Chicago: University of Chicago Press, 1963), 195.

but are incapable of distinguishing the identity of those who may be recipients of such an "evangel." In the age of the Wesleys, the people who attended "revivals" did so out of some specific interest the faith into which, with very few exceptions, they had been born; and the evangelists not only knew this but directed their messages precisely to such persons. It is very different in our present context. Billy Graham writes: "Each of my prime-time 'specials' is now carried by nearly 300 stations across the U.S. and Canada, so that in a single telecast I preach to millions more than Christ did in his lifetime."[22]

As this quotation signifies, evangelism in the North American situation has been identified with a particular segment of the Christian church which is by now able to claim almost exclusive rights to the concept. Where the vast majority of contemporary North Americans are concerned, the words "evangelism" and "evangelical" denote a particular form and content of Christianity; moreover, the words that are most associated with this "evangelical" content—key words of the faith, including the name of Jesus—are so colored by the association that (as we have seen at various points along the way) it is very hard to claim them for any other meaning or use. This strong identification with "evangelical" Christianity, together with the recognition of our multicultural and religiously pluralistic social profile, raises the question, Can evangelism as such still be considered by Christians who do not adhere to the "evangelical" churches a viable form of faith's confession?

No easy answer to this question presents itself to thoughtful Christians of the moderate and liberal churches of the "once-mainline" denominations. For them, the barriers to evangelism are formidable. From the perspective of the nuanced theology of Reformation Christianity, the strong association of evangelism with "evangelicalism" means in practical terms the reduction of the faith to what we designated in the first volume "religious simplism."[23] All of the major dogmas of the tradition are reduced to simplistic shadows of their classical expressions and "packaged" for quick delivery. *Thought* itself, which is the presupposition of every one of the primary teachings of the Reformation, is exchanged for the immediacy of the image and the slogan— an exchange that is almost a prerequisite of the electronic media preferred by popular evangelism. The fact that many who consider themselves evangelical Christians are also distressed by this reduction does little to alleviate its gravity.

The barrier presented by the religious diversity of our society, combined with the legitimate recognition on the part of thinking people that the imposition of beliefs, whether through direct proselytization or more subtle tactics,

---

22. Quoted in Neil Postman, *Amusing Ourselves to Death: Public Discourse in the Age of Show Business* (New York: Penguin, 1985), 118.
23. *Thinking the Faith*, chap. 3, §17, 228–37.

is offensive, is equally formidable. For Christians, this barrier consists not merely of adherence to some version of "political correctness" but of an evangel-inspired sense of the love of God for human beings and therefore of God's own respect for the integrity of the person. That love does not impose itself. Even when it comes to us as an "irresistible" grace, the divine *agape* commends itself powerfully precisely because it does not overpower. Christian respect for other faiths, and indeed for the refusal of faith of any kind, is a consequence of this understanding of the relation between grace and freedom. Evangelism as it is commonly practiced among us operates out of a quite different conception of this relation, and that is why the televangelists and others can blithely ignore the plurality of religions and religious choices in the United States and Canada today. A more thoughtful Christian faith is unable to do so, and not simply because of its "liberalism" but precisely because of its faith.

And perhaps the most formidable barrier to evangelism of them all is the one that has concerned us throughout this study: the fifteen hundred years of Christian triumphalism that guarantees in advance that any very explicit testimony to Christian faith will be received by many as an extension of Christendom's imperialistic past. This is a major factor in the previously named barrier as well, for neither members of non-Western religions nor Westerners who have adopted non-Christian or post-Christendom options can readily consider Christianity apart from its historical embodiment as the established religion of the West. The unassuming door-to-door Christian witness, the priest or minister with his clerical garb, the cross in public places—all cast shadows not their own, and the shadows are very long ones and, for many, very dark.

With such barriers, it is difficult to see how evangelism in any form can be entertained by serious Christians in our context, and certainly in the form most commonly understood and practiced among us it is not an option for such. Yet it cannot be discarded, either, because it emanates from the deepest impulses of the faith. The "evangel" itself, as we have insisted throughout, contains within itself an outward thrust: it must not be "hidden under a bushel," it must be shared. For the church not to share the message that called it into being is to court ghettoization and the elitism of the mystery cults and philosophies of the ancient world with which Christianity often became entangled. For the gospel's sake *and* for the church's own sake, if not for the world's, evangelism is a "must."

How, then, may we undertake this necessary form of faith's confession without overlooking the barriers to it? Without attempting very specific answers to that question (for specific answers can only be contextual in the most "local" sense of the term), the following conditions seem to me minimal requirements for evangelism in our larger context:

1. Modesty.   By modesty I do not refer only to deportment or demeanor; modesty of person ought simply to be assumed. Of far greater importance is the maintenance on the part of the confessing community of a modest attitude toward its confession of the faith itself. Karl Barth establishes the theological basis of this modesty when he writes, "Evangelical theology is *modest* theology, because it is determined to be so by its object, that is, by him who is its subject."[24] Only those who misunderstand the Word of God can imagine that *their words* are themselves unqualifiedly and absolutely true. Jesus Christ did not give his followers the truth, he gave them himself—his presence, his life; he promised them his Spirit, "the Comforter" (John 14–16). The language of possession, we repeat, is inappropriate to this tradition. The evangelist can only point to what infinitely transcends him or her. There is no authentic response to this reality other than one of great modesty. And in view of the *immodesty* of so much Christianity, both past and present, those who would be evangelists in our present context must even risk overemphasizing the modesty factor, or at least must exercise uncommon restraint and imagination.

2. Communality.   The evangelical work of the first Christians was not an individualistic labor. Even Paul, the first evangelist outside the boundaries of the parental faith, did not step forward as a single charismatic figure, as though his message were *his* message. He had companions in his mission— in a real sense, all of his mission churches themselves became his companions in evangelical witness. Moreover, he was particularly critical of those who attributed their "conversion" to himself or to some other individual. This was not only an affront to the divine Spirit, apart from whose "internal witness" no evangelical effort could succeed; it was also an affront to the Christian community, the *koinonia,* the body with its many members and their many different gifts.

Just as conversion is a highly individualistic conception among us, so is the evangelism that works for conversion. Genuine evangelism can be engaged in by thoughtful Christians in our context only if they recover the biblical sense of mission as belonging to the whole disciple community. The theological rationale behind this insistence is rather obvious: if the evangel is a gospel of reconciliation that not only puts one into a "right relationship with God" (a familiar concept among "evangelicals") but also into a new relationship with one's own kind ("the neighbor"), then only a new community of persons in process of being reconciled to one another can concretize such a message, lifting it above the status of theory. The communal dimension of evangelism is badly needed in our context to correct the impression, reinforced by the

---

24. Karl Barth, *Evangelical Theology,* trans. Grover Foley (New York: Holt, Rinehart and Winston, 1963), 7.

Elmer Gantry syndrome of so much evangelicalism, that evangelism is the work of gifted (or perhaps just exhibitionistic!) individuals.

3. Participation. The verbalization of faith in the post-Christendom context will be credible only where there is evidence of faith at the participatory level, that is, as sincere and committed involvement in the life of the world. As Lesslie Newbigen has written, our society, like the society into which the first Christian evangelists were sent, is a "pagan" society; but it is also vastly different from the society of the ancient world "because it is not a pre-Christian paganism, but a paganism born out of the rejection of Christianity." As such, "it is far tougher and more resistant to the Gospel than the pre-Christian paganisms with which foreign missionaries have been in contact during the past two hundred years."[25] It is a society that has some awareness of the enormous gap between Christian theories and Christian practice, and that mistrusts easy declarations of salvation. Many of its most illustrious and intelligent citizens of all classes, but more particularly the poor and marginalized, harbor a deep suspicion of Christian declarations of love and justice, and even of Christian deeds of charity; for they have had centuries to observe the quest for power that lurks beneath the rhetoric and tokenism of "concern."

Thus evangelism today must be in some sense "by invitation only." Christians must earn the right to confess the faith verbally by confessing the faith in our manner of being in the world. We must, as Newbigin insists, "understand the difference between bearing witness to the truth and pretending to possess the truth," remembering that "witness (*marturia*) means not dominance and control but suffering."[26] The "word of the cross" will be believable and compelling only if it comes as an answer to the worldly question, "Why, Christians, have you chosen to suffer with us?" It will not be less "evangelism" because it occurs in response to a question and invitation. We shall return to this discussion when we consider confession as deed and as stance.

b. Christian Apologetics. Christian apologetics refers to the practice, anticipated in certain well-known passages of the newer Testament[27] and adopted as a method in the 2nd century C.E., of attempting to explain and commend the faith by reasonable argumentation, that is, by providing "answers" that may be acceptable to those addressed. Apologetics is "the art of answering,"[28] whether of answering specific and perhaps antagonistic ques-

---

25. Lesslie Newbigin, "Can the West Be Converted?" in *The Princeton Seminary Review* 6, no. 1, new series (1985): 36.
26. Ibid.
27. Especially Romans 1–3 and Acts 17:16ff.
28. Tillich, *Systematic Theology,* vol. 3, 195.

tions (as was often the case with the second-century apologists) or of responding to questions and concerns that seem implicit in the social fabric.

Few Christian apologists have assumed that apologetics are a fully adequate means of presenting Christianity to the world, and therefore it may be questioned whether apologetics are sufficiently confessional to be considered in this place. In view, however, of the circumscription of direct evangelism in our present context, and because Christian *apologia* has always been at least partially a mode of faith's public articulation, it may be that its neglect in Protestantism especially should be questioned, and new applications of the apologetic approach explored in the post-Christendom situation.[29]

"Apologetics," writes John Macquarrie, "is not a branch of theology, but rather a style of theology, namely that style which defends faith against attacks."[30] This definition, while partially accurate, strikes me as much too restrictive. The apologist not only defends faith against its detractors, he or she also *interprets* the faith to those external to it, whether with a view to explaining otherwise puzzling or offensive aspects, or with the intention of commending the faith. The apologists of the second century emphasized the defensive aspect of the task, because their context was one of suspicion and, often, gross misunderstanding of the "new religion," especially with respect to its social and political attitudes. In the later traditions of Christian apologetics, however, and particularly in Britain, where the apologetic approach has often set the tone for academic and practical theology, apologetics has been virtually inseparable from that type of philosophical theology which assumes that what Christians believe is at least partially communicable to all, for humankind naturally seeks truth of a trancendental character.[31]

There are good reasons that those who adhere to continental Reformation traditions cannot be satisfied with apologetic theology as a sufficiently *confessional* form of the propagation of the faith. For by its nature such a theology must maximize the continuity and minimize the discontinuity between Christian revelation and ordinary human experience and reflection. If faith in the Christian sense means trust in an eternal Thou who reveals, not data but Self, and does so through historical event and spiritual presence, then it is only by encountering God that such a trust may be engendered. No amount of "preparation for the gospel" (*praeparatio evangelica*) can overcome the

---

29. See in this connection Howard Moody, "Toward a Religionless Church for a Secular World," in Stephen C. Rose, ed., *Who's Killing the Church?* (Chicago: Renewal Magazine; and New York: Association Press, 1966), 82–92. The following sentence from this essay captures, in my view, the essence of the apologist's approach: "Theology . . . is not a weapon to use against agnostics and atheists, but rather a means by which we clarify our own experience" (88).

30. John Macquarrie, *Principles of Christian Theology* (New York: Charles Scribner's Sons, 1966), 35.

31. William Temple's *Nature, Man, and God* (London: Macmillan, 1951), the Gifford Lectures of 1932–1934, is a good example of Christian apologetics understood in this broader sense.

"leap" (Kierkegaard) that must be made if one is to move from thought *about* God to believe *in* God and consequent discipleship.

It would seem, however, that most of those who are historically important in the development of apologetic theology and its practical applications have understood this. Few have not thought apologetics to be sufficient as faith's confession, but they have regarded this approach as a preliminary stage of witness, intended to prepare the ground, as it were, for the sowing of more direct testimony. It may, of course, be asked whether this preparatory work is either necessary or relevant. It may even be suggested (and by strict "kerygmatists" like Barth, it is) that apologetics deters genuine understanding of the faith by establishing an atmosphere of reflection that is incompatible with revelation, spiritual encounter, and conversion. Apologetic theology is predisposed by its very nature to suppose that the transition from disbelief or indifference to belief and involvement is gradual. Paul, according to the writer of Luke-Acts, was proceeding on that assumption in his famous address to the philosophically inclined on the Areopagus (Acts 17:16ff.). But if Paul's Mars Hill address began in that way, it ended with the Apostle's rediscovery of the very *skandalon* that he speaks of in 1 Corinthians 1 and 2. Between the abstract reasonableness of the beginning of his address (common belief in deity) and the concrete historical particularity of the Christology that he introduces in what we have as verse 31, there is indeed a "leap," and Paul's Athenian hearers were not slow in recognizing it.

This point, regularly aired by all advocates of the more kerygmatic approach to faith's confession, must be taken seriously. Yet Paul's listeners did not *all* leave or scoff at the mention of the "righteousness" and "resurrection" of that one man; "some," we are told, "joined him and became believers, including Dionysius the Areopagite and a woman named Damaris, and others with them" (v. 33). And, we may add, for one very short sermon, that is not an unimpressive result!

The point that was made in the first volume, which ought to be reinforced here, is that in the matter of deciding between the more apologetic and the more kerygmatic approach to theology and faith, contextual factors must be thought rather decisive.[32] "There is a time . . . and a time . . . " (Eccles. 3). Both positive and negative factors in our own context make it advisable for Christians, especially those inclined toward the kerygmatic posture, to reconsider Christian apologetics. The negative factors were already present in our discussion of evangelism. It is very difficult for kerygmatic applications of theology at the confessional level to avoid being identified straightforwardly with biblicism and fundamentalism in the North American context. Karl Barth, who was in fact almost wholly out of sympathy with American-style

---

32. *Thinking the Faith,* chap. 5, §27; 349–68.

religious conservativism, was and still is nevertheless frequently taken up by biblicists and fundamentalists as a champion of their cause; and only the more astute conservatives, such as Cornelius van Til, have understood that such a measure is like bringing a Trojan horse into the camp of the Bible Christians. There are, we claimed, occasions when direct address in the kerygmatic or proclamatory mode may be appropriate, and a time may come in our own continental history when this approach should be normative. But to adopt it as a norm under the present sociohistorical circumstances seems to me quixotic.

Positively speaking, we have noticed elsewhere in this series that there is in our midst a sufficient dissatisfaction with the secular status quo and a strong enough quest for transcendence that an apologetic approach to faith's confession may find greater sympathy than in the past. Sisyphus is better prepared for grace by his failure than Prometheus by his alleged successes![33] Not only among the general public but also among the learned (scientists, for example, who have rediscovered the vulnerability and the mystery of the natural order over which, formerly, they thought to attain control) there is an openness to connectedness, depth, and even metaphysics that would greatly surprise earlier generations of the secular society. The gods of modernity—especially the god "humanity"—have failed; therefore Christians and others may again be able to speak of God in ways not unlike Paul at Athens.

No human confession of the faith, however, is guaranteed a hearing. Between Christian witness and human hearing, there is a great gulf fixed, and only God can bridge it. Apologetic theology, and *especially* at times that seem favorable to its deployment, can too easily forget this discontinuity factor. The preacher-philosopher Paul did not by his cleverness secure the adherence of "some"; God the Spirit did. Apologetics as confession is always incomplete, and like all theology it comes replete with pitfalls—one of which is that it may beget a religious community whose intellectual theism remains once removed from life, an exercise in God-talk that is lacking "fire" (Pascal). Perhaps the wisest counsel would be that in the public sphere today the Christian community ought to develop its capacities of public interpretation and witness along apologetic lines, while in and around the edges of its own community accentuating the kerygmatic dimension.

c. Addressing Specific Issues. A third way in which Christians confess their faith verbally is by addressing specific problems and issues within their context. Recent examples of such confessional activity are the World Council of Church's "Justice, Peace, and the Integrity of Creation" process, to which attention has been drawn at various points in this series; the letters of Roman

---

33. See *Professing the Faith,* chap. 5, §17, 253–62.

Catholic bishops and other church leaders on peace, justice, and other matters of public importance (in Canada, for example, on the grave question of unemployment); various pronouncements of Christian bodies on such subjects as human sexuality, the rights of extrahuman species, the humiliation and marginalization of women; and racial, technological, environmental, and many other specific areas of concern.

Possibly faith's confession, as distinct from its *profession*, must always assume the existence of certain social realities that *evoke* the need of the disciple community to "take a stand." If one considers the history of confessions, this suggestion certainly presents itself strongly. The various confessions of the early church were issued in the face of problems and possibilities present in church and society. We have noted before the link between the earliest recorded confession, *"Jesus Christos Kurios"* (Jesus Christ is Lord) and the Roman cry, *"Kaiser Kurios"* (Caesar is Lord). What the Christian confession presupposes, apart from which this three-word slogan could be thought innocuous or even meaningless, is the idolatry of Roman society, with its resultant ills—scapegoatism, repression, and brutality. The false elevation of the Caesars induced the Christians to counter this destructive idolatry by bearing witness to a very different kind of sovereignty. Similarly, Barmen, which with others we have treated as an instance of Christian confession close enough at hand to serve as a paradigm, was occasioned by a specific set of circumstances. Given the entrenched character of the *Zwei Reiche Lehre* ("two kingdoms theory") of German Lutheranism and German respect for authority, it would have been unthinkable for such a confession to emerge apart from the quite extreme character of the crisis represented by Nazi power and policies.

It is a truism that there are *always* social and moral problems that ought to draw forth from the Christian church concrete declarations of its faith. If the confessional mode has been rare within Christendom—so rare, in fact, that an instance like Barmen becomes exceptional and conspicuous—it is due to the social positioning of Christianity, namely its establishment status, and to the lack of critical awareness and social imagination that this status has created amongst Christians. If we are to derive from the Barmen paradigm the truth that is in it, we must appropriate two of its aspects that are regularly neglected: (1) it expresses the position of a very small minority, which grasped the seriousness of the situation a decade in advance of the vast majority of people (Christians included) in Germany; (2) it did not satisfy itself with surface observations and the resistance of specific items in the program of Nazism, but sought and named the deeper causes of this threat to God's beloved world and did so in explicitly Christian, indeed christocentric, terms. These points require prolonged reflection on the part of Christians today who intend their stands on particular issues to be understood as confessional.

The first point relates to the "prophetic" dimension of Christian confession. As we have already noted, the prophets of Israel were not predicters of the future, but they were "seers" in the sense of anticipating the future consequences of human activity in the light of their understanding of the intentions of God. The "secret" of their insights into the future was no secret, really. To state the matter in rather horizontal terms, they were persons who contemplated the world from the perspective of a certain "story" or "system of meaning" or "creative illusion" (Becker); they were able, from that perspective, to recognize the deviation, incongruity, and loss, as well as the promise, healing, and recovery that were introduced into history by human actions and reactions. In terms of our primary metaphor in this work, they *professed* a faith, a "meditative core" of understanding, on the basis of which they were enabled to *confess* their faith in specific historical circumstances, and to do so in depth and with foresight.

We have expressed the opinion previously that the churches in North America tend to *reflect* rather than to *engage* our society, and that this is as much the case with the liberal and "radical" elements in the churches as it is with most conservative groupings. With exceptions, those who are regarded as radical are Christians who align themselves with issues and positions in society at large that are already considered radical; and while the Christian radicals may bring to these issues a particular motivation and passion, they too seldom bring either originality or foresight. What is lacking, surely, is a sufficiently integrated, contemplated and professed Christian perspective or 'meditative core' to enable both greater independence of understanding and an earlier grasp of the meaning of events.

The second observation about Barmen is of still greater significance. If specific issues are to become the occasion for the confession of the faith, then the confessing community must demonstrate that it has grasped something of the deeper problematic of which the specific issue is a manifestation, and it must attempt to interpret this in terms that relate to the core of its faith. Whether the community incorporates the latter requirement in its public witness (as Barmen did) is a matter for decision in each instance; but that it must do so *for itself* is a given of Christian obedience. For without clarifying "the *reason* for its hope" the disciple community will inevitably lack the wisdom that is needed to distinguish, in the first place, which amongst the many "issues" that are present in a given historical moment it must make its own. Whether its confessional stand includes or does not include an explicit public articulation of its basis in faith, the confessing community needs continually to rehearse and contemplate what it professes if it is to be able to recognize "the little point where the battle rages." It is quite possible to mistake effects for causes, or symptoms for the disease!

To exemplify: There are many active Christians in North America today (fortunately!) who lament the facts of economic disparity between rich and poor, unemployment and underemployment, the underdevelopment or erosion of social services in our society and such critical issues. Few, however, have probed deeply enough into the depths that are revealed by such surface problems to question the capitalistic system which fosters such problems or the individualism and consumerism that keeps them afloat. Or again: Many active Christians in our context (fortunately!) have become conscious of humanity's rapacious treatment of nature. No single cause in North America today has commanded so much public attention as concern for the environment. But few among the many (including Christians) who would have us learn friendlier ways of being-with the extrahuman creation have subjected their minds to profound analyses of the technocratic mindset that is the silent determiner of every policy from government to the households of our nations.

The disciple community *must* address itself to problems like abortion, euthanasia, racial and gender discrimination, unconcern and violence for the more vulnerable members of society, crime, military policy, pornography, and countless other difficult issues of present-day life. But if its address is to approximate faith's confession and not remain at the level of surface moral involvement, it must make the effort to get beneath the immediately visible *effects* of any or all such issues to their deeper *causes,* and it must attempt to understand and view these in the light of the wisdom of the tradition and not to be content to think them "the right issues" because they are popular issues, endorsed by many others.

Why? Not, certainly, in order that the Christian religion may have its "commercial at the end." The only reason for such probing is that there is *wisdom* in the tradition and that, if the Christian movement as such is to be persuaded of the appropriateness of this particular point of concentration, it must be to *that wisdom,* and not the popularity of the issue, or "humanitarian concern," or any other motivation that the appeal is made. The "radical" Christians who are dismayed by the moral lethargy or conservative reluctance of their churches ought to ask themselves whether they have made any effort to interpret and explain their stands to the churches in terms that are recognizably related to basic Christian belief, or whether they simply expect all Christians to embrace their kinds of causes as a matter of course.

Again to speak of Barmen, our paradigm, it is not incidental or merely a mark of piety that the first article of the Declaration accentuates the sovereignty of Jesus Christ "alone." The sense of Christ's "lordship" that was shared by the signers of the Declaration, just as amongst the early Christians who cried (whispered, rather!) "Jesus Christ is Lord," is precisely what enabled people to recognize the essential idolatry of Fascist theory and practice. And it was legitimate for Christian leaders to expect that other Christians—indeed, all Christians—would recognize the idolatry precisely on that basis, and not, for instance, because some might be more radically inclined or cynical about authority generally than were others. In the resistance against facism, Christians could and did make common cause with communists, humanists, existentialists, national patriots, and many others who had their own reasons for resisting. But Christians could not legitimately expect every professed Christian to be sympathetic to Marxism, humanism, existentialism, and the rest, or to find in any of these a sufficient compulsion to act. They could, however, expect and require the Christian conscience to recognize idolatry and the rank usurpation of God's sovereignty, and to resist.

It is this *theological* reflection that is lacking in so much issue-related Christian witnessing in our context. Those who are adamantly persuaded of the "right to life" in the abortion question expect every Christian to consent to their program, but for the most part they do not delve into the wisdom of the tradition, but make their case on the basis of outrage, sentiment, public trends, and arguments drawn from human rights and other positions that Christians may sometimes endorse but that are not as such Christian sources of authority. The same thing could be said, *mutatis mutandis,* of their opponents, the "right to choice" faction. Typically, neither group achieves any real depth of analysis, and neither makes the breakthrough into *theological* reflection. In consequence, these factions within the churches remain poised between personal or group bias and vague, half-formed religious and other ideologies. The call to confess the faith through focusing on such truly vital issues as abortion, euthanasia, and many other contemporary problems, is not a call to stand up for conventions associated with various religious and other organizations, codes, and lifestyles, but rather to regard human problems and possibilities from the perspective of the gospel, and to seek to understand and demonstrate how, as disciples of Jesus Christ, Christians ought to think, speak, and act.

In addition to evangelism, apology, and the addressing of specific issues, there are other ways in which, through language or symbol, Christians confess the faith. Especially where individual Christians are concerned, for example, the whole realm of dialogue within personal relationships and human contacts could be investigated. One hopes, also, that theological works like the present series might be thought, in part at least, works of faith's confession. We have concentrated, however, on three different *types* of direct address that belong, not to individual Christians but to the church as a whole.

We turn now to more indirect forms of confession, realizing as we do that the lines of distinction throughout this discussion are inevitably more theoretical than existential; our purpose, however, is to clarify and therefore hopefully to fructify Christian praxis.

25.2. Indirect Testimony.   It will be clear from the foregoing discussion of direct address that the author holds confession of the faith in that form to be both necessary and, in our context, in particular need of revitalization; yet if faith's confession were limited to direct testimony, something indispensable to Christian life would be missing, even where language and symbol are concerned. For, as we have affirmed throughout these volumes, Christian belief cannot be confined to explicitly theological aspects of the church's life and thought but opens itself to the whole of reality. The division of the world into sacred and secular dimensions is challenged in a fundamental way by the incarnation of the Word. Human words and symbolic forms of address are obliged, under the impact of this gospel, to serve the inclusive thrust of the eternal into time, and express the impact of divine judgment and love in relation to the whole of creaturely being—"everything," in the sense in which, in the first volume, we already characterized that term.

Usually this inclusive impulse of faith will articulate itself more indirectly than directly. Especially in the post-Christendom situation, indirect confession of the faith may have to be almost the norm. We have already begun to move in that direction with our discussion of evangelism and apologetics, and we shall become even more deliberate in embracing the indirect approach with the subsequent discussions of confession as deed and as stance. Words, especially words that are overtly religious, simply cannot stand on their own in a society like ours. Not only (to our great shame) are words of all sorts "cheap" in this society, but religious words, and particularly words associated in the public mind with an explicitly Christian piety, carry connotations that the most sensitive of their users will certainly not intend: the long shadows of centuries of monopolistic religion, as well as the continuing sentimentality, simplism, and bombast of their contemporary misuse. If direct address on the part of Christians is to be authentic or even useful in the communication of the faith today, it will have to be buttressed by Christian testimony at the level of *being;* and this includes not only the actual involvement of Christians in the life of the world (the subject of our discussion in sections 25 and 26), but also the capacity of mature Christian faith to perceive the implications of the gospel for every aspect of existence and to translate its perceptions into terms accessible to the consciousness and presuppositions of others who are "not of this fold."

This is by no means a new proposal. It has been understood and practiced by many throughout the history of the Christian movement, and especially since the breakdown of the Christian establishment in the West. Nevertheless, indirect confession of the faith has heretofore been left largely to individuals, whose imagination and experience taught them its necessity. What we have now to propose is that it should become a more intentional form of faith's confession within the church at large. As the once-mainline churches emerge from their establishment status, they will have to reconsider the whole matter of faith's confession and the communication of "gospel." Their expulsion from the center of social and political influence presents them with choices and necessities hitherto concealed from them by their position of supposed privilege. Since they cannot now presume upon any kind of real preeminence in society, ingenuity and imagination will be required of them. This is salutary, not only for the church itself but also for its host culture; for a church that could afford direct public address only because of its allegedly privileged position in society did not have to bother itself with profound reflection on either its own message or society's real needs, but could rely on its authority and the conventions of the past to provide an immediate platform and program for its witness. The broad way of immediate access having been closed, or being in the process of closure, "mainline" Christians are increasingly in the position of those who must discover other routes into the *civitas terrena;* and in searching for these no doubt narrower ways they are less likely to act out of real or assumed power and more likely to ask themselves both what, precisely, their gospel means for that time and place, and how it may serve the actual needs of humanity and creation.

What, concretely, is meant by indirect Christian confession or testimony? What kinds of activity would be included in this category? In every walk of life, Christians may be found who attempt to bring to their vocation a perspective that is recognizably Christian, although they may seldom if ever speak openly of their faith or explain how it leads them to act as they do. Instead, they learn how to translate the "fundamentals" of Christian belief into language and symbol appropriate to their situation. We may exemplify this form of faith's confession by considering the work of Christians in three areas of recent social history: political, intellectual, and literary.

a. Political Involvement. In the United States and Canada, there has been a long tradition of Christians who involve themselves in the political life of their countries *because* of their Christian identity and vocation. They are driven into politics by their understanding of the faith. This in itself indicates something like a confessional stance, for it implies that these persons are persuaded that the Christian message has directly to do with the "mending" and well-being of this world, and that, as we have had numerous occasions to notice already, is an assumption that has not always been evident in Christian history.[34]

How shall we interpret the obvious fact that Christianity has been able to inspire so many and such divergent types of political activity? On the one hand, it is claimed by militant political factions of the Right, so that among the staunchest advocates of corporate capitalism, free trade, and rampant globalization, many are avowed and vocal Christians. On the other hand, Christianity has produced important political expressions of socialism, including Marxism, to the point that it is frequently noted that Communism itself is an offshoot of Christianity or a Christian heresy.

When Christianity is claimed as the background and inspiration for such irreconcilable positions of the political Right and Left, as well as every conceivable position between the two, can it be thought meaningful at all to advance political involvement and testimony as an indirect form of faith's confession? Do not the overt politics of Christians in fact enshrine the confusion and chaos of the many divergent forms of Christianity itself? Are not those Christians correct, therefore, who insist that there should be no direct concourse between religion and politics?

The whole tenor of the present work will, I trust, have made it impossible to answer at least the latter question affirmatively. If, as we have maintained throughout, the gospel is inherently world oriented, this implies that faith in the Christian sense is political by definition. Christians who have felt themselves impelled to take up political work on account of their faith have already made a confession of faith. At least to that point, from the perspective of this trilogy, this is a right confession. To stand apart from the complex and often morally corrupt world of political involvement and responsibility in the name of Jesus Christ is to dishonor that name—the name of one who was hauled before the authorities precisely because his "saving work" was perceived to be (and really was!) political.

The world of human beings determined the shape which God himself took when he came into the world that first Christmastime. The world determined the very form of the death of the Son of God.

Death by crucifixion was the world's way of getting rid of a disturber. Christ made himself vulnerable to the world. The Church is to be vulnerable to the world. It is to take the shape that the world needs. We are not to be protected by our own power structures which are so strong that the world cannot crucify

---

34. I can think of no better example of such a person than T. C. ("Tommy") Douglas, the Baptist minister who became premier of the province of Saskatchewan and leader of the New Democratic Party in Canada. See Lewis H. Thomas, ed., *The Making of a Socialist* (Edmonton: University of Alberta Press, 1982).

us! Our faith says that the only way there can be rebirth is by death and that the Christian must always think in terms of death and resurrection.[35]

As for the divergency and contradictions conspicuous in the working out of this initial decision, it is impossible for anyone to legislate. All that responsible theological thought may say on the matter is contained in the test that Jesus, according to the record, articulated: "You will know them by their fruits" (Matt. 7:16). If anyone can demonstrate to the community of faith, on the grounds of Scripture and tradition, that the so-called "German Christians" who took up with enthusiasm Hitler's racial and other policies were acting as faithful disciples of the Jewish man whom faith confesses to be the Christ, I shall be astonished. I shall be almost equally astonished if North American Christians who favor nuclear stockpiling, the creation of enemy-images, or blatant racism and sexism can demonstrate from the Bible many of them claim to honor above all else how such practices are justified, Christianly speaking.[36] However, it can be no secret to the reader of these volumes that, with many others, I personally find that the whole communitarian thrust of biblical faith favors a politics of statecraft inherently oriented toward world peace; solidarity with the victims of power; compassion for the weak, poor, and marginalized; equal opportunities for all persons in education and employment; the institution of measures against racism, violence, and gender prejudice; the creation of medical and other programs conducive to the health and life of all people; and so forth—in short, I am led by faith to what is usually (although not very helpfully) designated the politics of the Left. Moreover, I am—not astonished, but at least surprised—when people argue that none of these social ideals is commensurate with Christian discipleship. Surely it is not accidental that socialistic and communistic political experiments, by no means all of which may be thought totalitarian, have arisen within societies influenced by the Judeo-Christian heritage. Nor is it surprising that the vast majority of the leading Christian thinkers of the immediate past, as well as contemporary liberationists, many Christian feminists, and others within the central streams of Reformation, Anglo-Catholic and Roman Catholic traditions, have sought to live out their Christian discipleship to the left of center.

---

35. Gordon Cosby, "Not Renewal, But Reformation," in Rose, ed., *Who's Killing the Church?* 55.

36. "There are Christians who cry down others in the name of a theology of the resurrection, and yet at the same time . . . feel able to justify the use of the atomic bomb. It sounds plausible: a bit of genocide and world-wide destruction contrived by men is no greater matter to those who are looking only to the new world. But with all their hope of resurrection, such Christians blaspheme against God who, in Jesus, sought man for the purpose of helping him not merely in the next world, but here and now" (Ernst Käsemann, *Jesus Means Freedom*, trans. Frank Clarke [London: SCM, 1969], 26).

At the same time, it must be said that Christian faith, when it is serious and responsible, does not seek to confess itself *in* or *as* socialism, liberalism, or any other political credo. I am in full agreement with Dorothee Sölle when she writes,

> When combined with theology, "political" does not mean that theology should now exchange its content for that of political science; precisely the same misjudgment was made a generation ago by those who attributed to existentialist theology an exchange of themes, asserting that it spoke only of man. Furthermore, political theology is not an attempt to develop a concrete political program from faith, nor is it another type of Social Gospel in which praxis simply swallows up theory. There are no specifically Christian solutions to world problems for which a political theology would have to develop the theory. Political theology is rather a theological hermeneutic, which, in distinction from a theology that interprets reality from an ontological or existentialist point of view, holds open an horizon of interpretation in which politics is understood as the comprehensive and decisive sphere in which Christian truth should become praxis.[37]

Christian citizens who are critically mature know well enough that they must make common cause with many others whose motivations are not their own. But their own foundations are not ideological ones, however they may find that a specific political program approximates at the level of certain important assumptions and ethical consequences what, as Christians, they also believe to be attainable. Cold War history abounds with stories of Christian socialists who, often in difficult totalitarian situations, were able to maintain a certain critical distance from party politics, and yet enjoy a measure of trust rare in any political arena. Christian socialists such as the founders and many of the subsequent leaders of the socialist party in Canada (the CCF/NDP) have been able on account of this trust to incorporate Christian dimensions of justice, fairness, compassion, and reconciliation into the policies and platforms of their party, and so to qualify the propensity of the ideological mind-set to drive toward consistency of theory regardless of the human suffering that such a drive always courts.

The political involvement of Christians, when it is genuinely Christian and not a cloak for personal ambition or class identity, is determined by discipleship: that is, it is an answer to the question, "How shall I implement my vocation as a Christian?" Its priority therefore is not allegiance to a political philosophy and organization, but allegiance to Jesus Christ. Christians profess the reality of human sin, and consequently they understand in advance

---

37. Dorothee Sölle, *Political Theology*, trans. John Shelley (Philadelphia: Fortress Press, 1974), 58–59.

that *every* political platform and organization will manifest signs of human pride, self-defense, exaggeration, and temptation to power for the sake of power. It is this ultimate allegiance and this tradition of wisdom concerning human possibilities and failings that constrains Christians who confess their faith through political testimony to maintain a critical vigilance with respect to *whatever* political party they associate with, while displaying a humane understanding and decency that does not hold itself aloof in the presence of sin.

To confess the faith indirectly through political involvement is always to recognize that one's confession is decidedly *in*direct, and will not suffice as confession. But in the give and take of worldly life, this indirect confession may, as it has done in an impressive number of instances in recent history, become the vehicle of a testimony that is more effective just because it is indirect.

b. Intellectual Involvement. A second example of indirect testimony comes from the intellectual world, specifically the world of the universities, colleges, and research institutions of our society. Historically, the intellectual life of the Western world is inseparable from Christianity. The idea of the university has its origin in the court and cathedral schools of the Middle Ages, and the church has maintained a continuing connection with higher education to the present time. Most of the older institutions of higher learning on this continent, like those of Europe, trace their histories to ecclesiastical foundations or associations, and the whole notion of a *uni*versity owes its existence to the Christian scholasticism that posited the unity and interconnectedness of all truth.

It is almost a truism, however, that today Christianity lives a peripheral existence in the university and among the intelligentsia. The cultural disestablishment of the Christian religion began, in fact, with the intellectuals of the modern West, and was visible in the studies of scholars and the classrooms of universities long before it was noticeable in the public arena. Enlightenment critique of institutional religion quickly assumed precedence even in most church-founded universities and colleges, and "science" became the critic of and alternative to "religion." The churches, to preserve a place for themselves in the academy, often felt compelled to create their own colleges and seminaries in, alongside of, or separate from the increasingly secular established institutions of higher learning. Such Christian schools sometimes managed to preserve the Christian tradition while carrying on a lively debate and dialogue with the evolving world of the natural sciences, the social sciences, and technology; but they also frequently devolved into islands of protective Christian piety and morality, where young people from Christian homes could be insulated from the harsh winds of skepticism and unbelief.

It is against this background that we should view the earlier work of Christian scholars, teachers, and students who opted to work within the secular intellectual milieu or who, finding themselves in such contexts, have attempted to engage in the indirect form of faith's confession. They have done this, usually, not as a deliberate tactic, but out of the conviction that truth really is one, and that whole dimensions of truth were being neglected by the growing tendency of modernity to pursue a one-dimensional scientism that reduced reality to empirically verifiable data. Through the period of high scientific optimism from the late 1800s until the outbreak of World War II, if some reminiscence of transcendence, mystery, and the integrity of creation was kept alive in communities of higher learning on this continent, it was at least in part because of Christian scholars who, in their various disciplines, refused to concede to the flatness of a rationality that was not only scornful of deity but willing to dispense with any view of the world other than the allegedly "scientific." In departments of literature, history, and classics, in fine arts, even in the sciences and technologies themselves, there were teachers throughout this period who kept alive an alternative conception of reality. They were not willing to reduce life to data or abstractions, to theories such as chance and evolution, or to ideologies of human personal and social behavior that robbed the world of its variety, unpredictability, and evidence of purpose.

In the second half of this century, the efforts of these teachers and students have been at least partially vindicated, both by negative and positive factors. Scientism and technologism have run aground, their bravado checked by environmental and other crises, most of which are attributable to their own premature and limited assumptions ("knowledge without love"—C. F. von Weizsäcker's summation of the "result" of the daring enterprise [of] the scientific and technical world").[38] Ideologies both political-economic and social have failed, and overt atheism is almost defunct as a viable "spiritual" alternative. In practical as well as theoretical ways, Western humanity has questioned the role assigned it by the Enlightenment, and asks again questions to which empiricism and humanism can provide few convincing answers. The secular universities themselves, in their curricula and their budgetary priorities, attempt within financial constraints to recognize—and much more openly than was the case fifty years ago—that human beings "do not live by bread alone"; that imagination and wisdom, and not just knowledge (*scientia*), are the proper goals of learning; that ethical questions affecting medicine, business, industry, and every area of life have arisen for which the intellectual pursuits of modernity have no aptitude; that thought itself is not

---

38. C. F. von Wiezsäcker, *The History of Nature*, trans. Fred D. Wieck (Chicago: University of Chicago Press, 1949), 190.

rightly defined if, being bound to verifiable data and given no guidance concerning the way in which it shall "process" the oceans of data now available, it can have nothing whatsoever to say to 95 percent of human experience.

This new openness to "transcendence," combined with recognition of the limitations of science and technology, is of course by no means unimpeded or universally embraced (the large grants still go to science and technology!); yet one cannot exist in a university today without realizing that broadly "religious" questions are being asked (or begged) in every phase of intellectual life. What is surely to be lamented, therefore, is that the Christian churches appear to be either unaware of this situation or else incapable of responding to it intentionally and creatively. On this continent, although there are countless Christians who engage in direct witness to the faith, very few seem to understand or be prepared to experiment with indirect confession of belief in the centers of study and reflection in which questions of "ultimate concern" (Tillich) are implicit and explicit at every juncture. This is, of course, part of the heritage of Christendom: being part of the establishment, the church of the centuries did not have to learn "indirectness." By contrast, Judaism, with its highly literate and involved sense of worldy vocation, has a very different history also in this connection.

There is, however, an important minority tradition of Christian involvement in the intellectual community that could serve as a model in the post-Christendom situation. It includes those persons and groups (for example, the World Student Christian Federation, Student Christian Movement, and the Inter-Varsity Christian Fellowship) that precisely through the almost-Dark Ages of scientism and modern progressivism continued to live and work among scholars and teachers. These small communities of students, professors, and staff did not begin with the assumption that they had a "right" to be in the universities and colleges by dint of their historic Christian "ownership" of the latter, nor did they assume that their secular associates would be ready to listen to, or to discuss with them, their Christian claims. On the contrary, they began with a sincere commitment to the life of the mind and to the mandate of the academic community to transmit to the young the best traditions of our civilization. Like those in the missionary movement of the churches who went abroad to serve and not to lord it over peoples and cultures, these individuals and movements learned first how to serve the best intentions of the academy. From a position of solidarity and the trust that can only be gained through years of service without ulterior motivation, they could discover how best to exercise their discipleship. No doubt their confessions have had more to do with the maintenance of meaning and mystery in the human project than, in an immediate way, with "God-talk." But they are no less confessions of the faith on that account; indeed, part of the indirectness of faith's confession today always concerns the necessity of translating into human and worldly terms the implications of what Christians believe about God.[39]

The future of "mainline" Christianity in North America, as well as the future of the university, will be profoundly affected by the way in which Christians, among others, relate to the intellectual project of the West at this critical juncture in its history (postmodernity).[40]

Unless the churches deepen their commitment to learning and their ability to cooperate with the persons, movements, and institutions in our society that are most concerned about education, they themselves will be increasingly drawn into the religious simplism and the anti-intellectualism of popular religion. But their reason for involvement in the intellectual community ought not to be mere self-preservation. The university today is also under attack. Both economic pressures and the lure of sophisticated technologies tempt institutions of higher learning to dispense with the very programs that have created them and made them, at their best, centers of holistic learning. Without history and the classics, ancient languages, fine arts, religious studies and the humanities in general, the university will produce technological and psychological experts who may be able to expand the "communications revolution" (for example) even beyond its present delirium, but will neither have very much of substance to communicate nor be able to distinguish significant from insignificant or injurious "data." Indirect confession of faith within the academy today and tomorrow begins with the recognition that it is a "field

---

39. See Sir Walter Moberley's *The Crisis in the University* (London: SCM, 1949), a book widely read and discussed in the university communities throughout the 1950s.

40. In an address to the Royal Society of Canada, Professor Bruce G. Trigger, F.R.C.S., soberly assessed the "long-range" prospects of the universities of this continent: "In a world of *laissez-faire* economic and social policies, university personnel find themselves being subjected as never before to external bureaucratic and ideological control, which seeks, in the name of efficiency and public accountability, to transform universities into command economies that will serve the interests of governments and industry. This has the general effect of tying scholarship ever more closely to the short-term goals of modern governments and commerce.

"Such an approach not only undermines longstanding university traditions of self-government, but also weakens the capacity of scholars to question the basic assumptions of an international consumer society. By subjecting university research increasingly to non-academic control, its innovative and critical potential is diminished. . . .

"Universities can abandon only at everyone's risk, including their own, their traditional role of pondering what is good for humanity. Maintaining this role requires a collective commitment to sustaining a critical dialogue in which existing beliefs and knowledge are examined in relation to new issues, not an obsession with mindless defence of tradition or the encouragement of innovation for its own sake. . . . Today the university's most valuable function may be to preserve a sense of the importance of ethical judgment in a world in which an extreme emphasis on technological innovation and commoditization is promoting moral illiteracy. . . .

"The survival of humanity may depend to no small degree on universities performing their traditional role of taking a long-term view of crucial issues" (presented at Carlton University, Ottawa, on May 22, 1992; reproduced by McGill University, Faculty of Arts, October 31, 1994).

that is white for harvest"—not for the conversion of souls to the Christian religion, but for the preservation of souls (including minds and bodies) from deprivation and, perhaps, perdition.

c. Literary Involvement.   A third instance of indirect verbal witness comes from the side of the literary arts. I am thinking in particular of imaginative literature (novels, short stories, essays), drama, and film. In a real sense, the great questions of humanity—the questions to which religious faith at its best always seeks to address itself: questions of being (ontology), meaning (teleology), and the good (ethics)—have been more consistently and imaginatively pondered in the literary arts than by contemporary philosophy, the traditional dialogue partner of theology. With the captivation of institutional philosophy by "technical reason" (Tillich) in the Anglo-Saxon world and by political ideologies in Europe and elsewhere, the perennial questions of human existence have found outlets in the arts. It is in part for this reason that we have seen in recent decades the emergence of such phenomena as "narrative theology," "story" as a major genre or metaphor in theology, biografhical and autobiographical theology, and whole departments devoted to religion and the arts, theology and literature, religion and film, and the like. Theology, and faith itself, requires a dialogue partner for reasons already established in the first volume. What faith looks for in such a partner is the articulation of what is here and now "blowing in the wind," that is, of the "mind of the age," "the *Zeitgeist*." The arts are considered by many Christian thinkers to be a better dialogue partner than either present-day formal philosophy or the social sciences. Both of the latter have their own theories to demonstrate, their own "axes to grind"; art is likely to be more directly revelatory of the spirit of a context. Besides, especially in its literary forms, art stands much closer to the biblical tradition, which, as Christian faith moved into the Greco-Roman world, was too quickly assumed to relate more immediately to the realm of philosophy.

That the confession of faith is to be discovered indirectly in literature, drama, and film today is thus not surprising. Not that every piece of modern literature, every drama, every film that has high significance for Christians in our time emanates from Christians themselves, as an expression of faith. Most in fact do not. Indeed, much that *is* intentionally Christian in its motivation and execution lacks sophistication as art, and may sometimes serve rather to discredit the faith than to foster curiosity about it. Nonetheless, there are numerous creative artists at work in our society who intend their work, not, certainly, as a cryptic form of Christian evangelism (in which case it would usually fail), but as being expressive of a deep concern for "keeping human life human" (Paul Lehmann)—a concern that is never far from the kingdom of God.[41]

Rather than enumerating examples of the kind of art to which I am referring (for the list would be very long and the reader will already know many of the works that would have to appear on it), I shall exemplify my meaning by quoting a brief passage from one recent work—Daniel Quinn's novel *Ishmael,* to which allusion has been made in the earlier text. The "Socratic" ape, "Ishmael," is speaking:

> "The people of your culture cling with fanatical tenacity to the specialness of man. They want desperately to perceive a vast gulf between man and the rest of creation. This mythology of human superiority justifies their doing whatever they please with the world, just the way Hitler's mythology of Aryan superiority justified his doing whatever he pleased with Europe. But in the end this mythology is not deeply satisfying. The Takers are a profoundly lonely people. The world for them is enemy territory, and they live in it everywhere like an army of occupation, alienated and isolated by their extraordinary specialness. . . .
>
> "The story the Takers have been enacting here for the past ten thousand years is not only disastrous for mankind and for the world, it's fundamentally unhealthy and unsatisfying. It's a megalomaniac's fantasy, and enacting it has given the Takers a culture riddled with greed, cruelty, mental illness, crime, and drug addiction."[42]

It would be difficult to find in works of explicit Christian testimony a more compelling statement of "that which threatens the life of the world."

The whole course of Western literature would not be what it is were it not for those who wrote explicitly as Christians and who, in some cases, intended their work as almost direct statements of faith (Bunyan). But with the secularization of the West, the vocation of the artist to remind humanity of the mystery of both its good and its evil has been lost to the churches. It is left to a few unusual individuals. Sadly, aesthetic mediocrity in the churches, which may be partly a consequence of the classical Protestant suspicion of art but is also a reflection of simplistic and sentimental forms of faith today, inhibits many Christians in our context from recognizing the profoundly "religious" themes and implications that are present in contemporary literature, drama, and film, and from realizing the possibilities for profound "confes-

---

41. A sterling example of what I mean are the drawings of Diedre Luzwick, which, in depicting so vividly "that which threatens the life of the world," come very close to the definition of faith's *confession* as established in this volume. See her *Endangered Species: Portraits of a Dying Millennium* (San Francisco: HarperSanFrancisco, 1992).

42. Daniel Quinn, *Ishmael,* 145, 147.

sion" inherent in all forms of art.[43] The question thus presents itself: Can the Christian movement create an atmosphere of sufficient depth and imagination within its ranks to encourage the emergence of new schools and expressions of literature and the related media, which may function indirectly as confession of the faith in a society that is not very receptive to direct address from the side of religious belief?

26. Confession as Deed

26.1. Not by Word Alone.   In spite of Luther's unkind quip about the Epistle of James, his own understanding of the relation between faith and "good works" does not differ in essence from that of James. Luther's objection to the "epistle of straw" was in reality an objection to those who *used* James's critique of "faith without works" to undermine the priority of the *sola gratia, sola fide* that had been for Luther, as we have seen, the breakthrough into gospel, beyond mere "religion." The Reformers were none of them ready to affirm that we are justified by right belief, doctrine, or faith isolated from *praxis*. In the first place, they understood faith relationally, as trust in God, involving the discipleship of Jesus Christ, mediated by the Holy Spirit; therefore they could not entertain the notion of a "faith" isolated from the triune God and from all the "horizontal" relationships of life. In the I-Thou relation called faith, the initiating "Thou" requires obedience of the trusting "I," and this obedience normally involves "love of the neighbor." Thus faith as such begets "good works," even though it never (if it is genuine faith!) holds up its good works to God or anyone else as if *they* were what constituted its "righteousness," its authenticity.

Faith "by itself, if it has no works, is dead" (James 2:17)—that is, it is not faith but something else. Perhaps it is religion, or doctrine, or ideology. As faith "drives to understanding" (*Fides quaerens intellectum*) (Anselm) so it drives to "works"; that is, it expresses itself in love. This is not only the particular teaching of James, it is as much Pauline (for example 1 Cor. 13) and Johannine (for example, 1 John 3 and 4) as it is Jamesian.

James's summary of the matter is perennially relevant as a corrective to every temptation to intellectualism and gnosticism:

> Be doers of the word, and not merely hearers who deceive themselves. For if any are hearers of the word and not doers, they are like those who look at themselves in a mirror; for they look at themselves and, on going away, immediately forget what they were like. But those who look into the perfect law, the

---

43. The fate of Margaret Laurence's novels, stories, and films among many "true-believing" Christians on this continent is a case in point.

law of liberty, and persevere, being not hearers who forget but doers who act—they will be blessed in their doing.

If any think they are religious, and do not bridle their tongues but deceive their hearts, their religion is worthless. Religion that is pure and undefiled before God, the Father, is this: to care for orphans and widows in distress, and to keep oneself unstained by the world.

(1:22–27)

Confession of the faith, then, is not by word alone. Must we not even say that it is *never,* legitimately, by word alone? Alone, words cannot be adequate vehicles of the Word. The Logos of God, according to John's prologue, "with" God from the beginning, presses from the beginning toward concretization, enfleshment, actualization. We have seen that the incarnation, however offensive it became to Judaism under the impact of Hellenistic and Constantinian-religious influences, nevertheless developed *within* the tradition of Jerusalem, and is a logical, if radical, continuance of the same earthward orientation of the divine *hesed* that can be noticed already with the creation narratives. It is a travesty of this tradition whenever Christians consider their words, dogmatic formulae, doctrines, theological systems, catechisms, sermons, and the like sufficient or more decisive than other forms of confession. That is to reverse the whole order of incarnational faith, and to disgrace the most rudimentary orientation of the biblical testimony by reducing faith's confession to verbiage. If Jesus castigated the Pharisees and others because of the no man's land they created between hearing and doing, a neutral zone where they could delight in reflection without the inconvenience of acting upon the truth they contemplated, how much more would he castigate Christians who advance theoretical Christologies, for example, as if this were their whole duty as disciples?[44]

One fears, however, that most North American Christians of the liberal and moderate Protestant traditions are likely to hear all this in a too self-congratulatory way. For there is an unmistakable preference for "the deed" running throughout the Anglo-Saxon world, and it manifests itself in English-speaking Christianity as in philosophic pragmatism and empiricism, the politics of "getting things done" and "American know-how." It despises nothing so much as idle talk and the spinning of worldviews (Gilbert and Sullivan's "sermons by mystical Germans"). By comparison with continental (and especially Germanic) Christianity, the Christianity of the English-speaking world is decidedly *practical,* and this practicality cuts across all denominational boundaries, incorporating even "high church" Anglicanism

---

44. See Dietrich Bonhoeffer's discussion of Pharisaism in *Ethics,* trans. Neville Horton Smith (London: SCM, 1955), 151–56, 166f.

and Anglo-Saxon Roman Catholicism. As our speech is dotted with maxims and proverbs extolling the virtues of the act over against mere theory and "good intentions,"[45] so our hymnology, liturgies, and catechesis invariably accentuate the importance of *doing* the faith. If the sermon in our "province" of the universal church regularly devolves into exhortation, as we have suggested in the discussion of preaching, this too is an extension of our practicality.

Within limits, one may be grateful for this emphasis. If it is necessary to choose between Germanic fascination with theory and Anglo-Saxon preference for practicality, the latter choice seems justifiable both historically and Christianly speaking. Theory is often both deceptive and, in the hands of the powerful (Hitler, Stalin, et al.!), dangerous. As Jean Martin Charcot (1825–1893) said, "*La théorie c'est bon, mais ça n'empêche pas d'exister*" (Theory is fine, but it doesn't prevent things from existing).[46] Undoubtedly the author of the Epistle of James would agree. One hopes, however, that it is not necessary, finally, to make such a choice; for Anglo-Saxon practicality has often begged the question "Why?" and not infrequently contributed not answers, but more problems. Besides, our highly practical Christianity has been accompanied by a dearth of theological reflection and depth, for in praising the deed the tendency (as one notes in proverbs such as those just footnoted) is to belittle thought. This introduces a vicious circle, for, without thought, deeds tend to become random and mutually contradictory. We begin our discussion of confession as deed, accordingly, by recognizing barriers to this form of confession in our own English-speaking context.

26.2. The Plight of Christian Activism. The penchant of North American Christianity for "doing" emanates not only from a genuine concern for practical obedience but also from a conspicuous hesitance in relation to thought, sometimes amounting to distaste and anti-intellectualism. In simplistic religious conservativism, thought is replaced by rote dogmas, pious clichés, and biblical sentences endlessly repeated. Even among the more sophisticated liberal and moderate denominations, there is often an impatience with study, reflection, and dialogue typical of the middle classes, whose whole way of life is built upon activity. After ten minutes spent in the discussion of any matter whatsoever, someone in a group of mainline Protestant church folk will want to know, "But what can we *do*?"

---

45. For example: "Handsome is as handsome does"; "Sticks and stones may break my bones, but words will never hurt me"; "The proof is in the pudding"; "I can't hear what you are saying; your deeds get in the way"; "Practice what you preach"; "It will all come out in the wash"; "The road to hell is paved with good intentions," and so on.

46. It was "one of Freud's favourite quotations," according to D. M. Thomas, in *The White Hotel* (Harmondsworth: Penguin Books, 1981), 111.

Christian activism ought not to be criticized lightly. There is far too little genuine activity in our churches and our society at large. The will to act, therefore, should always be encouraged. But part of the encouragement that is necessary if Christian activity is to have anything to do with obedience and the confession of Jesus Christ in the world, not to speak of contributing to the world's "mending," includes helping congregations to acquire the habit of disciplined reflection, meaning reflection that takes full advantage of the traditions of wisdom that are our heritage, as well as the dynamism that comes to us as a community convoked and sustained by the divine Spirit. Only such a recovery of the potentiality of Christian empowerment through the renewal of mind and spirit will enable the disciple community to act responsibly in the complex world that ours has become.

For the worldly arena in which faith must express itself in "good works" is today infinitely more complicated than that of either James or Luther. "Works" in such a world will prove "good" only if there is a sufficient understanding of the interrelatedness of the many threats that confront us to avoid the prospect of simply augmenting them. For instance, it is possible for church organizations, as for other groups in society, to become deeply concerned about the disturbing social phenomenon of violence toward women and children on the part of their male partners and fathers. This is an important issue and one that requires direct action; but unless there is a simultaneous investigation of the underlying causes of male violence (such as unemployment, the artificiality of urban life, the prevalence of violence in the "entertainment" industry, images of male and female behavior presented in education and the media, and so on), the energies of those concerned will be devoted to the care and treatment of symptoms and not of the underlying disease. To be sure, symptoms must be treated; the victims of violence must be protected and helped. The Good Samaritan did not wait to investigate the reasons the highways of his land were full of brigands before taking care of the man who had "fallen among" them. But since we are not speaking about individual obedience but the obedience of a "body," the church, should we not allow ourselves to assume that there are enough gifts within the body to enable it to be involved *simultaneously* with both the symptoms and the causes?

We are touching here, I believe, upon the two principal areas of need where Christian confession as deed is concerned today: the need for a theological perspective from which "the situation" may be considered, and the need to realize the fully corporate character of the disciple community so that Christian action arises out of the best efforts of a movement with a great variety of expertise and insight. We consider these points in the following two subsections.

26.3. Theology as Perspective. Christians have a vantage point, a window on the world, a heritage, a tradition of contemplation thousands of years in the making. And they have this as a perspective that, despite their many divisions and historical experiences and national, racial, class, or gender identities, is their *common* inheritance. But so long as most mainline Christianity is itself out of touch with the substance of that perspective, the church is as anchorless as everyone else. In the absence of a more holistic vision of the world as God intends it, according to this tradition of contemplation, contemporary Christians who are (rightly!) driven to act in the face of the human problems they encounter are reduced to acting on the basis of conventional humanitarian virtues vaguely associated with the language of faith: love, neighborliness, hospitality, justice, peace, kindness, hope, and so on. Actions so motivated may prove beneficial; but they may also be superficial and even detrimental to the genuine resolution of problems. Activity, even when it is well intentioned and relatively selfless, often ends by aggravating the very problems that it sought to address, or related problems that it did not notice because its perspective was not broad or deep enough.

The only way in which the plight of ecclesiastical activism on this continent can be resolved is through a concerted, sustained, and intentional effort on the part of serious Christians to regain a holistic theological perspective on the basis of which actions may emerge out of thought and vision, and not merely out of a humanitarian compulsion to act. What is needed is precisely *perspective* on the "here and now." No one, Christian or otherwise, can gain such a perspective from the context itself. It must be brought to the context from sources that transcend the constant flux of images and concerns and events of which the context is constituted. For Christians, those sources consist primarily of the Scriptures and theological traditions that have been "handed over" (*tradere*) to us. The ongoing encounter with these sources, reflected upon in the full awareness of our own time and place, is the indispensable presupposition of what is meant by "obedience."

Langdon Gilkey voiced this same concern three decades ago in a way that is still entirely pertinent because nothing in this respect has changed since he wrote, other than the deepening of the need:

If the congregation is to hear and obey the Word in its midst, the denominational church must lose its fear of and scorn for theology, and its resistance to the teaching of doctrine in the church. The life of historical American Protestantism has been based on the familiarity of the Bible to the congregation and the intelligibility and convincingness of its message to their several minds. Only thus has free-church Protestantism been able to dispense with creedal and theological requirements, and incidentally to free the mind to accept culture.

To the religiously untutored layman *in* modern culture, however, dominated as his thinking is by the casual order and worldly values of modern commercial and secular society, the Bible seems a strange, unbelievable, and largely irrelevant piece of writing. In the "real" world of commercial and technological life all happens by natural law, values are created by human effort, and he who looks after himself usually prospers. In the biblical world, on the contrary, most events seem to be the work of supernatural powers, man is portrayed as in desperate need of an invisible and intangible grace, and he who seeks his life will surely lose it. What, then, is modern man, conservative or liberal, honestly to make of this document, which seems so incompatible with what he knows of natural causality, and so opposite to all he values? How can he simply regard it as "true"? . . .

What is needed here—and desperately, if the Bible is to be any sort of authority in the church—is theological mediation.[47]

If the actions of Christians are to be confessions of faith, they must contain within themselves some glimpse of the *whole* vision out of which they have arisen. They need not be transparently Christian for all the world to see, and they do not have to come with Christian labels. Normally they will be anonymous as to their origins—which is part of that hiddenness of the Christian life of which we spoke earlier. But if, for the Christian community itself, they do not in themselves contain some definite reminiscence of that whole vision (let us call it "the reign of God"), then there will be some lack in them, and, over the long haul, the very habit of theological reflection giving rise to action will have been lost. We shall pursue this theme again, and more concretely, in the subsequent chapter on theological ethics.

26.4. The Corporate Nature of Obedience. Not only are Christians given the gift of a vantage point, they are also blessed with the gift of community, an extraordinary gift when contrasted with the isolation and alienation of most human beings in our society. Just as most North Americans are deprived of a perspective they can share with many both in and beyond the borders of this continent, so they are deprived of a community upon whose diverse wisdom and good will they may draw for support and guidance.

The solitary self, whether in the factory or the bureaucracy, does its work largely in isolation from other selves. The individual is often devoured by the monstrous mechanisms of industry and society. The state treats its citizens as instances of abstract categories, even of such ethical categories as equality, without regard to individual circumstances and needs. The result is . . . "moral-

---

47. Langdon Gilkey, *How the Church Can Minister to the World Without Losing Itself* (New York: Harper & Row, 1964), 85–96.

ized anonymity".... The upshot is a terrible anxiety and rage, a feeling of emptiness and impotence, an utter homelessness in the world.[48]

Without the support of others, people in our society can scarcely find the resources necessary to bind their own wounds, let alone consider the plight of whole nations, races, and classes. The importance of the corporate nature of the Christian life—the "body"—lies not only in its meaning for the individuals who are part of it, but in the promise that it provides for their shared work of world-mending.

That promise, one suspects, has scarcely been glimpsed by most of us. We almost automatically think of "the deed" in individualized terms.[49] If we hear a term such as the Reformation's "good works," we invariably see in our mind's eye the works of a Christian person. Moreover, these good works tend to accentuate the personal also with respect to their object: they are works done to or for some other person or small group of persons. With respect neither to the doer nor to the receiver of the deed have we learned how to think corporately. And yet that is a potent gift when seen from the contrasting perspective of secular isolation and the immense need, within the world today, to advance well beyond such isolation.

This is undoubtedly also related to the failure of a clerically and bureaucratically dominated ecclesiastical system to provide an adequate basis for the ministry of the laity. We have gone a little way toward incorporating the laity into the structures of church government, but few denominations have yet made the connection between the difficulty of acting as responsible and mature Christian witnesses in our complex society and the fact that in nearly every congregation there are human beings who, were they given a forum in which they could pool their varied experiences and expertise, would produce a community of reflection and action more promising than the average "think tank"—and more trustworthy!

We were reminded of this potential advantage of the corporate character of Christ's discipleship by the illustration of concern for violence against women and children being enacted simultaneously with investigations of the causes for such violence in males. This same observation can apply in nearly every area of human concern today. The limitations of single-issue orientation on the part of many good persons in the larger society do not *have* to be duplicated by the churches, and should not be. If and insofar as the church

---

48. Ralph C. Wood, "Peter Berger's Theology of Transcendence: A Review Article," in *Dialog* 33, no. 3 (Summer, 1994): 209, summarizing the thesis of Peter and Brigitte Berger in *The Homeless Mind* (New York: Random House, 1973).

49. Elisabeth Schüssler Fiorenza feels that this tendency is present in the biblical background—in Paul, who "necessarily privatizes Christian love and interiorizes it" (*In Memory of Her* [New York: Crossroad, 1992], 192).

makes good its status as "body," it is able on every issue both to do justice to specific problems and to consider such problems in the light of the larger *problematique* to which they belong. The deed, namely an act performed in response to some quite specific problem, can be truly confessional when it is undertaken as part of a sustained endeavor to see it within its greater context. It is far less likely, in that case, to prove a "solution" to one aspect of contemporary life only by aggravating problems that are present in other areas.

Is it purely idealistic to imagine that the church of Jesus Christ can develop a strong confession at the level of "the deed" because, among other things, it has access to sources of wisdom and courage that are so rare in our society? Is it utopian to posit a disciple community that is both engaged in pondering its worldly context from the perspective of a common theological heritage and doing so as a body whose members are able to combine their knowledge and experience of the world in order to act more responsibly within it? If we must respond in the affirmative, then we had better return to the initial considerations of this volume and ask ourselves precisely what is meant by the affirmation that the church is "the body of Christ," in whom the many members with their differing gifts are beginning to know how to be and to act as one.

For in neither of these observations are we assuming a purely voluntary situation, based on human ideals. If there is a community called Christian that searches the Scriptures and traditions in the light of the problems and possibilities of its context, and if this same community conducts its reflections in a corporate manner, drawing upon the variety of talents present in it, none of this is because this community is composed of especially studious and cooperative persons who have altruistically determined to "get together" and "do some research" in order to be able to act responsibly in the world. To the contrary! We suppose—on empirical grounds!—that in this community there is a good deal of reluctance, inertia, selfishness, personal ambition, jealousy, and most of the other faults that are present among human beings at large. We suppose that this is, in short, a community of sinners, and that their sin manifests itself in all aspects of their life and labor. But we also suppose—indeed, we *pre*suppose, having established the reasons for doing so in the first part of this volume—that this community is brought together and held together by a Spirit who is able to create something out of nothing: and therefore that what drives the members of this community to occupy themselves with ancient texts and difficult ideas that human lethargy would rather avoid, and to seek one another out with expectation and humility when human pride would prefer autonomy, is a grace that is more compelling than sin and more enduring than human determination.

Of such a grace-endowed community, deeds that bear witness to grace may be expected . . . together, of course, with much else that is not very gracious.

27. Confession as Stance

27.1. What Is Meant by Stance? The ordinary meaning of the word "stance," namely, a position of the body, provides an excellent entrée into the present discussion. If the church is "a body," Christ's *corpus,* what is the position of this body? Bodies and their "language" are taken very seriously in contemporary communications theory; and for a religious tradition in which the body is honored, as it is in the tradition of Jerusalem (1 Cor. 6:19), it ought not to be thought strange that there could be an ecclesiastical body language.

Institutions and movements, as well as individual persons, communicate with others through their physical embodiment and placement. The way an institution organizes itself; the shape of its gatherings; the positioning of various components within its ranks (men, women, children, visible minorities, the aged and infirm); the sorts of buildings it erects or uses; the characteristic dress of its officers and leaders; their gender, race, age, lifestyle; its manner of recognizing excellence or of correcting error: all such aspects of its life will "say" to those within and outside of the institution or movement in question something about its character and mission in the world. Indeed, as with the body language of persons, the messages communicated by the sheer physical behavior and ordering of institutional life may communicate more than its words do. Today great multinational corporations all wish to commend themselves to humane society through their assurances of concern over the technological rape of nature or the inequality of the sexes; but because their actual ordering of their affairs indicates to the observant that their love of nature and their feminist leanings are largely tokenism, their words *and their deeds* are belied by their actual stance. As Sir Kenneth Clark says in his well-known *Civilization* television series, "If I had to say which was telling the truth about society, a speech by a Minister of Housing or the actual buildings put up in his time, I should believe the buildings."[50]

More particularly, the stance of persons or institutions refers to their position vis-à-vis other persons, institutions, movements, and so on. An old adage warns, "One is known by the company one keeps." Individuals as well as institutions silently establish their identity and purpose through their associations. The church is by no means exempt from this rule of stance. Its embodiment and positioning is already a confession of its identity, intent, and faith. The way it orders its life contains easily decoded messages for all the world to read. Its leadership, their demeanor and dress, their sex, their

---

50. Kenneth Clark, *Civilization* (London: British Broadcasting Corporation and John Murray, 1969), 1.

economic standing; its placement of minorities, classes, and genders; its architecture (only consider how for masses of people the word "church" *means* a building, usual gothic);[51] and above all its associations in the larger human community: all these and related aspects of its life, which we may incorporate under the single term "stance," constitute the kind of self-declaration that is, if not directly confessional, paraconfessional or preconfessional in nature.

So important is such body language that it can either make or break the two other forms of confession to which we have devoted discussion previously. Like the industrial complex, which vows its intention to preserve the natural order while dumping effluent into the world's waterways, the church that announces its belief in (for example) "God's preferential option for the poor," yet parades itself in rich garments and lives in opulent buildings, enjoying the favor of the powerful, silently but effectively discredits itself and its verbal and active confessions. These latter will be regarded by the world as "tokenism," in much the same way as the promotional environmental literature of the multinationals is received by a knowing public.

Confession as stance is, of course, never a wholly satisfactory form of faith's confession, and never independent. For body language may also be misread. Besides, who among us is able to claim that his or her actual stance is wholly consistent with his or her intentions? Tolstoy, in his later years, after *Anna Karenina,* produced a spate of literature in which he advocated the most stringent and puritanical sort of sexual morality. In *The Kreuzer Sonata* and elsewhere, he even advocated celibacy within marriage. Meanwhile, as his wife Sofya knew very well (and divulged liberally), he himself was driven by lust and behaved toward his wife in an aggressive and almost rapacious manner. Does this destroy the power of Tolstoy's argument or its capacity to convict and convince? By the principle established above, we would have to

---

51. I do not intend this reference, or any other such that may have appeared in this series to suggest that church buildings are either unimportant or irrelevant. I have considerable sympathy for the point of view expressed in the following excerpt from a fine essay by the minister of Judson Memorial Church in New York City: "It is significant that *the Church happens in a space or place.* For some time, during the anti-building kick which accompanied the recovery of the truth that the Church is people, we felt very guilty about our Romanesque, rambling old brickpile. At times we were ashamed not to have sold it and gone 'on the road,' but as we saw *mission* 'happen' here we realized that the church must happen in a place or space. To deny this is to raise a serious question about the reality of the Incarnation. When the Church becomes a reality it is incarnate, visible, concrete, occupying a certain space at a certain time. Hans Schmidt says that the Holy Spirit is never a timeless manifestation:

"To illustrate: Remember that in the South it was church *buildings* that were bombed and burnt to the ground! We need not apologize for the building (whether it is irrelevant Gothic or hideous modern) but for what happens there. If the building is only a religious ghetto housing a holy enclave, it won't matter and nobody will bother to burn it or mark obscenities on its doors" (Howard Moody, "Toward a Religionless Church for a Secular World," in Rose, ed., *Who's Killing the Church?* 89).

say that it certainly vitiates his argument and should cause anyone to think twice about Tolstoy's reliability. But the whole story is not told, either, in the physical behavior of the great author. To assess the real character of his witness to truth as he understood it, we should also have to know about his remorse and chagrin over the discrepancy between his words and his behavior; and we should have to think, as well, about the others around him, including Sofya, who were still in most cases so committed to the status quo in Russia at the end of the Czarist era that they were incapable of questioning their aristocratic behavior either in sexual or economic and political matters.[52] Ultimate judgment of such questions of integrity does not belong to the human sphere.

The church at its best has felt obliged to confess in word and deed a gospel-intention for creaturely existence which, in its own existing, it could never perfectly attain and would in all likelihood often flagrantly contradict. But to know the whole story about this body we should also have to ask how the church feels about the discrepancy between its verbal and active confession of the faith and what its general posture in the world conveys. And we should also have to know about the others round about it, the commercial, social, and political segments of its host cultures, and their use and abuse of it, and so on. Body language does not "say" everything, and, like all language, it may conceal as well as reveal reality.

Nevertheless, the importance of stance being what it is, Christians and churches that consciously intend to confess the faith today are at least obliged to reflect truthfully upon this aspect of their common witness, because it has been greatly neglected in the past, and because the present is pregnant with the question, How, in this new situation in which the church of the ages is beginning to find itself—how, in this post-Christendom world, will the Christian community present itself? What kinds of buildings will it put up now? What kinds of people will it seek or appeal to for leadership? Above all, with whom will it now associate? Despite the real limits of body language or stance as a form of faith's confession, it may be that these questions are more decisive than the explicitly doctrinal and ethical questions that belong to the previously considered forms of confession. It would at least be well for serious Christians to consider the "stance" of Christendom in its past expressions, and to inquire whether this is the kind of pre-confessional message that they want the disciple community of the present and future to continue to convey.

27.2. The Stance of Christendom. In a real sense, the whole problem of Christendom, which has occupied much of our attention in this study and

---

52. See A. N. Wilson, *Tolstoy* (London: Penguin Books, 1988), chaps. 13–15, 295–392.

must, I believe, occupy the attention of Christians generally in this historical moment, can be summarized—or perhaps symbolized—by the metaphor of stance. It would be foolish for anyone to argue that throughout the entire period from 325 C.E. to (say) mid-nineteenth century Christendom failed utterly as a confessional faith, for there were wonderfully confessional words and deeds during all stages of that long history. But it would not be foolish to claim that the words of the great theologians and mystics and preachers, and the deeds of the great saints and activists, were regularly compromised by the general stance of Christendom in the Western world. Martin of Tours and Francis of Assisi engaged in lives of selfless solidarity with the poor and, in the case of Francis, the neglected nonhuman creatures of God; and their witness stands. But it stands in too close proximity to its antithesis to be dissociated altogether from the latter. When Pope Innocent III deigned to bless the *genuinely* innocent Francis, he engaged in an act of cooptation very familiar to power: incorporate dissent! Along with Francis's cooptation by nineteenth- and twentieth-century liberal Christian sentimentalism, the embrace of power has colored forever the manner in which the world could receive the confession of Giovanni Bernardoni (the birth name of St. Francis).

It is not altogether different with the theologians. St. Thomas, if and whenever his works can be read apart from their elevation to special authority under the auspices of a later cohort of ecclesiasts in need of a cohesive theological system to buttress the failing authority of the hierarchy, must be seen to offer us a daring and courageous interpretation of the faith that is by no means lacking in "critical theology." But as "the angelic doctor," whose teacher Albertus Magnus was canonized only in 1931 and in some proximity to the implementation of the concept of papal infallibility (1870), it is difficult to receive this testimony as it was clearly intended by its author. Protestant saints of the intellect are by no means exempt from this procedure. In their initial, protesting ministries, both Luther and Calvin brought to bear upon their respective contexts confessions of the faith that could grasp the most sensitive and learned as well as the most needful of their contemporaries. But in too short a time, both were taken up into the highest reaches of authority and became, with and in spite of their own consent and preference, legitimators of power and determiners of the fates of thousands.

The Christendom phenomenon is from start to finish one of stance—positioning, identity through association, power through proximity to power, and so on. At base, it is very simple: In the fourth century, the Christian movement ceases to be a movement and becomes an institution, reflecting in its own internal posture the posture of its host culture, and sustaining its life and work through the closest possible association with secular authority. When this becomes the fundamental assumption of the religion, little can be done, even by those who see the dilemma clearly, to alter the manner in which the Christian confession will always be caused to legitimate the status quo. Even prophetic critique can be absorbed into the structures of power, for every court has its critics—and its fools! Those who thoroughly defy the arrangement and refuse to be seduced can be excommunicated or summarily disposed of, and both partners in the concordat between the sacred and the secular will cooperate in the matter, for both are at risk—a fact that ought to give us new occasion today to examine the excluded parties, including individual heretics as well as whole movements such as the Anabaptists.

In the light of this history, and especially as we emerge from or are driven out of the Constantinian arrangement, it is profitable to reexamine the scriptural testimony to Jesus and the early church on the question of stance.

27.3. Jesus' Stance. When we do so, we discover rather soon that what we are calling stance is by no means an incidental aspect of the story that is told in the Gospels. We are apt to brush over this aspect of the narrative by assuming that it only indicates (what liberal Christians have always known) that Jesus has a particular sensitivity with respect to those who are pushed to the sidelines of society. But we should consider how the Gospel writers have apparently taken pains to depict for subsequent generations of Christians what today we would call Jesus' "lifestyle" and, especially, his associations. From the standpoint of the concern we are now investigating, that is, the way in which the sheer positioning of a person or organization constitutes a confessional or preconfessional statement, the "stance" of Jesus is almost as significant as his words; indeed, his words (or those attributed to him) lose their prophetic edge if they are separated from his positioning within his context.

In the first place, Jesus is born in obscurity—"of the house of David," as we are assured by Luke (1:27) for reasons that may not be entirely theological; but since Luke is also the source of the virgin birth concept, the connection with the important royal house, which is through Joseph, hardly secures any prestige. From the usual perspective, the child is illegitimate—the offspring of a "single mother"!

From the reference in Mark (6:3; par. Matt. 13:55) to the response to his public teaching on the part of people in "his own country," it is gathered that Jesus learned carpentry from his "supposed father" (Luther) and actually practiced that craft. The same reference makes it abundantly clear that carpentry then, as now, did not count for very much in the social sphere, and certainly was not considered a proper background for rabbinic or prophetic activity ("Where did this man get all this?"—v. 2).

For his closest associates, Jesus chooses ordinary working men, some of whom, such as the tax collector Matthew, enjoy unsavory reputations. He then associates himself with the wholly unorthodox movement of John the Baptizer and proceeds to conduct an itinerant ministry among the masses without benefit of cathedrals! He attracts to himself, and achieves a reputation for liking, classes of persons wholly unacceptable to good society:

> And as he sat at dinner in the house, many tax collectors and sinners came and were sitting with him and his disciples. When the Pharisees saw this, they said to his disciples, "Why does your teacher eat with tax collectors and sinners?" But when he heard this, he said, "Those who are well have no need of a physician, but those who are sick. Go and learn what this means, 'I desire mercy, not sacrifice.' For I have come to call not the righteous but sinners."
>
> (Matt. 9:10–13 NRSV)

Jesus is well aware, apparently, of the messages conveyed to his contemporaries through such associations:

> "John came neither eating nor drinking, and they say, 'He has a demon'; the Son of Man came eating and drinking, and they say, 'Look, a glutton and a drunkard, a friend of tax collectors and sinners.' Yet wisdom is vindicated by her deeds.'"
>
> (Matt. 11:18–19 NRSV)

Jesus' stance is visible not only in his association with lower classes and ostracized elements, but also in his fraternization with women, children, and foreigners. Some of the women are doubly unacceptable for public companionship with respectable males because they are prostitutes (Matt. 21:32). The Johannine story of Jesus' encounter with a woman taken in adultery, whatever its basis in fact, corresponds with the Synoptic judgment expressed by Matthew that "'the tax collectors and the prostitutes are going into the kingdom of God ahead of you'"—ahead, that is, of "the religiously correct" (Matt. 21:31).

That a Jewish man and "rabbi" of this period (even if he is only a very unofficial rabbi!) should hold major discourses with women, whether adulterous women or respectable women such as Mary and Martha, already tells one a great deal about him; and it is something unusual, not only for his own period and culture but for many centuries of "Christian" culture, well into our own epoch.

> Most of women's early Christian heritage is probably lost and must be extracted from androcentric early Christian records. However, since the Gospels were written at a time when other New Testament authors clearly were attempting to adapt the role of women within the Christian community to that of patriarchal society and religion, it is all the more remarkable that not one story or

statement is transmitted in which Jesus demands the cultural patriarchal adaptation and submission of women.[53]

The incident of the anointing at Bethany, which Elisabeth Schüssler Fiorenza has memorialized for present-day theological and biblical reflection,[54] would be as shocking to Christian congregations today as it was to Jesus' disciples then. So, in another way, is Jesus' encounter with the foreign woman, a Canaanite, who would not leave him alone and, while humbling herself, showed herself to be extremely resourceful and worldly wise:

> "I was sent only to the lost sheep of the house of Israel." But she came and knelt before him, saying, "Lord, help me." He answered, "It is not fair to take the children's food and throw it to the dogs." She said, "Yes, Lord, yet even the dogs eat the crumbs that fall from their masters' table." Then Jesus answered her, "Woman, great is your faith! Let it be done for you as you wish."
>
> (Matt. 15:21–28 NRSV)

It is as much the stance of Jesus as it is his teaching and his acts (the miracles, and so on) that wins him a hearing, and secures for him, at the same time, the kind of enmity that will lead inevitably to the cross. Or rather, it is the absolute correspondence between his words and deeds, on the one hand, and his bearing and positioning in his social context, on the other, that brings about that ending—for Christians, that beginning. It is entirely conceivable (for history corroborates the phenomenon with great regularity) that a person like this could have said and done what Jesus according to the record said and did, and, moving instead among the more reputable classes, with associates drawn from (say) the intelligentsia or the religious establishment, dressed conventionally and holding forth in the better public forums or the homes of influential persons, could without difficulty have survived into old age. He might even have been given honorary doctorates in our society; for the world knows how to honor prophets, critics, and mystics, provided they convey symbols and assurances of their essential "belonging."

Jesus did not do this. Not only by consistently refusing that kind of power and respectability (the temptations of the wilderness!) but by taking every opportunity to castigate such behavior as hypocrisy, disbelief, and blasphemy, he seems almost to have courted the rejection and violent renunciation that was his frequent prediction, like a self-fulfilling prophecy. The last earthly scene of this brief history, ordinarily understood, is a parabolic enactment of the whole of it: crucified between two thieves. His final associates, in

---

53. Elisabeth Schüssler Fiorenza, *In Memory of Her*, 52–53.
54. Ibid., 330–31.

the public eye, are not unlike the company that he has kept all the way through.

> What Christianity added to the classical account of justice was not any change in its definition but an extension of what was due to others and an account of how to fulfil that due. Christ added to the two great commandments the words that the second is "like unto" the first. At the height of the Gospels we are shown the moment when a tortured being says of his torturers that their due is to be forgiven. Despite all the horrors perpetrated by Christians, both in the west and more particularly outside the west, despite all the failures of Christians to understand the consequences of justice for the law, nevertheless the rendering to each being its due, in the light of the perfection of that rendering, could not be publicly denied among Christians.[55]

It is almost impossible for us to review the story of the crucified one, even in such a sketchy manner, without thinking it a gross exaggeration of the point! Did Jesus have to go so far out of his way to demonstrate the truth that his message contained implications, not only for the way that we are to speak and to act but for the way that we are to *be*? And *can* we be this way? The church of the ages has, on the whole, with a few exceptions that are notorious because they are so rare, answered that we cannot; that even when we learn to say those things and do those things with some consistency, we cannot be that way. And precisely this is the constant and repeated barrier to the reception of our verbal and our active confessions of the faith.

27.4. Another Chance?   It has been a recurring motif of this trilogy that today, with the winding down of the clock of Christendom, a new time opens up for Christian faith and life. Instead of regarding this ending as a tragic humiliation of the glorious institution whose *cultus* has been the cradle of Western culture, it is possible to regard it as the beginning of a new phase of Christian existence, full, to be sure, of uncertainty, disappointment, and perhaps "fear and trembling" (Kierkegaard), but also, perhaps, redolent of opportunities that were denied our Constantinian past just because of Christendom's majority status, its proximity to power, and its virtual monopoly on the souls of men and women.

At the core of this possibility for re-formation and renewal, there is most importantly the whole question of the Christian *stance* in the diaspora situation. The future of the church most certainly depends upon its words (proclamation, preaching, theology, and so on) and its deeds (ethics)—and it will not be denied that I have upheld these two forms of faith's confession in this

---

55. George P. Grant, *Technology and Justice* (Toronto: Anansi, 1986), 54–55.

discussion. But even if we Christians became better theologians, preachers, and "doers" of the truth, we would surely have failed to meet the challenge of the present were we to continue, as in the past, to position ourselves as favorably as possible in relation to the powerful, the rich, and the respectable. The great question facing us as "mainline" churches may not be whether there will be a theological renewal in our midst, or whether more Christians will become responsibly active in the great variety of life-and-death causes by which our civilization is confronted, but whether the Christian movement can survive its disestablishment in the very practical terms of being distanced from power. Can it find another *modus operandi* in the world besides the acquisition and retention of power through proximity to power?

Above all, and positively speaking, can the church that is coming to be associate itself more consistently than Christendom ever did with the excluded, the disenfranchised, the marginalized, the powerless, the poor? Without apotheosizing the human victim or romanticizing over the extrahuman, and without drawing attention to *itself,* can the church emulate the prophetic faith that pleads the cause of the widow and orphan and identifies with the groaning creation?

And the corollary of *that* dimension of the stance to which the diaspora church is called is stated by Jacques Ellul with utter clarity:

> Paul speaks about being weak with the weak but not about being strong with the strong. This is the real point. Jesus, too, says that he has not come to the healthy but to the sick. The respect which is demanded in love is respect for the weak, whether their weakness be corporal, mental, intellectual, social, moral, or spiritual. It is respect for the sick and the ugly, the lonely and the despised, the poor and the foolish, the exploited and the colonized, the overscrupulous and the confused.
>
> In contrast the gospel is always hard on the rich, for their wealth, whatever it may be, is power. For them Christian freedom may legitimately be an offense. If, then, our freedom shocks the mighty, the moral, the bigoted and violent capitalist or communist establishment, the ruling class, the absolutists, the men of intransigent principle, those who are sure of their principles or their authority, we can only rejoice in this. Offense is of profit for them. When we shake human certainty with our freedom, we are seeking the interest of these others. To introduce doubt and questioning where an equal conscience and tranquil self-righteousness reign, to shatter social, intellectual, and spiritual conformity, to jolt those who live by conventions and platitudes, to arouse uncertainty where security hold sway, is not this an extension of the saying of our Lord: "Go and sell that thou hast, and give to the poor . . . and come and follow me" (Matthew 19:21)?[56]

56. *The Ethics of Freedom,* trans. by Geoffrey W. Bromiley (Grand Rapids: Wm. B. Eerdmans, 1976), 205.

The body language of the emergent church will by no means constitute a whole and satisfactory form of faith's confession. Words will still be necessary—including the confession of sin that acknowledges the discrepancy between what is preached and what is practiced! And deeds will never be irrelevant. But apart from the adoption of a stance that is noticeably different from that of Christendom, neither our words nor our deeds will prove to be the confession of faith that is being required of us today, and that is newly possible for us on account of our own increasingly altered posture *vis-à-vis* power.

We shall continue this discussion, using other language and introducing different dimensions of the subject, as we turn to the consideration of theological ethics.

CHAPTER ▪ SEVEN
Theological Ethics

28. The Context of Christian Ethical Discussion

28.1. After Christendom—"Values." We confess the faith in word, deed, and stance; and in each of these forms of faith's confession, as in their inter-action, we encounter the question that is the basic concern of this chapter: What are Christian ethics? Many aspects of this question have been antici-pated and touched upon in the previous chapters of this book, and indeed throughout the trilogy.[1] Now we must address this subject more systemati-cally. If, as we have suggested in the preceding chapter, Christians today will frequently have to confess their faith through deed and stance rather than through verbal testimony that is explicitly "religious," then we shall have to clarify the manner in which they move between belief and obedience. If it is "the faith" that their ethical behavior confesses, and not merely their good will, their neighborliness, their concern as responsible citizens, and so forth, how shall we articulate the relation between theology, understood as intellec-tual reflection on "the faith" (*thinking* the faith), and ethics, understood as faith's *praxis*?

The three major sections of this chapter will address three questions that are implied in the basic question about the nature of Christian ethics: (1) How does the context in which we find ourselves affect our discussion of Christian ethics? (2) What makes Christian ethics Christian? And (3) how can the disciple community learn to live faithfully in a post-Christendom world?

In some ways, it would be preferable to begin with the second question, "What makes Christian ethics Christian?" We cannot do so, however, in a

---

1. In the present volume, ethics are explicitly discussed in chap. 5, §§20.5 and 22.1.

work that intends throughout to manifest a primary contextual concern. For our social context confronts us with challenges that would, if we ignored them, undermine our discussion throughout.

These challenges, although many and complex, should be considered from two different angles of vision, the one more abstract, the other altogether concrete. The *first* has to do with the loss of any shared assumptions concerning the possibility of ontological foundations for the contemplation of "the good." The *second* perspective focuses on the sheer moral chaos and lack of direction in private and public life in North America today—a condition that, for one thing, bespeaks the breakdown of Christendom and leaves Christians wondering whether, in the post-Christendom situation, there is such a thing as a peculiarly *Christian* ethic. We shall consider this latter in the two subsequent subsections; the present discussion concerns the confusion occasioned by the loss of ethical foundations.

From the outset and at varying levels of consciousness and significance throughout its history, the Christian movement has recognized that its ethic differs in important ways from the moral teachings of other communities. The early Christians were not particularly surprised by this, because they assumed that what they thought good in terms of human pursuits stemmed from their understanding of the nature and will of God as revealed in Jesus as the Christ, and that other systems of belief, whether religious or philosophic, would result in other types of behavior.[2] What they shared with all, or most, of the others, however, was a common assumption that any answer to the question "What ought we to do?" would have to emerge from reflection on the more basic question, "What is really real?" In other words, like most premodern systems of meaning, Christianity presupposes that an ethic requires a foundational ontology, that an "ought" requires an "is." One tries to behave in a certain way (for example, to love one's neighbor) because it is consistent with what one believes is ultimately real or true ("God is love.")

The confusion that underlies so much private and social behavior today, and that constitutes quite a new situation for many, especially in the once-mainline churches, is a consequence of the loss not only of ontological foundations but of the belief that such foundations are possible—or (as the optimists would say) necessary. This confusion already manifests itself in contem-

---

2. What really distinguishes the early Christian ethic according to both Wayne A. Meeks (*The Origins of Christian Morality: The First Two Centuries* [New Haven: Yale University Press, 1994]) and Willi Marxsen (*New Testament Foundations for Christian Ethics* [Minneapolis: Fortress Press, 1994]) should not be sought in specific points of morality but in the christological presupposition of Christian *being*. "There *is* a distinctively Christian ethic, but it must not be confused with any particular deeds or practices. Rather, it is a constituent part of the gospel, which is definitive of the Christian experience of God, of Christian community and of the community's calling in society" (Victor Paul Furnish, "Can Ethics Be Christian?" *The Christian Century* 111, no. 30 [October 26, 1994]: 993).

porary uncertainty concerning the term "ethic" (or "ethics") itself. Although this term is used with increasing frequency in public life today, its very usage on the whole renders it difficult or ambiguous for straightforward public application by Christians. In a vague way, the concept of ethics as employed by governments, think tanks, medical societies, industry and commerce, the media and other public agencies carries the connotation of distinguishing good and bad (rarely "evil"), or desirable and undesirable, or favorable and unfavorable, and so on. But part of the vagueness that attaches to the work of ethicists and committees on ethics in (for example) medicine or law stems from the ill-defined nature of what is expected of these persons. That such deliberation occurs at all belies the fact that in all areas of human concern today we are confronted by complicated decision-making that, to our considerable dismay, cannot be answered scientifically or objectively, yet can no longer be ignored or dismissed. Everyone knows that such ethical advisory groups are supposed to investigate the rectitude or advisability, or at least the consequences, of pursuing this or that course (for example, building a dam in a wilderness area traditionally occupied by indigenous peoples). But no one, and perhaps least of all the ethical experts themselves, can say with confidence on what grounds such decisions are to be made. As individuals, the ethical advisers to a government commission on euthanasia, for example, may have quite definite personal grounds for their views on the subject; but the pluralistic nature of such advisory groups and of the public they represent denies the possibility that any particular set of assumptions about "the good" might inform the work of a democratically representative committee of this kind.

The confusion felt by Christians who are asked to serve on such advisory committees is often acute. As Stanley Hauerwas has observed, what society wants from Christian ethicists are directives entirely divorced from the belief-basis upon which they depend. Writing of the "Enlightenment project" of creating a realm called "morality" independent of any metaphysic or ontology, Hauerwas notes that

> it is just this sense of ethics that Christians are called upon to embody in the interest of developing medical ethics, business ethics, professional ethics, and so on. We are asked to leave our theological convictions as much as possible behind and become casuists for liberal social order. We become technicians for the working out of basic principles of autonomy, justice, and beneficence for the quandaries of the profession . . . . Ethics now becomes an autonomous area of human behaviour that can be distinguished from religion and etiquette. . . . It is now assumed that morality, as such, must be autonomous.[3]

---

3. Stanley Hauerwas, *After Christendom* (Nashville: Abingdon Press, 1991), 28–29.

But is not the idea of an "autonomous morality" a contradiction in terms? Presumably, it means a morality that stands on its own and requires no foundation other than the power of its own persuasiveness—Kant's "categorical imperative." But while such a concept might hold in a relatively homogeneous society, such as Kant's society was,[4] it will hardly serve in a secularized and multicultural society such as ours. The neo-Kantian value theory that appeared in the nineteenth century to replace the breakdown of metaphysics as the basis of ethics quietly depended upon the residue of the Judeo-Christian religion that some of its advocates believed it could replace.[5] A system of morality may seem "autonomous" in a culture that shares a common history, culture, language, religion, and goals, and to some extent ours was such a culture prior to the end of World War II. But with the demise of Christendom and the enormous variety of historical memories, expectations, languages, artistic and literary traditions, ethnic and racial lifestyles, and religions represented on this continent today, it has become apparent that few if any moral imperatives are universally compelling.

The dilemma seems to be this: there is a sufficient anxiety about moral drift in our society to have caused thoughtful people to realize that morality cannot be autonomous or self-sustaining—left, as it were, to public convention, to "nature," or to chance. Yet we are prevented by our cultural variety, combined with our secular skepticism and relativism, from espousing any specific conception of ultimate reality (ontology) on which to base an ethic. No particular "worldview," not even those that can claim to be "scientific," may be imposed on the whole community; and the metaphysic that has enjoyed the status of dominance for centuries in the West, namely, the Christian belief system, is doubly suspect by many when it is drawn upon for ethical direction.

With the impasse created by this situation, many citizens, including educational policy makers, have turned to the consideration of "values." Accepting as a given of modern life the impossibility of basing morality on value-*free* verifiable data, people look to commonly accepted "values" for the moral guidance they cannot receive from "facts," and there is talk of "value-prioritizing" and even "value-engineering."

Everybody uses the word "values" to describe our making of the world: capitalists and socialists, atheists and avowed believers, scientists and politicians. The word comes to us so platitudinously that we take it to belong to the way things

---

4. For this reason, Nietzsche called Kant "the great delayer." See George P. Grant, *English Speaking Justice: The Josiah Wood Lectures of 1974* (Sackville, N.B.: Mount Allison University, 1974).

5. See Paul Tillich, *Systematic Theology*, vol. 3 (Chicago: University of Chicago Press, 1963), 28–30.

are. It is forgotten that before Nietzsche and his immediate predecessors, men did not think about their actions in that language. *They did not think they made the world valuable,* but that they participated in its goodness.[6]

The point is, values, too, require foundations. "If values have no *fundamentum in re* [foundation in reality] . . . , they float in the air of a transcendent validity, or else they are subjected to pragmatic tests which are arbitrary and accidental unless they introduce an ontology of essences surreptitiously."[7] The only foundation available, however, once one has adopted the language of values as the basis of morality, is public opinion. If enough people value a given practice (for example, public financial support of low-income families) it will continue, at least rhetorically, to inform public discourse; if they do not, it will be replaced by whatever else is consistent with majority opinion. Thus what passes for democratic process comes to fill the vacuum left by the demise of metaphysics, religion, and any allegedly universal "ought." In this way, a foundation of sorts is provided; but it is a very unstable and shifting foundation and it is subject to terrible abuses. Morality by consensus may guarantee that the moral preferences of the majority are satisfied on a fairly regular basis, as long as a democratic system of representative government exists, but it will also create perpetual uncertainty, frequent unhappiness, and potentially life-threatening dangers among minorities—and, on some matters, *everyone* will at some point find himself or herself among the latter.

To exemplify: In Canada at the present time, a celebrated trial has ended with the conviction of a father who, on grounds of profound compassion, effected the death of his severely handicapped young daughter. A groundswell of public opinion against the conviction indicates that large numbers of Canadians, perhaps the majority, favor legislation that would permit such "mercy killing" under certain circumstances. This in turn has alarmed a vocal minority—and understandably: the protesting group is composed chiefly of handicapped persons and those who care for them, who fear that any conceivable legislation of this nature would prove a lasting threat to the survival of such human beings as they.[8]

The incident illustrates that the only counterbalance to the dangers of morality by consensus is the continual vigilance of those harmfully affected by such a system. Thus the language of rights has emerged along with the

---

6. George P. Grant, *Time as History* (CBC Massey Lectures of 1969) (Toronto: Canadian Broadcasting System, 1969), 44–45. (My italics.)

7. Tillich, *Systematic Theology,* vol. 1 (Chicago: University of Chicago Press, 1951), 20.

8. On the question of euthanasia, see Katherine K. Young, *A Cross-Cultural Historical Case against Planned Self-Willed Death and Assisted Suicide* (McGill Law Journal, vol. 39, 1994), esp. 698–707.

language of values. Given the fact that values-thinking seems to have become normative and is perhaps the only short-term method of maintaining some kind of order in an otherwise potentially chaotic society, the struggle for their "rights" on the parts of minorities is a necessary corrective to the inordinate powers of the majority.

But can Christians accept, in the first place, the "values" approach to morality? George Grant believed that liberal Christian capitulation to modernity was nowhere more in evidence than in the uncritical adoption of the language of values:

> What is comic about the present use of "values," and the distinction of them from "facts," is not that it is employed by modern men who know what is entailed in so doing; but that it is used also by "religious" believers who are unaware that in its employment they are contradicting the very possibility of the reverence they believe they are espousing in its use. The reading of Nietzsche would make that clear to them.[9]

As the later discussion of the nature of Christian ethics will show, I am in full agreement with Grant. It is obvious enough that Christians, who by definition are committed to the life and well-being of God's creation, must make common cause today with a host of others whose rudimentary assumptions differ from our own. Among these will be persons, groups, and movements upholding "values" that can be seen to have something in common with Christian understanding of the nature of the good. But it is misleading and naive when Christians leap into the language-world of values without considering the shift that is involved in doing so. Wishing to bring their Christian "values" to bear upon the discussion, they fail to recognize that in their uncritical adoption of this very approach they are relinquishing the essence of the Christian ethic. Love (*agape*), which is that essence, is not a value. It is a reality, preceding us, directing us, judging and upholding us.

> God is love. In this the love of God was made manifest among us, that God sent his only Son into the world, so that we might live through him. In this is love, not that we loved God but that he loved us and sent his Son to be the expiation for our sins. Beloved, if God so loved us, we also ought to love one another. . . . We love, because he first loved us.
>
> (1 John 4:8b–19)

Christians indeed value love; but it is not our valuing of it that makes it real and viable. It would be real and "at work in the world" whether we valued it

---

9. Grant, *Time as History*, 45.

or not; and so would the justice, beauty, truth, and goodness that are born of this love and are the creatures of this "benificence" (Gustafson)[10]

It is not our mandate, as Christians, to persuade our contemporaries of the pathos or absurdity of the reduction of ethics to the morality of consensus, joining forces, perhaps, with others who on religious or philosophical grounds lament the substitution of values-language for the language of the good. It is also scarcely feasible, and least of all for a religion that for centuries imposed its morality on society without providing human beings with a convincing ontic foundation from which to weigh moral questions for themselves. After Christendom, the legislative and even the ethically persuasive powers of Christianity are limited and must, as we have insisted earlier, prove themselves anew indirectly by their fruits.[11]

But it *is* our Christian mandate to become sufficiently versed in the faith-foundations of our own ethic that we are able to gain perspective on the confusion that is introduced by the *loss* of foundations, as this loss affects both ourselves and our society at large. Only so will we avoid on the one hand the kind of liberalism that too easily embraces shallow secular alternatives to the failed ethical systems of the West and, on the other hand, the kind of conservativism that attempts to resuscitate and impose the moral codes of earlier phases of Christendom. Christian ethics in the post-Christendom situation must walk a narrow path between capitulation to the ever-changing trends of a society deprived of any compelling sense of what is real and good, and the defense of moralities whose presuppositions are inaccessible to the present. It is possible to walk that path only through a constantly renewed encounter with the foundational questions and assumptions of Christian faith itself, and not to settle for the seeming expediency of consensual solutions.

28.2. Bewilderment, Disarray, and Trauma. The three words of this heading have been chosen to describe what for many in our society and its churches is the moral state of our corporate life from the standpoint of its actual condition, as distinct from the discussion of ethical theory concerning its condition. As such, these words undoubtedly betray a vantage point that assumes both the necessity and the possibility of a "way of life" quite different from the one that North Americans on the verge of a new millennium seem to be pursuing. Such an assumption already runs headlong into one of the prominent features of our present condition, namely, the attitude on the part of

---

10. See James M. Gustafson, *Can Ethics Be Christian?* (Chicago: University of Chicago Press, 1975). See also my *Imaging God: Dominion As Stewardship* (Grand Rapids: Wm. B. Eerdmans, 1986), 122, 123, 128.

11. See my discussion of "Christendom ethics" in *The Steward: A Biblical Symbol Come of Age* (New York: Friendship Press, 1985), 133–35.

influential segments of the society that, in the absence of moral absolutes and normative patterns of life, one must simply accept what comes to be as natural and, probably, inevitable. That we have witnessed the emergence in this century not only of amoral individuals but of an amoral type of human being—a human type that no longer concerns itself with "the good" at either the individual or societal level, and even appears to enjoy the moral chaos of contemporary urban life—this is part of the reason for the "bewilderment, disarray, and trauma" that are felt by many people in our context, not only Christians.

It is not surprising, of course, that such alarmed reactions to the present are especially characteristic of older persons. Those of us who have any living memory of the immediate past (let us say, prior to 1960) are continuously made aware of the gap between what was considered normal or acceptable human behavior in our youth and what is allowed, or even encouraged, today. Is it simply an aspect of aging? Is each generation automatically shocked by the next? And is such shock little more, as some suggest, than a certain envy or indignation that one is oneself prevented by age or infirmity from participating in the "new morality"? Were our parents as shocked by our behavior as we are by our children's, and were their parents equally alarmed . . . and so on?

This kind of popular explanation of critical assessments of the morality of our context perhaps contains some truth, but not as much truth as it often assumes. For one thing, not all of those who lament our present disarray are senior citizens, and even among the latter there are few who wish to hold up the past as a golden age of human decency and responsibility. Many of us who remember a time before "the new morality" of the 1960s were ourselves "hurt" by the old morality—sometimes severely, and sometimes permanently scarred. Many, consequently, can rejoice in the various forms of "liberation" that have removed from whole classes of human beings the fetters that generations of self-righteousness and taboo fashioned for them.

The "bewilderment" is not all attributable, therefore, to the conservativism or the resentments of age. For the most part it is genuine bewilderment, because the sheer fact and extent of the change, especially when it is viewed by those with personal experience of *what* has changed, is simply very hard to assimilate. Engel's Law applies here: there is a point in quantitative change at which qualitative distinctions are introduced. One may assimilate without difficulty the knowledge that in a village of three hundred there were five broken marriages in 1945 when there were only two ten years earlier. But when almost half of present-day marriages in that same village *cum* suburban bedroom community now end in divorce, a whole new level of reflection is called for, and for many persons in our society there are no intellectual or spiritual criteria for "taking in" such a dramatically changed situation.

As this reference to divorce suggests, the altered moral condition of our society is most immediately visible in the sphere of personal ethics, and especially sexual ethics. That large numbers of people today regard any sort of formal marriage vows as being unnecessary and irrelevant ("a piece of paper"); that birth control should be discussed openly and frequently; that the majority of the populace should condone and regard as normal premarital sex (what is abnormal is chastity!); that it is necessary to indoctrinate little children in the dangers of sexually transmitted diseases and "safe-sex" practices; that primary school textbooks should depict "families" of many different kinds, those based on heterosexual cohabitation being presented as one among many "choices"; that films intended for public consumption should display explicit sex, and their producers fear for their box-office success without it; that Christian congregations should be asked to welcome into their manses, parsonages, and rectories gay or lesbian clergy and their partners; that denominations should consider devising ceremonies of marriage for same-sex couples, and so on and on: none of this was remotely conceivable in North America before 1950 at the earliest, not even in large cities.

The point in listing such items as the above in this connection is not to register any sort of evaluation of specific aspects of sexual ethics; one must assume the necessity of some of these changes (for example, education of the young concerning sexually transmitted diseases), and one may also laud *aspects* of most of these changes. But what I wish to convey at the moment is simply the enormity of the change, and therefore in some sense to justify the bewilderment that it engenders in many.[12] It is important for Christians, among others, to achieve some sympathic understanding of this bewilderment if they do not possess it already, because it is one of the most salient, if largely unspoken, reasons that many North Americans turn to the churches for refuge and, when they do not find it in the once-mainline churches, either attempt to alter these accordingly or turn, instead, to the more "conservative" churches. Moreover, the increasing popularity of the latter, as well as their political militancy, must be traced at least in some measure to this same bewilderment.

For that reason, any discussion of Christian ethics today must be undertaken in the awareness that what large numbers of avowed Christians in the United States and Canada wish to hear from Christian leaders and thinkers is that Christian morality means quite straightforwardly the morality that was dominant on this continent—at least quasi officially—prior to the eu-

---

12. Anyone who does not sympathize with the bewildered elderly, middle-aged, or young people described here would be well advised to view Hollywood and other films produced before about 1955 and to compare them with present-day cinematography. And the point is: *any* films will do!

phemistically designated "Age of Aquarius": in short, "the old morality," with its affirmation of the family, sexual fidelity in marriage, clean living (with or without a little alcohol!), and patriotic feeling. It is consistent with neither Christian compassion nor Christian wisdom to berate this quest for security on the part of the bewildered. Even when their collective bewilderment leads to such a phenomenon as the Christian Right, it behooves the perceptive to recognize, behind such militancy, the incipient anxiety and fear of persons who feel not only alienated from the cutting edge of their culture but personally disoriented and insecure. The liberal *cum* radical Christian rejection of this phenomenon may be quite right and necessary where powerful political movements like that associated with the Christian Right are concerned; but it is misguided and misleading when it fails to sympathize with the bewilderment of persons that is partly the cause of such movements. For from whatever specific motives these persons register their confusion and alarm, whether because of age or fear for their young or care for the future of their nation, their anxiety is not to be dismissed. Both its motivation and its attempts at resolution of the foreboding that it feels may be questioned, and usually should be. But *that* it feels foreboding, *that* it is alarmed, *that* it is bewildered, is entirely understandable. It may be reaction, but is it not a healthy reaction when human beings, sensing disintegration and death, recoil?

In fact, is it not possible that *not* to be bewildered by the present moral chaos of our society is the least life-affirming posture imaginable? One does not have to be an advocate of "the old morality," or a complacent member of the middle classes, or a prude or prig or bigot, to be astonished and fearful whenever one encounters concretely the many evidences of moral decay and amorality in our social context. One may just be, for example, a parent!

> To see the modern world from the point of view of a parent is to see it in the worst possible light. This perspective unmistakably reveals the unwholesomeness, not to put it more strongly, of our way of life: our obsession with sex, violence, and the pornography of "making it"; our addictive dependence on drugs, "entertainment," and the evening news; our impatience with anything that limits our sovereign freedom of choice, especially with the constraints of marital and familial ties; our preference for "nonbinding commitments"; our third-rate educational system; our third-rate morality; our refusal to draw a distinction between right and wrong, lest we "impose" our morality on others; our reluctance to judge or be judged; our indifference to the needs of future generations, as evidenced by our willingness to saddle them with a huge national debt, an overgrown arsenal of destruction, and a deteriorating environment; our unsated assumption, which underlies so much of the propaganda for

unlimited abortion, that only those children born for success ought to be allowed to be born at all.[13]

The trauma that is experienced by both "ordinary people" and keen observers of our society, such as the late Christopher Lasch, is real, and it is
based on evidence that is real. What ought this to mean for Christian ethics?
At the end of the previous subsection, I proposed that Christian ethics
must seek the narrow path that avoids, on the one hand, liberal capitulation
to the ever-changing mores of our society, and on the other conservative
attempts to resuscitate some version of "the old morality." Unfortunately,
since the 1960s, the impression seems to have been created in and around the
churches that there are only two alternatives, and they come very close to the
two approaches that I have indicated must be avoided: either one embraces
each new expression of "the new morality," finding in it some still finer expression of human liberation, or else one pits oneself against the stream of
"progressive" morality and clings to the old as steadfastly as possible, prefer-
ably in groups of the like-minded. These are both unfortunate and shallow
responses, and both should be resisted by serious Christians. In my opinion,
which is no doubt influenced by the fact that I belong to a liberal Christian
denomination, the liberal-radical response is far too often the shallower of
the two; for it fails to reckon with the ubiquitous reality of moral chaos, and
in the name of a misplaced and adolescent need to be thought *au courant*, it
endorses the latest popular alterations of the (scarcely existent!) moral code.
Conservative attempts to resist change are more justifiable wherever, to do
so, people must refuse popularity for the sake of integrity; but this perhaps
admirable refusal does not alleviate the problem of the inappropriateness of
attempts to reintroduce old forms of what has passed for Christian morality
in a post-Christendom society.

What is most unfortunate about the juxtaposition of these two approaches
and their increasing polarization in all of the historic Protestant churches as
well as Roman Catholicism is that they perpetuate a false understanding of
what the Christian ethic *is*. In identifying Christian ethics with a moral posture, the one liberal and malleable, the other conservative and unbending,
they further the impression that is already far too firmly fixed in the history
of Christendom, namely, that what Christians are called upon to obey "in
life and in death" (Barmen) is a moral posture, principle, or code. But that
is not what obedience means, Christianly understood. It is in fact the antithesis of what is intended by the term "discipleship."

---

13. Christopher Lasch, *The True and Only Heaven: Progress and Its Critics* (New York and
London: W. W. Norton, 1991), 33–34.

28.3. The Future as Enemy. "The most cunning and the strongest enemy is time, especially when it gathers itself for the attack and is called the future—for then it is like the mist which cannot be seen close at hand, but the farther away it is seen, the more terrible it seems."[14] Kierkegaard's words are more all-embracing today than when he wrote them. He was thinking in personal terms, but we hear such words as descriptive of the global situation, with its overwhelming and frighteningly interlacing problems. We sense that these problems have only begun to manifest their critical proportions, and in contemplating their unfolding we crouch in the shadows cast by their symptoms, hoping to avoid the full brunt of their "attack." Ironically and sadly, a people created by bright visions of the future now secretly suspects that the future is the enemy, and tries to ignore it or stave it off as long as possible. This, too, belongs to the context of our ethical deliberations today.

In the previous subsection, we concentrated chiefly on the challenges that come to Christian ethical concern from the side of personal life. If now, under the aegis of "future shock," we turn to social ethics, it is not because the future is lacking in shock value for individuals, nor ought this separation of subject matter be taken as a separation of reality. Individual life today is lived under the threat of a futureless future—a future in which it is not only likely that "I" shall have no part but in which it is at least possible that "we," humankind collectively, shall have no part. Individuals have always had to confront their own personal ending, but only in the past four or five decades have all thinking people been obliged to contemplate the ending of civilized life, or of the species, perhaps of the planet—namely (unlike apocalyptic scenarios ancient and modern), an ending not only cosmic and devastating but apparently lacking in purpose. Personal and social ethics here, as at every other point of observation, are inseparably intertwined. But the emphasis, where the "attack" of the future is concerned, must fall upon social ethics.

The great challenge that is put to Christianity (as to every other system of historical meaning) by the scope of this attack is whether Christian faith has the capacity both to absorb the impact of the threats under which earth and all of its creatures exist today, and to respond to these in ways that are consistent with the world-affirming faith we have claimed the Judeo-Christian tradition at its best to be. Even where open recognition of the threats to planetary survival is concerned, many would claim with some justification that the churches tend rather to shelter people from this awareness than to equip them for acknowledging and seeking to comprehend the problems associated with it. As for responding creatively and effectively to the cacophony of instabilities that hover on our near horizon, Christianity, even in its most sincere

---

14. Søren Kierkegaard, *The Gospel of Suffering,* trans. David Swenson and L. J. Swenson (Minneapolis: Augsburg Publishing House, 1948), 36.

endeavors, frequently gives more evidence of its complicity in the *problematique* than of its ability to "mend."[15]

That the critical character of global technological civilization will increase seems a conclusion that is now widely held. The following quotation from a document prepared for the centennial meetings of the Parliament of World Religions held in Chicago in 1993 is not untypical:

> If present beliefs and policies continue, the world in the 21st century will be more crowded, more polluted, less stable economically and ecologically, more vulnerable to violent disruption than the world we live in now . . . .
>
> For more than a billion desperately poor, the outlook for food and other necessities will be no better. For many it will be worse.[16]

It can be easy for the religious to give assurances and to issue ultimatums. The document quoted above goes on to affirm: "Life for most people on

---

15. The splendid endeavors of the World Council of Churches through its "Justice, Peace and Integrity of Creation" process, to which reference has been made throughout these volumes, were marred and perhaps rendered ineffectual by the inability of the Christians of the developed and developing worlds to agree even on the analysis of our global dilemma, to say nothing of engaging it in concert. (See my essay "The State of the Ark: Lessons from Seoul," in D. Premen Niles, *Between the Flood and the Rainbow* [Geneva: WCC Publications, 1992], 34–48.)

16. Quoted by Larry Rasmussen, "Current Trends, Permanent Questions" in *Christianity and Crisis* 53, no. 4 (April 12, 1993): 84. Almost any commentary on our civilization contains similar generalizations. They should of course be reinforced by as much concrete "data" as possible, but unless data is interpreted, it is little more than "part of the problem"—the problem, namely, of an overspecialized, fact-ridden intelligentsia incapable of saying what time it is! One of the best summaries of our global situation, in my view, is provided by Conor Cruise O'Brien in his 1994 Massey Lectures. In the excerpt that follows, O'Brien is quoting an earlier (1970) essay on Nietzsche, to whom he turns, in an ironic twist, at the end of the quotation: "The advanced world may well be like, and feel like, a closed and guarded palace, in a city gripped by the plague. There is another metaphor, developed by Andre Gide, one of the many powerful minds powerfully influenced by Nietzsche: This is the metaphor of the lifeboat, in a sea full of survivors of a shipwreck. The hands of survivors cling to the sides of the boat. But the boat has already as many passengers as it can carry. No more survivors can be accommodated, and if they gather and cling on, the boat will sink and all be drowned. The captain orders out the hatchets. The hands of the survivors are severed. The lifeboat and its passengers are saved.

"Something like this is the logic we apply, when we tighten our immigration laws, and in the general pattern of our relations with the so-called under-developed countries. . . . As this situation becomes more obvious it is likely to generate its own psychological and moral pressures. The traditional ethic will require larger and larger doses of its traditional built-in antidotes— the force of hypocrisy and cultivated inattention combined with a certain minimum of alms.

"But there will be minds, and probably some powerful minds among them, who will go in quest of a morality more appropriate to the needs of the situation and permitting, within the situation, both honesty and a good conscience. Such minds may well turn to Nietzsche, reading him, not in the gentle adaptations of Cold War scholarship, but for his bracing fierceness. There is much there for their comfort, not only in the general ethic, but also in specific applications. Nietzsche approves 'Annihilation of decaying races.' He also has this to say in *The Will to Power:* 'The great majority of men have no right to existence, but are a misfortune to higher men. I do not yet grant the failures (*den Missrathenen*) the right. There are also peoples that are failures (*missrathene Volker*)'" (*On the Eve of the Millennium* [Toronto: House of Anansi, 1994], 132–33).

Earth will be more precarious in the 21st century than it is now—*unless the faith traditions of the world lead the nations and peoples of the Earth to act decisively to alter current beliefs and policies.*"[17] Larry Rasmussen asks:

> What is to be done by "the faith traditions of the world" whether or not they answer the (wildly optimistic) call to "lead the nations and peoples of the Earth . . . to alter current beliefs and practices." For Christianity alone, the challenges are at least theological and pastoral. And monumental . . . . [18]

Not only are the major religions of the world torn by internal strife and still suspicious of one another, but nearly all of them contain conflicting beliefs that make it difficult for the world-affirming elements within them to achieve a hearing over racial, ethnic, gender-specific, and other narrowly conceived versions of belief.

In the case of Christianity, the barriers to an effective response to the challenges under discussion appear almost insurmountable: The influence of this faith tradition within the spheres of its former cultic hegemony is, as we have seen, greatly diminished. It is plagued by radically divergent attitudes toward this world, all the way from overly optimistic political theologies that are persuaded of their capacity to correct worldly injustice and establish the reign of peace and plenty, to otherworldly theologies that actually welcome the world's self-destructiveness and see in it a triumph of the divine will. Within the Protestant denominations that are the primary concern of this study, while minorities address themselves to specific issues of global survival, there is, as we have seen, a strong temptation throughout these churches to repress or ignore the problematic character of life today and to accentuate peace of mind. If such churches are to have any part in "altering current beliefs and policies," they will first have to be altered themselves. They will have to achieve a truth-orientation that is stronger than their apparently natural preference for comfort and the suppression of truth. Those who know these churches well are likely, in the face of such a prospect, to ask Jeremiah's question: "Can leopards change their spots?" (13:23).

Yet fatalism, although tempting in periods of decline, is not a Christian option. However improbable it may seem that middle-class Christianity in North America might renounce its well-practiced craft of providing insulation against the cold winds of the future, responsible Christians are commanded to think and to act as if change were actually possible.[19] Such determination is not the by-product of humanistic optimism, it is faith's response

---

17. Rasmussen, 84 (My italics.)
18. Ibid.
19. See Rosemary Radford Ruether, *To Change the World* (London: SCM, 1981).

to the reality of grace. It does not require rose-colored glasses. The challenges that are present at the level of both personal and social ethics, challenges whose depth is already manifested in contemporary theoretical reflection on the very possibility of ethics in a post-Christendom, postmodern world, must be faced squarely and without the dubious benefit of a priori religious assumptions concerning the ultimate victory of the good. The faith will be *confessed* in our ethical *praxis* only by those who have the courage to subject themselves unguardedly to the peculiar darkness of our own time and place and to trust that light enough will be given. For Protestant Christians who understood their own heritage, there have never been any "safety nets" (Grant).

For the theology of the cross begets not only an ecclesiology but also an ethic. That ethic does not require answers in advance of every problem, private or global. It does not rely on answers but on an Answerer—who carries us "whither we would not go": in this case, more deeply into the questions. Our task is now to inquire concerning the rudiments of that ethic.

29. Ethics as Discipleship

29.1. Foundations. What makes Christian ethics Christian? Challenges such as those we have discussed in the foregoing, combined with another contextual factor that we have noted earlier—the tendency of the North American churches to reflect rather than engage our society—prompt many Christians and others to wonder whether it is possible any longer to distinguish an explicitly Christian ethic. Perhaps Christianity is so thoroughly bound to the prescientific world that it is incapable of comprehending the kinds of problems that have emerged in late Western modernity. Perhaps its basic ethical principles are so vague and general as to be less than helpful in either personal or social ethics today. In that event, if Christians reflect the various mind-sets—conservative, liberal, radical—at work in our social context generally, it may be due to nothing more profound than their own incapacity for original thinking.

Jürgen Moltmann traces the ethical question to our deeper christological uncertainty:

> Is there such a thing as a specifically Christian ethic today? Does Christian faith involve a new life style? Can one know Christ at all without following him? In asking these questions we are not merely touching the fundamental nerve of Christian ethics. We are coming face to face with an unsolved problem of christology itself.[20]

---

20. Jürgen Moltmann, *The Way of Jesus Christ*, trans. Margaret Kohl (London: SCM, 1989; Minneapolis: Fortress Press, 1993), 116.

He acknowledges that "a number" of ethicists who identify themselves as Christians feel that it is impossible to derive an ethic that is explicitly Christian; hence that "Christians bring no greater insight to the solution of burning social and political problems than other members of society; consequently, all that is available to us is a common, natural or general human ethics, which Christians have to follow like other people."[21] If one follows the discussions of such important present-day concerns as environmental degradation, racial and gender conflict, sexuality, the crisis of Medicare and other social services, and so on, one is hard pressed, as we have noted previously, to discover any differences either of method or content between Christian and secular analysts.

> It is in fact true that the familiar patterns of Christian ethics have almost ceased to rest on any christological foundation. The ethics of natural law, the secular ethics of the Lutheran doctrine of the two kingdoms, the ethics of "orders"— whether it be the orders of creation, the orders of preservation, or the orders based on the covenant with Noah—are all conceived without any specific basis in christology. . . . [22]

But if Christian ethics do not have their foundation in what Christians believe concerning Jesus as the Christ, then not only Christian ethics but the core of the gospel is at stake: "If there is no specifically Christian ethic, then the acknowledgment of Christ is itself called in question; for then Jesus' message cannot have been ethically meant, in the sense of making a public claim."[23] In that case, the gospel becomes a purely "spiritual" message, apolitical, otherworldly in orientation, and perhaps apocalyptic in nature. This is indeed what many have made of it, but such an interpretation cannot satisfy those for whom the *sola scriptura* involves not only the Hebrew Bible but the ethical teaching of Jesus and his call to discipleship: "If any would come after me, let them deny themselves and take up their cross and follow me" (Matt. 16:24). "If [this] is taken seriously, then the confession of Jesus as the Christ also involves a practical discipleship that follows the messianic path his own life took; and that means an ethic which has to be made identifiably Christian."[24]

The ethic of discipleship is one of the most deeply submerged aspects of biblical faith. That this should be so is not surprising, for throughout the Christendom ages of the church, apart from minorities, Christians were obliged by the nature of their *modus operandi* with power to reflect the moral

---

21. Ibid.
22. Ibid., 117.
23. Ibid.
24. Ibid., 118.

preferences of their host societies. If Dietrich Bonhoeffer more than any other twentieth-century Christian thinker has recalled us to the ethics of discipleship, it is because in his context, given his kind of Christian devotion and seriousness, it was simply no longer possible to follow the rules of that "working arrangement." But Moltmann reminds us that the call to discipleship also belongs to the Reformation—especially to that so-called "radical" or "Left" wing, which had to discover the deepest biblical *radix* (roots) of membership in the "body of Christ" because it was denied membership in the establishment. As we cast about for a usable ethical past in the post-Christendom situation, we may find in that alternative expression of Reformation faith ethical guidance that points again to the christological heart of the faith of the early church:

> Ever since the Reformation, [the question of discipleship] has been the critical question put by Anabaptists, Mennonites and Moravians to the Protestant churches. As long as these churches followed Article 16 of the Augsburg Confession in maintaining the general responsibility of Christians for the world in civil "ordinances [which] are good works of God," the ethics of discipleship remained "a Cinderella of the Reformation." But in a "post-Christian" society, and especially in the deadly contradictions into which the modern social system has brought humanity and the earth, the special and identifiable Christian ethic of the discipleship of Jesus makes itself publicly evident. In this situation, faith in Christ can no longer be separated from ethics. The recognition that Christ alone is the Redeemer and Lord cannot be restricted to faith. It must take in the whole of life. . . . But this means that christology and christopraxis become one, so that a total, holistic knowledge of Christ puts its stamp not only on the mind and heart, but on the whole life in the community of Christ.[25]

This expresses quite precisely the point of view that has informed this trilogy from the outset.[26] With respect to Christian ethics, there is "no other foundation" (1 Cor. 3:11) than Jesus Christ. Although, as we have maintained throughout, Christians may and must make common cause with many others who "are not of this fold," the drumbeat to which they themselves march sounds from this source alone; and they are called to heed it, not as a matter of unquestioning and unreasoned obedience ("heteronomy," in Tillich's language); not merely as "law," but as gospel—that is, as possibility and hope neither effected nor glimpsed by human insight and inventiveness alone.

---

25. Ibid., 118–19.
26. See *Thinking the Faith,* in which the whole structure of the volume revolves around the relation between "the disciple community" and "the discipline"—namely, that of a thinking faith.

29.2. Gospel and Law. The Hebrew Bible does not begin with the Decalogue, nor does the newer Testament focus its attention upon the Sermon on the Mount. "The Bible is relentlessly ethical; but it is not a summary of ethics, however elevated. To drop in on the teachings of Jesus as if in their naked aphoristic simplicity they were self-evident, or even intelligible, is like dropping in on the coda of a Bach fugue having missed the polyphonic development."[27] Law is not and, according to biblical faith, cannot be foundational. An implication of the creation and fall sagas of Genesis that is usually overlooked is that the divine proscription concerning the tree that was in the midst of the garden has apparently no power whatsoever. It only detains the seeming inevitability of its abrogation long enough for an interesting exchange of ideas to occur. The point is that even in the imagined prelapsarian situation—even apart from the condition Christians call "original sin"—law is inadequate. The free creature seems almost bound to find in the proscription of the act the occasion to test the extent of its freedom—a commonplace experience of parents and teachers!

If even in the state of "dreaming innocence" (Tillich) law avails little or nothing by way of obedience to the divine intention, what must be said of the postlapsarian condition that is the condition of all historical life? What the Bible seems to answer, directly and indirectly, is that although law must certainly be given, it cannot create the conditions necessary to its fulfillment. Truly, it must be given: apart from the gift of the law, the will of the Creator, which is at the same time the essence of the creature, remains veiled from the sight of alienated humanity. God's intention for the creature must be made concrete; and if we follow the thread of the law in the continuity of the Testaments, what we find is surely that the concretization of God's will is more and more detailed and refined. This means both the elaboration of the divine will in an increasing number of laws affecting every aspect of life and (especially although not exclusively in the newer Testament) attention to the question of motivation. For implicit in the revelation and recording of the law of God is the insistence not only that it has implications for the whole of life, but that it entails right motives as well as right deeds. It is not enough to do what is commanded; one is obliged to do it "for the right reason."

And there is only one right reason: love. This is clear from the outset. When both Jesus and Paul summarize the whole intention of God in "the law" of love, they are by no means innovators. They only state explicitly what is assumed in the writings of the law-givers, historians, prophets, and wise ones of ancient Israel.

---

27. Joseph Sittler, "In the Light of Our Biblical Tradition," in The Religious Education Association, *What is the Nature of Man? Images of Man in Our American Culture* (Philadelphia: Christian Education Press, 1959), 190.

And just this is why law cannot be its own foundation. For love cannot be commanded—that is, it cannot be achieved in response to a command. Yet, because love of God, neighbor, and life itself is the condition and presupposition of true obedience, all human acts fall short of obedience—or, to say the same thing in other words, they fall short of the glory for which human life is intended. It would be possible, perhaps, to obey every one of the myriad commandments of the Scriptures with perfect attention to the letter of what is required and still to fail in relation to what God intends (1 Cor. 13). This is the implicit assumption of the law-givers themselves—for example, the Deuteronomist, who surrounded his codification of specific commandments with sermonic pieces whose function, among other things, is to say: these commandments are only the concretization of an inner vocation that is their presupposition.

The point is made with utter clarity in the incident of Jesus' encounter with the rich young ruler (Luke 18:18–30). In response to Jesus' recall of the Decalogue, the inquirer insists, "All these I have observed from my youth." While this may seem a boastful claim, the point of the incident is lost unless we accept the possibility of his having done just that. For the point is that "just that" is not enough. It is indeed the root of the man's frustration. Precisely his keen attention to the details of the Torah has alerted him to its internal implications, that is, to the demand for a frame of mind that no longer dwells upon such meticulous obedience but simply lives it, gladly and with a certain nonchalance. That he actually remembered his splendid obedience tells Jesus all he needs to know about this earnest human being, namely, that his great problem is his incapacity for self-forgetfulness. He will not have entered into life until his left hand no longer knows what his right hand is doing (Matt. 6:3)—that is, until he is immersed in love for "the other." Jesus names a condition through which, if he can manage it, the man may put himself in the way of being lost in love and love's service: "One thing you still lack. Sell all that you have and distribute to the poor . . . and come, follow me." (v. 22). But that condition, too, is law, and therefore it too must fail. We are not surprised (if we know our own ways!) when the inquirer, hearing this prescription, "became sad" and went away.

What this tells us is that Christian ethics do not begin with Christian ethics! Not only that, but it warns us that when we do try to begin with the ethical, we inevitably court either superficiality or sorrow. For nothing is shallower than moral precepts that concern themselves exclusively with externalities; and to go beyond the external and ask that the right deed be done for the right reason is to inflict upon the soul of the sensitive an unbearable burden. Perhaps such a burden may prove, in the end, the way to self-knowledge and thus to the recognition of that beggarly condition that is able to receive the grace that it cannot acquire or earn. Such was the "method" of Jesus, the teacher of the law;[28] and such has been the experience of many Christians, including Luther. But, "method" aside, what concerns us here is the relation between theology and ethics; and what we have seen so far is that the ethic is not and cannot be the point of departure, stage one. Theology is prior because it is descriptive of the foundation, that is, the ontological basis of all Christian prescription.

That priority is not to be construed to mean that theology is not first because it is theory, and, by implication, that the ethic is not *second* because it is practice. The recent language of praxis, although it may not warrant such misuse, has in many quarters created the impression that in the "old" systems of Christian thought the priority of dogmatic or systematic theology derived from its theoretical character as the ideational presupposition of all practical theology, including ethics; whereas, it is claimed, we must now think in terms of *praxis,* which refuses to divide theory and practice. Such a critique may be true of those systems of theology that really did proceed on the assumption that "systematic" theology was essentially theory; but not all the theology of the past indulged in such an assumption. The best of it never did! It was always a distortion of Christian theology when it was reduced to theory from which "applied theology" could be derived. The priority of theology over ethics has nothing to do with the distinction between theory and practice. Both aspects of the total theological task contain theoretical and practical elements, so far as this distinction is applicable to the discipline at all. The priority of theology over ethics has its only justification and necessity in the recognition of what we have claimed above: that the Christian ethic presupposes a *fundamentum* that cannot be contemplated adequately under the rubrics of ethics as it is usually understood; that to do any kind of justice to that upon which the house of ethics rests is to be carried, willy-nilly, into the whole subject matter of theology; or that (to use the shorthand of the Reformation) law presupposes gospel.[29]

Gospel, we have seen, is always *responsive;* that is, it is "good news" which contains within itself, and responds to, an existential awareness of the "bad news" that is present in the context in which it is uttered. For this reason we raised questions about the seemingly innocent inclusion of the definite article with the noun "gospel" (*the* gospel); for this suggests a static, unchanging articulation of the *euangellion* and so annuls both its contextual character and its basis in faith's relationship with its nonobjectifiable Subject. It is always *God's* Word, and therefore a Word that enters into dialogue and struggle

---

28. See *Professing the Faith*, §30.3, "Jesus as Prophetic Figure and Teacher," 408–13.

29. For an informative and helpful discussion of this subject, see Gerhard O. Forde, *The Law-Gospel Debate* (Minneapolis: Augsburg Publishing House, 1969).

with the "word" of those to whom it is addressed.[30] Given this contextual and relational understanding of gospel, it is certainly true that ethical reflection and concern impinges on theology all the way through and that *praxis* applies to the *whole* process. The gospel-foundation of Christian ethics will always therefore assume concrete forms, depending upon the ethical realities that have to be engaged.

In whatever form, however, one overriding thought will be predominant: namely, that *God the Spirit* is present, involved, and redemptive, bringing life out of death, creating something out of nothing, preventing the self-destruction that human creatures in their fallenness regularly court, mending the world. To say anything less than this would be to forget, disparage, or reduce to an abstraction the God who is self-revealed in Jesus Christ through the divine Spirit.

To claim that there is "no other foundation" for Christian ethics than Jesus Christ is to claim that this world-oriented God of love, in all the specificity of what love requires of lovers, is the rudimentary reality assumed by Christian ethics. As the late Paul Lehmann has stated it, ethics is being done "in a Christian context" when its basic presupposition is that God, namely the God revealed and redemptive in Jesus Christ, "is at work in the world." Lehmann believes that such a sense of the active presence of God in the world is of the essence of the theological ethics of the Reformation:

> The Protestant Reformation introduced into the Western cultural tradition a liberating grasp of the ways of God with men and thus also the possibility of ever fresh and experimental responses to the dynamics and humanizing character of the divine activity in the world. This meant for ethics the displacement of the prescriptive and absolute formulation of its claims by the contextual understanding of what God is doing in the world to make and to keep human life human.[31]

God's work in the world precedes ours. Our work, the subject of Christian ethics, can only be *a participation* in the divine work that is already well under way, and often in a manner least expected by us—like Luther's "hidden beneath its opposite."

How is God at work in the world? How can we recognize this work? Note Lehmann's answer: God is at work in the world "to make and to keep human life human." Perhaps if Professor Lehmann had been writing this work in

---

30. See Karl Barth, *The Word of God and the Word of Man,* trans. Douglas Horton (New York: Harper and Brothers, 1957).

31. Paul Lehmann, *Ethics in a Christian Context* (New York and Evanston: Harper & Row, 1963), 14.

1993 and not 1963, he would not have restricted God's prevenient work in the world to humanization but would have spoken in more broadly creational terms. Nevertheless, having asserted with the whole Judeo-Christian tradition that the human creature is central to the biblical story, both because of its unique vocation and its problematic nature, to speak of God's work as a "humanizing" work is not to fall into the trap of anthropocentrism but to engage the creation precisely at the point of its greatest vulnerability and its greatest potentiality. The assumption of the tradition is this: that if human beings are "truly human," human as God intends, the whole of creation will be more truly creaturely. Understood in this way, I find no better language for expressing the goal of God's work in the world than Lehmann's.

If one asks, as of course one must, what precisely "human" means in this usage, one notices that Lehmann refrains from definition. In her newly published study of this important and much too neglected American theologian and ethicist, Nancy J. Duff notes that Lehmann did not find it necessary to define precisely what he meant by "human"; he thought it self-evident.[32] It seems obvious that Paul Lehmann, the friend of Bonhoeffer, assumed what classical Protestant anthropology has characteristically believed, namely, that "human" must be defined by *that* humanity that God "puts forth" in the man, Jesus, called by faith the Christ. Here, as Chalcedon in its own way affirmed—here is "authentic humanity" (*vere homo*): "Behold, the man!" (John 19:5). The law and the prophets, Christians believe, all testify to that *kind* of humanity and therefore, at least in this respect, they all testify to the man, Jesus of Nazareth. Jesus' humanity is there, so to speak, before Jesus was there; it was "before Abraham was" (John 8:58); for it was nothing more, and nothing less, than the very humanity that the Creator had in mind before creation itself.

And now this humanity, lived by Jesus, is being offered us as gift. It is not only that Jesus *exemplifies* it—a favorite Liberal teaching—it is that having lived it, fulfilled its high intent, and "more" (Romans 5), this very humanity of the *vere homo* is being offered freely to those with whom Jesus identified and identifies himself, the human species as a whole. If Jesus is regarded only as a model or paradigm of the new humanity ("new creaturehood" [2 Cor. 5:17]), this does not go beyond the condition of law; in fact, it only makes the law more stringent by rendering "essential humanity" an ideal before which our "existential humanity" can only cower. The humanity of Jesus is therefore to be seen, not as a pattern to which we must attempt to conform, but as a gift that we are permitted to share, a "new creaturehood" into which we are graciously beckoned.

---

32. Nancy J. Duff, *Humanization and the Politics of God: The Koinonia Ethics of Paul Lehmann* (Grand Rapids: Wm. B. Eerdmans, 1992), 11.

Christian ethics begins just here—and it returns to this same foundation continuously. Therefore what dominates in this ethical tradition is not "thou shalt" but "thou art": Thou art the recipient of a new identity. Thou art forgiven and set upon a new path. Thou art no longer just thine own past, the image thou hast created by thy deeds, words and thoughts, the reputation thou hast acquired among thy neighbors and acquaintances, the possibilities thou hast entertained as such a one. Thou art befriended, liberated from the prisonhouse of thine own and thy neighbor's making;[33] thou art provided with spiritual food and clothing thou didst not possess, given a new family, new comrades, new resources. Thou art loved!

But not thou alone! The whole creation is loved. The *cosmos* in its totality is loved. And this love is effectual: the world is being changed by it. Its transformation may seem slow—the mere rumor of change! Do not be deceived by this. Life is being created over against death every day, every moment. Even if you see only death, you may trust that life is victorious over it.[34] Yes, death itself, together with the suffering that attends it, you may consider evidence of what is being born.[35]

We have resorted to direct address—to the sermonic, even. But this is essential. For the legalism and moralism that attends the whole discussion of Christian ethics in North America must be countered. The "thou shalt"/ "thou shalt not" must be put in its place, and its place is *after* the "thou art." So long as Christian moral teaching is thought to mean prescription, exhortation, nagging, wheedling, and the like it will be wholly misconceived. Christians perform no greater disservice in the world than when, in their

---

33. Nancy Duff notes that Lehmann was criticized by James Cone for not carrying his christological ethics to the "logical conclusion" of liberation of the oppressed. In response to Cone, Lehmann proposes that he means by "humanization" essentially the same thing that Cone means by "liberation." "While Lehmann does speak to the specifics of oppression, he does not *begin* with reference to a specific oppressed community. Furthermore, his poetic phrases sometimes obscure rather than clarify the specific references demanded by Cone" (Duff, *Humanization and the Politics of God*, 32–33.)

Without wishing to enter this debate in a major way, I would nevertheless suggest that Lehmann's reluctance simply to equate "humanization" with "liberation" was entirely justified. It is also contextually appropriate for James Cone to equate the two terms, or nearly so. But Lehmann was not writing for an oppressed minority! The trouble with focusing the process of humanization too explicitly is that it then limits the application of this quite necessary kind of language. For oppressed people, humanization means liberation (although it will, it is to be hoped, mean other things as well); but for oppressors, becoming human will require having to pass through a painful stage of judgment and self-knowledge before there can be any meaningful liberation!

34. The late William Stringfellow, one of the few North Americans who early saw the fate of cultural Protestantism, and who understood at a rudimentary as well as highly political level of consciousness the biblical dialectic of death and life, should be read in conjunction with this affirmation. See his *My People Is the Enemy: An Autobiographical Polemic* (New York: Doubleday, Anchor Books, 1964), esp. 30f., 150f.

35. See Rom. 8:18ff.; 2 Cor. 1; Phil. 3:10; Col. 1:24; Heb. 2; 1 Pet. 1, 4, 5, etc.

speech and, perhaps, in their whole bearing, they convey nothing but the imperative mood! It is said of John Calvin that his classmates named the young Calvin, brilliant Latinist and student of jurisprudence, "the accusative case."[36] Whether or not that is true, or fair, it cannot be denied that the Calvin*ism* that has been so influencial in the history of this continent acquired for itself a lasting reputation for a very dour and constricting version of morality.[37] Nor can it be denied that the liberalism that came as a reaction to Calvinism and other "thou shalt not" articulations of Christian morality did little to offset the fundamentally exhortational character of Christian preaching and teaching. It does not matter very much whether moralism is old or new, puritanical, sentimental, or "swinging": moralism is moralism. What the world is waiting to hear is not whether it should or not do this or that, but whether anything of significance has been done to it and for it, to alter the pathos or perhaps the tragedy of its condition. If there is no indicative, the imperatives that there are, whether negative or positive, will *always* be oppressive. Ultimately they will also be futile. If there is no gospel, the laws there are will be shallow, or they will lead to despair. The Christian ethic is a kerygmatic ethic: "Behold, I am making all things new" (Rev. 21:5)—beginning with you, who hear this.

29.3. "Follow Me."

> And passing along by the Sea of Galilee, he saw Simon and Andrew the brother of Simon casting a net in the sea; for they were fishermen. And Jesus said to them, "Follow me and I will make you become fishers of men." And immediately they left their nets and followed him. And going on a little farther, he saw James the son of Zebedee and John his brother. . . .
>
> (Mark 1:16f.)

There is something profoundly moving about the opening chapters of the Gospels, particularly of the three Synoptics. Dietrich Bonhoeffer captured this for a generation in his writings, especially *The Cost of Discipleship.* What I am referring to, however, is older than Bonhoeffer's unique exposition of it

---

36. Harry Emerson Fosdick, *Great Voices of the Reformation* (New York: Random House, 1952), 195. (Fosdick also notes, however, that Calvin has been recognized as "the only gentleman among the Reformers" [ibid.].)

37. Jonathan Edwards, the leading American theologian of the eighteenth century and one of the few North American Christian thinkers to be known throughout the Christian world, was dismissed from his parish in Northampton because his strict moral code was a source of humiliation and bitterness to his parishoners. (See Arthur Cushman McGiffer, Jr., *Jonathan Edwards* [New York and London: Harper and Brothers, 1932].)

under the dramatic circumstances of the third decade of this century.[38] It can be discovered in the devotional writings of some of the eighteenth-century pietists (Zinzendorf), in the chorales and prayers of the Reformation and post-Reformation period, in late medieval mysticism—indeed, throughout the history of Christianity. Reading these accounts of Jesus' call of his disciples, brief and almost matter-of-fact as they are, Christians throughout the ages have been touched and inspired—and perhaps not only Christians.

The reason for this is not to be construed as mere sentimentality, despite the fact that some of the pietistic language of the eighteenth century (and even of Bonhoeffer's earlier works) might lead contemporary readers to such a conclusion. The account of Christ's calling of his original disciples strikes a responsive chord in Christians because it echoes their own sense of "call." It reinforces for them the belief, which is never without its accompanying doubt, that the ultimate explanation of their attempts to pursue the Christian "way" is to be located, not in their own idealism, or religious convention, or peer pressure, or any other source than the fact that they, too, have been called by Jesus Christ to be his followers.

The ethics of discipleship are based upon that call, and upon the relationship that is initiated by it. They are in that sense not primarily "ethics," if by that term one means a code, a series of commandments, or the articulation of norms or principles or guidelines of human behavior. Not even the Sermon on the Mount, so revered (and often so sentimentalized!) by liberal piety, can be designated "the Christian ethic." Together with the Decalogue and the numerous imperatives of both scriptural Testaments, the Sermon on the Mount ought certainly to be honored as "a lamp unto my feet." (Ps. 119:105)—"law" in that sense, namely, as that which provides enough direction to keep one from falling into total moral confusion, enough light to stumble through the darkness. To those biblical sources some might wish to add "natural law," although this has not generally been appealing to Protestants.[39] But whatever explicit ethical directives may be and are available to Christians in scriptural and other traditional sources, the *foundational* as-

---

38. Bonhoeffer's *Nachfolge* was first published in 1937. The first English (abridged) edition, *The Cost of Discipleship,* did not appear until 1948.

39. Natural law, when used in theological discourse, refers to the law believed to be implanted in the human creature by the Creator and accessible to human understanding through the usual processes of reason. Its advocates have found in Romans 2:4 (where Paul speaks of the Gentiles having the law "written in their hearts"), a scriptural warranty for the concept, although as such it predates Christianity (especially in Stoicism). Classical Protestantism questioned natural law, as it questioned "natural theology," because it was thought to minimize the radical character of sin. For the modern—and even more the postmodern—mentality, it raises the question, "'natural' for whom?" Moral assumptions identified as "natural" on account of long usage within Western Christendom are not necessarily compatible with beliefs and practices considered "natural" in other cultures and civilizations. The natural law tradition ought not to be disdained or ignored by Christians; but contemporary Christians of every ecclesiastical

sumption of the ethics of discipleship is the relationship of the believer and the believing community with Jesus Christ. When in this tradition we employ the term "obedience" (a favorite word of Reformation theology), it is understood that the object of Christian ethical obedience is not, in fact, an object, but a living subject. One is obedient, not to a predetermined set of rules, but to "the Lord," "the Good Shepherd," "the living Spirit" who "proceedeth from the Father and the Son" (Nicene Creed). The various scriptural and traditional testimonies to what such obedience is likely to mean concretely are by no means to be set aside; yet they are not the *object* of obedience. One does not obey "the Ten Commandments," one obeys the Giver of the Ten Commandments. One does not obey the Sermon on the Mount, one obeys the One who taught it. And *if* one obeys that One, one should not be surprised to hear him saying to his disciples still today, "You have heard it said. . . . But I say unto you. . . ."

Three implications of this understanding of the christological foundations of Christian ethics need to be made explicit. *First,* these foundations make it clear that what has been claimed heretofore concerning all the basic concepts of this faith-tradition must also be claimed for Christian ethics as a whole, namely, a *relational* frame of reference. It is the disciple community's relationship with Jesus Christ that is presupposed in all Christian ethical discourse, and, when this is not understood, or when it is assumed to be a merely pious or poetic way of speaking, then quite naturally Christian ethics devolves into rules and regulations and quasi philosophic sophistry. For what is left when this relationship is overlooked or reduced to symbolic dimensions is little more than yet another "list" of moral precepts, which may or may not be unique, superior, or different from other "lists" that are available. This is not to minimize the genius of the Decalogue or the Sermon on the Mount or any of the other specific imperatives of the Scriptures. If not in general, certainly in many instances, the biblical injunctions (for example, "Love your enemies") may be shown to be wonderfully enlightened, compassionate, and wise. But although they function for faith as guides ("a lamp"), both providing specific positive direction and eliminating questionable alternatives, they are not to be substituted for the reality of the Presence whom we acknowledge as their source.

Second, the mystery and "hiddenness"[40] of that Presence and, consequently, of the life of discipleship that assumes that Presence, ought not to be turned into a mystique, a transworldly and suprahuman spirituality—in

---

background must surely recognize the *faith* dimension that it assumes, and therefore question the premodern tendency to distinguish sharply between "natural" and "revealed" law.

40. See Dietrich Bonhoeffer, *The Cost of Discipleship,* trans. R. H. Fuller with some revision by Irmgard Booth (London: SCM, 1959), chap. 16, "The Hiddenness of the Devout Life," 151–61.

short, a "religious" phenomenon. There is a very *human* dimension in the biblical view of discipleship. Real mystery and real "hiddenness" are there, but it is not the kind of mystery that simply bypasses human understanding and it is not the kind of hiddenness that bears no resemblance to ordinary experience.

Consider the call of the original disciples. It is inconceivable that Jesus was able through sheer hypnotic or charismatic power to wrest these working men away from their stations, their families and community, their routine. To attribute all this to his "divinity" is not only to step outside the parameters of biblical faith and to court pagan supernaturalism; it is, more importantly, to ignore the human reality that the Scriptures (and not the Scriptures only) assume: namely, the reality of human longing—of "waiting" (Weil)—for precisely such a "call." Humanity, as the best traditions of this faith have always understood, is not only in flight from God; it is also anxiously and hopefully waiting to be overtaken by God. That is what Augustine intended by his famous *cor inquietum*—the "restless heart," created "for Thyself," and full of unquietness until it again "reposes in Thee."

This anthropological assumption of the ethics of discipleship is decisive. If those persons named in the Markan pericope at the beginning of this subsection—the four fisherman brothers, the tax collector, and the others—did in fact leave their occupations and "follow," the reason is not to be found only in Jesus' extraordinary charisma but also in the waiting and longing that, as human beings, they too experienced in the depths of their beings. What is "natural" to human experience, I should say, is not so much (natural) "law" as it is the awareness—perhaps, in Augustinian terms, the "memory"—of a relationship that has been broken, a home that has been abandoned (the prodigal son), a destiny that has been forfeited in the name of what was imagined freedom. The Christ's "call to discipleship" is nothing more and nothing less than an invitation to resume that relationship, to recover that sense of "home," to reclaim the freedom that belonged to that destiny.[41]

Third, discipleship belongs to the tradition of the Bible's "covenant theology."[42] As we have seen in our discussion of that tradition, (*a*) it expresses a relationship in which (to call upon the terms just employed) human freedom and destiny are held in a creative tension, and (*b*) in which human beings, as covenant partners, are given a considerable measure of worldly responsibility.

Correspondingly, (*a*) with respect to human freedom and destiny, the discipleship upon which the Christian ethic is founded eschews both an ethic of absolute individual or corporate freedom, understood in the modern sense,

---

41. See M. C. D'Arcy, *The Mind and Heart of Love* (London: Faber and Faber, 1954).
42. See chap. 5, §20.

and an ethic of obedience conceived as the imposition of the will of Another (God). Again, Paul Tillich's categories are useful. The relationship called discipleship is not an "autonomous" one: that is, I do not volunteer to follow Jesus Christ, nor do I arbitrarily determine what following Jesus Christ means. Again, this relationship is not a "heteronomous" one: that is, I am not simply *caused* to follow, without any choice in the matter, nor am I told what following from day to day means concretely. The relationship, rather, is a "theonomous" one: that is, one in which what is asked of me by the Other corresponds with what I myself, at the deepest level of my being, will or wish to will. Here, so to speak, freedom and destiny meet, recognize, and embrace each other. This is not a theoretical resolution of these polar qualities of life. Theoretically, they cannot be resolved but remain in perpetual tension. Discipleship defines a practical resolution, that is, a resolution that occurs within this particular relationship. In the encounter with the Christ, I know that my real freedom is inseparable from my becoming servant (even *doulos*—slave!) to One "whose service is perfect freedom." What Jesus Christ asks of me (obedience) is nothing other than that which, being liberated by his Spirit from "bondage" (Luther) to a capricious will and false gods, I may freely desire.

This has decisive implications for Christian ethics. Voluntaristic ("autonomous") conceptions of what discipleship means always court legalistic versions of Christian morality, for they are the ethical side of soteriologies of self-salvation: "I have determined to follow Jesus Christ; therefore I am doing these good works." Deterministic ("heteronomous") conceptions of what discipleship means, on the other hand, equate divine grace with a nonrelational conception of destiny (really, fate) and overlook the biblical affirmation of human potentiality for responsible creaturehood as God's covenant partner (see below): "God has apprehended me and now acts through me in the performance of these good works." A "theonomous" understanding of disciplesip results in an ethic that combines recognition of the "otherness" of what is required of one with openness to change and the possibility of making it one's own: "I trust this Other who calls, and therefore I seek to obey even when what seems to be required of me does not immediately correspond with my own desires." It is the relationship with Jesus Christ that enables this approach and overcomes the tensions that are in it. In this relationship, as in the covenant concept generally, the disciple is not the initiating partner, and therefore "following" does entail adherence to the will of Another; but because the relationship is one of trust (faith) the disciple is disposed to an obedience in the performance of which real freedom may be experienced. Bonhoeffer expresses this quite precisely in the following excerpt from his *Ethics:*

432

The man [*sic*] who acts in the freedom of his own most personal responsibility is precisely the man who sees his action finally committed to the guidance of God. The free deed knows itself in the end as the deed of God; the decision knows itself as guidance; the free venture knows itself as divine necessity. It is the free abandonment of knowledge of his own good that a man performs the good of God.[43]

(*b*) As is true of covenant theology generally, discipleship entails a strong sense of human responsibility. The covenant partner—the disciple, the disciple community—is not passive. Obedience, far from being a blind adherence to prescribed commandments, entails imagination, ingenuity, involvement. It is not understood that this human activity is the ultimately decisive thing: God is not wholly dependent upon us! Yet faith in God's providential care does not give way to presumption and inaction: faith (as we have heard from St. James!) issues in "good works."

This, it will be recalled, is an important aspect of Irving Greenberg's advice to Christianity in its "second stage," its post-Christendom phase: "In this stage, Christianity would make the move from being out of history to taking power, i.e. taking part in the struggle to exercise power to advance redemption." It would manifest "a greater 'worldliness' in [its] holiness."[44] Bonhoeffer too spoke of the Christian's "responsibility for history."[45] Christian discipleship is after all a matter of "following" One who entered into the depths of the world's suffering and misery, with the object of overcoming it "from within." And in our discussion of "the marks of the Church"[46] we have affirmed, with Luther, that "the mark of the holy cross" is the church's one indispensable mark. In its post-Christendom phase, the disciple community is being liberated from the service of powerful empires and the pursuit of its own worldly power and success to participate in *this* kind of "responsibility for history." This leads us to the final consideration of the chapter.

30. The Ethics of a Prophetic Minority

30.1. The Need for an Independent Ethic. The question to be addressed here was announced at the outset in this way: How can the disciple community live faithfully in a post-Christendom world? If the ethic appropriate to Christianity is one of discipleship, and therefore one that is dependent upon the

---

43. Dietrich Bonhoeffer, *Ethics*, ed. Eberhard Bethge, trans. Neville Horton Smith (London: SCM, 1955), 218.
44. See chap. 4, §14.2.
45. Ibid.
46. Chap. 2, §4.7.

community's relationship with Jesus Christ, does this not suggest a certain *independence* of the social context in which the disciple community finds itself? And, in that case, how is the disciple community to exercise the "worldly responsibility" to which we have just referred?

We may begin to address these questions, indirectly at first, by considering a statement that was made about the churches of North America over sixty years ago. The opening sentence of Reinhold Niebuhr's *An Interpretation of Christian Ethics* reads:

> Protestant Christianity in America is, unfortunately, unduly dependent upon the very culture of modernity, the disintegration of which would offer a more independent religion a unique opportunity.[47]

This statement seems to me as true today as when it was written. It is true both in what it says about modernity, whose "disintegration" is even more visible now than it was in the 1930s, and in what it claims about the "unfortunate" dependency status of the mainline Protestant churches. While the latter are in some cases reduced by comparison with their size and influence at the time when Niebuhr wrote, they still (with important exceptions) cling to the culture with which they have been identified, providing for it what it seems to demand; therefore they are still ill-equipped to rise to the "unique opportunity" for wisdom and service that is present in the "disintegration" of that culture.

Niebuhr's further breakdown of the problematic character of the churches in this context requires only a little updating. He distinguishes two types of ecclesiastical failure, that of "orthodox Christianity" (that is, the churches that attempt to uphold what they take to be the fundamental teachings of classical Protestantism), and that of "Christian liberalism." The former, he avers, may have preserved a more independent identity, but it is so remote from the modern world that it provides no existential challenge or alternative to ailing modernity:

> Orthodox Christianity, with its insights and perspectives in many ways superior to those of liberalism, cannot come to the aid of modern man [*sic*] because its religious truths are still imbedded in an outmoded science and its morality is expressed in dogmatic and authoritarian moral codes. It tries vainly to meet the social perplexities of a complex civilization with irrelevant precepts, deriving their authority from their—sometimes quite fortuitous—inclusion in a sacred canon. It concerns itself with the violation of Sabbatarian prohibitions

---

47. Reinhold Niebuhr, *An Interpretation of Christian Ethics* (New York: Meridian Books [Living Age Books], 1956), 13. (This work was initially published by Harper and Brothers of New York and London in 1935.)

or puritanical precepts, and insights, figuratively, on tithing "mint, anise and cummin," preserving the minutae of social moral standards which may once have had legitimate or accidental sanctity, but which have . . . now lost both religious and moral meaning.[48]

Today, we might want to add that, remarkably enough, a higher percentage of Americans than could have been predicted in 1935 now turns to this outmoded "orthodoxy" (or its less sophisticated offspring) for guidance and refuge. This, however, does not diminish Niebuhr's judgment of its essential irrelevancy to the problems thrown up by an increasingly desperate modernity. It only shows the lengths to which the North American public will go to avoid the historical questioning of its social and political project and its foundational dream.

Niebuhr was predictably harder on liberalism than on orthodoxy, and his castigation of "Protestantism" is obviously intended primarily for liberal ears. "The religion and ethics of the liberal church," he writes, "is dominated by the desire to prove to its generation that it does not share the anachronistic ethics or believe the incredible myths of orthodox religion."

Its energy for some decades has been devoted to the task of proving religion and science compatible, a purpose which it has sought to fulfil by disavowing the more incredible portion of its religious heritage and clothing the remainder in terms acceptable to "the modern mind." It has discovered rather belatedly that this same modern mind, which only yesterday seemed to be the final arbiter of truth, beauty, and goodness, is in a sad state of confusion today, amid the debris of the shattered temple of its dreams and hopes. In adjusting itself to the characteristic credos and prejudices of modernity, the liberal church has been in constant danger of obscuring what is distinctive in Christian morality. Sometimes it fell to the level of merely clothing the naturalistic philosophy and the utilitarian ethics of modernity with pious phrases.[49]

Obviously, certain qualifications would have to be made to bring this part of the analysis up to date, although the basic point—the liberal quest for proximity to whatever seems *au courant*—is still eminently true. The liberalism and modernism of the earlier part of this century were attuned to the natural sciences in a way that is not on the whole the case today. Partly because liberalism did in some sense make its case in the dialogue with the sciences; partly because science itself, as we have suggested before, has been obliged to acquire a new modesty concerning its own capabilities and a new curiosity about what would have been considered almost "metaphysical"

---

48. Ibid., 14.
49. Ibid., 15.

questions sixty years ago; partly also because science no longer competes so openly with religion as a mode of salvation, but is perceived by the postmodern mind more ambiguously than by the modern; and partly because the center of dialogue has shifted to other arenas of concern, liberal Christianity now spends far less of its energy making itself amenable to the physical sciences. Indeed, that particular "interest" may now be said to have been taken over by some of the more conservative groupings within the churches.

That liberalism is marvelously sensitive to societal trends, however, is still its chief mark of identification. Today, that to which liberal Christianity seeks to accommodate the faith is represented more by some of the discourse of the social sciences than by the natural sciences. While it is difficult actually to name the worldview to which the liberal Christian spirit feels itself apologetically drawn ("postmodernity" is as yet too amorphous a concept), and while the attempt on the part of liberal *cum* radical elements in the churches to achieve proximity to this elusive phenomenon therefore assumes a variety of forms, it is clear that our "world" is shifting to some new "paradigm"; and the various and perhaps disparate components that seem to be involved in the latter (multiculturalism, religious pluralism, gender equality, an indefinite variety of acceptable sexual and familial patterns, nature-spirituality, and so on) evoke from the liberal spirit that is present in all of the once-mainline churches a predictable attempt to be part of the shift.

This attempt ought not to be disdained—and certainly not in the manner in which it is disdained by the inheritors of the "orthodoxy" of which Niebuhr wrote. There is, as we have insisted throughout this series, an *apologetic* dimension in responsible Christian faith and thought, and therefore all serious theology is called to aid and encourage those in the churches who endeavor to engage whatever is "blowing in the wind." Moreover, many of the changes that are evidently aspects of the emerging *Weltanschauung* (worldview) are, from a Christian standpoint, commendable; for they are humanly liberating, and far more deserving of the church's endorsement and cooperation than were many of the views, attitudes, and practices that they are replacing. For instance, it is far better, Christianly conceived, that homosexual persons should be received in both society and church as fully human beings, deserving of the same respect, the same social and legal benefits, the same job opportunities, and so on, as heterosexual persons—better, certainly, than the kind of prejudice and ostracization that has been practiced in both church and society heretofore.

The critical question about Christian liberalism must not, therefore, be raised at that level of discussion. Niebuhr would have said the same thing of the liberalism that he criticized: its morality was far more compassionate, and therefore closer to the One who said, "But I say unto you . . . ," than that of the older orthodoxies. Therefore he did not take liberalism to task for its affirmation of the human project (in that instance, the natural sciences) but for another reason: it seemed not to have anything of its own to bring to the dialogue with science. It was so *dependent* upon the culture that it wanted to address, or, to state it the other way around, so lacking in any sort of *independent* perspective, that it could only affirm its culture—a culture that, in the meantime, had begun to experience needs that it had not anticipated and problems that it had relegated to the Dark Ages!

This question must still be asked of the liberal spirit in the churches—a spirit that today, despising precisely the adjective "liberal," more often wishes itself to be thought "radical" (as some of the old liberals did also!). While involvement in the transforming influences and trends within society is to be expected and lauded, responsible theology must ask: What do Christians bring with them to this involvement? Do they imagine that their involvement itself is all that they are required to bring? Do they assume that the role of Christian faith and confession in the world is just to endorse what seems the latest thing—to assume that it is "the will of God," especially if it can be related to something "liberating" or "humanizing" or "fulfilling?"

That is what the old liberals thought, too. But, as Niebuhr points out, the culture that they were so happy to affirm (represented by the natural sciences, in that context) was already in a very bad state; and therefore liberal Christian dependence upon that same culture meant that it had nothing to offer the culture in its growing decadence and need. This failure, which was dismal, ought not to be forgotten! It is instructive for our learning.

What needs critical investigation today is not the alignment of Christian faith with various human quests for justice, liberation, equality, harmony, and similar ends. It should be taken as axiomatic that Christians *would* be involved in such quests. What has to be asked, rather, is why there is so little probing, so little critical vigilance, so little originality in the Christian endorsement of movements and trends associated with these goals. In Niebuhr's terms, why is there still so little evidence of *an independent Christian ethic*?

Let me exemplify this concern by considering three areas of contemporary life in which Christians are much involved. In doing so, I am well aware of the fact that in each of these areas there are individuals who *are* concerned that Christians should bring to these considerations something like an "independent" ethical perspective. I shall refer to some of these individuals. But I am also conscious of the fact that *in the churches* many of those who take up the causes in question are for all intents and purposes innocent of any specifically faith-based understanding of them and therefore tend to be driven by the trends themselves, uncritically identifying not only the end result of their actions but also their motivation for acting as "Christian," and depriving those with whom they associate in these causes of any depth and insight that might be brought to them from the posture of Christ's discipleship.

a. Many Christians today rightly espouse feminism. The liberation of women from debilitating and humiliating stereotypes, many of them propagated and perpetuated by Christendom, some of them emanating from the sacred writings of Israel and the church, is long past due. It is not only women who benefit from the work of feminists; men, too, and the society at large, need to be and are being significantly altered by the recognition of the patriarchal and androcentric assumptions and practices still operative in our civilization. Some of the results of the feminist critique have already changed the way we think about reality.

Many of these changes are such that informed Christians can only be grateful for them. The Christian tradition at its core, as distinct from Christendom's *use* of it, has affirmed and must affirm the full and equal humanity of women, who, contrary to much of the thinking of the church, are as truly *imago Dei* as are men. Moreover, as reference to the *imago* reminds us, the feminist critique has helped to restore the *relational* understanding of human existence and all existence, which throughout this series we have seen to be the primary assumption of the Bible's "ontology of communion." [50]

Christian feminism has been instrumental not only in introducing biblical, historical, and theological insights into the wider feminist discussion, but in bringing to bear upon the churches a new critical vigilance in relation to beliefs and practices that, while upholding certain well-established ecclesiastical conventions, in fact contradict the better wisdom of the tradition (for example, hierarchic, male-dominated structures of authority). All of the once-mainline Protestant churches today, to speak only of that sector, have been significantly transformed by this testimony, and it is obvious that the transformation will be and ought to be advanced.

As with all such movements of change, however, there is a tendency also of this movement to acquire its own momentum and its own internal rationale. This is inevitable and perhaps necessary. For Christians, however, it presents a certain quandary. For, as we have been arguing, Christian discipleship entails primary obedience to Jesus Christ; and it must always be asked whether the momentum and rationale of a transforming movement, any movement, when it is at work among Christians, is compatible with that primary allegiance, or whether Christian thinking, professing, and confessing of the faith is being replaced or displaced by the internal dynamics of the movement in question.

It is obvious enough to those who read theology and follow the deliberations of ecclesiastical councils that many Christian feminists today are themselves concerned precisely about this question. In the churches, where, in any case, as we have seen, there is a tendency to *reflect* rather than to *engage* our

---

50. See *Professing the Faith*, 213ff., 266ff., etc.

society, feminism, like some of the other "causes" of the present, can become a particular attraction for the liberal *cum* radical elements that seek to be on the forefront of what is or appears *au courant*. The danger implicit in this is the one that Niebuhr identified in the material cited earlier: that in the process of identifying with "the modern mind," Christians may lose touch with their own roots and, in the last analysis, bring little or nothing of their own to the dialogue of which they have striven to be part.

But Christian feminists *do* have something to bring to this dialogue and movement: they have, for instance, a theological heritage of mutuality based on the love of God in Jesus Christ for all creatures, regardless of race, class, gender, and all other distinctions; they have an ecclesiology in which "there is neither Jew nor Greek, there is neither slave nor free, there is neither male nor female; for you are all one in Jesus Christ" (Gal. 3:28); they have a hamartiology that, without dissolving into mere generalities, nonetheless refuses to indulge in easy distinctions between the good and the evil, the righteous and the unrighteous, the sinners and the sinned against; they have a "discipleship of equals" (Schüssler Fiorenza) that, over against sloganized and one-sided versions of both male and female preeminence, posits that the congregation is a sphere of human communality in which "dividing walls of hostility" are being overcome and ancient rivalries and suspicions laid to rest, and in which women and men together participate in a mission that transcends both sexes: the preservation and enhancement of all life.[51]

Such traditions as these contribute to an "independent Christian ethic" that can only enrich the necessary quest for human dignity and equality that is being undertaken today by persons and communities representative of many different perspectives and concerns.

b. During this century, particularly since the end of World War II, many Christians have understood as never before the necessity of overcoming racism, ethnocentrism, and jingoistic forms of nationalism. Partly because the two world wars provided the world with such terrifying displays of the violence that comes of these forms of human *hubris,* the struggle to end its most blatant expressions has been more successful on this continent than many would have predicted at the outset of the century. Christians have joined in

---

51. Writing of the "critical reconstruction of women's historical oppression within patriarchal biblical religion and community," Elisabeth Schüssler Fiorenza notes: "Such a historical reconstruction and theological revisioning is inspired not only by scholarly theoretical goals but . . . it is concerned . . . with changing the social reality of the Christian churches in which the religious oppression and eradication of women takes its specific historical patriarchal forms. In the last analysis, such a project is not just geared toward the liberation of women but also toward the emancipation of the Christian community from patriarchal structures and androcentric mind-sets so that the gospel can become again a 'power for the salvation' of women as well as men" (*In Memory of Her*, 30–31).

this struggle, and have often been at the forefront of campaigns against racial prejudice, economic and other forms of the subjugation of minorities, segregation of schools and other publicly funded agencies and services, and the like. They have helped to deconstruct and reconstruct the history of this continent in terms of its discovery by the white peoples of Europe, the cultures and histories of indigenous peoples, slavery and the African American experience, and many other aspects of a story that was told, heretofore, by "the winners."

Surely all Christians can be grateful for the fact that many of those involved in this struggle were Christians—persons whose faith was the primary motivation for their involvement and whose theological understanding informed their whole approach, including the refusal of most of them to resort to violence.

Yet here too it is necessary to realize that movements acquire their own momentum and evolve their own internal rationale. They also contain dimensions that can appeal to many—sometimes for less than noble, wise, or humane reasons. Many of the Christians who have been attracted to such movements have had little understanding of the profound struggles of mind and spirit that inspired a person such as the Rev. Martin Luther King Jr. Because of the generally humanistic orientation of liberal Christianity, Christians may just as unreflectively as other people of good will enter such movements with little thought about the faith-tradition in which they stand and the perspective that it might lend to their involvement. Although they may in some sense be said to act as Christians, beyond generalizations about love, peace, and justice, they do not think as Christians. Discipleship and the *nuanced* wisdom of the tradition play a much less important role in their involvement than do the more immediate rewards of the involvement itself. In consequence, the "independent" Christian perspective that they might have brought to their involvement is lacking. The movement or cause in question undoubtedly gains from the involvement of these persons as concerned individuals, but it does not receive from them whatever wisdom they might have contributed as Christians.

c. The multifaceted environmental problematic that has surfaced since Rachel Carson published her alarming study, *The Silent Spring*,[52] has claimed the attention of many Christians. In these volumes, I have referred several times to the World Council of Churches' decision at Vancouver in 1983 to pursue, as part of a seven-year program of study and action, the theme of the "integrity of creation." Ecology—first in the writings of Joseph Sittler, I

---

52. Rachel Carson, *The Silent Spring* (Boston: Houghton Mifflin, 1962).

believe—has become, almost, a theological term. No one seriously at work in systematic or ethical theology today can fail to treat this subject.

Through such biblical, historical, and theological research, Christians have been brought to understand—and in a way that is quite new—both the culpability of our own religious tradition in providing an ideational atmosphere on the basis of which the objectification and denigration of the extrahuman creation by Western technological civilization has been facilitated, and the submerged wisdom within that tradition by means of which we might now derive a better—indeed, a more Christian—awareness of the relation of human and extrahuman life. As we have seen throughout these volumes, and especially in our discussion of "creaturely being,"[53] it is no longer contexually responsible or faithful for Christians to elevate the human species at the expense of the other creatures and processes upon which, after all, the human species is dependent.

The ecological crisis has evoked a widespread and many-sided movement, to which people are attracted for a great variety of reasons. One prominent "wing" of this movement, in reaction not only to our anthropocentric Western past but also to the rampant technology that continues to plunder and despoil the earth, advances a worldview with variations on the theme that humankind is called to withdraw from its managerial stance and to blend into the natural world that it has tried to dominate. This is sometimes referred to as "deep ecology."

Many Christians, under the impact of New Age and other forms of fashionable "spirituality," are attracted to this (as we may call it) late-Romantic nature mysticism. But the accommodation of the Christian faith to such a position ignores or belittles that whole aspect of Christian anthropology which, in these volumes, we have identified as the human "vocation"[54] and, in the present chapter, "the ethics of responsibility." Without elevating the human species ontologically, the "ontology of communion" allows for (what the scriptural teachings concerning the covenant, stewardship, and discipleship in fact require) a representational calling on the part of the human creature vis-à-vis the other creatures of God, and what Bonhoeffer, as we have seen, called "responsibility for history."[55] Christians who are concerned for justice and peace (the other two "prongs" of the World Council's JPIC process) are entirely justified in protesting against the *kind* of Christian "ecologism" that would have human beings relinquish all stewardly concern for both nature and history. As Rosemary Radford Ruether has written recently,

---

53. *Professing the Faith*, Part II, esp. chap. 6, 301–62.
54. *Professing the Faith*, §§15, 25.
55. I have discussed this subject in several publications, including my three studies of the theology of stewardship. My critique of Christian 'nature romanticism' may be found in a series

The tendency of much New Age ecospirituality is toward a recreational frolic in paradise, which rebuffs awareness of the price of our holiday upon "native" residents as well as on their land. For many American seekers of consumer spirituality, "Gaia consciousness" means a pleasant turn-on of the psyche playing amid beautiful scenes of nature, not a confrontation with the costs of affluence for those on its underside.[56]

In our Scriptures and (often, neglected) theological traditions, Christians have a treasury of wisdom upon which to draw in their necessary involvement in environmental concerns.[57] There is no reason that the Christian community should not be able to glean from this long heritage of meditation a truly "independent" ecological ethic—one, namely, that could contribute greatly to an area of worldly concern that is very much in need of precisely some of the wisdom that Christians could bring to this subject.

30.2. In Search of Depth. Only a chauvinistic religion feels obliged to maintain its autonomy for its own sake. If Christians seek to enucleate and preserve an independent ethic there is only one legitimate reason for their doing so. That reason is alluded to implicitly in the statement of Reinhold Niebuhr that was quoted earlier: "Protestant Christianity in America is, unfortunately, unduly *dependent* upon the very culture of modernity, the disintegration of which would offer a more *independent* religion a unique opportunity."[58] Only by sustaining its independence from its host culture can the Christian movement serve its host culture. The truth of this observation surfaces particularly at moments of cultural societal "disintegration." If the church is simply a part of the problematic situation, it will have nothing to offer the world in its need for reordering or reintegrating its life. We are drawing here upon the same insight that was expressed in the earlier discussion of the demise of Christendom: the disciple community in its "awkward" transitional stage between establishment and disestablishment, we suggested, ought *intentionally* to disengage from its cultural context in order to be in a position to make the kind of contribution that it can make only if it is sufficiently distinguished from its context.

The "distinctive contribution" of religious faith to the ethical discourse of the world is signified in Niebuhr's thought by the word "depth": What faith

---

of papers and responses in the journal *Dianoia* 2, no. 2, (Spring 1992), published by Augustana University College in Camrose, Alberta.

56. Douglas John Hall and Rosemary Radford Ruether, *God and the Nations* (Minneapolis: Fortress Press, 1995), 91.

57. For example, the Eastern Orthodox traditions have much to contribute in this connection. See Vigen Guroian, *Ethics After Christendom: Toward an Ecclesial Christian Ethic* (Grand Rapids: Wm. B. Eerdmans, 1994).

58. Niebuhr, *An Interpretation of Christian Ethics*, 13. See text, xxx.

brings to human ethical deliberation "lies in its comprehension of the dimension of depth in life." Niebuhr explains what he means by depth in the following paragraph:

> A secular moral act resolves the conflicts of interest and passion, revealed in any immediate situation, by whatever counsels a decent prudence may suggest, the most usual counsel being that of moderation—"in nothing too much." A religious morality is constrained by its sense of a dimension of depth to trace every force with which it deals to some ultimate origin and to relate every purpose to some ultimate end. It is concerned not only with immediate values and disvalues, but with the problem of good and evil, not only with immediate objectives, but with ultimate hopes. It is troubled by the question of the primal "whence" and the final "wherefore." It is troubled by these questions because religion is concerned with life and existence as a unity and coherence of meaning. In so far as it is impossible to live at all without presupposing a meaningful existence, the life of every person is religious, with the possible exception of the rare skeptic who is more devoted to the observation of life than to living it, and whose interest in detailed facts is more engrossing than his concern for ultimate meaning and coherence. Even such persons have usually constructed a little cosmos in a world which they regard as chaos and derive vitality and direction from their faith in the organizing purpose of this cosmos.[59]

Remembering that this statement was published in 1935 and naturally, therefore, bears some of the earmarks of the concerns and language of that period,[60] it nevertheless summarizes in a permanently instructive way what is implied in an "independent Christian ethic." The "dimension of depth," to rephrase Niebuhr in terms that are undoubtedly more Barthian, means that, for Christians, every ethical question may and must be considered in the light of the larger vision of the world and its unfolding that is provided by the revelatory activity of the triune God. Or, to use the language of Bonhoeffer, the depth that Christians seek in their ethical reflections and actions entails an existential return to the "reality" that they glimpse in and through their encounter with Jesus Christ:

> The point of departure for Christian ethics is not the reality of one's own self, or the reality of the world; nor is it the reality of standards and values. It is the reality of God as He reveals Himself in Jesus Christ. It is fair to begin by demanding assent to this proposition of anyone who wishes to concern himself with the problem of a Christian ethic. . . .

---

59. Ibid., 15–16.
60. For example, the later Niebuhr would not have spoken so generally about "religion," but would have specified "biblical religion" or "prophetic faith" when he intended the kind of unambiguously positive connotation that he gives to the term here.

> The problem of Christian ethics is the realization among God's creatures of the revelational reality of God in Christ, just as the problem of dogmatics is the truth of the revelational reality of God in Christ. The place which in all other ethics is occupied by the antithesis of "should be" and "is," idea and accomplishment, motive and performance, is occupied in Christian ethics by the relation of reality and realization, past and present, history and event (faith), or, to replace the equivocal concept with the unambiguous name, the relation of Jesus Christ and the Holy Spirit.[61]

Considering the quest for depth in terms of the approach taken in the present work, we may say: Christian ethics are *confessional* ethics, undertaken by the disciple community in full consciousness of its worldly context and in the light of the ongoing dialogue and struggle of this community with the "meditative core" of its *profession* of the faith. The specific ethical question, which may well prove to be "the little point where the battle rages," is given very explicit attention. A contextual theology evokes a contextual ethic. There is no desire here to sweep all the moral problems of humankind, past, present, and future, into a common religious worldview from which both analyses and responses may without difficulty be drawn. Like its "eternal theologies," the successive moralities of Christendom are famous for their categorization and classification of ethical questions, so that with any of them—the medieval, the Victorian, the liberal bourgeois—one has the impression that there is indeed nothing new under the sun; all possible problems have been anticipated and all possible answers given. This is indeed a very major aspect of the theology of glory, which wishes above all to avoid the unpredictable and unanswered. The ethic that belongs to the theology of the cross knows neither questions nor answers in advance. It must therefore live with the questions—including the very difficult and wrenching social questions that we are experiencing in this time of global cultural upheaval. It lives with the questions as if they were entirely new—as, indeed, they always are for those who assume, as Christians do, a linear view of history. Faith is not only not in possession of immediate answers to all possible questions, it is not even insulated against the force of the questions!

The main difference between faith and unfaith or "bad faith"(Sartre) is that faith entertains a vision and a hope that emanates from the "reality" that it contemplates—the reality signified by the name Jesus, the Christ. Clinging to this reality, faith enters into the depths that are there behind every new problem that arises in human history and experience—every renewed "attack" of the future (Kierkegaard). Unlike those who concern themselves with "the immediate" (Niebuhr), seeking remedies for the symptoms of the

---

61. Niebuhr, *An Interpretation of Christian Ethics*, 56–57.

disease because they fear exposing themselves to Kierkegaard's "sickness unto death," Christians pray for the courage to pursue each problem to its foundations—while also attending to the symptoms. They do this, not because they fancy themselves "deep" or deeper than other people, but because they believe that the only finally satisfying responses to any of perplexities and ambiguities of existence are those that have wrestled with the interrelatedness of good and evil and have glimpsed something of the good of which evil deprives creation.

Today particularly, nothing is more needful than precisely such a holistic approach to human problems, especially in the realm of social ethics. In fact, one of the greatest problems of our period and, in particular, our context is that people—whole movements and segments of society, not only individuals—rush in with "answers" before they have lived long enough with the questions. Their answers to one problem, for example, pollution, in the end further complicate other problems, for example, the "population explosion." The incapacity of even (or perhaps especially!) the intelligentsia, with its overspecialization, to "see things whole" must at least in part be attributed to the lack of depth. Or should one not say, rather, to the *fear* of depth; for it requires courage (I did not use that word thoughtlessly earlier!) to follow even an apparently "minor" problem (waste, for example[62])through to its deepest causes. And in the long run, such courage cannot be sustained by human effort alone. I shall have the courage to go into the depths only if I can believe that going there will, in the end, make a difference. And I can believe that only if I can believe that there is something greater than my belief to sustain me. "A religious morality," writes Niebuhr, "is constrained by its sense of the dimension of depth to trace every force with which it deals to some ultimate origin and to relate every purpose to some ultimate end." In other words, the disciple community is "constrained" to do so—humanly speaking, one would rather not! But it is also emboldened by grace to do so. For, contemplating the core of its faith—the cross at the center—the disciple community dares to trust that light, the only light that really enlightens, will be found in the darkness that is found at the deepest level of causation.[63]

In recent experience, the best illustration of this quest for ethical depth on the part of the churches of the world was the aforementioned "process," as it

---

62. In this connection see the excellent essay of Wendell Berry entitled "Waste" in *What Are People For?* (San Francisco: North Point Press, 1990), 126–28. In this very brief essay, Berry illustrates concretely what is involved in the quest for *depth* in the analysis and tackling of any specific problem of social ethics. He does not go to what Christians could consider the deepest level, the theological, although his language (e.g., the use of the word "creation") suggests it; but he certainly demonstrates the errors of remaining at the level of "immediate" solutions.

63. A more developed discussion of this "courage" is found in *The Steward: A Biblical Symbol Come of Age* (Grand Rapids: Wm. B. Eerdmans, 1990) in a section titled "Beyond Christian Humanism" (114–18).

was called, undertaken by the World Council of Churches at its Sixth General Assembly. Only a detailed investigation of this seven-year-long undertaking can substantiate profoundly my use of the "Justice, Peace, and the Integrity of Creation" process for illustrative purposes here; the following generalizations may nevertheless serve to concretize what has been suggested above.

The significant "breakthrough" of the "Justice, Peace, and Integrity of Creation" process lay in the concerted efforts of Christians in every branch of the universal church to apply exactly the kind of "holistic" theological-ethical thinking described above to "the three great instabilities" (Charles Birch) of the epoch: injustice, unpeace, and the disintegration of the natural order under the impact of human use and abuse. In all of the discussions and symposia leading up to the "World Convocation" of 1990,[64] the point that was stressed again and again was the indivisible connectedness of all that is signified by the three categories named in the theme: There can be no justice without peace, no peace without justice, no justice *or* peace without respect for the integrity of creation.[65] These three "great instabilities," almost in trinitarian fashion, represent a seamless robe of evil that threatens global civilization, ergo any good that may come of Christian deliberation upon these inseparable "instabilities" must also be an integrated, cohesive response. Fragmentation, both at the level of analysis and cure, is of the essence of the instability as such. Depth, both in terms of understanding the whole *problematique* and in terms of responding to it meaningfully, presupposes a sustained refusal to address any *one* of these problematic areas without considering it in relation to the other two. It was, in short, a perfect illustration of Niebuhr's sentence: "[Faith] is troubled by [the questions "whence" and "wherefore"] because [it] is concerned with life and existence *as a unity and coherence of meaning.*"

The truth of the insistence that the quest for depth entails integration or wholeness of analysis and response is demonstrated not only by the many fine documents that emerged from conferences that were held during the seven-year period of this undertaking but also—and more instructively—by the final *failure* of the "JPIC process," about which we have thought heretofore. Precisely because the attempt at integrated thinking was abandoned at

---

64. The term "council" could not be used because of the Orthodox Christian restriction of that term to the seven councils of the early church. Nevertheless, it should be recognized very clearly that the "convocation" at Seoul came closer to being an ecumenical council of Christians than anything else that has occurred under the auspices of the World Council, and perhaps under Christian auspices of any sort.

65. See Carl Friedrich von Weizsäcker, *Die Zeit drängt: Eine Weltversammlung der Christen für Gerechtigkeit, Frieden und ei Bewahrung der Schöpfung* (München u. Wien: Carl Hanser Verlag, 1986).

the "World Convocation" in Seoul, the depth that was the *promise* of this process did not materialize. And if one asks why the attempt at holistic think-ing was abandoned at Seoul, then one has to answer: because *theological thinking* was abandoned at Seoul; because the meditative core of faith that constitutes the perspective ("lens," in Lindbeck's term) from which Christians view human problems and possibilities[66] was exchanged at Seoul for a variety of *ideological* commitments that were inevitably in conflict with one another; because the "seamless robe" of the threefold problematic named by the theme was divided, and Christians took up one or other of the "pieces" of this robe, depending upon their prior ideological commitment, as if it alone constituted the evil to be averted; because therefore there could be no inte-grated response to this evil from the side of a shared vision of the good— that is to say, there could be no *confession of the faith,* but only a rather sorry reflection of the world's own moral cacophony.

This must, I repeat, be attributed to a failure of *theology.* And the experi-ence of the World Council at Seoul in this respect especially mirrors faithfully the ethical confusion of the mainline Protestant churches at large today. It is only through constant renewal and struggle with the foundations of the faith—which is to say, through theology—that Christian ethical concern will result in faith's confession. Because the once-mainline Protestant churches of North America are suffering from a kind of theological amnesia, the ethical involvement in which minorities within them busy themselves seldom makes a breakthrough into the kind of confession that occurred here and there, for example, during the Civil Rights movement.[67] In other words, *depth* is not achieved. The darkness is not plumbed and therefore light is neither seen or given. With few exceptions, what is given by the churches is indistinguishable from what can be acquired from any number of other sources of moral con-cern, and often, it must be admitted, in greater depth.

We are led by this observation to what must be our conclusion.

30.3. On Moving "Beyond Ethics."   In his still-pertinent essay on Christian-ity in the United States of America, Dietrich Bonhoeffer wrote:

> American theology and the American church as a whole have never been able to understand the meaning of "criticism" by the Word of God and all that signifies. Right to the last they do not understand that God's "criticism"

---

66. See *Professing the Faith*, introduction, 1–42.
67. In this connection, see Stephen C. Rose's illuminating essay, "Whither The Gospel in Race Relations?" in Stephen C. Rose, ed., *Who's Killing the Church?* (Chicago: Renewal Maga-zine; New York: Association Press, 1966), 118–23.

touches even religion, the Christianity of the churches and the sanctification of Christians, and that God has founded his church beyond religion and *beyond ethics.*[68]

Bonhoeffer was right. The reduction of the Christian faith to "ethics" is a familiar pattern of ecclesiastical life on this continent. It is not exclusive to this continent, as Bonhoeffer's statement perhaps suggests, but it is conspicuous among us. The equation of faith with morality is in some ways the "natural" heresy, for it requires greater effort and commitment to comprehend the faith that causes people to act in the ways that they do than to observe (and perhaps to imitate) their acts. Second generations of believing communities usually tend to imitate to some extent the ethical results of belief even when they themselves do not believe or do not understand what was once believed.

This also indicates how Christian establishment affects the relation between theology and ethics. What is transmitted from generation to generation—in fact, all that can be transmitted or inculcated, humanly speaking—are the "results" of belief, or some of them. It is possible for authorities to establish the Christian religion, legally or culturally speaking; but what is really established are in truth only externalities—dogmas, ceremonials, moral codes. No human authority can establish Christian *faith.* Only the Holy Spirit can do so.

In case of North America, where, as we have seen, establishment was not and could not be at the level of legality, the externalities of dogma and ceremonial that in the European establishments have carried the very meaning of establishment were largely inapplicable. What has dominated in our context as official Christianity therefore has been morality. If we have seldom managed to get "beyond ethics," it has been because morality—in one or another of its constantly shifting forms—has been what parents, teachers, law courts, and other structures of authority could pass on as "Christianity."

Of course, the *churches* as such were not bound by this limitation. That is to say, within the confines of the congregation, clerical and lay educators could at least attempt to present the faith with greater concern for its fullness and its depth—beyond ethics. Our churches have known exceptional liberty with respect to what they *could* profess and confess. They have not been obliged by law to inculcate the ideology of the state. Preachers have not been compelled to preach only law and not gospel; Sunday schools have not been forced to avoid foundational questions of faith; congregational discipline and study have not had to concentrate on ethical "issues." But such has been the intrinsic power of our type of establishment that even though, legally and

---

68. Quoted in John de Gruchy, ed., *Dietrich Bonhoeffer: Witness to Jesus Christ*, The Making of Modern Theology (Minneapolis: Fortress Press, 1991), 216.

socially speaking, the churches of this continent have been remarkably "free," they have seldom ventured outside the regnant norms and expectations of the society but have faithfully performed the services of "culture religion." It is not accidental that Bonhoeffer associates his observation concerning our failure to get "beyond religion and beyond ethics" with our failure "to understand the meaning of 'criticism' by the Word of God." Of course, there have been exceptions! But the rule remains the one that the young Bonhoeffer intuitively recognized: morality—and, at that, a non-"critical" morality; a morality replicating the morality of the social strata (liberal or conservative) with which the churches identified—has been the hallmark of our Christianity.

But now, with our effective disestablishment, the opportunity presents itself that we shall be able, if we are willing, to go "beyond ethics." In the diaspora situation that is beginning to apply also to us, the church is being called to become a *disciple* community, a people engaged in original theological thinking as it attempts to follow its Lord into the far country of a complex and unpredictable future. Our past failure to achieve "depth" in our ethical concerns; the habitual identification of the faith with old moralities and new; the lack of an "independent ethic"—this old pattern *does not have to be continued.* If we are able to grasp and to accept our new situation, there are "unique opportunities" for once-mainline Protestantism in North America that were not visible when Niebuhr wrote his work on ethics. While we certainly have not *chosen* to be "a more independent religion," history has forced upon us conditions that could, if rightly appropriated, make for such independence. We might then become truly useful to our society. We might even manage to produce ethical counsel of a genuinely original character— ethics that are themselves "beyond ethics," beyond the usual moralities, beyond the solemn repetition of the "values" and "trends" set by others: *radical* ethics, in the true sense of the term—ethics that arise out of the roots of the ancient tradition that we have hardly begun to remember and appropriate.

PART IV

THE REIGN OF GOD AND CHRISTIAN HOPE

CHAPTER ▪ EIGHT
Confessing Hope

31. "Hope against Hope"

31.1. Eschatology and "Future Shock."   To confess Christian faith is to confess Christian hope. It would not be *Christian* faith if its confession did not contain an elemental future thrust. For faith in Jesus as the Christ is trust in him, not only as the sovereign of the present but as sovereign of the future as well. Indeed, Christians dare to confess that the future will reveal what the tradition called "the Kingship of Christ" in a way that the present does not and cannot. For the present, Christ's sovereignty is obscured. It can only be confessed, not demonstrated; more accurately, its right demonstration is its confession. The sovereignty of Jesus Christ is visible only to the eyes of faith, for it is the sovereignty of the crucified "King of the Jews." So far as sight is concerned, what is most obvious to everyone—including the disciple community—is a grim procession of events, the vast majority of which would appear to demonstrate nothing so conclusively as that death is indeed the "lord of the dance," as medieval art often depicted.

Let us be concrete: As I write, the former Yugoslavia is the scene of apparently interminable and inevitable ethnic, racial, and religious warfare. The United Nations, with Britain and the United States in the lead, now entertains the prospect that its peace-keeping operations will have to be supplemented by military "strikes" against strategic points in the Serbian territories, but some experts insist this will only escalate the conflict. In Somalia, tribally and criminally incited bloodshed and starvation continue to stalk the land; and lately it has been revealed that some Canadian soldiers, part of the U.N. peace-keeping forces, have been so unnerved by human degradation of a kind wholly foreign to their experience that they have resorted to shotgun discipline in their dealings with the marauding citizens of that land. In Washington, the President of the United States of America, so recently installed in office, is already the brunt of harsh criticism from the sides both of his predictable detractors and his erstwhile supporters. The largest demonstration in American history occurred there a few days ago as of this writing, and it tells us more than we should like to know about ourselves that it was a demonstration of gay and lesbian people demanding their rights. In Los Angeles, the conviction of two officers responsible for beating an African American citizen has momentarily placated the anger of those who wreaked havoc upon that city a year ago; but the news media assure us that the anger has not disappeared. In Montreal, where the unemployment rate in poorer parts of the city reaches as high as 30 percent of the workforce, police are still being accused of gross prejudice and unwarranted brutality in their dealings with members of the black community. Women invited to share their experiences of harassment and violence on "talk shows" almost without exception relate incidents that an earlier generation could only have read about, if anywhere, in *The Police Gazette.* The promised economic recovery is so slow in making itself felt that most people no longer believe the optimistic statements of the political and financial leaders, either in Canada or the United States.

The specifics of the world situation will have changed, of course, by the time these words reach my readers. (As I revise my work in October of 1995, they have already changed significantly). But the data that replace these data will not likely be more hopeful. One trusts that specific problems will be alleviated or even resolved; but one is conditioned by experience to expect new problems to fill the places of the old ones. So familiar has the litany of earth's sorrows become that those who follow world events have long since given up expecting anything like an upward trend toward global peace and justice to become audible in the reports of the media. The discrepancy between the carefree, prosperous, and beautiful people of the television advertisements and the scarred and broken bodies of those killed by bombs set off by some terrorist organization or the tormented, vacant faces of starving and disease-ridden African children verges on the obscene. Newscasters intentionally insert into their bleak reports on the state of the planet supposedly humorous incidents, the function of which is obviously presumed to be comic relief; but these "clips" are usually so trivial that they convey nothing so much as the world's feeble attempt to say something "nice": "Forget all this and 'have a nice day!'"

How, in such a world, can anyone dare to confess that the One who is *Dominus,* "Lord," is like a gentle shepherd with his sheep, a mother hen with her chicks, a healer of souls and bodies, a wise and compassionate ruler guiding his army of peace toward a victory that can already be celebrated in its anticipation? An earlier age, the age of progress, spurred on by social Darwinism and a mood of euphoria that seemed confirmed by wondrous new inventions and the opportunities they afforded for overcoming ancient foes of life—illness, ignorance, prejudice—produced Christians who believed it not only possible but mandatory to expect "the kingdom of God in this generation." The twentieth century, which was supposed to have been "the Christian century," has systematically eroded that assumption; so that now, although the churches still try to behave as if it were their duty to be "hopeful," it is very hard to discover sincere historical hope among the Christians or anyone else. The most "successful" and "growing" churches, whose success and growth are evidently related to just this fact, are those that have located their hopes in inner sanctuaries of spiritual peace or in posthistorical promises.

It has been the consistent theme of this trilogy, based on the theology of the cross understood as "God's abiding commitment to the world," that the God of the Jews and the Christians intends to mend the world; that redemption must mean the redemption of creation, not its destruction or replacement but its fulfillment; that the resurrection of Jesus Christ must not be turned into a *Deus ex machina* type of escape from history but is rather the source of Christian courage to enter all the more boldly into the process of history, time being something like the moving edge of the eternal. How can such a point of view be sustained in a historical context which, in contrast to both our remembered past and what we North Americans were taught to hope for the future, provides so little evidence of the sovereignty of divine love? Is it not time for Christians to relinquish whatever remains in their tradition of worldly hope? Would it not enhance the condition of the old, besieged liberal and moderate denominations of our continent if they, like the popular apocalypticists and otherworldly sectarian groups, began to accentuate the transhistorical meaning of the Lordship of Jesus Christ and the divine "Kingdom"?

Certainly this temptation exists in all the Christian denominations. In a manner that would shock and anger our social-gospel progenitors, apocalyptic cults are conspicuously on the increase in North America, and the societal impulses that create these cults infiltrate also the older denominations. For the most part, however, the remnants of classical Protestant churches in North America function rather as middle-class bulwarks against the impulses that create apocalypticism, and are practically silent in the whole area of eschatology.

They are silent because they are both repressive and doctrinally confused and ill informed. Their general confusion manifests itself in all phases of their enterprise, but nowhere perhaps more conspicuously than in their failure to develop a meaningful, communicable eschatology—an alternative to apocalypticism of the antiworld variety; an alternative also to old, lingering forms of liberal progressivism. Despite the fact that serious theology since Albert

Schweitzer's *The Quest for the Historical Jesus* or Karl Barth's *Römerbrief* has put eschatology at the forefront of Christian theological reflection, the term remains one of the great unknowns so far as the vast majority of Christians on this continent are concerned. This would not be so lamentable in itself, since theological terminology is universally too esoteric for the church-going public, and the scholars, most of them, do not bother to teach the church their language; but what has to concern every serious Christian in North America deeply is that what the term eschatology stands for is just as foreign to most Christians as the term itself.

This is in part because eschatology really is a complex dimension of Christian thought. Of all areas of the theological tradition, it is perhaps the most nuanced and difficult to grasp. For it concerns itself with what is probably the most complex *human* question, that of time. On the surface, time may seem the simplest of subjects: the ticking clock, that most characteristic and exuberant invention of the Enlightenment that has become a commonplace symbol of our civililzation, seems to tell us all that we need to know about time—that it moves only in one direction, that it cannot be stopped, that it can be measured but not controlled, that it conditions every aspect of our lives. But as soon as we ponder for an instant any one of those obvious factors, time becomes a mystery that is wonderful and terrifying, but mostly terrifying. "Time, like an ever-rolling stream, bears all its sons away" (Isaac Watts). Time at its simplest is just a quantity; but a quantity by which life itself is affected in every way is at once a quality.

And eschatology has to do with time, as we shall try to show later. It is the Christian attempt to explain how it is possible to live under the tyranny of time yet to do so freely and joyfully.

Such a statement already makes it obvious why eschatology is the most complex of Christian theological subjects; because that statement could only be made as the conclusion of a deep and prolonged reflection upon the whole subject-matter of the faith. It presupposes everything that has gone before in these three volumes, and much besides. It presupposes exposure to Scripture and tradition, theology, creation doctrine, pneumatology—and above all Christology and soteriology. And it presupposes all of this, not merely as a matter of intellectual exposure but also as meditation and prayer.

This is no doubt the reason that, in the conventional articulations of Christian dogmatics or systematic theology, eschatology was regularly identified as "the doctrine of last things": it had to be left until the last because it presupposes all the rest. But, unfortunately, its reputation for having to do with "last things" has obscured rather than promoted Christian understanding of the depth and breadth of this facet of Christian doctrine. For eschatology is not about what people naturally think of when they hear a term like "*last* things"; it is about *every*thing—"everything" in the manner in which, in the first volume, we already established the intent of that term. That is, eschatology is not "a doctrine" among doctrines, but a dimension of every other doctrinal area. Without this dimension they all—theology, Christology, anthropology, ecclesiology, and the rest—become flat and one-dimensional: they do not live. For everything that is exists under the impossibilities and the possibilities of time. Even the eternal One, time's Creator, insofar as God loves and wills to redeem creatures of time, is subject to time.

While the complexity of the subject thus partially explains its almost universal neglect in the "established" churches, there is also another and more contexually important reason for this neglect. It is a reason that has been close to the surface very often in these reflections, and therefore we need not dwell on it at length here; for it will be recognized immediately by those who have followed the course of this discussion. Let me put it in this way, if I may be forgiven a little irony: What need had the churches of North America to dabble in the complexities of biblical eschatology when modernity had made it plain, and our cultural milieu made it mandatory to believe, that time itself progressively redeems?[1]

In other words, we peoples of the so-called New World, who have no past other than the past of modernity, who did not listen to the older sages of our own civilization any more than we were ready to listen to the sages who were present on these shores when the ships brought our ancestors hither: we have had a powerful, appealing eschatology all along. It is a species of "realized" eschatology, that is, a view of history in which the goal of the march of time is already built into the process itself, is steadily unfolding beneath our very eyes, and is visibly *good*. More important still, it insists that *we*, "America," represent the cutting edge of this purposeful movement of time. The tired, hopeless, cynical Old World takes comfort as it looks upon us, the New, and sends us its poor and wretched—

> Give me your tired, your poor,
> Your huddled masses yearning to breathe free,
> the wretched refuse of your teeming shore.
> Send these, the homeless, tempest-tost to me,
> I lift my lamp beside the golden door![2]

That, by any other name, represents an eschatology, and a very decisive one. It has nobility and poignancy in its best expressions, as in the poem of

---

1. See Reinhold Niebuhr, *Faith and History: A Comparison of Christian and Modern Views of History* (New York: Charles Scribner's Sons, 1951), esp. chap. 2, "The History of the Modern Conception of History," 14–34.

2. Familiar lines from the sonnet "The New Colossus," by the American poet of immigrant (Russian Jewish) extraction Emma Lazarus, affixed to the pedestal of the Statue of Liberty in 1903.

Emma Lazarus. It seldom fails to stir the embers of idealism even in the most cynical of hearts; and in a world whose cynicism lies very close to the surface, such reminders of the dreams of earlier, more innocent cohorts of the race should neither be forgotten nor scorned.

Yet this New World eschatology, hardened into ideological and promotional forms, can be and has been very misleading—and even destructive. Unless it is held in dialectical tension with the most unflinching realism, it is gravely at odds with biblical faith! Liberal Christianity caused as much of the Bible and the Christian tradition as possible to buttress modernity's "religion of progress"; but—partly, it must be admitted, on account of the continuing witness of conservative, fundamentalist, and apocalyptic groups on this continent—there has always been in the churches a secret knowledge that our Christian authoritative sources simply do not support such a teleology, and can only do so if they are shamelessly manipulated and truncated. The ideology of progress is just not compatible with the "good news" of a redemption introduced into time from beyond time's relentless cycle of cause and effect. Neither the Scriptures nor the greater traditions of Christian theology, including the Reformation, could condone the belief that salvation is built into the very processes of history; indeed, in the face of such a claim, biblical faith can only give rise to a critical theology.

The eschatological reflections that have informed serious Christian theology from Schweitzer to Barth[3] and Reinhold Niebuhr to Moltmann, have not been kept from the Christian churches only on account of their complexity, then, but because the once-mainline churches of this continent, along with the classes that support them, have been pursuing an eschatology that is antithetical to everything suggested by those names (and others that could be included in the list). The merest hint of a concept of the procession of time that did not assume that it is "growing ever lighter" (Buber) and that America is the vanguard of that procession, has been enough, even though such hints could be nicely cloaked in biblical language, to ruin the careers of honest clergy on this continent. The "old theology" of progress has not, with us, been a merely secular religion; it has been the basic mood of our Christianity. To endorse any other eschatology than the eschatology of ever-upwardness was (as a U.S. Christian once said to the author) "anti-American, that is, anti-Christian."

---

3. Interestingly, when Karl Barth visited Chicago in 1962, although he had determined in advance to avoid any criticism of the United States, he could not resist in his closing remarks introducing a sly critique of just the American "eschatology" we have been characterizing. Referring to the Statue of Liberty, he quipped, "I have not seen that lady, except in pictures. Next week I shall see her in person. That lady needs a little or, perhaps, a good bit of demythologization" (*Criterion* [A Publication of the Divinity School of the University of Chicago] 2, no. 1 [Winter 1963]: 24).

But now, as we have seen, another, alien mood has swept over us. It has been called—perceptively—"future shock" (Toffler). It marks the death of the old eschatology, because the essence of that conception of time was belief in a redeemed future, already evident in the progressive unfolding of past and present events. Are we perhaps ready now, at least in the churches, to listen to the precepts of another mode of eschatological thought?

Even if we are not ready for it, we shall have to listen, despite our past and our preferences. For given the different evidence of time's procession cast up by present events, neither as North Americans nor as Christians in North America shall we be able to sustain any hope for the future unless we can learn how to disguish hope from the optimism that has been our "national philosophy" (Sydney Hook). Christian hope is "hope against hope" (Rom. 4:17).[4] It is hope (*spes*) that knows and dialogues with its antithesis, despair (*de* + *sperare* > *spes* = "without hope"). It is the very opposite of hope understood as a character trait or "natural" aptitude. It is the consequence not of nature but of grace. *Sola gratia.*

31.2. "The Reign of God." When Jesus began his ministry of preaching after being tempted in the wilderness, according to Mark's Gospel, his message was that "the reign of God"[5] would now begin and that his hearers ought to alter their ways accordingly. "'The time is fulfilled, and the kingdom of God is at hand; repent, and believe in the gospel'" (Mark 1:15).

This continued to be the thrust of Jesus' message, and not only of his spoken testimony but of his ministry as a whole. The miracles of healing and the casting out of devils (exorcisms) are understood by their recorders as signs and symbols of the divine reign. Many of the parables have been known for centuries as "parables of the kingdom," for they describe the nature of the divine reign and of its advent. Thus the parable of the seed, which grows quietly and secretly while its sower is asleep, demonstrates that the divine reign takes shape within the old order, develops unnoticed, "the earth producing of itself," and does not depend upon human ingenuity (Mark 4:26–

---

4. See my *Hope against Hope* (Geneva: WSCF, 1971); also *Lighten Our Darkness: Toward an Indigenous Theology of the Cross* (Philadelphia: Westminster Press, 1976).

5. Although the term "reign of God" has been introduced in recent theological discussion in order to avoid the sexist terminology of male monarchy ("kingdom"), it has long been recognized as being a more accurate rendition of the Greek, *basileia tou Theou,* for this term does not suggest a *place* but a *condition,* namely God's sovereignty.

The related term "kingdom of heaven," which has a special place in the piety of many North American Christians because of the transcendental as well as the personalistic connotations that have been read into it, is in reality nothing more than an alternative expression for the same "reign" or "kingdom" of God. Its usage is explained by the desire within Judaism to avoid demeaning the name of God (and thus breaking the third commandment); so one spoke of "heaven" instead.

29). In the parable that immediately follows this, the well-known "mustard-seed" analogy, an even more emphatic point is made concerning the hidden, insignificant beginnings of the divine reign: this seed is smaller than all others. But in the end—which is "not yet"—it will produce something surprisingly provident.

It is understood that although God's reign is not introduced by Jesus, in and through his ministry and his life, it is given a new direction and a new urgency. The time has come! And the appropriate response to this announcement is repentance, faith, and discipleship. Jesus' choice of his closest followers succeeds immediately the sentence-summary of his opening sermon repeated above (Mark 1:16f.). The ministry of Jesus is compared with the time of sowing. The harvest will come later. It is too soon to know what the harvest will amount to. The seed falls on different kinds of soil (Mark 4:3ff.). But now it is time to decide, to act, to follow. Laborers are being called into the vineyard (Matt. 20:1–16), and it may even now be the last opportunity to heed the call—the eleventh hour. To heed it, to follow, will not be easy; sacrifice is involved (Luke 14:28–32). But those who recognize the worth of the goal will be like one who heard of a fabulous, costly pearl and sold everything in order to obtain it (Matt. 13:45) . . . and so on.

What is intended here? What are we to gather from this after all strange admixture of metaphors and similies, signs and wonders? What *is* "the reign of God"?

It is perhaps best to begin by saying what it is not. First, it is not a program, a plan of action, a strategy for change. Obviously, the preacher of the imminent reign intends to involve his hearers. God's reign is not just a condition that is going to occur, willy-nilly. The whole point of Jesus' communication of the coming reign of God is surely to acquire participants. Yet the participants are neither the initiators of this new and decisive form of God's earthly sovereignty nor is it to be achieved through their efforts. Their participation matters—chiefly to them! But if they do not heed the call to involvement others will; it will occur, regardless of their individual responses.

Neither, second, is it an ideal or utopian vision. Jesus is not a visionary recruiting people for his dream, or a revolutionary bent upon displacing the tired and corrupt denizens of the old order, or a charismatic filled with zeal for the new. There are elements of all of these in the account of his life and teaching, but none of them serves to categorize him. He is too realistic to be utopian, too suspicious of power to be a revolutionary, and too conscious of others and their needs to be caught up in personal charism. The *basileia* whose advent he proclaims is for him not only a vision but a reality; it is to be inaugurated—has already been inaugurated—quietly and without the fanfare, tumult, and self-righteousness of revolutionaries; and although it is certainly cause enough for enthusiasm, it is far too practical a consciousness of the need for concrete forms of justice to be just another charismatic movement.

Third, the "reign of God" is not a merely subjective state, a *metanoia* of the heart, a "spiritual" disposition. The King James Version of the Bible, a translation the beauty of which has not been surpassed, is nevertheless often misleading. Confronted by the Pharisees' demand to know when the alleged "kingdom of God" should come, Jesus, in this version, answers: "'The kingdom of God cometh not with observation: neither shall they say, Lo here! or, lo there! for, behold, the kingdom of God is within you.'" (Luke 17:20b–21 KJV). Under the impact of eighteenth- and nineteenth-century pietism and North American religious privatism, this "within you" has achieved a marvelous reputation for truth—despite the fact that many editions of the KJV itself indicated marginally that an alternative reading would be "among you." The Revised Standard Version and most other modern translations render this difficult thought as "in your midst." The internalization or spiritualization of the kingdom in North American mainstream Christianity remains, however, the most powerful deterrent to the recognition of critical social and political overtones in this prominent symbol of the newer Testament.

The precise wording of the previous sentence needs to be borne in mind as we attempt now to define "the reign of God" in positive terms. To say that it *is* a social and political category seems to me to run the risk of identifying this theological symbol too quickly with some political ideology. Both the Social Gospel of the earlier part of this century and much liberation theology of the present have been ready, apparently, to take that risk. In my judgment, that must be regarded as being preferable to pietistic inwardness or a purely "religious" interpretation of the meaning of the symbol. Obviously both the Social Gospel and, in many of its expressions, liberation theology developed precisely over against these inveterate alternatives, which are themselves covertly and effectively political because they challenge nothing in existing systems and thus, whether intentionally or by default, regularly support unjust regimes.

In my judgment, however, *basileia tou Theou,* if it is to function as biblical faith intends, ought not to be heard as an overtly political category, or as an open invitation to invest it with specific political content. Rather, it must be kept free to be a vantage point of truth, justice, and courage from which any and every system and regime may be watched and assessed. Since every human "kingdom" creates its victims, the "kingdom of God" is above all the sovereignty of one who identifies with the excluded; and every political ideology and agenda excludes someone. This "King" was "reckoned with transgressors" (Luke 22:37; Mark 15:28).

Obviously enough, to provide the kind of perspective from which such vigilance can be acquired in the midst of history's ambiguities, the "reign of

God" cannot be empty of content—a mere form to which faith may resort indiscriminately for its ethic of resistance. We know from the whole literature of the Scriptures—we even know rather well!—what is intended. God's reign could hardly be identified with ideas, laws, or visions of the good in which one could not recognize any longer the objectives specified in the Decalogue, the Sermon on the Mount, the prophetic consciousness of "divine pathos," the passion for justice and truth, the sense of creational harmony contained in (say) the final chapter of the Apocalypse, and so forth. If we are speaking about *God's* reign, then we are speaking about a sovereignty that is continuous with the whole character and intention of God as these are presented in the continuity of the Testaments; and as Christians, we are speaking in particular about Jesus, the supreme exemplar and representative both of the divine sovereign and of human obedience.

This testimony to the positive content of the symbol is not inconsiderable. There is at least enough here for us to realize that certain systems, practices, and events are *not* acceptable to those whose perspective on the world can be associated with this symbol. The reign of God is *not* compatible with tyranny, gross economic disparity, the degradation of the earth and of human beings because of their skin pigmentation, or their gender, or their sexual orientation. It is *not* compatible with violence, war, slavery, "ethnic cleansing," indifference to those in need, personal greed and acquisitiveness, and so on and on. Such things may surely be said straightforwardly by anyone with only a slight knowledge of the background of Jesus' use of this term and of his own exemplification of its meaning.

In short, there is quite enough by way of positive content here to permit and necessitate the deployment of the "reign of God" symbol as a critical symbol, and to indicate how far I am ready to carry that claim, I shall confess without hesitation that I am convinced that both the Social Gospel and the liberationists are right in assuming that this symbol is incompatible with unchecked capitalism and economic, racial, gender, and other forms of oppression and exclusion. How much more evidence do we need?

At the same time, the critical functioning of this symbol and reality ought not to overshadow another of its important dimensions, one that has been present even in the few scriptural quotations we have been able to incorporate in this discussion: namely, the dimension of mystery. The divine reign is the *divine* reign, and therefore it partakes of the mystery of the deity, "whose ways are not our ways, nor whose thoughts our thoughts." The disciple community believes that God reigns, all contrary evidence notwithstanding. But God, as God is depicted in the continuity of the Testaments, is never quite predictable—or rather, only this is predictable about God: that God will be faithful. God's faithfulness, however, is not to be equated with our ideas of consistent behavior! The biblical God sometimes uses "the enemy" over against those who "name the Name," and reigns more effectively among those who have no knowledge or intention of obedience than among those who claim to be God's subjects and servants.

Thus Jesus warns his followers against those who find the divine sovereignty in this or that program or regime or system, and run after it as though no further questions need to be asked:

> "The days are coming when you will desire to see one of the days of the Son of man, and you will not see it. And they will say to you, 'Lo, there!' or 'Lo, here!' Do not go, do not follow them. For as the lightning flashes and lights up the sky from one side to the other, so will the Son of man be in his day. But first he must suffer many things. . . ."
>
> (Luke 17:22f., KJV)

The mystery of God's reign, like the mystery of God's person, is not for its own sake only. This is not the usual mysticism, the "abstract mysticism" (Tillich) that has sometimes also invaded the Christian church. The mystery of the divine reign exists for the sake of the life enhancement that is its object. *Life resists classification;* when it is subjected to definition, it is invariably stifled. Even to be a critical symbol, the "reign of God" must remain a transcendent one, for otherwise it will become the property of some power elite whose object is to control nature, eliminate chance, and cause life to conform to its ideal—usually, a high ideal. But however high, it will end—as did the high ideals of New England Puritanism—by substituting for the reign of God, which is the the divine stewarding of life, the dominion of death.

31.3. Confessing Hope in an Officially Optimistic Society. Despite the subterranean apprehension of the future that stalks our culture, the excessive optimism of which the American dream was fashioned continues to assert itself in both our private rhetoric and our public declarations. It is in fact more militant than ever, because it is so patently under seige. Candidates for political office who do not give off copious tokens of their personal hopefulness as well as their expansive "vision" for the future of the national enterprise cannot expect to win elections, no matter how poignantly the situation calls for truth and not bravado. It is ironic to the point of high comedy that persons whose expertise in problematic areas of our common life, such as environmental pollution or the debt crisis, are required by the very public opinion they are attempting to sway to sprinkle their analyses with affirmations of their personal optimism; for they know that, otherwise, their often extremely negative prognoses would be suppressed before they had penetrated the consciousness of their listeners. Optimism, and optimism of the most banal variety, is *de rigueur* behavior for all whose livelihood or advancement is dependent upon their public image. Millions of dollars are expended on the production of films depicting the most horrendous violence, because their producers can be sure of box-office successes if the violent heroes are "winners." Such "entertainment" mirrors too closely the recent political trends in both the United States and Canada. We are electing to office increasingly obdurate advocates of self-reliance. Evidently, we would rather facilitate the grand material ambitions of the few, and so perpetuate the mythology of "unlimited opportunity," than to witness any common lowering of lifestyles through economic policies that enhance the security of the many.

How is it possible to confess Christian hope in an officially optimistic society? Twenty-five years ago I raised this question in *Lighten Our Darkness* and other writings, and I raise it still; for the unanswered question continues to frustrate serious attempts at Christian theology and ecclesiastical renewal in this context. The intervening years have witnessed some theologically significant alterations of our context. More people have become conscious of the problems that had begun to dawn upon the Viet Nam generation. Important movements have emerged in our midst that constitute zones of truth and do not demand, in advance, easy answers for every difficult question. But such gains are offset by the advent of new social phenomena: smugness over the downfall of "the evil empire," New Age and similar admixtures of secular and quasi religious "spirituality," Yuppiedom and its consumerist variations. Also, the diminishment of secular optimism within significant segments of the population has been counterbalanced by its transference to new and sometimes bizarre forms of a religious optimism that no longer concerns itself with the fate of the earth.

What all of this has meant for the once-mainline denominations is that they are under even greater pressure to accentuate the positive. In a society that offers middle-class, relatively stable, family-oriented people few outlets for the confirmation of human hope, the historic denominations of North American Christendom become for many of those who turn to them havens of security, islands of "whatever is lovely and of good report." The more chaotic and threatening public life becomes, the more these churches are called upon to exemplify the conventional verities, or what are perceived as such; above all, they are looked to for order and decency, some sense of form, ritual, calm, communality.

Probably the churches must be willing to play that role. To refuse shelter to besieged and battered human spirits just because they are the spirits of the nonpoor is just as reprehensible as avoiding the more conspicuously needy. There is an ideological type of Christianity, a new sort of Puritanism, that will only have dealings with the visible victims of the times and is so myopic as to see nothing but "the enemy" in every family whose income slightly exceeds the minimum wage. I would be loath to have anything that I have said in these pages used in support of this type of "religious correctness." The evils that we have to combat are "principalities and powers" that cannot and must not be visited upon the heads of ordinary people, whatever their gender, race, or economic bracket. To try to raise a family in a society that has grown cynical about marriage and family life; to behave with human decency in cities filled with mutual suspicion, indifference, and rudeness; to sustain a moderate morality in the midst of a "culture" that celebrates vulgarity (all aims that are undoubtedly "middle class") may constitute challenges just as great, in their way, as the more abysmal struggles of the poor. The Christian organization that refuses to help people meet such challenges is not to be admired, no matter how impressive its solidarity with other victims may be. The once-established churches should not be surprised if they are sought out for precisely this kind of help; after all, their reputations have been built on such promises.

All the same, the middle-class membership base of these churches makes it particularly difficult to confess Christian hope within and through them; for it almost automatically happens that every positive sentiment uttered in such contexts is seized upon by spirits that are so eager for immediate rein-forcement of the positive that they will use facile affirmations of it to insulate themselves from sobering discourse with that which negates. And we are thinking of words like love, faith, and hope, to mention only three. The com-mon fate of these great, searching concepts of the faith is that they are quite likely to function repressively in our congregations. Biblically speaking, every one of these terms describes a dialogue with its antithesis. They do not elimi-nate the negative, they engage it. Each of them, as they are deployed by this tradition, implies its antithesis within itself. "Faith and doubt run like twin threads crosswise through the whole history of Israel," writes Pinchas Lap-ide.[6] Nor is there any "monism of love" (Kitamori) in these Scriptures. Even the love of God is dialogically related to God's hatred of the evil of those whom God loves; and in the long narrative of Scripture as in the "reality" (Bonhoeffer) to which it bears witness, "the line between love and hate is as thin as a razor's edge" (W. Somerset Maugham).

As for hope, the biblical dialogue partner of despair, it is the most difficult of all theological categories to preserve from cooptation by the desperately optimistic. The preacher needs only to say the word and it is grasped by eager souls who will do anything to avoid open confrontation with their incipient and controlled despair. Indeed, if the preacher does not use that word and its derivatives on a regular basis; if it is not worked into prayers and sung in hymns; if sermons, by point three, do not come out on the side of hope,

---

6. Pinchas Lapide, *The Resurrection of Jesus: A Jewish Perspective,* trans. Wilhelm C. Linss (Minneapolis: Augsburg, 1983), 127.

then the minister's neglect will register itself in diminished congregations and reduced givings.

We are thinking of a real dilemma, not an artificial one. Without hope life cannot go on; and there is such palpable, if covert, despair in our society, and on the part of people who for the most part have absolutely no spiritual or intellectual capacities for coping with it, that every responsible pastor knows that he or she must "confess the hope" regularly and unconditionally. Yet the responsible pastor who is also enough of a biblical scholar and theologian to know that hope is not another word for optimism will not be able to treat his calling in a demand-and-supply fashion. If such a pastor is also a sensitive observer of the human psyche, she will realize that the greatest disservice she could render her people would be to cater to their demand for instant hope.

It is primarily because of cheap hope—our peculiarly North American version of Bonhoeffer's "cheap grace"—that both our society and our churches find themselves in the dilemma they do. As North American Christians whose faith is tainted by ideological optimism, we are trying to answer all of our problems without exposing ourselves to them *as real problems.* There is not one crisis on our horizon—whether this means vast social problems such as poverty, unemployment, and racism, or intensely personal problems such as the search for meaning, vocation, or personal integrity—that can be resolved unless we are prepared to go much farther into the *depths*[7] of the question than we are apparently able or willing to do. In particular, the habit of seeking technological "quick fixes" will have to be unlearned. Most of the solutions that are offered on every hand only complicate the problems further, or postpone more catastrophic encounters with them to the generations that will follow ours. Few citizens of our nations are able to entertain the thought that there may be something so wrong with our "world" that its righting would require of us, individually and corporately, acute sacrifice and dramatically changed expectations.

In other words, our optimism is defensive, and what it seeks to defend us from is truth. By contrast, truth understood in Christian terms is the inseparable companion of hope. Biblically speaking, hope is *always* "hope against hope": that is, the hope that is the future dimension of faith in Jesus Christ will resist every preliminary suggestion of the too quickly hopeful spirit, because it will recognize the lack of truth in it. As credulity is the deadly enemy of faith and sentimentality of love, so is obsessive hopefulness the great enemy of hope. Hopefulness is undoubtedly a pleasant character trait, a virtue even, or at least a "noble temptation" (Chesterton). We are all attracted to hopeful personalities, just as, conversely, we are repelled by gloomy ones. But

---

7. See chap. 7, §29.2.

cultivated hopefulness is also a pathetic and sometimes a very dangerous proclivity—"the mania of maintaining that everything is well when we are wretched" (Voltaire). And when such hopefulness is encouraged and coddled by Christian churches, they ought not to be shocked when they are made an object of resentment by those whose deeper acquaintance with reality does not afford them the luxury of such a sunny mentality. Middle-class Christianity in North America has not achieved its wide reputation for superficiality without cause!

There is no way of overcoming this confusion of hope and optimism short of painful exposure to truth, including the truth both of our personal and our societal fictions. Such exposure belongs to the experience called by the Bible *metanoia*—repentance, conversion. To its credit, evangelical Christianity in North America has retained this awareness and assumes "conversion," involving overpowering consciousness of personal sin, as the normal mode of entry into the community of faith. Unfortunately, its retention of the individual dimensions of this experience is seldom accompanied by any profoundly social dimension ("I dwell in the midst of *a people* of unclean lips," Isa. 6:5), but at least the recognition that new hope entails a radical break with false hope and untruth is still present in this tradition. In the remnants of mainline churches, even personal *metanoia* is rare, and it is often caricatured or ridiculed. One can enjoy full membership in such communities of faith without ever having to confront the inauthenticity of one's own life, let alone the "unclean lips" of the "people" to which one belongs. Indeed, in such communities, the consciousness of sin, when it is genuine and vocal, usually seems out of place, excessive. The demand for hope is not accompanied by a demand for truth, and individuals in such communities who are driven by truth-orientation can be an embarrassment.

As long as there are classes of persons in our society who demand this kind of insulation from the world, there will be "churches" that are ready to provide it. If the Christian churches refuse to do so, substitutes will be found; they are already moving toward center stage.

Yet the demand for immediate hope cloaks a far deeper, if less frequently verbalized, need. Liberal and moderate Christianity in North America has so capitulated to the *surface* demands of its middle-class clientele that it is blind to the profound if usually unspoken yearning of that same middle class. Quietly desperate people ask for ersatz hope because they are deeply skeptical about the possibility of any other kind. If they could believe that there are grounds for a "hope that does not disappoint us," few would be satisfied with exhortations to a programmed cheerfulness and other solemn religious versions of the official optimism. Christians possess no absolutes where the future is concerned. Of all people, they are likely to distrust any such claim to absolutes. What they do have is a gospel. The only access that Christian

467

churches have to a hope that has foundations is through the proclamation of *gospel.*

The lesson to be learned here is an obvious one: If, in the liberal and moderate once-established churches, we covet anything that approximates genuine hope, we shall have to rediscover *gospel.* Only gospel will offer a love that transcends sentimentality, a faith that can live with doubt and a hope that is able to confront despair.

> We must . . . preach the gospel to this, as to every generation. Our gospel is one which assures salvation in the cross of Christ to those who heartily repent of their sins. It is a gospel of the cross; and the cross is a revelation of the love of God only to those who have first stood under it as a judgment. It is in the cross that the exceeding sinfulness of human sin is revealed. It is in the cross that we become conscious how, not only what is worst, but what is best in human culture and civilization is involved in man's rebellion against God. . . . Thus does the cross reveal the problem of all human culture and the dilemma of every human civilization.
>
> Repentance [*metanoia*] is the first key into the door of the Kingdom of God.[8]

One cannot be associated with any of the older denominations of Protestantism on this continent without feeling, in the presence of such an affirmation as the above, that (with exceptions) what we have really *lost* is gospel, hence also "repentance," hope, and much besides. For us, there is no easy way back to the kerygmatic foundations of Christian faith. It could require decades before there is even a sufficiently sincere and informed demand for such "depth" in the remnants of these churches. But that does not mean that those who are concerned for the equipping of the diaspora are without resources in the meantime. Part of the nurturing of the community that *waits for gospel* is sound teaching.

While the recovery of gospel may require a transformation of congregational life that cannot be engineered but must await the occasion that only the divine Spirit can create, preparation for such a moment may be undertaken by acquainting small groups within congregations with the basic constituents of the faith. At least there could be at this "awkward" (Lindbeck) stage of the journey a concerted effort on the part of clerical and lay educators to disabuse congregations of commonly held errors and misrepresentations of the faith. The false equation of Christian hope and New World optimism would be a very good place to start. By becoming more knowledgeable concerning Christian hope as it is understood biblically and within the theo-

---

8. Reinhold Niebuhr, "The Church in a Secular Age," in Robert McAfee Brown, ed., *The Essential Reinhold Niebuhr: Selected Essays and Addresses* (New Haven and London: Yale University Press, 1986), 83.

logically mature traditions of the faith, people are encouraged to bring to the surface of their consciousness aspects of their experience they have had to suppress because the optimism of their society silently forbade discussion of them. Apart from such an acquaintance with Scripture and tradition, the formerly established churches of the Protestant mainline are simply victimized by the most immediate demands of their "clientele."

Sound teaching in the area of eschatology, especially as we near the end of the millennium, could be a worthy project of any concerned congregation in our context. Although it is conceptually difficult, Christian eschatology is by no means impossible to understand at some basic level of comprehension. It should also be recognized that part of the reason that people have difficulty grasping this doctrinal area conceptually has less to do with the intellect than it does with the will. For, in contrast to *either optimistic or pessimistic* credos, Christian eschatology demands of us the kind of openness to the future that is able to hold together honest recognition of time's negating dimensions and an expectancy based on trust in the God who "gives life to the dead and calls into existence the things that do not exist" (Rom. 4:17). It asks us to be realistic about the tragedy of existence while trusting that the end of the matter is "beyond tragedy" (Niebuhr). To live consciously and intentionally within such a dialectical tension is difficult, perhaps impossible, for most human beings, perhaps because, in actuality, precisely such a tension comes close to describing where we do live and must live. For there is within all of us a strong compulsion to resolve just this tension—to choose one or the other alternative; to determine here and now that the future is either devoid of reasons to hope (the choice of the pessimists) or that it is going to confirm all our fond desires (the choice of the optimists). Only the trust in God that we call faith can enable us consistently to refuse either of these premature and "childish" (Heidegger) resolutions, and to submit ourselves knowingly and joyfully to the hope that belongs to the life of discipleship.

32. What *Is* Eschatology?

32.1. The Two Connotations of "End." The Greek word *eschatos,* like the simple English word "end," contains two connotations. The most common use of both words, for instance, in everyday discourse, is the idea of termination: something—a vacation, a war, a life—comes to an end. In most theological work prior to the present century, eschatology had primarily to do with this meaning. The "doctrine of last things" was intended to answer the question, What, according to Christian doctrine, is believed about the final termination of life, whether individual or cosmic? What shall we say about the end toward which (*terminus ad quem*) life and history are moving?

But it is hard to consider this ordinary, temporal meaning of "the end" without at least touching upon the second meaning, which concerns the *purpose* of the process that will end. The connection of the two meanings is not strange or complicated, really; we regularly, at least implicitly, connect the purpose of a thing with the end-stage to which it moves. In education, for example, the temporal end of a course of studies conditions and is conditioned by the goal of the enterprise.

"End" as goal is less commonly used in ordinary speech today, and its usage in earlier literature often seems to us slightly archaic—for instance, "What is the chief end of man?"—the most famous question of the Westminster Catechism. Yet whether we use the word or not, the thought is present also to us. Nothing ends without implicitly raising the question of its end, its purpose (in Greek, *telos*). The most dramatic and existential instance of this is, of course, the personal experience of death. It may be the boast of atheism that the teleological question is a vestige of the age of belief, but few atheists have been able to confront the reality of their own end or that of their loved ones without asking, Why? And the "why" of death is the "why" of life itself. To what end, all this struggle to be? to become? to endure?

Obviously enough, if the termination of anything is dismal or abysmal or apparently capricious, it raises all the more poignantly the question of the meaning of that entity and its whole course through time. In a real sense, secular disbelief, far from rendering teleology obsolete, has intensified the question of the *telos* or "inner aim" of existence. We argued in the second volume that the great question of our epoch and context is some variation on the theme, "What are people for?"[9] If anything, secularization and "working atheism" have made this question more persistent and agonizing than it ever was in periods of strong religious faith. As Homo sapiens has grown more and more knowledgeable about the inevitable termination of *all* things, including the planet, the other, qualitative side of the term *eschatos* has become all the more conspicuous.

This, in part, is why we have observed in Christian theology over the past century a shift in the connotation of the term "eschatology." While, as we have seen, it has never been possible fully to separate the two meanings of "the end," anyone who has followed the dialogue of scholarly theology over the past hundred years or so realizes that "the doctrine of last things" is no longer only or even chiefly about "last things." Particularly since Rudolf Bultmann "discovered" the centrality of eschatology in the kerygma of the newer Testament, what has come to dominate the discussion of "the eschaton" is not the first but the second meaning of the term.

---

9. *Professing the Faith,* chap. 4, §15, "Human Vocation," 232–38.

Within the world of Christian scholarship, then, as distinct from popular (and especially apocalyptic) religion, twentieth-century theology has reversed the prioritization of the two aspects of eschatology. Its great question is not, How will everything end and what will happen "afterwards"?—a question that always *begged* the question of how, after the end of time, there could be any afterwards in the first place. Now, rather, the question is, What is the purpose of this process that we must regard as having a beginning and an ending? Popular religion continues to be fascinated with the termination and its "aftermath";[10] but although Christian scholarship cannot, or ought not, ignore the chronological aspect of the eschatological question, it has been forced by its consciousness of the *Zeitgeist* as well as its own internal processes to devote its main energies to the teleological aspect of eschatology: What is this strange business—life, history, existence between beginning and ending?—and why is it? To what end?

This has, of course, vastly complicated the whole field of eschatology. By comparison, it was a fairly straightforward area of doctrine when it could be thought primarily a chronological question. Systems of theology could then begin with the beginning—the doctrine of creation—and end with the ending, "last things." But this schema was called into question not only by the Darwinian considerations that affected the beginning but also by certain societal mood changes with respect to the ending. The former were felt most keenly by conservative Christianity, with its tendency toward biblical literalism on the subject of creation. The latter—questions about the future— were felt most keenly by liberal Christianity, which in the meantime had embraced so enthusiastically the great expectations for history and civilization that were part of modern euphoria.

Contemporary eschatology in fact begins in earnest with the first intimations of that "future shock" mentioned above—particularly, in Europe, with the first World War. At that point, the liberal tendency to envision a rather straight line of progress toward the future kingdom of God on earth began to seem exaggerated and false, just as, earlier, the conservative Christian concept of the beginning was rendered questionable by scientific theory. With both the beginning and the end understood very differently from the past, our century has witnessed developments in eschatology quite unlike nearly everything informing the postbiblical Christian tradition.

Perhaps, however, these developments are in some ways more *biblical* than most of the eschatological doctrine of the tradition. The changed eschatological perspective registers most conspicuously, I think, in christological changes. The christological center of Christian faith, under the impact of

---

10. See, for example, Hal Lindsey's *The Terminal Generation* (New York: Bantam Books, 1976).

events such as the "Great War" and the economic depressions of the earlier part of the century, could simply not sustain the kind of future-thinking indulged in by liberal and modernist theology.

The liberals presented Jesus as the founder of a movement whose exemplary moral behavior would eventually lead to the redemption of history, God's "kingdom," in which "the brotherhood of man" would be the ethical consequence of humankind's new realization, through Jesus, of "the fatherhood of God." But with the catastrophic beginnings of this century, such a Christology seemed inadequate to minds sensitive to the shift in the "spirit of the times." How, then, should one understand the person and work of the Christ? If he is not the initiator of a process of transformation that will issue in this sort of happy ending, this fulfillment of the promises of historical time, how shall we consider him?

Under the tutelage, partly, of the father of existentialism, Søren Kierkegaard, and the novelist Fyodor Dostoevsky, and through a revisitation of the Pauline and Reformation traditions, Karl Barth in his commentary on Romans presented a Christology that was informed by eschatological thinking of a sort very different from anything produced by liberalism, or, for that matter, its conservative critics. It is said that Adolf von Harnack, the eminent historian of dogma, simply did not know what to make of Barth's *Römerbrief*.[11] On December 7, 1923, Barth's great friend, the pastor Eduard Thurneysen, in a letter to Barth characterized the impact of Barth's work upon the liberals:

> One had come to cherish the hope (they said) that we were sufficiently advanced in accord with critical results to speak "simply" of Jesus and of love in a way that would be comprehensible to all, and now comes the "new school" and revives the whole orthodox bibliolatry, shuts God up between the two covers of a book (canon!) and basically inserts merely its own speculations into the Bible and ancient dogma. We are no longer living in the sixteenth century, etc., etc. . . . [12]

Barth did not speak "simply" of Jesus. He saw Jesus Christ as the vehicle of an eternity that at once invades, judges, and qualifies time. In his earlier works especially, the emphases would have to fall on the first two verbs:

---

11. The first version of this work appeared in 1918. It was completely rewritten and reissued in 1921. The first English translation did not appear until more than a decade later (*The Epistle to the Romans,* trans. from the sixth edition by Edwyn C. Hoskyns [London: Oxford University Press, 1933]).

12. James D. Smart, *Revolutionary Theology in the Making: Barth-Thurneysen Correspondence, 1914–1925* (Richmond: John Knox Press, 1964), 155.

"invades" and "judges." Eventually, Barth's emphasis upon God's "complete otherness" would give way, in Barth himself and others who were influenced by him, to that side of the earlier dialectic that stresses eternity's *qualification* of time. Thus, by the time twentieth-century theology reaches Jürgen Moltmann and is expressed in Moltmann's first and most influential book, *Theology of Hope,*[13] the eschatological perspective of Christianity is one that depicts God as the sovereign of time-future, who, as it were, pulls historical time (*chronos*) toward the divine goal, breaking the vicious circle of cause and effect, causing time to produce possibilities of "the new" (*novum*) that, apart from the grace revealed and effected through the Christ, it could not produce.

What is vital for us to grasp here is the way in which, in serious twentieth-century Christian thought, eschatology is no longer a doctrine or a doctrinal area appearing at the end of systems of theology, but a dimension affecting all aspects of the Christian story. Christian theology, as an account of the world visited and transformed by the Word made flesh, is now by definition *eschatological:* that is, it is a commentary on reality seen from the perspective of the triune God, and therefore understood as the interface of time and eternity, with the meaning or purpose of the whole of history introduced by the Christ *in medias res* (in the midst of things).

32.2. *Chronos* and *Kairos.* We may begin to sort this out a little if we distinguish two aspects of the biblical conception of time, which are tangentially related to the two connotations of *eschatos*. The first is the chronological aspect: Time moves in a linear fashion for the tradition of Jerusalem. It is not cyclical or spiral, not endlessly repetitive but always new. Yesterday was yesterday, today is today, tomorrow will be tomorrow. To conceptualize time, and simply to live within it, you need all three basic tenses—past, present, and future. Each moment on the "time line" is unique, irrevocable. This moment—the split second in which I am writing this word—will not occur again; and even if in the next instant I should duplicate the action of writing this word, it will not constitute a real repetition; it will be new, however familiar. Time is clock time.

This conception of time is essential to the Hebraic sense of history. There was a time when Abraham was not. There was a time when Abraham *had been*, and therefore could be remembered, but was no more. The lovely, nos-

---

13. The preface to the German edition of September, 1964, clearly announces the change in emphasis: "The following efforts bear the title *Theology of Hope,* not because they set out once again to present eschatology as a separate doctrine and to compete with the well known textbooks. Rather, their aim is show how theology can set out from hope and begin to consider its theme in an eschatological light" (English translation by James W. Leitsch [London: SCM, 1967; Minneapolis: Fortress Press, 1993]).

talgic, and perhaps a little ominous sentence in the KJV translation of Exodus 1:8 always seems to me to say it all: "Now there arose up a new king over Egypt, which knew not Joseph." This sense of the mystery, poignancy, and irrevocability of time is of course by no means exclusive to the tradition of Jerusalem; one has it in Virgil, for example—*Sed fugit interea, fugit inreparabile tempus.*[14] The passing of time is an essential dimension of the Hebraic understanding of reality. Israel's story may contain mythic elements, that is, elements that seem timeless; but its primary mode throughout is historical, not mythic. *Chronos* is taken very seriously and is not despised, as it tends to be in Greek thought. The honoring of chronological time belongs to that whole Jewish respect for finitude and particularity that has been such a scandal to peoples who wanted to embrace religions and ideologies that locate "the really real" in the transcendent. The Hebraic commitment to God (to God!) requires a commitment to history as well; because God is not only the creator of time but its sovereign, and God's providence is inseparable from the events that happen, the particular people who shape these events, and the deeds and misdeeds, sufferings and rejoicings of these people.

At the same time, Hebraic faith cannot be said to be *founded* on the chronological experience in itself. The mere subjection of the self to the process of time does not elicit faith. On the contrary, as one sees in the Wisdom traditions and especially Ecclesiastes, *chronos* as such is more apt to elicit faith's antithesis, and therefore also hope's antithesis.

> All flesh is grass,
>> and all its beauty is like the flower of the field.
> The grass withers, the flower fades,
>> when the breath of the Lord blows upon it;
>> surely the people is grass.
>
> (Isa. 40:6–7)

Thus, alongside of and in dialectical tension with the chronological sense of time's passage, there occurs in this faith-tradition also another mode of conceiving of time. In twentieth-century systematics, this has been associated with the Greek term *kairos,* which some have translated as "filled time," others as "the right time."[15] Let us try to characterize this concept.

---

14. "Time meanwhile flies, flies never to return," *Georgics* II.

15. "*Kairos* in secular usage is the moment in time which is especially favorable for an undertaking. . . . The New Testament usage with reference to redemptive history is the same. Here, however, it is not human deliberations but a divine decision that makes this or that date a *kairos,* a point of time that has a special place in the execution of God's plan of salvation" (Oscar Cullmann, *Christ and Time: The Primitive Christian Conception of Time and History,* trans. by Floyd V. Filson [London: SCM, 1951], 39).

There are moments, events, constellations of occurrences within chronological time that seem to bear special significance. They do not exactly transcend time chronologically understood—no, they certainly occur within history, for that is our inescapable matrix. But they impress themselves upon the soul in ways that "ordinary" events do not. A person, a community, is taken up into them, and is exposed, through them, to dimensions of reality that are extraordinary.

The very existence of Israel and of the church is predicated upon such *kairoi*. For Israel, *the* kairotic event—the "root experience" (Fackenheim) of all such *kairoi*—is the Exodus.[16] For the Christian community the core event, the *kairos* that creates this community, is "the Christ event."[17] In neither case does this mean that *kairoi* are limited to these two "moments" of history. But as the foundational events, these tell us immediately something about what is involved in the *kairos* aspect of time.

First, they tell us that *kairoi* are not antithetical to chronological time but occur within it. Second, they indicate that for both Israel and the church, the *kairos* event involves something like an invasion of the time process—not its supercession, but its being entered into and in some way being taken over, used, and transformed by what transcends it. Third, these primary *kairoi* show that this aspect of time is strongly informed by the experience of change: something comes to be that was not ("a people," where before there was "no people"); possibilities open up that were formerly not possible (deliverance from Egypt; reconciliation and unity as at Pentecost); above all, meaning is given where before there was only the confusion of occurrences and inevitabilities. Fourth, these two primary kairos events illustrate how the experience belonging to such an event qualifies *all* time—not only the particular moment or period that is associated with the event itself. Thus the Exodus becomes a theme of the whole life of Israel, indeed, the ground of its life, so that the present, no matter how apparently lacking in transparency of the divine presence, becomes meaningful on account of the community's remembrance: "Our fathers were slaves in the land of Egypt, and the Lord led us out." What occurred in and through the Christ becomes, for the disciple community, a source of continuing hope, regardless of the circumstances in which this community finds itself, which may be quite hopeless according to the usual standards.

We may think of *chronos,* then, as *quantitative* time and *kairos* as *qualitative* time. Time as quantity, as the sheer progression of "the clock," does not

---

16. See Emil L. Fackenheim, *God's Presence in History: Jewish Affirmations and Philosophical Reflections* (New York: New York University Press, and London: University of London Press, 1970), 8ff.
17. See Cullmann, *Christ and Time,* 39ff., and Part II in its entirety.

contain the teleological dimension. It is commonly said that "time heals all," but, in fact, time heals nothing by itself. In time we may forget, or rationalize, or discover new significance in events that seemed at the moment only absurd or frightening or mournful. Time contains no power of its own. Left to itself—if it can even be thought of in that way—time moves toward nothingness.[18] What lends substance and meaning to *chronos* is the in-breaking of the eternal. As faith apprehends this gracious entry of the eternal into time, it finds that quantitative time itself is *qualified*. Time, which as such could never produce the sense of purpose, becomes the locus of meaning and expectancy. All time is hallowed by "that" time.

Eschatology refers to the attempt of human minds inspired by faith to keep these two almost naturally conflictual dimensions of time in juxtaposition. That means on the one hand maintaining an uncompromising realism about chronological time, and on the other sustaining the expectation that, despite and even through the incomprehensibilities and vanities of the daily round, what is really "going on" is significant because it is informed by the meaningful consummation toward which sovereign grace inclines the whole process.

It has seemed to me useful to illustrate these two dimensions of time graphically by borrowing the most ancient "teaching symbol" of the doctrine of the Trinity, the invention (some say) of Thomas Aquinas—the so-called Shield of the Trinity. The purpose of this symbol in trinitarian doctrine is to hold together the two seemingly impossible affirmations of that doctrine, the absolute unity of the Deity and the reality of distinctions within the Godhead. The same dual purpose informs the use of the "shield" when we apply to the form of it the two categories of temporality. The outer rim of the shield upholds *chronos:* the past *is not* the present; the present *is not* the future; the future *is not* the past, and so on. The inner structure then illustrates the *kairos*-quality of time. In the revelatory "moment" (to borrow a Kierkegaardian category), the moment of the "root experience," the "Now" of the divine

---

18. "While it is true that the historian always works in limited areas of history with limited methods, especially when he works analytically, he nevertheless always reaches points where he encounters the abyss of history which by no means is God, but the destructive *nihil.* Where this nothing, this absurdity, this absolute death encounters him, he has an 'experience of history,' the way everyone who is involved in history can have it every day. Here arises the question of the meaning and the meaninglessness of world history. It is not answered by history itself. The Christian resurrection faith in the coming God, born of the cross, begins in such experiences to speak of history. 'We are first of all historical beings before we are contemplators of history, and only because we are historical beings do we turn into the latter' (William Dilthey). It occasionally helps to remind oneself of this relationship between suffering history and knowing history" (Jürgen Moltmann, in Frederick Herzog, ed., *The Future of Hope* [New York: Herder and Herder, 1970], 164.

Presence (see, for example, Rom. 3:21),[19] all three time-tenses seem to converge: the past, present, and future all meet together in the "now" of faith, yet without negating their distinctions.[20]

A symbol more indigenous to the Christian life (and it is of course more than a symbol) is the Lord's Supper. In this most rudimentary communitarian sacrament, both the chronos and the kairos character of time are acknowledged and, in their convergence, celebrated. The eucharistic meal honors the chronological dimension: we remember ("Do this in remembrance of me"), and what we remember is an occurrence that is past: "It is finished." It is a once-and-for-all occurrence; we cannot recreate it and that is not our intention—not, at any rate, in Protestant ecclesiology and liturgy. But we remember it. We also hope: "inasmuch as you do this, you show forth the Lord's death until he comes." What we hope for is still in the future. It has not yet occurred. It is awaited, and we groan with the creation while we wait.

Yet in the remembering and the hoping, as we are met by the divine Presence and therefore are able, although separate, to meet and engage one another anew, the thing may happen that is no longer happening and has not yet happened. That is, there is already an anticipation of the eschatological unity, reconciliation, and fulfillment that was experienced by the community of the upper room. I do not think that this happens *always,* or automatically; and I am not among those who believe that the more frequently you engage in the sacrament, the more you are likely to experience this interfacing of time and eternity, chronos and kairos. Moreover, I believe we must recognize that the sacrament may often occur quite outside the precincts of the sacred and intentional, in very secular and ordinary circumstances.

Nevertheless, what is *intended* by this sacrament is that, in time, we should be able now and then to experience the intersection of time and eternity; or,

---

19. Cullmann writes of "the emphatic 'now' (*nun*), which we often find used in the New Testament to stress the fact that the present period of the Apostolic Age belongs in an outstanding way to the redemptive history and is thus distinguished from all other times. For example it is said in Col. 1:26 that 'the mystery which has been hidden for ages and generations has *now* been revealed to the saints, to whom God has willed to make it known. It is in a similar sense that the author of the Epistle to the Hebrews speaks of his own time as 'today' (*semeron,* ch. 3:7, 13, 15)" (Cullmann, *Christ and Time,* 44).

20. "Past and future meet in the present, and both are included in the eternal 'now.' They are not swallowed by the present; they have their independent and different functions. Theology's task is to analyze and describe these functions in unity with the total symbolism to which they belong. In this way the *eschaton* becomes a matter of present experience without losing its futuristic dimension: we stand *now* in face of the eternal, but we do so looking ahead toward the end of history and the end of all which is temporal in the eternal. This gives to the eschatological symbol its urgency and seriousness and makes it impossible for Christian preaching and theological thought to treat eschatology as an appendix to an otherwise finished system" (Paul Tillich, *Systematic Theology,* vol. 3 [Chicago: University of Chicago Press, 1963], 395–96).

more modestly stated, that we should at least sense that our lives, individually and communally, are part of a much larger story, with a past they did not themselves fashion and a future they could not themselves create.

But if this convergence of time and eternity applies to the the Lord's Supper, Protestants who remember and hope within their tradition will want to insist that it applies also to the sacrament of the Word. The poor, despised words of the preacher—words that are always thoroughly conditioned by *chronos*—may be vehicles of what by themselves they by no means can achieve. Through these words, now and then, here and there, it may be that one hears a Word that infinitely transcends while humbly dwelling with these words.

And if we take seriously this whole dialectic of the quantitative and the qualitative in time, faithfully understood, we shall have to think that *every* aspect of ordinary, everyday experience bears about it some mysterious connection with the holy; that the secular and the sacred are virtually inseparable, even if they are theoretically distinguishable.

> There is only one reality—the world. And we are all a part of that God-given and God-sustained reality. There is one holy place—the world. Holy worldliness is the stance of Christianity.[21]

32.3. Futuristic and Realized Eschatology. An important debate of the earlier part of this century centered in the distinction between futuristic and realized eschatology. In some respects, it seems to me to have been an unprofitable and misleading debate. Futuristic eschatology, as the term immediately suggests, accentuates the future realization of the salvation introduced through Jesus Christ, and it is right to do so. Those who employed the term "realized eschatology" believed that it was wrong to reserve the whole eschatological experience for the future because, they said, it is already realized by faith; and they were right to say so. Both positions preserve something that is essential to Christian hope, but when they separate the two dimensions of eschatology, they end with truncated views.

Futuristic eschatology came to be out of a concentration upon the chronological aspect of the biblical conception of time and history. The same approach to the faith that thinks of the beginning in a temporal sense considers the end in the same way. The fulfillment of the redemption wrought in the life,

---

21. Robert C. Strom, "A New Freedom for Ministry," in Stephen C. Rose, ed., *Who's Killing the Church?* (Chicago: Renewal Magazine; and New York: Association Press, 1966), 14. (Recall in this connection the discussion of Irving Greenberg's proposal for Christianity's "second stage," chap. 4, §14.2.)

death, and resurrection of Jesus remains to be accomplished, even though its character and reality are already visible to faith in Jesus Christ himself and, in a measure, in the church.

The appropriateness of this view lies in its potentiality for theological and ethical realism, in the modern sense of the term. As we remarked at the beginning of this chapter, if one looks about the world for concrete evidence of the victory of forgiving, reconciling love, one finds all too little of it. Already the writer of the Epistle to the Hebrews recognized this: "As it is, we do not yet see everything in subjection to him. But we see Jesus, who for a little while was made lower than the angels, crowned with glory and honor because of the suffering of death, so that by the grace of God he might taste death for everyone" (2:8–9). To point in this way to the crucified Christ as evidence of the divine fulfillment belongs to the theology of the cross; it is to see the triumph of grace "hidden beneath its opposite." In this respect, the emphasis on futurity ought to be retained.

The problem historically associated with futuristic eschatology, however, is that it has seldom articulated itself under the aegis of the theology of the cross; on the contrary, it was taken up very early by Christian triumphalism of the otherworldly variety. The fulfillment of redemption was transferred to the supramundane sphere, to "the afterlife." This may have been an understandable reaction of the early church as it faced the disappointment of its expectations for an imminent Parousia. It may also be a natural outlet for the faith of a relatively small community, such as the church was prior to its establishment, disheartened by the prospect of worldly transformation through its witness. Nevertheless, however understandable, this kind of futurism has helped to create one of the problems we highlighted in *Professing the Faith*: that the Christian faith historically seems to have had little to say to the question of the "fate of the earth." If the consummation or goal of the "root experience" of the church has nothing to do with this world, why, in the first place, is the incarnation of the Word so central? If the goal of history is the return of reality to a purely spiritual estate, surely the doctrine at the center of the faith ought to have been that of the Holy Spirit.

The strength of what C. H. Dodd and others named (over against the regnant futurism of the tradition) "realized eschatology" is that it is able to incorporate the here and now and not to transfer "the end" to an indeterminate and probably supramundane future. Realized eschatology concentrates on the second meaning of the term *eschatos,* and on time as *kairos* rather than *chronos.* It looks for the goal or purpose of time in the midst of time, experienceable as something that grasps the hearer existentially. The end is therefore already realized in the life of faith—the faith of individuals and the faith of the believing community.

The problem, as Macquarrie has noted,[22] is that realized eschatology tends to become individualized. Although it rightly relates the eschaton to the here and now of worldly existence, it is more applicable to the microcosm than to the macrocosm. Once again, therefore, the question of the future of history and of the world is held in abeyance.

It seems necessary, then, to retain both the future and the accomplished or realized aspects of biblical eschatology. It would be difficult to take in the whole witness of the newer Testament and to eliminate or minimize either of these dimensions. Clearly, for this testimony, something decisive *has happened,* and this decisive occurrence is already grasped in some definite sense by faith. Not everything is left to the future. Faith is not just hope, but also remembrance; and without remembrance, hope is foundationless and may be nothing more than wishful thinking, constitutional optimism.

On the other hand, for the biblical witness, something is still awaited. "We do not see everything put beneath his feet." Despite the decisive visitation and transformation of time by the eternal Word, everything seems to continue as usual—evil goes its way unaffected, like a prowling lion (1 Peter 5:8); it may even seem stronger than ever. And even our faith is unsatisfactory— is mingled with doubt; is longing for clear-headed sight. And even the church, the only "place" in which there is explicit consciousness of the triumph of grace, is imperfectly formed and informed by this consciousness; it is often faithless, and may be "last" in the divine kingdom—nothing is to be presumed!

It was in an effort to retain both of these emphases that Oscar Cullmann and others made use of the by now familiar juxtaposition "already/not yet." Cullmann used the metaphor of the battlefield:

> The decisive battle in a war may already have occurred in a relatively early stage of the war, and yet the war still continues. Although the decisive effect of that battle is perhaps not recognized by all, it nevertheless already means victory. But the war must still be carried on for an undefined time, until "Victory Day."[23]

Karl Barth employed another metaphor: the pendulum of the clock still swings on its own momentum, even though its mechanism has already stopped. Already/not yet.

---

22. Realized eschatology "is defective precisely because it gains most plausibility from being individualized, thus leaving out the whole cosmic and communal dimensions of New Testament teaching. As far as the cosmos as a whole is concerned, or even the human race, the eschatological expectations are far from being realized. There can be no doubt that the New Testament writers themselves intended much more than what is left when demythologizing has treated their eschatology as realized and individualized" (John Macquarrie, *Principles of Christian Theology* [London: SCM, 1966], 316–17).

23. Cullmann, *Christ and Time,* 84.

Such metaphors may be needed, because it is difficult to convey in language—even symbolic language—this experience that is nevertheless central and vital to faith. In the end, only the experience itself can convey its meaning. Just as time as a whole defies definition, although its strange paradoxes are the subject matter of our daily life and thought, so the eschatological character of the faith can be lived but never fully explained. Here, as perhaps nowhere else in Christian theology, the discipline has to admit its impossibility. The "already/not yet" language is useful, for we know of this dialectic in many of our life experiences; yet by itself it is an awkward linguistic tool, and it has become too much of a cliché to communicate, perhaps, what it once communicated. Its basic problem in most of its earlier exegetes, however, was its lack of a clear theological basis. It seemed a linguistic device without an adequate foundational theology.

The foundation that the device requires is the theology of the cross. Indeed, it could almost be said that the theology of the cross *is* an eschatology, except that this would too easily be heard as eliminating or rendering secondary Christology and all other doctrinal areas; and, as we have seen, the *theologia crucis* is a spirit and method affecting all doctrine. This theology does, however, imply and build upon a decisive eschatology; and it is precisely an eschatology in which the future and present or "realized" dimensions are held in a creative tension.

By contrast, both futuristic and realized eschatologies presuppose, imply, or court a theology of glory. Conventional eschatologies throughout the Christian centuries have accentuated the future *heavenly* consummation of redemption because, unable or unwilling to consider the redemption of creation, they could only ensure the triumph of omnipotence in a supernatural projection. Realized eschatology rightly wished to make the goal of existence accessible "already" here and now; but it, too, has for the most part presupposed a *theologia gloriae,* which it could only realize in individual faith.

The great service Jürgen Moltmann's earlier works performed for eschatology was to develop the whole theology of hope under the aegis of the theology of the cross. This was not obvious to many people in his first major work, *Theology of Hope;* and it was partly for that reason that he wrote *The Crucified God.* In his introduction to the latter work, Moltmann writes:

> I intend to show that the theology of the cross is none other than the reverse side of the Christian theology of hope, if the starting point of the latter lies in the resurrection of the *crucified* Christ. As I said in *Theology of Hope,* that theology was itself worked out as an *eschatologia crucis.* This book, then, cannot be regarded as a step back. *Theology of Hope* began with the *resurrection* of the crucified Christ, and I am now turning to look at the *cross* of the risen Christ. . . . Unless it apprehends the pain of the negative, Christian hope can-

not be realistic and liberating. In no sense does this theology of the cross "go back step by step"; it is intended to make the theology of hope more concrete, and to add the necessary power of resistance to the power of its visions to inspire to action.[24]

The dimension of "realization" in Moltmann's eschatology applies not only to individual faith or even the faith of the *koinonia;* it is, rather, in the tradition of Bonhoeffer, a worldly and indeed a cosmic realization. But Moltmann does not separate the aspect of completedness or realization from that of futurity; instead, he presents the work of the triune God as a proleptic triumph of the new (*novum*) which is coming to meet us from God's future and is being realized both in faith and in the reality of worldly change. Because Christian hope is the future dimension of a faith (trust) that is focused on the resurrection of the *crucified* one, it does not have to ignore or repress worldly negations in order to believe in the possibility of the negation of the negations. Hope is hope, and indeed hope against hope, and not fulfillment; the future is "not yet." But it is already coming to be—so long as this possibility is understood *sub specie Christi.*

---

24. Jürgen Moltmann, *The Crucified God,* trans. R. A. Wilson and John Bowden (London: SCM, 1974; Minneapolis: Fortress Press, 1993), 5.

CHAPTER ■ NINE
Creaturely Destiny

33. The Reign of God and History

33.1. Biblical Affirmation of History "In Spite Of." The Christian view of history is determined by the trinitarian presupposition that God is committed to the creation and its transformation. Although there have been powerful expressions of the Christian religion that depreciate history, and although, as we have seen, Christianity as a whole has rarely affirmed historical existence unambiguously, the conception of God and God's purposes informing the primary sources of this faith make it mandatory to embrace a view of historical time that insists upon the meaningfulness of history. Theories of history that understand it as being devoid of meaning or the mere shadow play of a meaning that is utterly transcendent of time must be rejected. As we have shown in the discussion of time, *chronos,* which is to say the chronological aspect of nature, takes on meaning because it is penetrated by *kairos,* which is to say by grace.

At many points in this trilogy we have had to recognize that the Christian religion, in its meeting with Hellenistic thought, was altered significantly. Perhaps no greater or more permanently damaging alteration can be noted than exists in the realm of historical hope. Although the tradition of Athens is by no means monolithic, it manifests a marked suspicion of historical existence. Most of the religions as well as the philosophical schools that evolved in that ancient classical atmosphere advance religious or quasi religious soteriologies that in effect save believers *from* history. Even Epicurus, who did not believe in any realm other than the material, was known as *Soter* (savior) by his disciples, because he taught them how to accept their materiality and no longer torment themselves with the quest for immortality.

Biblical faith is by no means unconscious of the precarious nature of the course of finite being in time. One could never say that the parental religion, Judaism, is naive about the negative side of historical existence. Even the theoretically optimistic Wisdom literature, with its pragmatism and celebration of the senses, is full of warnings against the snares of sensuality, acquisitiveness, jealousy, and the like. As for the allegedly pessimistic Wisdom literature, in some of it—particularly Koheleth (Ecclesiastes)—biblical Israel confronts openly the question of whether meaning could ever be found in life "under the sun"—

> Vanity of vanities! All is vanity.
>> What does man gain by all the toil at which he
>> toils under the sun?
> A generation goes, and a generation comes,
>> but the earth remains for ever.
> The sun rises and the sun goes down,
>> And hastens to the place where it rises.
> . . . .
> All the streams run to the sea
>> but the sea is not full;
> to the place where the streams flow,
>> there they flow again.
> All things are full of weariness,
>> a man cannot utter it;
> the eye is not satisfied with seeing,
>> nor the ear filled with hearing.
> What has been is what will be,
>> and what has been done is what will be done;
>> and there is nothing new under the sun.

I have seen the business that God has given to the sons of men to be busy with. He has made everything beautiful in its time; also he has put eternity into man's mind, yet so that he cannot find out what God has done from the beginning to the end.

(Eccles. 1:2ff; 3:10–11)

Here, specifically and boldly, but sporadically also, in the prophets, psalmists, and the letter writers of the newer Testament, biblical religion entertains the prospect that history as such is an eternal round of frantic, essentially unfathomable, and perhaps directionless activity. Yet biblical religion does not succumb to this temptation. The fact that it entertains the prospect and, particularly in Ecclesiastes, the poem of Job, and the Apocalypse, is tempted by it, makes biblical religion's affirmation of the meaningfulness of historical existence all the more profound. It is easy enough for those who never ask

484

whether life "under the sun" has any purpose to affirm its purposefulness! The Bible is well acquainted with Shakespeare's thought that history may be "a tale told by an idiot, full of sound and fury, signifying nothing." Think only of Sarah's laughter when she heard "those men" under the tree talking about her forthcoming pregnancy (Gen. 18). When Israel affirms that hope is a legitimate historical category, applicable to time, applicable to individual life as well as the life of the creation as a whole, it does not do so naively but in the full knowledge that this can never be done easily. It is a matter of trust in God, not in processes naturally favorable to human welfare.

Perhaps, as many affirm, the newer Testament has already been affected by Hellenistic skepticism about history. Certainly it is possible to find in it intimations of the all-too-human "world-weariness" to which Koheleth gives voice. But this skepticism about the applicability of hope to history is countered by what is after all the central affirmation of both the Gospels and the epistles—the Incarnation. The enfleshment of the divine Logos, which the Gospel writers themselves understand as the culmination of a long, painful, gracious movement on the part of God toward the groaning creation, curbs the temptation of the earliest forms of Christianty to capitulate to other-worldliness.

That such a temptation existed for the first Christians is entirely under-standable. A rejected, persecuted minority easily succumbs to the thought that its hope has little to do with the conditions under which its life is lived; that it is a pilgrim people, sojourning temporarily in a strange and foreign land; a people whose goal is "on the other side of Jordan," and so forth. Moreover, this thought readily translates into the belief that the object of the Christian life is to pass through history with as much fortitude (and perhaps as much haste) as possible, in order to attain the heavenly goal.

But this familiar temptation of religion is contraposed, surely, by the pri-mary message of the newer Testament, which is that God, far from wishing to supercede time and finitude, seeks proximity to fallen creation and finally, in Jesus as the Christ, enters into an unqualified state of identification with creation, with all the burden of vulnerability, anxiety, temptation, suffering, and death associated with that state. So decisive is this message for the earli-est disciple communities that even that gospel that is most tempted by Helle-nistic religion affirms in its central claim the incarnational thrust of a love that is directed toward the redemption *of the world.* "God so loved *the cosmos* . . . " (John 3:16).

The impulse to flee history is not only an ancient one. It is a human incli-nation, and as such it is present in every age. Even Euro-American modernity, which more than any previous age wished to celebrate history unambigu-ously, produced its Schopenhauers and its Hal Lindseys. And now, at the end of the modern epoch—perhaps one should say *as* the end of this epoch—

there is a socially pervasive temptation to escape from history that is all the more effective because it is mostly repressed and follows upon such an exaggerated outburst of historical optimism. While our churchgoing grandparents and great-grandparents were imbued with the thought of "the kingdom of God in this generation," what characterizes our cohort of North Americans is what Robert Lifton has called "a sense of radical futurelessness."

> From the standpoint of psychic impact, it does not matter much whether we imagine the end of *all* or merely *most* human life. Either way, we can no longer feel certain of biological posterity. We are in doubt about the future of *any* group—of one's family, geographical or ethnic confreres, people, or nation. The image is that of human history and human culture simply terminating. The idea of *any* human future becomes a matter of profound doubt. In that image we or perhaps our children are the last human beings. There is no one after us to leave anything to. We become cut off, collectively self-enclosed, something on the order of a vast remnant. The general human narrative would come to an end, and nothing in that narrative can justify to us or explain the reasons for that end.[1]

Paraphrasing the prophet, one may say that without a future, people perish. More devastatingly, when the future that appears on the horizon not only lacks promise but is full of pain, the impulse to avoid it is perhaps the most immediate reaction. Flight from history is attempted in many different ways. Less sophisticated methods of escape are alarmingly conspicuous in North America today. The so-called drug culture is inexplicable apart from this deep sociopsychic phenomenon. To imagine that widespread drug addiction is due only to organized crime, and that its cure will be found when the drug barons and their underlings have been delivered over to the law, is naive in the extreme. The demand for drugs would not be what it is if it were not for the fact that so many people find present existence unbearable and the future unthinkable. We could speak of suicide in a similar vein. There is a very high incidence of suicide in Canada and the United States, particularly among the young and more particularly still among the youth of the indigenous peoples. In any society, younger people are most susceptible to the loss of historical meaning. They are not likely to understand that this is what they are responding to, but they have not built up psychic resources of indifference or sublimation to deal with the negations they feel. Those negations are especially oppressive among native peoples, whose way of life has been taken from them by the encroachments of the technological society.

---

1. Robert Jay Lifton and Richard Falk, *Indefensible Weapons: The Political and Psychological Case Against Nuclearism* (Toronto: Canadian Broadcasting Corporation, 1982), 67.

But such obvious flights from history are probably not as damaging to the social fabric as the more subtle and indirect forms of escape. "The sense of radical futurelessness" is at least as strongly at work in consumerism as in drug use. Those who pursue the private life, who seek personal, material security above the vicissitudes of history, whose major energy is devoted to the perfecting of their own bodies, who stay away from the voting stations, or who advocate new versions of American isolationism in a global society that is no longer easily partitioned: such persons are also fleeing from history. Because they are relatively affluent, they do not have to numb their own minds or extinguish their own lives; they anaesthetize the rest of the world instead.

While therefore it may be true that Hellenistic religion and philosophy swayed Christianity historically, luring it away from Jerusalem's dogged determination to remain faithful to the creation, the human refusal of creaturehood has always provided a fertile soil for the abandonment of history. That refusal is rampant in our context. It is part of what we called the Sisyphus syndrome.[2] Although we continue to indulge in the rhetoric of progress, most of us expect little improvement in the public realm.

There can be no recovery of the biblical determination to affirm history "in spite of" everything unless representatives of biblical faith, whether Judaic or Christian, are willing to expose themselves at depth to the temptation to historical hopelessness and inarticulate despair by which our epoch is marked. The kind of bourgeois religion that subsists by helping people to conceal their incipient despair, that is, by superficial affirmations of the meaning of life, will never produce profound expressions of historical hope.[3] Here as elsewhere, the positive relation between hope and history can only be articulated by those who are sufficiently exposed to the antithetical prospect in all of the specificity of its current power. "The man who does not know what death is does not know either what resurrection is."[4] Christians

---

2. *Professing the Faith,* chap. 5, §17, 253–62.

3. "It is interesting how every religion which imparts a superficial meaning to life, and grounds that meaning in a dubious sanctity, finally issues in despair. Those who make the family their god must despair when the family is proved to be only a little less mortal than the individual. Those who make a god of their nation must despair when the might of their nation crumbles, as every creaturely and sinful might must: 'For we are consumed by thine anger and by thy wrath are we troubled' (Ps. 90:7). . . .

"Every humanistic creed is a cosmos of meaning sustained by a thin ice on the abysmal deeps of meaninglessness and chaos. Only the faith in God, who has been 'our dwelling place in all generations,' and who was God 'before the mountains were brought forth or ever the earth and the world were made' (Ps. 90:1–2), can survive the vicissitudes of history, can rescue human existence from the despair in which it is periodically involved by its sinful pretentions, and the tragic disappointment of its facile hopes" (Reinhold Niebuhr, in Robert McAfee Brown, ed., *The Essential Reinhold Niebuhr* [New Haven and London: Yale University Press, 1986], 84).

4. Karl Barth, *Dogmatics in Outline,* trans. G. T. Thomson (London: SCM, 1949), 154.

must ask themselves whether there is not some mysterious but not illogical relation between the extremely negative experiences of Judaism in our epoch and the Judaic renewal of hope in history. Emil Fackenheim, Canada's foremost Jewish theologian and philosopher, now living in Israel, has written that after Auschwitz, hope is for the Jew not an option but a "commandment." But hope is authentic only when the Jew remembers—that is to say, remembers not only the ancient "root experience" of the exodus but also the modern one, the Holocaust. If the data of despair is neglected, then hope—or what will be called hope—will revert to shallow hopefulness, a conditioned reflex of the well off.[5]

In the previous chapter, we argued that the great sin of white North American middle-class Protestantism is precisely that shallow hopefulness, "cheap hope." We cannot be said to have a gospel because we refuse to know enough of the bad news to prepare our collective soul for the good. Our insistence upon being and remaining positive and optimistic is what prevents us from exploring deeply the meaning of hope, biblically understood. We want to have Easter Sunday without Good Friday—or better, we desire a Friday so "good" that it is no longer for us a symbolic mode of identification with the suffering world.

Here, as at many other points of faith and understanding, Caucasian American and Canadian Christians need to learn from the African American experience. In his recent work, *We Have Been Believers: An African-American Systematic Theology*,[6] James H. Evans discusses the contrast between black and white American attitudes toward time, future and past. Even reflection on the African roots of black North Americans yields important distinctions: "The thoroughly modern notion of historical progress, which has been so essential to the development of Western societies, is not part of traditional African thought." He quotes John S. Mbibi on the subject:

"In traditional African thought, there is no concept of history moving 'forward' toward a future climax, or toward an end of the world. Since the future does not exist beyond a few months, the future cannot be expected to usher in a golden age, or a radically different state of affairs from what is in the Sasa and the Zamani. The notion of a messianic hope, or a final destruction of the world, has no place in the traditional concept of history. So African peoples have

---

5. Emil Fackenheim, *God's Presence in History: Jewish Affirmations and Philosophical Reflections* (New York: New York University Press, and London: University of London Press, 1970), chap. 3; 67ff.

6. James H. Evans, *We Have Been Believers: An African-American Systematic Theology* (Minneapolis: Fortress Press, 1992).

no 'belief in progress,' the idea that the development of human activities and achievements move from a low to a higher degree."[7]

As for the enslaved Africans in the New World, their perception of historical time was almost the antithesis of their white owners:

> Enslaved Africans had attitudes towards the past different from their enslavers. For its enfranchised inhabitants "the New World" was a place of new fortunes, new hope, new identity, where new ideas could be put into practice with minimal impediment. The past could be scuttled. . . . African slaves, on the other hand, had been robbed of both their past and their homeland. In their place was a history of degradation and a land not their own. Thus the content of any meaningful eschatological discourse in the African-American context must take into account the attempts to murder that history and reclaim their land.[8]

Since they could not derive hope immediately from their bleak experience of the present, the enslaved people looked to a transcendent source of hope; and since they could not even speak of their hope for God's care and deliverance directly, they "were compelled to find a language that would unmistakably express their hopes for a reversal in their fortunes and at the same time conceal that message from their slaveowners. The apocalyptic language found in the Bible was a ready vehicle."[9]

It is a mistake, Evans demonstrates, to believe that African Americans turned to "heaven" and abandoned hope for the transformation of earth. Their transcendent source of hope in its main expression did not produce the "otherworldliness" that can be read into some of their spiritual songs. Against such an interpretation, James Cone's first book, *Black Theology and Black Power,* "rejects the apparent otherworldliness of traditional Black religion. Black theology, [Cone] argues, cannot accept any perspective that does not compel the oppressed to deal with the evil in this world."[10] This, Evans feels, was stated somewhat too strongly, and he notes that "in Cone's theology, one can observe a movement from the rejection of otherworldliness to a critique of distorted otherworldliness, to an appreciation of the role of eschatological vision in the liberation struggle of the oppressed. However, the com-

---

7. Evans, *We Have Been Believers,* 143. (The quotation is from Mbibi's *African Religions and Philosophy* [Garden City, N.Y.: Doubleday, 1969], 21.)

8. Ibid., 146. (The quotation in the excerpt is from Bonnie J. Barthold, *Black Time: Fiction of Africa, The Caribbean, and the United States* [New Haven: Yale University Press, 1982], 23.)

9. Ibid., 146.

10. Ibid., 147.

mon element in this perspective is the relation of eschatology to the evil of the world, or the theodicy of the landscape."[11]

The parallels between the conclusions about hope and history drawn by African American slaves and those who knew slavery "in the land of Egypt" are so obvious as to need no commentary. Like the former, biblical faith affirms history, knowing that it is by no means obviously "good." For the most part it is a history of pain, and from this history none of us, finally, can escape. The source of faith's affirmation of history "in spite of" the pain is God's own participation in it. Through God's assumption of the searing negations of historical existence, history itself has been, is being, and shall be transformed.

33.2. Biblical, Classical, and Modern Views of History.   This biblical view of history rests, we have said, upon its theology and Christology. Stating the matter in another way, it rests upon a dialectical conception of the relation of meaning and time. It will help to explicate this relation if we follow the example of Reinhold Niebuhr and contrast the biblical view of history with two alternative positions, the classical and the modern. With each of these, Christianity has something in common besides its experienced connection with each; and it also diverges markedly from each.

The classical view, which receives expression in many different philosophic and religious systems associated with Hellenic and Hellenistic thought, tends not only to locate the principle of meaning outside of history but to leave it there.[12] Individuals and enlightened schools or worshiping communities are able to discover transcendent meaning and apply it to their lives, but it always transcends time as such. The temporal process is incapable of incorporating the eternal. Through wisdom, mystic identification with deities, or ascetic practices, finite beings may anticipate the infinite; but they shall only become

---

11. Ibid., 149.

12. "The classical culture, elaborated by Plato, Aristotle and the Stoics, is a western and intellectual version of a universal type of ahistorical spirituality. . . . The common characteristic in all of these approaches is that a rigorous effort is made to disassociate what is regarded as a timeless and divine element in human nature from the world of change and temporal flux. The mystical, predominantly oriental, versions, seek this divine and changeless element in a level of consciousness which transcends every particularity of finite existence, including the particularity of the individual ego. The rational, predominantly western-classical version finds the divine and immortal element in human nature primarily in the power of human reason, more specifically in man's capacity for conceptual knowledge. This capacity, when rigorously purged of the taints and corruptions of the passions and senses of man's physical existence, lifts man into a timeless realm. It relates him to the world of change only in the sense that conceptual knowledge enables him to discern the changeless patterns and structures which underlie the world of change, the world of 'coming-to-be' and 'passing away'" (Reinhold Niebuhr, *Faith and History: A Comparison of Christian and Modern View of History* [New York: Charles Scribner's Sons, 1951], 16).

fully aware of the eternal when they themselves have achieved complete liberty from finitude.

As for the temporal process itself, it circles about—seeking, as it were, its goal, but never finding it: "All the rivers run to the sea, yet the sea is not full" (Eccles. 1:7). In some systems, such as Neoplatonism, the temporal process is truly futile. It recurs aimlessly. In others (including some types of Christianity that have been deeply influenced by Platonism), while the process is not aimless, it is so inconclusive and so devoid of clear direction that in order to discover any teleological frame of reference for life one must so far as possible eschew the material and the finite and pursue the modicum of infinity that lingers in the embodied soul as memory of its original state.

The modern conception of history reverses this entirely. With the end of the medieval period and the beginnings, in the Renaissance, of modernity, there is a new determination to locate meaning within the historical process as such. At first this determination is qualified by the Renaissance propensity to look back, past the ignorance of "the Dark Ages," to the light of classical culture. Since classical culture included the suspicion of history, there is a kind of ambiguity in the early Renaissance: it wants to have the positive anthropological view of classical culture, especially including its high estimate of human rationality; but it cannot yet dissociate this from the tendency of classical culture to locate meaning outside the historical process.

With the seventeenth century, this hesitance begins to disappear, and with the eighteenth-century Enlightenment it is, for all intents and purposes, overcome. Aided by the industrial revolution and social Darwinism, the modern vision blossoms fully in the nineteenth century. At the heart of it is the insistence that the principle of meaning—the teleological principle—is built into the historical process itself. In other words, time progresses inevitably toward the unfolding of the good.

This is the "religion of progress" to which reference has been made throughout these volumes. As such, it certainly had its critics prior to our own century.[13] It is the twentieth century, however, that has produced the sharpest critics of this view of history, for the "great events" of this century have hardly confirmed such a positive worldview.

Modernity, as Robert Heilbronner and others have pointed out, embraced a strange and never-consistent admixture of determinism and voluntarism in its theory of history. The modern mind was in agreement that history prog-

---

13. Leo Tolstoy was one of them. In 1857, after he had witnessed an execution by guillotine in Paris, Tolstoy wrote: "When I saw the head part from the body and how it thumped separately into the box, I understood, not with my mind, but with my whole being that no theory of the reasonableness of our present progress could justify this deed, and that though everyone from the creation of the world, on whatever theory, had held it to be necessary, I knew it would be unnecessary and bad; and therefore the arbiter of what is good and evil is not what people say

resses, but it seemed unable to decide whether (to paraphrase Shakespeare's Malvoleo in *Twelfth Night*) we have greatness thrust upon us or whether we are to achieve greatness through determination and hard work. Does history progress *inevitably,* regardless of human deportment? Or do we humans, with our superior intellect and our technical skills, cause time to bring forth the good? Heilbronner's resolution of this question is to suggest that modernity wanted to retain both proposals: the winds of time are blowing in ways entirely favorable to the human project; it is our task to steer our ship intelligently so as to take best advantage of these fortuitous conditions.[14] Niebuhr, on the other hand, thinks that the contradiction between voluntarism and determinism remains, and that it in fact skews the whole modern project.[15] Since on the one hand the modern mind thinks the future dependent in some way upon its own activity, we find ourselves burdened with an impossible sense of our own divinity, so that when things go wrong we blame ourselves mercilessly. Since on the other hand modernity was also convinced that history was moving toward perfection all by itself, there has developed a tendency in the technological society to believe that we are not responsible, that technology will right itself, including its own problems, and that whatever we do will "come out right in the end." Thus modernity has wavered between two divergent pathways.

If we try to understand the biblcal view of history, it is didactically useful as well as apologetically necessary to contrast it with these related but quite different conceptions of the course of time. The biblical view has points of convergence with both of these views, but it is also in fundamental disagreement with both of them.

Against classical types of thought about historical existence, biblical faith insists that meaning, while it is certainly not (as modernity insisted) built into the process, nevertheless decisively *enters* the process, altering it, transforming it, orienting it toward the good. I repeat: *toward.* Biblical faith is in agreement with classical expressions of this subject insofar as it locates the teleological source of historical purpose outside the process of history itself. History itself does not contain its own redemptive principle, nor does that "principle" (if divine grace can be so named) ever simply merge into historical time. But biblical faith disagrees with classical culture where the latter refuses to let the eternal and transcendent principle of meaning into the time

---

and do, nor is it progress, but is my heart and I" (quoted by A. N. Wilson in his biography *Tolstoy* [London: Penguin Books, 1988], 146–47).

14. Robert Heilbronner, *The Future as History* (New York: Harper and Brothers, Harper Torchbooks, 1959), 34.

15. Niebuhr, *Faith and History,* 3.

process at all. As I shall try to say in a moment, this relates both to Christology and ecclesiology.

Biblical faith agrees with classical theory on the question of the locus of the teleological principle, namely, that it lies outside the historical process as such, and it disagrees with the modern conception of history precisely at this point. Both capitalist and communist theories of history are modern in that they both assume that purpose—indeed, salvation—inheres in the process. The quarrel of Christianity with both of these modern political-economic ideologies stems from the biblical and Reformation insight that grace and nature are not to be equated. Grace may penetrate, alter, and even perfect nature; but it does not *become* nature.

We know that certain forms of Christianity in the Western world adapted themselves precisely to the modern conception of history. At the heart of Christian liberalism lay the assumption that the workings of divine providence were for all intents and purposes identical with the laws of nature and history, and that the latter could be confidently interpreted as progressive in character. The "kingdom of God," whose imminence inspired enthusiastic liberal missionaries to devote lifetimes of service to its advent, seemed almost visibly on the way. As the previous sentence demonstrates, liberal Christians also suffered from the same ambiguity mentioned earlier: were they to usher in God's kingdom through their evangelical and social activity, or was the kingdom inevitable?

Neo-orthodoxy was not only an attack upon the optimistic anthropology of liberalism. It was also (and, I should judge, more so) inspired by the recognition that Christian liberals had been absurdly optimistic about the course of history. Liberalism could not account for the enormous setbacks to historical progress that were coterminous with the twentieth century, beginning especially with World War I. With modernity as a whole, Christian modernism, in its enthusiasm for progress, relinquished all the intellectual and spiritual tools of the tradition that could have helped Christianity to comprehend and deal with the overwhelmingly negative experiences that began to occur just at the point where, in the liberal scenario, the fine promises of the past ought to have begun manifesting themselves.

They had thrown out original sin, the sense of the tragic, the idea of divine judgment and wrath; they had accentuated what they imagined were the positive elements of the Christian gospel—but devoid of the negations in dialogue with which, in biblical faith, these positives could acquire depth and weight. It is now fashionable to think that neo-orthodoxy, so called, was itself an overreaction, and perhaps in some ways that is true; but with the downfall of Marxist-Leninist experiments and the implicit although not widely acknowledged failure of capitalism as well, it is necessary to recognize that the neo-orthodox theologians of the earlier part of this century anticipated the judgment of modernity that these events have confirmed. Modernity was superficial—and precisely in its assumption of history's inherent redemptive capacities.

The lesson that needs to be learned from these failures of modernity is not that believing Christians should retreat into theories and theologies of history that bear the stamp of classical culture, with its suspicion of any meaning in history (one of the temptations of "postmodernity"!); rather, they should explore more deeply the dialectical relation of time and meaning that is indigenous to their own biblical tradition. Here, too, the fact that Christianity is just at this point emerging from its Constantinian captivity means that Christians are afforded the opportunity of achieving a greater originality in their study of their own sources and neglected traditions, for they are under no obligation now to uphold specific cultural assumptions and beliefs.

But what would it mean to embrace such a dialectical view of the relation between meaning and history? I would answer as follows: First, it would mean to cultivate a compassionate but incisive skepticism with respect to every ideology of progress, especially those ideologies which, whether from the political right or the political left, employ a heavy ingredient of technologism.

The reason for such skepticism should not be located in a mere suspicion of machinery, a Luddite distaste for work-saving devices, and so on. The Luddites may indeed, as some have proposed, have been "the last human beings," yet I seriously doubt that much can be accomplished by destroying the machines. What has to be changed is not the machinery, but the attitude that assumes that machinery can solve all our problems and bring about the good life. It is the ideology of progress itself that has to be tempered.

The Christian view of history is not based on that ideology. Christians do not believe in progress, they believe in providence. The religion of progress is, as George Grant taught us, a secularized and one-dimensional version of the biblical conception of providence. Biblical faith insists that God has the good destiny of the world at heart—that God's Spirit is at work mending the world—and therefore it affirms a providential movement within history. But this movement is neither automatic nor humanly graspable in clear, logical forms. "God moves in a *mysterious* way, his wonders to perform." The biblical God, as distinct from the deistic God of eighteenth-century intellectuals such as Adam Smith, does not do "the providential thing" as a matter of course.

Some of the most depressing episodes in Christian history have been the spilling of much silly ink to show that the universe as a whole vouchsafed a representable purpose of design analogous to the way that the purpose of the automaker is given in the design of the automobile.

Nevertheless, it is obvious that faith cannot turn away from the idea of the good.[16]

Meaning is not guaranteed! There is no fixed plan, there are no inevitable patterns of history—as in dispensationalism. The story that is told in the continuity of the two Testaments is one of constant interaction, of meeting, of being-with; the activity of God may be directive, but it is also responsive. In response to human arrogance and presumption God acts in one way; in response to human discouragement and defeat, divine providence means something else.[17]

This is the prophetic logic of judgment and compassion, and if it is taken seriously it is the death of ideology. For the essence of every ideology is that it does and must assume patterns, fixed principles, and limited flexibility.[18] What we ought to have noticed from the dramatic end of the U.S.S.R. is that life itself is always larger, more unpredictable, more "mysterious" than any of our ideas about it. The ideologue—often, to be sure, for very admirable, humane, and rationally impressive reasons—having derived a theory of the way the world ought to "work," goes out into it to *make* it work that way. If the conditions are right (for instance, if there is sufficient confusion of spirit, economic hardship, or social chaos), then the ideologue will likely be able to find a hearing, especially if he can put his theory into communicable forms, with attractive slogans. No word appeared more often in the great red and white signs that were put up all over Eastern Europe in Marxist lands than the word "progress" (in German, *Fortschritt*). Ironically, but with impeccable logic, it is the same word that is most often heard on television commercials in the United States and Canada. What brought down the Soviet Union, however, was precisely this exaggeration of the movement of history. The human spirit may be exceptionally willing to be persuaded of its happy future, but, eventually, the human spirit will recognize the discrepancy between rhetoric and reality. Even if it is backed up with tens of thousands of stockpiled weapons and kept in place by sheer brutality, the ideology will fall as soon as it is noticed by a sufficient number of those who suffer under it that its high promises are insupportable.

Christianity does not despise ideologies because Christian realism, where it exists, understands that God may also use simplistic conceptions of the

---

16. George P. Grant, *Technology and Justice,* 44.

17. For a more detailed discussion of the theology of providence, see Douglas John Hall and Rosemary Radford Ruether, *God and the Nations* (Minneapolis: Fortress Press, 1995), chap. 1, "The Mystery of God's Dominion," 13–27.

18. See Dietz Lange, "Ideology and Tolerance in the Thought of Reinhold Niebuhr," in *Reinhold Niebuhr (1892–1971): A Centenary Appraisal,* ed. Gary A. Gaudin and Douglas John Hall (Atlanta: Scholars Press, 1995), 97–112.

good in order to achieve God's purposes. But any Christian today who does not cultivate a critical vigilance with respect to the ideological mindset, and especially the faith in *la technique* that today inevitably accompanies that mindset, will have failed to distinguish between progress and providence.

Second, on the other hand, rightly to grasp the dialectical relation of hope and history in biblical terms would mean to resist the continuing temptation to capitulate to historical cynicism. I think that we are particularly, although discretely and hiddenly, prone to historical cynicism as a people at this moment in history, although the rhetoric of modernity is still powerful and seductive. It is so seductive in its late, commercialized, and globalized phase that most people in our society will blame themselves for their individual failures before they will inquire seriously about the external social, economic, and political realities that condition their lives. They will also blame specific governments, manufacturers, social services, and so forth—and there is no doubt that such blame ought to be placed. But what needs to be questioned is the social vision itself, that is, the ideology of progress. For it is long since past the time when we ought to have noticed that there *are* limits, and that we have already transgressed them.[19]

The danger as we emerge from this long period of exaggerated expectations, however, is not that we shall become all the more Promethean but that we shall increasingly adjust ourselves to the Sisyphus role, and become a cynical people. As a covertly nihilistic society we are dangerous enough; but as an openly nihilistic society we would undoubtedly be more dangerous still.

The Christian conception of history sets itself against historical cynicism just as decisively as it sets itself against classical versions of history that deny

---

19. Although written from within the European context, Michael Welker's recently translated *God the Spirit* (trans. John F. Hoffmeyer [Minneapolis: Fortress Press, 1994]) powerfully describes the fate that is upon all of us as Western peoples: "The spirit of the Western world has made possible and solidified the development leading to self-imposed global danger. . . .

"The most striking collective incarnation of this is what Germans call 'the enterprise' (*das Unternehmen*), which in every operation for 'the general public,' the market of greatest possible extension, must pursue its own self-preservation. Specifically, it must do so by being attuned to 'the market's' resonance to its operations of self-preservation. Whether the autmobile industry, air travel, the tourism industry, deep-sea fishing, the chemical industry, or the power plant industry—powerful enterprises, in their every operation intent on their self-preservation and expansion, chew their way from many different directions into the ecological substance of the earth. In accord with the Western spirit, they must guard against all sensibilities and operations that endanger their *self-continuation,* that do not immediately or mediately affect their self-preservation, self-reproduction, and self-extension. They must—at least selectively—close themselves off from other domains and keep the horizons of ignorance closed if they do not want to endanger their 'success' and thus their own continued existence. Even the societal subsystems responsible for the 'common good,' even the 'nonprofit enterprises' must first gear their operations to their own self-preservation and to the 'political mood' in the land if they want to operate steadily and efficiently. . . . [Even the churches] are busy with their 'fleshly' self-preservation, are corrupted by the Western spirit, and are trapped in many forms of faintheartedness" (306–8).

meaning to the daily round. And this is not just a matter of ethics; it is a subject of foundational theology. For while Christianity agrees with classical culture in its insistence that meaning transcends history as to its source, it rejects the classical assumption that meaning has and can have no continuity with history. For biblical faith, history does not itself produce and nurture the teleological principles that drive it; but that *telos* (purpose, aim) is continually being introduced into history and pulling historical time toward itself. Christian hope does not lie in the process as such (this we must perhaps say over against process theology); it lies, rather, in God. But since it is hope in a God who loves the world, who is determined to redeem it, it is also historical hope. Even what is negative may be the bearer of meaning. Consider the story of Joseph. Consider the cross of Jesus, the Christ.

> Just as it is important to recognize the spirit of the Western world with sobriety and clarity, it is equally important to recognize the Spirit of God in the Spirit's nearness and world-overcoming power. The Spirit of God is not an ideal, a product of wishful thinking, a dream of a different future, or a general moral alternative to be uncovered or conjured up. Instead the Spirit is a reality that, to be sure, becomes recognizable and attested in various times and various surroundings and world situations with different degrees of determinacy and clarity, but one that is no less surely effective "in this world" than is the Western spirit. The world that endangers and destroys itself need not and must not be accepted, because human beings in the Spirit of Christ, in the Spirit of love, of righteousness and of peace in the communion of the sanctified belong . . . to a reality that is present in this world, one that works against the power of the spirit of the Western world.[20]

As the bombs of World War II were beginning to fall on the city of Edinburgh, where he was living as the Gifford Lecturer in 1939, Reinhold Niebuhr wrote:

> The new world must be built by resolute people who "when hope is dead will hope by faith"; who will neither seek premature escape from the guilt of history, nor yet call the evil, which taints all their achievements, good. There is no escape from the paradoxical relation of history to the Kingdom of God. History moves towards the realization of the Kingdom, but yet the judgement of God is upon every new realization.[21]

---

20. Michael Welker, *God the Spirit*, 307–8.
21. Reinhold Niebuhr, *The Nature and Destiny of Man*, vol. 1 (New York: Charles Scribner's Sons, 1953), 286.

34. The Journey of the Self

34.1. The Inescapability of the Question. No consideration of the future is ever wholly impersonal. The modern discipline of futurology, basking in the reflected glory of science, laces its predictions with brave attempts at detached objectivity; but no one can entertain scenarios of the type presented by most contemporary students of earth's future without experiencing personal concern, not to say anguish. The "fate of the earth" (Jonathan Schell) is never just earth's fate; it is our fate, my fate, the fate of those I love, the fate of my children's children. Only the illusion of remoteness, painstakingly preserved, prevents the dire prognostications about Western civilization by which we are now confronted on a daily basis from rendering us speechless and helpless. So long as there can seem to be a buffer of time between us and the point at which (for example) the population curve begins to go straight up or the ozone layer is finally exhausted, we can continue to observe the macrocosm as if the microcosm, namely, our personal existence, were not affected. But this is a sham detachment, and we know it—deeply.

Although Christian theology itself has not been guiltless where such attempts at detachment are concerned, a contextually sensitive theology today must acknowledge this intimate connection between the self and the cosmos. When, as Christians, we reflect upon the nature of historical hope, we beg the question, if we do not raise it explicitly, of what hope could mean for individual life; for history *is* the intermingling of persons. It is a capitulation to North American individualism if our thoughts concerning ultimate destiny revolve too prominently around the personal, and that indeed is the strongest temptation of the Christian church in our context, as we shall argue presently. But to ignore the question of individual destiny for the sake of a more impersonal approach to eschatology is to repress the obvious involvement of the self in all profound reflections upon the future, and to end in the same absurdity as do natural scientists who think they can analyze reality without entering into it personally or allowing "it" to enter into them.

Besides, for Christians there is ample positive reason for asking about the destiny of persons. As we have seen in our discussion, for example, of the dialectics of individuality and communality in the doctrine of the church,[22] any intentionally Christian consideration of *any* aspect of this tradition that, in effect, abandons the individual in favor of a more corporate approach to the faith will have to be questioned. For the individual person matters profoundly to this tradition.

---

22. See below, chap. 2, §6.

And not only *human* individuals matter. Even sparrows, we are assured (Matt.10:29) do not fall unknown, unloved. The universal is not uninteresting to the tradition of Jerusalem, but, unlike Athens, Jerusalem is not tempted to find reality in unembodied universals—*that is,* it is not so willing to overlook particulars or find them mere vehicles for the conveyance of the mind to absolutes; *that is,* it is governed by the ontology of communion; *that is,* it is determined by the foundational concept and reality of divine *agape.*

For this reason, eschatologies which have the effect of merging all particularities into an ultimate, undifferentiated whole are, if not altogether unacceptable, at least unsatisfactory where this tradition is concerned. For instance, Origen's doctrine of *apokatastasis* (the belief that through purging all souls will finally return to God and God will be "all in all") has the (perhaps unintended) effect of saying to those same individual "souls" in their struggle of life that what they are about is ultimately unimportant, for it will be swallowed up in the divine *apatheia.* [23]

> If everything is to return to an undifferentiated unity, then creation would have been pointless in the first place, and all the risk of creation, and its suffering and striving, would have been sheer waste. [24]

If confining eschatology to personal destiny is perhaps the ultimate egoism, discussing eschatology abstractly without reference to the ego (self) is perhaps the ultimate reduction of theology to bloodless theory.

Christian theology therefore not only may but must ask about the destiny of the individual. And when theology does not do so explicitly and seriously, it leaves a vacuum that popular religion and irreligion regularly and ambitiously fill. For the question of our personal "Whence?" is always present to us, if not directly then indirectly; no amount of general speculation about "the future" will satisfy it. Our lives being immersed from beginning to end in particularity, we are not likely to find either appealing or truthful theories about the ultimate from which every trace of the particular has been erased. Even those who have discovered how to deflect the sting of particularity by transforming all human concerns into abstractions, faced by the prospect of imminent death, are driven to wonder what will become of "me." We cannot

---

23. "The church rejected Origin's doctrine of the *apokatastasis panton* (the restitution of everything) because this expectation seemed to remove the seriousness implied in such absolute threats and hopes as 'being lost' or 'being saved.' A solution of this conflict must combine the absolute seriousness of the threat to 'lose one's life' with the relativity of finite existence" (Paul Tillich, *Systematic Theology,* vol. 3 [Chicago: University of Chicago Press, 1963], 407).

24. John Macquarrie, *Principles of Christian Theology* (New York: Charles Scribner's Sons, 1966), 321.

live intimately with partners, parents, children, close friends, colleagues—all persons with names, faces, unique characteristics, foibles, endearing traits, and so on; we cannot spend every day of our lives mingling with quite specific human beings, animals, trees, vistas; we cannot move through time bumping into particular beings that share our space, make claims upon us, respond and initiate—in short, we cannot exist under the conditions of history and find satisfactory the assurance that all the searing questions of that existence are answered by "eternity." It is not only the little child who wants to know "What happened to Gramma? Where is she now?" The child lives on in the adult—and perhaps more insistently than ever.

The question of personal destiny, then, cannot and should not be avoided. But how shall we discuss it intelligently, faithfully, responsibily—we, whose religious context is a society and church that have elevated precisely this question to the highest rank, making it the very touchstone of religious relevancy?

34.2. Conflicting Options in Our Context. No single aspect of the Christian religion is so prominent in North America as the essentially un-Christian belief in the immortality of the soul. When all else has been neglected and forgotten, this remains. People whose ecclesiastical connections have been so tenuous as to be practically nonexistent will insist upon their being, nonetheless, Christians because they hold firmly to the belief in the soul's immortality. Every funeral sees the unlikely emergence into the realm of what passes for divine service of persons who, although utter strangers to Christians beliefs and, perhaps, outspoken despisers of all dogma, are able without difficulty to participate in worship that celebrates the undying soul. Conversely, no piece of skepticism is more offensive to the religious public of this continent than the suggestion that the "soul" is just as mortal as the body, being indivisibly linked with the latter in a psychosomatic unity of personhood. (As a parish minister in my youth, the only sermon of mine that evoked the almost universal wrath of my little congregation was one, preached on the Sunday after Easter ["Low Sunday"!], in which I discussed the distinction between the concept of the immortality of the soul and the *Christian* teaching concerning the resurrection of the dead.)

The doggedness of this opinion concerning the ultimate destiny of persons may be, in part, a consequence of our being still a rather unsophisticated public. Our agrarian and working-class roots still show through in the vestiges of our religion, even when we have achieved an economic and educational status far more complex than that of our pioneer and other progenitors. There are ways in which we have more in common with medieval peasants than with the ultramodern people of our iconography; and these ways are nowhere more visible than in our thoughts and practices concerning death and the dead. Here, we give way to beliefs, superstitions, and imaginings of the most prescientific variety. The ubiquitous hold of the immortality of the soul concept is, by comparison with many of the afterlife fantasies entertained by the North American public, high philosophy!

In important historical ways, it *is,* of course high philosophy, for it can be traced to the great and golden age of Greek philosophic thought, notably to the Socratic tradition. For that tradition, the *psyche,* that is, the *essential* self, is confined in its earthly pilgrimage to a body (*soma*) which, being matter, inclines it toward that which detracts from its ultimate goal. Death, therefore, should be considered a release from the *soma sema* (body-tomb). The soul, liberated from its confinement by the body and its lusts and limitations, may now soar to the heights of being that consitute its true goal—a goal that, in some versions, it may attain only after successive "reincarnations."

The popular ballad about that most revolutionary of American abolitionists, John Brown (1800–1859), while celebrating more the spirit of his cause than affirming the continuance of his personal essence, nevertheless could assume without explanation this socially entrenched notion of the soul's immortality:

> John Brown's body lies a-mouldering in the grave,
> But his soul goes marching on. . . .

The soul, in this popular conception of the subject, is fundamentally unkillable. The thing that makes John Brown, John Brown, and John F. Kennedy, John F. Kennedy, simply cannot die. We *are* our souls, and our souls are not subject to the mutations that constantly assail the flesh, including the last great change, death itself.

Oddly, this same elevation of soul in its popular expression gives way to imagery that is by no means transphysical; for it begets language from which bodily allusion is not only not excluded, but plays the most vital role. Thus it happens that the fundamental properties of the soul turn out to be physical properties: bodily appearance, the voice, the eyes, the face—smoothed, no doubt, of the wrinkles of age and the worries of this world (an essentialization that the funeral industry in North America attempts, very successfully, to anticipate!).

This very necessity of clothing the belief in the soul's immortality in language borrowed from the body indicates the internal flaw of the whole approach; moreover, as we shall attempt to show, it indicates why the Christian belief in "the resurrection of the body," while scientifically incredible, is spiritually and theologically more consistent with Hebraic-Christian assumptions concerning both creature and Creator. We shall return to this subject in the next section.

First, however, it is necessary to consider the antithetical "option" concerning personal destiny powerfully at work in our society. Understanding the immortality concept as the spiritualization of the topic, we may describe this option as its materialization. And if it is supposed that we are dealing here with a case of social antithesis and polarization, the supposition is surely not amiss. For the strong secular rejection of what is assumed to be Christian teaching on this subject is in great measure a rejection of spiritualistic reductionism by those who feel committed to the empirical and the physical.

Like Epicurus, such persons are unwilling to abandon the obvious fact of our materiality in favor of either dualism or a monism of spirit. They feel they are "stuck with the body," however reluctant some may be to have it so. And why would they not feel this way? Not only is the body the only form of existence we know personally, so that even those who try to spiritualize ultimate destiny for human beings must resort, as we have seen, to bodily language, but our whole society, from its most exalted scientific assumptions to its daily rhetoric, is clearly fixated on the body. More, one suspects, than any known civilization past or present, contemporary North American society is a body-oriented society. This is obvious enough where our most physical and emotional preoccupations are concerned (food, sex, health, beauty, strength, pleasure, and so on); but it is also the case with our more intellectual and broadly spiritual concerns. We pursue most avidly *that* species of truth that can be acquired through empirical observation. We distrust hypotheses and propositions that are not empirically verifiable, measurable, quantifiable; we manifest unusual respect for "hard data." It would be very strange, therefore, if persons formed by such a social climate were able without any sense of inconsistency to become spiritualizers where only one phenomenon is concerned—death and its aftermath. In fact, the only possible explanation of the current turn toward "spirituality" on the part of many fully materialistic persons is that the material sphere, in which, like good moderns, they hoped for salvation, has lately proven less soteriologically promising. The gods of sex and health and beauty, along with the gods of science and technology, are greatly reduced in status, despite their continuing cults. Materialism offers far less by way of satisfaction to the young today than it did in the years immediately following World War II.

Concretely, this means that the materialistic response to the question of human destiny, namely, that it is probably confined to the here and now, can be conscientiously embraced today only in a reluctant manner. Materialism is not a joyous conclusion to which people are led, as were the disciples of Epicurus, who called him *Soter* (savior) because he delivered them from the vain frustrations of seeking after immortality. With contemporary materialism, it is rather a matter of resignation: "Sadly, there is nothing beyond the grave."

But in the first place, who can imagine "nothing"—and particularly where his or her own being is concerned; and in the second place, is this so very empirical a conclusion to have reached, after all? In an irony not unlike that of the spiritualizers, the secular materialists are driven to defeat their own empiricism in order to deliver themselves from the tensions of living indecisively between yes and no. They often resort to what is in fact spiritualistic, or at least poetic, language to articulate their melancholy conclusions concerning personal destiny. If death is a simple, verifiable "fact," and the evidence of anything beyond that fact nonexistent or so ambiguous as to be unhelpful, then why should not the matter be stated very simply? We die. Why add, even, an exclamation point? Albert Camus, who may have been the only great Epicurean of the twentieth century (I do not think Sartre's classification of him as "a classical pessimist" is true), *tried* to state the matter in just that way. But even Camus could not be consistent about it. Had he been, we should probably never have heard of him. As it is, all that he wrote stands as a kind of Noltean "primal scream" against precisely the "fact" that (as he summarized the human journey) "Men die, and they are not happy."

These two options, then, dominate our context as we attempt to articulate what Christianity teaches concerning the destiny of the self. They represent the extremes from which we shall have to distinguish what Christians *profess.* But how, in this matter, shall we *confess* the faith, given the persuasive power of both of these options and the captivation of our contemporaries by both?—including our fellow Christians, most of them.

34.3. "Nothing Can Separate Us. . . . " The first and indispensable presupposition of the Christian profession of faith concerning the destiny of the person is that we are speaking here of a matter of grace and of faith. Here the *sola gratia, sola fide* of the Reformation must be strictly adhered to. That the self has anything that may be called a destiny beyond its historical sojourn is a possibility given it from beyond its own potentialities, not an inevitability inherent in its very being. It is a thing of grace, not of nature. It is a work of the divine Spirit, not a property of the human spirit. It is a consequence of God's labor *pro nobis* in Jesus Christ, not a consequence of our "works."

For this reason, the concept of the immortality of the soul is *fundamentally* incongruous with biblical faith.[25] For the principal assumption of the immortality idea is precisely *not* grace but nature, *not* the Holy Spirit but the human spirit, not Jesus Christ but our being and our deserving. If the soul *is* immortal, then nothing has to be conferred upon it; it already contains within itself the wherewithal of its continuance. One may say that it is a matter of grace

---

25. One of Karl Barth's least known books, I have found, is his *The Resurrection of the Dead,* trans. J. H. Stenning (London: Hodder and Stoughton, 1933).

that this is so—that a gracious God made souls immortal. But to do so is to ignore and blur the distinction between nature and grace, and to subsume the whole discussion of personal destiny under the doctrine of creation. Redemption is superfluous if the soul's eternal destiny is already implicit in its being.

Some have argued that, although the immortality of the soul is not a biblical idea, it is nevertheless a Christian one, since from very early times the Christians adopted it as their own. This historical convention does not, however, legitimate the teaching. Christians adopted a great many things along the way, and very many of them—as we have seen throughout these volumes—have to be examined critically.

Another approach is suggested by Paul Tillich. He criticizes the theologians who reject the term "immortality" outright. It is acceptable, he believes, "If the term is used in the way in which 1 Timothy 6:16 applies it to God [for then] it expresses negatively what the term eternity expresses positively: it does not mean a continuation of temporal life after death, but it means a quality which transcends temporality."[26] Tillich acknowledges that when immortality is applied to "the soul," "it introduces a dualism between soul and body [and] is incompatible with the symbol 'resurrection of the body.'"[27] Yet he thinks that the Platonic teaching of the soul's immortality may be used legitimately by Christians if it is used symbolically rather than conceptually:

> As a symbol "immortality" has been used of the gods and of God, expressing the experience of ultimacy in being and meaning. As such it has the certainty of man's immediate finitude exactly in this awareness. The "immortal gods" are symbolic-mythical representations of that infinity from which men as mortals are excluded but which they are able to receive from the gods. The structure remains valid even after the prophetic demythologization of the sphere of the gods into the reality of the One who is ground and aim of everything that is. He can "clothe our mortality with immortality" (I Corinthians 15:33). Our finitude does not cease to be finitude but it is "taken into" the infinite, the eternal.
>
> The cognitive situation is totally changed when the conceptual use of the term immortality replaces its symbolic use. In this moment immortality becomes characteristic of the part of man called soul, and the question of the experiential ground for certainty of eternal life is changed into an inquiry into the nature of the soul as a particular object. . . . The natural theology of both Catholics and Protestants used old and new arguments for the immortality of the soul, and both demanded acceptance of this concept in the name of faith. They gave official standing to the confusion of symbol and concept, thus pro-

---

26. Tillich, *Systematic Theology,* vol. 3, 410.
27. Ibid.

voking the theoretical reaction of the philosophical critics of metaphysical psychology, of whom Locke, Hume, and Kant are examples. Christian theology should not consider their criticism as an attack on the *symbol* "immortality" but on the *concept* of a naturally immortal substance, the soul. If understood in this way, the certainty of Eternal Life has been liberated from its dangerous connection with the concept of an immortal soul.[28]

This nuance may render the idea of immortality in some way useable in Christian discourse, but it is a highly scholastic distinction that will not help us to move from faith's profession to its confession in our particular context. The very word "immortality," particularly in its connection with the word "soul," conjures up a whole religious ethos that is not only incompatible with Christian foundations but militates against their reinstatement within the churches.

What is at stake here is not only a question of the destiny of the self but a whole Theology and anthropology. For instance, given the widespread and historically important inference of this concept, that only humans have souls, there are very serious implications here for the development of a theology of creaturely being that does not automatically elevate the human above all creatures and so perpetuate the spirituality that has led to the exploitation and degradation of the biosphere. Even Tillich himself, writing in the early 1960s, intuited this and other dangers associated with this language and concluded his discussion of immortality with the remark that "in view of this situation it would be wise in teaching and preaching to use the term 'Eternal Life' and to speak of 'immortality' only if superstitious connotations can be prevented."[29] We shall argue presently that the more biblically based teaching of the "resurrection of the dead" can be subject to the same kind of misuse; but it contains inferences that militate against a too-facile anthropocentrism.

To reject the language of the soul's immortality is in some ways to register one's *agreement* with the materialists. Christianity is "the most avowedly materialist of all the great religions"[30] in part because it not only takes matter seriously as the locus of the real and the good, but because it refuses to indulge in a dualism of matter and spirit. Materialists are right when they locate the essence of selfhood in its materialization and concretization; and the early Christians who burned or otherwise disposed of the works of Epicurus were misguided by spiritualizing influences coming, not from the original community of Christian faith, but from another side of the same pagan culture to which Epicurus belonged. A faith that celebrates creaturehood and

---

28. Ibid., 410–11.
29. Ibid., 412.
30. William Temple, *Nature, Man and God* (London: MacMillan, 1951), 478.

understands redemption itself as entailing the "humanization" of God[31] cannot with integrity despise the flesh and look for salvation in its destruction, including the existential destruction wrought by a rigidly ascetic morality that is intended to "mortify" the body before its actual death and decay.

There is something altogether anticreational and anti*biblical* about a theology and ethic that assume the stance of a war against "the flesh," and this is true even when such an emphasis can, occasionally, be found in or near the biblical record itself. Whatever warnings must be uttered against sensuality and lust and gluttony and other allegedly "bodily" sins (and such warnings are needed, as we have again discovered in the post-permissive society!), this must not evolve out of or lead to an ontology that is inherently ashamed of our physicality. When it does, as it has so often done, then it opts for a religious matrix quite antithetical to that of the tradition of Jerusalem, no matter how "Christian" it may profess itself to be. For Jerusalem not only assumes human physicality and psychosomatic unity, but it locates distortion not in matter, but in a wrong turning of the mind and the will. Sin, in fact, is *spiritual,* even when it manifests itself in physical life—as it is bound to do, given the unity of spirit and body. Moreover, if we are going to allow the use of the term "sin" in the plural at all, and perhaps we should not, the great sins of the tradition, as Jesus also continually reminded his hearers, are not the so-called sins of the flesh but the subtle sins of spirit and will that may, in fact, be combined with an inordinate desire to *control* the flesh!

Thus, while it is true that historic Christianity has sided almost exclusively with the spiritualistic companions of its long history, from the mystery religions and ascetic sects of the early church to the romanticism and New Ageism of today, in its foundations Christianity has more in common with materialism, old and new, than its own history indicates. Moreover, an important part of the task of theology throughout the present century, from the Barthian attempt to dialogue with Marxism to the ecotheological attempts to recover humanity's earthiness, has been and is to reclaim the materialistic dimensions of the tradition and redeem them from reductionist interpretations put upon them by history's many spiritualizers.

All the same, Christians are not able—*qua* Christians—to embrace the materialistic response to the question of the self's ultimate destiny. There is a mystery about our being, and indeed about all being, that cannot be dispelled by the realization that we are finite and mortal. Even humanly speaking, quite apart from any faith stance, it is impossible to account for both "the grandeur and the misery" (Pascal) of humankind under the aegis of an undiluted materialism.

---

31. See Karl Barth, *The Humanity of God,* trans. John Newton Thomas and Thomas Wieser (Richmond: John Knox Press, 1960).

I am personally content to leave this problem of deathlessness in the frame of mystery, and to console myself with the fact that the mystery of human selfhood is only a degree beneath the mystery of God.[32]

That we *are* in the first place is astonishing to all but dull imaginations. That we are *such* as we are—creatures not only of thought and will and language, but of a myriad variations, an indefinite concretization of characteristics, an unpredictable and unrepeatable uniqueness, each one; and that we shall continue to be such even if earth's population should rise to ridiculous proportions: this alone brings skepticism into the midst of our incipient leanings toward materialism. That we are beings of memory, creators of art and music, tellers of tales, participants in a creative process that we know transcends us while making room for us—all this is lost to the strictly materialistic explanation of the self.

And precisely deep skepticism about that explanation is what must be seen beneath the surface of the disintegration of "the second world." Finally, the materialistic explanation is more incredible than the religious explanations that it fancied it would quite naturally and without violence supercede. As Hans Küng has incisively put it, "Not religion, but its dying off, was the grand illusion."[33]

Christians, then, are not under obligation to put forward arguments for the immortality of the soul or to find evidence of that sort—perhaps in the late testimonies of the "clinically dead" who have been revived; but neither are they obliged by their profession of human embodiment to conclude with classical or more recent forms of materialism that our destiny, personally, is confined to the story that could be chronicled between the two dates that will appear on our tombstones. With materialism, nontheistic existentialism, and all thought that recognizes the reality of matter and the body, Christians are bound to take with great seriousness both the life and the death of the human person. Their quarrel with materialism is not its fundamental commitment to matter; on the contrary, it is just this commitment that informs their ontology and ethic of world orientation (the "nonreligious" meaning of the theology of the cross, as we have established it in the first volume). Rather, their quarrel with materialism is its reductionism: namely, that in its (usually strangely theoretical—even spiritual!) commitment to matter it does not even do justice to matter, which is far too mysterious a phenomenon to be objectivized. In the end, the materialists tend to be as abstract as the spiritualists. The body that is called John Brown is neither a "mortal coil" that remains

---

32. Reinhold Niebuhr, "Epilogue: A View of Life from the Sidelines," in Brown, ed., *The Essential Reinhold Niebuhr*, 256.

33. Hans Küng, *Theology for the Third Millenium*, trans. Peter Heinegg (New York: Doubleday, Anchor Books, 1990), 7.

a-mouldering in the grave while the essence of the man "marches on," nor a random constellation of chemicals that for a short time wander upon the face of the earth! That body itself is composed of "stardust,"[34] and breathes the same oxygen as Cleopatra and Caesar and Jesus. Even if it can be thought of only in material terms, its materiality is the stuff of wonder, before which we should take off our shoes.

Of course! say Christians, for it was made by God: God the eternal One, not (with Arius) some lesser demi-urgos! And it is the temple of the Holy Spirit. It will not be abandoned by the One who made it, filled it with spirit-breath, and finally also inhabited it personally.

That is the basis of the Christian *confession* concerning the whole journey of the self, and Paul expresssed it in a way that has never, I think, been improved upon:

> What then shall we say to this? If God is for us, who is against us? He who did not spare his own Son but gave him up for us all, will he not also give us all things with him? Who shall bring any charge against God's elect? It is God who justifies; who is to condemn? Is it Christ Jesus, who died, yes, who was raised from the dead, who is at the right hand of God, who intercedes for us? Who shall separate us from the love of Christ? Shall tribulation, or distress, or persecution, or famine, or nakedness, or peril, or sword? . . .
>
> No, in all these things we are more than conquerors through him who loved us. For I am sure that neither death, nor life, nor angels, nor principalities, nor things present, nor things to come, nor powers, nor height, nor depth, nor anything else in all creation, will be able to separate us from the love of God in Christ Jesus our Lord.
>
> (Rom. 8:31–39)

34.4. "The Resurrection of the Body." The Bible is conspicuously silent about what happens to persons beyond the point of their death. Given the prescientific matrix of biblical literature, as well as the kind of speculation concerning the afterlife allowable at the time, newer Testamental literature must be considered almost agnostic where this subject is concerned. It seems content to affirm life beyond death, without either explaining *how* that could be, or *what* it is.

This lack of speculation in an area that has surely been the most fertile field of fantasy in all religious discourse should itself be contemplated. The authority of Holy Scripture for Christians refers not only to what the Bible

---

34. "The elements which are the raw materials of life have to be made in the nuclear furnaces of stars. Every atom of carbon inside your body was once inside a star. We are all made from the ashes of dead stars" (John Polkinghorne, "The Care of Creation," The Sproule Lectures, Faculty of Religious Studies, McGill University, Montreal, 1993 [unpublished], Lecture I, manuscript p. 17.)

says but also to what it does *not* say. The evident refusal of biblical writers to enter into the usual flights of imagination as soon as the gates of knowledge have been closed on the empirically demonstrable tells us something very important: namely, that here what matters is not *gnosis,* but *pistis*—trust, not information.

The truth is of course that we cannot *know;* and this refusal, scripturally understood, is not due only to the inability of the human mind to penetrate that mystery, it is also due to limits purposely imposed by the divine will: "Beloved, we are God's children now; what we will be has not yet been revealed" (1 John 3:2). It has not been *revealed.* The suggestion here is that it could have been revealed, but it has not been. In other words, there are reasons for this. The very absence of revelation in this key point of existence brings home to us a truth that might otherwise be kept from us by our own illusions of knowledge and power. As it is, the true character of our situation as creatures is made utterly clear by the reality of death and the limit that death imposes upon both our knowing and our willing.

> Now absolutely everything is taken from us. Now, even if we are in a good hospital and have all the necessary drugs, we are suspended with Christ between heaven and earth and are excluded from human society. . . .
> We can share our life with others, but not our death.[35]

In the prime of life we can often believe we are masterful beings; but death reveals what has been true of us all along—our utter dependency (Schleiermacher), our beggarliness (Luther). That is why the Bible senses a strange but ineluctable connection between death and the getting of wisdom—

> "But where shall wisdom be found?
>   And where is the place of understanding?
> Mortals do not know the way to it . . .
> The deep says, 'It is not in me,'
>   and the sea says, 'It is not with me.'
> It cannot be gotten for gold . . .
> Abbadon and Death say,
>   'We have heard a rumour of it with our ears.'"
>   (Job 28:12ff. NRSV)

In death—that is, in its existential anticipation—we are therefore thrust back upon the basic choice that sentient life presents: either we shall trust the creative Source of life, or we shall be lured by the fearful thought of oblivion,

---

35. Karl Rahner, *The Practice of Faith: A Handbook of Contemporary Spirituality* (New York: Crossroad, 1983), 295–96.

a thought that not only annuls our future but casts its long shadow over every present moment.

Undoubtedly, the usual response, avowals notwithstanding, is a vacillation between the two. We believe and disbelieve, trust and mistrust, simultaneously. *Simul justus et peccator.* A war transpires within us—the war that Paul alludes to in the famous seventh chapter of Romans, or an extension of the same. We desire with all our hearts to trust "the Lord and Giver of Life"; yet the very faithfulness that we try to live is besieged by doubt, and the moreso when we do not live, as Christians of the classical and medieval periods did, in a culture that assumes the supernatural.

The only possible Christian rejoinder to this vacillation and ambiguity is also, as we have just seen, the one that Paul offers in Romans 7, with its follow-through in the eighth chapter: "Who will rescue me from this body of death? Thanks be to God through Jesus Christ our Lord!"

This kind of confidence (not certitude!) was very early expressed in the confessional formula, "resurrection of the dead." Paul himself, basing his argument on the oral tradition attributed by the disciple community to Jesus but now seeking to explain the thought more fully, attempts in the first letter to the Corinthians, chap. 15, to show the meaning of this belief. It is a noble attempt—and one that is certain to court dangers, if not to fail altogether as *apologia*!

The primary danger in Paul's discussion is the one identified by Tillich in his commentary on the "resurrection of the dead" as in his discussion (touched upon earlier) of the "immortality of the soul": namely, the danger of moving from symbol to concept. Precisely in his desire to *explain* resurrection, and to do so conceptually, the Apostle risks sacrificing its symbolic significance. And when his argument in 1 Corinthians 15 is taken up by minds more literal than Paul's, as happens regularly in our religious context, the result is a crass trivialization of the subject.

To begin with, Paul's argument is circular: "If there is no resurrection of the dead, then Christ has not been raised; if Christ has not been raised, then our proclamation has been in vain and your faith has been in vain. . . . For if the dead are not raised, then Christ has not been raised. . . . But in fact Christ has been raised. . . . " and so on (vv. 12–20 NRSV). Evidently the author is trying to establish the necessary theological connection between the resurrection of Jesus Christ and that of the faithful; but you cannot prove one unverifiable assertion by putting forward another unverifiable assertion. In the end, Paul is reduced to confession, as we all are. Yet he is tempted to bolster the *confessio fide* with explanations that in fact require their author to step well outside the circle of faith.

This temptation becomes still more conspicuous (and for the reader more confusing!) when the author of 1 Corinthians 15 tries to explain "the resurrection body": "But someone will ask, '*How* are the dead raised? With what kind of body do they come?' Fool! What you sow does not come to life unless it dies. And as for what you sow, you do not sow the body that is to be, but a bare seed, perhaps of wheat or of some other grain. But God gives it a body as he has chosen. . . " (vv. 35ff. NRSV). In short, the Apostle is led by an apologetic impulse to explain grace by nature;[36] and this lures him (vv. 39–41) into the still more questionable idea of making distinctions between the "flesh" of creatures, with the suggestion that the *human* creature *qua* creature bears, implicitly, a higher potentiality for "glory" than do other creatures of flesh.

But this, he seems finally to recognize, is clearly tangential to his main argument, and he returns in verse 42 to the confessional mode, though mixed with a quasi naturalistic attempt to distinguish the "physical body" from the "spiritual body." The symbol and the concept vie for ascendency throughout the entire discussion, and one wishes that Paul had stayed with his declaration of the sufficiency of divine grace as in the Romans passage quoted earlier, and in this matter especially had not given way to apologetics. For the Corinthians passage, while containing some very beautiful symbolic language, fails as apologetics; and its failure is never more conspicuous than when it is read (as it regularly is) at funerals by persons devoid of poetry, who present the pericope as if it were a fully satisfactory answer to the awesome question implied in the apparent "victory" and "sting" of the ultimate negation.

If, however, we ask what is *foundational* for the author of this passage, what he is trying to preserve in the midst of all his frustrating logic, then we may be grateful also for this portion of the Pauline corpus. For what motivates the author throughout are principles that are vital to the symbolic significance of the confession concerning the resurrection of the dead. They are three in number.

First, the priority of divine grace: Despite Paul's temporary wanderings in the dangerous territory of hierarchic ontology (vv. 37–41), he is clear that what gives the possibility of life beyond death is not, after all, the different, perhaps higher form of "flesh" possessed by humans, but sheer grace: "God gives it a body as he has chosen." The "victory" over death is not ours, but God's, "through our Lord Jesus Christ" (v. 56).

Second, the priority and redemptive efficacy of God's raising of the Christ: Although Paul is tempted to use this as a kind of external proof of *our* resurrection, or vice versa, the main point of his argument is that because, in faith, we believe *Jesus* lives, we may certainly trust (trust!) that God will not aban-

---

36. See Jürgen Moltmann, *The Way of Jesus Christ,* trans. Margaret Kohl (London: SCM, 1989; Minneapolis: Fortress Press, 1993), 266.

don those with whom Jesus has identified himself in suffering love. It is the same point, in short, that the Apostle made in Romans 8.

Third, the essential unity of the person, body and soul: Paul was, after all, a Jew. He could not without renouncing his whole education and tradition embrace a spiritualistic theory of survival such as the "immortality of the soul" concept. If he undertakes what is a quite fantastic and confusing explanation of the personal *post mortem* estate of God's beloved, offering up what is almost an oxymoron—the term "spiritual body"—as a way of conceptualizing this estate, it is because he thinks holistically about the human person. Bodies are not *accidens* (inessentials), mortal shells to be cast off like the chrysalis of the butterfly. Spirits, souls, minds, or whatever nomenclature may be used, are inseparable from limbs, hair, stature, eyes, speech, and so forth.

To speak concretely, for Paul we are faces. If, beyond sheer trust in the love and grace of the triune God, it is worthwhile discussing the so-called afterlife at all, the discussion has to take account of that rudimentary reality. I am not interested in surviving my death if I cannot survive, so to speak, with my face, lined and unbecoming as it may have developed under the conditions of existence. What, without my face (and all that goes with it!) am I? I cannot think of anyone I know and love without seeing in my mind's eye a face. This is a homely and plain way of speaking, but it emerges from the same ethos as was lived by the Apostle Paul, the Jew. As Tillich wrote:

> The Christian emphasis on the "body of resurrection" also includes a strong affirmation of the eternal significance of the individual person's uniqueness. The individuality of a person is expressed in every cell of his body, especially his face. The art of portrait-painting continually calls to mind the astonishing fact that molecules and cells can express the functions and movements of a man's spirit which are determined by his personal centre and determine it in mutual dependence.[37]

The awkward distinction "physical body"/"spiritual body" is a consequence of this Jewish refusal to reduce the essential self to spirit/soul/mind, accompanied by an equally Jewish respect for the body and the particularity that it articulates so unmistakably. Paul knows as well as any materialist that the human body, being matter, is mortal. But he also knows that it is mortality created by the Immortal One, who will not abandon it. Or, to put the same thing into other words, he knows that, as the creation of such a Creator, the whole "ensemble" called person is a mystery greater than the sum of its parts, irreducible to ingredients, knowable only in the totality of its living

---

37. Tillich, *Systematic Theology,* vol. 3, 413.

presence—and, above all, loved as such. The love that called it into being in the first place, *ex nihilo,* will give it new being when it has been refined by exposure to the truth of its condition. The process is already well under way. It is what has begun with the baptism of fire and of water.

In the end, grace is the same whether it has to do with the creation of the world, the justification of sinners, or the resurrection of the dead. It is always a matter of "something out of nothing," for it is always a confession concerning the God "who gives life to the dead and calls into existence the things that do not exist" (Rom. 4:17). If ever one experiences this grace as that which "justifies," it is not a very great leap to believe that it could also create the world and raise the dead.

34.5. Heaven and Hell. If North American Christians hold fast to the idea of immortality long after they have lost touch with both religion and classical philosophy, they are also still strangely fixated on the ancient ideas of heaven and hell. Such a fixation is of course natural enough: if one clings to the assumption of life beyond death, one is bound to entertain thoughts about the character of such a survival. At its crassest, the heaven/hell contrast is little more than a projection into the afterlife of simplistic moral assumptions governing this life. Relative sophistication should not blind one to the fact that such assumptions rule the lives of vast numbers of people, and that heaven's rewards and hell's punishments still play a very significant role in both the religion and the morality of this Continent.

Responsible Christians are therefore obliged to enter a strong protest against popular heaven-and-hell mythology. It is not the product of innocent or merely "untutored" spirituality. It is one of the points at which a whole substructure of misunderstanding informs much folk religion (which in our context usually means some form of what is called "Christianity"). Beneath this mythology lie assumptions about God, humanity, salvation, and ethics that are frankly anti-Christian. It is the end product of a soteriology that not only virtually ignores Jesus Christ, or casts him in a false light, but it assumes that human good and human evil are easily distinguishable and separable: if our good outweighs our evil we will "go to heaven," and if not then hell is our destiny. For Roman Catholic piety, the concept of purgatory softens this stark dichotomy and at least introduces nuances that are both more compassionate and therefore, despite the unbiblical character of the teaching, more nearly compatible with biblical faith. For purgatorial teaching at least recognizes that good and evil are subject to subtle interpretation, and to change. Yet the dogma of purgatory too participates in an anthropocentric notion of salvation that places the emphasis upon what the Reformers called "works righteousness"; it is, besides, open to shocking forms of manipulation by religious authority, as church history all too amply demonstrates.[38]

The whole thrust of the heaven/hell approach to the ultimate destiny reflects and perpetuates an anthropology, an ethic, and an eschatology that are both naive and humanly destructive. The approach is naive because it fails to grasp the admixture of good and evil, saint and sinner, sheep and goat that all human beings under the conditions of history are:

> From the point of view of human nature, the doctrine of a twofold eternal destiny contradicts the fact that no human being is unambiguously on one or the other side of divine judgment. Even the saint remains a sinner and needs forgiveness and even the sinner is a saint in so far as he stands under the divine forgiveness. If the saint receives forgiveness, his reception of it remains ambiguous. If the sinner rejects forgiveness, his rejection of it remains ambiguous. . . .
> The qualitative contrast between the good and evil ones, as it appears in the symbolic language of both Testaments, means the contrasting quality of good

---

38. While the Eastern church has always prayed for the dead, the Latin church early in its history began to develop precise conceptions of the status of the dead, and appropriate liturgical practices for observing these. Purgatorial teaching is found in the early third-century *Passion of St. Perpetua,* a document possibly edited by Tertullian, and in more developed forms in the writings of Ambrose of Milan, Augustine, Gregory the Great, the Venerable Bede, Thomas Aquinas, and many other Western writers. The teaching was rejected by the Waldensians and Albigensians, as well as by the later reformers. The Protestant rejection of the dogma is based on its obvious incompatibility with the central Reformation message of "justification by grace through faith"; but it is also bound up with the protest of all the reforming movements against ecclesiastical and clerical abuse. Thus Tillich notes that "Protestantism abolished the doctrine of purgatory because of the severe abuses to which clerical greed and popular superstition subjected it" (*Systematic Theology,* vol. 3, 417).

The Tractarians of the early Oxford Movement attempted to introduce purgatory into Church of England practice, and some Anglican and even Protestant theologians remain open to the doctrine. Thus John Macquarrie writes: "It is hard to understand why Protestant theologians have such a violent prejudice against this conception, for it seems to me to be indispensable to any reasonable understanding of Christian eschatology. If, as in the present work, we think of heaven and hell as limits to be approached rather than final conditions in which to remain; if we try to visualize eschatology in dynamic rather than in static terms; if we refuse to draw any hard and fast line between the 'righteous' and the 'wicked' or between the 'elect' and the 'reprobate'; if we reject the idea that God's reconciling work is restricted to the people living at this particular moment and believe that his reconciliation can reach anywhere, so that it makes sense to pray for the departed; above all, if we entertain any universalistic hopes of salvation for the whole creation, then we are committed to the belief in an intermediate state, whether or not we call it 'purgatory.'

"The name 'purgatory' is, however, entirely appropriate, for it points to the process by which we are fitted for that union with God which is our ultimate destiny. Heaven, purgatory, and hell are not sharply separated, but form a kind of continuum through which the soul may move, perhaps from the near annihilation of sin to the closest union with God. Indeed, the concept of purgatory served the valuable purpose of introducing the dynamic, moving element into the traditional scheme, where heaven and hell could easily be mistaken for fixed immutable states" (*Principles of Christian Theology,* 328).

and evil as such (for example, truth and lie, compassion and cruelty, union with God and separation from God). But this qualitative contrast does not describe the thoroughly good or thoroughly evil character of individual persons. The doctrine of the ambiguity of all human goodness and the dependence of salvation on the divine grace alone either leads us back to the doctrine of double predestination or leads us forward to the doctrine of universal essentialization.[39]

In short, the confessional corrective to a heaven/hell mythology that enshrines the worst, most oppressive and, above all, most simplistic forms of moralism in North American popular religion is a theology of grace, which sees our destiny not as the consequence of an almost mathematical calculation of our private worth but as a gift discontinuous with both "the good that we would but do not and the evil that we would not, but do" (Rom. 7). The cross, which stands as judgment not only of our evil but also what passes for our goodness, cancels out all claims to eternal bliss on the basis of what we have been and done. If we have a destiny that transcends our historically ambiguous life story, it is the destiny of Another, into which by sheer grace we have been taken up, with all our ambiguities and duplicity.

But this christological corrective to the "natural" tendency of human beings to assess their own and one another's eternal worth on the basis of superficial calculations of good and evil introduces other problems for Christians—ancient problems that are by no means lessened by the religiously pluralistic situation in which North American Christians find themselves today. If Jesus Christ is our hope for eternal life, the door by which we enter the heavenly realm, what of all those millions who do not know and perhaps may not even have heard that Name?

It was, one suspects, more readily managed in the high days of Christendom to consign all such "souls" to damnation or oblivion. In the monolithically "Christian" context of premodern Europe, one did not meet these theoretical candidates for hell face to face on a daily basis! One might facetiously say that the Christians were too busy assessing one another's chances for reaching heaven to give much thought to the multitudes of mostly faraway races and kindreds who were surely on the road to outer darkness and the gnashing of teeth!

Our context, however, is very different in this respect. And it is in many ways salutary *theologically* that this is so! As Berkhof writes, "Fortunately, secularism and the intense contact with non-Christian worlds compel to a deeper and more careful consideration of this matter." He adds, however, that

---

39. Tillich, *Systematic Theology,* vol. 3, 408.

to date "little of that [deeper and more careful consideration] is noticeable in the study of the faith."[40] This leads us to the final consideration of this topic.

34.6. Judgment. Perhaps at its best, the heaven-and-hell preoccupation of much Christianity in North America reflects an incipient and greatly under-developed concern for justice. Intuitively, instinctively, the human spirit rebels at the thought of both goodness unrecognized and evil unpunished. Heaven, popularly conceived, is the "religious" answer to the first neglect, and hell to the second. If earth will not reward or punish according to recognizably just standards (and apparently it will not), then the thing must be transferred to a supramundane sphere. If heaven and hell do not exist, we shall invent them!

This sense of there being an ultimate assessment of persons, an assessment based upon standards of justice that, if they are not fully known by humans, are at least not wholly unknown, is not to be dismissed lightly. The "last judgment," so ubiquitously announced by street-corner evangelists and highway signs across this continent, is at very least a token of the insistence that there are norms of behavior that transcend our constantly shifting codes of morality and our convenient accommodation to circumstances. All things considered, this in itself is a remarkable vestige of moral absolutes in an epoch that has relativized everything and substituted the language of values for the language of the good. That people are *answerable* for their treatment of one another, their behavior as members of society, their deportment vis-à-vis the extrahuman creation: this is a societal presupposition that may be a *conditio sine qua non* of civilization itself. One has cause to wonder today whether such a presupposition of normative justice can be sustained at all apart from some religious sense of a righteous judgment that both undergirds and assesses human moral codification.

The danger attending the belief in a final judgment is implied in the language of the previous sentence. For while dominant classes and authorities are always pleased to think that their standards of conduct are *undergirded* by divine decree, they seldom entertain the prospect that their moral codes are *assessed* and judged by divine justice. The whole history of Christendom is the history of a triumphant religion whose triumphalism was made possible, theologically, by its failure to distinguish sharply between God's ways and its own. The theology of glory is nothing more nor less than the conse-

---

40. Hendrikus Berkhof, *An Introduction to the Study of the Faith,* trans. by Sierd Woudstra (Grand Rapids: Wm. B. Eerdmans, 1979), 531. (I would qualify this by noting the careful and imaginative exegetical work that Jürgen Moltmann has done on the subject in his *God in Creation,* chap. 7, "Heaven and Earth," 158–84.)

quence of an inordinate and finally quite ludicrous tendency on the part of moral and spiritual mediocrity to think itself worthy of ultimacy.

It belongs to the critical perspective of the *theologia crucis,* on the contrary, to live dialectically between the hope that our decisions, acts and judgments reflect transcendent good and the honest realization that they will also always distort God's righteousness, even when they approximate it. The consequence of this mode of reflection for any consideration of *ultimate* judgment is that it will retain, above all, a certain modest reserve—and expect to be surprised. The first may indeed be last, and the last first. Even that, however, should not be turned into a rule. The disciple community goes its way, practicing as much nonchalance as possible with respect to its ultimate "standing," refusing to keep a record of good and evil thoughts, words and deeds, and paying attention rather to the Voice that speaks through the silence—and to the neighbor. "Let not your right hand know what your left hand is doing."

The source of this nonchalance is neither sheer human presumption nor religious credulity. It is the consequence of trust in the One who judges, who is no other than the crucified one. "Whatever the significance of the teaching about the Last Judgment . . . it can never limit or modify what we have known as God's will in Jesus Christ. Judgment is never the *goal* of the divine Will—

> If it is objected that the Will of God is not merely the will to communicate Himself (love) but also to glorify Himself (holiness), that is indeed correct, but must at once be supplemented by the addendum that in the revelation of Christ the decisive thing is the unity, the coincidence of love and holiness. . . . What has come to our knowledge is clear, namely, the revelation of the un-conditional and therefore un-limited love of God in Jesus Christ.[41]

Under the sign of the cross and resurrection of Jesus Christ, the "end" (*telos*) of the *whole* process, including judgment, is life and not death. As Jürgen Moltmann has shown, the general effect of the concentration of both the theology and art ("especially medieval art") of the Christian church has been to accentuate so unconditionally the association of Christ's *Parousia* with judgment that it has overshadowed altogether the tradition of the *consummation* of all things, which is to say restoration and life:

> The one-sided way in which Christ's "second coming" was linked with the Last Judgment obscured the meaning of this judgment, which is solely the victory

---

41. Emil Brunner, *The Christian Doctrine of the Church, Faith and the Consummation* (Dogmatics, vol. 3), trans. David Cairns in collaboration with T. H. L. Parker (London: Lutterworth Press, 1962), 417.

of the divine righteousness that is to become the foundation of the new creation of all things. Of course judgment must be expected too, together with the consummation of Christ in the glory of God, for the perfecting of the kingdom includes the ending of injustice. There is no need to leave out the expectation of judgment, or to demythologize it as an antiquated apocalyptic concept. But neither is there any reason for giving way to fear and panic at the thought of it. . . . The Judge who is expected is the One who gave himself up for sinners and who suffered the pains and sicknesses of men and women. The crucified One will judge according to his gospel of the saving righteousness of God, and according to no other law.[42]

At the end of the day, one knows that one is an "unprofitable servant," even if one has done all that could reasonably be expected (which is surely seldom the case!). On the other hand, such knowledge does not reduce one to despair. A disciple in anguish over the sins of the day could not follow tomorrow. One knows that, whatever others may consider one's "worth," and however one may oneself esteem or not esteem oneself, the God of Abraham and Sarah, whom Jesus called "Abba," does not judge after the manner of humankind. *Whatever* one's story, compassion will be necessary. (And, in parentheses, faith whispers: It will be given.)

---

42. Moltmann, *The Way of Jesus Christ,* 315.

CONCLUSION

A contextual theology defies what is usually meant by a "conclusion," for it assumes that the task of theology goes on, and that it will require ever new and "original" reflection on the part of the disciple community—specifically, on the part of individuals who are called to that particular aspect of the whole work of the church. Even to write such a theology, and to have it published in books that will, some of them, outlast not only the author but the specifics of the time and place in which the author wrote, is in some real sense a contradiction in terms. The Christian gospel is intended for the "here and now," and theology, whose function is to help the church rediscover and articulate gospel, necessarily participates in the existential nature of the "hearing" that this involves.

The earliest Christians, most of them, probably did not know how to write. They undertook their work of theology and witness through speech; and when they were warned not to speak about these things any longer they said they could not do otherwise (Acts 4:20). In a way, the oral tradition that preceded the written Gospels and epistles remains a permanent judge of written theology, for it contains the irrepressible thought that *God's* Word, which cannot even be testified to adequately in the inspired spoken words of those who hear it, eludes even more adamantly the written word, which too easily gives the impression of permanency.

Nevertheless, one may feel some kinship with, as well as gratitude for, the second- or third-generation Christians, as well as the thousands who since then have felt compelled to "write it down." The best of them understood that writing was a sort of vanity, in Koheleth's sense—and also that what needed to be said could not be contained, finally, in a whole world full of books (John 21:25). Fortunately, few of them conceived of their labors as though they wrote in stone, however, and one is glad that they left us their testimony.

Were those ancients who wrote down their accounts of "the events that have been fulfilled among us" (Luke 1:1) able to enter the complex and harried discussions of the newer Testamental scholars today (for instance, to sit in on "The Jesus Seminar"), I have no doubt they would experience emotions ranging from astonishment to ire and amusement. For they would be amazed that their simple testimonies to events that had changed their lives or the lives of their mentors in the faith should have given rise to such an industry. What a terrific weight of responsibility they would have felt had they suspected that twenty and more centuries of thought concerning the faith would rest upon their every iota! Such knowledge would no doubt have ensured that their writings would never have seen the light of day. As for Paul, the first great Christian contextualist, who wrote different things to different churches, and even to the same churches at different times, I firmly believe that, although not particularly gifted with humor, he would have sympathized with a certain "dictum" that I found myself formulating one day in a class for beginners in systematic theology: "In Christian theology, you have to keep talking; otherwise, someone will believe your last sentence."

If one writes theology despite all such awesome deterrents, it is because one cannot do otherwise. "We cannot but *write* of what we have seen and heard!" Needless to say, this compulsion does not refer to the publish-or-perish mandate of the contemporary professional world, which with regularity demonstrates one of the principles espoused in these pages, namely, that without an indicative, an imperative ("Publish!") is a vain and shallow thing. For Christians, the need to write is an internal one. It emanates from a two-fold conviction: a sense of the liberating truth by which one has been grasped, and of responsibility for the community that has been formed around that truth.

Like those from whom I have learned my craft (that "great cloud of witnesses") I have been impelled by the manner in which all the many aspects and facets of the tradition we have received constitute, in the end, an integrated and clarifying account of reality. Truth *is* one. But more importantly, the one truth engages what is fragmented and duplicitous and divisive within our own and the world's existence—engages it and begins to heal it, lending to it an integrity that otherwise it would certainly not know. For me, as for thousands who preceded and have accompanied me in this discipline, Christian theology has meant a history of seeing connections. It would be absurd, and *easily* falsifiable, for anyone to claim that he or she had grasped all of the connecting links to which this "modest science" (Barth) opens one. For myself, I would only say that I have sensed from afar the wonder of their integrity. But even with that, I found that I could not avoid the attempt to point to that unity in words. At least to point! In that respect, I gladly acknowledge my continuity with all who have called themselves, or been called, systematic theologians.

The other prong of the *necessitas* that drives one who writes theology is a sense of responsibility to what is called by the much-beleaguered name of "church." As I have endeavored to show in these three volumes, as in other writings of mine, I am convinced that the church today is passing through one of the two great periods of transition in its nearly two-thousand-year history. What it is to become, what shapes it will assume in the future, none of us knows with any certainty. I have, however, the strong conviction that within the remnants of Christendom there could come to be—*is* coming to be!—a movement of peoples, a scattering, a diaspora, an ecumenical community of discipleship such as Jesus envisaged: salt, yeast, and light for a world whose own future is gravely uncertain.

For myself, I have come to believe that I belong to a relatively small community of professional students of the faith who understand themselves as theologians of the transitional period, the "awkward" time between Christendom and diaspora. That community holds for me much by way of hope and promise; but it is also going to be (and already is!) heir to some very serious temptations.

One of these is the danger of losing the very meaning of "theology" in the Christian sense by losing touch with the biblical and historical traditions that have given substance to that discipline. There is already a tendency to interpret theological reflection in so subjective a manner that the very idea of an integrated and integrating truth is lost. In its place there emerges a Babel of experiences and visions, and "values" and spiritualities that, far from illuminating and resolving the fragmentation of the world, only mirror and aggravate it. Reporting on a recent consultation of Christians, an ecclesiastical newspaper quotes one concluding statement as follows: "Theology is your life and how you deal with it." To the contrary! Theology is not "our life," it is a disciplined reflection upon that which addresses our life and is busy changing it: gospel! As such it requires a good deal of hard work, because we are neither born with historical knowledge nor do we engage in any sort of depth of thought without effort. "We" did not invent this gospel, and its subject matter, while not excluding "us," infinitely transcends "our life"!

It would be a sorrowful thing if an account of "reality" (Bonhoeffer) profound enough to alter the minds and hearts of people like Augustine of Hippo, Teresa of Avila, Thomas Aquinas, Hildegaard of Bingen, Søren Kierkegaard, and countless other such thought-full human beings, were reduced to the sloganized and experientially based platitudes of so much that now passes for Christian theologizing. A church that jettisons its theological past along with the triumphalistic organizational forms of that past will very soon be dissipated and unrecognizable. "We have these treasures in earthen vessels"—the vessels of a distorted and often corrupt ecclesiastical imitation of worldly pomp and woe. But they are, all the same, treasures, and they are not to be thrown out carelessly or exchanged for trinkets that are cheap and ephemeral.

Since I began to employ the term "contextuality," it has become a cliché of the ecclesiastical avant garde, and for the most part its usage suggests an attitude that is pretty scornful of the past. I wish to conclude this work, therefore, by noting my hope that whatever I have written in these pages about earlier expressions of the Christian faith will never be conceived as emanating from scorn. Contemplating what has been "handed over" (*tradere*), we must, I believe, hold together an attitude that is both critical and grateful. We are not here to perpetuate that past; we are here to perpetuate what the best representatives of that past tried to perpetuate: gospel.

On the other hand, if we forget that past; if we no longer struggle with it and demand that it bless us; if we discard it in favour of *le dernier cri*, we are bound not only to repeat it with all of its heresies and idiocies intact, but, worse than that, we shall have nothing with which to engage our present historical moment, or even to discern its character.

Traditional*ism*, like every other ideology, is the enemy of faith. But to stand within a tradition has always been a gift, and the condition without which civilization itself cannot be. How much more so, then, in a context like ours, whose greatest malaise is "cultural amnesia."*

---

* See the novel *Ishmael*, by Daniel Quinn (New York: Bantam/Turner Books, 1993), 200.

INDEX OF SUBJECTS

INDEX OF NAMES

530